The Perception of Risk

RISK, SOCIETY AND POLICY SERIES
Edited by Ragnar E Löfstedt

The Perception of Risk

Paul Slovic

Earthscan Publications Ltd, London and Sterling, VA

First published in the UK and USA in 2000
by Earthscan Publications Ltd

Reprinted 2001, 2002

ISBN: 1 85383 528 5 paperback

Typesetting by Composition & Design Service
Printed and bound in the UK by Creative Print and Design Wales, Ebbw Vale
Cover design by Yvonne Booth

For a full list of publications please contact:

Earthscan Publications Ltd
120 Pentonville Road, London, N1 9JN, UK
Tel: +44 (0)20 7278 0433
Fax: +44 (0)20 7278 1142
Email: earthinfo@earthscan.co.uk
http://www.earthscan.co.uk

22883 Quicksilver Drive, Sterling, VA 20166-2012, USA

Earthscan is an editorially independent subsidiary of Kogan Page Ltd and publishes
in association with WWF-UK and the International Institute for Environment and
Development

A catalogue record for this book is available from the British Library

Library of Congress Cataloging-in-Publication Data

Slovic, Paul, 1938—
        The perception of risk / Paul Slovic.
          p. cm. — (Risk, society, and policy series)
        Includes bibliographical references and index.
        ISBN 1-85383-527-7 (alk. paper) — ISBN 1-85383-528-5 (pbk.: alk. paper)
        1. Risk perception. 2. Risk assessment. 3. Risk —Sociological aspects. I. Title. II.
        Series.

        BF637.R57 S57 2000
        153.7'5—dc21

                                                                                    00-059305

Contents

List of Figures

List of Tables

Foreword

In a wide variety of ways contemporary society is enlarging the number and complexity of activities that are known to carry the risk of degrading the quality of human life and its natural environment. Technology is expanding, social organization is becoming more complex and interrelated, and scientific knowledge of some of the processes and consequences is deepening.

In response, measures to assess and manage the risks to people and natural systems are growing in number. The range of risks includes, for example: human disease impacts of polluted water; changed cancer death rates from chemical exposure; urban property damage from floods; health impacts from the transport of high-level nuclear waste; deterioration of ecosystems from changes in land use. In these and many other directions individual, group and government measures are being taken to assess and manage the risk. The results show in proliferating standards and requirements, such as environmental impact statements.

An essential part of such assessment and management is understanding how the affected individuals and groups judge and interpret available evidence on their possible losses and the particular vulnerability associated with the risk. This affects, in complex ways, the degree to which individual action is taken and to which support or opposition is offered for public management measures that may be proposed.

The authors represented in this volume are pioneers in investigating the processes by which the available evidence and experience are judged and enter into decisions. For a long time it was rare for scientists involved in risk analysis to investigate the judgments of people directly at risk. The efforts by Paul Slovic and his associates have brought those people into the picture of response. Thus, the innovative research efforts reported in this volume are to be welcomed as strengthening the scientific groundwork for sensitive and effective public action in dealing with hazards to the well-being of the planet.

Gilbert F White
University of Colorado
Boulder, Colorado

Acknowledgments

This book is the product of many years of exciting and gratifying collaboration with a great number of friends and scholars. In the Introduction, I attempt to convey my indebtedness to Clyde Coombs and Ward Edwards, my mentors at the University of Michigan; to Gilbert White and Howard Kunreuther, who stimulated me to look at risk beyond the confines of the psychological laboratory; to Sarah Lichtenstein and Baruch Fischhoff, who helped launch the psychometric paradigm as a way to study societal risk-taking and who contributed so skilfully to this effort; and to Amos Tversky and Danny Kahneman, whose brilliant experiments motivated and inspired much of our work. Behind the scenes in important roles were Paul J Hoffman, founder and director of the Oregon Research Institute, and Lew Goldberg, teacher, colleague and friend. There are also many, many others to whom I am grateful – their names grace the chapters in this book and the cited references to their work.

The innumerable critical steps and details that needed tending in assembling, revising, editing and producing the material in this book were handled with extraordinary skill by Kari Nelson, Janet Douglas, Janet Kershner and, especially, Leisha Mullican. I am profoundly grateful for their help.

It is important, also, to acknowledge the numerous public and private sources who funded the research reported in this book. Special thanks go to the Decision, Risk and Management Science Program and its predecessor at the National Science Foundation, the primary sponsor for research on risk- and decision-making. Other important sponsors of our research on risk have been the Alfred P Sloan Foundation, Ciba-Geigy Pharmaceuticals, the Environmental Protection Agency, Health and Welfare Canada, Dean Kathleen Hall Jamieson of the Annenberg School at the University of Pennsylvania, the John D and Catherine T MacArthur Foundation, David Dreman and the Dreman Foundation, the Electric Power Research Institute, Procter & Gamble and the Nuclear Waste Project Office of the State of Nevada (with particular thanks to Joe Strolin of that office).

Finally, I dedicate this book to Roz Slovic, a remarkable woman who has been at my side supporting me and this effort every step of the way since 1959, and to my children, Scott, Steven, Lauren and Daniel.

Paul Slovic
Eugene, Oregon,
August 2000

Acronyms and Abbreviations

ADR	adverse drug reaction
AIDS	acquired immune deficiency syndrome
ANOVA	analysis of variance
ARPA	Advanced Research Projects Agency (US Department of Defense)
AS	ankylosing spondylitis
BGH	bovine growth hormone
BSE	bovine spongiform encephalopathy ('mad cow disease')
¢	cent
CO	carbon monoxide
CO_2	carbon dioxide
DDT	dichlorodiphenyltrichloroethane
DES	diethylsilbestrol
df	degrees of freedom (statistical term)
DNA	deoxyribose nucleic acid
DOE	US Department of Energy
DOT	US Department of Transportation
EDB	ethylene dibromide
EMF	electric and magnetic fields
EPA	US Environmental Protection Agency
EPRI	Electric Power Research institute
F	test statistic of the F test (statistical term)
IUD	intrauterine device
LNG	liquified natural gas
LOWV	League of Women Voters
LP	large probability
LULU	locally unwanted land use
MRS	monitored retrievable storage
n	number of sampling units in a sample (statistical term)
N	number of sampling units in a population (statistical term)
NIMBY	not in my backyard
NO_x	nitrous oxide
NRC	either US Nuclear Regulatory Commission or National Research Council
NSAID	non-steroidal anti-inflammatory drug
NSF	National Science Foundation
ONR	Office of Naval Research
p	probability (statistical term)

PCB	polychlorinated biphenyl
PVC	polyvinyl chloride
r	product moment correlation coefficient (statistical term)
r^2	coefficient of determination (statistical term); also, percentage of variance accounted for
RAD-AR	risk assessment of drugs-analysis and response
RASS	Risk Assessment Summer School
rem	roentgen equivalent man
sd	standard deviation (statistical term)
SO_2	sulphur dioxide
SOT	Society of Toxicology
SP	small probability
SRI	Stanford Research Institute
SST	supersonic transport
STD	sexually transmitted disease
t	test statistic of the t test (statistical term)
TMI	Three Mile Island
TVA	Tennessee Valley Authority
UK	United Kingdom
US	United States
USC	University of Southern California
USGS	US Geological Survey

Introduction and Overview

HISTORY

This book is the product of a 25-year program of research on perception of risk that I have been fortunate to pursue with the help of many fine colleagues. The origins of this effort can be traced to 1959, my first year as a graduate student in psychology at the University of Michigan. I was assigned to work as a research assistant for Clyde Coombs and became fascinated by a study Coombs was doing in which he examined people's preferences among gambles. I replicated and extended this study for my first-year project. The following year I began to work with Ward Edwards who was doing experimental studies of risk-taking and decision-making. In Edwards' laboratory I met Sarah Lichtenstein and Amos Tversky, who were also students of Edwards. Lichtenstein, Edwards and I teamed up in a study of boredom-induced changes in preference among bets (Slovic, Lichtenstein & Edwards, 1965). Lichtenstein and I went our separate ways but were reunited in Eugene, Oregon, in 1966, and have worked together since then.

In 1970, I was introduced to Gilbert White, who asked if the studies on decision-making under risk that Lichtenstein and I had been doing could provide insight into some of the puzzling behaviors he had observed in the domain of human response to natural hazards. Much to our embarrassment, we realized that our laboratory studies had been too narrowly focused on choices among simple gambles to tell us much about risk-taking behavior in the flood plain or on the earthquake fault.

White's questions were intriguing, however, and, with Howard Kunreuther, we turned our attention to natural hazards, attempting to relate behavior in the face of such hazards to principles that had been emerging from psychological studies of probabilistic judgments and risky choices (Slovic, Kunreuther & White, 1974; see Chapter 1). We found the work that Amos Tversky and Danny Kahneman had been doing on heuristics and biases in probabilistic thinking (Tversky & Kahneman, 1974) to be particularly valuable in explaining people's responses to the threats posed by natural hazards. The mid 1970s was a time when concerns about pesticides and nuclear power were rapidly increasing and we soon found our attention drawn to technological hazards. Discovery of Chauncey Starr's stimulating article on 'Social Benefit versus Technological Risk' (Starr, 1969) led Lichtenstein, Baruch Fischhoff and I to begin a research program designed to study what we referred to as 'cognitive processes and societal risk-taking' (Slovic, Fischhoff & Lichtenstein, 1976; see Chapter 2). The findings from that research program make up the contents of this book.

Howard Kunreuther, Gilbert White and Paul Slovic (right)

The Psychometric Paradigm and Its Origins

Starr's paper sought to develop a method for weighing technological risks against benefits to answer the fundamental question: 'How safe is safe enough?'. His *revealed preference* approach assumed that, by trial and error, society arrives at an essentially optimum balance between the risks and benefits associated with any activity. Under this assumption, one may use historical or current risk and benefit data to reveal patterns of 'acceptable' risk–benefit trade-offs. Concerns about these assumptions in Starr's model and the difficulties of collecting data to test his approach motivated us to conduct an analogous study using questionnaires to ask people directly about their perceptions[1] of risks and benefits and their *expressed preferences* for various kinds of risk–benefit trade-offs (Fischhoff, Slovic, Lichtenstein, Read & Combs, 1978; see Chapter 5). This approach appealed to us for several reasons: it elicits current preferences; it allows consideration of many aspects of risks and benefit besides dollars and body counts; and it permits data to be gathered for large numbers of activities and technologies, allowing the use of statistical methods to disentangle multiple influences on the results. Over the years, many studies of risk perception have been carried out using this approach.

In our replication of Starr's study, and in much of our subsequent work, we went beyond merely asking about risk and benefit. Borrowing from personality theory, we also asked people to characterize the 'personalities of hazards' by rating them on various qualities or characteristics (eg, voluntariness, catastrophic potential, controllability, dread) that had been hypothesized to influence risk perception and acceptance (Starr, 1969; Lowrance, 1976).

Another distinguishing feature of our studies has been the use of a variety of psychometric scaling methods to produce *quantitative* measures of perceived risk, perceived benefit, and other aspects of perceptions (eg, estimated fatalities resulting from an activity). First we used magnitude estimation techniques (Stevens, 1958) to assess risks and benefits and perceived frequencies of fatal events (Fischhoff, Slovic, Lichtenstein, Read et al, 1978; Lichtenstein, Slovic, Fischhoff, Layman & Combs, 1978). Later, we moved to numerical rating scales. In subsequent studies, we have supplemented these measures with traditional attitude questions and non-traditional word association and scenario generation methods. We have referred to this general approach and the theoretical framework in which it is embedded as the *psychometric paradigm*.

Of course, the psychometric paradigm, with its elicitation of perceptions and expressed preferences, has its own assumptions and limitations. It assumes people can provide meaningful answers to difficult, if not impossible, questions ('What is the risk associated with the use of nuclear power?'). The results depend upon the set of hazards studied, the questions asked about these hazards, the types of persons questioned, and the data analysis methods. Furthermore, the questions typically assess affective feelings and cognitions – not actual behavior. Despite these and other limitations, the studies using this approach have invariably produced coherent and interesting results that have motivated further use of the paradigm.

In sum, the psychometric paradigm encompasses a theoretical framework that assumes risk is subjectively defined by individuals who may be influenced by a wide array of psychological, social, institutional and cultural factors. The paradigm assumes that, with appropriate design of survey instruments, many of these factors and their interrelationships can be quantified and modeled in order to illuminate the responses of individuals and their societies to the hazards that confront them.

EARLY RESULTS

One of the most exciting findings, to those of us who drafted the first questionnaires (and who realized their difficulty), was that people could and would answer them, making hundreds of judgments per person in sessions lasting up to several hours. Equally surprising to us was that the results seemed to make sense and provide insight into many of the puzzling phenomenon evident in societal risk management and its controversies. Perceived and acceptable risk appeared systematic and predictable. Psychometric techniques seemed well suited for identifying similarities and differences among groups with regard to risk perceptions and attitudes. Our results also showed that the concept 'risk' meant different things to different people. When experts judged risk, their responses correlated highly with technical estimates of annual fatalities. Laypeople could assess annual fatalities if they were asked to (and they produced estimates somewhat like the technical estimates). However, their judgments of 'risk' were sensitive to other factors as well (eg, catastrophic potential, controllability, threat to future generations) and, as a result, differed considerably from their own (and experts') estimates of annual fatalities.

Another consistent result from psychometric studies of expressed preferences was that people tended to view current risk levels as unacceptably high for most activities. The gap between perceived and desired risk levels suggested that, contrary to the assumptions of the revealed preference approach, our respondents were not satisfied with the way that market and other regulatory mechanisms had balanced risks and benefits. However, studies of expressed preferences did seem to support Starr's conclusion that people are willing to tolerate higher risks from activities seen as highly beneficial. Nevertheless, while Starr concluded that voluntariness of exposure was the key mediator of risk acceptance, studies of expressed preference have shown that other characteristics, such as dread, familiarity, control, catastrophic potential, equity and level of knowledge, also seem to influence the relationship between perceived risk, perceived benefit and risk acceptance.

Various models have been advanced to represent the relationships between perceptions, behavior and these qualitative characteristics of hazards. The picture that has emerged from this work is both orderly and complex.

Factor-analytic Representations

Early work with the psychometric paradigm, as described in Chapters 5, 6 and 8, led to the representation of hazards within a two-dimensional space derived from factor analysis. The factors in this space reflect the degree to which the risk from a particular hazard is understood and the degree to which the risk evokes a feeling of dread. Research showed that laypeople's perceptions of risk were closely related to the position of a hazard within the factor space.

Perceptions Have Impacts

Another direction taken by early work within the psychometric paradigm was to examine the role of perceptions in determining the degree of impact resulting from an 'unfortunate event' (eg, an accident, a discovery of pollution, sabotage, product tampering).

Early theories equated the magnitude of impact to the number of people killed or injured, or to the amount of property damaged. However, risk-perception studies showed that there were other impacts as well, analogous to the ripples from a stone dropped into a pond. These secondary impacts could be enormous and were found to depend upon characteristics of risk perception stimulated by the extensive media coverage that accompanies certain events.

A conceptual framework aimed at describing how psychological, social, cultural and political factors interact to 'amplify risk' and produce ripple effects was presented by Kasperson et al (1988; see Chapter 14). An important element of this framework is the assumption that the perceived seriousness of an accident or other unfortunate event, the media coverage it gets, and the long-range costs and other higher-order impacts on the responsible company, industry or agency are determined, in part, by what that event signals or portends. *Signal value* reflects the perception that the event provides new information about the likelihood of similar or more destructive future mishaps (Slovic, Lichtenstein & Fischhoff, 1984).

The pace of psychometric research accelerated over the years. The early work was replicated and extended with new and more interesting samples of respondents and with very different sets of hazards and characteristics (see, for example, Chapter 10). Important concepts from other domains, such as stigma (Chapter 21), were brought to bear upon risk perception and risk-impact analysis.

EXTENDING THE PARADIGM

New Respondents

Our early studies were limited, by financial constraints, to local populations of students and citizen groups (League of Women Voters; business clubs). In later years, the paradigm was applied internationally, sometimes with local groups and sometimes with representative national samples. International studies contrasted perceptions of college students in the United States, Hungary (Engländer, Farago, Slovic & Fischhoff, 1986), Norway (Teigen, Brun & Slovic, 1988), Hong Kong (Keown, 1989), Japan (Hinman, Rosa, Kleinhesselink & Lowinger, 1993; Kleinhesselink & Rosa, 1991; Kleinhesselink, 1992), Poland (Goszczynska, Tyszka & Slovic, 1991) and the Soviet Union (Mechitov & Rebrik, 1990). Some of the largest discrepancies were found between American and Hungarian students in the study by Engländer et al. The Hungarians perceived much lower risks from 84 of 90 activities. Within each country, the relative ordering of concerns was also different. Hungarians saw relatively greater risks from common hazards such as railroads, boating, home appliances and mushroom hunting, whereas the Americans were relatively more concerned with technological hazards pertaining to radiation and chemical technologies. Turning to non-student populations, Gould et al (1988) studied representative samples of 1320 individuals living in New England and the South-west US in a replication of our earlier studies. Kunreuther, Easterling, Desvousges and Slovic (1990) conducted a national telephone survey in the US, focusing on attitudes and perceptions associated with a nuclear waste repository. We have also conducted large psychometric surveys of the general public in Sweden (Slovic, Kraus, Lappe, Letzel & Malmfors, 1989), Canada (Slovic, Kraus, Lappe & Major, 1991; Krewski, Slovic, Bartlett, Flynn & Mertz, 1995a, 1995b), France (Slovic, Flynn, Mertz, Mays & Poumadère, 1996), and the US (Slovic et al, 1996; Flynn, Slovic & Mertz, 1994; Finucane, Slovic, Mertz, Flynn & Satterfield, 2000). An important finding to come from these studies was the large difference in risk perceptions of men and women (Flynn et al, 1994; see Chapter 25).

New Hazard Domains

The earliest psychometric studies were distinguished by their comparisons of large sets of hazards containing items as diverse as bicycles and nuclear power plants. Many subsequent surveys have been dedicated to hazards within the same domain – starting with Kraus and Slovic (1988b), who examined perceptions of 49 railroad accident scenarios. Slovic, MacGregor and Kraus (1987) examined perceptions of risk for 40 structural defects in automobiles of the kind that compel manufacturers to initiate a recall campaign (see Chapter 12). Still other studies within our program have concentrated on perceptions of risks from medicines (Slovic, 1989; see Chapter 15), risks to the natural environment (McDaniels, Axelrod & Slovic, 1995), risks associated with electric and magnetic fields (Morgan et al, 1985; MacGregor, Slovic & Morgan, 1994), risks from earthquakes (Flynn, Slovic, Mertz & Carlisle, 1999), risks in investing (MacGregor, Slovic, Berry & Evensky, 1999), risks from asteroids colliding with Earth (Morrison, Chapman & Slovic, 1994), other risks associated with automobiles (MacGregor & Slovic, 1989), risks from transferring materials between Mars and Earth (MacGregor & Slovic, 1995), and risks from the storage and transportation of nuclear wastes (Kunreuther et al, 1990; Slovic, Flynn & Layman, 1991 – see Chapter 17; Slovic, Layman, Kraus et al, 1991; MacGregor, Slovic, Mason et al, 1994). Benthin, Slovic and Severson (1993), Benthin et al (1995 – see Chapter 20), and Slovic (1998 – see Chapter 23) studied adolescents' perceptions of risk from activities that put them at risk, such as smoking, drinking alcohol and using drugs.

New Forms of Risk Impact – Stigma

In 1986, we were afforded the opportunity to work with an interdisciplinary team of social scientists in what was the largest social-impact assessment project ever attempted. The task was in some sense an impossible one – to forecast the social and economic impacts on residents and communities in southern Nevada in the event that the nation's high-level nuclear waste repository was sited, built and put into operation at Yucca Mountain, Nevada. As we sought to find some way to approach this daunting task, we came upon the concept of *stigma*. When we examined this concept, it became evident that stigmatization is closely associated with perception of risk (see Chapter 21).

Goffman (1963) noted that the word stigma was used by the ancient Greeks to refer to bodily marks or brands that were designed to expose infamy or disgrace – for example, to indicate that the bearer of the mark was a slave or criminal. As it is used today, the word denotes someone 'marked' as deviant, flawed, limited, spoiled or generally undesirable in the view of some observer. Such individuals have attributes that do not accord with prevailing standards of the normal and the good. They are denigrated and avoided.

Jones et al (1984) attempted to characterize the key dimensions of social stigma. The six dimensions or factors they proposed were as follows:

1   *Concealability*. Is the condition hidden or obvious? To what extent is its visibility controllable?
2   *Course*. What pattern of change over time is usually shown by the condition? What is its ultimate outcome?
3   *Disruptiveness*. Does the condition block or hamper interaction and communication?
4   *Aesthetic qualities*. To what extent does the mark make the possessor repellent, ugly or upsetting?
5   *Origin*. Under what circumstances did the condition originate? Was anyone responsible for it, and what was he or she trying to do?
6   *Peril*. What kind of danger is posed by the mark and how imminent and serious is it?

Dimension 6, peril, is the key link between stigma and perceived risk, but the other dimensions may also come into play in the stigmatization of hazards. It seems evident that stigmatization can be generalized from persons to products, technologies and environments. For example, nuclear and chemical waste-disposal sites may be perceived as repellent, ugly and upsetting (dimension 4) to the extent that they become visible (dimension 1). Such waste sites may also be perceived as disruptive (dimension 3). They are certainly perceived as dangerous (dimension 6).

'What is the potential for a high-level nuclear waste repository at Yucca Mountain to stigmatize the city of Las Vegas and the state of Nevada, thus harming the economy in those places?' To answer this question, we proposed a model in which stigma is based upon negative imagery that has become associated with places, products, technologies and, of course, people (Slovic, Layman, Kraus et al, 1991). When we think of the prime targets for stigmatization in our society – members of minority groups, the aged, homosexuals, drug addicts and persons afflicted with physical deformities and mental disabilities – we can appreciate the affect-laden images that are associated with such individuals.

To test this model of stigma, studies were designed to develop a measure of environmental imagery, assess the relationship between imagery and choice behavior, and describe economic impacts that might occur as a result of altered images and choices. The results supported the proposed relationship between images, affect, decision-making and stigma (Slovic, Layman, Kraus et al, 1991).

Specifically, this research supported three propositions pertaining to Yucca Mountain: images of cities and states, derived from a word-association technique, exhibited positive and negative affective meanings that were highly predictive of preferences for vacation sites, job and retirement locations, and business sites (proposition 1). The concept of a nuclear-waste storage facility evoked extreme negative imagery (proposition 2) indicative of stigmatization. Dominant associations to a repository were 'dangerous', 'death', 'pollution', 'bad', 'undesirable' and 'somewhere else'. The nuclear-weapons test site, which has been around far longer than the Yucca Mountain nuclear-waste project, resulted in a modest amount of nuclear imagery becoming associated with the state of Nevada. This provided indirect evidence for proposition 3, which asserts that nuclear-waste related images will also become associated with Nevada and Las Vegas if the Yucca Mountain project proceeds. Moreover, nuclear imagery, when present in a person's associations with Nevada, was found to be linked with a much lower preference for Nevada as a vacation site, indicative of a stigmatization response. Slovic, Layman, Kraus et al (1991) concluded that, were development and operation of the Yucca Mountain site to proceed, any problems associated with the repository would have the potential to link the repository, things nuclear and many other highly negative images with the state of Nevada and the city of Las Vegas. Increased negativity of imagery could possibly lead to serious impacts on tourism, migration and economic development in the southern Nevada region.

Nuclear facilities are not the only technologies with highly stigmatizing imagery. The image of chemical technologies is so stigmatized that when we asked college students or members of the general public to tell us what first comes to mind when they hear the word 'chemicals', by far the most frequent response was 'dangerous' or some similar response (eg, toxic, hazardous, poison, deadly, cancer); beneficial uses of chemicals were rarely mentioned (Slovic, 1992). It is, therefore, not surprising that national surveys have found that up to 75% of the public agrees with the statement: 'I try hard to avoid contact with chemicals and chemical products in my everyday life' (Krewski et al, 1995b).

Although stigmatizing images are created through direct experiences such as bad odors, ugly landscapes, accidents, illnesses, etc, the greatest contributor to stigma, by far, is the news media, through the social amplification process (see Chapter 14). Some well-known examples of events resulting in strong social amplification impacts include the chemical manufacturing accident at Bhopal, India; the disastrous launch of the space shuttle *Challenger*; the nuclear-reactor accidents at Three Mile Island and Chernobyl; the adverse effects of the drug Thalidomide; the *Exxon Valdez* oil spill; the adulteration of Tylenol capsules with cyanide; and the BSE (mad cow) scare in the United Kingdom. An important feature of social amplification is that the direct impacts need not be too large to trigger major indirect impacts. The seven deaths due to Tylenol tampering resulted in more than 125,000 stories in the print media alone, and inflicted losses of more than $1 billion upon the Johnson & Johnson Company, due to the damaged image of the product (Mitchell, 1989).

Therefore, we see that, just as environments can become stigmatized by risk problems, so can products (Tylenol, the IUD, the Pinto) and their manufacturers (Johnson & Johnson, A H Robbins, Ford Motor Company). Union Carbide undoubtedly became stigmatized because of the Bhopal accident and Exxon as well because of the oil spill at Valdez, Alaska.

Episodes of stigmatization such as the Tylenol, Alar and BSE scares are noteworthy because they illustrate a new form of societal vulnerability. While human health was the primary vulnerable commodity in the past, increasing technical and medical sophistication, combined with hypervigilant monitoring systems to detect incipient problems, make such problems less likely now. But the price of this vigilance, based in no small part upon the incredible ability of modern media to 'spread the word', is the impact that this information itself has upon social, political, industrial and economic systems. Thus we live in a world in which information, acting in concert with the vagaries of human perception and cognition, has reduced our susceptibility to accidents and diseases at the cost of increasing our vulnerability to massive social and economic catastrophes. Is this latter vulnerability inevitable? What might be done to reduce it without losing the benefits of hypervigilant warning systems? A number of potential strategies for reducing vulnerability to stigma are sketched by Kunreuther and Slovic (in press).

TOWARD DEEPER LEVELS OF PSYCHOLOGICAL ANALYSIS

Mental Models

One strength of the psychometric approach is its broad descriptive capability. This is illustrated, at the extreme, by the well-known plot of 81 hazards within the two-dimensional space defined by dread risk as one factor and unknown risk as the other (see Figure 13.1). This single figure represents a synthesis of more than 30,000 individual ratings. Such breadth carries with it, of necessity, a limitation. The analyses lack depth. They provide only a surface level of description that leaves many important questions unanswered. For example, why wouldn't motorists wear seat belts until they were mandated by law? Why do adolescents engage in so many dangerous activities, even those that they supposedly recognize as risky (eg, smoking cigarettes)? Why do we dread risks from chemicals (except for medicines) but not auto accidents? Why do we fear radiation exposures from nuclear wastes but not from radon in our homes? How, and why, do individuals differ in their perceptions of risks?

Answers to these sorts of questions require different methods of analysis – methods which may afford deeper understanding of specific issues rather than broad, but shallow, representations. One important approach, pioneered and successfully applied by researchers at Carnegie-Mellon University, has used extensive open-ended interviews to construct influence diagrams and 'mental models' depicting people's knowledge, attitudes, beliefs, values, perceptions and inference mechanisms with regard to specific hazards such as radon and global climate change (see, for example, Bostrom, Fischhoff & Morgan, 1992; Atman, Bostrom, Fischhoff & Morgan, 1994; Bostrom, Morgan, Fischhoff & Read, 1994).

One of our first attempts along this line aimed to provide insight into two questions:

1   Why are people reluctant to insure their property against natural hazards?
2   Why won't motorists wear seat belts?

Both of these questions involve insurance in the face of low-probability, high-consequence events. A combination of experimental studies and questionnaires, as described in Chapters 3 and 4, led us to conclude that perceived probability of loss was the critical factor for triggering both types of protective behaviors – purchasing insurance and buckling one's seat belt. The seat-belt question sensitized us to the importance of considering perceptions of risks that cumulate over a large number of exposures. For the driver, the probability of a serious accident on the very next trip is rather small, but the probability of such an accident occurring sometime during the approximately 50,000 trips taken in one's lifetime may be quite high. A similar concern regarding perception of risk for single versus multiple exposures also led us to examine the psychology of risk perceptions among adolescent smokers (Chapter 23). There we concluded that, in many important ways, young people did not really understand or appreciate the risks they were taking by smoking. They believed, often incorrectly, that they would smoke only for a short while and then quit before cigarettes caused them any serious harm.

Intuitive Toxicology

We have also gone beyond the psychometric approach in an attempt to describe and compare the mental models of experts and laypersons regarding the effects of chemicals on human health. Given the importance of chemical technologies in our daily lives, the extreme negative perceptions of chemical risks held by so many people is nothing short of astounding. This negativity of perceptions is especially significant in light of the immense scientific and regulatory efforts that have been designed to reduce public exposure to, and harm from, chemicals. Billions of dollars have been spent on risk-assessment studies by toxicologists and epidemiologists. Massive regulatory bureaucracies have been formed to oversee the use of these risk assessments for standard setting and risk management.

Yet, despite this enormous effort, people in the US and many other industrialized nations see themselves as increasingly vulnerable to the risks from chemical technologies and believe that the worst is yet to come. Regulatory agencies have become embroiled in rancorous conflicts, caught between a fearful and dissatisfied public on the one side and frustrated industrialists and technologists on the other. Industry sees an urgent need to communicate with the public but often does not know how to do so (see Chapter 11).

Nancy Kraus, Torbjörn Malmfors and I approached this problem from a perspective that we labeled 'intuitive toxicology' (see Chapters 18 and 25). Humans have always been intuitive toxicologists, relying on their senses of sight, taste and smell to detect unsafe food, water and air. The science of toxicology has been developed to supplement and, in many cases, replace our sensory systems. However, as an influential report by the National Academy of Sciences indicated (National Academy of Sciences, 1983), toxicological risk assessment itself is inherently subjective, relying heavily upon assumptions and judgment.

The objective of our research was to explore the cognitive models, assumptions and inference methods that comprise laypeople's 'intuitive toxicological theories' and to compare these theories with the cognitive models, assumptions and inference methods of scientific toxicology and risk assessment. Such comparisons have exposed the specific similarities and differences within expert communities as well as the similarities and differences between lay perceptions and expert views. For example, whereas toxicologists give great importance to considerations of exposure and dose when evaluating chemical risks, laypeople tend to believe that any exposure to a toxic substance or carcinogen, no matter how small, is likely to prove harmful. Another important finding was the divergence of opinion among toxicologists on questions pertaining to the reliability and validity of animal tests for assessing the risks that chemicals pose to humans (see Chapters 18 and 25). This lack of confidence in the science may be a significant cause of the public's anxiety and distrust. We also observed a strong 'affiliation bias' indicating that toxicologists who work for industry see chemicals as more benign than do their counterparts in academia and government. Compared to other experts, industrial toxicologists were somewhat more confident in the general validity of animal tests – except when those tests were said to provide evidence for carcinogenicity – in which case many of the industrial experts changed their opinions about the tests being valid. Similar results have been found in follow-up studies in Canada (Slovic et al, 1995) and in the UK (Slovic, Malmfors, Mertz, Neil & Purchase, 1997; see also Lynn, 1987). Together, these various studies clearly show the influence of personal and organizational values on risk assessment. In sum, the knowledge gained from these studies of intuitive toxicology appears to provide a valuable starting point around which to structure discussion, education and communication about chemical risk assessment.

The Affect Heuristic

Two important findings from the earliest psychometric studies were not adequately appreciated and lay somewhat dormant for two decades, until additional findings led them to be recognized as key links in a theory about the role of affective processes in judgment, decision-making and risk perception. Fischhoff, Slovic, Lichtenstein, Read et al (1978; see Chapter 5) noted in passing that perceived risk declined as perceived benefit increased. They also found that the characteristic most highly correlated with perceived risk was the degree to which a hazard evoked feelings of dread. The inverse relationship between perceived risk and perceived benefit and the importance of dread has subsequently been confirmed in numerous other studies (see, for example, McDaniels et al, 1997 and Slovic, Flynn & Layman, 1991 – Chapter 17).

Although risk perception was originally viewed as a form of deliberative, analytic information processing, over time we have come to recognize just how highly dependent it is upon intuitive and experiential thinking, guided by emotional and affective processes. This recognition has occurred as a consequence of many streams of research. One of these streams includes the work of psychologist Seymour Epstein (1994), who observed:

> There is no dearth of evidence in everyday life that people apprehend reality in two fundamentally different ways, one variously labeled intuitive, automatic, natural, non-verbal, narrative and experiential, and the other analytical, deliberative, verbal and rational (p710).

One of the characteristics of the experiential system is its reliance on affect. Affect is a subtle form of emotion, defined as positive (like) or negative (dislike) evaluative feelings toward an external stimulus (such as a cigarette, or the act of smoking).[2] Such evaluations occur rapidly and automatically – note how quickly you sense an affective response toward the word 'beautiful' or the word 'hate'. Although deliberation and analysis is certainly important in many decision-making circumstances, reliance on affect and emotion is a quicker, easier and more efficient way to navigate in a complex, uncertain and sometimes dangerous world.

In addition to Epstein, many other students of motivation, learning, memory and social cognition have long had an interest in affect. Particularly important has been the work of Hobart Mowrer (1960a, b) on images and conditioned emotions and the more recent work of neurologist Antonio Damasio (1994) on affective disorders in people with certain types of brain damage.

A strong early proponent of the importance of affect in decision-making was Zajonc (1980) who argued that affective reactions to stimuli are often the very first reactions, occurring automatically and subsequently guiding information processing and judgment. Other important work on affect and decision-making has been done by Isen (1993), Johnson and Tversky (1983), Janis and Mann (1977), Kahneman and Snell (1990), Mellers, Schwartz, Ho and Ritov (1996), Loewenstein (1996), Loewenstein, Weber, Hsee and Welch (1999), Rozin, Haidt and McCauley (1993), and Wilson et al (1993).

We can now see that affect is linked to risk perception in many ways. As noted above, feelings of dread and the many other influential characteristics linked with dread in the factor analysis of risk perception (eg, risks being involuntary, uncontrollable, inequitable, catastrophic, fatal) reflect the importance of affect. So does the work showing stigma to be driven by affect-laden images associated with nuclear power, nuclear waste, chemicals and other hazards (see Chapters 17 and 21). Research by Peters and Slovic (1996) examined data from a national telephone survey and found that affect-laden imagery was highly predictive of perceived risk from nuclear power and support for (or opposition to) that technology. Affect measures were created by asking people to produce word associations to the stimulus 'nuclear power' and then to rate these associations on an affective scale ranging from very bad to very good. Similarly, Benthin et al (see Chapter 20) also studied imagery derived from word associations and found that the affective valence of that imagery was useful for understanding what motivates adolescents to participate in health-threatening and health-enhancing behaviors.

A significant step toward understanding the importance of affect for risk perception was taken by Alhakami and Slovic (1994), who observed that the inverse relationship between perceived risk and perceived benefit was linked to an individual's general affective evaluation of a hazard. If an activity was 'liked', people tended to judge its benefits as high and its risks as low. If the activity was 'disliked', the judgments were opposite – low benefit and high risk.

Building upon the Alhakami and Slovic study, Finucane et al (see Chapter 26) collected experimental data supporting the proposal that people use an *affect heuristic* when judging risk. According to this model, people consult or refer to an 'affective pool' containing all the positive and negative images associated with the object or activity being judged. In other words, the inverse relationship between risk and benefit evaluations occurs because they are derived from a common affective source.

Although it is tempting to conclude that these studies demonstrate that laypeople's perceptions of risk are derived from emotion rather than reason, and hence should not be respected, such a conclusion is incorrect. Research shows that affective and emotional processes interact with reason-based analysis in all normal thinking and, indeed, are essential to rationality (Damasio, 1994). It is not surprising, therefore, to find evidence for these very same affective processes at work in the judgments of scientists such as toxicologists (see Chapter 25).

This is not to say, however, that our affective reactions might not, in some cases, mislead us. For example, studies of programs designed to save human lives, including the investigation by Fetherstonhaugh et al (Chapter 24), find that people's support for such programs is determined more by the proportion of lives saved (relative to the population at risk) than by the actual number of lives expected to be saved. Thus, for example, a program that is expected to save 4500 lives out of 11,000 at risk will likely be judged more favorably than a program that is expected to save 10,000 lives out of 100,000 at risk (assuming that the programs are judged individually by each of two separate groups of people). This may be due to our inability to respond differently in an emotional or affective sense to the prospects of 4500 versus 10,000 deaths – a phenomenon that Fetherstonhaugh et al labeled 'psychophysical numbing'. This affective miscalibration is well captured in the observation of Nobel laureate Albert Szent-Gyorgi:

> I am deeply moved if I see one man suffering and would risk my life for him. Then I talk impersonally about the possible pulverization of our big cities, with a hundred million dead. I am unable to multiply one man's suffering by a hundred million.

SOCIOPOLITICAL AND CULTURAL DETERMINERS OF PERCEIVED RISK

The study of risk perception began as an exercise in individual psychology and this perspective continues to develop through the study of mental models and affective processes. However, research has also demonstrated that there are important social, political and cultural factors that play important roles in the story.

Early work showed that the public has a broad, multidimensional conception of risk that incorporates into the risk equation considerations such as voluntariness, controllability, catastrophic potential, equity and threat to future generations. We subsequently came to appreciate that these considerations raise questions about social values that are relevant to risk-policy decisions. For example, is a risk imposed on a child more serious than a known risk accepted voluntarily by an adult? Are the deaths of 50 passengers in separate automobile accidents equivalent to the deaths of 50 passengers in one airplane crash? As our research, and research by others, proceeded, we observed that values interacted with worldviews, gender and trust in ways that further supported a sociopolitical and cultural perspective on risk.

Worldviews

According to Dake (1991; 1992) worldviews, defined as general attitudes toward the world and its social organization, are 'orienting dispositions', serving to guide people's responses in complex situations. As such, they were found by Dake and others to be instrumental in determining people's risk attitudes and perceptions.

Our studies extended and confirmed Dake's observations. A national survey analyzed by Peters and Slovic (1996) and reported in Chapter 25 found that people holding an egalitarian preference for wealth and power to be distributed equally in society had higher perceived risk for a wide range of hazards and were particularly concerned about nuclear power. People who prefer a hierarchical social order, in which experts and authorities are in control, had much lower perceptions of risk and more favorable attitudes toward nuclear power. Peters and Slovic concluded that both affect and worldviews functioned as orienting dispositions helping people assess and respond to risk. Experts' judgments, like those of laypersons, have also been found to be influenced by worldviews and affect (see Chapter 25).[3]

To the extent that our judgments and actions are influenced by 'non-technical' factors, such as worldviews and affect, we can appreciate why the communication of technical information often has little effect on citizens' attitudes toward hazards such as nuclear power plants or nuclear waste repositories. Our attitudes toward nuclear power are part of who we are. We cannot change these attitudes without changing our social worldviews and our emotional makeup as well.

Gender – the White Male Effect

Almost every study of risk perception has found that men seem to be less concerned about hazards than are women. What is less clear is why this should be the case. Hints about the origin of these differences come from a survey of 1500 Americans by Flynn, Slovic and Mertz (1994), which is described in Chapter 25. As expected, males perceived risks to be smaller than females for all 25 hazards studied. However, non-white males and females did not differ greatly in their perceptions – the gender effect was found to be driven by about 30% of the white male population who saw all risks as extremely small. This finding has subsequently been replicated in another national survey of the US population by Finucane et al (2000). In this study, white males differed significantly from others in perceived risk even when age, income and education were taken into account.

The gender effect does not seem to be a simple matter of biology. If it were, we would expect to see similar differences between males and females of all races. Also doubtful is an explanation based primarily upon differences in scientific literacy or education because men and women scientists have been found to differ in ways similar to the differences among laypeople.

Perhaps the best explanation may be that the roles of gender and race in perceived risk are strongly related to a range of social and political factors. When Flynn et al compared the low-risk white males with the rest of the respondents, they were found to hold very different attitudes, characterized by trust in experts and by anti-egalitarianism, including disinclination toward giving decision-making power to citizens in areas of risk management. Similar findings were found by Finucane et al.

These findings lead naturally to the hypothesis that differences in worldviews, trust, control and other sociopolitical factors could be key determinants of gender and race differences in risk judgments, and that risk perceptions may reflect deep-seated values about technology and its impact on society. White males may perceive less risk than others because they are more involved in creating, managing, controlling and benefiting from technology and other activities that are hazardous. Women and non-white men may perceive greater risk because they tend to have less control over these activities and benefit less from them. Indeed, risk perceptions seem to be related to individuals' power to influence decisions about the use of hazards (see also Gustafson, 1998).

Risk and Trust

The research described above has painted a portrait of risk perception influenced by the interplay of psychological, social and political factors. Members of the public and experts may disagree about risk because they define risk differently and have different worldviews, different affective experiences and reactions or different social status. Another reason why the public often rejects scientists' risk assessments is lack of trust. Trust in risk management, like risk perception, has been found to correlate with gender, race, worldviews and affect.

Social relationships of all types, including risk management, rely heavily on trust. Indeed, much of the contentiousness that has been observed in the risk-management arena has been attributed to a climate of distrust that exists between the public, industry and risk-management professionals (eg, Slovic, 1993; Slovic, Flynn & Layman, 1991 – Chapter 17). The limited effectiveness of risk-communication efforts can be attributed to the lack of trust. If you trust the risk manager, communication is relatively easy. If trust is lacking, no form or process of communication will be satisfactory (Fessenden-Raden, Fitchen & Heath, 1987).

Chapter 19 describes an empirical study by Slovic (1993) demonstrating an 'asymmetry principle'. Trust in risk management is easier to destroy than to create. The study goes on to argue that this asymmetry, which is based upon psychological reactions, is amplified through the workings of our open and highly participatory democratic system of government, with the media and special interest groups being quite skilled in bringing trust-destroying news to public attention. The problem is compounded by the fact that, in the US, risk-management tends to rely heavily upon an adversarial legal system that pits expert against expert, contradicting each other's risk assessments and further destroying the public trust.[4] In sum, our social and democratic institutions, admirable as they are in many respects, breed distrust in the risk arena.

RESOLVING RISK CONFLICTS: WHERE DO WE GO FROM HERE?

One certainly hopes that more than two decades of research on the perception of risk would lead to new insights and changes in perspective that would contribute to conflict resolution and improved risk management. I believe this has occurred. When we began this odyssey, risk assessment seemed rather straightforward and non-controversial – a matter of combining models and data to calculate probabilities, expected losses and actual injuries and fatalities. Perception studies, rooted in cognitive psychology and stimulated by new and exciting research on judgmental heuristics and biases, set out to investigate the degree to which these biases distorted judgments of risk (see, for example, Chapters 1, 2, 8 and 9). We accepted statistical data and model estimates as representative of 'real risks' that could be compared with risk perceptions.

As the technical approach to risk assessment blossomed, it became apparent that its depiction of the real risks did not always prevail in bitter and protracted controversies regarding the management of nuclear power plants, nuclear wastes, chemicals and new hazards such as those associated with biotechnologies. Studies of perception naturally began to focus on these conflicts in the 'risk assessment battlefield' where differences of opinion between experts and the public, as well as differences among experts and among laypersons, were striking and quite resistant to change.

Research on risk perception has gradually illuminated many of the causes of these conflicts. In doing so, it has exhibited a clear progression away from the simple views in the initial studies of perception to an increasingly complex conception of risk and its assessment as a socially constructed phenomenon. Chapter 25 entitled 'Trust, Emotion, Sex, Politics and Science: Surveying the Risk-assessment Battlefield', attempts to portray this new view and to describe some of its implications for risk management.

One of the most important conclusions in Chapter 25 is that risk is inherently subjective. In this view, risk does not exist 'out there', independent of our minds and cultures, waiting to be measured. Instead, human beings have invented the concept *risk* to help them to understand and cope with the dangers and uncertainties of life. Although these dangers are real, there is no such thing as real risk or objective risk. Even the simplest, most straightforward risk assessments are based on theoretical models, whose structure is subjective and assumption-laden and whose inputs are dependent upon judgment.

At the same time, risk-perception research has demonstrated that non-scientists have their own models, assumptions and subjective assessment techniques (intuitive risk assessments), which are sometimes very different from the scientists' models. Early studies showed that public concerns could be traced to sensitivity toward technical, social and psychological qualities of hazards that are not well modeled in technical risk assessments. The important role of social values in risk perception thus became apparent. Further research reinforced and extended this view, documenting the influence of worldviews, gender and trust, and their social and political overtones. Scientists' judgments of risk were also found to be sensitive toward some of these non-technical social and cultural factors, including affiliation effects.

Chapter 25 summarizes this complex view and argues for a new perspective on risk and new approaches to risk management. Whoever controls the definition of risk controls the rational solution to the problem at hand. If you define risk one way, then one option will rise to the top as the most cost effective, or the safest or the best. If you define it another way, perhaps incorporating qualitative characteristics and other contextual factors, you will likely get a different ordering of your action solutions (Fischhoff, Watson & Hope, 1984). Defining risk is thus an exercise in power.

Scientific literacy and public education are important, but they are not central to risk controversies. The public is not irrational. The public is influenced by emotion and affect in a way that is both simple and sophisticated. So are scientists. The public is influenced by worldviews, ideologies and values. So are scientists, particularly when they are working at the limits of their expertise.

The limitations of risk science, the importance and difficulty of maintaining trust, and the subjective and contextual nature of risk point to the need for a new approach – one that focuses on introducing more public participation into both risk assessment and risk decision-making to make the decision process more democratic, to improve the relevance and quality of technical analysis, and increase the legitimacy and public acceptance of the resulting decisions.

Drawing upon insights from the study of risk perception, scholars and practitioners in Europe and North America have begun to lay the foundations for improved methods of risk decision-making using deliberative processes that include negotiation, mediation, oversight committees and other forms of public input and involvement (National Research Council, 1996). Recognizing interested and affected citizens as legitimate partners in the exercise of risk assessment is no short-term panacea for the problems of risk management. But serious attention to participation and process issues may, in the long run, lead to more satisfying and successful ways to manage risk.

Paul Slovic
Eugene, Oregon

Notes

1. The word *perception* is used here and in the literature to refer to various kinds of attitudes and judgments.
2. Affect may be viewed as a feeling state that people experience, such as happiness or sadness. It may also be viewed as a quality (eg, goodness or badness) assigned to a stimulus. These two conceptions tend to be related. The research described here has been concerned with both of these aspects of affect.
3. Some researchers have observed that the correlations between worldviews and risk perceptions are weak since they account for a rather small percentage of variance when looked at from the perspective of r^2 (see, for example, Sjöberg, 1997, or Brenot, Bonnefous & Marris, 1998). However, Slovic and Peters (1998) demonstrated that r^2 is not a proper measure of the strength of such relationships. When more appropriate measures are used, the magnitude of worldview effects is often substantial (see, for example, Table 25.3 and Figure 25.6 in this book).
4. This is, of course, a simplified version of the trust story. For an alternative view, the reader is encouraged to examine the work of Earle and Cvetkovich (1995).

1 Decision Processes, Rationality and Adjustment to Natural Hazards

Paul Slovic, Howard Kunreuther and Gilbert F White

The distress and disruption caused by extreme natural events has stimulated considerable interest in understanding and improving the decision-making processes that determine a manager's adjustment to natural hazards. Technological solutions to the problem of coping with hazards have typically been justified by a computation of benefits and costs that assume the people involved will behave in what the policy-maker considers to be an economically rational way. However, it has slowly become evident that technological solutions, by themselves, are inadequate without knowledge of how they will affect decision-making. In reviewing the wide range of adjustments to Gangetic floods or Nigerian drought or Norwegian avalanche, it has been observed that attempts to control nature and determine government policy will not succeed without a better understanding of the interplay among psychological, economic and environmental factors as they determine the adjustment process.

Throughout this chapter we shall use the terms 'decision-maker' and 'manager' synonymously. Managers are defined as individuals who act in the management of an establishment. An establishment is defined as a single residence, agricultural, commercial or public-service organization that has distinct use of an area. The term 'adjustments' refers to the many courses of action available to the manager for coping with natural hazards. For example, in the case of floods, potential adjustments include bearing the loss, insurance, land elevation, structural works (such as dams) and public relief.

By assuming that managers are rational and that they act according to the same decision criteria that public agencies prescribe, government programs to reduce hazards have been based upon predictions that often failed to materialize. These failures have been attributed to the ignorance and irrationality of the occupants of a hazard zone; but recent work suggests that adjustments to hazards may be understandable and, in a sense, reasonable, within the framework of decision models different from the traditional optimization models. One such model is that of 'bounded rationality', which takes into account limitations of the decision-maker's perceptual and cognitive capabilities. The need for an improved understanding of the decision-making process is urgent and is at the heart of systematic improvement of public policy. Such improvement becomes increasingly significant as man intervenes still further in natural processes and thereby opens himself to further hazard from their variability and uncertainty.

AIMS AND ORGANIZATION

This chapter focuses on cognitive elements of decision-making under risk that are important for understanding adjustment to natural hazards in a modern technological society. It includes such topics as human understanding of probabilistic events, perception of hazards and the processes involved in balancing risks and benefits when choosing among alternative modes of adjustment to hazard. The phenomena to be reviewed are, for the most part, likely to generalize across cultures and across individuals and are likely to increase understanding of adjustments to man-made hazards as well as natural ones. This cognitive emphasis is not meant to deny the obvious importance of personality, cultural and social factors in determining adjustments to natural hazards. The influence of culturally ingrained attitudes toward nature and toward fate is illustrated by Burton and Kates (1964), Baumann and Sims (1972), Parra (1971) and others. The effects of community organization are reviewed by Barton (1970). Individual personality factors that influence adjustment to hazards are discussed by Schiff (1970) and Burton (1972). The reader interested in a model of the interrelationships among cognitive, personality and cultural factors in the context of adjustment to natural hazards should see Kates (1970).

The organization of the chapter is as follows. It begins with a brief overview of the leading normative and descriptive theories of decision-making. Particular emphasis is given to a comparison between a decision theory that espouses maximization of expected utility as a normative guideline and a conceptualization of bounded rationality that has both normative and descriptive intent. The next section presents evidence from the psychological laboratory and data from field observations of adjustment to natural hazards to document the usefulness of the notion of bounded rationality as a framework for understanding adjustment to hazards. Whenever possible, related data from laboratory and field are juxtaposed to highlight the generality and importance of these phenomena. The picture that emerges from this work illustrates some rather startling limitations in the ability of the decision-maker to think in probabilistic terms and to bring relevant information to bear on his or her judgments. However, the knowledge gained about human cognitive limitations has implications for improving the decision-making process. These implications are discussed in the latter part of the chapter.

Theories of Decision-making under Risk

Maximization of Expected Utility

The objective of decision theory is to provide a rationale for making wise decisions under conditions of risk and uncertainty. It is normative in intent, concerned with prescribing the course of action that will conform most fully to the decision-maker's own goals, expectations and values. Since good expositions of decision theory are available elsewhere (Coombs, Dawes & Tversky, 1970; Dillon, 1971; Luce & Raiffa, 1957; Savage, 1954), the coverage here will be quite brief.

Decisions under uncertainty are typically represented by a payoff matrix, in which the rows correspond to alternative acts that the decision-maker can select and the columns correspond to possible states of nature. In the cells of the payoff matrix are one set of consequences contingent upon the joint occurrence of a decision and a state of nature. A simple illustration for a traveler is given in Table 1.1.

Since it is impossible to make a decision that will turn out best in any eventuality, decision theorists view choice alternatives as gambles and try to choose according to the 'best bet'. In 1738, Bernoulli defined the notion of a best bet as one that maximizes the 'expected utility' of the decision. That is, it maximizes the quantity:

$$EU(A) = \sum_{i=1}^{n} P(E_i) U(X_i)$$

where $EU(A)$ represents the expected utility of a course of action which has consequences $X_1, X_2, \ldots X_n$ depending on events $E_1, E_2, \ldots E_n$, $P(E_i)$ represents the probability of the ith outcome of that action, and $U(X_i)$ represents the subjective value or utility of that outcome. If we assume that the parenthesized values in the cells of Table 1.1 represent the traveler's utilities for the various consequences, and if the probability of sun and rain are taken to be .6 and .4 respectively, we can compute the expected utility for each action as follows:

$$EU(A_1) = .6(+1) + .4(+1) = 1.0$$
$$EU(A_2) = .6(+2) + .4(0) = 1.2$$

In this situation, leaving the umbrella has greater expected utility than taking it along. The same form of analysis can be applied to computing the expected utility of heeding a flood warning (Shrewsbury, 1974), planting drought-resistant

Table 1.1 *Example of a Payoff Matrix*

	State of nature	
Alternatives	*Sun* (E_1)	*Rain* (E_2)
A_1 Carry umbrella	(+1) stay dry carrying umbrella	(+1) stay dry carrying umbrella
A_2 Leave umbrella	(+2) dry and unburdened	(0) wet and unburdened

maize in Kenya (Wisner & Mbithi, 1974) or protecting against frost in Florida (Ward, 1974).

A major advance in decision theory came when von Neumann and Morgenstern (1947) developed a formal justification for the expected utility criterion. They showed that if an individual's preferences satisfied certain basic axioms of rational behavior, then his decisions could be described as the maximization of expected utility. Savage (1954) later generalized the theory to allow the $P(E_i)$ values to represent subjective or personal probabilities.

Maximization of expected utility commands respect as a guideline for wise behavior because it is deduced from axiomatic principles that presumably would be accepted by any rational man. One such principle, that of *transitivity*, is usually defined on outcomes but applies equally well to actions or probabilities. It asserts that, if a decision-maker prefers outcome A to outcome B and outcome B to outcome C, it would be irrational for him to prefer outcome C to outcome A. Any individual who is deliberately and systematically intransitive can be used as a 'money pump'. You can say to him: 'I'll give you C. Now, for a penny, I'll take back C and give you B'. Since he prefers B to C, he accepts. Next you offer to replace B with A for another penny and again he accepts. The cycle is completed by offering to replace A by C for another penny; he accepts and is 3¢ poorer, back where he started and ready for another round.

A second important tenet of rationality, known as the *extended sure-thing principle*, states that, if an outcome X_i is the same for two risky actions, then the value of X_i should be disregarded in choosing between the two options. Another way to state this principle is that outcomes that are not affected by your choice should not influence your decision.

These two principles, combined with several others of technical importance, imply a rather powerful conclusion – namely that the wise decision-maker chooses that act whose expected utility is greatest. To do otherwise would violate one or more basic tenets of rationality.

Applied decision theory assumes that the rational decision-maker wishes to select an action that is logically consistent with his basic preferences for outcomes and his feelings about the likelihoods of the events upon which those outcomes depend. Given this assumption, the practical problem becomes one of listing the alternatives and scaling the subjective values of outcomes and their likelihoods so that subjective expected utility can be calculated for each alternative. Another problem in application arises from the fact that the range of theoretically possible alternatives is often quite large. In addition to carrying an umbrella, the risk-taking traveler in our earlier example may have the options of carrying a raincoat, getting a ride, waiting for the rain to stop and many others. Likewise, the outcomes are considerably more complex than in our simple example. For example, the consequences of building a dam are multiple, involving effects on flood potential, hydroelectric power, recreation and local ecology. Some specific approaches that have been developed for dealing with the additional complexities of any real decision situation will be discussed later.

Descriptive Decision Theory and Bounded Rationality

Although the maximization theory described above grew primarily out of normative concerns, a good deal of debate and empirical research has centered around the question of whether this theory could also describe both the goals that motivate actual decision-makers and the processes they employ when reaching their decisions. The leading critic of utility maximization as a descriptive theory has been Simon (1959, p272), who observed:

> The classical theory is a theory of a man choosing among fixed and known alternatives, to each of which is attached known consequences. But when perception and cognition intervene between the decision-maker and his objective environment, this model no longer proves adequate. We need a description of the choice process that recognizes that alternatives are not given but must be sought; and a description that takes into account the arduous task of determining what consequences will follow on each alternative.

As an alternative to the maximization hypothesis, Simon introduced the theory of 'bounded rationality', which asserts that the cognitive limitations of the decision-maker force him to construct a simplified model of the world to deal with it. The key principle of bounded rationality is the notion of 'satisficing', whereby an organism strives to attain some satisfactory, though not necessarily maximal, level of achievement. Simon (1956) conjectured that 'however adaptive the behavior of organisms in learning and choice situations, this adaptiveness falls far short of the ideal of "maximizing" postulated in economic theory. Evidently organisms adapt well enough to "satisfice"; they do not, in general, optimize' (p129).

The 'behavioral theory of the firm' proposed by Cyert and March (1963) elaborated the workings of bounded rationality in business organizations. Cyert and March argued that to understand decision-making in the firm we must recognize that there are multiple goals and we must understand the development of these goals, the manner in which the firm acts to satisfy them, and the procedures the firm employs to reduce uncertainty. They described how uncertainty is avoided by following fixed decision rules (standard operating procedures) whenever possible and reacting to short-run feedback rather than trying to forecast the future (which is too uncertain). Firms avoid the uncertainties of depending on other persons by negotiating implicit and explicit arrangements with suppliers, competitors and customers. A firm's search for new alternatives is triggered by a failure to satisfy one or more goals; thus a crisis is often required to spur corrective action. Cyert and March claim this short-run behavior is adaptive, given the complexity of the environment and the decision-maker's cognitive limitations.

At about the same time that Simon and Cyert and March were developing their ideas, Lindblom (1964) came to a similar conclusion on the basis of his analysis of governmental policy-making. Lindblom argued that administrators avoid the difficult task of taking all important factors into consideration and weighing their relative merits and drawbacks comprehensively by employing what he calls *the method of successive limited comparisons*. This method drastically simplifies decisions by comparing only those policies that differ in relatively small degree from policies already in effect. Thus, it is not necessary to undertake fundamental inquiry into an alternative and its consequences; one need study only those respects in which the proposed alternative and its consequences differ from the status quo. As an example, Lindblom cites the similarity between the major political parties in the US. They agree on fundamentals and offer only a few small points of difference. Lindblom refers to this conservative method as 'muddling through' and defends it as efficient and effective, although he admits that its use may cause good new policies to be overlooked, or worse – never even to be formulated.

Just as Cyert and March's business firms act and react on the basis of short-term feedback, Lindblom's policy-maker recognizes his inability to avoid error in predicting the consequences of policy moves. He thus attempts to proceed through a succession of small changes, oriented toward remedying a negatively perceived situation, rather than attaining a preconceived goal:

> His decision is only one step, one that if successful can quickly be followed by another...He is in effect able to test his previous predictions as he moves on to each further step. Lastly, he often can remedy a past error fairly quickly – more quickly than if policy proceeded through distinct steps widely spaced in time (Lindblom, 1964, p166).

Comparison of the Two Theories

Although utility theory is primarily normative in intent and bounded rationality has a descriptive character, this distinction is not completely accurate. There are those who argue that utility theory has some relevance for describing how decisions are actually made and, as we shall see later, the notion of bounded rationality has normative as well as descriptive implications.

Utility theory is concerned with probabilities, payoffs and the merger of these factors – expectation. The problem of comparing the worth of one consequence with the worth of another consequence is faced directly by translating both into a common scale of utility. The theory of bounded rationality, on the other hand, postulates that decision-makers do not think probabilistically and that they try to avoid the necessity of facing uncertainty directly. Likewise, they avoid the problems of evaluating utilities and comparing incommensurable features. The goal of the decision-maker is assumed to be the achievement of a satisfactory, rather than a maximum, outcome. Because he is constrained by limitations of perception and intelligence, the boundedly rational decision-maker is forced to proceed by trial and error, modifying plans that do not yield satisfactory outcomes and maintaining those that do until they fail.

Bounded Rationality and Adjustment to Natural Hazards

Several lines of evidence illustrate the workings of bounded rationality in the context of adjustment to natural hazards.

Limited range of alternatives

It is clear that the resource manager never has available the full range of alternatives from which to make a decision (White, 1961; 1964; 1970). Local regulations or cultural traditions eliminate some alternatives from consideration, and lack of awareness eliminates the others. Early studies of individual and public decisions regarding flood damage reduction, for example, revealed that the traditional choice for users of floodlands in the US has been simply to bear the loss or to encourage the government to construct engineering works to protect against flooding. Other adjustments such as structural changes in buildings and land-use changes were practiced, until recently, by relatively few managers and were typically ignored in public action.

Misperception of risks and denial of uncertainty

There are extensive data indicating that the risks of natural hazards are misjudged. For example, Burton and Kates (1964) pointed out that the estimates of hazards made by technical experts often fail to agree. As an illustration of this, they noted that three highly regarded methods of flood frequency analysis placed the long-run average return period of the largest flood on record in the Lehigh Valley as 27, 45 and 75 years.

Misperception of hazards by resource users is further illustrated by an extensive study of flood perception by Kates (1962), who interviewed occupants of locations for which detailed records of flood occurrences were available. The major findings related to the difficulties these floodplain dwellers had in interpreting the hazard within a probabilistic framework. Unlike the technical personnel, who never entirely discounted the possibility of a flood recurring in a previously flooded location, 84 out of 216 floodplain dwellers indicated they did not expect to be flooded in the future.

Close examination of the residents' views illustrated several systematic mechanisms for dispelling uncertainty. The most common of these was to view floods as repetitive, and even cyclical, phenomena. In this way, the randomness that characterizes the occurrence of the hazard is replaced by a determinate order in which history is seen as repeating itself at regular intervals (Burton & Kates, 1964). Another common view was the 'law of averages' approach, in which the occurrence of a severe flood in one year made it unlikely to recur the following year. Other occupants reduced uncertainty by means of various forms of denial. Some thought that new protective devices made them 100% safe. Others attributed previous floods to a freak combination of circumstances unlikely to recur. Still others denied that past events were floods, viewing them instead as 'high water'. Another mechanism was to deny the determinability of natural phenomena. For these people, all was in the hands of a higher power (God or the government). Thus, they did not need to trouble themselves with the problem of dealing with the uncertainty.

Crisis orientation

Just as Cyert and March's business firms and Lindblom's policy analysts appear to need direct experience with misfortune as a stimulus to action, so do resource managers. It has been observed: 'National catastrophes have led to insistent demands for national action, and the timing of the legislative process has been set by the tempo of destructive floods' (White, 1945, p24). Burton and Kates (1964) commented that, despite the self-image of the conservation movement as a conscious and rational attempt at long-range policy and planning, most of the major policy changes have arisen out of crises generated by catastrophic natural hazards. After interviewing floodplain residents, Kates (1962) concluded that it is only in areas where elaborate adjustments have evolved by repeated experiences that experience has been a teacher rather than a prison. He added: 'Floods need to be experienced, not only in magnitude, but in frequency as well. Without repeated experiences, the process whereby managers evolve emergency measures of coping with floods does not take place' (Kates, 1962, p140).

Individual versus collective management

It is tempting to draw generalizations embracing individuals and groups such as firms and community organizations, but the evidence for doing so is slim. The situational factors vary and the methods of handling information may be different for individuals than for groups with corporate memories and organized analysis. Nevertheless, it appears that there are a number of parallels among the bounded rationality of business firms, the behavior of political policy-makers, the responses of organizations under stress, and the behavior of individuals with regard to the hazards in their environment. Specifically, decision-makers in all these settings exhibit limited awareness of alternatives; they tend to misperceive probabilistic events and employ numerous mechanisms to reduce uncertainty and avoid dealing with it. Finally, they exhibit a short-run, crisis-oriented approach to adaptation.

PSYCHOLOGICAL RESEARCH: FURTHER EVIDENCE FOR BOUNDED RATIONALITY

Thus far the evidence for a theory of bounded rationality within the contexts of business, policy-making and adjustment to natural hazards has been reviewed. In doing so, little that is new or that has not been reviewed by others has been noted. However, most of the evidence has been anecdotal in nature, coming from close observation of behavior and interviews in natural settings. Although this type of analysis has the benefit of realism and relevance, it lacks rigor. Moreover, most of the evidence for bounded rationality in hazard adjustment comes from studies of floodplain residents, and the generality of these conclusions as applied to other types of hazards has not been fully demonstrated. Current efforts are underway to extend the studies of floods in the US to other cultures and to other hazards. As the detailed analyses of that additional evidence about avalanches, droughts, earthquakes, frost, snow, tropical storms, volcanoes and winds proceed, it is helpful to ask how the evidence from the field may be compared with that from the laboratory. This question is vital to understanding the complex processes by which man comes to terms with risk in nature, and it has wider implications. It bears upon the degree to which experience with natural hazards can be extrapolated to other sectors of behavior. Should comparable evidence be obtained from laboratory and field research, the validity and importance of both endeavors will be enhanced.

In keeping with these points, the recent psychological literature is examined here for evidence bearing upon man's information-processing limitations since it may relate to hazard adjustment. This work differs from that previously discussed in that it comes primarily from controlled laboratory research. Also, its relevance to hazard adjustment has not been reviewed before. Although Burton and Kates (1964) contended that the artificiality of the laboratory seemed to provide only limited insights into decision strategies and the perception of probabilities, it is our belief that the results of many recent laboratory studies merge nicely with the observations of geographers in their field studies, and help provide a more complete understanding of bounded rationality as it impinges upon adjustments to natural hazards.

The format to be followed in this section is as follows. The psychological principles and data will be reviewed, followed by speculations about the relevance of this work for understanding adjustment to natural hazards. Wherever possible, evidence from field surveys of human response to natural hazards will be presented to further highlight the relevance and generality of these phenomena.

The description of research on information processing is organized around several basic issues of concern to a decision-maker. First, he wonders what will happen or how likely it is to happen, and his use of information to answer these questions involves him in probabilistic tasks such as inference, prediction, probability estimation and diagnosis. He must also evaluate the worth of objects or consequences, and this often requires him to combine information from several components into an overall judgment. Finally, he is called upon to integrate his opinions about probabilities and values within the selection of some course of action. What is referred to as 'weighing risks against benefits' is an example of the latter combinatorial process.

Studies of Probabilistic Information Processing

As anyone who has ever planned a picnic understands, nature epitomizes uncertainty. The uncertainties of natural hazards are compounded by the need to plan for periods of time far longer than those considered in other endeavors. The usual damaging flood in urban areas, for example, has a recurrence interval of 50 to 100 years, and the great floods are less frequent.

Efficient adjustment to natural hazards demands an understanding of the probabilistic character of natural events and an ability to think in probabilistic terms. Because of the importance of probabilistic reasoning to decision-making in general, a great deal of recent experimental effort has been devoted to understanding how people perceive, process and evaluate the probabilities of uncertain events. Although no systematic theory about the psychology of uncertainty has emerged from this literature, several empirical generalizations have been established. Perhaps the most widespread conclusion is that people do not follow the principles of probability theory in judging the likelihood of uncertain events. Indeed, the distortions of subjective probabilities are often large, consistent and difficult to eliminate. Instead of applying the correct rules for estimating probabilities, people replace the laws of chance by intuitive heuristics. These sometimes produce good estimates, but all too often yield large systematic biases. Given these findings, Kates' observations that individuals refuse to deal with natural hazards as probabilistic events are not surprising. To do otherwise may be beyond human cognitive abilities.

The law of small numbers

A series of recent studies of subjective probability has been reported by Tversky and Kahneman (1971), who analyzed the kinds of decisions psychologists make when planning their scientific experiments. Despite extensive formal training in statistics, psychologists usually rely upon their educated intuitions when they make their decisions about how large a sample of data to collect or whether they should repeat an experiment to make sure their results are reliable.

After questioning a number of psychologists about their research practices, and after studying the designs of experiments reported in psychological journals, Tversky and Kahneman concluded that these scientists had seriously incorrect notions about the amount of error and unreliability inherent in small samples of data. They found that the typical psychologist gambles his research hypotheses on small samples, without realizing that the odds against his obtaining accurate results are unreasonably high; second, he has undue confidence in early trends from the first few data points and in the stability of observed patterns of data. In addition, he has unreasonably high expectations about the replicability of statistically significant results. Finally, he rarely attributes a deviation of results from his expectations to sampling variability because he finds a causal explanation for any discrepancy.

Tversky and Kahneman summarized these results by asserting that people's intuitions seemed to satisfy a 'law of small numbers', which means that the 'law of large numbers' applies to small samples as well as to large ones. The 'law of large numbers' says that very large samples will be highly representative of the population from which they are drawn. For the scientists in this study, small samples were also expected to be highly representative of the population. Since his acquaintance with logic or probability theory did not make the scientist any less susceptible to these cognitive biases, Tversky and Kahneman concluded that the only effective precaution is the use of formal statistical procedures, rather than intuition, to design experiments and evaluate data. People are not always incautious when drawing inferences from samples of data. Under somewhat different circumstances they become quite conservative, responding as though data are much less diagnostic than they truly are (Edwards, 1968).

In a related study, this time using Stanford University undergraduates as subjects, Kahneman and Tversky (1972) found that many of these subjects did not understand the fundamental principle of sampling – namely, the notion that the error in a sample becomes smaller as the sample size gets larger. To illustrate, consider one of the questions used in this study:

A certain town is served by two hospitals. In the larger hospital about 45 babies are born each day, and in the smaller hospital about 15 babies are born each day. As you know, about 50% of all babies are boys. The exact percentage of baby boys, however, varies from day to day. Sometimes it may be higher than 50%, sometimes lower.

For a period of one year, each hospital recorded the days on which more than 60% of the babies born were boys. Which hospital do you think recorded more such days?

Check one:

☐ the larger hospital;

☐ the smaller hospital;

□ about the same (ie, number of days were within 5% of each other).

About 24% of the subjects chose the first answer, 20% chose the second answer and 56% selected the third. The correct answer is, of course, the smaller hospital. A deviation of 10% or more from the 50% proportion in the population is more likely when the sample size is small.

From these and other results, Kahneman and Tversky (1972, pp444–5) concluded that 'the notion that sampling variance decreases in proportion to sample size is apparently not part of man's repertoire of intuitions... For anyone who would wish to view man as a reasonable intuitive statistician, such results are discouraging.'

What are the implications of this work for adjustment to natural hazards? We hypothesize that those in charge of collecting data for the purposes of making inferences about degree of hazard would fall prey to the same tendency to overgeneralize on the basis of small samples as do the research psychologists, unless they employ formal statistical procedures to hold their intuitions in check. Although it is common for scientists concerned with recurrence intervals of extreme natural events to lament the short periods of recorded data, we suspect that once the computation is made, whether it is on the basis of data from 20 years or from 70 years, the results will be treated with equal confidence. One rather dramatic example of overgeneralization on the basis of a ridiculously small amount of evidence is given by Burton and Kates (1964), who describe how the occurrence of two earthquakes in London in 1750, exactly one lunar month apart (28 days), with the second more severe than the first, led to predictions that a third and more terrible earthquake would occur 28 days after the second. A contagious panic spread through the city, which led to its being almost completely evacuated.

Perception of randomness

A number of experiments bear ample testimony to the fact that people have a very poor conception of randomness; they do not recognize it when they see it and they cannot produce it when they try (Chapanis, 1953; Cohen & Hansel, 1956; Jarvik, 1951). The latter conclusion is illustrated in a study by Bakan (1960) where subjects were asked to generate a series of outcomes representing the tosses of a coin. Subjects' sequences showed more alternation than would be expected in a truly random sequence. Thus triples of responses, *HHH* and *TTT*, occurred less often than expected; alternating sequences, *HHT, TTH, HTH* and *THT*, were produced too often. Ross and Levy (1958) found that subjects could not behave randomly even when warned of the types of biases to expect in their responses. The tendency to expect a tail to be more likely after a head, or series of heads, and vice versa, is a common finding, and is known as the negative recency effect. Others call it the gambler's fallacy. This basic result is found also in the views of some of the floodplain residents interviewed by Kates (1962). These individuals believed that a flood was less likely to occur in year $x + 1$ if one had occurred in year x.

Judgments of Correlation and Causality

Another important facet of intuitive thinking is the perception of correlational relationships between pairs of variables that are related probabilistically. Correlation between two such variables implies that knowledge of one will help you to predict the value of the other, although perfect prediction may not be possible.

Chapman and Chapman (1969), studying a phenomenon they have labeled illusory correlation, have shown how one's prior expectations of probabilistic relationships can lead an individual to perceive relationships in data where they do not really exist. They presented naive subjects with human-figure drawings, each of which was paired with a statement about the personality of the patients who allegedly drew the figures. These statements were randomly paired with the figure drawings so that the figure cues were unrelated to the personality of the drawer. They found that most subjects learned to see what they expected to see. In fact, naive subjects discovered the same relationships between drawings and personality that expert clinicians report observing in clinical practice, although these relationships were absent in the experimental materials. The illusory correlations corresponded to commonly held expectations, such as figures with big eyes being drawn by suspicious people and muscular figures being drawn by individuals who worried about their manliness.

The Chapmans noted that in clinical practice the observer is reinforced in his observation of illusory correlations by the reports of his fellow clinicians, who themselves are subject to the same illusions. Such agreement among experts is, unfortunately, often mistaken as evidence for the truth of the observation. The Chapmans concluded that the clinician's cognitive task may exceed the capacity of the human intellect. They suggested that subjective intuition may need to be replaced, at least partly, by statistical methods of prediction.

Will illusory correlation influence perceptions of natural hazards? Remarks by Kates (1962, p141) suggest it may:

> For some managers, a belief that floods come in cycles reduces an uncertain world into a more predictable one. They might be expected to develop interpretive mechanisms that would enable them to transform any hazard information by selective abstraction into a buttress for their existing belief. Managers in LaFollette appear to do this with their observed experience and might find it even easier to do so with information conveyed by maps or printed word.

Several studies have investigated people's perceptions of correlation or causality in simple probabilistic situations involving two binary variables. Consider a 2 x 2 table of frequencies in which variable X is the antecedent or input variable and Y is the consequent or output variable (see Table 1.2). The small letters are the frequencies with which the levels of these variables occur together, thus X_1 is followed by Y_1 on a occasions, is followed by Y_2 on b occasions, and so forth. A correlation exists between X and Y to the extent that the probability of Y_1, given X_1, differs from the probability of Y_1, given X_2 – that is, to the extent that $a/(a + b)$ differs from $c/(c + d)$. In other words, if Y_1 is as likely to occur after X_2 as it is after X_1, there is no correlation between X and Y. Causal relationships can sometimes be inferred from tables such as these. If X_1 causes Y_1, we would expect the

Table 1.2 *Frequency of Levels of Y Occurring Jointly with Levels of X*

Input	Output	
	Y_1	Y_2
X_1	a	b
X_2	c	d

occurrence of Y_1 to be more probable after X_1 had occurred than after X_2 had occurred, other considerations being equal.

Research indicates that subjects' judgments of correlation and causality are not based on a comparison of $a/(a + b)$ versus $c/(c + d)$. For example, Smedslund (1963) had students of nursing judge the relation between a symptom and the occurrence of a particular disease across a series of trials where the symptom was either present or absent and the disease was either present or absent. He found that the judgments were based mainly on the frequency of joint occurrence of symptom and disease (cell *a* in the matrix), without taking the frequency of the other three event combinations into account. As a result, the judgments were unrelated to statistical correlation. Similar results were obtained by Jenkins and Ward (1965) and by Ward and Jenkins (1965).

The tendency for people to misperceive the degree to which causation is present in a probabilistic environment has important implications for decisions regarding natural hazards. For example, Boyd et al (1971), in discussing the decision to modify a hurricane by cloud seeding, pointed out that observed changes in seeded hurricanes can result from both the effect of seeding and from the natural variability of the storm. Suppose that a seeded hurricane intensifies, changes course and causes damage to a point not on the apparent trajectory before seeding. Would the public react to the joint occurrence of seeding and this unfortunate outcome by assuming that the seeding caused the unfortunate result? Would they conclude that meteorologists are irresponsible? The research described above strongly implies that the initiators of a cloud-seeding enterprise would be blamed for any unfavorable change in a hurricane, even though such changes would occur as frequently, or even more frequently, in the absence of human intervention. As Boyd et al indicated, the government must be prepared to be held liable for damages occurring from a seeded hurricane, and this possibility must be weighed carefully in its decisions concerning the general feasibility of hurricane modification programs. This clearly is a situation in which it will be imperative to educate the public on the uncertainty involved in such circumstances, lest a bad outcome be equated with a bad decision.

Judgment of probability by availability

Tversky and Kahneman (1973a) have proposed that people estimate probability and frequency by a number of heuristics, or mental strategies, which allow them to reduce these difficult tasks to simpler judgments. One such heuristic is that of availability, according to which one judges the probability of an event (eg, snow in November) by the ease with which relevant instances are imagined or by the number of such instances that are readily retrieved from memory.

Our everyday experience has taught us that instances of frequent events are easier to recall than instances of less frequent events, and that likely occurrences are easier to imagine than unlikely ones; thus, mental availability will often be a valid cue for the assessment of frequency and probability. However, availability is also affected by recency, emotional saliency and other subtle factors, which may be unrelated to actual frequency. If the availability heuristic is applied, then factors that increase the availability of instances should correspondingly increase the perceived frequency and subjective probability of the events under consideration. Therefore, use of the availability heuristic results in predictable systematic biases in judgment.

Consider, for example, sampling a word (containing three or more letters) from an English text. Is it more likely that the word starts with a *k*, or that it has a *k* in the third position? To answer such a question, people often try to think of words beginning with a *k* (eg, 'key') and words that have a *k* in third position (eg, 'like'), and then compare the frequency or the ease with which the two types of words come to mind. It is easier to think of words that start with a *k* than of words with a *k* in the third position. As a result, the majority of people judge the former event more likely despite the fact that English text contains about twice as many words with a *k* in the third position. This example, and many others, are presented by Tversky and Kahneman to document the pervasive effects of availability.

The notion of availability is potentially one of the most important ideas for helping us understand the distortions likely to occur in our perceptions of natural hazards. For example, Kates (1962, p140) writes:

> A major limitation to human ability to use improved flood hazard information is a basic reliance on experience. Men on flood plains appear to be very much prisoners of their experience... Recently experienced floods appear to set an upward bound to the size of loss with which managers believe they ought to be concerned.

Kates further attributes much of the difficulty in achieving better flood control to the 'inability of individuals to conceptualize floods that have never occurred' (p92). He observes that, in making forecasts of future flood potential, individuals 'are strongly conditioned by their immediate past and limit their extrapolation to simplified constructs, seeing the future as a mirror of that past' (p88). In this regard, it is interesting to observe how the purchase of earthquake insurance increases sharply after a quake, but decreases steadily thereafter, as the memories become less vivid (Steinbrugge, McClure & Snow, 1969).

Some hazards may be inherently more memorable than others. For example, one would expect drought, with its gradual onset and offset, to be much less memorable, and thus less accurately perceived, than flooding. Kirkby (1972) provides some evidence for this hypothesis in her study of Oaxacan farmers. Kirkby also found that memory of salient natural events seems to begin with an extreme event, which effectively blots out recall of earlier events and acts as a fixed point against which to calibrate later points. A similar result was obtained by Parra (1971), studying farmers in the Yucatan. Parra found that perception of a lesser drought was obscured if it had been followed by a more severe drought. He also observed that droughts were perceived as greater in severity if they were recent and thus easier to remember.

Natural catastrophes are, typically, rare events. For example, Holmes (1961) found that 50% of the damage due to major floods was caused by floods whose probability of occurrence at that place in any year was less than .01. The city of Skopje was leveled by earthquakes in 518, 1555 and 1963. The mudflow that took 25,000 lives in Yungay, Peru, had similarly swept across the valley between 1000 and 10,000 years before. Adequate decision-making regarding natural hazards obviously requires a realistic appreciation of the likelihood of these rare events, yet such appreciation is likely to be especially sensitive to the effects of mental availability. For example, ease of imagination almost certainly plays an important role in the public's perception of the risks of injury and death from attack by a grizzly bear in the national parks of North America. In view of the widespread public concern over the dangerousness of these bears, it is indeed surprising that the rate of injury is only 1 per 2 million visitors and the rate of death is even smaller (Herrero, 1970). Imaginability of death by the claws of an enraged grizzly is heightened by newspaper stories and movies that only portray attacks, while the multitude of favorable public experiences go unpublicized.

The availability hypothesis implies that any factor that makes a hazard highly memorable or imaginable – such as a recent disaster or a vivid film or lecture – could considerably increase the perceived risk of that hazard. The Tennessee Valley Authority (TVA) apparently recognizes this, at least at an intuitive level. Kates (1962) noted that the TVA goes to considerable lengths to bring home the graphic reality of potential floods. It plots potential floods on easily read maps, and shows flood heights on photographs of familiar buildings. In a similar vein, a recent film entitled 'The City that Waits to Die' depicts the vast death and destruction that would occur in San Francisco's next major earthquake. The film was promoted by a group attempting to prohibit the building of new skyscrapers in the city, but was initially banned from public showings. As Kates noted, there is a great need for well-designed studies investigating the effects of such graphic presentations on hazard perception. A decade after Kates's remarks, the need remains unmet.

One additional comment on availability seems warranted. Subtle changes in an individual's mental set are likely to alter the images and memories he brings to bear when evaluating hazard, with profound influence on his judgments. For example, an analyst who attempts to evaluate the likelihood of a flood of given magnitude may do so by recalling hydrologic conditions similar to those of the present or by recalling previous floods. The latter are easier to remember because they are more sharply defined, whereas hydrologic states are more difficult to characterize and, therefore, harder to recall. The resulting probability estimate is likely to be greatly dependent upon which of these two sets the analyst adopts. Even the form of the question may be important. Consider the following questions:

1 How likely is it that there will be a flood this season?
2 How likely is it that, given the present hydrologic state, there will be a flood this season?

The first question may focus attention on past instances of flood, whereas the latter may cause the analyst to think about previous hydrologic conditions. The answers to the two questions may be quite different.

Anchoring and adjustment in quantifying uncertainty

Another heuristic that seems useful in describing how humans ease the strain of integrating information is a process called anchoring and adjustment. In this process, a natural starting point is used as a first approximation to the judgment – an anchor, so to speak. This anchor is then adjusted to accommodate the implications of the additional information. Typically, the adjustment is a crude and imprecise one which fails to do justice to the importance of additional information.

Application of the anchoring and adjustment heuristic is hypothesized to produce an interesting bias that occurs when people attempt to calibrate the degree to which they are uncertain about an estimate or prediction. Specifically, in studies by Alpert and Raiffa (1968) and Tversky and Kahneman (1973b), subjects were given almanac questions such as the following:

> How many foreign cars were imported into the US in 1968?
> * Make a high estimate such that you feel there is only a 1% probability that the true answer would exceed your estimate.
> * Make a low estimate such that you feel there is only a 1% probability that the true answer would be below this estimate.

In essence, the subject is being asked to estimate an interval such that he or she believes there is a 98% chance that the true answer will fall within the interval. The spacing between the high and low estimates is the subject's expression of his uncertainty about the quantity in question. We cannot say that this single pair of estimates is right or wrong. However, if the subject were to make many such estimates, or if a large number of persons were to answer this question, we should expect the range between upper and lower estimates to include the truth about 98% of the time – if the subjective probabilities were unbiased. What is typically found, however, by Alpert and Raiffa and by Tversky and Kahneman is that the 98% confidence range fails to include the true value from 40 to 50% of the time, across many subjects answering many kinds of almanac questions. In other words, subjects' confidence bands are much too narrow, given their state of knowledge. Alpert and Raiffa observed that this bias persisted even when subjects were given feedback about their overly narrow confidence bands and urged to widen the bands on a new set of estimation problems.

These studies indicate that people believe they have a much better picture of the truth than they really do. Why this happens is not entirely clear. Tversky and Kahneman tentatively hypothesize that people approach these problems by searching for a calculational scheme or algorithm by which to make a best estimate. They then adjust this estimate up and down to get a 98% confidence range. For example, in answering the above question, one might proceed as follows:

> I think there were about 180 million people in the US in 1968. There is about one car for every three people thus there would have been about 60 million cars. The lifetime of a car is about 10 years. This suggests that there should be about 6 million new cars in a year, but since the population and the number of cars is increasing let's make that 9 million for 1968; foreign cars make up about 10% of the US market, thus there were probably about 900,000 foreign imports. To set my 98% confidence band, I'll add and subtract a few hundred thousand cars from my estimate of 900,000.

Tversky and Kahneman argue that people's estimates assume that their computational algorithms are 100% correct. However, there are two sources of uncertainty that plague these algorithms. First, there is uncertainty associated with every step in the algorithm and there is uncertainty about the algorithm itself. That is, the whole calculational scheme may be incorrect. It is apparently quite difficult to carry along these several sources of uncertainty and translate them intuitively into a confidence band. Once the 'best guess' is arrived at as an anchor (eg, the 900,000 figure above), the adjustments are insufficient in magnitude, failing to do justice to the many ways in which the estimate can be in error.

The research just described implies that our estimates may be grossly in error – even when we attempt to acknowledge our uncertainty. This may have profound implications for many kinds of judgments about the risks associated with natural hazards or the benefits of plans for coping with those hazards. It is likely, for example, that an individual's intuitive estimates of the size of a flood that would be exceeded only one time in 100 will be conservative (ie, too close to his estimate of the 'most likely' flood magnitude), and he thus would allow too small a margin of safety in his protective adjustments.

Problems in Integrating Information from Multiple Sources

Thus far, our review of laboratory research has been concerned with the assessment of risks and the estimation of uncertain quantities. A somewhat different problem is as follows. Suppose that we have good information about both risks and benefits. How capable is the decision-maker of balancing these several factors and coming up with an optimal decision? By optimal, we do not mean a decision that will, necessarily, turn out well. Some good decisions work out poorly and vice versa. We are thinking of optimal decisions in the sense that such decisions faithfully reflect the decision-maker's personal values and opinions.

Information processing biases in risk-taking judgments

As if we did not have enough problems with our tendencies to bias probability judgments, there is some evidence to the effect that difficulties in integrating information may often lead people to make judgments that are inconsistent with their underlying values. An example of this within a risk-benefit context comes from two experiments (Lichtenstein & Slovic, 1971; 1973), one of which was conducted on the floor of the Four Queens Casino in Las Vegas. Consider the following pair of gambles used in the Las Vegas experiment:

Bet A
11/12 chance to win 12 chips
1/12 chance to win 24 chips

Bet B
2/12 chance to win 79 chips
10/12 chance to lose 5 chips

where the value of each chip has been previously fixed at, say, 25¢. Notice that bet *A* has a much better chance of winning, but bet *B* offers a higher winning payoff. Subjects were shown many such pairs of bets. They were asked to indicate, in two ways, how much they would like to play each bet in a pair. First they made a simple choice, *A* or *B*. Later they were asked to assume that they owned a ticket to play each bet, and they were to state the lowest price for which they would sell this ticket.

Presumably, these selling prices and choices are both governed by the same underlying quality, the subjective attractiveness of each gamble. Therefore, the subject should state a higher selling price for the gamble that he prefers in the choice situation. However, the results indicated that subjects often chose one gamble, yet stated a higher selling price for the other gamble. For the particular pair of gambles shown above, bets *A* and *B* were chosen about equally often. However, bet *B* received a higher selling price about 88% of the time. Of the subjects who chose bet *A*, 87% gave a higher selling price to bet *B*, thus exhibiting an inconsistent preference pattern.

What accounts for the inconsistent pattern of preferences? Lichtenstein and Slovic concluded that subjects use different cognitive strategies for setting prices than for making choices. Subjects choose bet *A* because of its good odds, but they set a higher price for *B* because of its large winning payoff. Specifically, it was found that, when making pricing judgments, people who find a gamble basically attractive use the amount to win as a natural starting point. They then adjust the amount to win downward to take into account the less-than-perfect chance of winning and the fact that there is some amount to lose as well. Typically, this adjustment is insufficient and that is why large winning payoffs lead people to set prices that are inconsistent with their choices. Because the pricing and choice responses are inconsistent, it is obvious that at least one of these responses does not accurately reflect what the decision-maker believes to be the most important attribute in a gamble.

A 'compatibility' effect seems to be operating here. Since a selling price is expressed in terms of monetary units, subjects apparently found it easier to use the monetary aspects of the gamble to produce this type of response. Such a bias did not exist with the choices, since each attribute of one gamble could be directly compared with the same attribute of the other gamble. With no reason to use payoffs as a starting point, subjects were free to use any number of strategies to determine their choices.

Compatibility bias

The overdependence on payoff cues when pricing a gamble suggests a general hypothesis to the effect that the compatibility or commensurability between a dimension of information and the required response affects the importance of that information in determining the response. This hypothesis was tested further in an experiment by Slovic and MacPhillamy (1974), who predicted that dimensions common to each alternative in a choice situation would have greater influence upon decisions than would dimensions that were unique to a particular alternative. They asked subjects to compare pairs of students and to predict which would get the higher college grade-point average. The subjects were given each student's scores on two cue dimensions (tests) on which to base their judgments. One dimension was common to both students, and the other was unique. For example, student A might be described in terms of his scores on 'Need for Achievement and Quantitative Ability', while student B might be described by his scores on 'Need for Achievement and English Skill'.

In this example, since need for achievement is a dimension common to both students, the compatibility hypothesis suggests it will be weighted particularly heavily. The rationale for this prediction is as follows: a comparison between two students along the same dimension should be easier, cognitively, than a comparison between different dimensions, and this ease of use should lead to greater reliance on the common dimension. The data strongly confirmed this hypothesis. Dimensions were weighted more heavily when common than when they were unique. Interrogation of the subjects after the experiment indicated that most did not wish to give more weight to the common dimension and were unaware that they had done so.

The message in these experiments is that the amalgamation of different types of information and different types of values into an overall judgment or decision is a difficult cognitive process and, in our attempts to ease the strain of processing information, we often resort to judgmental strategies that may do an injustice to our underlying values. In other words, even when the risks and benefits are known and made explicit, as in the gambling situation, subtle aspects of the decision we have to make, acting in combination with our intellectual limitations, may bias the balance we strike between the many relevant attributes.

Relevance to decisions regarding natural hazards

The research on information integration described above suggests that simplified strategies for easing the strain of making decisions about natural hazards may be used by experts and laymen alike. Although this hypothesis has not been studied systematically, a few relevant examples exist. Perhaps the simplest way to minimize the strain of integrating information is to avoid making decisions. Kates (1962) found that many floodplain managers wanted to abdicate their responsibilities and leave the decision-making to the experts. White (1966) noted that, when attention turned to the possibility of setting aside floodplains for open space, some municipalities adopted the blanket policy of buying up valley bottoms for recreational use without even attempting to weigh the alternatives in any given instance. And Kates (1962) observed that three structures in different sites in a town were each elevated by 0.3 meter (1 foot), despite a wide variation in hazard among the sites. One foot is a convenient number, and these decisions suggest that a crude approximation rule was used to determine the elevation changes, much as these approximations were used in the risk-taking studies described above. One wonders also about the depth of analysis that led to the selection of the '100-year flood' as a standard criterion in the design of flood-protection structures.

It is interesting to compare these observations with another example of how simplistic thinking can influence even the most important decisions. With regard to the decision to place a 1.0-megaton (one million-ton) nuclear warhead atop the first *Atlas* missile, physicist Herbert York (1970, pp89–90) commented:

Why 1.0 megaton? The answer is because and only because one million is a particularly round number in our culture. We picked a one-megaton yield for the *Atlas* warhead for the same reason that everyone speaks of rich men as being millionaires and never as being ten-millionaires or one hundred-thousandaires. It really was that mystical, and I was one of the mystics. Thus, the actual physical size of the first *Atlas* warhead and the number of people it would kill were determined by the fact that human beings have two hands with five fingers each and therefore count by tens.

Even technical persons, whose job is to aid the decision-making process, can be accused of grossly oversimplified use of information. Their chief tool, cost-benefit analysis, has focused primarily on the dollar values of various adjustments, presumably because these are readily measured and commensurable. The tendency is to ignore non-economic considerations such as aesthetic and recreational values, or the emotional costs of leaving friends and familiar surroundings when moving to a less hazardous location.

One mechanism that is useful for bringing disparate considerations to bear upon a decision without actually attempting to make them commensurable is to employ a lexicographic decision rule in which one dimension of information is considered at a time. The most important dimension is considered first. Only if this first dimension does not lead to a clearly preferred alternative is the next most important dimension considered. An example of lexicographic behavior in the laboratory that led people to be systematically intransitive in their preferences is presented by Tversky (1969). A natural hazards example is provided in a study of how people, drawing water for household use in a rural area, choose among alternative sources (White, Bradley & White, 1972). It was found that the users classified the sources as good or bad solely on the basis of health effects. If more than one source was satisfactory on this primary dimension, the remaining 'good' sources were then discriminated on the basis of the economic costs of transporting the water. There was little indication that they were willing to 'trade off' lower quality water with accompanying health hazard for lower economic costs. The two dimensions were simply not compensatory.

Another non-compensatory mode of processing diverse dimensions of information is to set a criterion level on one or more of these dimensions. Alternatives that do not promise to meet that criterion are rejected. For those alternatives that remain, another dimension can then be employed as a basis for discrimination. This sort of mechanism has been observed in a laboratory study of risk taking by Lichtenstein, Slovic and Zink (1969). A natural hazards example is given by Kunreuther (1972), who hypothesized that peasant farmers seek reasonable assurance of survival when deciding how to allocate their resources among crops varying in risk and expected yield. Only for those allocation plans in which survival needs are likely to be met is it likely that maximizing expected yield becomes a consideration. What happens when none of the alternatives meet all of the decision-maker's requirements? Something must be sacrificed, and Kunreuther (1974) hypothesizes that this sacrifice occurs by means of a lexicographic process whereby the decision-maker proceeds sequentially, trying always to satisfy his more important goals, while relaxing those of lesser importance. Kunreuther again uses a crop-allocation decision in the face of natural disasters to illustrate the process.

Investigating Bounded Rationality in Field Settings

On the preceding pages we have described a number of aspects of bounded rationality that have been demonstrated in laboratory experiments. Some of the results have close parallel with findings from field studies of floodplain residents. However, most fieldwork has not been oriented toward cognitive processes and, therefore, has not provided data relevant to the phenomena described above. We believe it would be profitable to look for illustrations of bounded rationality in future field surveys, much as one would examine personality, cultural or institutional influences upon behavior in the face of natural disaster. The following serves as an overview of the research described above and a brief guide to the kinds of phenomena one might wish to examine in the field.

The law of small numbers

Do individuals overgeneralize on the basis of small samples of evidence? Do they fail to discriminate between short and long periods of record when evaluating evidence or making decisions? Do they take conclusions on faith without questioning the amount of data upon which those conclusions were based?

Judgments of causality and correlation

Do people attribute a bad outcome to a bad decision and a good outcome to a good decision? Do they interpret evidence as supporting a preconceived hypothesis when it does not (illusory correlation)? That is, do they perceive relationships that they expect to see in the data, even when these relationships are not present?

Availability

Do factors of imaginability or memorability influence perception of hazards or actions regarding the hazard? Does rephrasing a question about the likelihood of a hazard to influence memorability also influence the answer? Do vivid films, lectures or newspaper articles influence perception of rare events? Hazards differ in characteristics that may affect their memorability or imaginability. Some have more sudden onset and offset than others. Duration varies. Contrast a flash flood, for example, with a drought. Do these characteristics systematically affect perception of the hazard? Are people prisoners of their experience, seeing the future as a mirror of the past? Do they predict the future by describing the past?

Anchoring and insufficient adjustment

Do individuals use simple starting-point and adjustment mechanisms when making estimates about quantities? When they attempt to calibrate their uncertainty by placing confidence bounds on their estimates, are those bounds too narrow, thus resulting in rare events occurring more often than they were expected to occur?

Information processing shortcuts

Is there evidence for simple decision strategies that avoid the weighing of multiple considerations? Do people avoid making decisions by relying on experts, authority, fate, custom and so forth? Is there evidence for lexicographic processes or other non-compensatory decision modes in the evaluation of adjustments?

Additional needs for research

Finally, there are a number of important situational factors about which we have neither laboratory nor field data. For example, we need to better understand the effects of savings and reserves, time horizon and amount of diversification upon perception of alternatives and efficiency of adjustment. Will larger amounts of reserves make it more likely that an individual will consider alternatives that have greater risk but also greater expected payoffs? Similarly, will diversification of farming activity reduce the risk of failing to meet one's goals of subsistence and thus permit the farmer to consider risky but profitable alternatives?

We need to know more about the condition of decision as it affects behavior. Will individuals become aware of a wider range of perceived alternatives if they are required to make a decision with respect to a given risk as opposed to conditions where the decision is voluntary?

Finally, we need theoretical models of boundedly rational behavior which, from reasonable assumptions about the constraints pertinent to a given natural hazards decision, yield testable hypotheses about the effects of income reserves, insurance, time horizon and so forth, on factors such as range of perceived alternatives, criteria for choice and level of aspiration.

Comment

The experimental work described in this chapter documents man's difficulties in weighing information and judging uncertainty. Yet this work is quite recent in origin and still very much in the exploratory stage. In addition, its implications do not fit with the high level of confidence that we typically accord our higher mental processes. Consider, for example, the statement by a famed economist: 'We are so built that what seems reasonable to us is likely to be confirmed by experience or we could not live in the world at all' (Knight, 1921; 1965, p227). Since the laboratory results greatly contradict our self-image, it is reasonable to question whether the observed information processing difficulties will persist outside the confines of the laboratory in situations where the decision-maker uses familiar sources of information to make decisions that are personally important to him or her.

In light of this natural skepticism, and since our coverage of the psychological experiments was necessarily rather brief, we would like to point out that evidence for cognitive limitations pervades a wide variety of tasks where intelligent individuals served as decision-makers, often under conditions designed to maximize motivation and involvement. For example, the subjects studied by Tversky and Kahneman (1971) were scientists, highly trained in statistics, evaluating problems similar to those they faced in their work. Likewise, Alpert and Raiffa (1968) found it extremely difficult to reduce the biased confidence judgments in their subjects, who were students in the advanced management program at a leading graduate school.

In many of the experiments reported above, extreme measures were taken to maximize the subjects' motivation to be unbiased. When Lichtenstein and

Slovic (1971) observed inconsistent patterns of choices and prices among college student subjects who were gambling for relatively small stakes, they repeated the study, with identical results, on the floor of a Las Vegas casino. It should also be noted that their experiments involving selling-price responses employed a rather elaborate procedure devised by Becker, De Groot and Marschak (1964) to persuade subjects to report their true subjective value of the bet as their lowest selling price; any deviations from this strategy, any efforts to 'beat the game', necessarily resulted in a game of lesser value to the subjects than the game resulting when they honestly reported their subjective valuations. Tversky and Kahneman have also resorted to extreme measures to motivate their subjects to behave in an unbiased manner.

Finally, the laboratory conclusions are congruent with many observations of non-optimal decision-making outside the laboratory – in business, governmental policy setting and adjustment to natural hazards. The belief that people can behave optimally when it is worthwhile for them to do so gains little support from these studies. The sources of judgmental bias appear to be cognitive, not motivational. They have a persistent quality not unlike that of perceptual illusions.

It is interesting to speculate about why we have such great confidence in our intuitive judgments, in the light of the deficiencies that emerge when they are exposed to scientific scrutiny. For one thing, our basic perceptual motor skills are remarkably good, the product of a long period of evolution, and thus we can process *sensory* information with remarkable ease. This may fool us into thinking that we can process *conceptual* information with similar ease. Anyone who tries to predict where a baseball will land by calculating its impact against the bat, trajectory of flight and so forth will quickly realize that their analytic skills are inferior to their perceptual motor abilities. Another reason for our confidence is that the world is structured in such a complex, multiply determined way that we can usually find some reason for our failures, other than our inherent inadequacies – bad luck is a particularly good excuse in a probabilistic world. In many situations, we get little or no feedback about the results of our decisions and, in other instances, the criterion for judging our decisions is sufficiently vague that we can not tell how poorly we are actually doing. Finally, when we do make a mistake and recognize it as such, we often have the opportunity to take corrective action – thus, we may move from crisis to crisis but, in between crises, we have periods of fairly effective functioning. When we have the opportunity to learn from our mistakes, and can afford to do so, this may be a satisfactory method of proceeding. When we cannot, we must look toward whatever decision aids are available to help us minimize errors of judgment.

IMPLICATIONS FOR FUTURE POLICY: HOW CAN WE IMPROVE ADJUSTMENT TO NATURAL HAZARDS?

Research, in both natural and laboratory settings, strongly supports the view of decision processes as boundedly rational. Given this awareness of our cognitive limitations, how are we to maximize our capability for making intelligent decisions about natural hazards?

Two answers to this question are considered here. The first is primarily non-analytic in character and works within the framework of bounded rationality. The second is an analytic approach that accepts the notion that human beings are fallible in processing information, but strives to help them come as close as possible to an ideal conception of rational decision-making.

Implications of Bounded Rationality

Knowledge of the workings of bounded rationality forms a basis for understanding constraints on decision-making and suggests methods for helping the decision-maker improve as an adapting system. For example, Cyert and March (1963) describe how policy inputs can trigger a search for new alternatives by introducing constraints which make old habits of adjustment unacceptable. Within the context of business decision-making, Cyert and March point to three ways in which the firm's decision-making behavior can be altered via policy changes. The first changes the inputs to standard decision rules as exemplified by changes in the product specifications or work regulations. The second use of policy is to force a failure in meeting some valued goal by setting explicit constraints on costs, prices, profits or the like. The third use of policy is to modify the consequences of potential solutions to problems to enhance the attractiveness of solutions that would otherwise be unacceptable.

How might we apply knowledge of bounded rationality to improving adjustment to natural hazards? Consider two key aspects of the problem – the need to make the decision-maker's perceptions of the hazard more accurate and the need to make him aware of a more complete set of alternative courses of action.

To improve probabilistic perception of hazards, it is essential that complete historical records be kept, analyzed and made available in understandable form to all resource managers. Technical experts should be taught how to express hazards probabilistically and their opinions should be made available in a format that attempts to be comprehensible to individuals not particularly skilled in probabilistic thinking. Records should be continually updated and, when a new development occurs that might render the historical data invalid, the technical expert should estimate the effect of this change on the hazard.

There has been a small amount of experimentation with physical formats for expressing probabilities of natural extremes: the US Geological Survey (USGS) and the Corps of Engineers have tried several ways of presenting flood frequencies, including historical summaries, graphs of recurrent intervals, eyewitness accounts, photographs and maps. An elaborate set of maps showing susceptibility to geophysical hazards such as earthquake and landslide are under preparation by the USGS and the Department of Housing and Urban Development for the San Francisco Bay region. However, there has been no serious effort to find out what effect, if any, the different formats have upon the understanding of probability. Perhaps the only relatively searching attempt has been in connection with public interpretation of weather forecasts which use probability estimates (Murphy & Winkler, 1971).

Of course, given our limited ability to comprehend probabilistic information, imaginative presentations of records may not be enough. Creative new devices will be necessary to facilitate imaginability and to break through the 'prison of experience' that shackles probabilistic thinking. One procedure worth exploring is that of informing decision-makers of the biases that are likely to distort their interpretation and use of information. Another device is simulation, which might be particularly effective in conveying an appreciation of sampling variability and probabilities. Consider the important practical situation where a farmer in a frequently drought-stricken area must decide whether or not to plant drought-resistant maize. Such maize will provide greater yield than regular maize if a drought occurs, but will do worse in the event of normal rainfall. The farmer can be shown a historical record of rainfall for the past 50 years, but from what we know of the Tversky and Kahneman experiments and geographical surveys by Kates, it is unlikely that he will be able to use this information properly. The farmer's problem is increased by the difficulty of taking into account the utilities of various yields, as well as their probabilities. It is here that simulation can be particularly valuable. A farming game can give the decision-maker realistic and appropriate experience with this type of decision and its consequences. The farmer begins with a specific amount of cash. In year one he makes the decision about what percent of his maize crop to plant with drought-resistant seed. Nature runs its course and the farmer receives an appropriate bounty. Our subject plays against nature and quickly gains experience that would ordinarily accrue only over many years. Simulations such as this have already been introduced as teaching aids in high-school and college geography courses (High & Richards, 1972; Patton, 1970). Kates (1962) observed: 'Without frequent experience, learned adjustments wither and atrophy with time' (p140). Simulation might be a quick and painless way to provide the concrete experiences needed to produce adjustments that are maximally adaptive.

With regard to widening the range of perceived alternatives, several possibilities exist. For example, since we know that perception is typically incomplete, we can take special measures to inform resource managers of the range of available options. Although there have been frequent pleas for encouraging people to consider a wider range of alternatives in coping with hazards (National Research Council, 1966) the means of doing so have been explored only casually. Thus, the National Environmental Protection Act of 1969 specifies that environmental impact statements will indicate alternative measures for resource allocation, but it does not indicate how this should be done. The principal measures now being tried are survey reports, public hearings, public discussions and informational brochures. With the exception of the studies of Corps of Engineers' public consultations (Borton et al, 1970), these have not been evaluated.

Another way to widen the range of perceived choice is to employ policy to modify the potential consequences of an alternative, thus making a previously unattractive alternative worthy of consideration. Compulsory insurance is a good example of a policy that can play a role in improving hazard perception and widening the range of alternatives. By guaranteeing individuals a minimum level of income if they adopt an innovative adjustment, insurance can decrease the risk entailed by the innovation, thereby enhancing its attractiveness. Probably the most significant role that may be played by insurance is in requiring explicit, conscious attention to risk by the individual concerned. He or she is faced with an estimate of risk expressed by an annual premium charge, and in some cases may also be provided with a schedule of reduced premiums contingent upon taking certain actions, such as flood proofing his or her home. A government scheme that fails to base premiums on risk may have undesirable effects (O'Riordan, 1974). For a more detailed discussion of the role of insurance in the context of natural hazards, see Kunreuther (1974), Kunreuther (1968), Dacy and Kunreuther (1969) and Lave (1968).

How safe is safe enough?

There are some who believe that, given a static environment, man learns by trial, error and subsequent corrective actions to arrive at a reasonably optimal balance between the benefit from an activity and its risk. One such individual is Starr (1969; 1972), who has developed a quantitative measure of the acceptable risk-benefit ratio for an activity, based on this belief. Starr assumes that historical national-accident records adequately reveal consistent patterns in risk-benefit ratios and that these historically revealed social preferences are sufficiently enduring to predict what risk levels will be acceptable to society when setting policies or introducing new technologies. Implicit in this approach is yet another assumption, that what is best for society is approximately equivalent to what is traditionally acceptable.

Starr distinguishes between voluntary activities, which individuals can evaluate via their own value system, and involuntary activities, where the options and criteria of evaluation are determined for individuals by some controlling body. His measure of risk is the statistical expectation of fatalities per hour of exposure to the activity under consideration. For voluntary activities, his measure of benefit is assumed to be approximately equal to the amount of money spent on an activity by the average individual. For involuntary activities, benefit is assumed to be proportional to the contribution that activity makes to an individual's annual income.

Analysis of a number of natural and man-made risks, according to these considerations, points to several important conclusions:

- the public seems willing to accept voluntary risks roughly 1000 times greater than involuntary risks at a given level of benefit;
- the acceptability of a risk is roughly proportional to the real and perceived benefits;
- the acceptable level of risk is inversely related to the number of persons participating in an activity.

Starr's assessment technique falls within the purview of bounded rationality approaches because, rather than assuming that individuals can indicate directly an optimal risk-benefit trade-off, it merely assumes that across a large group of individuals, given an opportunity to learn from their mistakes, a satisfactory level will emerge.

The importance of knowing the acceptable risk level for an activity cannot be overestimated. The Starr technique thus promises to be a valuable aid for decisions regarding natural hazards; and, in fact, a similar approach has already been used to guide the development of a new earthquake building code for the city of Long Beach, California (Wiggins, 1972). However, several reservations bear mentioning. First, the psychological research described above points to the prevalence of systematic biases in risk-taking decisions. It is unlikely that all such biases will be eliminated as a result of experience. Therefore, just as an individual's decisions may not accurately reflect his or her 'true preferences', historical data may not necessarily reflect the underlying preferences of a group of people. Second, the validity of historical data as an indication of preference assumes that the public has available a wide selection of alternatives and, furthermore, that these alternatives are perceived as being available. Can we really assume, for example, that the public will demand automobiles that are as safe as they would wish, given the available benefits? Unless the public really knows what is possible from a design standpoint, and unless the automobile industry cooperates in making available information that may not necessarily serve its own profit maximization interests, the answer is likely to be no. (For a more detailed discussion of the limitations of the public's 'market' behavior as an indicator of its risk values, see Schelling, 1968.) Finally, the Starr approach does not consider the question of who should bear the costs of damages from natural hazards. As Kunreuther (1973) has pointed out, individuals and communities might adopt quite different risk levels if they were forced to bear the costs of disasters rather than relying on liberal government relief.

With these qualifications, the Starr approach would seem to merit serious consideration as a method for designing and evaluating adjustments to natural hazards.

The Analytic Approach to Improving Adjustments

Bounded rationality, with its emphasis on short-run feedback and adaptation triggered by crises, may work satisfactorily in some settings, particularly in static environments where the same decision is made repeatedly and the consequences of a poor decision are not too disastrous. However, where natural hazards are concerned, we may prefer not to rely upon learning from experience. First, relevant experiences may be few and far between; and second, mistakes are likely to be too costly. With so much at stake, it is important to search for methods other than the clever ways of 'muddling through' and 'satisficing' advanced by the advocates of bounded rationality.

The alternative to muddling through is the application of scientific methods and formal analysis to problems of decision-making. The analytic approach originated during World War II from the need to solve strategic and tactical problems in situations where experience was either costly or impossible to acquire. It was first labeled 'operations analysis' and later became known as 'operations research'. Operations research is an interdisciplinary effort, bringing together the talents of mathematicians, statisticians, economists, engineers and others. Since the war, its sphere of application has been extended primarily to business, but its potential is equally great for all areas of decision-making.

Simon (1960) outlined the stages of an operations research analysis as follows: the first step is to construct a mathematical model that mirrors the important factors in the situation of interest. Among the mathematical tools that have been particularly useful in this regard are linear programming, dynamic programming and probability theory. The second step is to define a criterion function that compares the relative merits of the possible alternative actions. Next, empirical estimates are obtained for the numerical parameters in the model for the specific situation under study. Finally, mathematical analysis is applied to determine the course of action that maximizes the criterion function.

During recent years, a number of closely related offshoots of operations research have been applied to decision problems. These include systems analysis and cost-benefit analysis. Systems analysis is a branch of engineering whose objective is capturing the interactions and dynamic behavior of complex systems. Cost-benefit analysis attempts to quantify the prospective gains and losses from some proposed action, usually in terms of dollars. If the calculated gain from an act or project is positive, it is said that the benefits outweigh the costs, and its acceptance is recommended (see, for example, the application of cost-benefit analysis to the study of auto-safety features by Lave & Weber, 1970).

Decision analysis

What systems analysis and operations-research approaches lacked for many years was an effective normative framework for dealing either with the uncertainty in the world or with the subjectivity of decision-makers' values and expectations. The emergence of decision theory provided the general normative rationale missing from these early analytic approaches. By the same token, systems analysis and operations research had something to offer to applied decision theory. There is an awesome gap between the simple decisions that are typically used to illustrate decision theoretic principles (eg, whether or not to carry an umbrella) and the complex real-world problems one wishes to address. Systems analysis attempts to provide the sophisticated modeling of the decision situation needed to bridge the gap. The result of the natural merger between decision theory and engineering approaches has been labeled 'decision analysis'. Our review of decision analysis will be brief. For further details, see the tutorial papers by Howard (1968a; 1968b) and Matheson (1969; 1970), and the books by Raiffa (1968) and Schlaifer (1969).

A thorough decision analysis takes a great deal of time and effort and thus should be applied only to important problems. Typically, these problems involve a complex structure where many interrelated factors affect the decision, and where uncertainty, long-run implications and complex trade-offs among outcomes further complicate matters.

A key element of decision analysis is its emphasis on *structuring* the decision problem and *decomposing* it into a number of more elementary problems. In this sense, it attempts a simplification process that – unlike the potentially detrimental simplifications the unaided decision-maker might employ – maintains all the essential ingredients necessary to make the decision and ensures that they are used in a manner logically consistent with the decision-maker's basic preferences. Raiffa (1968, p271) expresses this attitude well in the following statement:

> The spirit of decision analysis is divide and conquer: decompose a complex problem into simpler problems, get your thinking straight in these simpler problems, paste these analyses together with a logical glue, and come out with a program for action for the complex problem. Experts are not asked complicated, fuzzy questions, but crystal clear, unambiguous, elemental hypothetical questions.

Decision analysis of hurricane modification

The technique of decision analysis is best communicated via a specific example. Fortunately, there is a detailed example available in the analysis of hurricane modification prepared by the decision analysis group of Stanford Research Institute (SRI) on behalf of the National Oceanic and Atmospheric Administration (Boyd et al, 1971; Howard, Matheson & North, 1972). An overview of this analysis is presented below.

In the case of hurricane modification, one important decision is strategic: 'Should cloud seeding ever be performed?' If the answer is yes, then tactical decisions concerning which hurricanes are to be seeded become important. The SRI analysis focuses on the strategic decision. The basic approach is to consider a representative severe hurricane bearing down on a coastal area and to analyze the decision to seed or not to seed this hurricane. Maximum sustained surface wind speed is used as the measure of the storm's intensity, since it is this characteristic (which is the primary cause of destruction) that seeding is expected to influence. The analysis assumes that the direct consequence of a decision on seeding is the property damage caused by the hurricane.

However, property damage alone is insufficient to describe the consequences of hurricane seeding. There are indirect social and legal effects that arise from human intervention; thus, the government might have some legal responsibility for the damage from a seeded hurricane. The trade-off between accepting the responsibility for seeding and accepting higher probabilities of severe property damage is viewed as the crucial issue in this decision.

The first step in the SRI analysis was to merge current experimental evidence with the best prior scientific opinion to obtain a probability distribution over changes in the intensity of the representative hurricane as measured by its maximum surface wind speed. This was done for both alternatives – seeding and not seeding. Then, data from past hurricanes were used to infer the relationship between wind speed and property damage. On the basis of this information, the expected loss in terms of property damage was calculated to be about 20% less if the hurricane is seeded. Varying the assumptions of the analysis over a wide range of values caused this reduction to vacillate between 10 and 30%, but did not change the preferred alternative.

The above analysis favors seeding but does not take the negative utility of government responsibility into account. The assessment of responsibility costs entails considerable introspective effort on the part of the decision-maker, who must make judgments such as 'Estimate x such that the government would be indifferent between a seeded hurricane that intensifies 16% between time of seeding and landfall and an unseeded hurricane that produces x% more damage than that of the seeded hurricane'.

On the basis of estimates such as the above, it was inferred that the responsibility costs needed to change the decision were a substantial fraction (about 20%) of the property damage caused by the hurricane. This, and further analyses, led to the conclusion that on the basis of present information, the probability of severe damage is less if a hurricane is seeded, and that seeding should be permitted on an emergency basis and encouraged on an experimental basis.

Critique of decision analysis

It is difficult to convey in a summary the depth of thinking and the logic underlying the decision analysis. The brief description necessarily simplifies the
analysis and highlights a chief objection to decision analysis in general – the
claim that it oversimplifies the situation and thus misleads. Nevertheless, even
those who read the complete analysis may have concerns over its validity. They
may note that Howard, Matheson and North (1972) have constrained their analysis to ignore the beneficial and detrimental aspects of hurricanes in their major
contribution to the water balance of the areas affected. The analysis also ignores the possibility that knowledge of an operational seeding program will give
residents a false sense of security, thus inviting greater damages than might occur
without seeding. The critics argue that such decision analyses are inevitably
constrained by time, effort and imagination, and must systematically exclude
many considerations. A second major objection to decision analysis is the possibility that it may be used to justify, and give a gloss of respectability to, decisions made on other, and perhaps less rational, grounds.

Decision analysts counter these attacks by invoking one of their basic tenets – namely, that any alternative must be considered in the context of other
alternatives. What, they ask, are the alternatives to decision analysis, and are
they any more immune to the criticisms raised above? The analysts point out
that traditional modes of decision-making are equally constrained by limits of
time, effort and imagination, and are even more likely to induce systematic
biases (as illustrated earlier in this chapter). Such biases are much harder to
detect and minimize than the deficiencies in the explicit inputs to decision
analysis. Furthermore, they argue, if some factors are unknown or poorly understood, can traditional methods deal with them more adequately than decision
analysis does? Traditional methods also are susceptible to the 'gloss of respectability' criticism noted above. We often resort to expertise to buttress our decisions without really knowing the assumptions and logic underlying the experts'
judgments. Decision analysis makes these assumptions explicit. Such explicit
data are easy for knowledgeable persons to criticize and the explicitness thus
focuses debate on the right issues.

Decision analysts would agree that their craft is no panacea, that incomplete
or poorly designed analyses may be worse than no analyses at all, and that analysis may be used to 'overwhelm the opposition'. It seems clear, however, that
the main task for the future is not so much to criticize decision analysis but rather
to see how it can be used most appropriately.

CONCLUSION

In coping with the hazard of natural events, man enlarges the social costs of
those events and tends to make himself more vulnerable to the consequences
of the great extremes. His response to uncertainty in the timing and magnitude
of droughts, earthquakes, floods and similar unusual events has led to increases
in the toll of life and property which they take.

Understanding why this is so is essential in wisely designing new policies.
Much of the improved policy necessarily will depend upon action by individuals

within public constraints. Here it is important to recognize how people make their choices in the face of uncertainty in nature and how they might be expected to respond within a different set of constraints.

Enough is known about the process of choice to be sure that it cannot be accurately described as a simple effort to maximize net marginal returns. Nor can it be explained solely in terms of the culture or the personality of the decision-makers. It is not easily predicted as a product of particular environmental or organizational conditions. It is a complex, multidetermined phenomenon. The need for relatively clear analysis of its essential elements is urgent and is at the heart of systematic improvement of public policy.

The present chapter attempted to show that:

- Convergent evidence from psychology, business, governmental policy-making and geography documents the usefulness of bounded rationality as a framework for conceptualizing decision processes.
- An understanding of the workings of bounded rationality can be exploited to improve adjustment to natural hazards.
- Decision analysis, though still in an early stage of development, promises to be a valuable aid for the important decisions man must make regarding natural hazards.

Measures needed to increase understanding of the decision process and provide opportunities for improving it require a combination of theoretical, laboratory and empirical approaches. Determining a rationale for optimal behavior in the face of a capricious nature requires theoretical development. The basic modes of assessing probabilities of rare natural events and of assigning values to consequences involve cognitive processes that may be discerned most clearly in controlled laboratory experiments. Recognizing ways in which cultural and situational factors may influence decisions calls for observation in field settings.

ACKNOWLEDGMENTS

Principal support for this chapter came from Grant 6S-2882X from the National Science Foundation to the University of Colorado. Additional support was provided by grants to the Oregon Research Institute from the National Science Foundation (Grant GS-32505) and the US Public Health Service (Grant MH-21216).

2

Cognitive Processes and Societal Risk Taking

*Paul Slovic, Baruch Fischhoff and
Sarah Lichtenstein*

Our world is so constructed that the physical and material benefits we most desire are sprinkled with the seeds of disaster. For example, the search for fertile fields often leads us to floodplains, and our attempt to make less fertile fields productive forces us to rely, at some risk, on fertilizers, pesticides and fungicides. The wonder drugs that maintain our health carry side effects proportional to their potency and the benefits of energy are enjoyed at the risk of damage from a host of pollutants. People today have some control over the level of risk they face, but reduction of risk often entails reduction of benefit as well.

The regulation of risk poses serious dilemmas for society. Policy-makers are being asked, with increasing frequency, to 'weigh the benefits against the risks' when making decisions about social and technological programs. These individuals often have highly sophisticated methods at their disposal for gathering information about problems or constructing technological solutions. When it comes to making decisions, however, they typically fall back on the technique that has been relied on since antiquity – intuition. The quality of their intuitions sets an upper limit on the quality of the entire decision-making process and, perhaps, the quality of our lives.

The purpose of this chapter is to explore the role that the psychological study of decision processes can play in improving societal risk taking. Over the past 25 years, empirical and theoretical research on decision-making under risk has produced a body of knowledge that should be of value to those who seek to understand and improve societal decisions. After we review relevant aspects of this research, we will focus on some of the many issues needing further study.

The chapter is organized around three general questions:

Note: reprinted from 'Cognitive Processes and Societal Risk Taking', by P Slovic, B Fischhoff and S Lichtenstein, in *Cognition and Social Behavior* (pp165–184), by J S Carroll & J W Payne (eds), 1976, Potomac, MD: Lawrence Erlbaum Associates. Copyright 1976 by Lawrence Erlbaum Associates, Inc. Reprinted with permission.

1　What are some of the basic policy issues involving societal risk?
2　What do psychologists already know about how people behave in decision-making tasks that is relevant to these issues?
3　What more do we need to know and how may we acquire that knowledge?

BASIC POLICY ISSUES

The issues involved in policy-making for societal risks can best be presented within the contexts of specific problem areas. Two such areas, natural hazards and nuclear power, are discussed in this section.

Natural Hazards

Natural hazards constitute an enormous problem. Their mean cost in the US is approaching US$10 billion annually (Wiggins, 1974). A major earthquake in an urban area could cause $20 billion in property damage (Gillette & Walsh, 1971), not to mention the accompanying human misery, anguish and death.

The question facing public policy-makers is: what sorts of measures should be employed to maximize the benefits of our natural environment, while at the same time minimizing the social and economic disruption caused by disasters? In the case of floods, policy options that have been tried or considered include compulsory insurance, flood control systems, strict regulation of land usage and massive relief to victims.

Not surprisingly, modern industrial countries have opted for technological solutions, such as dams. It is now recognized, however, that these well-intended programs have often exacerbated the problem. Although the US government has spent more than $10 billion since 1936 on flood control structures, the mean annual total of flood losses has risen steadily (White, 1964). The damage inflicted on Pennsylvania in 1972 by flooding associated with Hurricane Agnes exceeded $3 billion despite the area being protected by 66 dams. Apparently, the partial protection offered by dams gives residents a false sense of security and promotes overdevelopment of the flood plain. As a result of this overdevelopment, when a rare flood does exceed the capacity of the dam the damage is catastrophic. Perpetuating the problem, the victims of such disasters typically return and rebuild on the same site (Burton, Kates & White, 1968). The lesson to be learned is that technological solutions are likely to be inadequate without knowledge of how they affect the decision-making of individuals at risk.

Current debate over public policy is focused on whether disaster insurance should be compulsory. Kunreuther (1973) has noted that, whereas few individuals protect themselves voluntarily against the consequences of natural disasters, many turn to the federal government for aid after suffering losses. As a result, the taxpayer is burdened with financing the recovery for those who could have provided for themselves by purchasing insurance. Kunreuther and others argued that both the property owners at risk and the government would be better off financially under a federal flood-insurance program. Such a program would shift the burden of disasters from the general taxpayer to individuals living in hazard-prone areas and would thus promote wiser decisions regarding use of floodplains. For example, insurance rates could be set proportional to the magnitude of risk in order to inform residents of those risks and deter development of high-risk areas.

Without a better understanding of how people perceive and react to risks, however, there is no way of knowing what sort of flood-insurance program would be most effective. To take another example, it seems reasonable that lowering the cost of insurance would encourage people to buy it. Yet there is evidence that people do not voluntarily insure themselves even if the rates are highly subsidized. The reasons for this are unknown. Knowledge of how psychological, economic and environmental factors influence insurance purchasing may suggest ways to increase voluntary purchases – or indicate the need for a compulsory insurance program.

Nuclear Power

The problem of determining our level of dependence on nuclear energy is so well known as to require little introduction. Policy decisions must weigh the risks and benefits of a technology for which relevant experience is so limited that technicians must extrapolate far beyond available data. Policy-makers must also guess how the public is going to react to their analyses and decisions.

One major issue in the nuclear power controversy involves determining the locus of decision-making authority and the nature and amount of public input. At one extreme are those who argue that decisions about nuclear development should be left to technical experts and to policy-makers trained in sophisticated decision-analytic techniques. Resistance to this view is exemplified by Denenberg (1974), who insisted that 'Nuclear safety is too important to be left to the experts. It is an issue that should be resolved from the point of view of the public interest, which requires a broader perspective than that of tunnel-visioned technicians.'

At present, the weighing of benefits versus risks has degenerated into a heated controversy over the magnitude of the risks from loss of coolant accidents, sabotage, theft of weapon's grade materials and long-term storage of wastes. Some experts argue that nuclear power is extraordinarily safe; others vigorously dissent and have mobilized numerous public interest groups in opposition to the nuclear menace. If the opponents of nuclear power are right about the risks, every reactor built is a catastrophe. If they are wrong, following their advice and halting the construction of reactors may be equally costly to society.

What contributions can cognitive psychologists make toward resolving this controversy? Several possibilities exist. First, they can help develop judgmental techniques to assist engineers in assessing probabilities of failure for systems that lack relevant frequentistic data. Second, they can attempt to clarify, from a psychological standpoint, the advantages and disadvantages of various methods of performing risk-benefit evaluations and determining acceptable levels of risk. Third, they can assist the layman in trying to understand what the professionals' analyses mean. Even the most astute technical analysis is of little value if its assumptions and results cannot be communicated accurately to the individuals who bear ultimate decision-making responsibility. Fourth, psychological study of man's ability to think rationally about probabilities and risks is essential in determining the appropriate roles of expert and layman in the decision-making process. Fifth, such study can help the public understand how much faith to put into experts' subjective judgments. Given the biases to which these judgments are susceptible, the public may sometimes decide that the experts' best guesses are not good enough.

PSYCHOLOGICAL KNOWLEDGE RELEVANT TO SOCIETAL RISK TAKING

Early Work

The classic view of peoples' higher mental processes assumes that we are intellectually gifted creatures. A statement typical of this esteem was expressed by economist Frank Knight (1921–1965): 'We are so built that what seems reasonable to us is likely to be confirmed by experience or we could not live in the world at all' (p227).

With the dawn of the computer era and its concern for information processing by man and machine, a new picture of man has emerged. Miller (1956), in his famous study of classification and coding, showed that there are severe limitations on people's ability to process sensory signals. About the same time, close observation of performance in concept formation tasks led Bruner, Goodnow and Austin (1956) to conclude that their subjects were experiencing a condition of 'cognitive strain' and were trying to reduce it by means of simplification strategies. The processing of conceptual information is currently viewed as a serial process that is constrained by limited short-term memory and a slow storage in long-term memory (Newell & Simon, 1972).

In the study of decision-making, too, the classic view of behavioral adequacy, or rationality, has been challenged on psychological grounds. For example, Simon's (1957) theory of 'bounded rationality' asserts that cognitive limitations force decision-makers to construct simplified models in order to deal with the world. Simon (1957, p198) argued that the decision-maker:

> ...behaves rationally with respect to this [simplified] model, and such behavior is not even approximately optimal with respect to the real world. To predict his behavior, we must understand the way in which this simplified model is constructed, and its construction will certainly be related to his psychological properties as a perceiving, thinking and learning animal.

Research providing empirical support for the concept of bounded rationality is discussed next.

Recent Studies of Probabilistic Information Processing

Because of the importance of probabilistic reasoning to decision-making, a great deal of recent experimental effort has been devoted to understanding how people perceive and use the probabilities of uncertain events. By and large, this research provides dramatic support for Simon's concept of bounded rationality. The experimental results indicate that people systematically violate the principles of rational decision-making when judging probabilities, making predictions or otherwise attempting to cope with probabilistic tasks. Frequently, these violations can be traced to the use of judgmental heuristics or simplification strategies. These heuristics may be valid in some circumstances, but in others they lead to biases that are large, persistent and serious in their implications for decision-making. Because much of this research has been summarized elsewhere (Slovic et al, 1974; Tversky & Kahneman, 1974), coverage here is brief.

Misjudging sample implications

After questioning a large number of psychologists about their research practices and studying the designs of experiments reported in psychological journals, Tversky and Kahneman (1971) concluded that these scientists seriously underestimated the error and unreliability inherent in small samples of data. As a result, they:

- had unreasonably high expectations about the replicability of results from a single sample;
- had undue confidence in early results from a few subjects;
- gambled their research hypotheses on small samples without realizing the extremely high odds against detecting the effects being studied; and
- rarely attributed any unexpected results to sampling variability because they found a causal explanation for every observed effect.

Similar results in quite different contexts have been obtained by Berkson, Magath and Hurn (1940) and Brehmer (1974). However, people are not always incautious when drawing inferences from samples of data. Under certain circumstances they become quite conservative, responding as though data are much less diagnostic than they truly are (Edwards, 1968).

In a study using Stanford undergraduates as subjects, Kahneman and Tversky (1972) found that many of these individuals did not understand the fundamental principle of sampling – that the variance of a sample decreases as the sample size becomes larger. They concluded that 'for anyone who would wish to view man as a reasonable intuitive statistician, such results are discouraging' (p445).

Errors of prediction

Kahneman and Tversky (1973) contrasted the rules that determined peoples' intuitive predictions with the normative principles of statistical prediction. Normatively, the prior probabilities, or base rates, which summarize what we knew before receiving evidence specific to the case at hand are relevant even after specific evidence is obtained. In fact, however, people seem to rely almost exclusively on specific information and neglect prior probabilities. Similar results have been obtained by Hammerton (1973), Lyon and Slovic (1976), and Nisbett, Borgida, Crandall and Reed (1976).

Another normative principle is that the variance of one's predictions should be sensitive to the validity of the information on which the predictions are based. If validity is not perfect, predictions should be regressed toward some central value. Furthermore, the lower the validity of the information on which predictions are based, the greater the regression should be. Kahneman and Tversky (1973) observed that otherwise intelligent people have little or no intuitive understanding of the concept of regression. They fail to expect regression in many situations when it is bound to occur and, when they observe it, they typically invent complex but spurious explanations. People fail to regress their predictions toward a central value even when they are using information that they themselves consider of low validity.

A third principle of prediction asserts that, given input variables of stated validity, accuracy of prediction decreases as redundancy increases. Kahneman and Tversky (1973) have found, however, that people have greater confidence in predictions based on highly redundant or correlated predictor variables. The effect of redundancy on confidence is, therefore, opposite of what it should be.

Availability bias

Another form of judgmental bias comes from use of the 'availability' heuristic (Tversky & Kahneman, 1973). This heuristic involves judging the probability or frequency of an event by the ease with which relevant instances are imagined or by the number of such instances that are readily retrieved from memory. In life, instances of frequent events are typically easier to recall than instances of less frequent events and likely occurrences are usually easier to imagine than unlikely ones. Therefore, mental availability is often a valid cue for the assessment of frequency and probability. However, because availability is also affected by subtle factors unrelated to actual frequency, such as recency and emotional saliency, relying upon it may result in serious errors.

Availability bias is illustrated in an experiment we conducted to study people's perceptions of low-probability, high-consequence events. Our stimuli were 41 causes of death, including diseases, accidents, homicide, suicide and natural hazards. The probability of a randomly selected US resident's dying from one of these causes in a year ranges from about 1.0×10^{-8} (botulism) to 8.5×10^{-3} (heart disease). We constructed 106 pairs of these events and asked a large sample of college students to indicate, for each pair, the more likely cause of death and the ratio of the greater to the lesser frequency.

We found that:

- Our subjects had a consistent subjective scale of relative frequency for causes of death.
- This subjective scale often deviated markedly from the true scale.
- The subjects could consistently identify which of the paired events was the more frequent cause of death only when the true ratio of greater to lesser frequency was greater than 2:1.

At true ratios of 2:1 or below, discrimination was poor. A subset of the detailed results is presented in Table 2.1.

According to the availability hypothesis, any incident that makes the occurrence of an event easy to imagine or to recall is likely to enhance its perceived frequency. For example, one's direct experiences with a lethal event should

Table 2.1 *Judgements of Relative Frequency for Selected Pairs of Lethal Events*

Less likely	More likely	True ratio	Correct discrimination (%)	Geometric mean of judged ratios [a]
Asthma	Firearm accident	1.20	80	11.00
Breast cancer	Diabetes	1.25	23	0.13
Lung cancer	Stomach cancer	1.25	25	0.31
Leukemia	Emphysema	1.49	47	0.58
Stroke	All cancer	1.57	83	21.00
All accidents	Stroke	1.85	20	0.04
Pregnancy	Appendicitis	2.00	17	0.10
Tuberculosis	Fire and flames	2.00	81	10.50
Emphysema	All accidents	5.19	88	269.00
Polio	Tornado	5.30	71	4.26
Drowning	Suicide	9.60	70	5.50
All accidents	All diseases	15.50	57	1.62
Diabetes	Heart disease	18.90	97	127.00
Tornado	Asthma	20.90	42	0.36
Syphilis	Homicide	46.00	86	31.70
Botulism	Lightning	52.00	37	0.30
Flood	Homicide	92.00	91	81.70
Syphilis	Diabetes	95.00	64	2.36
Botulism	Asthma	920.00	59	1.50
Excess cold	All cancer	982.00	95	1490.00
Botulism	Emphysema	10,600.00	86	24.00

[a] Geometric means less than 1.00 indicate that the mean ratio was higher for the less likely event. A geometric mean of 0.20 implies the mean was 5:1 in the wrong direction.

certainly influence one's judgments. So should one's indirect exposure to the event, via movies, television, newspaper publicity and so forth. Examination of events most seriously misjudged lends indirect support to this hypothesis. The frequencies of accidents, cancer, botulism and tornadoes, all of which get heavy media coverage, were greatly overestimated; asthma and diabetes are among the events whose frequencies were most underestimated. Both of these events are relatively common in their non-fatal form and deaths are rarely attributed to them by the media. Similarly, the spectacular event, fire, which often takes multiple victims and which gets much media coverage, was perceived as considerably more frequent than the less spectacular single-victim event, drowning, although both are about equal in terms of actual frequency.

In addition to demonstrating availability bias, this study implies that, contrary to the assumptions of some policy-makers, intelligent individuals may not have valid perceptions about the frequency of hazardous events to which they are exposed.

Anchoring biases

Bias also occurs when a judge attempts to ease the strain of processing information by following the heuristic device of 'anchoring and adjustment'. In this process, a natural starting point or anchor is used as a first approximation to the judgment. This anchor is then adjusted to accommodate the implications of additional information. Typically, the adjustment is crude and imprecise and fails to do justice to the importance of additional information. Recent work by Tversky and Kahneman (1974) demonstrates the tendency for adjustments to be insufficient. They asked subjects such questions as: 'What is the percentage of people in the US today who are age 55 or older?' They gave the subjects starting percentages that were randomly chosen and asked them to adjust these percentages until they reached their best estimate. Because of insufficient adjustment, subjects whose starting points were high ended up with higher estimates than those who started with low values. Other biases caused by anchoring and adjustment have been described by Slovic (1972).

Hindsight biases

A series of experiments by Fischhoff (1974; 1975; Fischhoff & Beyth, 1975) have examined the phenomenon of hindsight. Fischhoff has found that being told some event has happened increases our feeling that it is inevitable. We are unaware of this effect, however, and tend to believe that this inevitability was apparent in foresight, before we knew what happened. In retrospect, we tend to believe that we (and others) had a much better idea of what was going to happen than we actually did have. Fischhoff (1974) showed how such misperceptions can seriously prejudice the evaluation of decisions made in the past and limit what is learned from experience.

DISCUSSION

Because these experimental results contradict our traditional image of the human intellect, it is reasonable to ask whether these inadequacies in probabilistic thinking exist outside the laboratory in situations where decision-makers use familiar sources of information to make decisions that are important to themselves and others.

Much evidence suggests that the laboratory results will generalize. Cognitive limitations appear to pervade a wide variety of tasks in which intelligent individuals serve as decision-makers, often under conditions that maximize motivation and involvement. For example, the subjects studied by Tversky and Kahneman (1971) were scientists, highly trained in statistics, evaluating problems similar to those they faced in their own research. Overdependence on specific evidence and neglect of base rates has been observed among psychometricians responsible for the development and use of psychological tests (Meehl & Rosen, 1955). When Lichtenstein and Slovic (1971) observed anchoring bias in subjects' evaluations of gambles, they repeated the study, with identical results, on the floor of a Las Vegas casino (Lichtenstein & Slovic, 1973).

Particularly relevant to this chapter is evidence illustrating these sorts of biases in individuals attempting to cope with natural disasters. For example, availability biases are apparent in the behavior of residents on the floodplain. Kates (1962, p140) writes:

> A major limitation to human ability to use improved flood hazard information is a basic reliance on experience. Men on flood plains appear very much to be prisoners of their experience... Recently experienced floods appear to set an upward bound to the size of loss with which managers believe they ought to be concerned.

Kates further attributes much of the difficulty in achieving better flood control to the 'inability of individuals to conceptualize floods that have never occurred' (p88). He observes that, in making forecasts of future flood potential, individuals 'are strongly conditioned by their immediate past and limit their extrapolation to simplified constructs, seeing the future as a mirror of that past' (p88). A more detailed linkage between psychological research, bounded rationality and behavior in the face of natural hazards is provided by Slovic et al (1974).

One additional implication of the research on people's limited ability to process probabilistic information deserves comment. Most of the discussions of 'cognitive strain' and 'limited capacity' that are derived from the study of problem solving and concept formation depict a person as a computer that has the right programs but cannot execute them properly because its central processor is too small. The biases from availability and anchoring certainly are congruent with this analogy. However, the misjudgment of sampling variability and the errors of prediction illustrate more serious deficiencies. Here we see that people's judgments of important probabilistic phenomena are not merely biased but are in violation of fundamental normative rules. Returning to the computer analogy, it appears that people lack the correct programs for many important judgmental tasks.

How can it be that we lack adequate programs for probabilistic thinking? Sinsheimer (1971) argues that the human brain has evolved to cope with certain very real problems in the immediate, external world and so lacks the framework with which to encompass many conceptual phenomena. Following Sinsheimer's reasoning, it may be argued that we have not had the opportunity to evolve an intellect capable of dealing conceptually with uncertainty. We are essentially trial-and-error learners, who ignore uncertainty and rely predominantly on habit or simple deterministic rules. It remains to be seen whether we can change our ways in the nuclear age when errors may be catastrophic.

Where Do We Go from Here? Psychological Considerations in Risk-Benefit Analysis

Our society has, with increasing frequency, sought help from technical experts trained in the application of formal, analytical methods to problems of decision-making. The scientific approach originated during World War II from the need to solve strategic and tactical problems in situations where experience was costly or impossible to acquire. One of the offshoots of this early work has been the technique called cost-benefit analysis, which attempts to quantify the expected gains and losses from some proposed action, usually in monetary terms. If the calculated gain from an act or project is positive, it is said that the benefits outweigh the costs and its acceptance is recommended, providing no other alternative affords a better cost-benefit ratio. A good example of this is the analysis of auto-safety features by Lave and Weber (1970). Risk-benefit analysis is a special case of cost-benefit analysis in which explicit attention is given to assessing the probabilities of hazardous events and quantifying costs from loss of life or limb, pain and anguish.

Risk-benefit analysis, still in its early stages of development, is being counted on to provide the basic methodological tools for societal risk-taking decisions. Psychological research can contribute to this nascent methodology by identifying the major sources of error in societal risk-taking decisions and by devising techniques to minimize those errors. In the remainder of this chapter we shall speculate about some of the directions this research may take.

Evaluating Low-probability, High-consequence Events

The most important public hazards are events with extremely low probabilities and extremely great consequences. For example, Holmes (1961) found that 50% of the damage from major floods was caused by floods with probabilities of occurrence in any year of less than .01. The city of Skopje, Yugoslavia, was leveled by earthquakes in the years AD 518, 1555 and 1963, and the mudflow that took 25,000 lives in Yungay, Peru, had swept across the same valley between 1000 and 10,000 years before. The probability of serious radiation release from a nuclear power reactor has been estimated at between 10^{-4} and 10^{-9} per reactor year. Despite the obvious significance of understanding how (and how well) experts and laymen estimate probabilities for such events, there has been little or no systematic study of this problem other than that by Selvidge (1975) and the 'causes of death' study described above.

This section considers the manner in which psychological analysis may help technical experts using two sophisticated analytic techniques for assessing the probabilities of rare hazards: fault-tree analysis and scenario construction.

Fault-tree analysis

When frequentistic data regarding failure rates of a complex system are unavailable, estimates can be obtained analytically by means of a fault tree. Construction of the tree begins by listing all important pathways to failure, then listing all possible pathways to these pathways, and so on. When the desired degree of detail is obtained, probabilities are assigned to each of the component pathways and then combined to provide an overall failure rate. For example, major pathways in a fault tree designed to evaluate the probability of a car failing to start would include defects in the battery, starting system, fuel system, ignition system and so forth. Battery deficiency could then be traced to loose terminals or weak battery charge. The latter could be further analyzed into component causes, such as lights left on, cold weather or a defective generator. The likelihoods of these separate events are combined to produce an estimate of the overall probability of starting failure.

The importance of fault-tree analysis is demonstrated by its role as the primary methodological tool in a recently completed study assessing the probability of a catastrophic loss of coolant accident in a nuclear power reactor (Rasmussen,

1974) The study, sponsored by the Atomic Energy Commission at a cost of US$2 million, concluded that the likelihood of such an accident ranged between 10^{-5} (for an accident causing ten deaths) and 10^{-9} (for a 1000-death accident) per reactor year. Fault-tree analysis, however, has recently come under attack from critics who question whether it is valid enough to be used as a basis for decisions of great consequence (eg, Bryan, 1974).

Psychologists may be able to improve the effectiveness of fault trees by identifying biases that may afflict fault-tree users and by shoring up tile methodology. One methodological problem that psychologists surely can address is deciding by what technique (eg, direct estimation, paired comparisons, Delphi methods) failure rates for component parts should be estimated. One possible source of bias worth investigating arises from the fact that one rarely has complete empirical failure rates on every component part of a complex system. The rates used are typically estimated from slightly different parts or parts that have been developed for a different purpose. Anchoring and adjustment may well play a role here, possibly leading to estimates more suitable for the original part or original context than for the one in question.

Another possible bias would arise from the omission of relevant pathways to failure or disaster. A tree used to estimate starting failure in an automobile could, for example, be seriously deficient if it failed to include problems with the seat-belt system (for 1974 models), theft of vital parts or other vandalism. The dangers of omitting relevant pathways to disaster should not be underestimated. The cartoon by Mauldin (Figure 2.1) dramatizes this problem, reflecting the recent reports that the ozone layer, which protects the earth from solar radiation, may be damaged by the fluorocarbons released by aerosol products. In the innumerable scenarios that have been created to evaluate the major risks of technology to mankind, who has thought prior to this discovery to include hair sprays and deodorants as lethal agents?

We suspect that, in general, experts are not adequately sensitive to those avenues to disaster that they have failed to consider because of ignorance, forgetfulness, or lack of imagination. People who are unaware of their own omissions are likely to seriously underestimate the true failure rate. This hypothesis can surely be tested experimentally.

Even if technical experts could be helped to produce better estimates, problems with the fault tree would not be over. With most societal decisions, ultimate responsibility lies with either the general public or political policymakers. The finest analysis is of little value if it cannot be communicated to these people. Considerations of availability suggest that fault-tree analysis is a technique the results of which are particularly prone to creating misconceptions. For example, naive observers of a fault tree may be startled by the variety of possible pathways to disaster, some of which are likely to be new and surprising to them. Unless they combat the increased imaginability of disaster pathways by properly discounting the less probable paths, they may overreact, perceiving the risk to be greater than it is. Furthermore, the larger and bushier a tree is – in the detail with which specific components of each major pathway are presented – the greater the misperception may be. Therefore, analyses intended to clarify decision-makers' perceptions may instead distort them.

Critics of nuclear power often appear to be playing on these proclivities. Consider this message from Alfven (1972): 'Fission energy is safe only if a number of critical devices work as they should, if a number of people in key positions all follow their instructions, if there is no sabotage, no hijacking of the transports... No acts of God can be permitted' (p6).

Although Alfven's statement is an extreme position, it suggests that availability effects may make it difficult to engage in unbiased attempts at discussing low-probability hazards without, at the same time, increasing the perceived probability of those hazards. This may explain, in part, why continued discussions of nuclear power risks have led to increased resistance to this technology. Ultimately, public acceptance of new, high-risk technologies may be determined more by psychological considerations than by the opinions of technical experts.

"SO **THAT'S** THE ONE MOST LIKELY TO GET US."

Source: Reprinted with special permission from *The Chicago Sun Times, Inc.*© 2000.

Figure 2.1 *'So that's the one most likely to get us'*

Evaluating scenarios

Forecasts and predictions of high-consequence events are often developed with the aid of scenarios. Some recent examples are 'The Day They Blew Up San Onofre' (Schleimer, 1974), describing the sabotage of a nuclear reactor and its consequences, and 'The Oil War of 1976' (Erdmann, 1975), describing how the world as we know it comes to an end when the Shah of Iran decides to take it over with Western arms.

A scenario consists of a series of events linked together in narrative form. Normatively, the probability of a multievent scenario's happening is a multiplicative function of the probabilities of the individual links. The more links there are in the scenario, the lower the probability of the entire scenario's occurrence. The probability of the weakest link sets an upper limit on the probability of the entire narrative.

Human judges do not appear to evaluate scenarios according to these normative rules. We have begun to collect data suggesting that the probability of a multilink scenario is judged on the basis of the average likelihood of all its links. Subsequent strong links appear to 'even out' or compensate for earlier weak links, making it possible to construct scenarios with perceived probabilities that increase as they become longer, more detailed and normatively less probable. Consider the following example of such a scenario, taken from one of our experiments:

> Tom is of high intelligence, although lacking in true creativity. He has a need for order and clarity, and for neat and tidy systems in which every detail finds its appropriate place. His writing is rather dull and mechanical, occasionally enlivened by somewhat corny puns and by flashes of imagination of the sci-fi type. He has a strong drive for competence. He seems to have little feel and little sympathy for other people and does not enjoy interacting with others.
>
> In the light of these data, what is the probability that (a) Tom W will select journalism as his college major (b) but quickly become unhappy with his choice and (c) switch to engineering?

When subjects were given the initial conditions contained in the first paragraph and asked to estimate the probability of subsequent event *a*, Tom's selection of journalism as his college major, their mean estimate was .21. When they were asked to estimate the compound probability of statements *a* and *b*, given the same initial conditions, the mean probability rose to .39. When they were asked to estimate the compound event consisting of statements *a*, *b* and *c*, the mean probability rose to .41. These results suggest that scenarios which tell a 'good story' by burying weak links in masses of coherent detail may be accorded much more credibility than they deserve.

Experiments are needed to clarify the cognitive processes that determine whether a scenario appears plausible, to identify biases in scenario evaluation and to develop techniques for combatting such biases. An obvious first step toward debiasing is simply educating or warning judges about the problem. If this fails or merely adds noise and confusion to their judgments, more sophisticated techniques must be devised. For example, it may be necessary to decompose the scenario into its component events, estimate conditional probabilities for individual events given preceding developments, and then combine these conditional probabilities mathematically to produce an overall evaluation (see Edwards & Phillips, 1964, for details of a similar approach to combat a different bias). Alternatively, one could insist on the production of several alternative scenarios on any given topic and use an adversary approach in which the merits and disadvantages of each are debated.

How Safe Is Safe Enough?

Any risk-benefit analysis must ultimately answer the question: how safe is safe enough? Starr (1969) has proposed a quantitative technique for answering this question based on the assumption that society arrives by trial and error at a reasonably optimal balance between the risks and benefits associated with any activity. Therefore, one may use historical accident and fatality records to reveal patterns of 'acceptable' risk-benefit ratios. Acceptable risk for a new technology becomes that level of safety associated with ongoing activities having similar benefit to society.

Starr illustrates his technique by examining the relationship between risk and benefit across a number of common activities. This measure of risk for these hazardous activities is the statistical expectation of fatalities per hour of exposure to the activity under consideration. Benefit is assumed to be equal to the average amount of money spent on an activity by an individual participant or, alternatively, to the average contribution that activity makes to an individual's annual income.

From this type of analysis, Starr concludes that:

1   the acceptability of a risk is roughly proportional to the real and perceived benefits;
2   the public seems willing to accept voluntary risks (eg, skiing) roughly 1000 times greater than it tolerates involuntary risks (eg, natural disasters) that provide the same level of benefit; and
3   the acceptable level of risk is inversely related to the number of persons participating in an activity.

Noting the similarity between risks accepted voluntarily and the risks of disease, Starr (1969) conjectures that 'the rate of death from disease appears to play, psychologically, a yardstick role in determining the acceptability of risk on a voluntary basis' (p1235).

The Starr approach provides an intuitively appealing solution to a problem facing all risk-benefit analyses and, in fact, a similar approach has already been used to develop a building code regulating earthquake risk in Long Beach, California (Wiggins, 1972). There are, however, a number of serious drawbacks to this method. First, it assumes that past behavior is a valid indicator of present preferences. Second, it ignores recent psychological research revealing systematic biases that may prevent an individual from making decisions that accurately reflect his or her 'true preferences' (eg, Lichtenstein & Slovic, 1971; 1973; Slovic & MacPhillamy, 1974). Third, the Starr approach assumes that the public has available a wide selection of alternatives from which to choose. Is it reasonable to assume, for example, that the public's automobile-buying behavior accurately reflects its preferences concerning the trade-off between safety and other benefits? Unless the public really knows what is possible from a design standpoint, and unless the automobile industry cooperates in making available information that may not necessarily serve its own profit-maximization interests, the answer is likely to be no. Finally, the misperception of risks as observed in the 'causes of death' study described above casts doubt on Starr's hypothesis regarding the 'yardstick role' of disease rates. It also suggests that revealed historical preferences reflect the forces of the market place rather than the conscious weighing of risks and benefits based on full and accurate information. If so, the justification for using them as a guide for the future is not 'this is what people want' but 'this is what people have come to accept'.

One avenue of research that might help circumvent these difficulties would be to examine risk-benefit trade-offs via judgmental techniques. Psychological measures of perceived risk and perceived benefit could be developed for major classes of activities. Judgments of desired risk could be elicited in addition to judgments of actual risk. Analysis of these data would focus on the degree to which judged risk and benefit agreed with empirical calculations of these factors. In addition, Starr's results regarding voluntary as opposed to involuntary activities, level of perceived benefit, and number of persons participating in an activity could be re-examined by repeating his analyses within the judgmental risk-benefit space.

Perceived Risk

It is surprising that, with the exception of a few studies using simple gambles as stimuli (see, for example, Coombs & Huang, 1970; Payne, 1975), the determinants of perceived risk remain unexplored. Yet there is anecdotal and empirical evidence of a number of risk phenomena meriting serious psychological study. One is society's apparent willingness to spend more to save a known life in danger than to save a statistical life. Is this really true and, if so, why? A second is the speculation that repeated 'uneventful' experience with a hazard reduces its perceived risk more than it should. Study of this question may provide insight into why the public tolerates levels of risk from some hazards (eg, radiation from medical X-rays) that they do not tolerate from nuclear power plants. A third untested notion is that hazards with delayed consequences (eg, smoking) are discounted. Finally, perceived risk may depend greatly on the way in which the relevant information is presented. For example, risks from radiation may appear negligible when described in terms of 'average reduction in life expectancy for the population within a given radius of a nuclear power plant'. However, when this figure is translated into the equivalent number of 'additional cancer deaths per year', risk may take on quite a different perspective.

Research on these phenomena may also help us to understand how the public responds to scientific information about risk. Growing concern over environmental risks has increased scientific research on the effects of such hazards as herbicides, fertilizers, pesticides, pollution and radiation. It has been assumed that publication of scientific information about these hazards is sufficient to

elicit appropriate public action. In fact, although scientific information sometimes leads to hasty public action, it often goes unheeded (Lawless, 1975).
Although the determinants of societal response are undoubtedly complex, cognitive factors related to the communication of information and perception of risk
are likely to play an important role.

Value of a Life

Although the economic costs stemming from property damage, disruption of
production, medical expenses, or loss of earnings can be estimated, we have no
suitable scheme for evaluating the worth of a human life to society. Despite the
aversion to thinking about life in economic terms, the fact is inescapable that
by our actions we put a finite value on our lives. Decisions to install safety features, to buy life insurance or to accept a hazardous job for extra salary all carry
implicit values for a life.

Economists have long debated the question of how best to quantify the value
of a life (see, for example, Hirshleifer, Bergstrom & Rappaport, 1974; Mishan,
1971; Rice & Cooper, 1967; Schelling, 1968). The traditional economic approach has been to equate the value of a life with the value of a person's expected future earnings. Many problems with this index are readily apparent.
For one, it undervalues those in society who are underpaid and places no value
at all on people who are not in income-earning positions. In addition, it ignores
interpersonal effects where the loss suffered by the death of another bears no
relation to the financial loss caused by the death. A second approach, equating
the value of life with court awards (Holmes, 1970; Kidner & Richards, 1974), is
hardly more satisfactory.

Bergstrom (1974) argues that the question 'What is a life worth?' is ill formed
and what we really want to know is 'What is the value placed on a specified
change in survival probability?' As with the Starr approach to assessing risk-
benefit trade-offs, Bergstrom argues that the best way to answer this second
question is by observing the actual market behavior of people trading risks for
economic benefits. For example, Thaler and Rosen (1973) studied salary as a
function of occupational risk and found that a premium of about $200 per year
was required to induce men in risky occupations (eg, coal mining) to accept an
annual probability of .001 of accidental death. From this, they inferred that the
value of life, at the margin, is equivalent to about $200,000. Certainly, the same
criticisms leveled earlier at the Starr approach apply to this method. It assumes
that individuals have enough freedom of choice and perceptiveness of risks so
that their preferences are valid indicators of their values.

We believe this question is too important for psychologists to ignore. They
can contribute by testing the cognitive assumptions on which the economic
measures rest and by providing alternative methods of assessing the value of a
life, such as direct questions or other psychophysical techniques. Preliminary
attempts at this by Acton (1973) and Torrance (1970) have been downgraded by
economists on the grounds that 'Time and again, action has been found to contradict assertion. Since surveys always elicit some degree of strategic behavior
(what do they want me to say?), we would be better advised to observe what
people choose under actual conditions' (Rappaport, 1974, p4). Whether

attitudes or behaviors provide a more accurate reflection of people's values needs to be examined utilizing the broader perspective and expertise that psychology can provide.

Justification

Decision-makers will employ the new tool of risk-benefit analysis to the extent that they believe that such a tool leads to good decisions. What are the perceived characteristics of a good decision? Tversky (1972) and Slovic (1975) have found evidence that decision-makers rely on procedures that are easy to explain and easy to justify to themselves and others. If this is generally true, it may be that decisions are made by searching for or constructing a good justification, one that minimizes lingering doubts and can be defended no matter what outcome occurs. For people accustomed to relying on such justifications, risk-benefit analysis may not be satisfactory. The early steps of such techniques, which involve structuring the problem and detailing alternatives and their attributes, may be useful devices for helping the decision-maker think deeply and in relevant ways about his problem. However, the latter steps, involving quantification, may be forcing people to produce information at a level of precision that does not exist.

An alternative conceptualization, possibly more in tune with people's natural predilections, would have decision-makers act like debaters, marshalling thorough and convincing arguments relevant to the decision at hand, rather than act like computers, making decisions on the basis of arithmetic (for a similar argument, see Mason, 1969).

These speculations lead naturally to the following questions. What are the components of justifiability? What makes a good justification? Although we do not have any firm answers, we do have some hypotheses about factors that may not be viewed as adequate justifications. We think subjective factors – which are the cornerstones for sophisticated decision aids, such as trade-off functions or probability judgments unsupported by frequentistic data – are perceived as weak justifications for decisions in the face of risk. Subjective probabilities, for example, leave one vulnerable to second guessing – imagine the designers of the Edsel explaining in 1961 that their carefully constructed opinions about the market indicated that it was likely to be a big seller. Expected value computations may also make weak justifications because of their dependence on 'long-run' estimates; such estimates may not appear relevant for decisions viewed as one-shot affairs.

Will people view decisions based on shallow but nice-sounding rationales (clichés, universal truths, adages) as better than decisions based on complex, thorough decision-analytic techniques? The answer to this question obviously has important implications for understanding and predicting public decision-makers' responses to information bearing on technological risk. Roback (1972, p1331), in discussing the defeat of the Supersonic Transport (SST) subsidy, provides anecdotal evidence in support of this conjecture:

> There was not ... a nice weighing of risk and benefit... What counted most in the balance, I daresay, was the question that enough congressmen put to themselves before casting a vote: 'How will I explain to my constituents, the majority of whom

have never even been on an airplane or traveled far from home, why we need an SST to save two or three hours' travel time between New York and Paris?'

If these hypotheses are true, the risk-benefit analyst may be preparing analyses merely for his own edification, since few others are likely to use them. In this event, research is vital for teaching us how to communicate risk-benefit and other valuable analytic concepts in ways that enable such material to be woven into the fabric of convincing justifications.

CONCLUDING REMARKS

We have tried to summarize, briefly and from our own perspective, the state of psychological knowledge regarding decision-making under risk; we have also attempted to convey our sense of excitement regarding the potential contributions of this branch of cognitive psychology to basic knowledge and societal well-being.

Our knowledge of the psychological processes involved in risk-taking decisions has increased greatly in recent years. However, we still have only a rudimentary understanding of the ways in which bounded rationality manifests itself. We know much about certain types of deficiencies and biases, but we do not know the full extent of their generality across tasks and across individuals of varying expertise. Nor do we know how to combat these biases. We still do not understand the psychological components of value and how they determine, or depend upon, decisions. We know little about perceived risk, the determinants of societal response to threat, modes of communicating information about risk, or the role of justifications in decision processes. Research in these problem areas is vital to the development of methodologies for societal decision-making that can accommodate the limitations and exploit the specialties of the people who must perform and consume these analyses.

H G Wells once commented: 'Statistical thinking will one day be as important for good citizenship as the ability to read and write.' That day has arrived. Our discussion points to the need for educating both the technical experts and the public regarding the subtleties of statistical thinking. Such education should be incorporated into the curriculum of the schools, perhaps as early as in the lower grades. We need to teach people to recognize explicitly the existence of uncertainty and how to deal rationally with it. We must become accustomed to monitoring our decisions for consistency. We need to understand that the quality of a decision cannot by gauged solely by the quality of its outcome. We must recognize the distortions of hindsight when we evaluate the past.

Although the concept of bounded rationality has arisen within the mainstream of cognitive psychology (eg, Miller's and Simon's work), research on decision processes has made little subsequent contact even with such closely related fields as the study of non-probabilistic information processing. It should. Certainly, the phenomena described here cannot be fully understood without consideration of their underlying cognitive mechanisms. Likewise, some of these phenomema may provide stimulating inputs for general theories of cognition. The hindsight results, for example, indicate one way in which semantic memory is reorganized to accommodate new information. The bias here called 'availability' suggests a need to better understand the process of constrained associates production. No theory of cognitive development appears to relate to the acquisition of judgmental biases and heuristics as conceptualized here. Without such knowledge, we have no idea when it is best, or when it is even possible, to begin teaching children to think probabilistically.

Although this chapter has emphasized what psychologists can do to facilitate societal decision-making, clearly a multidisciplinary approach, involving cooperative efforts with physicists, economists, engineers, geographers and – perhaps most importantly – decision-makers, is necessary. Only by working hand in hand with decision-makers can we learn what their problems are – both those they perceive and those they do not. Only continued multidisciplinary interaction can alert us to the narrowness of our own perspective and enable us to develop practical tools for decision-makers.

ACKNOWLEDGMENTS

Support for this chapter was provided by the Advanced Research Projects Agency of the Department of Defense (ARPA Order No 2449) and was monitored by the Office of Naval Research (ONR), under Contract No N00014-73-C-0438 (NR 197-026). We are indebted to Berndt Brehmer, Daniel Kahneman, Howard Kunreuther and Amos Tversky for stimulating our thinking on many of the issues discussed here.

3 Preference for Insuring Against Probable Small Losses: Insurance Implications

Paul Slovic, Baruch Fischhoff, Sarah Lichtenstein, Bernard Corrigan and Barbara Combs

What determines whether people will act to protect themselves from the severe consequences arising from a low-probability event? The answer to this question is vital for understanding how people cope with the risks from accidents, diseases and natural hazards and for helping them manage their lives more effectively in the face of such risks.

The importance of this question has motivated a major research project concerned with one class of risks, those from natural hazards (floods and earthquakes), and one class of protective mechanisms, insurance. The project staff, under the direction of Howard Kunreuther, interviewed 2000 homeowners residing in flood-prone areas, half of whom were insured and half uninsured. In addition, 1000 homeowners residing in earthquake-prone areas, also divided equally between insured and uninsured, were interviewed.

The general goal of the survey was to provide an understanding of behavior useful for guiding public policy regarding the role of insurance in mitigating losses from floods and earthquakes. One specific issue under consideration was whether insurance coverage should be voluntary or compulsory. A second was whether utility theory provides a description of behavior adequate for guiding policy decisions. Survey questions considered socioeconomic variables; awareness of the hazard; knowledge about the availability, costs and coverage of insurance; and previous experience with both the hazard and insurance. The study and its results are discussed in detail by Kunreuther (1976) and Kunreuther et al (1977). The experimental work described here was intended to test, in rigorously controlled settings, some hypotheses derived from the Kunreuther field survey.

UTILITY THEORY OF INSURANCE

To date, nearly all thinking about insurance behavior has been within the framework of utility theory. This theory has been proposed both as a prescriptive model, indicating when insurance should be purchased, and as a descriptive model, indicating how insurance decisions are made (Friedman & Savage, 1948; Murray, 1971; Neter, Williams & Whitmore, 1968).

Expected utility theory originally was formulated by Bernoulli (1738) and first axiomatized by von Neumann and Morgenstern (1947). The basic principle of the theory is that decisions under risk are made so as to maximize expected utility, the sum of the products of the utilities of outcomes and the probabilities that they will be obtained.

Traditionally, it has been assumed that individual utility functions are concave (monotonically increasing and negatively accelerated) functions of wealth, as in Figure 3.1. The concavity of the utility function embodies the property of risk aversion, which is assumed to characterize responsible people who buy insurance and diversify investments. Risk aversion is defined as the tendency to prefer any sure outcome X, over any gamble with an expected value of X. Thus, a risk-averse person would prefer to receive a sure $50 rather than accept a gamble offering a 50:50 chance to win $100 or win $0. Alternatively, a risk-averse person would prefer to pay any amount Y, rather than to play a gamble with an expected value equal to $-Y$. Such individuals always should be willing to buy insurance at actuarially fair rates.

Arrow (1971) has observed that the predominance of the risk aversion hypothesis is due 'to its success in explaining otherwise puzzling examples of

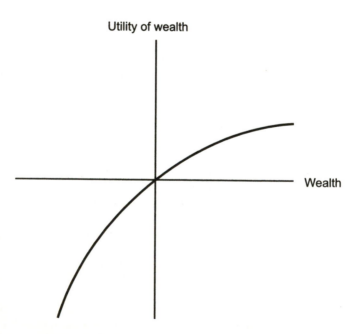

Figure 3.1 *Traditional risk-averse utility function*

economic behavior. The most obvious is insurance, which hardly needs elaboration' (p91).

Despite the widespread acceptance of utility theory, there are reasons to question its descriptive adequacy. First, the few controlled experimental studies of insurance buying have observed behavior contrary to the theory. For example, Murray (1971, 1972) and Neter and Williams (1971) found that utility functions scaled individually for each of their subjects failed to predict insurance preferences. Schoemaker (1977), studying clients of an insurance agency, found preferences for low-deductible policies, context effects and scale effects, all of which ran counter to the theory.

An experiment by Williams (1966) showed that people's preferences among gambles offering no chance of gain were unrelated to their preferences among speculative gambles, which have a chance of loss or gain. Neither of these preferences predicted people's insurance behavior outside of the laboratory (for similar results, see Greene, 1963; 1964). A recent review of laboratory studies by Slovic, Fischhoff and Lichtenstein (1977) found that the expected utility theory accounts poorly for preferences among speculative gambles except in some simple situations.

Field studies, too, have shown that some aspects of people's insurance behavior run counter to utility theory. One is the preference for low-deductible policies despite their disproportionately high premiums (Pashigian, Schkade & Menefee, 1966). Another is the failure of individuals to purchase insurance even when the premiums have been highly subsidized (Anderson, 1974).

Kunreuther et al (1977) found that many residents of hazard-prone areas had no information or wrong information about many factors relevant to the expected utility model (eg, premium rates, subsidies, deductible levels). Even more telling was the fact that, when survey respondents' perceptions of flood and earthquake probabilities, likely monetary damage and premium rates were incorporated into an expected utility analysis, some 30–40% of their insurance decisions were inconsistent with predictions from the theory. These and other data led Kunreuther et al to stress the sequential nature of insurance purchase decisions. Individuals first must consider the hazard to be a problem (stage 1) and then must be aware of insurance as a coping mechanism (stage 2) before they even begin to collect and process information relevant to insurance (stage 3).

This chapter describes a series of laboratory studies of insurance decision-making. Although the authors have manipulated only a few of many possible determinants of insurance decisions, the data are believed to indicate clear and important violations of the risk-aversion assumption of utility theory. These results, in conjunction with those from the Kunreuther field survey, have significant implications for both insurance theory and policy-making.

METHODOLOGICAL CONSIDERATIONS

The Experimenter's Problem

How does one create a laboratory situation analogous to that faced by property owners threatened by natural hazards? It is not difficult to create risks with comparable probabilities of occurrence. Simulating the loss of a home or business is another matter. Certainly, it is immoral for an experimenter to threaten a subject's economic well-being, even in return for a substantial reward for engaging in risk; it also would be improper to exploit an existing risk situation for the sake of scientific knowledge (eg, willfully manipulating the policies offered to subjects living in hazard-prone areas). In principle, one could stake subjects to substantial assets which could then be put at risk. But even if the economics of scientific research enabled staked assets to be substantial, losing someone else's money might not be the same as losing one's own funds.

The Urn Solution

The response to these problems was to pose insurance questions in the abstract. The hazard that the subjects faced was the drawing of a blue ball from an urn composed predominantly of red balls. Their potential losses and the premiums of insurance policies which they could purchase to protect themselves against such losses were measured in undefined 'points'. Subjects never played these abstract games; rather, they were asked what insurance they would purchase were they to participate. Thus, all the 'urn' studies described below reflect the way people believe that they would insure themselves in a particular hypothetical situation.

As an isolated research tool, such urn studies clearly would be inadequate. However, in conjunction with the Kunreuther field survey and a more realistic paradigm called the farm game (described later), they comprise part of a multimethod research program. If these three different approaches produce similar results, one can have much greater confidence in the conclusions than would be justified solely on the basis of any one research design. In the field survey, control is traded for realism; in the laboratory experiment, the trade-off is reversed. The package of studies should indicate what results would be obtained in that realistic and controlled study that is beyond the authors' power to conduct.

EXPERIMENTS WITH THE URN GAME

General Instructions

Each urn experiment was prefaced with the following introduction:

> In the present booklet, we are going to describe a series of gambling games. Each game has the possibility of negative outcomes. Each allows you to buy insurance against the negative outcomes, although it is not compulsory. We are not going to ask you to play any of the games. Instead, we are going to ask you to consider each and then tell us how you would play were they for real. Try to take each as seriously as possible even though nothing is at stake.

Subjects were then told that each game consisted of drawing one ball from each of a set of urns; each urn contained a different mixture of red and blue balls. Drawing a blue ball incurred a loss, unless the subject had purchased insurance at some fixed premium. Unless otherwise noted, the cost of the premium was

Table 3.1 *A Typical Urn Game*

Urn number		Ball color		Insurance premium	Would you buy insurance? (yes or no)
		Blue	Red		
1	No of balls	1	999		
	No of points	−1000	0	1	_____
2	No of balls	5	995		
	No of points	−200	0	1	_____
3	No of balls	10	990		
	No of points	−100	0	1	_____
4	No of balls	50	950		
	No of points	−20	0	1	_____
5	No of balls	100	900		
	No of points	−10	0	1	_____
6	No of balls	250	750		
	No of points	−4	0	1	_____

set at one point for each urn and the loss (L) and probability of loss, $P(L)$, were adjusted so that the expected loss $[P(L)\,L]$ from drawing one ball from the urn was also one point. For example, an urn might contain one blue ball in one thousand balls, and drawing it incurred a loss of 1000 points. Thus, in each case, subjects were offered insurance for the loss cost only, known as the 'pure premium'. In real life situations, the premium would be greater than the expected loss to include an allowance for expenses and additions to retained earnings.

To clarify the subjects' goals in the game, they were told:

> As you can see, you can only lose in this sort of game (either by drawing a blue ball or by buying insurance). Your object is to lose as little as possible. For each game figure out what insurance you would buy to end up with the fewest negative points.

A typical game is presented in Table 3.1. In such a game:

1   Subjects incur only losses and no gains.
2   Subjects have no accrued assets (or nest egg) to protect.
3   Only one ball is to be drawn from each urn.
4   There are six urns, comprising a portfolio of risks.
5   The premium is the same for each urn.

In these features the urn game resembles some real-life situations and differs from others. The effects of changes in some of these features are investigated below; the effects of other changes await further research.

Subjects

About 700 individuals participated in these experiments. Most were volunteer subjects recruited through advertisements in either the University of Oregon student paper or the general circulation local newspaper. All were paid for their participation. They were typically between 20 and 25 years' old, although the range of ages extended from 18 to 72. One exception was a study in which members of the Eugene, Oregon, chapter of the League of Women Voters and their spouses served as subjects. This group was studied to determine whether the results obtained from the younger subjects would generalize to a population of socially concerned homeowners responsible for making insurance decisions in their daily lives.

The Basic Experiment: Varying Probability of Loss

The urn game presented in Table 3.1 systematically varies loss and probability of loss, the one increasing as the other decreases. Different theories lead to different predictions about which of these six urns will be insured. The risk aversion property of utility theory postulates a concave relationship between (negative) utility and loss; the disutility of a loss increases faster than does the loss. Subjects behaving in accordance with this theory should purchase all insurance in which only the loss cost is charged (ie, every policy offered in Table 3.1). However, it is reasonable to suppose that subjects occasionally will not purchase insurance, because of transaction costs or error in the subjective assessments of utility or because they may believe that the experimenter implicitly wants them to choose some but not all policies. In such a situation, utility theory predicts that subjects would most likely insure against the lowest probability, highest loss urns because these provide the largest difference between the disutility of the premium and the expected disutility of the uninsured urn.

In contrast, a threshold model would predict that subjects will not buy insurance unless they view the hazard as a problem worthy of concern. Thus, they may ignore urns for which the probability of loss is too low to constitute a threat. Presumably, such a threshold would vary among individuals. For some, it might lie between urns 1 and 2 (ie, between $P(L) = .001$ and .005), for others, between urns 4 and 5 and so on. If this hypothesis is correct, then one should find, over a group of subjects, a greater propensity to insure against high-probability, low-loss events.

Results

The solid curve in Figure 3.2 presents the pooled responses of 109 subjects who were presented the game in Table 3.1. Contrary to the predictions derived from utility theory, a strong preference was found for insuring against high-probability, low-loss events: events which are relatively likely to happen, but incur only minor losses. Whereas only about 20% of the subjects were willing to insure against the urn with $P(L) = .001$, over 80% insured against the urn with $P(L) = .25$. Thus, four times as many subjects were willing to insure against a likely loss of 4 points as would insure against an unlikely loss of 1000 points.

Preference patterns of individual subjects were also examined. Each subject's responses were classified into one of six categories:

1   buy all six policies;
2   buy no policies;

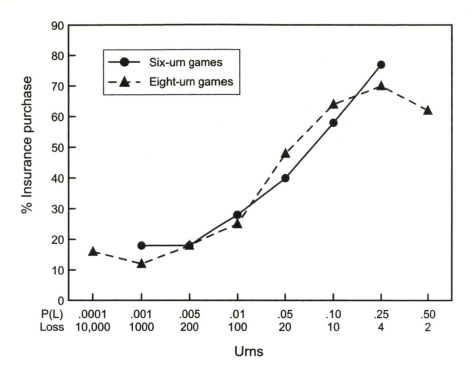

Figure 3.2 *Percent of subjects purchasing insurance for urns varying in probability and amount of loss*

3   insure against some subset of least likely losses (ie, urns 1; 1 and 2; 1, 2 and 3; 1, 2, 3 and 4; or 1, 2, 3, 4 and 5);
4   insure against some subset of the most likely losses (eg, urns 6; 5 and 6; 4, 5 and 6; etc);
5   buy insurance for some subset of contiguous middle likelihood losses (eg, urns 2 and 3); and
6   other patterns (eg, urns 3 and 5; 1 and 4).

The results of this analysis, shown in line 1 of Table 3.2, further demonstrate the strong preference for insuring against the most likely losses rather than

Table 3.2 *Patterns of Insurance Purchase*

			Buy some subset of:			
	Buy all	*Buy none*	*Least likely losses*	*Most likely losses*	*Middle likely losses*	*Other patterns*
6 Urns	12.6	19.6	6.7	46.0	3.7	11.4
8 Urns	6.7	9.6	5.3	48.4	16.6	14.4
Farm Game I	30.0	8.0	11.8	27.3	13.1	9.8
Farm Game II	33.3	9.4	17.2	24.7	7.7	7.7

Note: All entries show the percent of subjects exhibiting each purchasing pattern.

against the least likely ones. Nearly half of the subjects insured against some subset of the most likely losses, compared with only about 7 per cent who insured against some subset of the least likely losses. About one subject in five bought no insurance, while one in eight purchased all available policies.

To extend the solid curve shown in Figure 3.2, this experiment was repeated with two urns added, one at each end of the probability (or loss) continuum. One urn had $P(L) = .0001$ and $L = 10,000$; the other had $P(L) = .50$, and $L = 2$. Both premiums were 1 unit. The responses of 178 subjects to this urn game are shown as the broken curve in Figure 3.2. The pattern found with six urns is substantially replicated in the $P(L) = .001$ to .25 range. At the low end of the probability continuum, no further decline was found in insurance purchases with the $P(L) = .0001$ urn. At the high end, there was a slight decline in demand with the increase of $P(L)$ from .25 to .50. For this last urn, the premium was half as large as the possible loss. Again, nearly half the people insured against some subset of the most likely losses (Table 3.2, line 2, column 4).

Robustness of the Probability Effect

However dramatic the results depicted in Figure 3.2, one might ask whether they are not, at least in part, an artifact of the particular subjects or the particular version of urn game used. One would like evidence showing that these results are sufficiently resilient to withstand changes in subject population and in experimental format.

Subjects

To test for the generality of results over subject populations, the 8-urn study was replicated with 46 members and spouses from the Eugene, Oregon, Chapter of the League of Women Voters (33 women; 13 men). Only individuals who participated in making insurance decisions for their household were studied. The results (not shown) were similar to those obtained with the younger subjects, recruited through newspaper ads. Again, insurance purchasing increased as probability of loss increased and possible loss decreased. Whereas only 33% said they would purchase insurance at $P(L) = .0001$, 63% would purchase insurance at $P(L) = .50$.

Order of presentation

One aspect of the experimental format that may have introduced some bias is the order in which the urns were presented in the questionnaire. In the foregoing experiments, subjects considered first those urns with the lowest $P(L)$, as in Table 3.1. Perhaps they favored insuring against the most likely losses because of some perspective acquired while considering the least likely ones. To test this conjecture, 44 additional subjects were asked to consider the most likely losses first when making decisions about each of the eight urns. Although this sequential change produced a slight across-the-board increase in insurance buying (not shown), it had no effect on the subjects' preference for insuring against the more likely losses.

Expected value manipulation

Another possibility is that these responses were atypical because subjects were considering insurance whose premium equaled the expected loss of the gamble, a situation seldom encountered in real life. Figure 3.3 compares the results of offering 178 subjects several different urn games for which the expected loss of the gamble was greater than, less than or equal to the premium. These premiums reflected insurance that was subsidized, commercially offered and offered at pure loss cost, respectively. Subsidized insurance was created by decreasing the premium by 20% or 50% (and holding loss constant), or by decreasing the loss by 20% or 50% (and holding the premium constant). Commercially offered insurance situations were created by 20% or 50% increases in premium or 20% or 50% decreases in the loss. The same eight loss probabilities were used as before. The results of these variations, averaged across the four types of subsidized and commercial insurance, are shown in Figure 3.3. While the subjects were sensitive to these expected-value manipulations, the preference for insuring against high-probability, low-loss risks remained strong under all conditions.

Simultaneous versus separate urns

Another aspect of the experimental design considered was the appearance of all six or eight urns in a single game. One might argue that presenting subjects with such a portfolio of risks all at one time might induce some peculiar

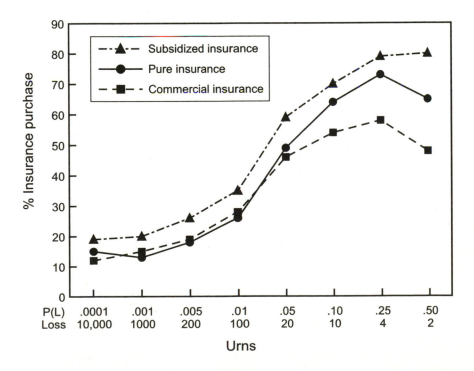

Figure 3.3 *Effect of varying relationship between premium and expected loss of gamble*

Table 3.3 *Effect of Simultaneous versus Separate Presentation of Urns*

Probability of loss P(L)	Amount of loss	Premium	Proportion purchasing insurance	
			Urns presented together (N = 134)	Urns presented separately (N = 36)
.001	5000	5	.13	.28
.01	200	2	.20	.25
.25	200	50	.57	.47
.25	5000	1250	.43	.42
.50	1000	500	.64	.53

strategies not found when risks are considered one by one. Table 3.3 shows the results of presenting urns separately (to 36 subjects) as opposed to presenting them simultaneously in one game (to 134 subjects). The particular urns used in this experiment were different from those used in the previous ones; they were adopted from the work of Amos Tversky and Daniel Kahneman at the Hebrew University in Jerusalem. With separate presentation, the differential preference for insuring likely losses was slightly reduced, but by no means eliminated.

Note that of the two urns for which $P(L) = .25$, subjects were less likely to insure against the urn with the highest loss and highest premium. Schoemaker (1977) has reported a similar finding. This result, too, is inconsistent with concave utility functions such as that in Figure 3.1.

PROMOTING INSURANCE AGAINST UNLIKELY CALAMITIES

Compounding with Other Risks

How can one get people to insure against low-probability, high-consequence events? Perhaps disaster insurance should be treated as an unmarketable commodity and ways sought to package it more effectively. One such possibility is that if people prefer to insure against high-probability, low-loss events, perhaps they will also insure against unlikely disasters if such insurance is sold along with insurance against likely losses, at a reasonable extra cost. A test of this hypothesis was attempted by offering subjects a comprehensive policy, in which the only insurance available protected against all eight urns (those in Figure 3.2) for a premium of eight points. Of 35 subjects, only 11 bought this policy.

Whereas the previous studies offering insurance against eight urns individually 'sold' an average of 3.3 points' worth of insurance per subject, here only 2.5 points per subject were sold. The proportion of subjects insuring against the least likely losses increased from about 1 in 6 to about 1 in 3 (11 of 35 subjects), at the cost of greatly reduced purchases of insurance against high and medium likelihood losses.

With the eight-urn comprehensive insurance policy, subjects were asked to buy more than twice as much insurance as they ordinarily would have purchased (8 versus 3.3 points). Perhaps greater success would be achieved with a relatively less expensive insurance package. In a subsequent experiment, 151 new subjects were shown three urn games. One consisted of a single urn offering a high (.20) probability of losing 10 points and an insurance premium of 2 points. The second game also had one urn, carrying a .001 chance of losing 1000 points with a 1-point premium. The third game included both of these urns and a combined (3 point) premium; here subjects had to draw once from each urn and could insure only against both.

The three games were presented to subjects in varying orders, none of which affected the results. Pooled results appear in Table 3.4. Again, when considering each urn separately, subjects were twice as likely to insure against the high-probability as against the low-probability loss. However, more people were willing to buy the compound insurance than either single urn policy, resulting in over twice as many people being insured against the low-probability loss. The subjects were willing to spend 30% more for compound insurance than the sum of their expenditures for the two single-urn policies. If it is in society's best interest for people to insure themselves against unlikely calamities, then adding protection against a small but likely loss might help accomplish this purpose.

Compounding over Time

Another variation that might change one's attitude toward insuring against an unlikely loss is to extend the time span over which that risk is faced. This extension can be accomplished in an experiment by increasing the number of times the urn must be sampled, and in life by selling multiyear policies. Perhaps when one faces repeated chances for possible disaster, the increase in subjective probability of loss may outweigh the increase in premium, making insurance more attractive.

This hypothesis was tested with 72 subjects, assigned to four groups of approximately equal size. Group 1 was exposed to a gamble offering 1 chance in 100 of losing $100. Group 2 faced 1 chance in 20 of losing $20. Subjects in both groups could take their chances or purchase insurance at a premium of $1 which reflected loss cost only. Groups 3 and 4 saw these same gambles, but were told that they had to play the gamble five times. Group 3 was told that over all five plays, each having a 1 in 100 chance to lose $100, they faced a .05 probability of losing $100 at least one time. Group 4 was told that five plays, each having a 1 in 20 chance to lose $20, provide a .23 probability of losing $20 at least once. Subjects were allowed either to go uninsured on all five plays or purchase insurance for all five plays for a $5 premium.

Multiple exposure to the .01 gamble did not affect the proportion of subjects who bought insurance (63% for single play, 65% for the five-play condition).

Table 3.4 *Insurance Purchases for Single and Compound Urns*

Urn game	P(L)	L	Premium	Proportion purchasing	Points sold per subject
Low probability	.001	1000	1	.24	.24
High probability	.20	10	2	.47	.94
Compound	both of above		3	.51	1.53

However, whereas 58% of the subjects purchased insurance against a single chance of 1 in 20 to lose $20, 94% paid the $5 premium to insure against 5 plays of this gamble. (This difference in proportions was statistically significant at $p < .01$.) Thus it does appear possible that multiple exposures can induce people to purchase insurance by boosting the overall probability of loss.

Insurance as an Investment

Other approaches to marketing insurance are suggested by the notion that people view insurance as an investment; that is, they like to receive some money back for their premium. The probability effect could be due, at least in part, to this preference; insuring against high-probability, low-loss urns gives people a good chance of getting a monetary return (reimbursement of a loss).

One way to improve the possibility of a monetary return with low-probability losses is to offer to reimburse subjects who make no claims. Of the many possible refund arrangements, the one selected for this study was a comprehensive insurance plan (one premium for eight urns) which refunded all of a subject's premium if no claims were made (ie, if no blue balls were drawn). Insurance offering this option must carry a higher premium than that for insurance which reimburses only when losses occur. For the 8-urn situation, the premium based on the loss cost and the possibility of a full premium refund is 11.7 points.

Each of the 35 subjects offered the comprehensive, no-refund insurance described above subsequently was offered the opportunity to purchase 'money back if nothing goes wrong' insurance, for a 12-point (11.7 rounded upward) premium. Twenty-two subjects purchased this insurance, twice as many as purchased the no-refund comprehensive. This amounted to 7.54 insurance points per subject or 62.8% of all insurance possible, compared with 31.4% of all comprehensive insurance possible and 41.3% of all non-comprehensive insurance purchased in the earlier 8-urn games. Examination of the subjects' reasons for purchasing this policy showed that they felt they could not lose; either they would suffer a loss and be reimbursed or they would receive a full return of their premiums. They appeared to neglect the likely possibility that they would be reimbursed for losses smaller than the premium.

Experiments with the Farm Game

In the experiments with urns, the subjects considered well-defined insurance problems in isolation and without real stakes at risk. To increase confidence in these results a farm game was designed presenting a much more realistic task, in which insurance was not the sole object of attention.

Details of the Game

On the topic of instructions and format, subjects were told:

> Farming is a business that requires decisions. In this game, the number of decisions has been reduced considerably from the number that must be made on a

real farm; however, the principles are the same. The decisions you will make at the beginning of each play year are:

1 what crops you are going to plant;
2 what and how much fertilizer you will purchase and apply to those crops; and
3 what insurance you will buy, if any, against certain natural hazards.

Participants played the game for 15 rounds; each round represented one year. Their income for each year was determined by the wisdom of their decisions, by random fluctuations in crop yield and market price, and by the randomly determined occurrences of the natural hazards. At the beginning of the game, each subject was given a 240-acre farm with a permanent concrete pipe irrigation system, a variety of farm equipment and $80,000 of debt, leaving an initial net worth of about $200,000. The instructions, which took one to 1.5 hours to complete, described the characteristics of the seven crops available (mean yield per acre, standard deviation of yield, mean and standard deviation of market price), the efficacy of two types of fertilizer for each crop, the fixed costs of growing each crop (machinery, labor and water), and the risks they faced.

For each round, the subjects' decisions were entered into a computer, which then prepared a year-end report. This report showed the subjects' predecision financial situation, production results (yield and market price), hazards incurred, yearly expenses and a year-end list of assets and debts.

The hazards

Table 3.5 shows the natural hazards faced by the subjects. The hazards were left unnamed, to render irrelevant any particular knowledge or beliefs subjects might have had about the probabilities or losses associated with real hazards such as hail or hurricanes. This decision afforded control over the perceived probability of each hazard. The probability values were chosen to cover the range that had produced the greatest differences in insurance purchases in the urn studies. Losses and premiums were established so that (a) the largest loss equaled or exceeded the value of the farm, thus ending the game should the largest loss be incurred; and (b) the cost of the premium would be significant. The average subject's net profit was approximately $6,000 per year. Thus, the purchase of insurance at $500 per hazard was a significant expense.

Table 3.5 *Farm Game Hazards*

Hazard number	Probability	Loss ($)
1	.002	247,500
2	.01	49,500
3	.05	9900
4	.10	4950
5	.25	1980

Note: Premium for each hazard equals $500.

Subjects

Thirty subjects were recruited through an advertisement in the local city newspaper offering $2.25 per hour for participation in a 5-hour decision-making experiment. Applicants were screened to eliminate those uncomfortable or unfamiliar with working with numbers. There were 19 men and 11 women, with a mean age of 25.

Results

The clearest comparison between the farm game and the urn study is afforded by the farm game subjects' first-round responses. On that round, they, like urn subjects, had no direct experience with the possible disasters, knowing them only in the abstract. Figure 3.4 shows that the first-round responses of the farm game subjects were similar to the responses of the urn game subjects in avoiding insurance against low-probability, high-loss hazards and preferring insurance against high-probability, low-loss hazards. Farm game subjects were much more willing to spend $500 to insure against a $1980 loss than they were to spend the same amount of money to insure against the loss of their whole farm.

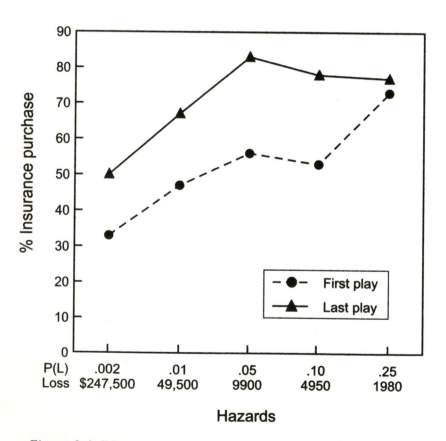

Figure 3.4 *Effect of probability of loss on insurance purchasing in first farm game*

Figure 3.4 also shows the subjects' responses on the last (15th) round of this game. Here, a marked increase is found in the subjects' willingness to insure against all but the most likely losses. This increase is due largely to an increase in the number of subjects who bought all policies (from 5 on the first round to 15 on the last one). Indeed, all but one of the subjects who insured against the least likely loss on the last round also insured against all other losses, suggesting that the attractiveness of insuring against the rarest event increased only as a result of the increase in 'buy all' strategies.

There are several possible reasons for the increased purchase of insurance over time:

1   As subjects became more familiar with the game, they may have devoted relatively more attention to insurance decisions (as opposed to crop and fertilizer decisions) and thereby discovered the wisdom of insurance.
2   As the farms gained in value over time, the subjects may have become more conservative, wishing to protect their increased assets.
3   The differentially greater increase in purchasing low- and middle-probability insurance may have been due to a ceiling effect. There is more room for increase when the starting rate is 33% than when it is 73%.
4   Subjects may have believed that the lower probability disasters, which rarely occurred, were 'due to happen soon', while high-probability disasters, which occurred more frequently, had 'already had their share' of occurrences. This interaction between the occurrence of disasters and purchase of insurance is examined more closely below.

Over all rounds, farm-game subjects bought much more insurance than urn subjects; 30% of the time they insured against all five disasters, compared to 12.6% of the subjects buying full coverage for the 6-urn games and 6.7% for the 8-urn games. Nevertheless, farm game subjects still were more than twice as likely to buy insurance against some subset of the most likely losses as against some subset of the least likely losses (see Table 3.2, row 3, columns 3 and 4).

Farm Game II

Rationale
One possibly important difference between the farm game and real-life decisions is that subjects were not rewarded for managing their farm properly. Although subjects appeared to be intrinsically motivated by the game, intrinsic motivation may have induced some strategy other than profit maximization (eg, experimenting with different crop fertilizer combinations to see what would happen).[1] A final experiment explored this possibility with 31 new subjects whose earnings for participating in the experiment depended upon their farm earnings. They were paid from $2.50 to $20, depending on their net worth at the end of round 15.

Results
Figure 3.5 shows first play and last play decisions. Hourly pay (Game I) and pay-by-farm-earnings (Game II) produced remarkably similar patterns. The only

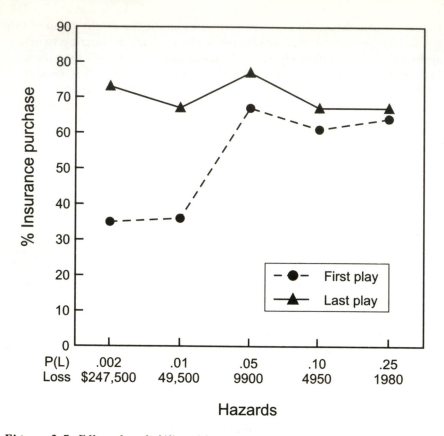

Figure 3.5 *Effect of probability of loss on insurance purchasing in second farm game*

marked difference was the increased purchase of insurance against the greatest possible loss on the last play. This result appears to have been due to specific end-game behavior, with some subjects taking care not to lose the farm on the last round before 'cashing out'.

In as realistic a context as may be possible in a laboratory experiment, where insurance was not the subjects' sole consideration, there was unwillingness to insure against low-probability, high-loss events. Although this aversion was weaker than with the urn games, these results still clearly violated the predictions of utility theory.

Effect of Experience

What effect did the occurrence or non-occurrence of a disaster have on subsequent insurance behavior? Table 3.6 shows insurance purchases as a function of whether a hazard was incurred on the previous round. Looking at the last two columns of line 1, one sees that when no hazard occurred on the previous round, only 9% of the decisions on the next round were changes from the previous decision. These changes were about equally divided between buying a policy against a previously uninsured hazard (4.9%) and canceling an existing policy (4.1%).

Table 3.6 *Effect of Hazard Experience on Round N upon Decisions for Round N + 1*

Outcome on Round N	Number of decisions	Decisions on Round N + 1			
		Keep existing policy	Remain uninsured	Buy a new policy	Cancel existing policy
1 No hazard	2485	58.0	33.0	4.9	4.1
2 Hazard occurred	1840	57.0	33.5	5.8	3.8
2a Hazard occurred: decision for same hazard	368	55.7	29.9	5.4	9.0
2b Hazard occurred: decision for different hazard	1472	57.3	34.3	5.8	2.5

Note: Numbers are the percent of all decisions made on Round N + 1. These results are combined over both farm games.

In examining decisions after the occurrence of a hazard (line 2), it is instructive to divide the data into two categories – decisions made relevant to the hazard that had just occurred (line 2a) and decisions for the other hazards, which had not just occurred (line 2b). Here, one sees that there was a much greater rate of cancellation of existing policies for hazards that had just occurred (9%) than cancellation of other policies (2.5%). This suggests a belief that, as the hazard has just happened, it is unlikely to repeat soon. This belief, known as the 'gambler's fallacy', often has been found in laboratory studies as well as among residents of hazard areas (Slovic et al, 1974).

A slightly different way of looking at the effect of hazard experience is to examine people's behavior toward hazards on which they have just incurred an uninsured loss. On the round following such losses, 15.4% purchased insurance for that hazard. This percentage is only slightly higher than the rate of new insurance purchases on hazards other than the one that just occurred (14.5%) or the rate of new insurance on rounds that were not preceded by hazards (13.0%). Thus, people did not markedly increase their insurance holdings after an uninsured hazard, a result that conflicts with observations of actual insurance behavior in the aftermath of a disaster (eg, Kunreuther et al, 1977, Chapter 2). The reasons for this difference are unclear. One possibility is that the odds in the farm game are well defined and unchanging, whereas in the real world the occurrence of a disaster may greatly increase the perceived probability of its recurrence.

DISCUSSION

Explaining the Probability Effect

A *utility explanation*

The most striking result of the experiments just described is that people buy more insurance against moderate- or high-probability, low-loss events than against low-probability, high-loss events. How might this behavior be explained? Two possible explanations come to mind, both of which are contrary to traditional utility theory. The first postulates a utility function that is convex over losses, as shown in Figure 3.6, instead of the traditional concave (risk averse) curve shown in Figure 3.1.

A convex curve, implying diminishing marginal utility over losses, has solid empirical support beyond the present study. Galanter has repeatedly obtained convex functions in carefully performed psychophysical experiments aimed at scaling the subjective value of various monetary and non-monetary losses (Galanter, 1975; Galanter & Pliner, 1976). Swalm (1966) observed convex functions over monetary losses with corporate executives, a result apparently neglected by other theorists and practitioners. Most recently, Kahneman and Tversky (1979) have observed preferences among gambles that could be explained only by a convex utility function for losses. Kahneman and Tversky noted that diminishing marginal utility is compatible with well substantiated principles of perception and judgment, according to which sensitivity to changes decreases as one moves away from a neutral point (here, no change in asset position).

Taken at face value, a convex utility function for losses implies that people never will buy insurance (just as a concave function implies that they always will buy insurance). Anderson (1974) has extensively discussed people's reluctance to purchase insurance. He cited the following testimony by George Bernstein, the federal insurance administrator, before a US senate subcommittee:

> Most property owners simply do not buy insurance voluntarily, regardless of the amount of equity they have at stake. It was not until banks and other lending institutions united in requiring fire insurance from their mortgagers that most

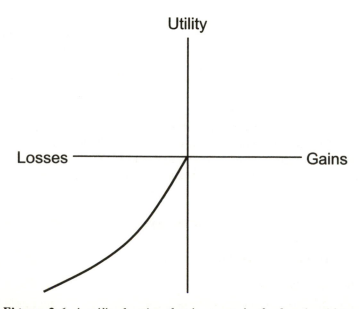

Figure 3.6 *A utility function that is convex in the domain of losses*

people got around to purchasing it. It was also many years after its introduction that the now popular homeowners' insurance caught on. At one time, too, insurers could not give away crime insurance, and we just need look at our automobile insurance laws to recognize that unless we force that insurance down the throats of the drivers, many, many thousands of people would be unprotected on the highways. People do not buy insurance voluntarily unless there is pressure on them from one source or another (Bernstein, 1972, p23).

If Bernstein is correct, then utility theory should be modified not only by postulating a convex disutility function, but also by adding factors such as social or sales pressures, errors and so on.

A *threshold explanation*

An alternative hypothesis invokes the notion of a probability threshold to explain the tendency to buy less insurance as probability of loss decreases. As suggested above, people may refuse to worry about losses whose probability is below some threshold. Probabilities below the threshold are treated as though they were zero.

When asked why they made their decisions about insurance purchases, most of the subjects in the foregoing experiments referred to some sort of threshold notion. For example:

- Only in urns number 7 and 8 were the probabilities high enough to warrant buying insurance.
- I thought the odds of my coming up with a blue ball had grown sufficiently by urn number 4 to start taking insurance.
- I bought insurance only if the chance of selecting a blue ball was significant.
- In the first two, the chances of picking the blue ball are too small to worry about. The remainder caused increasing concern for me.

Judging by these comments and the experiment results, the threshold apparently varies across individuals. Whether it also varies within individuals across situations is a topic for future research. If the threshold is affected by factors other than probability, then it might best be viewed as defined on a variable called 'worry' or 'concern'. The worry generated by a particular situation could be a function of several variables, including probability. The threshold concept makes good intuitive sense. There are only so many things in life one can worry about. Without some sort of threshold for concern, people would spend their entire lives obsessively protecting themselves against a 'Pandora's urn' of rare horrors.

Ideas similar to the threshold notion have appeared in previous discussions of people's failure to protect themselves against natural hazards. Haas (1971, p78) classed people's inattention to earthquake risks with their failure to check the air pressure in their spare tire before a long auto trip or to examine their house roof yearly for leaks. He commented:

What do people attend to most of the time? They pay attention to that which is most pressing, that which must be attended to, that which has deadlines, that which is generally considered most critical, that which one would be severely criticized for if he or she didn't attend to.

Senator Robert Taft Jr (1972, p18) observed:

> The most difficult obstacle for the flood insurance program to overcome, how-
> ever, does not relate to the difficulties of certifying communities for insurance.
> Instead, it relates directly to the psychological outlook of individual homeowners
> and businessmen in the flood plain areas. People just do not buy the insurance.
> The probability that a flood will damage their property once in a hundred years is
> apparently not a matter of concern to most individuals.

The notion of a threshold protecting a finite reservoir of concern helps explain
why so many respondents in the Kunreuther field survey were unconcerned
about floods or earthquakes and collected little information about the hazards
or about protective measures such as insurance.

The influence of perceived probability provides insight into the failure of
premium subsidization to facilitate the purchase of hazard insurance (Anderson, 1974). It may be that subsidization does not work because the hazards seem
so unlikely that insurance is not even considered. If the event is not going to
happen, it does not matter how inexpensive the insurance is. The role of perceived probability might also explain the inconsistency of insurance behavior
across situations where probability of loss varies (Vaughn, 1971) and the inability to predict insurance decisions on the basis of risk aversion indices obtained
from gambling preferences (Green, 1963, 1964; Williams, 1966).

The popularity of low-deductible insurance plans (Pashigian, Schkade &
Menefee, 1966; Schoemaker, 1977) and appliance service contracts is further
evidence of the preference for insuring against high-probability events. Although
the authors are attracted to the threshold hypothesis, it should be noted that the
idea that people view insurance as an investment (and like to be able to make
claims, thereby getting a return on their money), is also consistent with most of
these results.

IMPLICATIONS FOR PUBLIC POLICY

Though changing rapidly in certain insurance markets, it is axiomatic in the insurance industry that 'insurance is sold, not bought'. People's reluctance to
purchase insurance voluntarily has long been a matter of concern and debate
(Anderson, 1974). The experiments reported above suggest that people's natural
predisposition is to protect against high-probability hazards and to ignore rare
threats. Individuals will not use insurance to protect themselves against rare, large
losses if most of their attentional capacity is devoted to dealing with likely events.

The policy-maker, on the other hand, has a different perspective on hazards
and insurance. For example, when one considers natural hazards aggregated
over many individuals and locations, over a long period of time, the probability
of disaster becomes high. This difference in perspective from that of the individual resident of a hazard area, who is concerned with one particular house and
a shorter time horizon, may be a source of conflict and mutual frustration between the policy-makers and the public.

The present study, however, not only highlights the policy-maker's problem, but also suggests some remedies. In particular, it seems that in order for

individuals to insure themselves against low-probability, high-consequence events, they must believe that these events are likely enough to warrant protective action. Two methods of changing people's perspective on hazard probability suggested by the foregoing experimental results are:

1   combine low-probability hazards with higher probability threats in one insurance 'package'; and
2   compound the hazard over time.

Thus, for the latter, instead of describing the chances of a 100-year flood as .01 per year, one could note that an individual living in a particular house for 25 years faces a .22 chance of suffering 100-year damage at least once. Either technique might make the probability of loss (and the chances of collecting on one's premiums) high enough to warrant insuring.

It is also known that the probability of an event is determined, in part, by the ease with which relevant instances are imagined or remembered (Tversky & Kahneman, 1973a). Memorability and imaginability may be increased by publicity or use of visual displays like the Tennessee Valley Authority's device of plotting flood heights on photographs of familiar buildings (Kales, 1962). It might also help to persuade the public to view insurance and other protective measures as problems of community risk and welfare rather than from their own limited and subjectively safer point of view.

Although the foregoing results appear to tell a coherent story, the surface of understanding the insurance decision process has just been scratched. A number of variables (hazard probability, size of loss, realism, order of presentation, etc) have been studied, but many other factors that may play important roles have been neglected. For example, Kunreuther's subjects apparently were influenced by communications with friends and neighbors; they may have been following social norms regarding insurance without engaging in any sort of analytic thinking. Other research has shown that subtle changes in problem formulation can have marked effects upon risk taking and insurance decisions (Lichtenstein & Slovic, 1971; 1973; Williams, 1966). Even within the urn and farm game paradigms, issues have only begun to be explored – issues such as premium and deductible rates, refund plans, information costs, requirements for insurance coverage, and information about qualitative aspects of hazards and the losses they entail. Until further research has clarified the roles of such factors, knowledge of the determinants of insurance behavior will be incomplete.

Acknowledgments

This research was supported by NSF-RANN Grant ATA 73-03064-A03 to the Wharton School of the University of Pennsylvania under subcontract to the Oregon Research Institute. We thank Howard Kunreuther, Daniel Kahneman and Amos Tversky for their invaluable contributions to this project. Frank Conklin supplied us with a prototype for the farm game.

NOTE

1   It should be noted that because subjects in the first farm game were paid by the hour, they should have been particularly motivated to avoid losing their farm, thus terminating the game early. This pecuniary consideration should have increased their readiness to insure against the least-likely (greatest loss) hazard.

4 Accident Probabilities and Seat Belt Usage: A Psychological Perspective

Paul Slovic, Baruch Fischhoff and Sarah Lichtenstein

Research has demonstrated that seat belts effectively reduce injury and death in automobile accidents (Campbell, O'Neill & Tingley, 1974; Fhanér & Hane, 1973; Green, 1976; Hodson-Walker, 1970; Preston & Shortridge, 1973) and that most people are aware of this fact (Knapper, Cropley, & Moore, 1976; Marzoni, 1971). It is, therefore, perplexing that only a small percentage of motorists wear lap belts or shoulder harnesses. Forgetfulness, laziness, inconvenience, discomfort and low perceived risk are reasons given for not wearing belts (Fhanér & Hane, 1973; Knapper et al, 1976). Numerous media campaigns, employing the full armamentarium of 'Madison Avenue' have failed to persuade people to 'buckle up for safety' (Robertson, 1976).

Recently, psychologists have begun to study how people react to low-probability, high-consequence threats. Some of these results suggest reasons why motorists refuse to use seat belts voluntarily. These results and their implications are discussed below.

PSYCHOLOGICAL CONSIDERATIONS

Over the years, as the number of vehicle miles driven per year in the US has increased, the death rate per 10^8 vehicle miles has steadily decreased, reaching a low of 3.31 in 1976 (National Safety Council, 1977). We estimate that approximately 1 in every 3.5 million person trips ends in a fatal accident, and about 1 in every 100,000 person trips results in a disabling injury.[1] Thus, the probability of death or injury on any given trip is extremely low. Considered in the light of basic principles of learning and cognition, these probabilities make it

Note: reprinted from *Accident Analysis and Prevention*, vol 10, P Slovic, B Fischhoff and S Lichtenstein, 'Accident Probabilities and Seat Belt Usage: A Psychological Perspective', pp281–5, 1978, with permission from Elsevier Science.

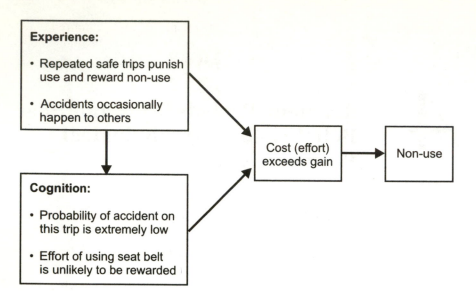

Figure 4.1 *Psychological considerations in the non-use of seat belts*

unreasonable to expect people to use seat belts voluntarily. Figure 4.1 presents the rationale behind this assertion schematically.

Attitudes and behaviors reflect people's experience. In particular, it has long been known (eg, Thorndike, 1913) that rewarded actions tend to be repeated while non-rewarded behavior diminishes in frequency. Fortunately, the overwhelming majority of driving experiences are accident free. Each safe trip rewards (reinforces) the non-use of seat belts; the expense of buckling up has been saved without incurring any cost. On the other hand, travelers who do use belts are punished (negatively reinforced) by the effort, inconvenience and discomfort they have incurred without any concrete reward. Peace of mind, usually considered the immediate tangible reward for insuring oneself, may seem a pale compensation and one that is hard to enjoy while driving. Thus, safe driving experiences can be expected to lead to non-use of seat belts.

Other factors may further reduce people's belief in the efficacy of buckling up:

- the knowledge that seat belts are not 100% effective (Fhanér & Hane, 1974);
- drivers' tendencies to view vehicle risks as under their control (Fischhoff, Slovic, Lichtenstein, Read et al, 1978), coupled with the fact that perceived control produces exaggerated feelings of confidence (Langer, 1975); and
- the fact that 75–90% of the drivers in various countries consider themselves to be better than average (Svenson, 1977).

We do occasionally see or read about accidents, but the victims are *other* people.

The failure to use seat belts surprises us because of the extremely high value people place on their lives. Even a very small probability of saving one's life or avoiding serious injury should make the expected gain from using a seat belt exceed the costs. Such reasoning assumes that people have the unlimited time, energy and attentional capacities needed to have an infinite reservoir of concern. In fact, however, there are only so many things people can worry about and protect themselves against. Unless many hazards are ignored, obsessive preoccupation with risk would preclude any sort of productive life.

When choosing which life-threatening events to ignore, those with probabilities near zero are obvious candidates. Indeed, there are many threats that we routinely ignore in order to go on with the business of living: elevators falling, dams bursting, televisions exploding and so forth. For many people, auto accidents may seem so improbable that they fail to incite concern.[2]

INSURANCE BEHAVIOR: SUPPORTING EVIDENCE

An instructive analog to the seat-belt problem can be found in another type of protective activity: buying insurance. People's resistance to purchasing insurance is well known (see Chapter 3). Consider, for example, the following testimony by George Bernstein, then federal insurance administrator, before a US senate subcommittee:

> Most property owners simply do not buy insurance voluntarily, regardless of the amount of equity they have at stake. It was not until banks and other lending institutions united in requiring fire insurance from their mortgagers that most people got around to purchasing it ... and we just need look at our automobile insurance laws to recognize that unless we force that insurance down the throats of the drivers, many, many thousands of people would be unprotected on the highways. People do not buy insurance voluntarily unless there is pressure on them from one source or another (Bernstein, 1972, p23).

Efforts by the government and private companies to induce people to insure their property against earthquakes and flood damage have been spectacularly unsuccessful (Anderson, 1974), much like the seat-belt campaigns. Even strong economic incentives, such as 90% premium subsidies, have not stimulated flood insurance sales.

Concern about the viability of insurance as a mechanism for coping with risks from natural hazards has led to several recent field surveys and laboratory studies of insurance decision-making (Kunreuther et al, 1978; Schoemaker, 1977; Slovic, Fischhoff, Lichtenstein, Corrigan & Combs, 1977). One robust finding from this research has been that people are more willing to insure against small losses with relatively high probabilities than against large but unlikely losses. Table 4.1 illustrates this effect with data from an experiment performed by Slovic et al (1977) in which people played an elaborate farm management game. One of their many decisions was whether to insure against each of five natural hazards. The probability of occurrence of these hazards ranged from .002 to .25. The magnitude of loss varied inversely with the probability of occurrence such that the expected loss (ie, probability multiplied by loss) was the same for each. Premiums were set slightly above the expected loss. As the table shows, people were much more likely to insure against relatively high-probability, low-loss hazards than against low-probability, high-loss hazards. This behavior, which has

Table 4.1 *Effect of Probability of Loss on Insurance Purchase Decisions in a Farm Management Game*

Probability of loss	Magnitude of loss ($)	Persons insuring (%)
.002	$247,500[a]	33
.01	49,500	45
.05	9900	52
.10	4950	49
.25	1980	73

Note: Compiled from Slovic, Fischhoff, Lichtenstein, Corrigan and Combs (1977). Insurance premium for each decision is US$500.
[a] A loss of this magnitude would cost the individual the farm.

also been obtained in other experiments, runs counter to that postulated by the traditional economic theories of insurance (eg, Friedman & Savage, 1948). Those theories assume that people wish to protect themselves against rare, catastrophic losses that they could not bear themselves. Outside the laboratory, the popularity of low-deductible insurance plans (Fuchs, 1976; Pashigian, Schkade & Menefee, 1966) which offer expensive coverage for small, but likely, losses is consistent with results from the experiments.

Two considerations seem to dominate these insurance decisions, both inside and outside the laboratory. One is the disinclination to worry about low-probability hazards. The second is a propensity to view insurance as an investment. Insuring against probable losses increases the probability of making a claim and getting something tangible for one's premium dollars.

IMPLICATIONS

Given these results, we might expect that many motorists would find it irrational to bear the costs (however slight) of buckling up in return for partial protection against an overwhelmingly unlikely accident. On the other hand, public safety officials, who must consider an entire population of drivers taking many trips, view the problem quite differently. Whereas the probability of seat-belt usage being beneficial on any one trip is minuscule, any increment in the percentage of trips on which seat belts are worn is certain to save many lives and prevent many injuries. Such differing perspectives may trigger much of the conflict and mutual frustration between public officials and motorists, each believing (with some justice) that their analysis of the situation is correct.

It follows from the psychological considerations described above that appeals based on either the efficacy of seat belts (in the event of an accident) or lurid descriptions of accidents will be ineffective unless they somehow raise the perceived probability of accidents. Indeed, such appeals have not worked in practice (eg, Robertson, Kelley, O'Neill, Wixom, Elswirth & Haddon, 1974). As long as accidents are viewed as virtually impossible, efficacy and damage mean little. In his review of 15 years of research on fear arousal and the failure of threat appeals, Higbee (1969, p440) reached a similar conclusion. He noted:

The severity of the consequences (threat level) and the probability of their occurrence may be negatively related. Thus, a highly threatening consequence (eg, paralysis or blindness) may not be seen as too likely to result from not brushing one's teeth, whereas it may be seen as more likely that not brushing one's teeth could lead to cavities. If such a negative relationship exists, then increases in fear level could lead to decreases in perceived probability of occurrence of the threat and thus to decreased persuasiveness.

Our analysis suggests that the voluntary use of seat belts depends on motorists believing that their personal likelihood of being in an accident is high enough to make wearing a belt sensible. As long as the chances of accident on any given trip remain minuscule, the only hope may be to get people to think about the risks faced over a lifetime of driving. The 1969 Nationwide Personal Transportation Study indicates that the average US citizen makes about 800 automobile trips per year. This suggests that the probability of a fatal accident sometime within a 50-year period of driving (40,000 trips) is about .01, while the probability of experiencing at least one disabling injury is about .33.[3] Perhaps presentation of these probabilities, along with the admonition that 'no one knows when that accident will come', might trigger concern and increase the use of seat belts.

In our laboratory experiments, we found that people could be induced to purchase insurance against rare threats by lengthening their time perspective (Slovic et al, 1977). Supporting evidence more germane to seat belts comes from an exploratory study we recently conducted. The participants in this study were 38 men and 41 women who responded to an advertisement placed in the University of Oregon newspaper. Most were students; their range of ages was 17 to 50 years, with a median age of 21 years. Participants were assigned randomly to one of two groups. One group was given the probabilities of death and injury per single trip along with the following statement: 'Because the probability that any particular automobile trip will end in death or serious injury is so very small, the wearing of seat belts is just not necessary. Any effort or inconvenience involved in wearing seat belts, however slight, is unlikely to be repaid'. The second group was given the probabilities of death and injury in the course of 40,000 trips. They were then told: 'Because these probabilities of death or serious injury are so high, the wearing of seat belts is quite important. Any effort or inconvenience involved in wearing seat belts is likely to be repaid.'

After being exposed to the single trip or lifetime (40,000 trips) statistics and the statements that accompanied them, both groups were asked several questions about the likely impact of this information on their use of seat belts and their attitude toward enactment of laws requiring the use of some sort of protection, either the wearing of seat belts or the installation of air bags.

Prior to presenting any information about accident probabilities, we examined our participants' opinions about the effectiveness of seat belts. We also asked them to indicate the frequency with which they wore seat belts. There were no differences between the two groups on either of these measures. However, differences between groups did appear after the statistics were presented. Few respondents (4 out of 41) believed their use of seat belts would be changed as a result of exposure to the single-trip statistics, but 39% of those exposed to the lifetime probabilities said they expected their use of seat belts to increase because of this information. Whereas 54% of the persons who received single-trip information favored mandatory protection, 78% of those exposed to lifetime statistics favored such a law. Participants in both groups were later shown both single-trip and lifetime information accompanied by the respective anti- and pro-seat belt statements. When asked to compare the statements and indicate which was more convincing, 80% of the participants selected the pro-seat belt argument based on the probabilities over the course of 40,000 trips.

While this study is promising, we have no assurance that the favorable attitudes toward seat belts engendered by a lengthened time perspective will be maintained and translated into behavior, especially in light of people's repeated safe experiences with automobile trips. If a favorable perspective cannot be maintained, public safety officials will have to reassess the problem. Strictly enforced legislation requiring seat belts (eg, Freedman, Wood & Henderson, 1974) or passive devices such as air bags may be the only way to ensure that the majority of motorists are adequately protected.

CONCLUSION

The small probability of accidents, continually reinforced by safe experiences, in conjunction with people's limited capability to attend to rare threats, helps explain the non-use of seat belts. While this perspective on the problem indicates one approach toward increasing voluntary use of seat belts, it also suggests that there is an element of rationality in people's behavior that may keep voluntary use at its current low rate.

ACKNOWLEDGMENTS

This study was supported by the National Science Foundation under Grant No ENV77-15332 to Perceptronics, Inc. Any opinions, findings and conclusions or recommendations expressed in this publication are those of the authors and do not necessarily reflect the views of the National Science Foundation. We are indebted to Ward Edwards for his comments on an earlier draft of this paper.

NOTES

1   Our calculations of injury and fatality probabilities are based on the 1969 Nationwide Personal Transportation Study (US Department of Transportation), which estimated the total annual number of person trips in passenger cars and trucks at 163.282 billion. Traffic fatality rates used here exclude fatalities involving pedestrians or pedal cycles. The probability of a disabling injury (disabling beyond the day of the accident) is estimated as about 40 times higher than fatality probability, based on data presented in *Accident Facts* (National Safety Council, 1977).

2   There are, of course, some unlikely hazards to which people react quite strongly, nuclear reactor accidents being a prime example. We believe this reaction occurs because people perceive the probability of a catastrophic

accident to be quite high. People have no first-hand experience with (the safety of) nuclear power; instead, they must rely on the news media which typically pay more attention to breakdowns and potential accidents than to the successful day-to-day operations of power plants.

3   These probabilities were based on assumed rates of one fatality per 3.5 million trips and one disabling injury per 100,000 trips, combined with the assumption that these events are randomly and independently distributed. Given these assumptions, the probability of experiencing a fatality in 40,000 trips is $1-[1-(1/3,500,000)]^{40,000}$ and the probability of experiencing one or more disabling accidents in 40,000 trips is $1-[1-(1/100,000)]^{40,000}$.

5

How Safe Is Safe Enough? A Psychometric Study of Attitudes Toward Technological Risks and Benefits

*Baruch Fischhoff, Paul Slovic,
Sarah Lichtenstein, Stephen Read and
Barbara Combs*

Citizens of modern industrial societies are today learning a harsh and discomforting lesson – that the benefits from technology must be paid for not only with money but with lives. Whether it be ozone depletion and consequent skin cancer from the use of spray cans, birth defects induced by tranquilizing drugs or radiation damage from nuclear energy, every technological advance carries some risks of adverse side effects.

Reduction of risk typically entails reduction of benefit, thus posing serious dilemmas for society. With increasing frequency, policy-makers are being required to 'weigh the benefits against the risks' when making decisions about technological enterprises. To do this, they have been turning to risk-benefit analysis, an offshoot of cost-benefit analysis that is still in its early stages of development, as the basic decision-making methodology for societal risk taking (Fischhoff, 1977).

The basic question that risk-benefit analysis must answer is: is this product (activity, technology) acceptably safe? Alternatively, how safe is safe enough? There are, at present, two main approaches to answering these questions. One, the 'revealed preference' method advocated by Starr (1969), is based on the assumption that by trial and error society has arrived at an 'essentially optimum' balance between the risks and benefits associated with any activity. One may therefore use economic risk and benefit data from recent years to reveal patterns of acceptable risk-benefit trade-offs. Acceptable risk for a new technology is defined as that level of safety associated with ongoing activities having

Note: this is a slightly revised version of 'How Safe Is Safe Enough? A Psychometric Study of Attitudes Towards Technological Risks and Benefits', by B Fischhoff, P Slovic, S Lichtenstein, S Read and B Combs, 1978, *Policy Sciences*, 9, pp127–52. Copyright 1978 by Kluwer Academic Publishers; with kind permission from Kluwer Academic Publishers.

similar benefit to society. The present study investigates an alternative approach, called 'expressed preferences', which employs questionnaires to measure the public's attitudes toward the risks and benefits from various activities. Both approaches have their proponents and critics (eg, Kates, 1978; Linnerooth, 1975; Otway & Cohen, 1975).

Starr (1959) illustrated the potential usefulness of revealed preferences by examining the relationship between risk and benefit across a number of common activities. His measure of risk for these hazardous activities was the statistical expectation of fatalities per hour of exposure to the activity. Benefit was assumed to be equal to the average amount of money spent on an activity by an individual participant, or alternatively, equal to the average contribution that the activity makes to a participant's annual income.

From this analysis, Starr derived what might be regarded as 'laws of acceptable risk' – namely, that:

- the acceptability of risk is roughly proportional to the third power (cube) of the benefits;
- the public seems willing to accept risks from voluntary activities (eg, skiing) roughly 1000 times greater than it would tolerate from involuntary activities (eg, food preservatives) that provide the same level of benefit;
- the acceptable level of risk is inversely related to the number of persons exposed to that risk; and
- the level of risk tolerated for voluntarily accepted hazards is quite similar to the level of risk from disease.

On the basis of this last observation, Starr (1969) conjectured that 'the rate of death from disease appears to play, psychologically, a yardstick role in determining the

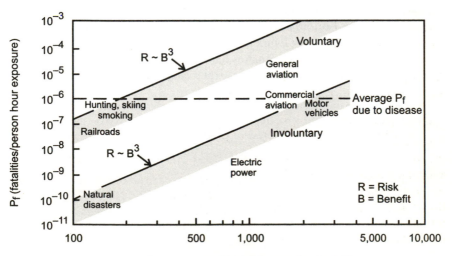

Source: taken from Starr, 1969

Figure 5.1 *Revealed risk-benefit relationships*

acceptability of risk on a voluntary basis' (p1235). Figure 5.1 depicts the results of Starr's analysis in a *revealed preference* risk-benefit space.

Starr's approach has the advantage of dealing with public behavior rather than with attitudes. It has, however, a number of serious drawbacks. First, it assumes that past behavior is a valid indicator of present preferences. In Starr's words, 'The ... assumption is that historically revealed social preferences and costs are sufficiently enduring to permit their use for predictive purposes' (Starr, 1969, p1232). However, Starr and his colleagues have subsequently acknowledged that 'The societal value system fluctuates with time, and the technological capability to follow fast-changing societal goals does not exist' (Starr et al, 1976, pp635–6). Second, Starr's approach 'does not serve to distinguish what is "best" for society from what is "traditionally acceptable"' (Starr, 1969, p1232). What is accepted in the marketplace may not accurately reflect the public's safety preferences. Consider the automobile, for example. Unless the public really knows what is possible from a design standpoint, and unless the automobile industry provides the public with a varied set of alternatives from which to choose, market behavior may not indicate what 'a reflective individual would decide after thoughtful and intensive inquiry'. A revealed preference approach assumes that people not only have full information, but also can *use* that information optimally, an assumption that seems quite doubtful in the light of much research on the psychology of decision-making (Slovic et al, 1977). Finally, from a technical standpoint, Otway and Cohen (1975) have shown that the quantitative conclusions one derives from an analysis of the type Starr performed are extremely sensitive to the way in which measures of risk and benefit are computed from the historical data.

Although only a few questionnaire studies have specifically considered levels of acceptable risk (eg, Maynard et al, 1976), or the value of a life at risk (Acton, 1973; Torrance, 1970), direct questioning procedures have been used to scale the perceived seriousness of a wide variety of natural and man-made hazards (see, for example, Golant & Burton, 1969; Lichtenstein et al, 1978; Otway, Maderthaner & Gutmann, 1975; Otway & Pahner, 1976; Wyler, Masuda & Holmes, 1968).

Use of psychometric questionnaires has been criticized on the grounds that answers to hypothetical questions bear little relationship to actual behavior.

> Time and time again, action has been found to contradict assertion. Since surveys always elicit some degree of strategic behavior ('what do they want me to say?'), we would be better advised to observe what people choose under actual conditions (Rappaport, 1974, p4).

Such criticisms of psychometric studies appear to us to be overstated. Attitudes elicited in surveys often correlate highly with behavior (Liska, 1975). Furthermore, they elicit present values rather than historical preferences.

The goal of the present study is to evaluate the usefulness of questionnaire techniques for investigating issues pertaining to risk-benefit trade-offs. Psychometric procedures were used to elicit quantitative judgments of perceived risk and benefit from various activities and technologies as well as judgments of acceptable risk levels. Participants in our experiment also judged the degree of voluntariness of each activity or technology. These judgments were used to determine whether people do, indeed, judge the acceptability of risks differently for voluntary and involuntary activities. The influence of other potential moderators of perceived and acceptable risk were also studied. These included familiarity with the risk, its perceived controllability, its potential for catastrophic (multiple-fatality) consequences, the immediacy of its consequences, and the extent of scientists' and the public's knowledge about its consequences. Various authors have speculated on the influence of these factors (eg, Green, 1974; Lowrance, 1976; Otway, 1975; Otway & Pahner, 1976; Rowe, 1977; Starr et al, 1976), but little empirical data is available.

METHOD

Design

The participants in our study evaluated each of 30 different activities and technologies with regard to (a) its perceived benefit to society; (b) its perceived risk, (c) the acceptability of its current level of risk; and (d) its position on each of nine dimensions of risk. Because tasks (a) and (b) were quite arduous and we were interested in independent judgments of perceived risk and benefit, participants performed either tasks (a), (c) and (d) or tasks (b), (c) and (d). Which of the two combinations of tasks they faced was determined randomly. As part of their general instructions, participants were told: 'This is a difficult, if not impossible, task. Nevertheless, it is not unlike the task you face when you vote on legislation pertaining to nuclear power, handguns or highway safety. One never has all the relevant information; ambiguities and uncertainties abound, yet some judgment must be made. The present task should be approached in the same spirit.'

Items

The 30 activities and technologies included the eight items used by Starr (1969) and 22 others chosen to vary broadly in the quality and quantity of their associated risks and benefits. They appear in Table 5.1.

Tasks

Perceived benefit

People given this task were asked to 'consider all types of benefits: how many jobs are created, how much money is generated directly or indirectly (eg, for swimming, consider the manufacture and sale of swimsuits), how much enjoyment is brought to people, how much of a contribution is made to the people's health and welfare, and so on'. Thus, they were told to give a global estimate of all benefits, both tangible and intangible. They were specifically told:

> Do not consider the costs of risks associated with these items. It is true, for example, that swimmers sometimes drown. But evaluating such risks and costs is not your present job. Your job is to assess the *gross benefits*, not the net benefits which remain after the costs and risks are subtracted out. Remember that a beneficial activity affecting few people will have less gross benefit than a beneficial activity affecting many people. If you need to think of a time period during which

Table 5.1 *Mean Judgments of Risk and Benefit from 30 Activities and Technologies*

Activity or technology	Perceived benefit	Perceived risk	Risk adjustment factor [a]		Acceptable level of risk [b]	
			Risk subjects	Benefit subjects	Risk subjects	Benefit subjects
	(Geometric mean)		(Geometric mean)			
1 Alcoholic beverages	41	161	4.7	4.2	34	38
2 Bicycles	82	65	1.6	1.4	41	46
3 Commercial aviation	130	52	1.2	1.4	43	37
4 Contraceptives	113	50	2.1	1.9	24	26
5 Electric power (non-nuclear)	274	52	1.2	0.9	43	58
6 Fire fighting	178	92	1.2	1.0	77	92
7 Food coloring	16	31	2.7	3.4	11	9
8 Food preservatives	44	36	2.6	2.8	14	13
9 General (private) aviation	53	114	2.3	1.8	50	63
10 Handguns	14	220	17.1	17.5	13	13
11 High-school and college football	35	37	1.8	1.6	21	23
12 Home appliances	133	25	1.1	1.0	23	25
13 Hunting	30	82	2.9	2.1	28	39
14 Large construction (dams, bridges, etc)	142	91	2.0	1.4	46	65
15 Motorcycles	29	176	5.1	5.5	35	32
16 Motor vehicles	187	247	7.3	4.9	34	50
17 Mountain climbing	28	68	1.1	0.9	62	76
18 Nuclear power	52	250	32.2	25.9	8	10
19 Pesticides	87	105	10.5	8.5	10	12
20 Power mowers	30	29	1.7	1.3	17	22
21 Police work	178	111	2.3	1.3	48	85
22 Prescription antibiotics	209	30	1.4	1.2	21	25
23 Railroads	185	37	1.4	1.1	26	34
24 Skiing	38	45	1.1	1.0	41	45
25 Smoking	20	189	15.2	15.3	12	12
26 Spray cans	17	73	8.6	6.9	8	11
27 Surgery	164	104	2.2	1.6	47	65
28 Swimming	68	52	1.2	0.9	43	58
29 Vaccinations	194	17	1.0	0.7	17	24
30 X-rays	156	45	2.1	1.3	21	35
All responses	69	69	2.7	2.2		
Coefficient of concordance	0.77	0.50	0.50	0.50		

[a] Values greater than one mean that the item should be safer; values less than one mean that the item could be riskier.

[b] Acceptable levels of risk were calculated by dividing column 2 by columns 3 and 4, respectively.

the benefits accrue, think of a whole year – the total value to society from each item during one year.

To make the evaluation task as easy as possible, each activity appeared on a 3x5-inch card. Participants were told first to study the items individually, thinking of the benefits accruing from each; then to order them from least to most beneficial; and finally, to assign numerical benefit values by giving a rating of 10 to the least beneficial and scaling the other ratings accordingly. They were also given additional suggestions, clarifications and encouragement to do as accurate a job as possible. For example, they were told 'a rating of 12 indicates that the item is 1.2 times as beneficial as the least beneficial item (ie, 20% more beneficial). A rating of 200 means that the item is 20 times as beneficial as the least beneficial item, to which you assigned a 10 ... Double check your ratings to make certain that they are consistent. For example, if one activity is rated 50 and a second 100, the second item should seem twice as beneficial as the first. Adjust the numbers until you feel that they are right for you.'

Perceived risk

Participants in this task (who, it will be remembered, did not judge perceived benefit) were told to 'consider the risk of dying as a consequence of this activity or technology. For example, use of electricity carries the risk of electrocution. It also entails risk for miners who produce the coal that generates electricity. Motor vehicles entail risk for drivers, passengers, bicyclists and pedestrians, etc'. They were asked to order and rate these activities for risk with instructions that paralleled the instructions for the perceived benefit task, giving a rating of ten to the least risky item and scaling the other items accordingly.

Note

These measures of risk and benefit differ from Starr's in several respects other than their source in attitudes rather than in behavior. Our subjects were asked to evaluate total risk per year to participants, not risk per hour of exposure, the unit of measurement used by Starr (1969). Several considerations motivated this change of unit, the most important of which is that the definition of 'hour of exposure' is extremely equivocal for some items (eg, handguns, pesticides). Excluding activities and technologies for which such measurement is problematic would introduce a systematic bias into our sample of items. Although the shape or magnitude of the relationship may vary with choice of measure, there is no a priori reason why people's historical risk-benefit trade-offs are best revealed with one particular measure of risk. Starr, himself (1972, p28), apparently believed that total risk per year was a more appropriate measure but rejected it because of measurement difficulties and because of his belief that 'the hour of exposure unit [is] more closely related to the individual's intuitive process in choosing an activity than a year of exposure would be'. In any case, he found that use of either unit 'gave substantially similar results'.

A second difference in unit is that we have considered total benefit and risk to society rather than *average* benefit and risk per person involved. For activities and technologies whose risks and/or benefits are shared by all members of society, this change is inconsequential. For the others, our risk and benefit measures should be weighted by the proportion of individuals participating in the activity in order to achieve strict comparability with Starr's measures.

A third difference from Starr is that relying on our participants' ability to consider all types of benefits relieved us of the restriction that Starr imposed on himself to consider only benefits to which a dollar value could be readily assigned.

Risk adjustment factor

After rating risks or benefits, both groups of participants were asked to judge the acceptability of the level of risk currently associated with each item. The instructions included the following:

> This is not the ideal risk. Ideally, the risks should be zero. The acceptable level is a level which is 'good enough,' where 'good enough' means you think that the advantages of increased safety are not worth the costs of reducing risk by restricting or otherwise altering the activity. For example, we can make drugs 'safer' by restricting their potency; cars can be made safer at a cost, by improving their construction or requiring regular safety inspection; we may, or may not, feel restrictions are necessary.
>
> If an activity's present level of risk is acceptable, no special action need be taken to increase its safety. If its riskiness is unacceptably high, *serious action*, such as legislation to restrict its practice, should be taken. On the other hand, there may be some activities or technologies that you believe are currently safer than the acceptable level of risk. For these activities, the risk of death could be higher than it is now before society would have to take serious action.

On their answer sheets, participants were provided with three columns labeled:

- 'Could be riskier: It would be acceptable if it were _____ times riskier';
- 'It is currently acceptable'; and
- 'Too risky: to be acceptable, it would have to be _____ times safer'.

These risk adjustment factors were used to establish levels of acceptable risk.

Rating scales

As their final task, participants were asked to rate each activity or technology on nine 7-point scales, each of which represented a dimension that has been hypothesized to influence perceptions of actual or acceptable risk (eg, Lowrance, 1976). These scales, in the order and wording in which they were described, were:

1 Voluntariness of risk: Do people get into these risky situations voluntarily? If for a single item some of the risks are voluntarily undertaken and some are not, mark an appropriate spot towards the center of the scale (the scale was labeled 1 = voluntary; 7 = involuntary).
2 Immediacy of effect: To what extent is the risk of death immediate – or is death likely to occur at some later time (1 = immediate; 7 = delayed)?
3 Knowledge about risk: To what extent are the risks known precisely by the persons who are exposed to those risks (1 = known precisely; 7 = not known)?
4 Knowledge about risk: To what extent are the risks known to science (1 = known precisely; 7 = not known)?
5 Control over risk: If you are exposed to the risk of each activity or technology, to what extent can you, by personal skill or diligence, avoid death while engaging in the activity (1 = uncontrollable; 7 = controllable)?

6   Newness: Are these risks new, novel ones or old, familiar ones (1 = new; 7 = old)?

7   Chronic–catastrophic: Is this a risk that kills people one at a time (chronic risk) or a risk that kills large numbers of people at once (catastrophic risk) (1 = chronic; 7 = catastrophic)?

8   Common–dread: Is this a risk that people have learned to live with and can think about reasonably calmly, or is it one that people have great dread for – on the level of a gut reaction (1 = common; 7 = dread)?

9   Severity of consequences: When the risk from the activity is realized in the form of a mishap or illness, how likely is it that the consequence will be fatal (1 = certain not to be fatal; 7 = certain to be fatal)? Green (1974) has referred to this as the 'sporting chance' factor.

Participants rated all 30 activities and technologies on each scale before proceeding to the next.

Participants

Members of the Eugene, Oregon, League of Women Voters and their spouses were asked to participate in the study in return for a contribution to the organization's treasury. In all, 76 individuals (52 women and 24 men) returned completed, anonymous questionnaires. Spouses received the same set of questionnaires and were instructed not to discuss the tasks until they were completed. They indicated having spent an average of two hours on the three tasks. Although League members and spouses are by no means representative of all American adults, they do constitute an extremely thoughtful, articulate and influential group of private citizens. If there are systematic relationships between people's judgments of risk and benefit, they should be found in these participants' responses. While the particular relationships found here might differ from those found with other populations, the opinions of League members may be quite similar to those of many of the private citizens most heavily engaged in the public policy-making process.

RESULTS

Perceived Risk and Benefit

Because arithmetic means tend to be unduly influenced by occasional extreme values, geometric means were used to describe the data. They are calculated by taking the log of each score, finding the arithmetic mean of those logs and then finding the antilog of the arithmetic mean. Columns 1 and 2 of Table 5.1 present the geometric means of all risk and benefit judgments for each item.

Many of the substantive results in this table appear to be accurate reflections of the attitudes of a generally liberal, environmentally minded group: the League of Women Voters. Especially interesting is the low benefit attributed to food coloring, spray cans and handguns, and the great difference between the evaluations of non-nuclear and nuclear electric power. Although these specific judgments are quite revealing, the main purpose of this study was not to poll the

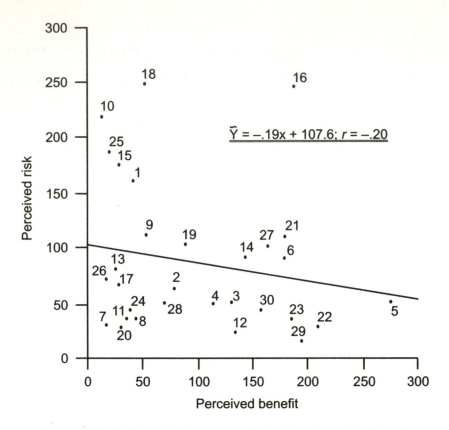

Figure 5.2 *Relationship between perceived risk and perceived benefit*

attitudes of any particular group of citizens, but to examine the relationships between perceived benefit and risk.

Figure 5.2 presents these judgments in a perceived risk-benefit space analogous to Starr's revealed risk-benefit space (see Figure 5.1). In general, perceived risk *declined* slightly with overall benefit, motor vehicles being the only item which was rated high on both scales. The overall best-fit line had a negative slope ($y = -.19x + 107.6$; $r = -.20$; $p > .25$). The axes in Starr's Figure 5.1 are logarithmic. Replotting our data in Figure 5.2 using log geometric means left the relationship unchanged ($y = -.18x + 2.18$; $r = -.23$).

Examination of columns 1 and 2 in Table 5.1 provides insight into the nature of the perceived risk-benefit relationship. Society currently tolerates a number of activities that our participants rated as having very low benefit and very high risk (eg, alcoholic beverages, handguns, motorcycles, smoking) as well as a number of activities perceived to have great benefit and relatively low risk (eg, prescription antibiotics, railroads, vaccinations).

Could these differences between our results and Starr's be artefacts of technical differences between our research procedures? In particular, are they due to our use of additional technologies and different units of measurement? We will consider these factors in turn. We can, however, make no statement about the degree to which our results depend upon the participant population studied.

Different items

Figure 5.3 compares the perceived (bottom figure) and revealed (top figure) risk-benefit spaces for the 8 of our 30 items used also by Starr (1969). The computed space is Otway and Cohen's (1975) recalculation of Starr's original data. Although the scale differences make it difficult to compare the two figures directly, it is clear that both the nature of the relationship and the relative costs and benefits of the various items were quite different. For this subset, as for the full set of items, risk decreased somewhat with benefit in the perceived space.

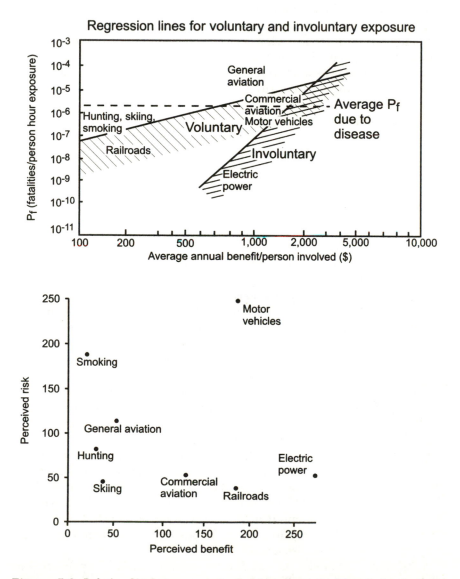

Figure 5.3 *Relationship between perceived risk and perceived benefit for the items studied by Starr (1969) and Otway and Cohen (1975) (above) and the present subjects (below)*

Different units

Allowing people to consider all benefits accruing from an activity, not just those readily expressed in dollars, may have been responsible for some of the differences between our results and Starr's. For example, railroads and electric power appear to be relatively more beneficial in the perceived space, perhaps reflecting the not-readily-quantifiable environmental benefits of the former and the 'great flexibility in patterns of living' (Starr, 1972, p29) conferred by the latter. Here, we believe that there are advantages to using the comprehensive measure of benefit.

Another difference between our units of measurement and Starr's was that we considered total risk and benefit to society, not just consequences per person exposed. Of the 30 activities and technologies used in this study, 25 have risks and/or benefits for all or almost all members of society. For these, use of risk and benefit per participant (Starr's measure) would produce a figure whose pattern is identical to that in Figure 5.2 ($y = -.20x + 109.7$; $r = -.21$ without those items, compared to $y = -.19x + 107.6$; $r = -.20$ with them).

Finally, we have argued that the unit 'risk per year' exposure used here is equal or superior to the unit 'risk per hour' exposure used by Starr. Whether this change of unit was responsible for differences in our results is a topic for future research. Starr reported that the change made little difference in his computations, although that need not also be the case with subjective estimates.

Risk Adjustment Factor

Columns 3 and 4 of Table 5.1 present the geometric means of our participants' judgments of the acceptability of the risk levels associated with the various items. As indicated by the preponderance of items for which the mean adjustment factor is greater than one, people thought that most items should be made safer; this occurred despite instructions emphasizing that such a rating indicated the need for serious societal action. Of the 2280 acceptability judgments, roughly half indicated that the item in question was too risky; 40% indicated that its current risk level was appropriate, and 10% indicated that it could be riskier still. There were, however, relatively few items that people believed should be made *much* safer, namely alcoholic beverages, handguns, motorcycles, motor vehicles, nuclear power, pesticides, smoking and spray cans.

Perceived risk was correlated .75 and .66 with risk adjustment factor ratings for the risk and benefit groups, respectively. Thus, both groups felt that the higher the risk, the more it should be reduced.

Participants in our study made these risk adjustment ratings after ordering and rating the 30 items for either perceived benefits or perceived risks. Comparing columns 3 and 4 shows that for 24 of the 30 items, the current risk level was judged more acceptable (less in need of change) by those people who had previously considered benefits than by those who had previously dwelt on risks. Thus, the way in which activities and technologies are considered may affect the acceptability of their risk levels.

A 'level of acceptable risk' was determined for each item by dividing its perceived risk (column 2 of Table 5.1) by the geometric mean adjustment factor (column 3 or 4 of Table 5.1). This was done separately for people who had previously judged risk first and those who had judged benefit first. The results are shown in columns 5 and 6 of Table 5.1. For example, for alcoholic beverages, the level of acceptable risk was 161/4.7 = 34.2 for perceived risk participants and 161/4.2 = 38.3 for perceived benefit participants. In general, the level of acceptable risk increased with the level of perceived benefit, although the relationship was not strong. According to this inferred relationship, participants in our study believed that more risk should be tolerated with more beneficial activities.

Interparticipant Agreement

In order to assess how well participants agreed with one another in their judgments, Kendall's coefficient of concordance was computed for each task. This index reflects the average rank-order correlation between the judgments of all pairs of participants (Siegel, 1956). The values shown at the bottom of Table 5.1 are moderate to high (all being significantly different from zero at $p < 0.001$) and indicate that people substantially agreed in their rankings, particularly when they evaluated benefits (column 1).

Rating Scales

Table 5.2 presents the arithmetic mean ratings of the nine risk characteristics for the 30 items. Since people in the perceived risk and perceived benefit groups produced very similar judgments (difference in means less than 1.00 in almost every case), their responses were pooled. There was also considerable agreement among people within each of the two groups, as reflected by the moderately high coefficients of concordance.

Perceived risk and benefit

Correlations between the nine risk characteristics and perceived risk and benefit are shown in Table 5.3. None of the risk characteristics correlated significantly with perceived benefit (column 1). Perceived risk was found to correlate with dread and severity but not with any of the other characteristics.

Starr (1969) hypothesized that the trade-off between risk and benefit is mediated by degree of voluntariness. If so, we would expect a tendency for voluntary activities to lie above the common regression line shown in Figure 5.2 and involuntary activities to lie below it. This was not the case. When the 30 items were dichotomized into the 15 most and 15 least voluntary, regression lines for the voluntary and involuntary subsets were virtually identical.

If voluntariness is conceptualized as a continuous rather than a dichotomous variable, then according to Starr's hypothesis an item lying high above the common regression line should be very voluntary (with a rating near 1); an item lying far below that line should be very involuntary (with a rating near 7). Let us define a deviation score as the signed vertical distance between each point in the risk-benefit space and the regression line; positive deviation scores belong to points above the line. These deviation scores reflect the variance in the risk scores that cannot be accounted for by the benefit scores. The correlation between these deviation scores and the voluntariness ratings indicates the proportion of this unexplained variance which can be accounted for by the

Table 5.2 Mean Ratings for Nine Characteristics of Risk

	Voluntariness	Immediacy	Known to exposed	Known to science	Controllability	Newness	Chronic-catastrophic	Common-dread	Severity of consequences
	1 = voluntary	1 = immediate	1 = precisely	1 = precisely	1 = can't be controlled	1 = new	1 = chronic	1 = common	1 = certain not to be fatal
1 Alcoholic beverages	2.10	5.34	3.77	1.98	5.57	6.61	1.79	1.92	4.40
2 Bicycles	1.90	2.82	3.27	2.80	4.99	5.19	1.30	1.74	3.77
3 Commercial aviation	2.80	1.85	3.24	2.12	2.18	4.24	6.09	3.39	5.72
4 Contraceptives	2.74	5.69	4.66	3.88	3.11	2.25	1.49	3.14	4.08
5 Electric power (non-nuclear)	4.40	2.82	3.98	2.68	4.25	5.09	2.66	1.72	4.52
6 Fire fighting	2.40	2.33	1.98	2.25	4.03	6.01	2.84	2.62	4.42
7 Food coloring	5.86	6.26	6.40	4.77	2.70	2.66	2.82	3.24	3.59
8 Food preservatives	5.65	6.18	6.39	4.76	2.70	2.73	2.82	3.32	3.66
9 General aviation	2.20	1.66	2.96	2.60	3.99	4.08	3.40	3.15	5.63
10 Handguns	3.42	1.65	2.64	2.41	4.05	5.69	2.10	4.40	5.67
11 High-school/college football	1.90	3.52	3.66	3.11	4.15	4.78	1.40	1.95	3.15
12 Home appliances	3.61	2.97	4.47	2.90	4.85	4.39	1.38	1.43	3.08
13 Hunting	2.01	1.66	2.62	2.64	4.45	6.14	1.59	2.79	4.91
14 Large construction	3.07	2.23	2.77	2.51	3.91	5.04	3.04	2.61	4.77
15 Motorcycles	1.87	1.76	2.69	2.17	4.08	4.31	1.59	3.02	5.19
16 Motor vehicles	4.04	2.33	3.14	2.31	4.19	4.73	3.28	3.04	4.57
17 Mountain climbing	1.15	1.78	1.83	2.49	4.98	5.63	1.32	2.57	4.80
18 Nuclear power	6.51	5.08	5.85	4.83	1.36	1.35	6.43	6.42	5.98
19 Pesticides	5.77	5.57	5.50	4.41	2.14	2.22	4.75	5.21	4.87
20 Power mowers	2.23	2.99	3.31	2.60	5.13	3.70	1.16	1.75	2.75

Table 5.2 *continues*

	Voluntariness 1 = voluntary	Immediacy 1 = immediate	Known to exposed 1 = precisely	Known to science	Controllability 1 = can't be controlled	Newness 1 = new	Chronic–catastrophic 1 = chronic	Common–dread 1 = common	Severity of consequences 1 = certain not to be fatal
21 Police work	2.44	2.14	2.05	2.25	3.76	5.50	2.07	3.05	4.35
22 Prescription antibiotics	4.44	4.33	5.40	3.91	2.77	2.87	2.35	2.19	3.82
23 Railroads	3.42	2.91	3.66	2.68	3.22	5.49	4.49	1.75	3.60
24 Skiing	1.28	2.45	2.47	2.51	4.73	4.69	1.06	1.92	3.15
25 Smoking	1.85	6.11	2.86	2.15	4.43	5.04	1.68	2.89	5.01
26 Spray cans	3.80	6.06	5.43	4.16	3.60	1.89	3.82	3.62	4.27
27 Surgery	4.28	2.71	3.84	2.86	2.39	4.95	1.14	4.04	4.68
28 Swimming	1.64	1.76	2.87	2.68	5.17	6.50	1.16	1.89	4.78
29 Vaccinations	3.82	3.71	4.84	2.82	2.53	4.50	1.88	2.03	3.62
30 X-rays	4.38	6.15	5.05	3.28	2.37	4.02	1.99	2.58	4.20
Mean	3.24	3.49	3.78	2.98	3.73	4.41	2.50	2.85	4.37
Standard deviation	1.47	1.70	1.33	0.87	1.10	1.41	1.43	1.12	0.85
Coefficient of concordance:									
Benefit Ss	.59	.59	.53	.30	.40	.59	.58	.45	.45
Risk Ss	.62	.66	.61	.35	.42	.65	.57	.47	.50

Table 5.3 *Correlations between Rating Scales and Perceived Risk and Benefit*

Scale	Perceived benefit	Perceived risk	Deviations from perceived benefit – perceived risk regression line [a]
Voluntariness (1 = voluntary)	.24	.08	.13
Immediacy (1 = immediate)	−.15	−.07	−.11
Known to exposed (1 = known precisely)	.04	−.20	−.22
Known to science (1 = known precisely)	−.16	−.17	−.21
Controllability (1 = uncontrollable)	−.29	−.04	−.06
Newness (1 = new)	.14	.05	.08
Chronic (1 = chronic)	.12	.30	.29
Common/dread (1 = common)	−.26	.64*	.54*
Severity of consequences (1 = certain not to be fatal)	−.10	.67*	.66*

[a] As shown in Figure 5.2.
*$p < .001$.

voluntariness measure. Starr's hypothesis suggests that this correlation would be negative (high positive deviations going with low voluntariness ratings). As can be seen from column 3 of Table 5.3, this was not the case ($r = .13$).

However, two other risk characteristics, dread and severity, did correlate with the deviations from the regression line. If we drew a figure for each of these scales, we would find two roughly parallel regression lines, one lying above the other. With the scale common/dread, we would find that items whose consequences are more dreaded tend to have higher perceived risk, at all levels of benefit, than items with more common consequences. Similarly, the line for the more severe (certain to be fatal) risks would lie above the line for less severe risks.

Acceptable risk

The fact that *perceived* risk was unrelated to voluntariness does not necessarily contradict Starr's claim that the voluntary nature of an activity influences its acceptable risk level. Table 5.4 presents the correlations between each risk characteristic and various aspects of acceptability. The significant correlations in the first column indicate that activities with the most dread and certainly fatal consequences were deemed most in need of risk reduction. The significant correlations in the second column show that if risks were adjusted to an acceptable level, then higher risk levels would be tolerated for old, voluntary activities with well-known and immediate consequences. The correlations in the third column show the extent to which each qualitative risk characteristic accounts for variance in acceptable risk unexplained by perceived benefit. These correlations were significant for each of the first six characteristics. Thus, for any given level of benefit, greater risk was tolerated if that risk was voluntary, immediate, known precisely, controllable and familiar.

Table 5.4 *Correlations between Rating Scales and Measures of Acceptable Risk*

Scale	Risk adjustment factor	Level of acceptable risk [a]	Deviations from perceived benefit – level of acceptable risk regression line [b]
Voluntariness (1 = voluntary)	.38*	–.47**	–.64***
Immediacy (1 = immediate)	.28	–.64***	–.64***
Known to exposed (1 = known precisely)	.21	–.68***	–.75***
Known to science (1 = known precisely)	.29	–.57***	–.58***
Controllability (1 = uncontrollable)	–.30	.40*	.48**
Newness (1 = new)	–.34	.60***	.60***
Chronic (1 = chronic)	.45*	.22	–.25
Common/dread (1 = common)	.75***	–.29	–.24
Severity of consequences (1 = certain not to be fatal)	.54***	.17	.22

Note: Perceived risk and perceived benefit groups combined.

* $p < .05$, ** $p < .01$, *** $p < .001$.

[a] perceived risk divided by risk adjustment factor

[b] as shown in Figure 5.3

The relationship between voluntariness and acceptable risk level is further illustrated in Figure 5.4, which shows the separate regression lines for the 15 most and least voluntary activities and technologies. Figure 5.4 clearly shows a double standard in risk tolerance for voluntary and involuntary activities, such as that found by Starr (see Figure 5.1). Note, however, that the y-axis in Figure 5.4 is 'acceptable risk level' and not 'current risk level'. The participants in our study believed that a double standard would be appropriate if risk levels were made acceptable. This was also reflected in the large negative correlation between voluntariness scores and deviations from the perceived benefit-acceptable risk regression line noted above. Figures such as 5.4 would show a similar double standard for each of the first six risk characteristics in Table 5.4.

Factor analysis of risk characteristics

Ratings of the various task characteristics tended to be highly intercorrelated, as shown in Table 5.5. For example, risks faced voluntarily tended to be known to the exposed individual ($r = .83$); new risks tended to be judged less controllable ($r = .64$), and so forth. The intercorrelations were sufficiently high to suggest that they might be explained by a few basic dimensions of risk underlying the nine characteristics. In order to identify such underlying dimensions, we conducted principal-components factor analyses (Rummel, 1970) for risk participants and for benefits participants, separately. The unrotated factor loadings for the two groups were so similar (the mean absolute difference between loadings was .05) that they were averaged (see Table 5.6).[1] Two orthogonal factors appeared sufficient to account for the intercorrelations shown in Table 5.5. The

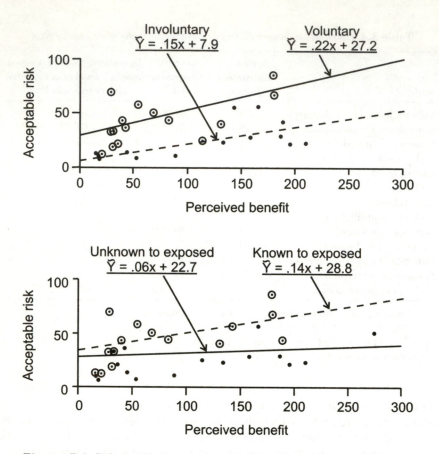

Figure 5.4 *Relationship between perceived benefit and acceptable risk for voluntary (circled)–involuntary and known (circled)–unknown items*

factor loadings shown in Table 5.6 indicate the degree to which each risk characteristic correlated with each of the two underlying factors. The first factor correlated highly with all characteristics except severity of consequences. The second factor was associated with severity of consequences and, to a lesser extent, with common/dread and chronic/catastrophic. The communality index in Table 5.6 reflects the extent to which the two factors accounted for each of the ratings. The communalities were high, indicating that this two-factor solution did a good job of representing the ratings for the nine scales.

Just as each of the 30 items had a (mean) score on each of the nine risk characteristics, we can obtain a score for each item or each factor. These factor scores enable us to plot the 30 items in the space defined by the two factors. As might be expected from the similarity of the factor solutions for risk and for benefit participants, these plots were very similar for the two groups. The mean absolute difference between factor scores was .10 for factor 1 and .18 for factor 2. The correlations between factor scores for the two groups were .99 for factor 1 and .98 for factor 2. Given the extraordinary similarity of the plots for these two independent groups, their factor scores were averaged. Figure 5.5 plots these scores for the 30 items.

Table 5.5 *Rating Scale Intercorrelations*

Scale	Voluntariness	Immediacy	Known to exposed	Known to science	Controllability	Newness	Chronic	Common/dread	Severity
Voluntariness		.54*	.83*	.75*	–.76*	–.65*	.5	.5:	.0(
Immediacy			.78*	.68*	–.42	–.63*	.1	.2:	–.2:
Known to exposed				.87*	–.63*	–.78*	.3	.3	–.2:
Known to science					–.60*	–.83*	.3	.4(	–.1<
Controllability						.64*	–.6	–.6<	–.2<
Newness							–.4	–.5:	.0!
Chronic								.6(	.4(
Common/dread									.6:
Severity of consequences									

Note: These correlations were computed separately for the risk and benefits groups and then averaged (using Fisher's Z transformation).
* *p* < .001.

Table 5.6 *Factor Loadings Across Nine Risk Characteristics*

Characteristic	Factor 1	Factor 2	Communality
Voluntariness	.89	.03	.79
Immediacy	.70	–.45	.69
Known to exposed	.88	–.39	.93
Known to science	.88	–.28	.86
Controllability	–.83	–.24	.75
Newness	–.87	.14	.78
Chronic	.62	.55	.69
Common/dread	.67	.60	.81
Severity of consequences	.11	.91	.84
λ	5.30	1.90	
Percent of variance accounted for:	58.90	21.10	

Note: Risk and benefit subjects averaged.

This plot helps to clarify the nature of the two factors. The upper extreme of factor 1 was associated with new, involuntary, highly technological items, which have delayed consequences for masses of people. Items low on the first factor were familiar, voluntary activities with immediate consequences at the individual level. High scores (right-hand side) on factor 2 were associated with events whose consequences are certain to be fatal (often for large numbers of people) should something go wrong. It seems appropriate to label factors 1 and 2 as 'technological risk' and 'severity', respectively.

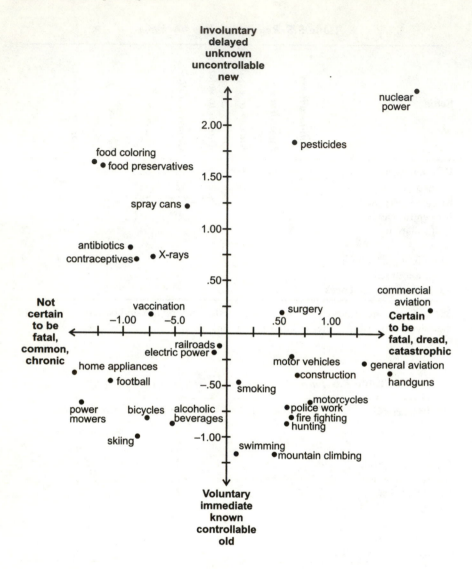

Figure 5.5 *Location of risk items within the two-factor space*

One of the more remarkable features of this factor space was the unique position (isolation) of nuclear power. Clearly, the participants in our study viewed the risks from nuclear power as qualitatively different from those of the other activities. Figures 5.6a and 5.6b highlight these differences by comparing the risk ratings for nuclear power and two ostensibly similar technologies, X-rays and non-nuclear electric power. Although X-rays and nuclear power both rely on radioactivity, nuclear power was perceived as markedly more catastrophic and dreaded. For those who believe that nuclear power is just another kind of energy, the discrepancies shown in Figure 8b should be very surprising. How widely these perceptions are shared by people other than members of the League of Women Voters and their spouses is a matter for future research.

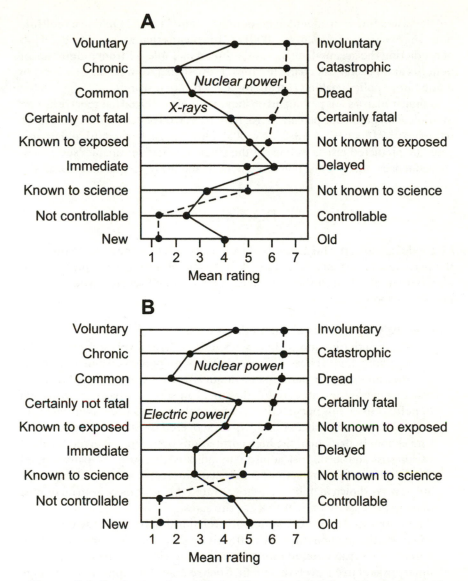

Figure 5.6 *Qualitative characteristics of perceived risk for nuclear power and related technologies*

Multivariate Determination of Acceptable Risk Levels

In Figure 5.1, Starr's goal was to show a way to predict the level of acceptable risk as a function of benefit and voluntariness. Rowe (1977) has done a similar analysis using qualitative aspects of risk other than voluntariness. A generalization of these approaches would be a formula specifying acceptable risk level as a function of benefit and all relevant qualitative aspects of risk. We have done this using the two risk dimensions derived by the factor analysis of the nine qualitative risk scales. A multiple regression equation predicting acceptable risk level as a function of perceived benefit, factors 1 and 2 yielded a multiple R of .76 [$F = 19.2$; $df = 3, 26$; $p < .0001$]. This means that we can do a good job of predicting the acceptable risk levels shown in Table 5.1 from judgments of benefits and several risk characteristics. How such a formula may be used to guide future policy-making is also a topic for future research.

A similar analysis was performed on judgments of perceived (current) risk. The multiple R for predicting perceived risk from perceived benefit and the two factor scores was .67 [$F = 6.96$; $df = 3, 26$; $p < .005$]. However, perceived risk judgments could be predicted just as well using the single qualitative variable 'severity of consequences' and ignoring perceived benefit and the other qualitative scales.

Discussion

Methodologically, the main result of this study was that the task we posed to the participants was tractable. That is, it was possible to ask people for complex judgments about difficult societal problems and receive orderly, interpretable responses.

Substantively, the most important findings were:

1   For many activities and technologies, current risk levels were viewed as unacceptably high. These differences between perceived and acceptable risk indicated that the participants in our study were not satisfied with the way that market and other regulatory mechanisms have balanced risks and benefits. Given this perspective, such people may also be unwilling to accept revealed preferences of the type uncovered by Starr as a guide for future action. In particular, the high correlations between perceived levels of existing risk and needed risk adjustment indicated that our participants wanted the risks from different activities to be considerably more equal than they are now. As shown in Table 5.1, they wanted the most risky item on our list of 30 to be only 10 times as risky as the safest.

2   There appeared to be little systematic relationship between the perceived existing risks and benefits of the 30 activities and technologies considered here. Nor are risks entered into voluntarily perceived as greater than involuntary risks at fixed levels of benefit. Such relationships appeared to emerge in Starr's revealed risk-benefit space.

3   However, there was a consistent, although not overwhelming, relationship between perceived benefit and acceptable level of risk. Despite their desire for more equal risks from different activities, our respondents believed that society should accept somewhat higher levels of risk with more beneficial activities. They also felt that society should tolerate higher risk levels for voluntary, than for involuntary activities. Thus, they believed that Starr's hypothesized relationships should be obtained in a society in which risk levels are adequately regulated. In addition, other characteristics of risk besides voluntariness, namely perceived control, familiarity, knowledge and immediacy, also induced double standards for acceptable risk. Thus, these expressed preferences indicate that determining acceptable risk may require consideration of other characteristics than benefits.

4   The nine characteristics hypothesized by various authors to influence judg-
    ments of perceived and acceptable risk were highly intercorrelated. They
    could be effectively reduced to two dimensions. One dimension apparently
    discriminated between high- and low-technology activities, with the high
    end being characterized by new, involuntary, poorly known activities, often
    with delayed consequences The second dimension primarily reflected the
    certainty of death given that adversity occurs. Consideration of these two
    factors in addition to perceived benefit made acceptable risk judgments
    highly predictable. Conceivably, policy-makers might use such relationships
    to predict public acceptance of the risk levels associated with proposed tech-
    nologies.

Given the contrasts between our study and Starr's, the question arises: 'Who is
right?' We believe that neither approach is, in itself, definitive. The particular
relationships that Starr uncovered were based on numerous ad hoc assumptions
and applied to only a small set of possible technologies. Our own study used
but one of the psychophysical measurement procedures possible, applied to a
rather special participant population.[2] We are, at present, engaged in additional
studies employing different types of respondents and different judgment methods. Answering the question 'How safe is safe enough?' is going to require a
multimethod, multidisciplinary approach, in which the present work and Starr's
are but two components.

Balancing the results of these various approaches also depends on one's
conceptualization of the policy-making process. A definitive revealed-preference
study would be an adequate guide to action only if one believed that rational
decision-making is best performed by experts formalizing past policies as pre-
scriptions for future action. A definitive expressed-preference study would be an
adequate guide only if one believed that people's present opinions should be
society's final arbiter and that people act on their expressed preferences. The
obvious reservation that many people would have about the former approach is
that it is highly conservative, enshrining current economic and social relationships; an obvious problem with the latter approach is that it allows people to
change planning guidelines at will, possibly resulting in social chaos.

For most people, presumably, both current opinions and past behavior are
relevant to social policy. The believer in expressed preferences cannot ignore
existing economic arrangements. On the other hand, the public will resist even
the best-laid plans if they feel that policy-makers have not adequately considered their desires. Assume that future research finds that a representative sample
of properly informed citizens, queried by means of appropriate methods, evaluates the seriousness of hazards not only by their statistical and 'economic' risks,
but also according to qualitative features such as voluntariness and controllability. The legitimacy of these desires will have to be explored and debated. For
example, implementing a double standard for voluntary risks may prove, on
analysis, to be acceptable while the desire to make dreaded technologies especially safe may be found to have unreasonable consequences. Even if the public's
desires are ignored, either with or without analysis, there is no guarantee that
they will go away. Pressure on politicians and regulators may force laws based
on more 'rational' economic considerations to be implemented in accordance

with these 'irrational' desires. Indeed, the current functioning of our regulatory system might be better understood as a partial reflection of such pressures.

Although we have de-emphasized the substance of our respondents' judgments about specific technologies in order to concentrate on more general relationships between those judgments, such opinions from members of the League of Women Voters are quite likely to appear in regulatory hearings and elsewhere. If League members believe that nuclear power has low benefit relative to its level of risk, it is as much a political fact of life as the League members' failure to see any systematic trade-off between existing risks and benefits.[3]

The present study raised several questions worthy of further investigation. One intriguing finding was that people viewed current risk levels as more acceptable after they had ordered current benefits in depth (Table 5.1, columns 3 and 4). Does this imply that the way technologies are presented, say, in regulatory hearings, can affect the way in which they are evaluated? More research is needed on how to present the public with the information needed to give new technologies a fair hearing.

A second question is triggered by the observed inverse relationship between perceived risks and benefits. Could this have occurred because participants in the benefit group were unable to estimate gross benefits rather than net benefits? If people in the benefit group did take risk into consideration, high-risk activities would have been rated as relatively lower in benefit, and low-risk activities would have been viewed as relatively higher in benefit, much like the observed pattern. Future work should consider the advantages of having people judge multiple aspects of benefit (eg, economic aspects, physical and mental health, convenience, etc) separately. These could then be weighted and amalgamated into an overall, multi-attribute measure. This approach may reduce or eliminate possible contamination from the risk side.

Finally, what is the relationship between these attitudes about risk and people's responses to measures designed to ameliorate risks? If people believe that motor vehicles should be five times safer, does this mean that they would accept any immediate, Draconian step designed to attain that goal? Does it mean that a fivefold reduction in risk is a long-term goal for society and that meaningful (but not necessarily drastic) steps should be taken until that goal is reached; or does it mean that the adjustment ratios expressed here only measure relative concerns about the risk levels of various activities? A more behaviorally relevant scale of acceptability should be developed, with clearer implications for regulatory actions.

ACKNOWLEDGMENTS

This research was supported by National Science Foundation Grant OEP75-20318 to the University of California, Los Angeles, under subcontract No K559081-0 to Oregon Research Institute. We thank Robyn Dawes, Lew Goldberg, David Okrent, Ola Svenson and Chris Whipple for comments on an earlier draft.

NOTES

1 A varimax rotation was applied to these factors, but it produced no improvement in interpretability and will not be discussed.

2 Preliminary results indicate that the risk-benefit relationships obtained with the League of Women Voters subjects replicated almost exactly when a group of university students made the same sorts of judgments. A second study asked students to judge acceptable risks directly, instead of using an adjustment factor. The direct ratings correlated about .77 with ratings produced by another group using the indirect adjustment method of the present study. These results indicate an encouraging degree of cross-method consistency.

3 In November 1976, half a year after distribution of our questionnaire, Oregon voters decided the fate of a nuclear safeguards ballot measure that, if passed, would have curtailed, and perhaps stopped, the development of nuclear power in Oregon. In response to a survey preserving their anonymity, 95% of the participants in our study indicated voting in favor of the safeguards measure (ie, against nuclear power) compared with 42% supporting it statewide. Thus, the voting behavior of our League subjects matches the anti-nuclear sentiments they expressed in their risk and benefit judgments.

6 Rating the Risks

*Paul Slovic, Baruch Fischhoff and
Sarah Lichtenstein*

People respond to the hazards they perceive. If their perceptions are faulty, efforts at public and environmental protection are likely to be misdirected. In order to improve hazard management, a risk assessment industry has developed over the last decade that combines the efforts of physical, biological and social scientists in an attempt to identify hazards and measure the frequency and magnitude of their consequences. (We have not attempted here to review all the important research in this area. Interested readers should see Green, 1980; Kates, 1978; and Otway, Maurer & Thomas, 1978.)

For some hazards extensive statistical data is readily available; for example, the frequency and severity of motor vehicle accidents are well documented. For other familiar activities, such as the use of alcohol and tobacco, the hazardous effects are less readily discernible and their assessment requires complex epidemiological and experimental studies. But in either case, the hard facts go only so far and then human judgment is needed to interpret the findings and determine their relevance for the future.

Other hazards, such as those associated with recombinant DNA research or nuclear power, are so new that risk assessment must be based on theoretical analyses such as fault trees (see Figure 6.1), rather than on direct experience. While sophisticated, these analyses, too, include a large component of human judgment. Someone, relying on educated intuition, must determine the structure of the problem, the consequences to be considered and the importance of the various branches of the fault tree.

Once the analyses have been performed, they must be communicated to the various people who are actually responsible for dealing with the hazards, including industrialists, environmentalists, regulators, legislators and voters. If these people do not see, understand or believe these risk statistics, then distrust, conflict and ineffective hazard management can result.

Note: this is a slightly revised version of 'Rating the Risks' by P Slovic, B Fischhoff and S Lichtenstein, *Environment*, vol 2, issue 3, pp14–20, 36–9, 1979. Reprinted with permission of the Helen Dwight Reid Education Foundation. Published by Heldref Publications, 1319 18th St NW, Washington, DC 20036–1802. Copyright 1979.

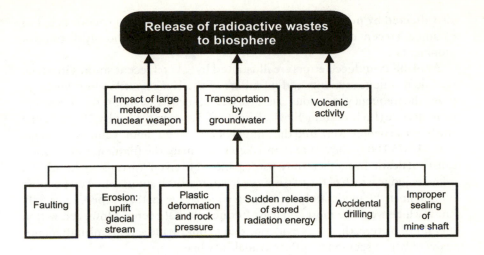

Note: Fault trees are used most often to characterize hazards for which direct experience is not available. The tree shown here indicates the various ways in which radioactive material might accidentally be released from nuclear wastes buried within a salt deposit.

To read this tree, start with the bottom row of possible initiating events, each of which can lead to the transportation of radioactivity by groundwater. This transport can in turn release radioactivity to the biosphere. As indicated by the second level of boxes, release of radioactivity can also be produced directly (without the help of groundwater) through the impact of a large meteorite, a nuclear weapon, or a volcanic eruption.

Fault trees may be used to map all relevant possibilities and to determine the probability of the final outcome. To accomplish this latter goal, the probabilities of all component stages, as well as their logical connections, must be completely specified.

Source: McGrath (1974).

Figure 6.1 *Illustration of a fault tree*

JUDGMENTAL BIASES

When laypeople are asked to evaluate risks, they seldom have statistical evidence on hand. In most cases they must rely on inferences based on what they remember hearing or observing about the risk in question. Recent psychological research has identified a number of general inferential rules that people seem to use in such situations (Tversky & Kahneman, 1974). These judgmental rules, known technically as *heuristics*, are employed to reduce difficult mental tasks to simpler ones. Although valid in some circumstances, in others they can lead to large and persistent biases with serious implications for risk assessment.

Availability

One heuristic that has special relevance for risk perception is known as 'availability' (Tversky & Kahneman, 1973). People who use this heuristic judge an event as likely or frequent if instances of it are easy to imagine or recall. Frequently occurring events are generally easier to imagine and recall than rare events. Thus, availability is often an appropriate cue. However, availability is also affected by numerous factors unrelated to frequency of occurrence. For example, a recent disaster or a vivid film such as 'Jaws' can seriously distort risk judgments.

Availability-induced errors are illustrated by several recent studies in which we asked college students and members of the League of Women Voters to judge the frequency of various causes of death, such as smallpox, tornadoes and heart disease (Lichtenstein, Slovic, Fischhoff, Layman & Combs, 1978). In one study, these people were told the annual death toll for motor vehicle accidents in the US (50,000); they were then asked to estimate the frequency of 40 other causes of death. In another study, participants were given two causes of death and asked to judge which of the two is more frequent. Both studies showed people's judgments to be moderately accurate in a global sense; that is, people usually knew which were the most and least frequent lethal events. However, within this global picture, there was evidence that people made serious misjudgments, many of which seemed to reflect availability bias.

Figure 6.2 compares the judged number of deaths per year with the annual number according to public health statistics. If the frequency judgments were

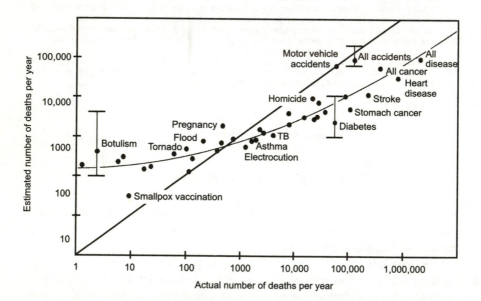

Note: If judged and actual frequencies were equal, the data would fall on the straight line. The points, and the curved line fitted to them, represent the averaged responses of a large number of lay people.

While people were approximately accurate, their judgments were systematically distorted. As described in the text, both the compression of the scale and the scatter of the results indicate this. To give an idea of the degree of agreement among subjects, vertical bars are drawn to depict the 25th and 75th percentile of individual judgment for botulism, diabetes and all accidents. Fifty percent of all judgments fall between these limits. The range of responses for the other 37 causes of death was similar.

Source: Redrawn from Lichtenstein et al. (1978).

Figure 6.2 *Relationship between judged frequency and the actual number of deaths per year for 41 causes of death*

accurate, they would equal the actual death rates, and all data points would fall on the straight line making a 45 degree angle with the axes of the graph. In fact, the points are scattered about a curved line that sometimes lies above and sometimes below the line of accurate judgment. In general, rare causes of death were overestimated and common causes of death were underestimated. As a result, while the annual death toll varied over a range of one million, average frequency judgments varied over a range of only 1000.

In addition to this general bias, many important specific biases were evident. For example, accidents were judged to cause as many deaths as diseases, whereas diseases actually take about 15 times as many lives. Homicides were incorrectly judged to be more frequent than diabetes and stomach cancer. Homicides were also judged to be about as frequent as stroke, although the latter annually claims about 11 times as many lives. Frequencies of death from botulism, tornadoes and pregnancy (including childbirth and abortion) were also greatly overestimated.

Table 6.1 lists the lethal events whose frequencies were most poorly judged in our studies. In keeping with availability considerations, overestimated items were dramatic and sensational whereas underestimated items tended to be unspectacular events which claim one victim at a time and are common in non-fatal form.

In the public arena, the availability heuristic may have many effects. For example, the biasing effects of memorability and imaginability may pose a barrier to open, objective discussions of risk. Consider an engineer demonstrating the safety of subterranean nuclear waste disposal by pointing out the improbability of each branch of the fault tree in Figure 6.1. Rather than reassuring the audience, the presentation might lead individuals to feel that 'I didn't realize there were so many things that could go wrong'. The very discussion of any low-probability hazard may increase the judged probability of that hazard regardless of what the evidence indicates.

In other situations, availability may lull people into complacency. In one study (Fischhoff, Slovic & Lichtenstein, 1978), we presented people with various versions of a fault tree showing the 'risks' of starting a car. Participants were asked to judge the completeness of the representation (reproduced in Figure 6.3). Their estimate of the proportion of no-starts falling in the category

Table 6.1 *Bias in Judged Frequency of Death*

Most overestimated	*Most underestimated*
All accidents	Smallpox vaccination
Motor vehicle accidents	Diabetes
Pregnancy, childbirth and abortion	Stomach cancer
Tornadoes	Lightning
Flood	Stroke
Botulism	Tuberculosis
All cancer	Asthma
Fire and flames	Emphysema
Venomous bite or sting	
Homicide	

Note: To control for the general systemic biases observed in Figure 6.2, these comparisons are made relative to the curved line.

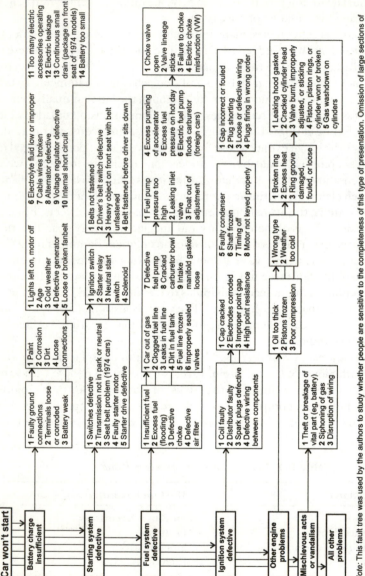

Note: This fault tree was used by the authors to study whether people are sensitive to the completeness of this type of presentation. Omission of large sections of the diagram was found to have little influence on the judged degree of completeness. In effect, what was out of sight was out of mind. Professional automobile mechanics did not do appreciably better on the test than did lay people.

Source: Fischhoff, Slovic and Lichtenstein (1978).

Figure 6.3 *Fault tree indicating the ways in which a car might fail to start*

labeled 'all other problems' was about the same when looking at the full tree of Figure 6.3 or at versions in which half of the branches were deleted. Such pruning should have dramatically increased the judged likelihood of 'all other problems'. However, it did not. In keeping with the availability heuristic, what was out of sight was effectively out of mind.

Overconfidence

A particularly pernicious aspect of heuristics is that people are typically very confident about judgments based on them. For example, in a follow-up to the study on causes of death, participants were asked to indicate the odds that they were correct in their judgment about which of two lethal events was more frequent (Fischhoff, Slovic & Lichtenstein, 1977). Odds of 100:1 or greater were given often (25% of the time). However, about one out of every eight answers associated with such extreme confidence was wrong (fewer than 1 in 100 would have been wrong if the odds had been appropriate). About 30% of the judges gave odds greater than 50:1 to the incorrect assertion that homicides are more frequent than suicides. The psychological basis for this unwarranted certainty seems to be people's insensitivity to the tenuousness of the assumptions on which their judgments are based (in this case, the validity of the availability heuristic). Such overconfidence is dangerous. It indicates that we often do not realize how little we know and how much additional information we need about the various problems and risks we face.

Overconfidence manifests itself in other ways as well. A typical task in estimating failure rates or other uncertain quantities is to set upper and lower bounds so that there is a 98% chance that the true value lies between them. Experiments with diverse groups of people making many different kinds of judgments have shown that, rather than 2% of true values falling outside the 98% confidence bounds, 20% to 50% do so (Lichtenstein, Fischhoff & Phillips, 1982). People think that they can estimate such values with much greater precision than is actually the case.

Unfortunately, experts seem as prone to overconfidence as laypeople. When the fault tree study described above was repeated with a group of professional automobile mechanics, they too, were insensitive to how much had been deleted from the tree. Hynes and Vanmarcke (1976) asked seven 'internationally known' geotechnical engineers to predict the height of an embankment that would cause a clay foundation to fail and to specify confidence bounds around this estimate that were wide enough to have a 50% chance of enclosing the true failure height. None of the bounds specified by these experts actually did enclose the true failure height. The multimillion dollar Reactor Safety Study (*Rasmussen Report*, US Nuclear Regulatory Commission, 1975), in assessing the probability of a core melt in a nuclear reactor, used a procedure for setting confidence bounds that has been found in experiments to produce a high degree of overconfidence. Related problems led the recent review committee, chaired by H W Lewis of the University of California, Santa Barbara, to conclude that the Reactor Safety Study greatly overestimated the precision with which the probability of a core melt could be assessed (US Nuclear Regulatory Commission, 1978b).

Another case in point is the 1976 collapse of the Teton Dam. The US Committee on Government Operations has attributed this disaster to the unwarranted confidence of engineers who were absolutely certain they had solved the many serious problems that arose during construction (US Committee on Government Operations, 1976). Indeed, in routine practice, failure probabilities are not even calculated for new dams even though about 1 in 300 fails when the reservoir is first filled. Further anecdotal evidence of overconfidence may be found in many other technical risk assessments. Some common ways in which experts may overlook or misjudge pathways to disaster include the following:

- Failure to consider the ways in which human errors can affect technological systems. Example: the disastrous fire at the Brown's Ferry Nuclear Plant was caused by a technician checking for an air leak with a candle, in violation of standard operating procedures.
- Overconfidence in current scientific knowledge. Example: the failure to recognize the harmful effects of X-rays until societal use had become widespread and largely uncontrolled.
- Insensitivity to how a technological system functions as a whole. Example: though the respiratory risk of fossil-fueled power plants has been recognized for some time, the related effects of acid rains on ecosystems were largely missed until very recently.
- Failure to anticipate human response to safety measures. Example: the partial protection offered by dams and levées gives people a false sense of security and promotes development of the floodplain. When a rare flood does exceed the capacity of the dam, the damage may be considerably greater than if the floodplain had been unprotected. Similarly, 'better' highways, while decreasing the death toll per vehicle mile, may increase the total number of deaths because they increase the number of miles driven.

Desire for Certainty

Every technology is a gamble of sorts and, like other gambles, its attractiveness depends on the probability and size of its possible gains and losses. Both scientific experiments and casual observation show that people have difficulty thinking about and resolving the risk-benefit conflicts even in simple gambles. One way to reduce the anxiety generated by confronting uncertainty is to deny that uncertainty. The denial resulting from this anxiety-reducing search for certainty thus represents an additional source of overconfidence. This type of denial is illustrated by the case of people faced with natural hazards, who often view their world as either perfectly safe or as predictable enough to preclude worry. Thus, some flood victims interviewed by Kates (1962) flatly denied that floods could ever recur in their areas. Some thought (incorrectly) that new dams and reservoirs in the area would contain all potential floods, while others attributed previous floods to freak combinations of circumstances, unlikely to recur. Denial, of course, has its limits. Many people feel that they cannot ignore the risks of nuclear power. For these people, the search for certainty is best satisfied by outlawing the risk.

Scientists and policy-makers who point out the gambles involved in societal decisions are often resented for the anxiety they provoke. Borch (1968) noted how annoyed corporate managers get with consultants who give them the probabilities of possible events instead of telling them exactly what will happen. Just before a blue-ribbon panel of scientists reported that they were 95% certain that cyclamates do not cause cancer, Food and Drug Administration Commissioner Alexander Schmidt said, 'I'm looking for a clear bill of health, not a wishy-washy, iffy answer on cyclamates' (*Eugene Register Guard*, 1976). Senator Edmund Muskie has called for 'one-armed' scientists who do not respond 'on the one hand, the evidence is so, but on the other hand...' when asked about the health effects of pollutants (David, 1975).

The search for certainty is legitimate if it is done consciously, if the remaining uncertainties are acknowledged rather than ignored, and if people realize the costs. If a very high level of certainty is sought, those costs are likely to be high. Eliminating the uncertainty may mean eliminating the technology and foregoing its benefits. Often some risk is inevitable. Efforts to eliminate it may only alter its form. We must choose, for example, between the vicissitudes of nature on an unprotected floodplain and the less probable, but potentially more catastrophic, hazards associated with dams and levées.

ANALYZING JUDGMENTS OF RISK

To be of assistance in the hazard management process, a theory of perceived risk must explain people's extreme aversion to some hazards, their indifference to others, and the discrepancies between these reasons and experts' recommendations. Why, for example, do some communities react vigorously against locating a liquid natural gas terminal in their vicinity despite the assurances of experts that it is safe? Why do other communities situated on floodplains and earthquake faults or below great dams show little concern for the experts' warnings? Such behavior is doubtless related to how people assess the *quantitative* characteristics of the hazards they face. The preceding discussion of judgmental processes was designed to illuminate this aspect of perceived risk. The studies reported below broaden the discussion to include more *qualitative* components of perceived risk. They ask, when people judge the risk inherent in a technology, are they referring only to the (possibly misjudged) number of people it could kill or also to other, more qualitative, features of the risk it entails?

Quantifying Perceived Risk

In our first studies we asked four different groups of people to rate three different activities and technologies according to the present risk of death from each (Fischhoff, Slovic, Lichtenstein, Read et al, 1978). Three of these groups were from Eugene, Oregon; they included 30 college students, 40 members of the League of Women Voters (LOWV), and 25 business and professional members of the 'Active Club'. The fourth group was composed of 15 persons selected nationwide for their professional involvement in risk assessment. This 'expert' group included a geographer, an environmental policy analyst, an economist, a lawyer, a biologist, a biochemist and a government regulator of hazardous materials.

All these people were asked, for each of the 30 items, 'to consider the risk of dying (across all US society as a whole) as a consequence of this activity or technology'. In order to make the evaluation task easier, each activity appeared on a 3x5 inch card. Respondents were told first to study the items individually, thinking of all the possible ways someone might die from each (eg, fatalities from non-nuclear electricity were to include deaths resulting from the mining of coal and other energy production activities as well as electrocution; motor vehicle fatalities were to include collisions with bicycles and pedestrians). Next, they were to order the items from least to most risky and then assign numerical risk values by giving a rating of 10 to the least risky item and making the other ratings accordingly. They were also given additional

Table 6.2 *Ordering of Perceived Risk for 30 Activities and Technologies*

	Group 1: LOWV	Group 2: College students	Group 3: Active Club members	Group 4: experts
Nuclear power	1	1	8	20
Motor vehicles	2	5	3	1
Handguns	3	2	1	4
Smoking	4	3	4	2
Motorcycles	5	6	2	6
Alcoholic beverages	6	7	5	3
General (private) aviation	7	15	11	12
Police work	8	8	7	17
Pesticides	9	4	15	8
Surgery	10	11	9	5
Fire fighting	11	10	6	18
Large construction	12	14	13	13
Hunting	13	18	10	23
Spray cans	14	13	23	26
Mountain climbing	15	22	12	29
Bicycles	16	24	14	15
Commercial aviation	17	16	18	16
Electric power	18	19	19	9
Swimming	19	30	17	10
Contraceptives	20	9	22	11
Skiing	21	25	16	30
X-rays	22	17	24	7
High school and college football	23	26	21	27
Railroads	24	23	20	19
Food preservatives	25	12	28	14
Food coloring	26	20	30	21
Power mowers	27	28	25	28
Prescription antibiotics	28	21	26	24
Home appliances	29	27	27	22
Vaccinations	30	29	29	25

Note: The ordering is based on the geometric mean risk ratings within each group. Rank 1 represents the most risky activity or technology.

suggestions, clarifications and encouragement to do as accurate a job as possible. For example, they were told 'A rating of 12 indicates that that item is 1.2 times as risky as the least risky item (ie, 20% more risky). A rating of 200 means that the item is 20 times as risky as the least risky item, to which you assigned a 10'. They were urged to cross-check and adjust their numbers until they believed they were right.

Table 6.2 shows how the various groups ranked the relative riskiness of these 30 activities and technologies. There were many similarities between the three groups of laypersons. For example, each group believed that motorcycles, other motor vehicles and handguns were highly risky, and that vaccinations, home appliances, power mowers and football were relatively safe. However, there were strong differences as well. Active Club members viewed pesticides and spray cans as relatively much safer than did the other groups. Nuclear power was rated as highest in risk by the LOWV and student groups, but only eighth by the Active Club. The students viewed contraceptives and food preservatives as riskier and swimming and mountain climbing as safer than did the other lay groups. Experts' judgments of risk differed markedly from the judgments of lay persons. The experts viewed electric power, surgery, swimming and X-rays as more risky than the other groups, and they judged nuclear power, police work and mountain climbing to be much less risky.

What Determines Risk Perception?

What do people mean when they say that a particular technology is quite risky? A series of additional studies was conducted to answer this question.

Perceived risk compared to frequency of death

When people judge risk, as in the previous study, are they simply estimating frequency of death? To answer this question, we collected the best available technical estimates of the annual number of deaths from each of the 30 activities included in our study. For some cases, such as commercial aviation and handguns, there is good statistical evidence based on counts of known victims. For other cases, such as the lethal potential of nuclear or fossil-fuel power plants, available estimates are based on uncertain inferences about incompletely understood processes. For still others, such as food coloring, we could find no estimates of annual fatalities.

For the 25 cases for which we found technical estimates for annual frequency of death, we compared these estimates with perceived risk. Results for experts and the LOWV sample are shown in Figure 6.4 (the results for the other lay groups were quite similar to those from the LOWV sample). The experts' mean judgments were so closely related to the statistical or calculated frequencies that it seems reasonable to conclude that they viewed the risk of an activity or technology as synonymous with its annual fatalities. The risk judgments of laypeople, however, showed only a moderate relationship to the annual frequencies of death (the correlations between perceived risk and the annual frequencies of death were .92 for the experts and .62, .50, and .56 for the League of Women Voters, students and Active Club samples, respectively), raising the possibility that, for them, risk may not be synonymous with fatalities. In

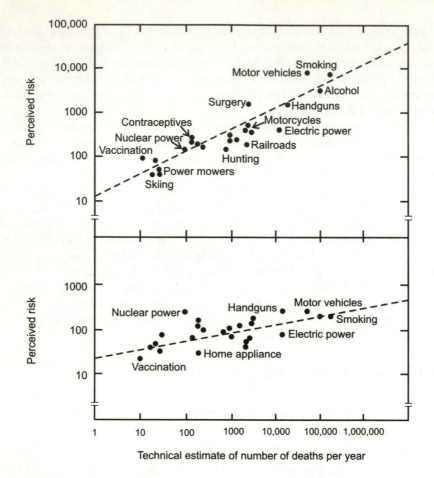

Note: Each point represents the average responses of the participants. The dashed lines are the straight lines that best fit the points. The experts' risk judgments are seen to be more closely associated with annual fatality rates than are the lay judgments.

Figure 6.4 *Judgments of perceived risk for experts (top) and laypeople (bottom) plotted against the best technical estimates of annual fatalities for 25 technologies and activities*

particular, the perceived risk from nuclear power was disproportionately high compared to its estimated number of fatalities.

Lay fatality estimates

Perhaps laypeople based their risk judgments on annual fatalities, but estimated their numbers inaccurately. To test this hypothesis, we asked additional groups of students and LOWV members 'to estimate how many people are likely to die in the US in the next year (if the next year is an average year) as a consequence of these 30 activities and technologies'. We asked our student and LOWV samples to consider all sources of death associated with these activities.

The mean fatality estimates of LOWV members and students are shown in columns 2 and 3 of Table 6.3. If laypeople really equate risk with annual fatalities, one would expect that their own estimates of annual fatalities, no matter how inaccurate, would be very similar to their judgments of risk. But this was not so. There was a moderate agreement between their annual fatality estimates and their risk judgments, but there were important exceptions. Most notably, nuclear power had the *lowest* fatality estimate and the *highest* perceived risk for both LOWV members and students. Overall, laypeople's risk perceptions were no more closely related to their own fatality estimates than they were to the technical estimates (Figure 6.4).

Table 6.3 *Fatality Estimates and Disaster Multipliers for 30 Activities and Technologies*

Activity or technology	Technical fatality estimates	Geometric mean fatality estimates, average year		Geometric mean multiplier, disastrous year	
		LOWV	Students	LOWV	Students
Smoking	150,000	6900	2400	1.9	2.0
Alcoholic beverages	100,000	12,000	2600	1.9	1.4
Motor vehicles	50,000	28,000	10,500	1.6	1.8
Handguns	17,000	3000	1900	2.6	2.0
Electric power	14,000	660	500	1.9	2.4
Motorcycles	3000	1600	1600	1.8	1.6
Swimming	3000	930	370	1.6	1.7
Surgery	2800	2500	900	1.5	1.6
X-rays	2300	90	40	2.7	1.6
Railroads	1950	190	210	3.2	1.6
General (private) aviation	1300	550	650	2.8	2.0
Large construction	1000	400	370	2.1	1.4
Bicycles	1000	910	420	1.8	1.4
Hunting	800	380	410	1.8	1.7
Home appliances	200	200	240	1.6	1.3
Fire fighting	195	220	390	2.3	2.2
Police work	160	460	390	2.1	1.9
Contraceptives	150	180	120	2.1	1.4
Commercial aviation	130	280	650	3.0	1.8
Nuclear power	100 [a]	20	27	107.1	87.6
Mountain climbing	30	50	70	1.9	1.4
Power mowers	24	40	33	1.6	1.3
High-school and college football	23	39	40	1.9	1.4
Skiing	18	55	72	1.9	1.6
Vaccinations	10	65	52	2.1	1.6
Food coloring	—[b]	38	33	3.5	1.4
Food preservatives	—[b]	61	63	3.9	1.7
Pesticides	—[b]	140	84	9.3	2.4
Prescription antibiotics	—[b]	160	290	2.3	1.6
Spray cans	—[b]	56	38	3.7	2.4

[a] Technical estimates for nuclear power were found to range between 16 and 600 annual fatalities. The geometric mean of these estimates was used here.
[b] Estimates were unavailable.

These results lead us to reject the idea that laypeople wanted to equate risk with annual fatality estimates but were inaccurate in doing so. Instead, we are led to believe that laypeople incorporate other considerations besides annual fatalities into their concept of risk.

Some other aspects of laypeople's fatality estimates are of interest. One is that they were moderately accurate. The relationship between the LOWV members' fatality estimates and the best technical estimates is plotted in Figure 6.5. The lay estimates showed the same overestimation of those items that cause few fatalities and underestimation of those resulting in the most fatalities that was apparent in Figure 6.2 for a different collection of hazards. Also, as in Figure 6.2, the moderate overall relationship between lay and technical estimates was marred by specific biases (eg, the underestimation of fatalities associated with railroads, X-rays, electric power and smoking).

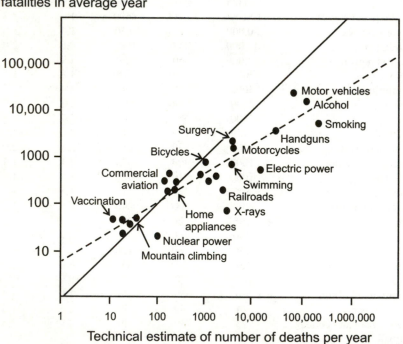

Note: The solid line indicates accurate judgment, while the dashed line best fits the data points. These results have much the same character as those shown in Figure 6.2 for a different collection of hazards. Low frequencies were overestimated and high ones were underestimated. The overall relationship is marred by specific biases (eg, the underestimation of fatalities associated with railroads, X-rays, electric power and smoking).

Figure 6.5 *Laypeople's judgments of the number of fatalities in an average year plotted against the best estimates of annual fatalities for 25 activities and technologies*

Disaster potential

The fact that the LOWV members and students assigned very high-risk values to nuclear power along with very low estimates of its annual fatality rates is an apparent contradiction. One possible explanation is that LOWV members expected nuclear power to have a low death rate in an average year but considered it to be a high-risk technology because of its potential for disaster.

In order to understand the role played by expectations of disaster in determining laypeople's risk judgments, we asked these same respondents to give a number for each activity and technology indicating how many more deaths would occur if next year were 'particularly disastrous' rather than average. The averages of these multipliers are shown in Table 6.3. For most activities, people saw little potential for disaster. For the LOWV sample all but five of the multipliers were less than 3, and for the student sample all but six were less than 2. The striking exception in both cases is nuclear power, with a geometric mean disaster multiplier in the neighborhood of 100.

For any individual an estimate of the expected number of fatalities in a disastrous year could be obtained by applying the disaster multiplier to the estimated fatalities for an average year. When this was done for nuclear power, almost 40% of the respondents expected more than 10,000 fatalities if next year were a disastrous year. More than 25% expected 100,000 or more fatalities. These extreme estimates can be contrasted with the Reactor Safety Study's conclusion that the maximum credible nuclear accident, coincident with the most unfavorable combination of weather and population density, would cause only 3300 prompt fatalities (US Nuclear Regulatory Commission, 1975). Furthermore, that study estimated the odds against an accident of this magnitude occurring during the next year (assuming 100 operating reactors) as about two million to one.

Apparently, disaster potential explains much or all of the discrepancy between the perceived risk and frequency of death values for nuclear power. Yet, because disaster plays only a small role in most of the 30 activities and technologies we have studied, it provides only a partial explanation of the perceived risk data.

Qualitative characteristics

Are there other determinants of risk perceptions besides frequency estimates? We asked experts, students, LOWV members, and Active Club members to rate the 30 technologies and activities on nine qualitative characteristics that have been hypothesized to be important (Lowrance, 1976).

Examination of 'risk profiles' based on mean ratings for the nine characteristics proved helpful in understanding the risk judgments of laypeople. Nuclear power, for example, had the dubious distinction of scoring at or near the extreme on all of the characteristics associated with high risk. Its risks were seen as involuntary, delayed, unknown, uncontrollable, unfamiliar, potentially catastrophic, dreaded and severe (certainly fatal). Its spectacular and unique risk profile contrasts with non-nuclear electric power and with another radiation technology, X-rays, both of whose risks were judged to be much lower. Both electric power and X-rays were judged much more voluntary, less catastrophic, less dreaded and more familiar than nuclear power.

Across all 30 items, ratings of dread and of the severity of consequences were found to be closely related to laypersons' perceptions of risk. In fact, ratings of dread and severity along with the subjective fatality estimates and the disaster multipliers in Table 6.3 enabled the risk judgments of the LOWV and student groups to be predicted almost perfectly.[1] Experts' judgments of risk were not related to any of the nine qualitative risk characteristics.[2]

Judged seriousness of death

In a further attempt to improve our understanding of perceived risk, we examined the hypothesis that some hazards are feared more than others because the deaths they produce are much 'worse' than deaths from other activities. We thought, for example, that deaths from risks imposed involuntarily, from risks not under one's control, or from hazards that are particularly dreaded might be given greater weight in determining people's perceptions of risk.

However, when we asked students and LOWV members to judge the relative 'seriousness' of a death from each of the 30 activities and technologies, the differences were slight. The most serious forms of death (from nuclear power and handguns) were judged to be only about two to four times worse than the least serious forms of death (from alcoholic beverages and smoking). Furthermore, across all 30 activities, judged seriousness of death was not closely related to perceived risk of death.

Reconciling Divergent Opinions

Our data show that experts and laypeople have quite different perceptions about how risky certain technologies are. It would be comforting to believe that these divergent risk judgments would be responsive to new evidence so that, as information accumulates, perceptions would converge toward one 'appropriate' view. Unfortunately, this is not likely to be the case. As noted earlier in our discussion of availability, risk perception is derived in part from fundamental modes of thought that lead people to rely on fallible indicators such as memorability and imaginability.

Furthermore, a great deal of research indicated that people's beliefs change slowly and are extraordinarily persistent in the face of contrary evidence (Ross, 1977). Once formed, initial impressions tend to structure the way that subsequent evidence is interpreted. New evidence appears reliable and informative if it is consistent with one's initial belief; contrary evidence is dismissed as unreliable, erroneous or unrepresentative. Thus, depending upon one's predisposition, intense effort to reduce a hazard may be interpreted to mean either that the risks are great or that the technologists are responsive to the public's concerns. Likewise, opponents of a technology may view minor mishaps as near catastrophes and dismiss the contrary opinions of experts as biased by vested interests.

From a statistical standpoint, convincing people that the catastrophe they fear is extremely unlikely is difficult under the best conditions. Any mishap could be seen as proof of high risk, whereas demonstrating safety would require a massive amount of evidence (Green & Bourne, 1972). Nelkin's (1977) case history of a nuclear siting controversy provides a good example of the inability of technical arguments to change opinions. In that debate each side capitalized on technical ambiguities in ways that reinforced its own position.

THE FALLIBILITY OF JUDGMENT

Our examination of risk perception leads us to the following conclusions:

- Cognitive limitations, coupled with the anxieties generated by facing life as a gamble, cause uncertainty to be denied, risks to be distorted and statements of fact to be believed with unwarranted confidence.
- Perceived risk is influenced (and sometimes biased) by the imaginability and memorability of the hazard. People may, therefore, not have valid perceptions even for familiar risks.
- Our expert's risk perceptions correspond closely to statistical frequencies of death. Laypeople's risk perceptions were based in part on frequencies of death, but there were some striking discrepancies. It appears that for laypeople, the concept of risk includes qualitative aspects such as dread and the likelihood of a mishap being fatal. Laypeople's risk perceptions were also affected by catastrophic potential.
- Disagreements about risk should not be expected to evaporate in the presence of 'evidence'. Definitive evidence, particularly about rare hazards, is difficult to obtain. Weaker information is likely to be interpreted in a way that reinforces existing beliefs.

The significance of these results hinges on one's acceptance of our assumption that subjective judgments are central to the hazard management process. Our conclusions mean little if one can assume that there are analytical tools which can be used to assess most risks in a mechanical fashion and that all decision-makers have perfect information and the know-how to use it properly. These results gain in importance to the extent that one believes, as we do, that expertise involves a large component of judgment, that the facts are not all in (or obtainable) regarding many important hazards, that people are often poorly informed or misinformed, and that they respond not just to numbers but also to qualitative aspects of hazards.

Whatever role judgment plays, its products should be treated with caution. Research not only demonstrates that judgment is fallible, but it shows that the degree of fallibility is often surprisingly great and that faulty beliefs may be held with great confidence.

When it can be shown that even well-informed laypeople have difficulty judging risks accurately, it is tempting to conclude that the public should be removed from the hazard-management process. The political ramifications of such a transfer of power to a technical elite are obvious. Indeed, it seems doubtful that such a massive disenfranchisement is feasible in any democratic society.

Furthermore, this transfer of decision-making would seem to be misguided. For one thing, we have no assurance that experts' judgments are immune to biases once they are forced to go beyond their precise knowledge and rely on their judgment. Although judgmental biases have most often been demonstrated with laypeople, there is evidence that the cognitive functioning of experts is basically like that of everyone else.

In addition, in many if not most cases effective hazard management requires the cooperation of a large body of laypeople. These people must agree to do without some things and accept substitutes for others. They must vote sensibly on ballot measures and for legislators who will serve them as surrogate hazard managers. They must obey safety rules and use the legal system responsibly. Even if the experts were much better judges of risk than laypeople, giving experts an exclusive franchise on hazard management would involve substituting short-term efficiency for the long-term effort needed to create an informed citizenry.

For those of us who are not experts, these findings pose an important series of challenges: to be better informed, to rely less on unexamined or unsupported judgments, to be aware of the qualitative aspects that strongly condition risk judgments, and to be open to new evidence that may alter our current risk perceptions.

For the experts, our findings pose what may be a more difficult challenge: to recognize their own cognitive limitations, to temper their assessments of risk with the important qualitative aspects of risk that influence the responses of laypeople, and somehow to create ways in which these considerations can find expression in hazard management without, in the process, creating more heat than light.

ACKNOWLEDGMENTS

The authors wish to express their appreciation to Christoph Hohenemser, Roger Kasperson and Robert Kates for their many helpful comments and suggestions. This work was supported by the National Science Foundation under Grant ENV77-15332 to Perceptronics, Inc. Any opinions, findings and conclusions or recommendations expressed herein are those of the authors and do not necessarily reflect the views of the National Science Foundation.

NOTES

1   The multiple correlation between the risk judgments of the LOWV members and students and a linear combination of their fatality estimates, disaster multipliers, dread ratings, and severity ratings was .95.

2   A secondary finding was that both experts and laypersons believed that the risks from most of the activities were better known to science than to the individuals at risk. The experts believed that the discrepancy in knowledge was particularly great for vaccinations, X-rays, antibiotics, alcohol and home appliances. The only activities whose risks were judged better known to those exposed were mountain climbing, fire fighting, hunting, skiing and police work.

7

Weighing the Risks:
Which Risks Are Acceptable?

*Baruch Fischhoff, Paul Slovic and
Sarah Lichtenstein*

The bottom line in hazard management is usually some variant of the question, 'How safe is safe enough?' It takes such forms as: 'Do we need additional containment shells around our nuclear power plants?' 'Is the carcinogenicity of saccharin sufficiently low to allow its use?' 'Should schools with asbestos ceilings be closed?' Lack of adequate answers to such questions has bedeviled hazard management.

Of late, many hazard management decisions are simply not being made – in part because of vague legislative mandates and cumbersome legal proceedings, in part because there are no clear criteria on the basis of which to decide. As a result, the nuclear industry has ground to a halt while utilities wait to see if the building of new plants will ever be feasible (*Business Week*, 1978); the Consumer Product Safety Commission has invested millions of dollars in producing a few puny standards (Bick & Kasperson, 1978); observers wonder whether the new Toxic Substances Control Act can be implemented (Culliton, 1978); and the Food and Drug Administration is unable to resolve the competing claims that it is taking undue risks and that it is stifling innovation.

The decisions that are made are often inconsistent. Our legal statutes are less tolerant of carcinogens in the food we eat than of those in the water we drink or in the air we breathe. In the UK, 2500 times as much money per life saved is spent on safety measures in the pharmaceutical industry as in agriculture (Sinclair, Marstrand & Newick, 1972). US society is apparently willing to spend about $140,000 in highway construction to save one life and $5 million to save a person from death due to radiation exposure (Howard, Matheson & Owen, 1978).

Frustration over this state of affairs has led to a search for clear, implementable rules that will tell us whether a given technology is sufficiently safe. Four ap-

Note: reprinted from 'Weighing the Risks: Which Risks Are Acceptable?' by B Fischhoff, P Slovic and S Lichtenstein, *Environment*, vol 2, issue 4, pp17–20, 32–38, 1979. Reprinted with permission of the Helen Dwight Reid Educational Foundation. Published by Heldref Publications, 1319 18th St NW, Washington, DC 20036–1802. Copyright 1979.

proaches are most frequently used in attempting to make this assessment. They are cost-benefit analysis, revealed preferences, expressed preferences and natural standards. Respectively, they would deem a technology to be safe if its benefits outweigh its cost; if its risks are no greater than those of currently tolerated technologies of equivalent benefit; if people say that its risks are acceptable; if its risks are no greater than those accompanying the development of the human species. Each of these approaches has its pros and cons, its uses and its limitations. (Other discussions of acceptable risk criteria may be found in Lowrance, 1976.)

COST-BENEFIT ANALYSIS

Cost-benefit analysis attempts to answer the question of whether the expected benefits from a proposed activity outweigh its expected costs. The first steps in calculating the expected cost of a project are to enumerate all the adverse consequences that might result from its implementation; to assess the probability of each such consequence; and to estimate the cost or loss to society whenever the consequence occurs. Next, the expected cost of each possible consequence is calculated by multiplying the cost of the consequence by the probability that it will be incurred. The expected cost of the entire project is computed by summing the expected losses associated with the various possible consequences. An analogous procedure produces an estimate of the expected benefits (see Table 7.1 and Fischhoff, 1977; or Stokey & Zeckhauser, 1978). The most general form of cost-benefit analysis is decision analysis, in which the role of uncertainty, the subjective nature of costs and benefits and the existence of alternative actions are made explicit (Brown, Kahr & Peterson, 1974; Howard, Matheson & Miller, 1976).

These procedures, and decision analysis in particular, are based on appealing premises and are supported by sophisticated methodology. Furthermore, they permit considerable flexibility; analyses are readily revised to incorporate new options and new information. An important advantage of these methods for decision-making in the public sphere is that they are easily scrutinized. Each quantitative input or qualitative assumption is available for all to see and evaluate, as are the explicit computational rules that combine them.

However, decision analysis and its variants have a number of potentially serious limitations, perhaps the most important of which are their unrealistic assumptions about the availability of the data needed to complete the analysis. Performing a full-dress analysis assumes, among other things, that all possible events and all significant consequences can be enumerated in advance; that meaningful probability, cost and benefit values can be obtained and assigned to them; and that the often disparate costs and benefits can somehow be made comparable to one another.

Unfortunately, it is sometimes impossible to accomplish some of these tasks, while in the case of others, the results are hardly to be trusted. Despite the enormous scientific progress of the last decade or two, we still do not know all or even most of the possible physical, biological and social consequences of any large-scale energy project (Fischhoff, Hohenemser, Kasperson & Kates, 1978).

Table 7.1 *Cost-Benefit Analysis*

Consider a fictitious new product, Veg-E-Wax, designed to coat fresh fruits and vegetables. Its demonstrated advantages are reducing losses in storage and preserving nutritive value. Aside from the cost of application, its disadvantages are making food look less appetizing and possibly causing cancer to workers who apply it and to consumers who fail to wash fruit. A highly simplified cost-benefit analysis of the decision to apply Veg-E-Wax to a $10 million (market value) shipment of pears bound for storage might appear as follows:

Advantages (benefits)	*$ million*
Guaranteed reduction in storage loss from 30% to 20%	1.0
Improved nutritive value (translating into a 10% increase in market value in the 80% that is not lost in storage)	0.8
Total benefits	1.8
Disadvantages (costs)	
Cost of application	0.1
Cancer in .1% of 100 workers (@ $1 million per case)	0.1
Cancer to users (one million consumers, of whom 10% fail to wash fruit, of whom .0001% contract cancer as a result, @ $1 million per case)	0.1
Unappetizing appearance (20% loss in market value of pears not lost in storage)	1.6
Total costs	1.9

In this calculation, the costs slightly outweigh the benefits and the packer should decide not to use Veg-E-Wax. The viability of this conclusion depends upon its capacity to withstand small changes in the figures. If there were only an 18% loss in market value due to the waxy look of the fruit (translating into a cost of $1.44 million), the balance would tip the other way. It might be impossible to predict this loss with the precision needed to take confident action.

Even larger effects may accompany changes in fundamental assumptions. A packer with no social conscience might decide not to worry about the $200,000 in cancer costs, reducing total costs to $1.7 million. Other interested parties, such as consumers interested in maximizing value and minimizing personal risk, might structure the problem entirely differently.

Even when we know what the consequences are, we often do not, or cannot, know their likelihood. For example, although we know that a nuclear reactor core melt-down is unlikely, we will not know quite how unlikely until we accumulate much more on-line experience. Even then, we will be able to utilize that knowledge only if we can assume that the reactor and the attendant circumstances remain the same (eg, no changes in the incidence of terrorism or the availability of trained personnel). For many situations, even when a danger is known to be present, its extent cannot be known. Whenever low-level radiation or exposure to toxic substances is involved, consequences can be assessed only by tenuous extrapolation from the consequences of high-level exposure to human beings or from observation of exposure in animals (Najarian, 1978).

In all these instances, we must rely on human judgment to guide or supplement our formal methods. Research into the psychological processes involved in producing such judgments offers reason for concern, because this research demonstrates that people (including experts forced to go beyond the available data and rely on their intuitions) have a great deal of difficulty both in comprehending complex and uncertain information and in making valid inferences from such information (Slovic, Fischhoff & Lichtenstein, 1979). Frequently, these problems can be traced to the use of judgmental heuristics – mental strategies whereby people try to reduce difficult tasks to simpler judgments. These strategies may be useful in some situations, but in others they lead to errors that are large, persistent and serious in their implications. Furthermore, individuals are typically unaware of these deficiencies in the judgments.

Even if all the consequences could be enumerated and their likelihood assessed, placing a price tag on them poses further difficulties. Consider, for example, the problems of placing a value on a human life. Despite our resistance to thinking about life in economic terms, the fact is that, by our actions, we actually do put a finite value on our lives. Decisions about installing safety features, buying life insurance or accepting a more hazardous job for extra salary all carry implicit judgments about the value we place on a life.

Economists have long debated the question of how best to quantify the value of a life (Linnerooth, 1975). The traditional economic approach has been to equate the value of a life with the value of a person's expected future earnings. Many problems with this index are readily apparent. For one, it undervalues those in society who are underpaid and places no value at all on people who are not in income-earning positions. In addition, it ignores the interpersonal effects of a death which may make the loss suffered much greater than any measurable financial loss. A second approach, which equates the value of life with court awards, can hardly be considered to be more satisfactory (Holmes, 1970; Kidner & Richard, 1974).

Some have argued that the question, 'What is a life worth?' is poorly phrased and what we really want to know is, "What is the value placed on a particular change in survival probability?" (Linnerooth, 1975). One approach to answering this second question is to observe the actual market behavior of people trading risks for economic benefit. For example, one study examined salary as a function of occupational risk and claimed to find that a premium of about $200 per year was required to induce workers in risky occupations (eg, coal mining) to accept an increase of .001 in their annual probability of accidental death (Thaler & Rosen, 1976).

From this finding it was inferred that society should be willing to pay about $200,000 to prevent a death. A replication of this study by Rappaport (1981) produced a value of $2 million, thus, even if one accepts the assumptions underlying this approach, a definitive value may still elude us. (These assumptions are essentially those underlying the revealed preference approach, described next.)

Decision analysis attempts to accommodate the uncertainties inherent in assessing problems and the values of the variables involved through the judicious use of sensitivity analysis. The calculations of expected costs and benefits are repeated using alternative values of one troublesome probability, cost or benefit. If each reanalysis produces the same relative preponderance of expected costs or benefits, then it is argued that these particular differences do not matter. In the Veg-E-Wax example (see Table 7.1), changing the estimate of lost market value from 20% to 18% is a sensitivity analysis. The fact that it tipped the balance from rejection to acceptance of Veg-E-Wax suggests that neither recommendation can be strongly supported.

Unfortunately, however, there are no firm guidelines regarding which of the data might be in error or what range of possible values ought to be tested. A further problem with sensitivity analysis is that it typically tells us little about how the uncertainty from different sources of error is compounded or about what happens when different data are subject to a common bias. The untested assumption is that errors in different inputs will cancel one another, rather than compound in some pernicious way (Fischhoff, 1980).

In the end, determining the quality of an analysis is a matter of judgment. Someone must use intuition to determine which inputs are of doubtful validity and which alternative values should be incorporated in sensitivity analyses. Essentially, that someone must decide how good his or her own best judgment is. Unfortunately, an extensive body of research suggests that people tend to overestimate the quality of such judgments (Slovic, Fischhoff & Lichtenstein, 1979).

REVEALED PREFERENCES

An alternate approach to determining acceptable risks is the method of revealed preferences advocated by Chauncey Starr (1969). This approach is based on the assumption that, by trial and error, society has arrived at an 'essentially optimum' balance between the risks and benefits associated with any activity. As a result, it is assumed that economic risk and benefit data from recent years will reveal patterns of acceptable risk-benefit trade-offs.

Acceptable risk for a new technology is defined as that level of safety associated with ongoing activities having similar benefit to society. Starr argued the potential usefulness of revealed preferences by examining the relationship between risk and benefit across a number of common activities.

Figure 7.1 depicts the results of Starr's analysis, while Figure 7.2 shows our own expanded replication of Starr's study, in which we examined 25 activities and technologies, including the eight he used.

In this replication somewhat different methods have been employed. Whereas Starr estimated risk in terms of fatality rate per hour of exposure, we have used annual fatalities. This change is motivated in part by the greater availability of data for the latter measure, and in part because the definition of exposure to some hazards (ie, handguns, smoking, antibiotics) is elusive. Whereas Starr measured benefit either by the average amount of money spent on an activity by a single participant or the average contribution the activity made to a participant's annual income, we have used the single measure of total annual consumer expenditure.

Like any other economic measure of benefit, expenditure has its limitations. It includes 'bad' as well as 'good' expenditures; for example, money spent on the abatement of pollution caused by an industry is weighted as heavily as the value of the product it manufactures. A second problem is that this measure ignores distributive considerations (who pays and who profits). A third problem is that the market price may not be responsive to welfare issues that are critical to social planning. Does the price of cigarettes take account of smokers' higher probability of heart disease or cancer? Does the price of pesticides adequately reflect the increased probability of various deleterious effects on the one hand and the increased yield of foodstuffs on the other?

Expenditures for private goods (whose purchase is the result of the decisions of individual consumers) were obtained from trade and manufacturing associations, while public services, such as police work or fire fighting, were estimated by using government expenditures on payroll and equipment. No attempt was

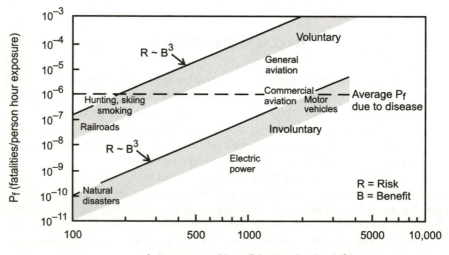

Note: Risk is measured by fatalities per person per hour of exposure. Benefit reflects either the average amount of money spent on an activity by an individual participant or the average contribution an activity makes to a participant's annual income. The best-fitting lines were drawn by eye with error bands to indicate their approximate nature.

Source: Starr (1972).

Figure 7.1 *A comparison of risk and benefit to US society from various sources*

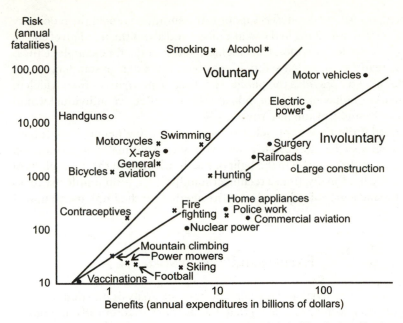

Figure 7.2 *One possible assesment of current risks and benefits from 25 activities and technologies*

made to calculate the secondary and tertiary economic benefits of a product or service (eg, the increase in agricultural yield attributable to the use of pesticides), or the present value of past structural investments (eg, airport terminals, acquisition of wilderness areas), or contributions to distributional equity.

Despite the differences in procedure, our analysis produced results similar to Starr's. Overall, there was a positive relation between benefits and risks (slope = .3, correlation = .55). Furthermore, at any given level of benefit, voluntary activities tended to be riskier than involuntary ones (compare alcohol and surgery or swimming and nuclear power).

To apply these results to Veg-E-Wax (see Table 7.1), consider this technology to be an involuntary activity (imposed on consumers) with a total economic benefit to the food industry of $1 billion. Its risks would be tolerable if the expected annual toll were less than 40 lives.

Although based on an intuitively compelling logic, the method of revealed preferences has several drawbacks. It assumes that past behavior is a valid predictor of present preferences, perhaps a dubious assumption in a world where values can change quite rapidly. It is politically conservative in that it enshrines current economic and social arrangements. It ignores distributional questions (who assumes what risks and who gets what benefits). It may underweigh risks to which the market responds sluggishly, such as those involving a long-time lag between exposure and consequences (as in the case of carcinogens).

It makes strong (and not always supported) assumptions about the rationality of people's decision-making in the marketplace and about the freedom of choice that the marketplace provides. Consider the automobile, for example. Unless the public really knows what safety is possible from a design standpoint, and unless the industry provides the public with a set of alternatives from which to choose, market behavior may not indicate what a reflective individual would decide after thoughtful and intensive inquiry.

A revealed preference approach assumes not only that people have full information but also that they can use that information optimally, an assumption which seems quite doubtful in the light of much research on the psychology of decision-making. Finally, from a technical standpoint, it is no simple matter to develop the measures of risks and benefits needed for the implementation of this approach.

EXPRESSED PREFERENCES

Both cost-benefit analysis and revealed preference analysis must infer public values indirectly, using procedures that may be both theoretically and politically untenable. The expressed preference approach tries to circumvent this problem by asking people directly what levels of safety they deem acceptable.

The appeal of this approach is obvious. It elicits current preferences; thus, it is responsive to changing values. It also allows for widespread citizen involvement in decision-making and therefore should be politically acceptable. It allows consideration of all aspects of risks and benefits, including those not readily converted into dollars and body counts. Some ways of obtaining expressed preferences are through referenda, opinion surveys, detailed questioning of selected groups of citizens, interviewing 'public interest advocates', and hearings.

Recently, we conducted a series of expressed preference studies paralleling Starr's revealed preference study (Fischhoff, Slovic, Lichtenstein, Read et al, 1978). We asked people to judge the total risk and benefit for each of 30 activities and technologies, including those used by Starr. Contrary to Starr's presumption, our respondents did not believe that society had managed these activities and technologies in order to allow higher risk only when higher benefit is obtained. In their view, society currently tolerates a number of activities with very low benefits and very high risks (eg, alcoholic beverages, handguns, motorcycles, smoking). Some very safe activities were judged to have very great benefits (eg, use of antibiotics, railroads, vaccinations).

When we asked people what level of safety would be acceptable for each of the 30 activities and technologies, they responded that current levels were too safe 10% of the time, about right 40% of the time, and too risky about 50% of the time ('too risky' was defined as 'indicating the need for serious societal action'). Thus, for these individuals, the historical record used by the revealed preferences approach apparently would not be an acceptable guide to future action.

When acceptable levels of safety were compared with perceived benefits, a relationship emerged much like the one obtained by Starr. Participants believed that greater risk should be tolerated for more beneficial activities and that a double standard is appropriate for voluntary and involuntary activities.[1] Similar studies were conducted with students, members of the (generally liberal) League of Women Voters, and members of a (generally conservative) community service club. Although the groups disagreed on the evaluation of particular items, their judgments showed the same general pattern of results.

One frequent criticism of the expressed preferences approach is that safety issues are too complicated for ordinary citizens to understand. However, the results just cited suggest that, in some situations at least, motivated laypeople can produce orderly, interpretable responses to complex questions.

A related criticism is that, when it comes to new and complex issues, people do not have well-articulated preferences. In some fundamental sense their values may be incoherent – not thought through (Fischhoff, Slovic & Lichtenstein, 1980). In thinking about acceptable risks, people may be unfamiliar with the terms in which the issues are formulated (eg, social discount rates, minuscule probabilities, megadeaths). They may have contradictory values (a strong aversion to catastrophic losses of life and a realization that they are not more moved by a plane crash with 500 fatalities than one with 300). They may occupy different roles in life (parents, workers, children) which produce clear-cut but inconsistent values. They may vacillate between incompatible, but strongly held, positions (freedom of speech is inviolate but it should be denied to authoritarian movements). They may not even know how to begin thinking about some issues (how to compare the opportunity to dye one's hair with a vague, minute increase in the probability of cancer 20 years from now). Their views may change over time (say, as the hour of decision or the consequence itself draws near), and they may not know which view should form the basis of a decision.

In such situations, where people do not know what they want, the values they express may be highly unstable. Subtle changes in how issues are presented – how questions are phrased and responses are elicited – can have marked effects on their expressed preferences. The particular question posed may evoke a central concern or a peripheral one; it may help to clarify the respondent's opinion or irreversibly shape it; it may even create an opinion where none existed before.

Three features of these shifting judgments are important. First, people are typically unaware of the extent of such shifts in their perspective. Second, they often have no guidelines as to which perspective is the appropriate one. Finally, even when there are guidelines, people may not want to give up their own inconsistency, creating an impasse.

NATURAL STANDARDS

A shared flaw of the approaches described above is that all of them are subject to the existing limitations of society and its citizens. It might be desirable to have a standard of safety independent of a particular society, especially for risks whose effects are collective, cumulative or irreversible. One such alternative is to look to 'biological wisdom' to insure the physical well-being of the species (not to mention the well-being of other species; Tribe, Schelling & Voss, 1976). Rather than examining (recent) historical time for guidelines, one might look to geological time, assuming that the optimal level of exposure to pollutants is that characteristic of the conditions in which the species evolved.

Specific proposals derived from this approach might be to set allowable radiation levels from the nuclear-fuel cycle according to natural background radiation and to set allowable levels of chemical wastes according to the levels found in archaeological remains (Ericson, Shirahata & Patterson, 1979). These standards would not constitute outright bans, as some level of radiation-induced mutation is apparently good for the species and traces of many chemicals are needed for survival. Because exposure has varied from epoch to epoch and from place to place, one could establish ranges of tolerable exposure.

Perhaps the best-known criteria for risk acceptability based on natural standards are those for ionizing radiation set by the International Commission on Radiological Protection. The standards set by this small, voluntary international group are subscribed to by most countries in the world. Their underlying assumptions include the following statements. The maximum permissible dose levels should be set in such a way that, in the light of present knowledge:

- They carry a negligible probability of severe somatic or genetic injuries; for example, leukemia or genetic malformations that result from exposure to individuals at the maximum permissible dose would be limited to an exceedingly small fraction of the exposed group.
- The effects ensuing more frequently are those of a minor nature that would not be considered unacceptable by the exposed individual and by the society of which he or she is a part. Such frequently occurring effects might be, for example, modifications in the formed elements of the blood or changes in bone density. Such effects could be detected only by very extensive studies of the exposed individual. Effects such as shortening of life span, which may be proportional to the accumulated dose, would be so small that they would be hidden by normal biological variations and perhaps could be detected only by extensive epidemiological studies (Morgan, 1969).

Natural standards have a variety of attractive features. They avoid converting risks into a common monetary unit (such as dollars per life lost). They present issues in a way that is probably quite compatible with people's natural thought processes. Among other things, this approach can avoid any direct numerical reference to very small probabilities, for which people have little or no intuitive feeling (Lichtenstein, Slovic, Fischhoff, Layman & Combs, 1978). Use of natural standards should produce consistent practices when managing the same emission appearing in different sources of hazards.

As a guide to policy, natural standards are flawed by the fact that our natural exposure to many hazards has not diminished. Thus, whatever new exposure is allowed is an addition to what we are already subjected to by nature and thereby constitutes excess 'unnatural' exposure (although conceivably within the range of toleration).

A second problem is that most hazards increase some exposures and reduce others. Trading off different exposures brings one back to the realm of cost-benefit analysis. Another problem arises when one considers completely new substances for which there is no historical tolerance (saccharin, for example). In such cases, a policy based on natural standards would tolerate none of the substance at all, unless it involved no risk. The Delaney Amendment, which outlaws the addition of any known carcinogen to food, is consistent with this approach.

The technical difficulties of performing this type of analysis are formidable. Indeed, while there may be some hope of assessing natural exposure to chemicals and radiation that leave traces in bone or rock, appraising the natural incidence of accidents and infectious disease is probably impossible. Furthermore, should such an analysis be completed, it would quickly become apparent that the ecology of hazard in which humans live has changed drastically over the eons – mostly for the better, as in the case of the reduced incidence of infectious disease (Harriss, Hohenemser & Kates, 1978). The biological wisdom (or importance) of restoring one component of the mix to its prehistoric values would demand careful examination.

In addition to whatever difficulties there may be with their internal logic and implementation, natural standards are likely to fail as a sole guide to policy because they ignore the benefits that accompany hazards and the costs of complying with the standards.

MULTIPLE HAZARDS

Our discussion so far has focused on the acceptable risk associated with individual hazards. What additional problems are created by considering many hazards at once? There are some 60,000 chemicals and 50,000 consumer products in common use in the US (Bick & Kasperson, 1978; Maugh, 1978). If even a small fraction of these presented the legal and technical complexities engendered by saccharin or flammable sleepwear (not to mention nuclear power), it would take legions of analysts, lawyers, toxicologists and regulators to handle the situation. If hazards are dealt with one at a time, many must be neglected. The instinctive response to this problem is to deal with problems in order of importance. Unfortunately, the information needed to establish priorities is not available; the collection of such data might itself swamp the system.

Even if legions of hazard managers were available, the wisdom of tackling problems one at a time is questionable. Responsible management must ask not only which dangers are the worst but also which are the most amenable to treatment. A safety measure that is reasonable in a cost-benefit sense may not seem reasonable in a cost-effectiveness sense. That is, if our safety dollars are limited, finding that the benefits of a particular safety measure outweigh its costs does not preclude the possibility that even greater benefits could be reaped with a like expenditure elsewhere. The hazard-by-hazard approach may cause misallocation of resources across activities (ie, giving greater protection to nuclear plant operators than to coal miners) or even within activities (protecting crop dusters but not those in the fields below; Berman, 1978).

The cumulative danger from a problem that appears in many guises may be hidden from a society that tackles hazards one by one. The current cancer crisis seems to reflect an abrupt realization of the cumulative impact of a risk distributed in relatively small doses over a very large number of sources. The nuclear industry has only recently been alerted to the possibility that temporary workers who receive their legal limit of radiation exposure in one facility frequently move on unnoticed to another and another (US Nuclear Regulatory Commission, 1978a).

Proponents of new products or systems can often argue persuasively that the stringent risk standards imposed on them by the public constitute an irrational resistance to progress. After all, many currently tolerated products have much greater risks with appreciably less benefit. The public may, however, be responding to its overall risk burden, a problem outside these proponents' purview. From that perspective, one of the obvious ways to reduce a currently intolerable risk level is to forbid even relatively safe new hazards unless they reduce our dependence on more harmful existing hazards.

Treating hazards individually may obscure solutions as well as problems. Hazard managers must worry not only about how to trade lives and health for dollars but also about how to do so in an equitable fashion. Resolving equity issues in the context of an individual hazard often demands either heroic theoretical assumptions or considerable political muscle. Looking at the whole portfolio of hazards faced by a society may offer some hope of circumventing these problems. No one escapes either the risks or the benefits of all aspects of a society. Indeed, they are often implicitly traded between individuals: I live below the dam that provides you with hydroelectric power in the summer while you live near the nuclear power plant that provides me with electricity in the winter. In this example, the participants might view the trade as equitable, without recourse to complex distributional formulas. While such simple dyads may be rare, looking at the total distribution of risks and benefits in a society may produce clearer, sounder guidelines for resolving equity issues than would solutions generated for individual hazards.

FACING POLITICAL REALITIES

Models that do not capture the critical facts about a hazard will not pass muster before the scientific community. Approaches that fail to represent the political realities of a situation will be rejected by those interests that are underrepresented. No one method can serve the needs of all the environmentalists, industrialists, regulators, lawyers and politicians concerned with a particular hazard. These people appropriately view each specific decision as an arena in which broader political struggles are waged.

In theory, any of the approaches described here should find some support among 'public interest' advocates and some resistance among technology proponents, because all of them make the decision process more open and explicit than it was in the dark ages of hazard management when matters were decided behind closed doors. However, the enchantment of the public wanes when closed doors are replaced by opaque analyses that effectively transfer power to the minute technical elite who perform them (McGinty & Atherly, 1977). In such cases, 'public interest' advocates may resist formal analysis, feeling that avoiding disenfranchisement is more important than determining acceptable levels of risk. The battle brewing in the US over the use of cost-benefit analysis to regulate toxic substances and other hazards may largely hinge on these concerns (Carter, 1979; *Chemical and Engineering News*, 1978).

For other members of the public, the openness itself is a sham, because each of these approaches makes the political ideological assumption that society is sufficiently cohesive and common goaled that problems can be resolved by reason and without confrontation. Sitting down to discuss a decision analysis would, in this view, itself constitute the surrender of important principles. Co-operation may even be seen as a scheme to submerge the opposition in paper work and abrogate its right to fight the outcome of an analysis not to its liking (Fairfax, 1978). Such suspicions are most easily justified when the workings of the decision-making process are poorly understood. It is not hard to imagine the observers of a decision analysis accepting its premises but balking at its conclusions when the results of the analysis are complex or counterintuitive. At the extreme, this would mean that people will only believe analyses confirming their prior opinions.

Proponents of a technology would probably prefer to have the determination of risk acceptability left to their own corporate consciences. Barring that (or the equivalent captive regulatory system), proponents may find it easier to live with adversity than with uncertainty. As a result, one would expect industry increasingly to advocate routinized approaches with rigorous deadlines for making decisions. From this perspective, the zenith of the influence of the Toxic Substances Control Act may have been reached immediately after its enactment. At that moment, industry practice could respond only by making all products as safe as possible, not knowing which substances would actually be dealt with nor how stringently. Cynically speaking, the sooner and more precisely the rules are laid down, the more efficacious the search for loopholes can be.

One could draw similar caricatures of the hidden agendas of other (would-be) participants in hazard management. The point of such an assessment is not to argue that reasonable management is impossible but that all approaches must be seen in their political contexts. Such a broadened perspective may help us to understand the motives of the various participants and the legitimacy that should be assigned to their maneuvers.

In so doing, a crucial issue will be deciding whether society should have higher goals than maximizing the safety of particular technologies. Such goals might include developing an informed citizenry and preserving democratic institutions. In this case, the process could be more important than the product, and it would be necessary for society to provide the resources needed to make meaningful public participation possible (Casper, 1976). Such participation would require new tools for communicating with the public – both for presenting technical issues to laypeople and for eliciting their values (Slovic, Fischhoff et al, 1979). It might also require new social and legal forms, such as hiring representative citizens to participate in the analytic process, thereby enabling them to acquire the expertise needed by the governed to give their informed consent to whatever decision is eventually reached. Such a procedure might be considered a science court with a lay jury. It would consider any or all of the analytic techniques described here as possible inputs to its proceedings. It might also place the logic of jurisprudence above the logic of analysis, acknowledging that there is no single way to determine what risks are acceptable.

The forums in which safety issues are currently argued were not designed to deal with such problems. H R Piehler has, in fact, argued that the legal system could hardly have been designed more poorly for airing and clarifying the technical considerations that arise in product liability suits (Piehler, Twerski, Weinstein & Donaher, 1974). Much public opinion about hazards derives from the testimony of experts. Often this testimony is offered in rancorous debates between experts trying to cast doubt on the probity of their opponents (Mazur, 1973). In addition to creating negative attitudes toward scientists, such spectacles tend to destroy public confidence in the possibility of ever understanding or satisfactorily resolving these issues.

Natural disagreements in areas of incomplete knowledge are aggravated by the feeling that 'bad evidence drives out good'. A two-handed scientist ('on the one hand ... while on the other') may be bested by a two-fisted debater intent on acquiring converts. Decisions about controversial technologies might be improved if all participants publicly subscribed to an established code of behavior. Some possible rules might be:

- Never cite a research result without having a complete, accessible reference.
- Never cite as fact a result supported only by tenuous research findings.
- Acknowledge areas in which you are not an expert (but are still entitled to an opinion).

Like rules of parliamentary procedure, this code would formalize values that many people espouse but have difficulty upholding in practice (fairness, mutual respect, etc).

MUDDLING THROUGH INTELLIGENTLY

No approach to acceptable risk is clearly superior to the others. To exploit the contributions each of these methods can make, careful consideration must be given to the social and political world in which they are used and to the natural world in which we all live. Our social world is characterized by its lack of orderliness. Because hazards are not the only consideration in hazard management decisions, the best we can hope for is some intelligent muddling through. Recognizing this, we should develop and apply the various approaches to hazard management not as inviolate ends in themselves but as servants to that process. The openness of formal analyses must be assured to avoid suspicion and rejection of whatever conclusions are finally reached. When the available numbers are not trustworthy, we should content ourselves with digitless structuring of problems. When good numbers are available, but the issues are unfamiliar, great care must be taken in designing suitable presentations. When we do not know what goal we want to reach, value issues should be framed in a variety of ways and their implications carefully explored.

A distinctive characteristic of our natural world is that it typically is not and cannot be known to the desired degree of precision. We must not only acknowledge this uncertainty but also devote more of our efforts to determining its extent. The most critical input to many hazard management decisions may be how good our best guess is. The real alternatives may be: 'If we don't understand it, we shouldn't mess with it' and 'If we don't experiment, we'll never know what it means' (Goodwin, 1978).

Uncertainty about facts and uncertainty about values both imply that determining the acceptability of a hazard must be an iterative process, partly because, as time goes on, we learn more about how a hazard behaves and how much we like or dislike its consequences. In other words, it takes experience which acknowledges the experimental nature of life to teach us what the facts are and what we really want.

Iteration is essential to any well-done formal analysis. A measure of the success of any analysis is its ability to inform (as well as to reflect) our beliefs and values. Once the analysis is completed, we may then be ready to start over again, incorporating our new and better understandings. In this light, many of the non-political critiques generated by the Reactor Safety Study (the *Rasmussen Report*, Atomic Energy Commission, 1975) reflect its success in deepening the respondents' perspectives. As an aid to policy, the study's main weakness was in attempting to close the books prematurely and thereby failing to take adequate account of these criticisms.

While a good analysis should be insightful, it need not be conclusive. At times, it may not be possible to reach any analytic conclusion, for example, when inter and intrapersonal disagreements are too great to be compromised. If people do not know what they want or if a topic is so politicized that no solution will ever be acceptable, analysis should perhaps best be treated as a process for deepening knowledge and clarifying positions. Performing the sort of calculations that lead to a specific recommendation would, in such cases, only create an illusion of analyzability.

A COMBINED APPROACH

The disciplinary training of scientists shows them how to get the right answers to a set of specially defined problems. The problems raised by hazard management are too broad to be solved by any one discipline. No one knows how to get the right answer. All we can do is avoid making the particular mistakes to which each of us is attuned. The more scientific and lay perspectives applied to a problem, the better chance we have of not getting it wrong.

Just as no single discipline has all the answers, no one of the approaches discussed above provides a sufficient basis for determining what levels of safety are acceptable. In attempting to solve the problems inherent in the other methods, each approach engenders problems of its own.

Are better approaches likely to come along? Probably not, since it seems as though all attempts to rule on the safety of particular hazards share common conceptual and operational difficulties whose source lies in the very attempt to reduce the problem to manageable size. What we can hope for is to understand the various approaches well enough to be able to use them in combination so that they complement one another's strengths rather than compound each other's weaknesses.

ACKNOWLEDGMENTS

This research was supported by the National Science Foundation under Grant ENV77-15332 to Perceptronics, Inc. Any opinions, findings and conclusions or recommendations expressed in this publication are those of the authors and do not necessarily reflect the views of the National Science Foundation. We are grateful to Bob Kates and Richard Wilson for comments on an earlier draft of the manuscript and to Michael Enbar for much of the analysis in Figure 7.2.

NOTE

1   One complication of this latter relationship is that the degree of voluntariness of some activities proved to be rather ambiguous – such as handguns. A second is that double standards were also observed with other qualitative aspects of risk, such as perceived control, familiarity, knowledge and immediacy.

8 Facts and Fears: Understanding Perceived Risk

Paul Slovic, Baruch Fischhoff and
Sarah Lichtenstein

AN EXTENDED STUDY OF RISK PERCEPTION

Our recent work extends early studies of risk perception to a broader set of hazards (90 instead of 30) and risk characteristics (18 instead of 9). Although the data have thus far been collected only from college students, the results appear to provide further insights into the nature of risk perception. In addition, they suggest that some accepted views about the importance of the voluntary–involuntary distinction and the impact of catastrophic losses may need revision.

Design of the Study

The extended study is outlined in Table 8.1. The 90 hazards were selected to cover a very broad range of activities, substances and technologies. To keep the rating task to a manageable size, some people judged only risks, others judged only benefits and others rated the hazards on five of the risk characteristics. Risks and benefits were rated on a 0–100 scale (from 'not risky' to 'extremely risky' and from 'no benefit' to 'very great benefit').

After rating the hazards with regard to risk, respondents were asked to rate the degree to which the present risk level would need to be adjusted to make the risk level acceptable to society. The instructions for this adjustment task read as follows:

> The acceptable level of risk is not the ideal risk. Ideally, the risks should be zero. The acceptable level is a level that is good enough, where 'good enough' means you think that the advantages of increased safety are not worth the costs of reducing risk by restricting or otherwise altering the activity. For example, we can make drugs 'safer' by restricting their potency; cars can be made safer, at a cost,

---

Note: excerpts from a paper by P Slovic, B Fischhoff and S Lichtenstein that appeared in R C Schwing and W A Albers, Jr (eds) *Societal Risk Assessment: How Safe is Safe Enough?* New York, Plenum, 1980. Copyright 1980 by Plenum Press. Reprinted with permission.

Table 8.1 *Overview of the Extended Study*

I The Hazards

1	Home gas furnaces	31	Food coloring	61	Darvon
2	Home appliances	32	Saccharin	62	Morphine
3	Home power tools	33	Sodium nitrite	63	Oral contraceptives
4	Microwave ovens	34	Food preservatives	64	Valium
5	Power lawn mowers	35	Food irradiation	65	Antibiotics
6	Handguns	36	Earth orbit satellite	66	Prescription drugs
7	Terrorism	37	Space exploration	67	Boxing
8	Crime	38	Lasers	68	Downhill skiing
9	Nerve gas	39	Asbestos	69	Fireworks
10	Nuclear weapons	40	Police work	70	Football
11	National defense	41	Firefighting	71	Hunting
12	Warfare	42	Christmas tree lights	72	Jogging
13	Bicycles	43	Cosmetics	73	Mountain climbing
14	Motorcycles	44	Fluorescent lights	74	Mushroom hunting
15	Motor vehicles	45	Hair dyes	75	Recreational boating
16	Railroads	46	Chemical	76	Roller coasters
17	General aviation		disinfectants	77	Scuba diving
18	Supersonic transport	47	DNA research	78	Skateboards
	(SST)	48	Liquid natural gas	79	Sunbathing
19	Jumbo jets	49	Smoking	80	Surfing
20	Commercial aviation	50	Tractors	81	Swimming pools
21	Anaesthetics	51	Chemical fertilizers	82	Fossil electric power
22	Vaccinations	52	Herbicides	83	Hydroelectric power
23	Pregnancy, childbirth	53	DDT	84	Solar electric power
24	Open-heart surgery	54	Pesticides	85	Non-nuclear electric
25	Surgery	55	Aspirin		power
26	Radiation therapy	56	Marijuana	86	Nuclear power
27	Diagnostic X-rays	57	Heroin	87	Dynamite
28	Alcoholic beverages	58	Laetrile	88	Skyscrapers
29	Caffeine	59	Amphetamines	89	Bridges
30	Water fluoridation	60	Barbiturates	90	Dams

II Judgments made for each hazard
  A Perceived risk of death (0 – 100 scale)
  B Perceived benefit (0 – 100 scale)
  C Risk adjustment (necessary to make perceived risk equal acceptable risk)
  D Ratings on 18 risk characteristics
      1 – 8 Eight characteristics from an earlier study.
        9 Can mishaps be prevented?
       10 If a mishap occurs, can the damage be controlled?
       11 How many people are exposed to this hazard?
       12 Does the hazard threaten future generations?
       13 Are you personally at risk from this hazard?
       14 Are the benefits equitably distributed among those at risk?
       15 Does the hazard threaten global catastrophe?
       16 Are the damage-producing processes observable as they occur?
       17 Are the risks increasing or decreasing?
       18 Can the risks be reduced easily?

by improving their construction or requiring regular safety inspection. We may, or may not, believe such restrictions are necessary.

If an activity's present level of risk is acceptable, no special action need be taken to increase its safety. If its riskiness is unacceptably high, *serious action*, such as legislation to restrict its practice, should be taken. On the other hand, there may be some activities or technologies that you believe are currently safer than the acceptable level of risk. For these activities, the risk of death could be higher than it is now before society would have to take serious action.

On their answer sheets, participants were provided with three columns labeled:

- 'Could be riskier: it would be acceptable if it were __ times riskier';
- 'It is presently acceptable'; and
- 'Too risky: to be acceptable it would have to be__ times safer'.

The 18 risk characteristics included eight from the earlier study (see Chapter 5). The ninth characteristic from that study, controllability, was split into two separate characteristics representing control over the occurrence of a mishap (preventability) and control over the consequences given that something did go wrong. The remaining characteristics were selected to represent additional concerns thought to be important by risk-assessment researchers. As in the earlier study, all characteristics were rated on a bipolar 1–7 scale representing the extent to which the characteristics described the hazard. For example:

15 To what extent does pursuit of this activity, substance or technology have the potential to cause catastrophic death and destruction across the whole world?

| VeryLow Catastrophic Potential | 1 | 2 | 3 | 4 | 5 | 6 | 7 | Very High Catastrophic Potential |

RESULTS

Risk Characteristics

The mean ratings for the 18 risk characteristics revealed a number of interesting findings. For example, the risks from most of these hazards were judged to be at least moderately well known to science (63 had mean ratings below 3 where 1 was labeled 'known precisely'). Most risks were thought to be better known to science than to those who were exposed. The only risks for which those individuals exposed were thought to be more knowledgeable than scientists were those from police work, marijuana, contraceptives (judged relatively unknown to both science and those exposed), boxing, skiing, hunting and several other sporting activities.

Only 25 of the hazards were judged to be decreasing in riskiness; two of them (surgery and pregnancy–childbirth) were thought to be decreasing greatly. Risks from 62 hazards were judged to be increasing, 13 of these markedly so. The risks from crime, warfare, nuclear weapons, terrorism, national defense, herbicides and nuclear power were judged to be increasing most. None of the

Table 8.2 *Intercorrelations among 18 Risk Characteristics in the Extended Study*

	1 Severity not controllable	2 Dread	3 Globally catastrophic	4 Little preventive control	5 Certain to be fatal	6 Risks & benefits inequitable	7 Catastrophic	8 Threatens future generations	9 Not easily reduced	10 Risks increasing	11 Involuntary	12 Affects me personally	13 Not observable	14 Unknown to those exposed	15 Effects immediate	16 New (unfamiliar)	17 Unknown to science	18 Many people exposed
1 Severity not controllable																		
2 Dread	.82																	
3 Globally catastrophic	.78	.83																
4 Little preventive control	.86	.72	.71															
5 Certain to be fatal	.80	.82	.73	.77														
6 Risks & benefits inequitable	.75	.76	.84	.63	.65													
7 Catastrophic	.77	.66	.77	.74	.67	.77												
8 Threatens future generations	.62	.76	.86	.52	.64	.81	.63											
9 Not easily reduced	.59	.67	.64	.67	.66	.59	.56	.59										
10 Risks increasing	.51	.63	.76	.48	.58	.76	.57	.75	.60									
11 Involuntary	.68	.58	.69	.52	.42	.77	.74	.62	.33	.44								
12 Affects me personally	.57	.64	.77	.43	.50	.71	.64	.78	.35	.67	.61							
13 Not observable	-.04	-.14	.04	-.19	-.28	.08	.00	.24	-.15	-.10	.33	.10						
14 Unknown to those exposed	.14	.05	.22	-.05	-.12	.28	.24	.35	-.20	.05	.63	.31	.79					
15 Effects immediate	.21	.15	.00	.34	.36	-.08	.11	-.29	.22	.01	-.25	-.14	-.87	-.77				
16 New (unfamiliar)	.32	.29	.32	.22	.20	.25	.18	.44	.13	.06	.36	.20	.63	.56	-.48			
17 Unknown to science	-.10	-.10	-.04	-.07	-.15	-.02	-.04	.02	-.23	.02	.13	.00	.43	.50	-.44	.32		
18 Many people exposed	-.04	.04	.23	-.14	-.11	.32	.23	.47	.03	.26	.34	.56	.37	.46	-.52	.07	-.01	

Conclusion: Characteristics 1–12 and 13–17 form clusters. Items within each cluster are highly correlated with one another. Correlations are low between items from different clusters. Thus, although these characteristics are distinct, there is much commonality among them.

hazards was judged to be easily reducible. The lowest of the 90 means on this characteristic was 3.2 (where 1 was labeled 'easily reduced'); it was obtained for home appliances and roller coasters.

The ratings of the various risk characteristics tended to be rather highly intercorrelated, as shown in Table 8.2. For example, risks with catastrophic potential were also judged as quite dread ($r = .83$). Application of a statistical technique known as factor analysis showed that the pattern of intercorrelations could be represented by three underlying dimensions or factors. The nature of these factors can be seen in Table 8.2 in which the characteristics are ordered on the basis of the factor analysis. The first 12 characteristics represent the first factor; they correlate highly with one another and less highly with the remaining 6 characteristics. In other words, these data suggest that risks whose severity is believed to be uncontrollable tend also to be seen as dread, catastrophic, hard to prevent, fatal, inequitable, threatening to future generations, not easily reduced, increasing, involuntary and threatening to the rater personally. The nature of these characteristics suggests that this factor be called 'dread'. The second factor primarily reflects five characteristics that correlate relatively highly with one another and less highly with other characteristics. They are: observability, knowledge, immediacy of consequences and familiarity (see Table 8.2). We have labeled this factor 'familiarity'. The third factor is dominated by a single characteristic, the number of people exposed. This characteristic can be seen in Table 8.2 to be relatively independent of the other characteristics.

Just as each of the 90 hazards has a mean score on each of the 18 risk characteristics, each hazard also has a score on each factor. These scores give the location of each hazard within the factor space. Figure 8.1 plots the hazards on factors 1 and 2. Items at the high end of factor 1 are all highly dreaded. Items at the negative end of factor 1 are seen as posing risks to individuals and being injurious rather than fatal. The placement of items on the vertical dimension, factor 3, intuitively fits the theme of familiarity and observability associated with the dimension label. Hazards lying at the extremes on factor 3 (number exposed) are shown in Table 8.3.

This three-dimensional factor structure is of interest because it differs considerably from the two-dimensional structure obtained from ratings of 30 hazards on 9

Table 8.3 *Extreme Scores on Factor 3 (Degree of Exposure to the Hazard)*

High exposure	Factor score	Low exposure	Factor score
Alcoholic beverages	2.9	Nerve gas	−1.2
Caffeine	2.0	Supersonic Transport	−1.2
Smoking	1.8	Surfing	−1.4
Food preservatives	1.8	Laetrile	−1.5
DDT	1.6	Boxing	−1.5
Herbicides	1.5	Roller coasters	−1.6
Motor vehicles	1.5	Scuba diving	−1.8
Food irradiation	1.4	Open-heart surgery	−1.8
Pesticides	1.3	Lasers	−1.8
Sunbathing	1.2	Space exploration	−2.0
		Solar electricity	−2.0

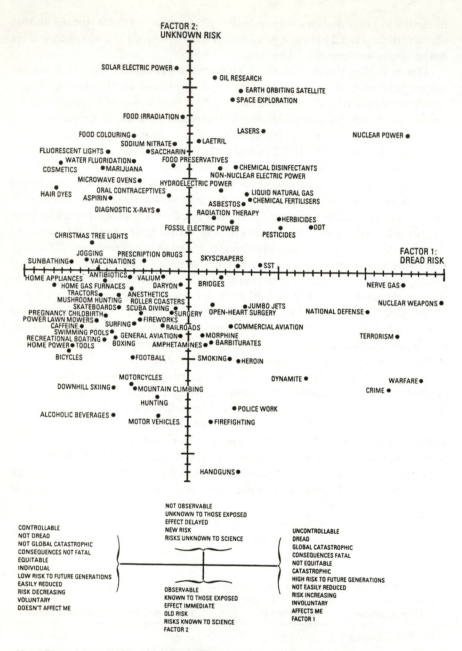

Note: Factor 3 (not shown) reflects the number of people exposed to the hazard.

Figure 8.1 *Factors 1 and 2 of the three-dimensional structure derived from interrelationships among 18 risk characteristics in the extended study*

characteristics (Fischhoff, Slovic, Lichtenstein, Read et al, 1978). That structure, in which one factor was labeled 'severity' (ie, certain to be fatal) and the other was labeled 'technological risk', has been found to be remarkably consistent across four different groups of lay and expert respondents (Slovic, Fischhoff &

Lichtenstein, 1980a). The present results indicate that the particular set of hazards and the particular set of risk characteristics under study can have an important effect on the nature of the observed 'dimensions of risk'.

One point of commonality between the present analysis and the previous one is that nuclear power is an isolate in both. Although activities such as crime, nerve gas, warfare and terrorism are seen as similarly dreaded (factor 1), none of these is judged to be as new or as unknown (factor 2) as nuclear power.

Risks and Benefits

Table 8.4 shows the mean judgments of perceived risk, perceived benefit and need for risk adjustment. Rather than discuss the details of the ratings for specific hazards, we shall focus on their intercorrelations and their relation to the risk characteristics and factor scores.

Our earlier study showed that perceived risk could be predicted from knowledge of an item's judged dread and severity. Table 8.5 shows this pattern was

Table 8.4 *Mean Risk and Benefit Judgments for 90 Activities, Substances and Technologies*

		Perceived risk	Perceived benefit	Adjusted risk
1	Nuclear weapons	78	27	49.1
2	Warfare	78	31	26.2
3	DDT	76	26	8.8
4	Handguns	76	27	15.2
5	Crime	73	9	19.2
6	Nuclear power	72	36	22.2
7	Pesticides	71	38	4.2
8	Herbicides	69	33	6.3
9	Smoking	68	24	6.6
10	Terrorism	66	6	26.3
11	Heroin	63	17	7.6
12	National defense	61	58	4.7
13	Nerve gas	60	7	17.4
14	Barbiturates	57	27	4.8
15	Alcoholic beverages	57	49	2.9
16	Chemical fertilizers	55	48	2.8
17	Motor vehicles	55	76	3.1
18	Amphetamines	55	27	4.9
19	Open-heart surgery	53	50	2.1
20	Morphine	53	31	4.4
21	Radiation therapy	53	36	3.6
22	Darvon	52	38	3.9
23	Oral contraceptives	51	67	3.8
24	Asbestos	51	51	4.9
25	Liquid natural gas	50	56	1.5
26	Chemical disinfectants	49	47	2.2
27	Valium	48	37	2.6
28	Surgery	48	64	2.4

Table 8.4 *continued*

		Perceived risk	Perceived benefit	Adjusted risk
29	Dynamite	47	30	2.0
30	Diagnostic X-rays	44	54	2.2
31	Fire fighting	44	83	2.7
32	Motorcycles	43	43	2.5
33	Police work	43	75	2.5
34	Lasers	42	34	1.5
35	Food preservatives	42	36	2.7
36	DNA research	41	41	2.2
37	Prescription drugs	41	73	1.5
38	Fossil electric power	40	65	1.7
39	Food irradiation	39	42	2.1
40	Sodium nitrite	38	31	3.0
41	Microwave ovens	36	34	1.7
42	Power lawn mowers	35	39	1.5
43	Laetrile	35	30	2.6
44	Saccharin	35	25	1.9
45	Home power tools	33	52	1.1
46	Hunting	33	47	1.8
47	Supersonic transport	33	30	1.5
48	Jumbo jets	32	48	1.4
49	Dams	31	64	1.5
50	Aspirin	31	63	1.1
51	Commercial aviation	31	54	1.4
52	Fireworks	31	42	1.4
53	General aviation	30	39	1.6
54	Caffeine	30	42	1.0
55	Hydroelectric power	30	66	1.1
56	Football	30	54	1.7
57	Antibiotics	30	68	1.5
58	Pregnancy, childbirth	30	60	1.1
59	Anesthetics	29	55	1.5
60	Home gas furnaces	29	49	1.0
61	Railroads	29	48	1.1
62	Food coloring	29	19	1.6
63	Tractors	29	61	0.9
64	Mountain climbing	28	47	1.3
65	Bridges	27	69	1.4
66	Christmas tree lights	27	44	1.0
67	Skateboards	27	37	1.7
68	Scuba diving	26	41	1.3
69	Skyscrapers	26	39	1.5
70	Non-nuclear electric power	26	75	1.1
71	Swimming pools	26	57	1.2
72	Home appliances	26	72	0.8
73	Downhill skiing	26	57	1.1
74	Space exploration	25	51	0.9
75	Bicycles	24	68	0.9

Table 8.4 *continued*

		Perceived risk	Perceived benefit	Adjusted risk
76	Vaccinations	24	77	1.0
77	Water fluoridation	24	44	1.2
78	Hair dyes	23	28	1.2
79	Mushroom hunting	23	32	1.1
80	Boxing	23	34	1.2
81	Recreational boating	22	45	1.2
82	Earth orbit satellite	22	54	0.7
83	Fluorescent lights	21	46	1.0
84	Surfing	21	41	1.0
85	Marijuana	21	53	1.1
86	Roller coasters	20	33	1.3
87	Cosmetics	20	49	0.9
88	Sunbathing	20	49	0.9
89	Jogging	14	65	0.6
90	Solar electric power	12	56	0.6

Table 8.5 *Correlations between Perceived Risk, Risk Adjustment, and Risk Characteristics*

	Perceived risk	Adjusted risk	Correlations with Adjusted Risk holding the effects of Perceived Risk constant
Dread	.83	.87	.47
Future generations	.80	.77	.15
Global catastrophe	.78	.82	.41
Fatal	.74	.74	.23
Increasing	.73	.76	.35
Affects me	.70	.65	.05
Inequitable	.68	.73	.38
Not easily reduced	.63	.69	.34
Uncontrollable	.63	.65	.25
Not preventable	.51	.57	.30
Catastrophic	.50	.54	.24
Involuntary	.39	.42	.18
Many exposed	.25	.14	−.23
New	.17	.16	.02
Immediate	.10	.17	.18
Unknown to exposed	−.06	−.09	−.09
Not observable	−.19	−.23	−.16
Unknown to science	−.27	−.22	.07
Factor 1	.74	.79	.43
Factor 2	−.22	−.22	−.04
Factor 3	.41	.29	−.21
Perceived Benefit	−.42	−.54	−.44
Adjusted Risk	.91		

repeated with perceived risk also being closely related to threat to future generations, potential for global catastrophe, personal threat and inequity. Among the factors, factor 1 was the best predictor of perceived risk. Perceived risk was inversely related to perceived benefit, a finding that has been obtained consistently in previous studies (Slovic et al, 1980a); our respondents do not believe that societal mechanisms have worked to limit risks from less beneficial activities, contrary to claims by Starr and others (Starr, 1969).

The greater the perceived risk, the larger the adjustment judged necessary to bring the risk to an acceptable level ($r = .91$). Because of this close relationship, some risk characteristics that predicted perceived risk also predicted the adjustment ratings. Note also that the more beneficial items were thought to need less risk adjustment ($r = -.54$).

Perceived risk is obviously the primary determiner of the risk-adjustment rating. Would the adjustment rating continue to correlate with the other risk characteristics if the influence of perceived risk were partialed out? The right-hand column of Table 8.5 indicates that the answer is yes. Although correlations between the risk characteristics and the adjustment ratings are much reduced once perceived risk is held constant, dread, global catastrophe, equity, factor 1 and perceived benefit still show moderate relationships. In other words, adjustments are mostly determined by perceived risk but they are somewhat sensitive to benefit and certain risk characteristics.

Table 8.5 shows that certain characteristics can do a good job, by themselves, of predicting perceived and adjusted risk. We have also used multiple regression analysis to develop simple equations involving combinations of characteristics. These produced multiple correlations in the range of .89 to .95. In other words, perceived and adjusted risk are quite predictable from knowledge of other risk characteristics.

SPECIAL ISSUES

The Voluntariness Hypothesis

By examining statistical and economic indicators of benefit and risk for eight hazards, Starr (1969) proposed several hypotheses about the nature of acceptable risk as discussed in Chapters 1, 2 and 5.

Although Starr acknowledged the preliminary nature of his data and hypotheses, his voluntary/involuntary distinction has been widely cited as relevant for standard setting (Council for Science and Society, 1977; Kinchin, 1978; Rowe, 1977). Attempts to derive quantitative criteria for acceptable levels of risk often recommend stricter standards on hazards imposed involuntarily.

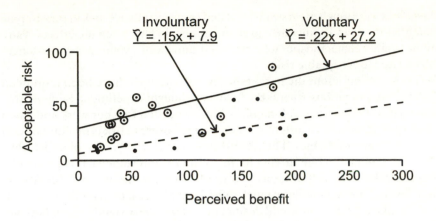

Source: Fischhoff, Slovic, Lichtenstein, Read et al (1978).

Figure 8.2 *Comparison between judgments of acceptable risk levels and judgments of benefits for voluntary and involuntary activities*

The judgments of current and acceptable risks in our own studies provide a test of Starr's hypotheses with very different methodology and data. Our first study (Fischhoff, Slovic, Lichtenstein, Read et al, 1978), in which members of the League of Women Voters rated the risks and benefits of 30 hazards, produced results supportive of Starr's (see Figure 8.2). Our respondents appeared to believe that greater risk should be tolerated for more beneficial activities and that a double standard is appropriate for voluntary and involuntary activities. However, these people also seemed to desire similar double standards based on characteristics such as controllability, knowledge, familiarity and immediacy. We concluded that in addition to benefits and voluntariness, a number of other psychological and physical characteristics of risk might need to be incorporated into risk standards.

The results of our extended (90-hazard) study have clarified these tentative conclusions. Consider first the role of voluntariness: the correlation matrix in Table 8.2 shows that involuntariness is closely related to many other risk characteristics and particularly to lack of control ($r = .68$), global catastrophe ($r = .69$), inequity ($r = .76$) and catastrophe ($r = .74$). For example, six of the ten most involuntary hazards (nuclear weapons, nerve gas, terrorism, warfare, nuclear power and DDT) are also among the ten most catastrophic hazards. These relationships suggest that much, if not all, of the observed aversion to involuntary risks may be due to other characteristics that are closely associated with voluntariness.

Support for this interpretation comes from the following data analyses conducted on the extended study. An estimate of the acceptable level of risk was calculated for each of the 90 hazards by dividing the hazard's mean risk level by its mean adjustment factor. This index of acceptable risk was found to correlate positively with perceived benefit ($r = .58$) as Starr hypothesized and as our previous studies had also demonstrated. Furthermore, deviations from the best-fit line relating benefit and acceptable risk were significantly correlated with voluntariness, in the direction predicted by Starr's hypothesis. However, these deviations were much more strongly related to characteristics such as catastrophic potential, dread and equity than to voluntariness. In fact, when the effects of any of these other characteristics were removed statistically, voluntariness no longer was related to acceptable risk.

These doubts about the importance of voluntariness have been reinforced by other considerations, such as the following thought experiment. Suppose that you own and ride in two automobiles. One is needed for your work and when you ride in it, you are chauffeured (thus your exposure to risk is involuntary and relatively uncontrollable). The second auto is driven by you for pleasure, thus the risks you take while driving it are voluntary and somewhat controllable. Consider the standards of safety you would wish for the two vehicles. Would you demand that standards be much safer for the first car than for the second? If you are like us, then you would desire equivalent safety standards for both vehicles.

Lave (1972) expressed similar doubts about the intrinsic significance of involuntary risks. He noted that involuntary hazards typically affect larger numbers of people so that stricter safety standards for such hazards merely reflect the greater amount of money that groups would be willing to pay for safety, relative to what an individual would be willing to pay.

We conclude that society's apparent aversion to involuntary risks may be mostly an illusion, caused by the fact that involuntary risks are often noxious in more important ways, such as being inequitable or potentially catastrophic.

THE IMPORTANCE OF CATASTROPHIC POTENTIAL

Whereas too much significance may have been attributed to voluntariness, our research suggests that more attention needs to be focused on the role played by catastrophic potential in determining societal response to hazards. As noted above, catastrophic potential appears to be a major determiner of judgments of perceived and acceptable risk and may account for the presumed importance of voluntariness. In similar fashion, it seems likely that catastrophic potential may also account for some of the other double standards observed by Fischhoff, Slovic, Lichtenstein, Read et al (1978). That is, the finding that, at any constant level of benefit, acceptable risk was lower for unknown, unfamiliar and uncontrollable activities may have been due to the expectation that such activities could lead to a great many deaths. This hypothesis would seem to merit careful examination.

Nuclear Power

The importance of catastrophic potential may be seen most clearly in the case of nuclear power. Our early studies with students and the League of Women Voters showed that these groups believed nuclear power to pose greater risks of death than any of the 29 other hazards under consideration. Further research linked this perception to the perceived potential for disaster (which was extremely high).

Like nuclear power, diagnostic X-rays produce invisible and irreversible contamination which leads to cancer and genetic damage. However, X-rays are not similarly feared. One reason for this difference may be found in the risk profile in Figure 5.6 and the disaster multipliers of Table 6.3 which show that X-rays are not seen as having much potential for catastrophe.

We are led to conclude that beliefs about the catastrophic nature of nuclear power are a major determinant of public opposition to that technology. This is not a comforting conclusion because the rarity of catastrophic events makes it extremely difficult to resolve disagreements by recourse to empirical evidence. Demonstrating the improbability of catastrophic accidents requires massive amounts of data. In the absence of definitive evidence, weaker data tend to be interpreted in a manner consistent with the individual's prior beliefs. As a result, the 'perception gap' between pro-nuclear experts and the anti-nuclear public is likely to persist, leaving frustration, distrust, conflict and costly hazard management as its legacy. We suspect that the potential for similar disputes exists with other low-probability, high-consequence hazards such as liquified natural gas (LNG), pesticides, industrial chemicals and recombinant-DNA research.

Weighing Catastrophes

Any attempt to control accidents must be guided by assessments of their probability and severity. As we have seen, probability assessment poses serious difficulties, particularly for rare events. Unfortunately, weighing of the severity or social cost of an accident is also problematic.

Society appears to react more strongly to infrequent large losses of life than to frequent small losses. This has led analysts to propose a weighting factor that accommodates the greater impact of N lives lost at one time relative to the impact of one life lost in each of N separate incidents. Risk-benefit analysts would then apply this weighting factor when evaluating the expected social costs of a proposed activity.

The precise nature of the fatality weighting factor has been the subject of some speculation. Wilson (1975) suggested that N lives lost simultaneously were N^2 times more important than the loss of one life. Ferreira and Slesin (1976) hypothesized, on the basis of observed frequency and severity data, that the function might be a cubic one.

We believe that a single weighting function cannot adequately explain, predict or guide social response to catastrophe. For one, we have found that people hold, simultaneously, several conflicting attitudes about the weighting function (Fischhoff, Slovic & Lichtenstein, 1980). They believe that the function relating social impact to N lives lost should be:

- concave, because they recognize that the same additional number of lives lost seems more important in a small accident than in a large accident;
- linear, because each unidentified life is equally important; and
- convex, because large losses of life have important higher-order consequences and may even threaten the resilience of a community or society.

Clearly, any attempt to model the impact of a multiple fatality event will need to consider how situational factors will interact with these multiple values (for a start on this problem, see Keeney, 1977).

Signal Value

Another complication is that the occurrence of a rare, catastrophic event contains information regarding the probability of its reoccurrence. As a result, the impact of an accident may be determined as much by its signal value as by its toll of death and destruction.

The importance of accidents as signals is demonstrated by a study in which we asked 21 women (median age = 37) to rate the seriousness of ten hypothetical accidents. Several aspects of seriousness were rated including:

- the total amount of suffering and grief caused by the loss of life in each mishap;
- the number of people who need to be made aware of the mishap via the media;
- the amount of effort (and money) that should be put into investigating the cause of the mishap and preventing its recurrence; and
- the degree to which hearing about the mishap would cause one to be worried and upset during the next few days.

The accident scenarios were constructed so as to vary on total fatalities and informativeness (see Table 8.6). The five uninformative accidents represented single incidents, generated by reasonably well-known and understood processes, and limited to a particular time and locale. The high-information mishaps were designed to signal a change in riskiness, potential for the proliferation of similar mishaps, or some breakdown in the system controlling the hazard. Thus, a bus skidding on ice represented a low-information mishap because its occurrence did not signal a change in motor-vehicle risks, whereas an accident caused by a poorly designed steering system in a new model automobile would be informative about all such vehicles. To check our intuitions our respondents also judged informativeness, defined as the degree to which the mishap told them (and society) something that may not have been known about the hazardousness of the specific activity.

All ratings were on a seven-point scale. The means ratings are shown in Table 8.6. Note that the five mishaps designed to be high in signal value were all judged more informative than the most informative mishap in the low-information category. As expected, the judged amount of suffering and grief was closely related to the number of people killed. However, all other aspects of seriousness were more closely related to the information content of the accident. Accidents signaling either a possible breakdown in safety-control systems or the possibility that the mishap might proliferate were judged more worrisome and in need of greater awareness and greater public effort to prevent reoccurrences. The number of people killed appeared to be relatively unimportant in determining these aspects of seriousness.

Table 8.6 *Effect of Informativeness on the Impact of Catastrophic Mishaps*

	Informative-ness	Suffering and grief	Need for awareness	Effort to prevent recurrence	Worry
Less Informative Mishaps:					
Bus skids on ice and runs off road (27 killed)	1.8	4.4	2.5	3.1	1.8
Dam collapse (40 killed)	4.7	4.9	4.7	5.9	3.8
Two jumbo jets collide on runway (600 killed)	4.8	6.1	5.8	6.5	4.5
Hundred year flood (2700 killed)	2.8	6.1	5.3	3.5	2.7
Meteorite hits stadium (4000 killed)	2.2	6.2	5.7	2.1	2.5
More Informative Mishaps:					
Nuclear reactor accident: Partial core meltdown releases radiation inside plant but not to outside (1 killed)	6.5	4.5	6.5	7.0	6.1
Botulism in well-known brand of food (2 killed)	5.7	3.7	5.2	6.1	4.6
New model auto steering fails (3 killed)	5.2	3.8	5.2	6.3	4.6
Recombinant DNA workers contract mysterious illness (10 killed)	6.1	4.6	5.9	6.3	5.1
Jet engine falls off on takeoff (300 killed)	5.7	6.0	6.1	6.9	5.5

For this study we conclude that risk analyses, designed to anticipate public reaction or to aid in decision-making, need to consider what accidents indicate about the nature and controllability of risk. An accident that takes many lives may have little or no impact on perceived risk if it occurs as part of a familiar, well-understood and self-limiting process. In contrast, a small accident may greatly enhance perceived risk and trigger strong corrective action because it increases the judged probability of future accidents. The great impact of the accident at Three Mile Island (which caused no immediate fatalities) would seem to reflect such considerations.

CONCLUSIONS

Although research into the nature of perceived risk is still incomplete, we offer the following tentative conclusions:

1   Perceived risk is quantifiable and predictable.
2   Groups of laypeople sometimes differ systematically in their perceptions. Experts and lay persons also differ, particularly with regard to the probability and consequences of catastrophic accidents.
3   Cognitive limitations, biased media coverage, misleading experience and the anxieties generated by the gambles life poses cause uncertainty to be denied, risks to be misjudged and judgments to be believed with unwarranted confidence.
4   Experts' risk assessments are also susceptible to bias, particularly underestimation due to omitting important pathways to disaster.
5   Differences in the judged seriousness of various modes of death are slight and do not seem responsible for discrepancies between public and expert assessments of risk.
6   The degree of adjustment judged necessary to make risk levels 'acceptable' is strongly determined by the perceived level of current risk; the greater the perceived risk, the greater the desired reduction. Perceived benefit plays a secondary role; all else being equal, somewhat less reduction in risk is deemed necessary to make highly beneficial activities 'acceptable'.
7   Many of the 18 characteristics of risk hypothesized to be important to the public do correlate highly with perceived risk and desire for risk reduction. Certain clusters of characteristics are highly interrelated across hazards, indicating that they can be combined into higher-order characteristics or 'factors'. Three factors, labeled dread, familiarity and exposure, seem able to account for most of the interrelations among the 18 characteristics.
8   The perceived potential for catastrophic loss of life emerges as one of the most important risk characteristics, responsible for: (a) the belief that people want involuntary hazards to be less risky than voluntary hazards of equal benefit; (b) the irresolvable disputes between experts and the public which lead to frustration, distrust, conflict and ineffective hazard management; and (c) the fear of nuclear power.
9   Disagreements about risk should not be expected to evaporate in the presence of evidence. Definitive evidence, particularly about rare hazards, is difficult to obtain. Weaker information is likely to be interpreted so as to reinforce existing beliefs.
10 The social impact of losing N lives in a single mishap cannot be adequately represented by a simple weighting function. People believe simultaneously in several different functional relationships. In addition, accidents serve as signals regarding the probability of further mishaps. The alarm created by an accident signal is a strong determiner of its social impact and is not necessarily related to the number of people killed.

POSTSCRIPT: WHO SHALL DECIDE?

The research described in this chapter demonstrates that judgment of risk is fallible. It also shows that the degree of fallibility is often surprisingly great and that faulty estimates may be put forth with much confidence. Since even well-informed laypeople have difficulty judging risks accurately, it is tempting to conclude that the public should be removed from the risk-assessment process. Such action would seem to be misguided on several counts. First, we have no assurance that experts' judgments are immune to biases once they are forced to go beyond hard data. Although judgmental biases have most often been demonstrated with laypeople, there is evidence that the cognitive functioning of experts is basically like that of everyone else.

Second, in many if not most cases, effective hazard management requires the cooperation of a large body of laypeople. These people must agree to do without some things and accept substitutes for others. They must vote sensibly on ballot measures and for legislators who will serve them as surrogate hazard managers. They must obey safety rules and use the legal system responsibly. Even if the experts were much better judges of risk than laypeople, giving experts an exclusive franchise for hazard management would mean substituting short-term efficiency for the long-term effort needed to create an informed citizenry.

ACKNOWLEDGMENTS

The authors wish to express their appreciation to Christoph Hohenemser, Roger Kasperson and Robert Kates for their helpful comments and suggestions on portions of this manuscript. This work was supported by the National Science Foundation under Grant PRA79-11934 to Clark University and under subcontract to Perceptronics, Inc. Any opinions, findings, and conclusions or recommendations expressed in this publication are those of the authors and do not necessarily reflect the views of the National Science Foundation.

9 Response Mode, Framing and Information-processing Effects in Risk Assessment

Paul Slovic, Baruch Fischhoff and
Sarah Lichtenstein

A chapter on framing by Tversky and Kahneman (1982) demonstrated that normatively inconsequential changes in the formulation of choice problems significantly affect preferences. These effects are noteworthy because they are sizable (sometimes complete reversals of preference), because they violate important tenets of rationality, and because they influence not only behavior but also how the consequences of behavior are experienced. These perturbations are traced (in prospect theory; see Kahneman & Tversky, 1979) to the interaction between the manner in which acts, contingencies and outcomes are framed in decision problems and to general propensities for treating values and uncertainty in nonlinear ways.

This chapter begins by providing additional demonstrations of framing effects. Next, it extends the concept of framing to effects induced by changes of response mode, and it illustrates effects due to the interaction between response mode and information-processing considerations. Two specific response modes are studied in detail: judgments of single objects and choices among two or more options. Judgments are prone to influence by anchoring-and-adjustment processes, which ease the strain of integrating diverse items of information. Choices are prone to context effects that develop as a result of justification processes, through which the deliberations preceding choice are woven into a rationalization of that action. As we shall see, these processes often cause judgments and choices to be inconsistent with one another.

Response mode, framing and information-processing considerations apply to all decision problems. However, like Tversky and Kahneman, we shall focus primarily on risk-taking decisions ranging from choices among simple gambles

Note: reprinted from 'Response Mode, Framing and Information-processing Effects in Risk Assessment' by P Slovic, B Fischhoff and S Lichtenstein in *New Directions for Methodology of Social and Behavioral Science: Question Framing and Response Consistency*, pp21–36, by R Hogarth (ed), San Francisco: Jossey-Bass, 1982. Copyright 1982 by Jossey-Bass Inc. Reprinted with permission.

to complex decisions about protective actions, such as insurance, vaccination and the use of seat belts. The studies to be described demonstrate the extreme sensitivity of judgments and decisions to subtle changes in problem format and response mode.

CONCRETENESS AND THE FRAMING OF ACTS

Decision options can often be viewed in a variety of perspectives. For example, Tversky and Kahneman (1982) showed that concurrent decision problems are dealt with independently, rather than as an integrated combination. Thus, choosing both a sure gain of $240 and a gamble offering a 75% chance of losing $1000 and a 25% chance of losing nothing is not viewed as equivalent to its conjunctions: a 25% chance of winning $240 and a 75% chance of losing $760.

By failing to integrate concurrent acts, Tversky and Kahneman's subjects responded to the explicit characteristics of each act and did not perform the simple transformations necessary to effect their merger. Similar behavior has been observed in two experiments that examined the effects of explicit representation of the variance of outcomes of simple gambles. In one experiment, specially constructed gambles manipulated variance without changing the probabilities and payoffs that were explicitly displayed to the subject (Slovic & Lichtenstein, 1968). To illustrate this, consider the upper half of Figure 9.1, which shows two bets: a duplex bet and a standard bet, which can be termed parallel because both have the same stated probabilities and the same payoffs, namely .6 chance to win $2 and .4 chance to lose $2. Imagine that the bets can be played by spinning pointers on the circular discs shown in Figure 9.1 such that one wins or loses the amount indicated by the final position of the pointer. To play a duplex bet, one must spin the pointer on both discs. Thus, one can win and not lose, lose and not win, both win and lose, or neither win nor lose. As a consequence, the duplex bet has much less variance than its parallel standard bet. That is, the standard bet leads either to a gain or loss of $2; however, by playing the duplex bet, one has a fairly high probability of breaking even. Most subjects perceived duplex bets and their parallel standard bets as equally attractive, which suggests that their judgments were based only on the explicitly stated probabilities and payoffs. The characteristics of the underlying distribution for the duplex bet did not exert any significant influence.

The second experiment (Payne & Braunstein, 1971) nicely complements the first. This experiment used pairs of duplex gambles with equal underlying distributions but different explicit probability values as illustrated in the lower half of Figure 9.1. Subjects showed strong preferences for one member of such pairs over the other, which further demonstrates the dominance of explicit or surface information.

These two experiments illustrate a form of concrete thinking (Slovic, 1972) whereby decision-makers appear to use only the information that is explicitly displayed in the formulation of the problem. Information that has to be inferred from the display or created by some mental transformation tends to be ignored. The tendency for considerations that are out of sight to be out of mind (see also

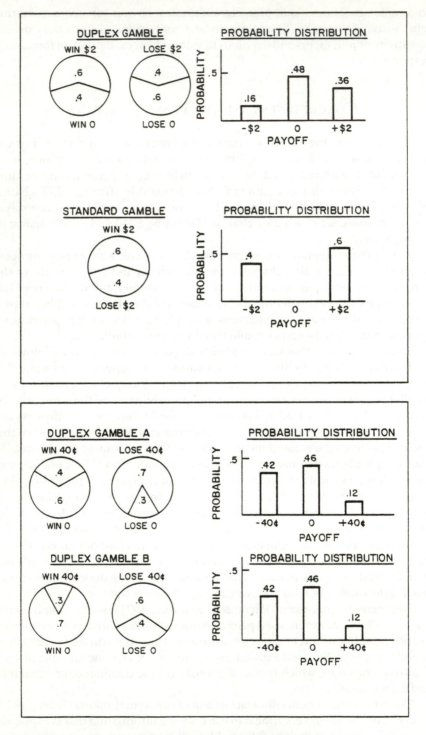

Source: Slovic and Lichtenstein (1968); Payne and Braunstein (1971).

Figure 9.1 *Experimental gambles*

Fischhoff, Slovic & Lichtenstein, 1978) imposes a serious burden on those entrusted with the presentation of risk information.

PROTECTIVE ACTION AND THE FRAMING OF CONTINGENCIES

Pseudocertainty

According to prospect theory, outcomes that are merely probable are underweighted in comparison with outcomes that are obtained with certainty. As a result, any protective action that reduces the probability of harm from, say, .01 to zero will be valued more highly than an action that reduces the probability of the same harm from .02 to .01.

Tversky and Kahneman (1982) noted that mental representations of protective actions can easily be manipulated so as to vary the apparent certainty with which they prevent harm. For example, an insurance policy that covers fire but not flood can be presented either as full protection against the specific risk of fire or as a reduction in the overall probability of property loss. Prospect theory predicts that the policy will appear more attractive in the former perspective, labeled *pseudocertainty*, in which it offers unconditional protection against a restricted set of problems.

We have tested this conjecture in the context of one particular kind of protection, vaccination. Two forms of a vaccination questionnaire were created. Form I (probabilistic protection) described a disease that was expected to afflict 20% of the population, and it asked people whether they would volunteer to receive a vaccine that protected half the people to whom it was administered. According to Form II (pseudocertainty), there were two mutually exclusive and equiprobable strains of the disease, each of which was expected to afflict 10% of the population; vaccination was said to give complete protection against one strain and no protection against the other. The 211 participants in this study were recruited by an advertisement in the University of Oregon student newspaper. Half received Form I; the other half received Form II. After reading the description, they rated the likelihood that they would get vaccinated in such a situation, using a 7-point scale ranging from 1 ('almost certainly would not get vaccinated') to 7 ('almost certainly would get vaccinated').

Although both forms indicated that vaccination reduced one's overall risk from 20% to 10%, we expected that vaccination would appear more attractive to those who received Form II (pseudocertainty) than to those who received form I (probabilistic insurance). The results confirmed this prediction: 57% of those who received Form II indicated that they would get vaccinated, compared to 40% for those who received Form I.

The pseudocertainty effect highlights the contrast between reduction and elimination of risk. As Tversky and Kahneman (1982) have indicated, this distinction is difficult to justify on normative grounds. Moreover, manipulations of certainty would seem to have important implications for the design and description of other forms of protection, such as medical treatments, insurance and flood- and earthquake-proofing activities.

Seat Belts

Research has demonstrated that seat belts are effective in reducing death and injury in automobile accidents and that most people are aware of this fact. However, the percentage of motorists who wear them is small, and numerous and expensive media campaigns have failed to persuade people to 'buckle up for safety' (Robertson, 1976).

The reluctance of motorists to wear seat belts is puzzling to many safety officials, in light of the high personal costs of a serious accident. One clue to motorists' reluctance is the finding of Slovic and others (1977) that perceived probability of loss was a key determinant of protective action in the context of insurance decisions. Extrapolating from insurance to seat belts, Slovic et al (1978) argued that resistance to the wearing of seat belts was understandable in light of the extremely small probability of an accident on a single automobile trip. Because a fatal accident occurs only about once in every 3.5 million person trips and a disabling injury only once in every 100,000 person trips, refusing to buckle one's seat belt prior to a single trip is not unreasonable.

The risks of driving can be framed differently, however. During the course of a 50-year lifetime of driving, the average motorist will take some 40,000 or more trips. The probability that one of these trips will end in a fatality is .01, and the probability of experiencing at least one disabling injury during this period is .33. It is as appropriate to consider these cumulative probabilities of death and disability as it is to consider the odds on a single trip. Slovic et al (1978) conducted a pilot study in which subjects were induced to adopt either a lifetime or a trip-by-trip perspective. Subjects in the lifetime condition responded more favorably toward the use of seat belts and toward the enactment of laws requiring the wearing of seat belts or the installation of air bags. As a result of exposure to single-trip risk statistics, fewer than 10% of the college students surveyed claimed that their use of seat belts would be changed, but 39% of those exposed to the cumulative probabilities said that they expected their use of seat belts to increase. Whereas 54% of the persons who received single-trip information favored mandatory protection, 78% of those exposed to lifetime probabilities favored such a law. Whether the favorable attitudes toward seat belts engendered by a lengthened time perspective will be maintained and translated into behavior remains to be determined.

INSURANCE DECISIONS AND THE FRAMING OF OUTCOMES

Traditionally, explanations of insurance decisions have been based on utility theory (Friedman & Savage, 1948), on the assumption that insurance can be conceptualized as a choice between acceptance either of a small probability of a large loss or of a certain small loss (the insurance premium). Recent research casts doubt on this conceptualization by showing that certain losses are more attractive when framed as insurance premiums rather than monetary losses.

We first began thinking about this issue when we noticed that preference data presented in an early paper on prospect theory (Kahneman & Tversky, 1975) differed from results that we had obtained with similar preferences portrayed as insurance problems (Slovic et al, 1977). Specifically, Kahneman and Tversky presented people with a choice between a certain loss, such as $50, and a probability of losing a larger amount, such as a .25 chance to lose $200. For each pair of options, the expected loss from the gamble was equal to the certain loss from its alternative. Our study had used similar problems in the context of insurance and called the certain loss an insurance premium. Whereas Kahneman and Tversky's subjects preferred the gambles for moderate or high probabilities of loss, ours preferred the insurance.

Intrigued by this discrepancy, we decided to explore the effects of context (insurance versus preference) more systematically. Two situations were studied. In one, people were presented with a choice between accepting a .001 chance of losing $5000 and a certain loss of $5; in the other, they were asked to choose between accepting a .25 chance of losing $200 and a certain loss of $50. The 208 subjects were paid volunteers who responded to an ad in a university newspaper. Each responded to only one problem situation (.001 or .25 chance of loss), which they initially received in only one context (insurance or preference). The results shown in Table 9.1 clearly indicate that the certain loss was more likely to be selected in the insurance as opposed to the preference context.

About one hour after the subjects had made these choices, they were presented again with the same problem, sometimes in the same context, sometimes in the other. When the context remained unchanged, so did choices: only 5% of the subjects changed their responses. However, when the second problem was framed differently, 29% changed their responses. In 85% of the cases when subjects changed their responses, subjects chose the gamble in the preference setting and the insurance premium in the insurance setting. Moreover, people who first saw the problem in the preference context were three times more likely to change as just described than those who saw it first in the insurance context. This suggests that people are more likely to realize that an insurance premium implies a certain loss than they are to realize that a certain loss represents an insurance premium. Varying probabilities and losses in a more systematic way than we did, Schoemaker and Kunreuther (1979) and Hershey and Schoemaker (1980) have obtained similar context effects with a wide variety of problems.

What causes this strong context effect? One explanation is that paying an insurance premium is not psychologically equivalent to choosing a sure loss. The insurance context forces an individual to acknowledge that he or she is at

Table 9.1 *Proportions of Subjects Choosing the Certain Loss in Insurance and Preference Contexts*

Context	Probability of loss	
	.001	*.25*
Insurance	37/56	26/40
	66%	65%
Preference	28/72	8/40
	39%	20%

risk. Paying a premium is an instrumental action that provides a benefit: it removes the risk; it buys safety. In contrast, accepting a certain loss is not perceived as saving one from an unattractive gamble. The logic of this interpretation is illustrated by the comments of a subject who chose the gamble in the preference condition and the premium in the insurance condition. When confronted with this inconsistency, the subject refused to change his preference, asserting that paying the premium seemed less aversive than choosing the certain loss. Asked whether he thought the preference and insurance problems were the same, he replied, 'Yes, they're the same, but they look different.'

A related interpretation is based on prospect theory, according to which one evaluates an option according to the change that it would make in one's position vis-à-vis some reference point. The theory also asserts that:

- Losses are valued more heavily than gains of the same magnitude.
- The individual becomes increasingly less sensitive to a given change in outcome as the stakes get larger (that is, the value function is concave above the reference point and convex below it).
- Low-probability events tend to be overestimated, although special weight is given to events that are certain.

If the preference context is interpreted as a comparison between a gamble and a certain loss, the reference point is the individual's status quo. The gamble would seem less aversive than the certain loss, both because large losses are somewhat discounted in comparison to small losses (the second point above) and because consequences that are certain to happen are given special weight (the third point above).

In the insurance context, however, the reference point is loss of the premium. The choice is then between paying the premium or accepting the gamble. For example, consider paying a $50 premium to avoid a .25 chance of losing $200. Accepting the gamble provides a 3/4 chance of gaining $50 (not paying the $50 premium and not losing on the gamble) and a 1/4 chance of losing $150 (losing $200 on the gamble but saving the $50 premium). Because losses loom larger than gains and small probabilities tend to be overestimated, this gamble should be valued negatively; that is, it should seem less attractive than staying at the reference point of the insurance policy.

A third (and much simpler) explanation proposed by Kahneman and Tversky (1979) and by Hershey and Schoemaker (1980) is that the insurance context may trigger social norms about prudent behavior that are not associated with the preference context. The latter, they claim, may actually stimulate a gambling orientation.

If the interpretations proposed here are validated by further investigations, they would have important implications for insurance decision-making and for protective behavior in general. The results suggest that people will be more likely to protect themselves from a probable hazard if they recognize that they are at risk and remain so unless they take protective action. Indeed, data from an extensive survey of people who did and did not insure themselves against flood or earthquake hazards support this notion (Kunreuther et al, 1978).

RESPONSE MODE, FRAMING AND INFORMATION PROCESSING

The way in which an individual has to respond to the decision problem is an important aspect of framing. Although people are sometimes free to choose their response mode, more often some external source defines the problem either as one of judgment (evaluating individual options) or as one of choice (selecting one from two or more options). Many theories of decision-making postulate an equivalence between judgment and choice. Such theories assume that each option X has a value $v(X)$ that determines its attractiveness in both contexts (eg, Luce, 1977). However, the descriptive validity of these theories is now in question. Much recent research has demonstrated that the information-processing strategies used prior to making choices are often quite different from the strategies employed in judging single options. As a result, choices and evaluative judgments of the same options often differ, sometimes dramatically. The conditions under which judgment and choice are similar or different need to be better understood (Einhorn & Hogarth, 1981).

Justification and Choice

One conception asserts that much of the deliberation prior to choice consists of finding a concise, coherent set of reasons that justify the selection of one option over the others. For example, Tversky (1972) provided evidence to support an 'elimination by aspects' model of choice. According to this model, options are viewed as sets of aspects; that is, a car has a price, a model, a color and so forth. At each stage in the choice process, one aspect is selected, with probability proportional to its importance. The options that are not adequate for each selected aspect are eliminated from the set of options considered at the following stage. Tversky argued that elimination by aspects is an appealing process because it is easy both to apply and to justify. It permits a choice to be resolved in a clear-cut fashion without reliance on relative weights, trade-off functions or other numerical computations, and eases demands on the decision-maker's limited capacity for intuitive calculation.

Another example of justification processes comes from a study of difficult choices (Slovic, 1975). Each of two options was defined by two dimensions differing in importance. To maximize the difficulty of choice, these paired options were designed to have equal value by making the option that was superior on the more important dimension to be so inferior on the lesser dimension that its advantage was canceled. The equating of options was done judgmentally. For example, one set of options involved gift packages with two components, cash and a coupon book offering miscellaneous products and services. The subject was shown two such gift packages with one component missing (see Table 9.2). The subject was asked to supply a value for the missing component large enough to make the two options equally attractive. Many different types of stimuli were used (eg, gift packages, pairs of jobs, routes to work), and the missing component was varied within each pair. Subjects were asked to equate various pairs of options and then to choose between them.

Contrary to the predictions of most choice theories, choices between these equally attractive alternatives were not made randomly. Rather, most subjects

Table 9.2 *A Typical Choice Pair*

	Cash ($)	Coupon book worth ($)
Gift package A	10	—
Gift package B	20	18

Source: Slovic 1975

consistently selected the option that was superior on the more important dimension. For the example in Table 9.2, cash was generally viewed as more important than the coupon book, and, among pairs of equated gift packages, the option that offered more cash was selected 79% of the time. Apparently, reliance on the more important dimension makes a better justification ('I chose this gift package because it provided more cash') than random selection ('They looked about equally attractive, so I flipped a coin').

Another demonstration of justification in choice comes from a study that presented college students and members of the League of Women Voters with both of the tasks shown in Figure 9.2 and Table 9.3 (Fischhoff, Slovic & Lichtenstein, 1980).

In the first task (Table 9.3), subjects chose between a high variance and a low variance option involving the loss of life. In the second task, they were asked to evaluate three functions representing the way in which society should evaluate lives in multifatality situations. The instructions for the second task provided elaborate rationales for adopting each of the functional forms over a range between zero and 100 lives lost in a single accident. Curve 1, the linear form, represents the view that every life lost is equally costly to society. Curve 2, the exponentially increasing function, represents the view that large losses of life are disproportionately serious – for example, that the loss of 20 lives is more than twice as bad as the loss of 10 lives. Curve 3 represents a reduced sensitivity to large losses of life; for example, the loss of 20 lives is less than twice as bad as the loss of 10 lives. Subjects were asked to study each curve and its rationale and then to indicate the ones with which they agreed most and least.

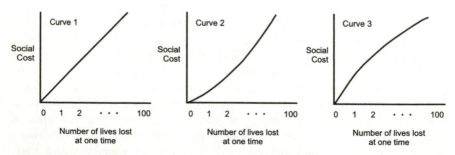

Note: subjects were asked to rank the three proposals in order of preference.

Figure 9.2 *Task 2: The impact of catastrophic events*

Table 9.3 *Task 1: Emergency Response*

A committee in a large metropolitan area met recently to discuss contingency plans in the event of various emergencies. One emergency threat under consideration posed two options, both involving some loss of life. These are described below. Read them and indicate your opinion about the relative merits of each.

> **Option A** carries with it a .5 probability of containing the threat with a loss of 5 lives and a .5 probability of losing 95 lives. It is like taking the gamble: .5 lose 5 lives, .5 lose 95 lives.

> **Option B** carries with it a .5 probability of containing the threat with a loss of 40 lives and a .5 probability of losing 60 lives. It is like taking the gamble: .5 lose 40 lives, .5 lose 60 lives.

Which option would you select? Option A _____   Option B _____

More than half of all subjects chose option *A* in task 1 (Table 9.3) and agreed most with curve 2 in task 2 (Figure 9.2). However, option *A* indicates a risk-seeking attitude toward loss of life, whereas curve 2 represents risk aversion. Choice of option *A* would be consistent with curve 3, which was the least favored view. These inconsistent results did not change appreciably when the degree of elaboration in the rationales given for the three curves was changed.

Subjects who were confronted with the inconsistency in their responses refused to change. They claimed to see no connection between the two tasks. Most appeared to be relying on some variant of this justification offered for choosing option *A*: 'It would be immoral to allow the loss of 40 lives or more when option *A* presents a good chance of coming out of the situation with little loss of life.' This perspective was evoked by the structure of the choice problem but not by the task of evaluating the three functional relationships.

Because many theorists have proposed to use such choices as these to infer people's value functions (eg, Johnson & Huber, 1977; Raiffa, 1968), the results presented here may give cause for concern about this practice.

Anchoring and Adjustment

Just as choice problems trigger justification processes, single numerical judgments are prone to being influenced by anchoring and adjustment. In this process, a natural starting point is used as a first approximation or anchor for the judgment. This anchor is then adjusted to accommodate the implications of additional information. Often, the adjustment is smaller than it should be, considering the importance of the new information. An example of how anchoring can lead to strong differences between evaluation and choice comes from two experiments (Lichtenstein & Slovic, 1971; 1973), one of which was conducted on the floor of the Four Queens Casino in Las Vegas. Consider the following pair of gambles used in the Las Vegas experiment: bet *A*: 11/12 chance to win 12 chips, and 1/12 chance to lose 24 chips; bet *B*: 2/12 chance to win 79 chips, and 10/12 chance to lose 5 chips, where the value of each chip was 25¢. Notice that bet *A* had a much better chance of winning and that bet *B* offered a higher winning payoff. Subjects indicated, in two ways, the attractiveness of each bet in many such pairs. First, they made a simple choice, A or B. Later, they were asked to assume that they owned a ticket to play each bet, and they were to state the lowest price for which they would sell this ticket.

Presumably, both these selling prices and choices were governed by the same underlying factor, the attractiveness of each gamble. Therefore, subjects should have stated higher selling prices for the gambles that they preferred in the choice situation. In fact, subjects often chose one gamble yet stated a higher selling price for the other. For the particular pair of gambles just mentioned, bets A and B were chosen about equally often. However, bet B received a higher selling price about 88% of the time. Of the subjects who chose bet A, 87% gave a higher selling price to bet B, thus exhibiting an inconsistent preference pattern. Grether and Plott (1979), two skeptical economists, replicated this study with numerous variations designed to show that the observed inconsistencies were artifactual. They obtained essentially the same results as Lichtenstein and Slovic.

What accounts for this inconsistent pattern of preferences for gambles? Lichtenstein and Slovic concluded that subjects used different cognitive strategies when setting prices and making choices. Subjects often justified the choice of bet A in terms of its good odds, but they set a higher price for B because they anchored on its large winning payoff. For example, people who found a gamble basically attractive used the amount to win as a starting point. They then adjusted the amount to win downward to accommodate the less-than-perfect chance of winning and the fact that there was some amount to lose as well. Typically, this adjustment was small and, as a result, large winning payoffs caused people to set prices that were inconsistent with their choices.

Another way of looking at these results is in terms of the notion of compatibility. Because a selling price is expressed in terms of monetary units, subjects apparently found it easier to use the monetary aspects of the gamble to produce this type of response. Compatibility made the amount to win an anchor, which caused that aspect to dominate the response. Such bias did not exist with the choices, because each attribute of one gamble could be compared directly with the same attribute of the other. With no reason to use payoffs as a starting point, subjects were free to use other rules to determine (or to justify) their choices.

Compatibility Bias

A compatibility hypothesis was tested directly in a study by Slovic and MacPhillamy (1974). They predicted that dimensions common to each option in a choice situation would have greater influence than dimensions that were unique to a particular option. They asked subjects to compare pairs of students and to predict, on the basis of scores on two cue dimensions (tests), which student would get the higher college grade point average. One dimension was common to both students, while the other was unique. For example, student A might be described in terms of scores on tests of English skill and quantitative ability, whereas student B might be described by scores on tests of English skill and need for achievement.

In this example, the compatibility hypothesis implies that English skill will be weighted particularly heavily, because it is common to both students. The rationale is that a comparison between two students along the same dimension should be cognitively easier than a comparison between two students along different dimensions. The data strongly confirmed this hypothesis. Dimensions were weighted more heavily when common than when unique. After the experiment, most subjects indicated they had not wanted to give more weight to the common dimension and they were unaware of having done so.

There is, of course, no common dimension when students are judged one at a time; hence, one would expect a dimension that was common in choice to be given less weight in a judgment task. Evidence for this was also found. For example, consider student A, who scored 470 on English skill and 674 on quantitative ability and whose need-for-achievement score was missing. Twenty-four of 26 subjects gave student A a higher rating (that is, judgment) than student B, who had scored 566 on English and 474 on need for achievement, but whose quantitative score was missing. However, when choosing between students A and B, 10 subjects who had given a higher rating to student A chose B but only two reversed in the other direction. Many other such differences between judgment and choice can be found in Slovic and MacPhillamy's (1974) data.

IMPLICATIONS FOR RISK ASSESSMENT

The message of this research is that the amalgamation of different types of information and values in an overall judgment or decision is a difficult cognitive process. Even when all factors are known and made explicit, subtle aspects of problem formulation, acting in combination with our intellectual predispositions and limitations, affect the balance that we strike among them. These effects seem endemic to a wide range of behaviors. Here, we discuss briefly their implications for two important components of risk assessment.

Eliciting Labile Values

Value judgments indicating the desired trade-offs between important decision outcomes lie at the heart of individual and societal risk assessment. For example, a person considering either surgery or radiation therapy as treatment for lung cancer must balance the enhanced life expectancy that surgery confers against the greater risk of sudden death that it entails (McNeil, Weichselbaum & Pauker, 1978). The evaluation that society makes of different energy technologies can be guided, in part, by whether it decides to give particularly great weight to potentially catastrophic accidents. Many observers advocate making such values explicit to help individuals and society to make better decisions. Some observers call for direct elicitation of values through surveys, hearings and the like, whereas others prefer to infer values from the preferences revealed by actual decisions. Both approaches assume that people know their own values and that elicitation methods are unbiased channels that translate subjective feelings into analytically usable expressions.

We doubt these assumptions. First, decision problems with high stakes tend to be unique and unfamiliar. They take us into situations in which we have never thought through the implications of values and beliefs acquired in simpler, more familiar settings. Second, due to the strong effects of framing and information-processing considerations, elicitation procedures become major forces in shaping the expression of values, especially when such values are ill defined (Fischhoff, Slovic & Lichtenstein, 1980). In such cases, the method becomes the message. Subtle aspects of how problems are posed, questions are phrased and responses are elicited can have substantial impact on judgments that supposedly express people's preferences.

One could hope that further research and analysis would identify better ways to ask questions about values. Although some methods distort values and should be avoided, others educate and deepen the respondent's perspectives. If we are interested in what people really feel about a value issue, there may be no substitute for an interactive elicitation procedure, one that employs multiple methods and acknowledges the elicitor's role in helping the respondent to create and enunciate values.

Informing People About Risk

One dramatic change in recent years is growing public awareness of the risks encountered in daily experience. Radiation hazards, medicinal side effects, occupational disease, food contaminants, toxic chemicals and mechanical malfunctions increasingly seem to fill our newspapers and our thoughts. A consequence of this growing awareness has been pressure on designers and regulators of hazardous enterprises to inform people about the risks that they face (Morris, Mazis & Barofsky, 1980; Slovic, Fischhoff & Lichtenstein, 1980b).

Clearly, better information about risk is crucial to making better personal decisions and to participating more effectively in the political processes through which societal standards are developed and enforced. Despite good intentions, however, it may be quite difficult to create effective informational programs. Doing an adequate job means finding cogent ways of presenting complex, technical material that is clouded by uncertainty and subject to distortion by the listener's preconceptions – or misconceptions – about the hazard and its consequences. Moreover, as we have seen, people are often at the mercy of the way in which problems are formulated. Those responsible for determining the content and format of information programs thus have considerable ability to manipulate perceptions. Moreover, because these effects are not widely known, people may inadvertently be manipulating their own perceptions by casual decisions they make about how to organize their knowledge.

The stakes in risk problems are high – product viability, jobs, energy costs, willingness of patients to accept treatments, public safety and health and so forth. Potential conflicts of interest abound. When subtle aspects of how (or what) information is presented make a significant difference in people's responses, one needs to determine the formulation that should be used. Making that decision takes one out of psychology and into the domains of law, ethics and politics.

Acknowledgments

The authors wish to thank Amos Tversky for comments on an earlier draft of this chapter. The writing was supported by the National Science Foundation under

Grant PRS79-11934 to Clark University under subcontract to Perceptronics, Inc. All opinions, findings, conclusions and recommendations expressed in this chapter are those of the authors and do not necessarily reflect the views of the National Science Foundation.

10 The Nature of Technological Hazard

Christoph Hohenemser, Robert W Kates and Paul Slovic

Each year the hazards associated with technology lead to illness and death, as well as varying environmental, social and economic impacts; these effects correspond to a significant fraction of the gross national product (Harriss et al, 1978; Tuller, 1985). Despite the burden imposed by technological hazards and the broad regulatory effort devoted to their control, there have been few studies comparing the nature of technological hazards in terms of generic characteristics. Most investigators have produced case studies (Lawless, 1977), comparative risk assessments of alternative technologies (Inhaber, 1979; National Research Council, 1980b), comparative lists of hazard consequences (Wilson, 1979; Cohen & Lee, 1979), or comparative costs of reducing loss (US Department of Transportation, 1976; Schwing, 1979; Lave, 1981).

A first step in ordering the domain of hazards should be classification. Today technological hazards are classified by the source (automotive emissions), use (medical X-rays), potential for harm (explosions), population exposed (asbestos workers), environmental pathways (air pollution), or varied consequences (cancer, property loss). One scheme is chosen, usually as a function of historical or professional choice and the relevant regulatory organizations, even though most technological hazards fall into several categories. For example, a specific chemical may be a toxic substance, a consumer product, an air or land pollutant, a threat to worker health or a prescription drug. Indeed, a major achievement has been the cross-listing of several of these domains of hazardous substances by their environmental pathways (Greenwood, Kingsbury & Cleland, 1979).

We have sought to identify common differentiating characteristics of technological hazards in order to simplify analysis and management of them. Technological hazards may be thought of as involving potentially harmful releases of energy and materials. We characterized the stages of hazard causation by 12 physical, biological and social descriptors that can be measured quantitatively;

Note: reprinted with permission from 'The Nature of Technological Hazard' by C Hohenemser, R W Kates and P Slovic in *Science*, 220, 1983, pp378–84. Copyright 1983 American Association for the Advancement of Science.

we then scored 93 technological hazards and analyzed the structure of correlations among them. In this article we present a highly condensed account of our analysis (Hohenemser et al, 1983).

MEASURES OF HAZARDOUSNESS

We should first distinguish between the terms hazard and risk. Hazards are threats to humans and what they value, whereas risks are quantitative measures of hazard consequences that can be expressed as conditional probabilities of experiencing harm. Thus, we think of automobile usage as a hazard but say that the lifetime risk of dying in an auto accident is 2 to 3 percent of all ways of dying.

We conceive of technological hazards as a sequence of causally connected events leading from human needs and wants to the selection of a technology, to the possible release of materials and energy, to human exposure, and eventually to harmful consequences (Figure 10.1). To differentiate among types of hazards, we defined 12 measures for individual hazards and applied them to the appropriate stage in this chain. We selected descriptors (Figure 10.1 and Table 10.1) that would be applicable to all technological hazards, comprehensible to ordinary people and could be expressed by common units or distinctions.

One variable describes the degree to which hazards are intentional, four characterize the release of energy and materials, two deal with exposure, and five apply to consequences (Figure 10.1). Only one descriptor, annual human mortality, is closely related to the traditional idea of risk as the probability of dying; the others considerably expand and delineate the quality of hazardousness. Four descriptors require categorical distinctions and eight use logarithmic scales (Table 10.1). Logarithmic scales are practical for cases where successive occurrences range over a factor of 10 or more in magnitude and where estimated errors easily differ by the same amount. Logarithmic scales may also match human perception better than linear scales, as seen by the success of the decibel scale for sound intensity and the Richter scale for earthquake intensity.

Hazards were selected from a variety of sources (Lawless, 1977; US Department of Transportation, 1976; Slovic, Lichtenstein et al, 1979; Slovic, Fischhoff & Lichtenstein, 1985) and, after scoring, were found to be well distributed on the 12 scales (Figure 10.2). Where appropriate, hazards were scored by reference to the scientific literature. Many cases were discussed by two or more individuals, or referred to specialists for clarification. When the results of this scoring were checked for consistency, changes of 1 or 2 points were made in 8% of the scores and 3 points or more in a few scores (< 1%). We therefore believe replicability to be within ± 1 scale point in most cases.

HAZARD CLASSIFICATION

Many investigators have developed descriptive classifications of technological hazards (Starr, 1969; Burton et al, 1968; Lowrance, 1976; Rowe, 1977; Litai, Lanning & Rasmussen, 1983; Slovic, Fischhoff & Lichtenstein, 1980c). Though

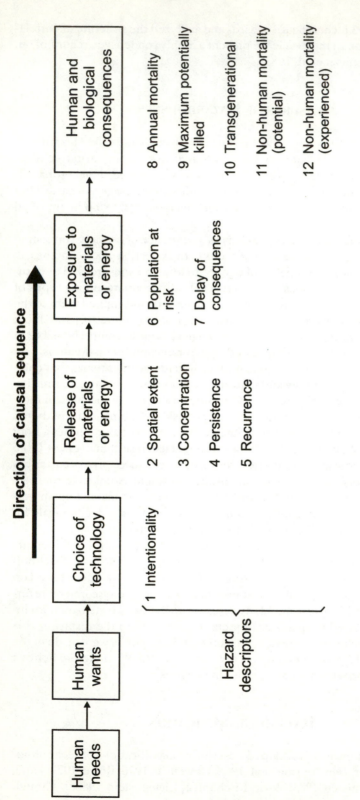

Figure 10.1 *Causal structure of technological hazards illustrated by a simplified causal sequence (Hazard descriptors used for classifying hazards are shown below the stage to which they apply)*

Table 10.1 *Hazard Descriptor Scales*

Technology descriptor

1   Intentionality. Measures the degree to which technology is intended to harm by a categorical scale: 3, not intended to harm living organisms; 6, intended to harm non-human living organisms; 9, intended to harm humans.

Release descriptors

2   Spatial extent. Measures the maximum distance over which a single event has significant impact on a logarithmic scale, $1 < s < 9$, where $s = \log_{10} d + 1$ rounded to the nearest positive integer, and d is the distance in meters.

3   Concentration. Measures the concentration of released energy or materials relative to natural background on a logarithmic scale, $1 < s < 8$. For materials and non-thermal radiation $s = \log_{10} R + 2$ rounded to the nearest positive integer, where R is the average concentration of release divided by the background concentration. For mechanical energy, $s = \log_2 a + 0.68$ rounded to the nearest positive integer, where a is the acceleration to which individuals are exposed measured in units of the acceleration of gravity. For thermal energy, $s = \log_2 f + 0.68$ rounded to the nearest positive integer, where f is the thermal flux expressed in units of the solar flux.

4   Persistence. Measures the time over which a release remains a significant threat to humans on a logarithmic scale, $1 < s < 9$, with $s = \log_{10} t + 1$ rounded to the nearest positive integer where t is the time measured in minutes.

5   Recurrence. Measures the mean time interval between releases above a minimum significant level on a logarithmic scale identical to that used for persistence.

Exposure descriptors

6   Population at risk. Measures the number of people in the US potentially exposed to the hazard on a logarithmic scale, $1 < s < 9$, with $s = \log_{10} P$ rounded to the nearest integer where P is the population.

7   Delay. Measures the delay time between exposure to the hazard release and the occurrence of consequences on the logarithmic scale defined for persistence.

Consequence descriptors

8   Human mortality (annual). Measures average annual deaths in the US due to the hazard on the logarithmic scale defined for population at risk.

9   Human mortality (maximum). Measures the maximum credible number of deaths in a single event on the logarithmic scale defined for population at risk.

10   Transgenerational. Measures the number of future generations at risk from the hazard on a categorical scale: 3, hazard affects the exposed generation only; 6, hazard affects children of the exposed generation and no others; 9, hazard affects more than one future generation.

11   Non-human mortality (potential). Measures the maximum potential of non-human mortality on a categorical scale: 3, no potential non-human mortality; 6, significant potential non-human mortality; 9, potential or experienced species extinction.

12   Non-human mortality (experienced). Measures non-human mortality that has actually been experienced on a categorical scale: 3, no experienced non-human mortality; 6, significant experienced non-human mortality; 9, experienced species extinction.

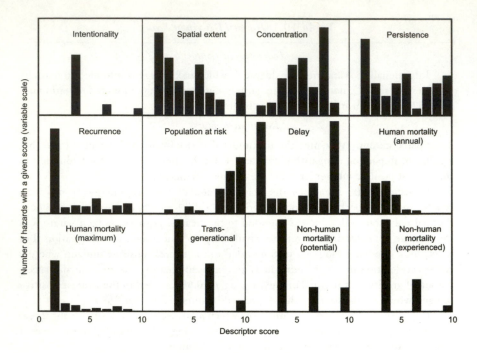

Figure 10.2 *Descriptor frequency distributions for 93 hazards*

mindful of this work, we based our classification entirely on the causal structure descriptors defined in Table 10.1.

Energy versus Materials Hazards

A simple, but significant, distinction is the division of hazards into those resulting from energy releases and those from materials releases. Comparison of 33 energy hazards and 60 materials hazards reveals four striking differences (Hohenemser et al, 1983).

1 Energy releases persist for short periods, averaging less than a minute; materials releases persist on average for a week or more.
2 Energy hazards have immediate consequences, with exposure-consequence delays of less than a minute; materials hazards have exposure-consequence delays averaging one month.
3 Energy hazards have only minor transgenerational effects; materials hazards affect on average one future generation.
4 Energy hazards have little potential non-human mortality; materials hazards significantly affect potential non-human mortality.

Reducing the Number of Dimensions

In addition to simple division of hazards by release class, we explored the extent to which hazards may be grouped according to causal structure. Using principal component factors analysis, we derived five orthogonal composite dimensions

Table 10.2 *Factor Structure*

Factor	Variance explained	Name	Factor loading [a]
		Hazard descriptors	
Biocidal	.21	Non-human mortality (experienced)	.87
		Non-human mortality (potential)	.79
		Intentionality	.81
Delay	.21	Persistence	.81
		Delay	.85
		Transgenerational effects	.84
Catastrophic	.18	Recurrence	.91
		Human mortality (maximum)	.89
Mortality	.11	Human mortality (annual)	.85
Global	.11	Population at risk	.73
		Concentration	−.73
Residual		Spatial extent	

[a] Factor loadings are the result of varimax rotation.

(factors) that account for 81% of the variance of the sample.[1] This means that the causal structure of each of the 93 hazards, and probably others to be scored in the future, can be described by 5 variables, rather than by 12.

The relation of the derived factors to the original set of descriptors is summarized in Table 10.2. The names given to the factors – biocidal, delay, catastrophic, mortality and global – are intended to aid the intuition and are related to the descriptors that define each factor. The first four factors use descriptors whose scores increase as the factor increases (positive factor loadings), but the factor global is different. Because of negative loading of concentration, hazards scoring highest on global are high in population at risk and low in concentration (that is, diffuse) (Table 10.2). The factor global thus defines a special combination of hazardousness with widespread exposure and a concentration of release that is modest with respect to background.

Several tests indicate that the factor structure does not change significantly when hazards are added and deleted from the sample, or when scoring changes comparable to the estimated scoring errors are made. Thus, an initially chosen set of 66 hazards yielded the same factor structure as the final 93; changing 10% of the scores by 1 to 3 scale points had no significant effect. Furthermore, removal of 24 hazards with the most extreme factor scores produced only minor changes in factor structure, an unexpected finding since extreme scores often dominate the analysis.

Scores of the 93 hazards and the derived factor structure are summarized in Table 10.3. Individual descriptor scores have been grouped by factor into a 12-digit descriptor code, and extreme scores on each factor have been identified through a five-digit factor code, with the use of truncated factor scores (Hohenemser et al, 1983).

Table 10.3 *Descriptor and Factor Codes for 93 Hazards*

Hazard	Descriptor Code [a]	Factor Code [b]
ENERGY HAZARDS		
1 Appliances – fire	333-333-42-3-95-2	00000
2 Appliances – shock	333-113-21-3-95-1	00000
3 Auto – crashes	333-113-11-5-96-2	00010
4 Aviation – commercial – crashes	333-113-63-3-97-4	00100
5 Aviation – commercial – noise	333-213-11-1-85-5	00000
6 Aviation – private – crashes	333-113-32-4-97-4	00010
7 Aviation – supersonic transport noise	333-313-41-1-76-5	00000
8 Bicycles – crashes	333-113-11-3-84-2	00000
9 Bridges – collapse	333-113-53-1-95-3	00000
10 Chainsaws – accidents	666-113-11-1-74-2	10000
11 Coal mining – accidents	333-233-53-3-64-3	00000
12 Dams – failure	693-423-74-2-85-5	10100*
13 Downhill skiing – falls	333-113-21-2-63-1	00000
14 Dynamite blasts – accidents	333-113-32-2-65-3	00000
15 Elevators – falls	333-113-52-2-96-2	00000
16 Fireworks – accidents	333-113-31-1-83-2	00000
17 Handguns – shootings	369-113-41-4-96-1	10010*
18 High construction – falls	333-113-71-1-28-2	00000
19 High voltage wires – electric fields	333-173-11-1-74-3	00000
20 Liquefied natural gas – explosions	363-213-85-1-86-5	00100
21 Medical X-rays – radiation	333-189-11-4-92-2	00011*
22 Microwave ovens – radiation	333-173-11-1-84-2	00000
23 Motorcycles – accidents	333-113-11-4-76-2	00010
24 Motor vehicles – noise	333-213-11-1-83-3	00000
25 Motor vehicles – racing crashes	333-113-52-2-67-2	00000
26 Nuclear war – blast	699-213-87-4-98-6	10110*
27 Power mowers – accidents	333-113-21-2-73-2	00000
28 Skateboards – falls	333-113-11-3-73-1	00000
29 Skydiving – accidents	333-113-51-2-48-1	00000
30 Skyscrapers – fire	333-423-53-3-85-4	00000
31 Smoking – fires	333-433-32-3-85-1	00000
32 Snowmobiles – collisions	333-113-41-2-73-2	00000
33 Space vehicles – crashes	333-313-84-1-98-5	00100
34 Tractors – accidents	333-113-41-2-74-2	00000
35 Trains – crashes	333-213-53-3-84-3	00000
36 Trampolines – falls	333-113-51-1-74-2	00000
MATERIALS HAZARDS		
37 Alcohol – accidents	333-313-11-4-95-2	00010
38 Alcohol – chronic effects	333-486-11-5-85-1	00010
39 Antibiotics – bacterial resistance	666-563-11-3-97-1	10000
40 Asbestos insulation – toxic effects	333-583-11-3-56-3	00000
41 Asbestos spray – toxic effects	333-583-11-1-83-3	00000
42 Aspirin – overdose	333-456-11-3-97-1	00000
43 Auto – CO pollution	333-346-11-2-94-4	00000
44 Auto – lead pollution	663-976-11-2-95-5	01000
45 Cadmium – toxic effects	663-986-11-2-74-6	01000

Table 10.3 *continued*

Hazard	Descriptor Code [a]	Factor Code [b]
46 Caffeine – chronic effects	333-566-11-1-95-1	00000
47 Coal burning – NO_x pollution	693-566-11-3-95-7	10000
48 Coal burning – SO_2 pollution	693-563-11-4-94-7	10010*
49 Coal burning – black lung	333-483-11-4-64-3	00010
50 Contraceptive IUDs – side effects	333-763-11-2-67-1	00000
51 Contraceptive pills – side effects	333-586-11-3-74-1	00000
52 Darvon – overdose	333-556-11-4-77-1	00010
53 DDT – toxic effects	996-886-32-1-87-5	11000*
54 Deforestation – CO_2 release	696-993-11-1-91-9	10001*
55 Diesthylstilbestrol (DES) – animal feed – human toxicity	333-586-11-1-93-1	00001
56 Fertilizer – NO_x pollution	393-686-11-1-93-9	00001
57 Fluorocarbons – ozone depletion	393-883-11-1-97-9	00000
58 Fossil fuels – CO_2 release	393-993-11-1-92-9	00001
59 Hair dyes – coal tar exposure	333-286-11-1-87-1	00000
60 Hexachlorophene – toxic effects	666-363-11-2-87-1	10000
61 Home pools – drowning	333-223-41-3-83-1	00000
62 Laetrile – toxic effects	333-553-11-1-55-1	00000
63 Lead paint – human toxicity	333-773-11-3-75-2	00000
64 Mercury – toxic effects	663-986-13-2-85-5	01000
65 Mirex pesticide – toxic effects	696-886-22-1-67-5	11000*
66 Nerve gas – accidents	669-836-73-1-77-5	10100*
67 Nerve gas – war use	699-836-87-3-97-7	10100*
68 Nitrite preservative – toxic effects	636-786-11-1-91-1	00001
69 Nuclear reactor – radiation release	363-969-86-1-96-7	01100*
70 Nuclear tests – fallout	663-989-73-3-91-9	01101*
71 Nuclear war – radiation effects	699-989-88-4-97-9	11110*
72 Nuclear waste – radiation effects	363-989-15-1-82-6	01001*
73 Oil tankers – spills	663-763-61-1-15-6	00000
74 PCBs – toxic effects	663-976-13-1-97-6	01000
75 Pesticides – human toxicity	996-886-12-2-97-5	11000*
76 PVC – human toxicity	333-486-11-2-77-4	00000
77 Recombinant DNA – harmful release	393-869-97-1-97-9	01100*
78 Recreational boating – drowning	333-223-51-4-83-2	00010
79 Rubber manufacture – toxic exposure	333-986-11-3-57-4	01000
80 Saccharin – cancer	333-486-11-1-87-1	00000
81 Smoking – chronic effects	333-486-11-6-85-1	00010
82 Supersonic transport – ozone depletion	393-893-11-1-93-9	00001
83 Taconite mining – water pollution	663-983-11-1-67-6	00000
84 Thalidomide – side effects	333-456-51-1-17-1	00000
85 Trichloroethylene – toxic effects	333-983-11-1-87-4	00000
86 2, 4, 5-T herbicide – toxic effects	696-886-22-1-77-5	11000*
87 Underwater construction – accidents	333-223-61-1-44-3	00000
88 Uranium mining – radiation	333-989-12-2-64-5	01000

Table 10.3 *continued*

Hazard	Descriptor Code [a]	Factor Code [b]
89 Vaccines – side effects	696-556-11-2-84-1	10000
90 Valium – misuse	333-566-11-3-87-1	00000
91 Warfarin – human toxicity	666-653-11-1-87-1	10000
92 Water chlorination – toxic effects	666-583-11-1-97-5	10000
93 Water fluoridation – toxic effects	333-786-11-1-82-5	00001

[a] Consists of a digit for each descriptor, and represents scores on the scales defined in Table 10.1. To help visualize the factor structure, descriptors have been grouped by factor in the order defined in Table 10.2.
[b] Consists of a single digit for each factor, and identifies extreme scores by '1' and non-extreme scores by '0', and also follows the order defined in Table 10.2. Hazards with two or more extreme factors are identified with an asterisk (*).

Inspection of Table 10.3 permits quick identification of dimensions that dominate hazardousness in specific cases. For example, commercial aviation (crashes) is high in the catastrophic factor and non-distinctive in the other four; power mower accidents are extreme in none of the five factors; nuclear war (radiation effects) is extreme in four.

The results of the coding in Table 10.3 led naturally to a seven-class taxonomy with three major groupings (Table 10.4). The first major group, multiple extreme hazards, includes cases with extreme scores in two or more factors; the second, extreme hazards, has cases with extreme scores on one factor; the third group, hazards, contains all the other cases. The group into which a hazard falls depends, of course, on the cutoff for the designation extreme. Although the location of the cutoff is ultimately a policy question, our preliminary definition is arbitrary.[1]

How appropriate and useful is our approach to hazard classification? To succeed it must describe the essential elements that make specific hazards threatening to humans and what they value, reflect the concerns of society and offer new tools for managing hazards. On the first point, we invite the review and evaluation of specialists; on the second and third points, we have additional evidence that we discuss below.

Table 10.4 *A Seven-class Taxonomy*

Class	Examples
Multiple extreme hazards	Nuclear war (radiation), recombinant DNA, pesticides
Extreme hazards	
Intentional biocides	Chainsaws, antibiotics, vaccines
Persistent teratogens	Uranium mining, rubber manufacture
Rare catastrophes	LNG explosions, commercial aviation (crashes)
Common killers	Auto crashes, coal mining (black lung)
Diffuse global threats	Fossil fuel (CO_2 release), SST (ozone depletion)
Hazards	Saccharin, aspirin, appliances, skateboards, bicycles

COMPARING PERCEPTIONS

Although the scores for 93 hazards are the result of judgments, we relied on explicit methods, a scientific framework and deliberate efforts to control bias. These attributes are not necessarily part of the judgments made by the general public. Indeed, many scientists believe that lay judgments about hazards vary widely from scientifically derived judgments (Kasper, 1980).

Because policies governing various types of hazards are determined to a large extent by people who are not scientists or hazard-assessment experts, it is important to know whether laypeople are able to understand and judge our hazard descriptors and whether these descriptors capture their concerns. The results of a pilot study that we conducted with 34 college-educated people (24 men and 10 women, mean age 24) living in Eugene, Oregon, are interesting.

To test the perceptions of these people we created non-technical definitions and simple scoring instructions for the causal descriptors of hazards and asked the subjects to score our sample of 93 hazards (Hohenemser et al, 1983). After an initial trial, concentration was judged to be too difficult for our respondents to score. For similar reasons, 12 of the less familiar hazards were omitted. The subjects then scored 81 hazards on 11 measures from our instructions and their general knowledge, reasoning and intuition.

The results indicate reasonably high correlations between the scores derived from the scientific literature and the mean judgments of our lay sample ($r = .65$ to .96; Hohenemser et al, 1983). But despite these high correlation coefficients, deviations of a factor of 1000 between scientific and lay estimates were encountered, suggesting that there were strong biases among our subjects for some descriptors and some hazards. The subjects also tended to compress the hazard scale, systematically overvaluing low-scoring hazards and undervaluing high-scoring hazards. Because this effect appeared in the scores of individual subjects, it was not an artifact of regression toward the mean. Similar effects were reported by Lichtenstein et al (1978) in comparisons of perceived risk with scientific estimates of annual mortality.

To test whether our descriptors by causes of hazards would capture our subjects' overall concern with risk, we collected judgments of perceived risk, a global risk measure whose determinants have been explored in other psychometric studies (Slovic, Lichtenstein et al, 1979, 1985; Slovic, Fischhoff & Lichtenstein, 1980c). Subjects were asked to consider 'the risk of dying across all of US society', as a consequence of the hazard in question, and to express their judgment on a relative scale of 1 to 100. Moderate positive correlations between perceived risk and our descriptor scores were obtained in 9 of 12 cases (Table 10.5).

The five factors from Table 10.2 also showed modest positive correlations with perceived risk. Because the factors are linearly independent, the summed variance of the factors may be used to determine the total variance explained. With the sample of 34 Oregonians we find that our descriptors account for about 50% of the variance in perceived risk.

Perhaps the most striking aspect of these results is that perceived risk shows no significant correlation with the factor mortality. Thus, the variable most frequently chosen by scientists to represent risk appears not to be a strong factor in the judgment of our subjects.

Table 10.5 *Correlation of Causal Structure Descriptors with Psychometrically Determined Values of Perceived Risk for 81 Hazards*

Causal Structure Descriptors		r
Technology descriptor:	Intentionality	.28
Release descriptors:	Spatial extent	.57
	Concentration	—
	Persistence	.42
	Recurrence	—
Exposure descriptors:	Population at risk	.42
	Delay	.30
Consequence descriptors:	Human mortality (annual)	—
	Human mortality (maximum)	.53
	Transgenerational	.43
	Nonhuman mortality (potential)	.53
	Nonhuman mortality (experienced)	.30
Factors:	Biocidal	.32
	Delay	.41
	Catastrophic	.32
	Mortality	—
	Global	.30
	Variance explained (Σr^2)	.50

Note: Only values of *r* at greater than 95% confidence level are given.

When average ratings from the 34 subjects were used instead of descriptor scores, correlations with perceived risk increased substantially, and factor scores derived from the subjects' descriptor ratings explained 85% (not 50%) of the variance in perceived risk. It appears, therefore, that the hazard descriptors were well understood by our non-expert subjects and that they captured most of the global concern with risk that is expressed in the variable perceived risk. Larger and more representative groups must be tested before the results can be generalized.

APPLICATIONS TO MANAGING HAZARDS

In addition to improving our understanding of hazards, our conceptualization of hazardousness may help society select social and technical controls to ease the burden of hazards. Though detailed discussion of hazard management is beyond the scope of this chapter, we can suggest three ways of improving this process.

Comparing Technologies

Basic to hazard management are comparisons and choices among competing technologies. For example, for electricity generation, coal and nuclear power are frequently compared, and the hazards of each are invariably couched in terms of mortality estimates. Inhaber (1979) has estimated that mortality rates

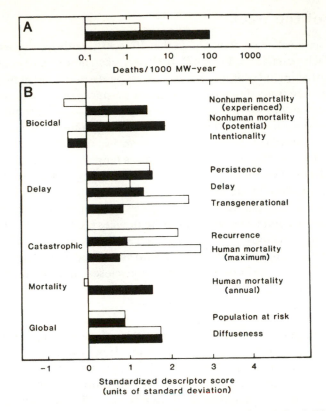

Figure 10.3 *Comparison of nuclear (light bars) and coal-fired (black bars) electric power by using Inhaber's analysis (A) and our hazardousness factors and descriptors (B)*

associated with coal technology are 50 times those for nuclear power technology (Figure 10.3a). Such one-dimensional comparisons have created considerable dissatisfaction because they ignore other important differences, including other aspects of hazardousness, between the two technologies (Holdren, 1982).

Our factors and descriptors for hazardousness offer a partial solution by allowing a multidimensional hazard profile to be applied to coal and nuclear power (Figure 10.3b). This profile was obtained from combined descriptor scores for each of several hazard chains that make up the total hazard of coal and nuclear power (Hohenemser et al, 1983). Coal still exceeds nuclear in human mortality, as expected from Inhaber's analysis, and it also exceeds nuclear in nonhuman mortality – that is, environmental effects. Nuclear power, on the other hand, dominates in possible transgenerational effects and the catastrophic factor. The two technologies show little difference in persistence, delay, population at risk and diffuseness.

The profile of hazardousness developed from the 12 hazard descriptors seems to capture the complexity of choice in energy risk assessment and management better than the common mortality index. The problem of choice remains, as does the question of how society should weight the different dimensions of hazardousness.

Hazard of the Week

Analysis of national news media shows that 40 to 50 hazards receive widespread attention each year (Kates, 1977, p7). In theory, each new hazard goes through a sequence that includes problem recognition, assessment and managerial action. Often there is need for early managerial response of some kind. Our descriptors of hazardousness provide a quick profile that allows new hazards to be grouped and compared with others that have similar profiles. Such comparisons may provide industrial or governmental managers some immediate precedents, as well as a warning of unexpected problems, a range of suggested managerial options and, at the very least, a measure of consistency in public policy.

We tested this use of the profile by scoring a new hazard, tampons – toxic shock syndrome. The profile of this hazard was most similar in structure to that of the profiles of contraceptive intrauterine devices (IUDs) – side effects; and then to aspirin – overdose; Valium – misuse; and Darvon – overdose. Indeed, subsequent regulatory response to the hazard associated with tampons has paralleled that of IUDs, the hazard in our inventory closest in structure to tampons.

Triage

As a society we cannot make extraordinary efforts on each of the 100,000 chemicals or 20,000 consumer products in commerce. If our causal structure and descriptors reflect key aspects of hazard – threats to humans and what they value – then our taxonomy provides a way of identifying those hazards worthy of special attention. Cases with multiple extreme scores (Table 10.3) lead naturally to a proposal for triage: extraordinary attention for multiple extreme hazards, distinctive effort for each of the groups of extreme hazards, and an ordered, routine response for the remainder.

Although we regard the suggestion of triage as an important outcome of our analysis, it is well to remember that many of the extreme hazards, such as nuclear weapons, are among a group that has defied solution for a long time; special efforts expended on them may produce few concrete results. This leads some to argue that society should focus its effort on cases of proven cost effectiveness – cases with the maximum reduction in hazardousness per unit expenditure.

We regard neither triage nor adherence to cost-effectiveness criteria as adequate foundations for managing hazards; rather, we see them as the horns of a familiar dilemma – whether to work on the big questions where success is limited, or to work on the normal, where success is expected.

SUMMARY AND CONCLUSIONS

All taxonomies are based on explicit or implicit assumptions, and ours is no different. We assume that technological hazards form a single domain, that they are defined by causal sequences, and that these are usefully measured by a few physical, biological and social descriptors. Our picture leads us to distinguish between energy and materials releases and provides a method for constructing profiles of hazardousness that considerably extend the conventional concept of risk as annual human mortality. Our profiles of hazardousness appear to be comprehensible to laypeople and to capture a significant fraction of our subjects' concern with hazardousness. This suggests that some conflict between experts and laypeople may be resolved by clarifying the definition of hazardousness.

We expect that our approach can improve the quality and effectiveness of hazard management. In particular, it may help in comparing the hazards expected from competing technologies as well as provide a quicker, more orderly response to new hazards and offer society a rational approach to triage. Yet to be resolved is the assignment of weights to the different descriptors of hazard.

ACKNOWLEDGMENTS

The research reported in this article was conducted by an interdisciplinary team including P Collins, R Goble, A Goldman, B Johnson, C Hohenemser, J X Kasperson, R E Kasperson, R W Kates, M P Lavine, M Morrison and B Rubin at Clark University, and B Fischhoff, M Layman, S Lichtenstein, D MacGregor, and P Slovic at Decision Research (a branch of Perceptronics). The research team received help in conceptualizing hazards from R C Harriss, NASA Langley Research Center, and T C Hollocher, Brandeis University. Research support was provided by NSF grants ENV77-15334, PRA79-11934, and PRA81-16925.

NOTES

1 Factor analysis was done using the package Biomedical Computer Program (1979). Orthogonal rotation was performed according to the varimax criterion, which maximizes the variance of the squared factor loadings.
2 We defined extreme hazards as those with truncated factor scores 1.2 to 1.5 standard deviations above the mean.

11

Informing and Educating the Public about Risk

Paul Slovic

To effectively manage ... risk, we must seek new ways to involve the public in the decision-making process... They [the public] need to become involved early, and they need to be informed if their participation is to be meaningful (Ruckelshaus, 1983, p1028).

INTRODUCTION

In a bold and insightful speech before the National Academy of Sciences at the beginning of his second term as Environmental Protection Agency (EPA) administrator, William Ruckelshaus called for a government-wide process for managing risks that thoroughly involved the public. Arguing that government must accommodate the will of the people, he quoted Thomas Jefferson's famous dictum to the effect that, 'If we think [the people] not enlightened enough to exercise their control with a wholesome discretion, the remedy is not to take it from them, but to inform their discretion.'

Midway into his tenure as EPA administrator, Ruckelshaus' experiences in attempting to implement Jefferson's philosophy led him to a more sober evaluation: 'Easy for *him* to say. As we have seen, informing discretion about risk has itself a high risk of failure' (Ruckelshaus, 1984).

This chapter attempts to illustrate why the goal of informing the public about risk issues, which seems easy to attain in principle, is surprisingly difficult to accomplish. To be effective, risk communicators must recognize and overcome a number of obstacles that have their roots in the limitations of scientific risk assessment and the idiosyncrasies of the human mind. Doing an adequate job of communicating means finding comprehensible ways of presenting complex technical material that is clouded by uncertainty and is inherently difficult to understand. Awareness of the difficulties should enhance the chances of designing successful informational programs.

Note: reprinted from 'Informing and Educating the Public about Risk' by P Slovic, 1986, *Risk Analysis*, 6(4), pp403–15. Copyright 1986 Society for Risk Analysis. Reprinted with permission.

LIMITATIONS OF RISK ASSESSMENT

Risk assessment is a complex discipline, not fully understood by its practioners, much less the lay public. At the technical level, there is still much debate over terminology and techniques. Technical limitations and disagreements among experts inevitably affect communication in the adversarial climate that surrounds many risk issues. Risk communicators must be fully aware of the strengths and limits of the methods used to generate the information they are attempting to convey to the public. In particular, communicators need to understand that risk assessments are constructed from theoretical models that are based on assumptions and subjective judgments. If these assumptions and judgments are deficient, the resulting assessments may be quite inaccurate.

Nowhere are these problems more evident than in the assessment of chronic health effects due to low-level exposures to toxic chemicals and radiation. The typical assessment uses studies of animals exposed (relatively briefly) to extremely high doses of the substance to draw inferences about the risks to humans exposed to very low doses (sometimes over long periods of time). The models designed to extrapolate the results from animals to humans and from high doses to low doses are controversial. For example, some critics have argued that mice may be from 3×10^4 to 10^9 times more cancer prone than humans (Gori, 1980). Different models for extrapolating from high-dose exposures to low doses produce estimated cancer rates that can differ by factors of 1000 or more at the expected levels of human exposures (which themselves are often subject to a great deal of uncertainty). Difficulties in estimating synergistic effects (interactions between two or more substances, such as occur between cigarette smoking and exposure to asbestos) and effects on particularly sensitive people (eg, children, pregnant women, the elderly) further compound the problems of risk assessment. In light of these various uncertainties, one expert concluded that: 'Discouraging as it may seem, it is not plausible that animal carcinogenesis experiments can be improved to the point where quantitative generalizations about human risk can be drawn from them' (Gori, 1980).

In the adversarial climate of risk discussions, these limitations of assessment are brought forth to discredit quantitative risk estimates. To be credible and trustworthy, a communicator must know enough to acknowledge valid criticisms and to discern whether the available risk estimates are valid enough to help the public gain perspective on the dangers they face and the decisions that must be made. On the positive side, there are some hazards (eg, radiation, asbestos) whose risks are relatively well understood. Moreover, for many other hazards, risk estimates are based on a chain of conservative decisions at each choice point in the analysis (eg, studying the most sensitive species, using the extrapolation model that produces the highest risk estimate, giving benign tumors the same weight as malignant ones). Despite the uncertainties, one may have great confidence that the 'true risk' is unlikely to exceed the estimate resulting from such a conservative process. In other words, uncertainty and subjectivity do not imply chaos. Communicators must know when this point is relevant and how to make it when it applies.

Parallel problems exist in engineering risk assessments designed to estimate the probability and severity of rare, high-consequence accidents in complex systems such as nuclear reactors or chemical plants. The risk estimates are devised from theoretical models (in this case fault trees or event trees) that attempt to depict all possible accident sequences and their (judged) probabilities. Limitations in the quality or comprehensiveness of the analysis, the quality of the judged risks for individual sequences, or improper rules for combining estimates can seriously compromise the validity of the assessment.

LIMITATIONS OF PUBLIC UNDERSTANDING

Just as they must understand the strengths and limitations of risk assessment, communicators must appreciate the wisdom and folly in public attitudes and perceptions. Among the important research findings and conclusions are the following.

People's Perceptions of Risk Are often Inaccurate

Risk judgments are influenced by the memorability of past events and the imaginability of future events. As a result, any factor that makes a hazard unusually memorable or imaginable, such as a recent disaster, heavy media coverage or a vivid film, could seriously distort perceptions of risk. In particular, studies by Lichtenstein et al (1978), Morgan et al (1985) and others have found that risks from dramatic or sensational causes of death, such as accidents, homicides, cancer and natural disasters, tend to be greatly overestimated. Risks from undramatic causes such as asthma, emphysema and diabetes, which take one life at a time and are common in non-fatal form, tend to be underestimated. News media coverage of hazards has been found to be biased in much the same direction, thus contributing to the difficulties of obtaining a proper perspective on risks (Combs & Slovic, 1979).

Risk Information May Frighten and Frustrate the Public

The fact that perceptions of risk are often inaccurate points to the need for warnings and educational programs. However, to the extent that misperceptions are due to relying on imaginability as a cue for riskiness, such programs may run into trouble. Merely mentioning possible adverse consequences (no matter how rare) of some product or activity could enhance their perceived likelihood and make them appear more frightening. Anecdotal observation of attempts to inform people about recombinant DNA hazards supports this hypotheses (Rosenberg, 1978), as does a controlled study by Morgan et al (1985). In the latter study, people's judgments of the risks from high voltage transmission lines were assessed before and after they read a brief and rather neutral description of findings from studies of possible health effects due to such lines. The results clearly indicated a shift toward greater concern in three separate groups of subjects exposed to the description. Whereas mere mention and refutation of potential risks raises concerns, the use of conservative assumptions and worst-case scenarios in risk assessment creates extreme negative reactions in people because of the difficulty of appreciating the improbability of such extreme but imaginable consequences. The possibility that imaginability may blur the distinction between what is (remotely) possible and what is probable obviously poses a serious obstacle to risk information programs.

Other psychological research shows that people may have great difficulty making decisions about gambles when they are forced to resolve conflicts generated by the possibility of experiencing both gains and losses, and uncertain ones at that (Slovic, 1982; Slovic & Lichtenstein, 1983). As a result, wherever possible, people attempt to reduce the anxiety generated in the face of uncertainty by denying that uncertainty, thus making the risk seem either so small that it can safely be ignored or so large that it clearly should be avoided. They rebel against being given statements of probability, rather than fact; they want to know exactly what will happen.

Given a choice, people would rather not have to confront the gambles inherent in life's dangerous activities. They would prefer being told that risks are managed by competent professionals and are' thus so small that one need not worry about them. However, if such assurances cannot be given, they will want to be informed of the risks, even though doing so might make them feel anxious and conflicted (Alfidi, 1971; Fischhoff, 1983; Weinstein, 1979).

Strong Beliefs Are Hard to Modify

It would be comforting to believe that polarized positions would respond to informational and educational programs. Unfortunately, psychological research demonstrates that people's beliefs change slowly and are extraordinarily persistent in the face of contrary evidence (Nisbett & Ross, 1980). Once formed, initial impressions tend to structure the way that subsequent evidence is interpreted. New evidence appears reliable and informative if it is consistent with one's initial beliefs; contrary evidence is dismissed as unreliable, erroneous or unrepresentative.

Naive Views Are Easily Manipulated by Presentation Format

When people lack strong prior opinions, the opposite situation exists – they are at the mercy of the way that the information is presented. Subtle changes in the way that risks are expressed can have a major impact on perceptions and decisions. One dramatic recent example of this comes from a study by McNeil, Pauker, Sox and Tversky (1982), who asked people to imagine that they had lung cancer and had to choose between two therapies, surgery or radiation. The two therapies were described in some detail. Then, some subjects were presented with the cumulative probabilities of surviving for varying lengths of time after the treatment. Other subjects received the same cumulative probabilities framed in terms of dying rather than surviving (eg, instead of being told that 68% of those having surgery will have survived after one year, they were told that 32% will have died). Framing the statistics in terms of dying dropped the percentage of subjects choosing radiation therapy over surgery from 44% to 18%. The effect was as strong for physicians as for laypersons.

Numerous other examples of framing effects have been demonstrated by Tversky and Kahneman (1981), and Slovic, Fischhoff and Lichtenstein (1982b). The fact that subtle differences in how risks are presented can have such marked effects suggest that those responsible for information programs have considerable ability to manipulate perceptions and behavior. This possibility raises ethical problems that must be addressed by any responsible risk-information program.

PLACING RISKS IN PERSPECTIVE

Choosing Risk Measures

When we know enough to be able to describe risks quantitatively, we face a wide choice of options regarding the specific measures and statistics used to describe the magnitude of risk. Fischhoff, Lichtenstein, Slovic, Derby and Keeney (1981) point out that choosing a risk measure involves several steps:

* defining the hazard category;
* deciding what consequences to measure (or report); and
* determining the unit of observation.

The way the hazard category is defined can have a major effect on risk statistics.

Crouch and Wilson (1982) provide some specific examples of how different measures of the same risk can sometimes give quite different impressions. For example, they show that accidental deaths per million tons of coal mined in the US have decreased steadily over time. In this respect, the industry is getting safer. However, they also show that the rate of accidental deaths per 1000 coal-mine employees has increased. Neither measure is the 'right' measure of mining risk. They each tell part of the same story.

The problem of selecting measures is made even more complicated by the framing effects described earlier. Thus, not only do different measures of the same hazard give different impressions, the *same* measures, differing only in (presumably) inconsequential ways, can lead to vastly different perceptions.

Sharlin's (1986) case study in the communication of information about the risks of the pesticide ethylene dibromide (EDB) points to an important distinction between macro and micro measures of risk. The Environmental Protection Agency, which was responsible for regulating EDB, broadcast information about the aggregate risk of this pesticide to the exposed population. While the media accurately transmitted this macro analysis, newspaper editorials and public reaction clearly indicated an inability to translate this into a micro perspective on the risk to the exposed individual. In other words, the newspaper reader or TV viewer had trouble inferring an answer to the question, 'Should I eat the bread?' from the aggregate risk analysis.

Basic Statistical Presentations

This section describes a few of the statistical displays most often used to educate people about general and specific risks. I do not mean to endorse these

Table 11.1 *Annual Fatality Rates per 100,000 Persons at Risk*

Risk	Rate	Risk [a]	Rate
Motorcycling	2000	Police work (nonclerical)	22
All ages	1000	Boating	5
Aerial acrobatics (planes)	500	Rodeo performer	3
Smoking (all causes)	300	Hunting	3
Sport parachuting	200	Fires	2.8
Smoking (cancer)	120	One diet drink/day (saccharin)	1.0
Fire fighting	80	Four tbs. peanut butter/day (aflatoxin)	0.8
Hang gliding	80	Floods	0.06
Coal mining	63	Lightning	0.05
Farming	36	Meteorite	0.000006
Motor vehicles	24		

[a] *Source:* Adapted from Crouch and Wilson (1982)

presentations as optimal. They simply represent the favored formats of statisticians and risk assessors.[1] To date, there has been little systematic effort to develop and test methods for maximizing clarity and understanding of quantitative risk estimates. As a result, we know of no 'magic displays' that guarantee understanding and appreciation of the described risks at the 'micro level'.

Among the few 'principles' in this field that seem to be useful is the assertion that comparisons are more meaningful than absolute numbers or probabilities, especially when these absolute values are quite small. Sowby (1965) argued that to decide whether we are responding adequately to radiation risks, we need to compare them to 'some of the other risks of life'. Rothschild (1978) observed: 'There is no point in getting into a panic about the risks of life until you have compared the risks which worry you with those that don't, but perhaps should.'

Familiarity with annual mortality risks for the population as a whole or as a function of age may provide one standard for evaluating specific risks. Sowby (1965) took advantage of such data to observe that one hour riding a motorcycle was as risky as one hour of being 75 years' old. Table 11.1 provides annual mortality rates from a wide variety of causes.

Mortality rates fail to capture the fact that some hazards (eg, pregnancy, motorcycle accidents) cause death at a much earlier age than others (eg, lung cancer due to smoking). One way to provide perspective on this consideration is to calculate the average loss of life expectancy due to exposure to the hazard, based on the distribution of deaths as a function of age. Some estimates of loss of life expectancy from various causes are shown in Table 11.2.

Yet another innovative way to gain perspective was devised by Wilson (1979), who displayed a set of activities (see Table 11.3), each of which was estimated to increase one's chance of death (during any year) by one in a million.

Comparisons within lists of risks such as those in Tables 11.1 to 11.3 have been advocated not just to gain some perspective on risks but as guides to decision-making. Thus Cohen and Lee (1979) argued that 'to some approximation, the ordering [in Table 11.2] should be society's order of priorities', and

Table 11.2 *Estimated Loss of Life Expectancy due to Various Causes*

Cause	Days	Cause	Days
Cigarette smoking (male)	2250	Diabetes	95
Heart disease	2100	Being murdered (homicide)	90
Being 30% overweight	1300	Drowning	41
Being a coal miner	1100	Job with radiation exposure	40
Cancer	980	Falls	39
Stroke	520	Natural radiation (BEIR)	8
Army in Vietnam	400	Medical X-rays	6
Dangerous jobs, accidents	300	Coffee	6
Motor vehicle accidents	207	All catastrophes	3.5
Pneumonia, influenza	141	Reactor accidents (USC)	2[a]
Accidents in home	95	Radiation from nuclear industry	0.02[a]
Suicide	95		

Source: Cohen and Lee (1979)

[a] These items assume that all US power is nuclear. USC is Union of Concerned Scientists, the most prominent group of critics of nuclear energy.

Table 11.3 *Risks Estimated to Increase Chance of Death in Any Year by .000001 (One Chance in One Million)*

Activity	Cause of death
Smoking 1.4 cigarettes	Cancer, heart disease
Spending 1 hour in a coal mine	Black lung disease
Living 2 days in New York or Boston	Air pollution
Traveling 10 miles by bicycle	Accident
Flying 1000 miles by jet	Accident
Living 2 months in Denver on vacation from New York	Cancer caused by cosmic radiation
One chest X-ray taken in a good hospital	Cancer caused by radiation
Eating 40 tbs of peanut butter	Liver cancer caused by aflatoxin B
Drinking 30 12-oz cans of diet soda	Cancer caused by saccharin
Drinking 1000 24-oz soft drinks from recently banned plastic bottles	Cancer from acrylonitrile monomer
Living 150 years within 20 miles of a nuclear power plant	Cancer caused by radiation
Risk of accident by living within 5 miles of a nuclear reactor for 50 years	Cancer caused by radiation

Source: R. Wilson (1979)

Wilson (1979) claimed that the comparisons in Table 11.3 'help me evaluate risk and I imagine that they may help others to do so, as well. But the most important use of these comparisons must be to help the decisions we make, as a nation, to improve our health and reduce our accident rate.' However, Slovic et al (1980b) argued that such claims could not be logically defended. Although carefully prepared lists of risk statistics can provide some degree of insight, they yield only a small part of the information needed for decision-making. As a minimum, inputs to decision-making should include a detailed account of the costs and benefits of the available options, as well as an indication of the uncertainty in these assessments. As we have seen, uncertainties in risk estimates are often quite large. Failure to indicate uncertainty not only deprives the recipient of information needed for decision-making, but it also spawns distrust and rejection of the analysis.

Some hazards, such as radiation, are present in nature and in many commonplace activities. For these hazards, comparisons of 'non-natural' exposures (eg, medical X-rays) with the natural or 'everyday' exposures may prove instructive.

BEYOND NUMBERS: A BROADER PERSPECTIVE ON RISK PERCEPTION AND COMMUNICATION

A stranger in a foreign land would hardly expect to communicate effectively with the natives without knowing something about their language and culture. Yet, risk assessors and risk managers have often tried to communicate with the public under the assumption that they and the public share a common conceptual and cultural heritage in the domain of risk. That assumption is false and has led to failures of communication and rancorous conflicts.

The Psychometric Paradigm

Evidence against the 'commonality assumption' comes from sociological, psychological and anthropological studies directed at understanding the determinants of people's risk perceptions and behaviors. In psychology, research within what has been called the 'psychometric paradigm' has explored the ability of psychophysical scaling methods and multivariate analysis to produce meaningful representations of risk attitudes and perceptions (see, for example, Brown & Green, 1980; Gardner, Tiemann, Gould, DeLuca, Doob & Stolwijk, 1982; Green, 1980; Green & Brown, 1980; Johnson & Tversky, 1984; Lindell & Earle, 1983; MacGill, 1983; Renn, 1981; Slovic, Fischhoff & Lichtenstein, 1980c, 1981a; Vlek & Stallen, 1981; von Winterfeldt, John & Borcherding, 1981).

Researchers employing the psychometric paradigm have typically asked people to judge the current riskiness (or safety) of diverse sets of hazardous activities, substances and technologies, and to indicate their desires for risk reduction and regulation of these hazards. These global judgments have then been related to judgments about the hazard's status on various qualitative characteristics of risk.

Among the generalizations that have been drawn from the results of the early studies in this area are the following:

1 Perceived risk is quantifiable and predictable. Psychometric techniques seem well suited for identifying similarities and differences among groups with regard to risk perceptions and attitudes.
2 Risk means different things to different people. When experts judge risk, their responses correlate highly with technical estimates of annual fatalities. Laypeople can assess annual fatalities if they are asked to (and produce estimates somewhat like the technical estimates). However, their

judgments of risk are sensitive to other characteristics as well and, as a result, often differ markedly from experts' assessments of risk. In particular, perception of risk is greater for hazards whose adverse effects are uncontrollable, dread, catastrophic, fatal rather than injurious, not offset by compensating benefits, and delayed in time so the risks are borne by future generations.

A useful concept that has emerged from this research is the notion that the societal cost of an accident or mishap is determined to an important degree by what it signifies or portends (Slovic, Lichtenstein, et al, 1984). The informativeness or 'signal potential' of a mishap, and thus its potential social impact, appears to be systematically related to the characteristics of the risk. An accident that takes many lives may produce relatively little social disturbance (beyond that which is caused to the victims' families and friends) if it occurs as part of a familiar and well-understood system (eg, a train wreck). However, a small accident in an unfamiliar system (or one perceived as poorly understood), such as a nuclear reactor or a recombinant DNA laboratory, may have immense social consequences if it is perceived as a harbinger of further and possibly catastrophic mishaps.[2]

Other Paradigms

Other important contributions to our current understanding of risk perception have come from geographers, sociologists and anthropologists. The geographical research focused originally on understanding human behavior in the face of natural hazards, but it has since broadened to include technological hazards as well (Burton, Kates & White, 1978). The sociological work (Mazur, 1984c; Moatti, Stemmelen & Fagnani, 1984) and the anthropological studies (Douglas & Wildavsky, 1982) have shown that the perceptions of risk that have been identified within the psychometric paradigm may have their roots in social and cultural factors. Mazur argues that, in some instances, response to hazards is caused by social influences transmitted by friends, family, fellow workers and respected public officials. In these cases, risk perception may form afterwards, as part of one's post hoc rationale for his or her behavior. In a similar vein, Douglas and Wildavsky assert that people, acting within social organizations, downplay certain risks and emphasize others as a means of maintaining the viability of the organization.

Implications for Risk Communication

Risk perception research has a number of direct implications for communication efforts. Psychometric studies imply that comparative examination of risk statistics, such as those in Tables 11.1–11.3 will not, by themselves, be adequate guides to personal or public decision policies. Risk perceptions and risk-taking behaviors appear to be determined not only by accident probabilities, annual mortality rates or mean losses of life expectancy, but also by numerous other characteristics of hazards such as uncertainty, controllability, catastrophic potential, equity and threat to future generations. Within the perceptual space defined by these and other characteristics, each hazard is unique. To many people, statements such as 'the annual risk from living near a nuclear power plant is equivalent to the risk of riding an extra 3 miles in an automobile' appear ludicrous because they fail to give adequate consideration to the important differences in the nature of the risks from these two technologies.

Psychometric research indicates that attempts to characterize, compare and regulate risks must be sensitive to the broader conception of risk that underlies people's concerns. Fischhoff, Watson and Hope (1984) have made a start in this direction by demonstrating how one might go about constructing a more adequate definition of risk. They advocated characterizing risk by a vector of measures (eg, mortality, morbidity, concern due to perceived uncertainty, concern due to dread).

The concept of accidents as signals indicates that, when informed about a particular hazard, people's concerns will generalize beyond the immediate problem to other related hazards. For example, with regard to the EDB scare, one newspaper editor wrote: 'The cumulative effect – the "body burden count" as scientists call it – is especially worrisome considering the number of other pesticides and carcinogens humans are exposed to' (*The Sunday Star-Bulletin and Advertiser*, Honolulu, 5 February, 1984). On the same topic, another editor wrote: 'Let's hope there are no cousins of EDB waiting to ambush us in the months ahead'. (*San Francisco Examiner*, 10 February, 1984).

As a result of this broad (and legitimate) perspective, communications from risk managers pertaining to the risk and control of a single hazard, no matter how carefully presented, may fail to alleviate people's fears, frustrations, and anger. If people trust the ability of the risk manager to handle the broader risk problems, these general concerns will probably not surface.

Whereas the psychometric research implies that risk debates are not merely about risk statistics, the sociological and anthropological work implies that some of these debates may not even be about risk. Risk may be a rationale for actions taken on other grounds or it may be a surrogate for social or ideological concerns. When this is the case, communication about risk is simply irrelevant to the discussion. Hidden agendas need to be brought to the surface for open discussion, if possible (Edwards & von Winterfeldt, 1984).

Perhaps the most important message from the research done to date is that there is wisdom as well as error in public attitudes and perceptions. Laypeople sometimes lack certain information about hazards. However, their basic conceptualization of risk is much richer than that of the experts and reflects legitimate concerns that are typically omitted from expert risk assessments. As a result, risk communication efforts are destined to fail unless they are structured as a two-way process (Renn, 1991). Each side, expert and public, has something valid to contribute. Each side must respect the insights and intelligence of the other.

THE ROLE OF THE NEWS MEDIA IN INFORMING PEOPLE ABOUT RISK

Critics of the Media

The mass media exert a powerful influence on people's perceptions of the world, the world of risk being no exception. Each morning's paper and each evening's TV newscast seems to include a report on some new danger to our food, water, air or physical safety. It is not surprising, given the actual and perceived influence of the media and the stakes involved in risk issues, that media coverage of risk has been subjected to intense scrutiny and harsh criticism. Content analysis of media reporting for specific hazards (DNA research, nuclear power, cancer) and the domain of hazards in general (eg, diseases, causes of death) has documented a great deal of misinformation and distortion (Burger, 1984; Combs & Slovic, 1979; Friemuth, Greenberg, DeWitt & Romano, 1984; Kristiansen, 1983), causing critics such as Cirino (1971) to assert: 'No one can be free from the effects of bias that exist in the mass media ... Decisions based on distorted views of the world resulting from [such] ... bias have resulted in tragically mistaken priorities, death and suffering' (p31).

More than a few observers have blamed the media for what they see as public overreaction to risk. Among the most vehement is physicist Bernard Cohen (1983b, p73), who argued that:

> Journalists have grossly misinformed the American public about the dangers of radiation and of nuclear power with their highly unbalanced treatments and their incorrect or misleading interpretations of scientific information... This misinformation is costing our nation thousands of unnecessary deaths and wasting billions of dollars each year.

In Defense of the Media

A balanced examination of media performance needs to consider the difficulties faced by the media in reporting risk stories. Journalists operate under many constraints, including tight deadlines, the pressure of competition to be first with a story and limitations on space or time (for TV reports). But the major difficulty stems from the inherent complexity of risk stories as outlined in the section of this chapter dealing with the limitations of risk assessment. Because of the technical complexity of the subject matter, journalists must depend upon expert sources. But a risk story may involve such diverse problems that the journalist might need to interview specialists in toxicology, epidemiology, economics, hydrology, meteorology, emergency evacuation and so forth, not to mention a wide variety of local, state and federal officials. Even then, there is no assurance of completeness. No one may know what all the pieces are, or recognize, the limits of their own understanding (Fischhoff, 1985a). Few journalists have the scientific background to sort through and make sense of the welter of complex and often contradictory material that results from such a search.

Improving Media Performance

Despite the difficulties, there seem to be a number of actions that might help the media improve in communicating risk information. Some of these actions are professional, others involve research. At the professional level, the following steps may be useful.

Acknowledge the problem

The first step in addressing any deficiency is to recognize it as an important problem. We now know that an understanding of risk is central to decisions that are of great consequence to individuals and to society, that risk and uncertainty are inherently difficult to communicate, and that the media are a dominant source of risk information. The combination of these factors highlights the role of the media as a problem worthy of explicit, sustained attention, in high-level meetings between journalists, scientists and risk managers.

Enhance science writing

Reporters obviously need to be educated in the importance and subtleties of risk stories. Fischhoff (1985b) suggests a number of checklists and protocols that a reporter might use as a guide to understanding and clarifying risk issues. One of these, entitled 'Questions to Ask of Risk Analyses', is shown in Table 11.4. There should be scholarships to induce students and young journalists to pursue science writing as a profession, accompanied by awards and prizes to recognize and reward good science journalism when it occurs.

Table 11.4 *Questions to Ask of Risk Analyses*

Reporters should consider the following questions whenever a risk analysis is produced for use in policy decisions. If the answer to any of these questions is 'no', then the use of that risk analysis should be questioned.

1　Does the risk analysis state the *probability* of the potential harm as well as the amount of harm expected?
2　Does the risk analysis disclose forthrightly the points at which it is based on assumptions and guesswork?
3　Are various risk factors allowed to assume a variety of values depending upon uncertainties in the data and/or various interpretations of the data?
4　Does the risk analysis multiply its probabilities by the number of people exposed to produce the number of people predicted to suffer damage?
5　Does the risk analysis disclose the confidence limits for its projections and the method of arriving at those confidence limits?
6　Are considerations of individual sensitivities, exposure to multiple hazards and cumulative effects included in the risk analysis?
7　Are all data and processes of the risk analysis open to public scrutiny?
8　Are questions of (a) involuntary exposure, (b) who bears the risks and who reaps the benefits, and (c) alternatives to the hazardous activity considered in the risk analysis?
9　Are the processes of risk analysis and risk policy separate?

Source: Adapted from Fischhoff (1985)

Develop science news clearinghouses

Science journalists need access to knowledgeable and cooperative scientists. A few organizations, such as the Scientists' Institute for Public Information, have performed an important service along this line; and some professional societies, such as the American Psychological Association, maintain offices that provide journalists with the name of scientists who specialize in specific topics. More needs to be done to help journalists get reliable information about risk topics.

RESEARCH DIRECTIONS

Although much progress has been made toward understanding risk attitudes, perceptions and behaviors, we still lack definitive understanding of many important issues relevant to risk communication. Some recommended research directions are described in this section.

Informed Consent

The right of citizens, patients and workers to be informed about the hazards to which they are exposed from their daily activities, their medical treatments and their jobs provides the motivation behind much of the efforts to communicate information about risks. Within the context of any information program, research is needed to determine what people know and what they want to know about the risks they face and how best to convey that information. Moreover, there is need for a deeper understanding of the concept of consent (MacLean, 1982), as well as for a theory of informed consent that sets out criteria for evaluating the adequacy of information presentations. Fischhoff (1983; 1985a) has made a start in the latter direction by characterizing the problem of informed consent as a decision problem. In this view, the goal of informed consent is to enable the individual to make decisions that are in his or her best interests. Fischhoff points out that there are both cognitive and institutional barriers to achieving informed consent. Research is needed to understand these barriers and overcome them.

To facilitate the process of informed consent, we need better ways to convey quantitative risk information. There is widespread agreement that casting individual risks in terms such as 10^{-x} per year is not helpful to people. We need creative new indices and analogies to help individuals translate risk estimates varying over many orders of magnitude into simple, intuitively meaningful terms. The task will not be easy. Ideas that appear, at first glance, to be useful, often turn out, on testing, to make the problem worse. For example, an attempt to convey the smallness of 1 part of toxic substance per billion by drawing an analogy to a crouton in a 5 ton salad seems likely to enhance one's misperception of the contamination by making it more easily imaginable. The proposal to express very low probabilities in terms of the conjunction of two or more unlikely events (eg, simultaneously being hit by lightning and struck by a meteorite) also seems unwise in light of experimental data showing that people greatly overestimate the likelihood of conjunctive events. Perhaps we can learn, by studying people's understanding of commonly used measures, such as distance, time and speed, whether and how their understanding of quantitative risk can be improved.

The sensitivity of risk communications to framing effects points to another avenue for research. We need a better understanding of the magnitude and generality of these effects. Are people's perceptions really as malleable as early results suggest? If so, how should the communicator cope with this problem? One suggestion is to present information in multiple formats – but does this help or confuse the recipient? Finally, the possibility that there is no neutral way to present information, coupled with the possibility that people's preferences are very easily manipulated, has important ethical and political implications that need to be examined.

Because of the complexity of risk communications and the subtlety of human response to them, it is extremely difficult, a priori, to know whether a particular message will adequately inform its recipients. Testing of the message provides needed insight into its impacts. In light of the known difficulties of communicating risk information, it could be argued that an informer who puts forth a message without testing its comprehensibility is guilty of negligence. This assertion raises a host of research questions. How does one test a message? How does the communicator judge when a message is good enough in light of the possibility that not all test subjects will interpret it correctly? Can testing be used against the communicator by providing evidence that not everyone understood the message?

Risk is brewed from an equal dose of two ingredients – probabilities and consequences. But most of the attention pertaining to informed consent seems to focus on the probabilities. It is assumed that once the potential consequence is named – lung cancer, leukemia, pneumoconiosis – one need say little else about it. We believe that neglecting to educate people about consequences is a serious shortcoming in risk-information programs. For example, an adequate discussion of risk cannot assume that people have good knowledge of what it is like to experience a certain disease, the pains, the discomforts, the treatments and their effects, and so forth. This sort of information might best come from those who are the victims of such diseases. Research is needed to determine how best to deepen perspectives about the novel, unfamiliar consequences associated with the outcomes of illnesses, accidents and their treatments.

Information Relevance

What lessons do people draw about their own vulnerability to a hazard on the basis of risk information? For example:

- What do residents living near the Union Carbide pesticide plant at Institute, West Virginia, infer about their personal risk as a result of the Bhopal accident?
- What does a heterosexual individual infer about personal vulnerability to AIDS from statistics based on homosexuals?
- What does a resident of the West Coast infer about his or her risk from cancer due to polluted groundwater upon receiving risk estimates for residents of the East Coast?

Obviously, the personal message one draws from risk information will depend upon the perceived relevance of that message – but the determinants of relevance are by no means understood. There are always differences between the time, place and population (or species) from which risk information is derived and the time, place and population with which the recipient identifies. When are these differences magnified into barriers justifying denial or relevance ('those statistics don't really pertain to me'), and when are the barriers made permeable and the message assimilated? Such questions are fundamental to the process of risk communication, yet we know virtually nothing about them.

Cognitive Representations of Perceived Risk

People's cognitive representation of risk dictates the sorts of information they will find necessary for participating in risk-management decisions. Thus, if characteristics of risk influence perceptions and behaviors, we will need to provide people with information about how well a hazard is known to science, the extent of its catastrophic potential and other important considerations. If people examine accident reports for their signal value, then methods are needed to assess this factor and communications techniques are needed to express it meaningfully. However, we still lack a full understanding of the ways in which people characterize risk. Research is needed to provide a clearer picture of the multiple ways to represent perceptions and the variations of these representations across different individuals and groups (Harding & Eiser, 1984; Kraus & Slovic, 1988b; Kuyper & Vlek, 1984).

The multivariate characterizations that have emerged from psychometric studies demonstrate that there are many things to be considered when thinking about risk and many (possibly incommensurable) factors to bear in mind when assessing the riskiness of different hazards. The need for some convenient general summary measure of risk seems apparent. Reliance on multiattribute utility theory to construct such an index (Fischhoff et al, 1984) provides one approach, but research is needed to determine if people can provide the explicit judgments needed to create such an index. Given an index, can people absorb the information it summarizes in a way that is meaningful, and will they make or accept decisions based upon it? Would they feel more comfortable being shown, in matrix or vector form, the component information it summarizes?

Risk and the Media

We need a theoretical framework to understand and improve the media's role in communicating risk. Some theorists, such as Gans (1980), have proposed that one major role of journalism is to report events that threaten or violate important values – such as preserving a stable social order. In this light, things that 'go awry' and thereby threaten natural, technological, social or moral disorder become prime news topics. The relation between hazard characteristics and news coverage should be examined to discern more precisely how the media interpret their responsibility to warn society.

One possibility is that coverage of risk incidents is systematically related to threat potential or signal value. If so, such coverage (as measured by frequency, size and prominence of reports) should be related to the same characteristics that predict other risk perceptions and attitudes. Thus, incidents involving hazards perceived as unknown, dread and potentially catastrophic would be expected to receive much greater coverage than incidents involving hazards with other characteristics. Data reported by Kristiansen (1983) provide some support for these notions. Her study of seven British daily newspapers found that threats with high signal value, such as infectious diseases, food poisoning and rabies, were disproportionately reported relative to their frequency of occurrence.

Content analyses of media reports need to be supplemented by more controlled studies. An intriguing example of a controlled study was done by Johnson and Tversky (1983), who asked subjects to judge the perceived frequency of death from various causes after reading a single newspaper-style story about a tragic incident involving the death of a young man. The cause of death was either leukemia, homicide or fire, depending upon the story. They expected to find that a story would increase perceived frequency most for the specific hazard involved in the story, with somewhat smaller increases for similar hazards. Instead, the results indicated large increases in perceived frequencies for all hazards, with size of increase being unrelated to similarity. They hypothesized that the stories aroused negative affect which had a general influence on perception. This hypothesis is an important one, in need of further study, because it implies that media coverage might influence our perceptions of threat in subtle and pervasive ways.

Other topics that could be studied by means of controlled news simulations are the reporting (or deletion) of uncertainties in risk estimates and the treatment given experts' disagreements. How, for example, would journalists report a story in which 20 experts argued one way and one argued another? Would it matter if the ratio were higher or lower or if the dissenter had more or less prestigious credentials? Would experienced journalists or their editors treat the story differently than inexperienced reporters? Would the type of medium (TV, radio, print) make a difference? In sum, studies such as these could point out biases or inadequacies in reporting, about which journalists would need to be informed.

CONCLUSIONS

Some observers, cognizant of the communication difficulties described above, have concluded that they are insurmountable. This seems an unreasonably pessimistic view. Upon closer examination it appears that people understand some things quite well, although their path to knowledge may be quite different from that of the technical experts. In situations where misunderstanding is rampant, people's errors can often be traced to biased experiences, which education may be able to counter. In some cases, people's strong fears and resistance to experts' reassurances can be traced to their sensitivity to the potential for catastrophic accidents, to their perception of expert disagreement about the probability and magnitude of such accidents, to their knowledge of serious mistakes made by experts in the past, and to their sensitivity to many qualitative concerns not included in technical risk analyses. Even here, given an atmosphere of trust in which both experts and laypersons recognize that each group has something to contribute to the discussion, exchange of information and deepening of perspectives may well be possible.

ACKNOWLEDGMENTS

This chapter draws heavily upon the author's joint work with his colleagues Baruch Fischhoff and Sarah Lichtenstein. Support for the writing of this paper was provided by the National Science Foundation under contract No PRA-8419168 to the University of Southern California.

NOTES

1   We make no attempt to defend the validity of the statistics presented in this chapter. We take them directly from various published studies. Earlier in this chapter we pointed out the problems that one must be aware of when using and interpreting risk data.

2   The concept of accidents as signals was eloquently expressed in an editorial addressing the tragic accident at Bhopal India:

> What truly grips us in these accounts [of disaster] is not so much the numbers as the spectacle of suddenly vanishing competence, of men utterly routed by technology, of fail-safe systems failing with a logic as inexorable as it was once – indeed, right up until that very moment – unforeseeable. And the spectacle haunts us because it seems to carry allegorical import, like the whispery omen of a hovering future (*The New Yorker*, 18 February, 1985).

12 Perception of Risk from Automobile Safety Defects

Paul Slovic, Donald G MacGregor and Nancy N Kraus

INTRODUCTION

Automobile safety decisions reflect a complex blend of manufacturer initiatives (Svenson, 1984) and government regulations (Bick, Hohenemser & Kates, 1979). Despite the obvious importance of automobile safety, we know of no systematic attempt to develop a socially comprehensive theory of safety design that might guide manufacturers and regulators. The closest we have to such a guide is the suggestion that cost-benefit analysis may be a useful framework for organizing risk information as part of a larger, complex process of making decisions about safety (eg, Coleman, 1976; Lave & Weber, 1970). There are, however, indications that cost-benefit calculations alone are an incomplete basis for safety decisions. One dramatic illustration of this is the case of the Ford Pinto, whose fuel tank was prone to rupture and fire when the vehicle was struck from behind. Analyses done by Ford concluded that the cost of correcting this defect by changing the design of the fuel tank greatly exceeded the expected safety benefits. Nevertheless, unsympathetic jurors found Ford guilty in a massive liability suit brought by relatives of Pinto victims (*Grimshaw versus Ford Motor Co*, 1978), and the National Highway Traffic Safety Administration subsequently ordered a recall of the defective vehicles.

Another indication that safety design needs to be guided by more than cost-benefit considerations comes from research on risk perception. MacGregor and Slovic (1986) asked people to evaluate the logical and moral adequacy of various approaches to making product-safety decisions. Cost-benefit analysis and a close relative, risk-benefit analysis, were not judged favorably when they were used as the sole basis for decision-making. However, these quantitative methods were seen as much more appropriate when their calculations were used as inputs to a more qualitative, deliberative process for making decisions. Research

Note: reprinted from *Accident Analysis & Prevention*, 19, P Slovic, D G MacGregor and N N Kraus, 'Perception of Risk from Automobile Safety Defects', 359–73, with permission from Elsevier Science. Copyright (1987).

on risk perception indicates that laypeople want risk decisions to be based on additional considerations besides expected damages, injuries and dollar costs (Slovic, Fischhoff & Lichtenstein, 1984; 1985). These considerations include voluntariness of exposure to the hazard; the degree to which the risks are dread, controllable or catastrophic; the degree of uncertainty surrounding the risk estimates; and possible inequities in the distribution of benefits among persons who bear the risks (Slovic, Fischhoff et al, 1984; 1985). May (1982), arguing from an ethical perspective, has come to a similar conclusion.

A primary contribution of risk perception research has been to demonstrate that these additional qualities of risk, which are not usually represented in cost – risk-benefit analyses, nevertheless determine important aspects of societal response to hazards. For example, hazards posing risks that are judged to be particularly uncertain, dread and catastrophic, such as chemical manufacturing or nuclear power, also tend to be judged most in need of strict government regulation. And when these 'worrisome' technologies experience an accident, the mishap is likely to be interpreted as a signal that the responsible company, and perhaps also the industry, is not properly managing the risks (Slovic, Lichtenstein et al, 1984). This signal triggers strong societal reactions (public opposition, liability suits, stricter government regulation) that can inflict massive costs on the company or industry. A dramatic example of these signal effects followed the accident at the Three Mile Island nuclear reactor. This mishap is estimated to have cost tens (perhaps hundreds) of billions of dollars as a result of reduced output from nuclear reactors worldwide, costs of using more expensive alternative fuels, stricter regulation of the industry, and so forth. (EPRI, 1980; Evans & Hope, 1984). The Pinto is an obvious example of an ultra-serious and costly defect for the automobile industry, both in terms of the monetary costs of litigation and intangible losses of good will and public regard for the manufacturer.

Early studies of perceived risk aimed to account for differential reactions to diverse hazards, such as the strong concerns about nuclear power and the lack of concern about living below a dam. A recent study by Kraus and Slovic (1988b) showed that the methods used to analyze judgments of diverse hazards could be applied as well to a more homogeneous set of hazards from the same industry. Kraus and Slovic asked people to evaluate 49 scenarios describing railroad hazards. They found that risk characteristics and overall levels of perceived risk varied widely from one scenario to the next. For example, the derailment of a train carrying toxic chemicals was perceived much as nuclear reactors were perceived in studies of diverse sets of hazards; it was greatly feared and appeared likely to have costly repercussions for the rail company. In contrast, a derailment involving a train carrying non-toxic freight did not generate such a high level of concern.

The success of Kraus and Slovic's study in differentiating rail-transport hazards has encouraged us to apply similar methods to examine motorists' perceptions of the risks associated with various kinds of automobile defects. Such methods might enable us to identify defects whose seriousness and potential higher-order costs are likely to be underestimated by typical cost-benefit and risk-benefit approaches.

METHOD

Subjects

The subjects for this study were 19 men and 26 women who responded to a newspaper ad. Their mean age was 23 years (range 17 to 38); 77% had a driver's license and 57% owned a car. On average, they had been driving for seven years. Only four individuals (9%) had ever received a recall notice. They were paid $6 for their participation, which took about 1–1/2 hours.

Recall Scenarios

Subjects were asked to evaluate 40 scenarios describing automobile defects that had led to the vehicles being recalled by the manufacturer for correction. These scenarios were selected for their diversity. Each scenario consisted of a short paragraph indicating the nature of the defect and the consequences to vehicle operation that might result should the defect go uncorrected.

Thirty-nine of the scenarios were selected from automobile recall listings compiled by the US Department of Transportation (DOT; 1967–1983). The descriptions of each defect were edited slightly to improve readability and standardize their length and content.

One scenario was not taken from actual DOT records, but was instead constructed to represent the fuel-tank defect that plagued the Pinto. This scenario read as follows:

> The fuel tank, placed directly behind the rear axle, may lack adequate protection from the rear axle mounting brackets. In the event of a rear end collision, the fuel tank could be pushed into the mounting brackets with sufficient force to cause it to rupture, allowing fuel to escape. This could create the possibility of a fire and/or burn injuries to vehicle occupants and bystanders.

The full set of scenarios is shown in Appendix 12A. Also included in the table is the code name for each scenario, to be used in subsequent tables and figures, the year that the recall was initiated, the number of cars recalled, and the compliance rate (indicating the percentage of defective vehicles that had been brought to the manufacturer for repair). Because average compliance seemed to vary with different manufacturers, compliance is listed for only 21 scenarios, all involving the same manufacturer. Analyses of compliance were based on only these 21 scenarios.

Questionnaire

Subjects were asked to rate each of the 40 defect scenarios on six characteristics of risk similar to those found to be important in prior studies by Slovic, Fischhoff et al (1984; 1985) and Kraus and Slovic (1988b). These six characteristics were anticipatory knowledge of the defect (on the part of the manufacturer), dread of the potential mishap, likelihood of a great amount of property damage, likelihood of severe personal injuries to vehicle occupants or bystanders, ability to control the vehicle if the defect caused a mishap, and likelihood of the driver observing the defect before it could cause an accident.

In addition to these characteristics, subjects rated the centrality or importance of the defective system for safe vehicle operation. Finally, they rated four characteristics that served as dependent variables in the subsequent analysis. These were the overall riskiness of the defect; the likelihood that they, personally, would comply with a recall notice to correct this defect; the likelihood that others would comply with such a notice; and the degree to which such a recall would reduce their likelihood of buying another car from the same manufacturer.

The full set of rating scales is shown in Table 12.1. All 40 defect scenarios were rated on one characteristic before the next characteristic was considered.

Table 12.1 *Scales on which Recall Scenarios were Rated*

Knowledge

To what degree should the manufacturer have been able to anticipate this defect when the automobile was designed?
  Scale: *Manufacturer couldn't have anticipated* (1); *Manufacturer should have anticipated* (10)

Dreadedness

How much do people dread the type of mishap that this defect might cause?
  Scale: *Mishap not dreaded* (1); *Mishap dreaded* (10)

Severity of Consequences – Property

Consider the entire *range* of possible consequences to property (vehicles, land, buildings and so on) if this defect were to cause a mishap. How likely is it that a mishap resulting from this defect would cause a great amount of property damage?
  Scale: *Certain* not *to cause a great amount of property damage* (1); *Certain to cause a great amount of property damage* (10)

Severity of Consequences – Personal

How likely is it that a mishap resulting from this defect would cause severe injury or death to vehicle occupants or bystanders? Consider the entire *range* of possible consequences for the driver of the vehicle, passengers, occupants of other vehicles, bystanders and so on.
  Scale: *Consequences not severe* (1); *Consequences severe* (10)

Control of Severity

How likely is it that the driver can remain in control of the vehicle (steer it, stop it, control speed, etc) in the event that this defect causes a mishap?
  Scale: *Driver has little control over the vehicle* (1); *Driver has much control over the vehicle* (10)

Observability

How likely is it that the driver would notice the defect well before it could cause an accident?
  Scale: *Extremely unlikely that the defect would be noticed* (1); *Extremely likely that the defect would be noticed* (10)

Centrality

How important is the affected system or equipment for safe vehicle operation?
  Scale: *Not at all important for safe vehicle operation* (1); *Extremely important for safe vehicle operation* (10)

Table 12.1 *continued*

Riskiness

Overall, how risky is driving an automobile that may have this defect?
    Scale: *Not at all risky* (1); *Extremely risky* (10)

Personal Compliance

How likely is it that you, personally, would comply with a recall notice for this defect and take your automobile to a dealer to have the defect corrected?
    Scale: *Very unlikely* (1); *Very likely* (10)

General Compliance

What percentage of all people involved in a recall campaign for this defect do you think would comply with the recall notice and take their automobile to a dealer to have the defect corrected?
    Scale: Percentage 10 20 30 40 50 60 70 80 90 100

Likelihood of Future Purchase

If your car was recalled for this defect, to what extent would this reduce the likelihood of you buying another car from this manufacturer in the future?
    Scale: *Would* not *reduce the likelihood of future purchase* (1); *Would greatly reduce the likelihood of future purchase* (10)

RESULTS

Means

Table 12.2 presents the means and standard deviations, across all 40 defect scenarios, for each measure. The knowledge scale had the highest mean (7.49) and smallest range (5.33 to 9.04) among the risk characteristics, indicating that our respondents thought most of the defects should have been anticipated (and presumably corrected) by the manufacturer. The rather low mean for observability (3.88) reflected the perception that most of these defects would catch the driver by surprise, without advance warning. In other words, most of these defects were

Table 12.2 *Means and Standard Deviations*

Variable	Mean	Standard deviation
Knowledge	7.49	0.54
Dread	6.24	1.01
Property damage	5.83	0.89
Personal injury	6.43	1.24
Controllability	5.31	0.99
Observability	3.88	0.92
Centrality	7.30	0.72
Riskiness	6.78	0.84
Self compliance	8.10	0.71
General compliance (%)	64.60	7.11
Future purchase	6.39	0.65
Actual compliance (%)	72.60	12.61

judged to be known to the manufacturers of the vehicles but not to the motorists operating them.

Because all of the 40 scenarios involved actual recalls, one might expect them to be judged quite risky. This was not the case. The mean perceived risk of the various defects varied greatly, from 3.49 to 8.53 on the 10-point scale. The defect causing a locking of the steering wheel was judged to be most risky, followed by the fuel-tank rupture (Pinto scenario), locking of the rear brakes, transfer of carbon monoxide into the passenger compartment, and a defective accelerator pin. The defects perceived as least risky involved problems with the heater, defroster, bumper jack, turn signals, and the omission of the tire rim size from a front door decal.

Table 12.3 presents the scenarios whose mean ratings were extreme on each of the ten remaining judgment scales. The scenario portraying a fuel-tank rupture on impact occurs repeatedly as one of the five most negatively rated defects, as do scenarios involving gas fumes or leaks, carbon monoxide fumes and steering or brake locking. Problems involving the turn signals, the heater or defroster and the tire information decal were consistently rated toward the less serious pole of each scale.

Table 12.3 *Extreme Scenarios for 10 Judgment Scales*

Scale	Five Highest Scenarios		Five Lowest Scenarios	
1 Knowledge	CO fumes	9.04	Windshield wipers	6.49
	Gas fumes	8.71	Loose steering	6.42
	Fuel-tank rupture	8.69	Power steering	6.38
	Seat-belt retractor	8.56	Signal switch	5.91
	Suspension damage	8.47	Exhaust pipe	5.33
2 Dread	Fuel-tank rupture	8.62	Power steering	4.09
	Gas fumes	7.98	Decal information	3.58
	CO fumes	7.78	Heater lever	3.58
	Fuel line leak	7.53	Defroster	3.40
	Rear brakes lock	7.49	Signal switch	3.04
3 Property damage	Steering lock	7.76	Power steering	3.91
	Fuel-tank rupture	7.71	Seat-belt retractor	3.89
	Fuel-tank leak	6.98	Defroster	3.09
	Fuel line leak	6.74	Signal switch	2.93
	Rear brakes lock	6.65	Heater lever	2.66
4 Personal injury	Fuel-tank rupture	8.69	Power steering	3.58
	CO fumes	8.18	Defroster	3.20
	Seat-belt retractor	7.98	Decal information	2.98
	Gas fumes	7.93	Heater lever	2.96
	Fuel-tank leak	7.87	Signal switch	2.60
5 Control of vehicle	Signal switch	8.52	Front-axle damage	4.02
	Decal information	8.23	Fuel-tank rupture	4.00
	Heater lever	8.19	Jack falls	3.84
	Defroster	8.09	Rear brakes lock	3.71
	Exhaust pipe	7.18	Steering lock	2.78

Table 12.3 *continued*

Scale	Five Highest Scenarios		Five Lowest Scenarios	
6 Observability	Defroster	6.76	Suspension damage	2.87
	Decal information	6.04	Rear-window	2.73
	Heater lever	5.91	Front windshield	2.69
	Signal switch	5.87	Steering lock	2.49
	Windshield wipers	5.86	Airbag	1.91
7 Centrality	Steering lock	8.93	Exhaust pipe	5.27
	Fuel-tank rupture	8.33	Decal information	4.93
	Rear brakes lock	8.18	Defroster	4.24
	Fuel line leak	8.18	Heater lever	4.20
	Accelerator pin	7.93	Signal switch	4.09
8 Personal compliance	CO fumes	8.89	Heater lever	6.76
	Fuel-tank rupture	8.84	Defroster	6.73
	Steering lock	8.78	Exhaust pipe	6.53
	Rear brake lock	8.76	Signal switch	6.30
	Gas fumes	8.73	Decal information	5.31
9 General compliance	Fuel-tank rupture	79.3	Front seat slide	47.3
	Gas fumes	76.4	Heater lever	41.2
	Steering lock	75.8	Exhaust pipe	39.8
	CO fumes	72.0	Decal information	38.9
	Rear brake lock	71.8	Signal switch	36.0
10 No future purchase	Fuel-tank rupture	8.33	Defroster	4.76
	Steering lock	7.38	Exhaust pipe	4.60
	Front windshield	7.13	Heater lever	4.40
	Gas fumes	7.13	Signal switch	4.11
	Fuel line leak	7.07	Decal information	4.00

Intercorrelations

Table 12.4 presents the intercorrelations among the 11 judgment scales. As one might infer from Table 12.3, there were extremely high intercorrelations among many of the variables, particularly among centrality, riskiness, personal and general compliance and future purchase. The median correlation within this cluster was .91 and the range was .86 to .94, indicating that the defects were ordered almost identically on these scales. The other characteristics were less similar to one another, except for dread and personal injury ($r = .92$). Ratings of dread correlated most highly with the dependent variables (perceived risk, compliance and decreased likelihood of future purchase). Knowledge and observability correlated least highly with these variables.

One slight surprise was that the likelihood of severe property damage correlated only .61 with the likelihood of severe personal injury. This was because a number of defect scenarios were judged to have the potential for far greater personal harm than property damage. These included problems with seat belts

Table 12.4 *Intercorrelations Among 11 Judgment Scales*

	Knowledge	Dread	Property damage	Personal injury	Control of severity	Observability	Centrality	Riskiness	Personal compliance	General compliance
1 Knowledge										
2 Dread	.61									
3 Property damage	.09	.62								
4 Personal injury	.52	.92	.61							
5 Control of severity	-.39	-.72	-.74	-.71						
6 Observability	-.22	-.47	-.56	-.51	.64					
7 Centrality	.42	.81	.81	.75	-.86	-.57				
8 Riskiness	.48	.84	.75	.83	-.82	-.54	.94			
9 Personal compliance	.48	.80	.64	.73	-.77	-.52	.87	.86		
10 General compliance	.54	.83	.65	.72	-.75	-.49	.91	.88	.94	
11 Future purchase	.57	.85	.68	.79	-.78	-.62	.89	.91	.93	.94

and airbags (defects 17, 30 and 34), and penetration of the passenger compartment by gas fumes (defect 28) or carbon monoxide (defect 16). The defective tire rim-size decal was a problem judged to be somewhat more likely to cause property damage than to cause personal harm. Table 12.4 also reveals that the likelihood of severe personal consequences was correlated somewhat more highly with the overall risk, compliance and future-purchase scales than was the likelihood of great property damage.

Factor Analysis

The intercorrelations among five of the risk characteristics (knowledge, property and personal damage, control and observability) were subjected to a principle components factor analysis. Judgments of dread were omitted from this analysis because they correlated so highly with judgments of personal injury. The analysis produced two uncorrelated factors, with the first factor accounting for 62% of the variance among the risk characteristics and the second factor accounting for 21% of the variance. No other potential factor accounted for more than 9% of the variance. Rotated factor loadings, indicating the degree to which each risk characteristic correlated with each factor, are shown in Table 12.5. The pattern of loadings indicates that factor 1 was determined by the likelihood of great property damage, inability to control the vehicle, and inability to observe the defect in advance of a mishap. Factor 2 was determined primarily by the manufacturer's anticipatory knowledge. The likelihood of severe personal injury was associated with both factors. We have chosen to name factor 1 'uncontrollable damage' and factor 2 'foreseeable injury'. Factor 1 represents the perceived inability of the driver to anticipate the defect and to control the vehicle once the defect manifests itself. Factor 2 represents the failure of the manufacturer to correct what was perceived to be a foreseeable and potentially injurious problem.

Factor scores were computed for each of the recall scenarios by weighting the ratings on each risk characteristic proportional to the importance of the characteristic for the factor and summing over all characteristics. This weighted sum gives a particular defect a score that is an amalgamation of its ratings on the variables that define the factor. The factor scores for each defect are plotted in Figure 12.1. As one moves from left to right in the space, the defects are judged to produce less controllable mishaps, occurring with less warning to the driver and resulting in more severe harm to persons and property. As one goes from the bottom to the top of the space, the defects are judged to be more knowable

Table 12.5 *Rotated Factor Loadings for Five Risk Characteristics*

Characteristic	Factor 1	Factor 2
Property damage	.91	−.01
Control	−.85	−.34
Observability	−.80	−.12
Personal injury	.67	.58
Knowledge	.07	.97

Table 12.6 *Correlations with Factor Scores*

Variable	Factor 1	Factor 2	R
Riskiness	.76	.46	.89
Personal compliance	.68	.46	.81
General compliance	.65	.50	.82
Future purchase	.72	.53	.89

or foreseeable to the manufacturer and more likely to produce severe personal injury or death.

Previous studies have found that important attitudes and perceptions tend to be closely related to a hazard's location in the factor space (Slovic, Fischhoff et al, 1984; 1985). The present study is no exception. Table 12.6 shows that perceived risk, judged compliance and likely effect on future purchase are all highly

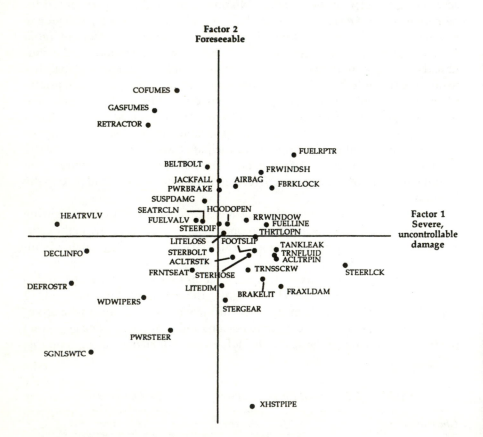

Note: Refer to Appendix 12.A for full description of scenario codes.

Source: Redrawn from Slovic, MacGregor and Kraus (1987)

Figure 12.1 *Location of 40 safety defects within a two-factor space derived from interrelationships among five risk characteristics*

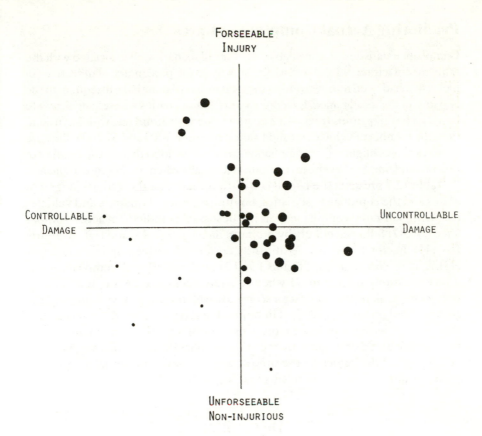

Figure 12.2 *Relationship between perceived risk and location of a defect in the hazard space. (The larger the point the greater the perceived risk)*

correlated with a defect's score on each factor. A linear combination of both factors would predict these variables with an *R* ranging from .81 to .89. Figure 12.2 demonstrates this predictability for perceived risk. As one goes from right to left in the factor space, and (to a lesser extent) from bottom to top, perceived risk (size of dot) increases. Factor 2, which is predominantly determined by manufacturer foreseeability, gets its link to risk from its secondary association with the likelihood of severe personal harm. This is why carbon monoxide and gas fumes, and problems with seat belts, are judged as highly risky, despite their negative scores on factor 1. They are all seen to lead to severe personal harm.

Of particular interest is the location of the Pinto scenario (FUELRPTR) in the upper-right quadrant of the factor space (severe and foreseeable damage). Much like nuclear power in the factor space derived from judgments of diverse activities and technologies (Slovic et al, 1985), the FUELRPTR scenario was located in the most ominous region of the taxonomy. In this sense, the present analysis shows the Pinto scenario to be the 'nuclear power' of the automobile defect space. Defects leading to locking of the rear brakes (RBRKLOCK) or disengagement of the front windshield (FRWINDSH) appear to be rather close to the Pinto scenario in the space. The defect perceived to be most risky, steering lock (STEERLCK), was most extreme on factor 1, but was judged to be relatively unforeseeable.

Predicting Actual Compliance Rates

Compliance statistics were available for 21 recall scenarios, all associated with the same manufacturer. These statistics represented the percentage of defective vehicles that had been repaired during the 6 quarters (18 months) subsequent to the issuance of the recall notice. Exceptions were four scenarios whose statistics were based on fewer quarters (two with 2 quarters, one with 3, and one with 5). In addition, the number of vehicles recalled varied between 9000 and 519,000. Because these variables might affect compliance rates, we decided to hold the number of quarters and number of vehicles constant statistically when predicting compliance.

Table 12.7 presents the partial correlations between the various judgment scales and the compliance statistics, holding number of quarters and vehicles constant. Self-rated compliance was the best single predictor of actual compliance ($r = .47$) followed closely by property damage ($r = .46$) and lack of control ($r = .44$). Factor 1 was also significantly correlated with compliance rate ($r = .43$). A linear combination of factors 1 and 2 correlated .61 with compliance rate. The correlation jumped to .71 when self-rated compliance was added to the predictor set, along with the factor scores. Also of interest is the finding that the riskiness judgment or perceived likelihood of serious injury did not correlate significantly with compliance rates. Considering that there are many uncontrolled variables that might influence the compliance rate – such as type of car and the age of the vehicle at the time of recall – these substantial correlations with compliance rate are quite encouraging.

DISCUSSION

A critical challenge to the automobile industry is to develop guidelines for the safety engineering of automobiles that address not only monetary and statistical

Table 12.7 *Correlations with Actual Compliance*

Variable	Correlation
Knowledge	−.24
Dread	.08
Property damage	.46*
Personal injury	−.05
Controllability	−.44*
Observability	−.16
Centrality	.40*
Riskiness	.18
Self compliance	.47*
General compliance (%)	.34
Future purchase	.31
Factor 1	.43*
Factor 2	−.34

* $p < .01$, 1 tailed
Note: these are partial correlations, holding number of cars and time since recall constant.

concerns but also incorporate elements of social accountability. Such a theory would draw on a number of sources for its components, including cost-benefit and risk analysis, and would be supplemented by methods that identify safety-related engineering defects whose seriousness and higher-order costs are likely to be underestimated by typical economic analysis.

The methodology proposed here as a step toward achieving that goal is based on techniques developed to study psychological perceptions of risk. These techniques were applied in the context of evaluating the type of automobile safety defects that result in manufacturers' issuing recall notices to vehicle owners. The results were encouraging. Motor-vehicle defects were found to be highly diverse in terms of the perceived qualities or characteristics of their risks. Differences among defect scenarios could be represented within a two-factor space defined in terms of the manufacturer's foreseeability of injury and the driver's controllability of damage. Location of a defect within this factor space was closely associated with (hence predictive of) perceived riskiness, perceived likelihood of compliance with a recall notice, attitudes toward purchasing another car from the same manufacturer and, to a surprising extent, actual compliance rates. The characterization of the Pinto scenario as extremely problematic on both factors (foreseeable and un-controllable damage) is reminiscent of the characterization of nuclear power in previous studies of risk perception (Slovic et al, 1985). It may be that the methods of risk-perception research can enable analysts to spot future 'Pinto scenarios' early enough to ensure that they do not harm people and manufacturers.

As noted earlier, the concept of signal potential reflects the interpretation that is given to a mishap, such as the discovery of a design defect. If the mishap is interpreted as a sign that the risks are not being managed properly, the cost-liness of the defect to the manufacturer can be extremely great. The enormous costs that can arise from social reactions (eg, liability suits, stricter regulation, damaged reputation, loss of sales) produce an incentive to manufacturers to prevent or mitigate 'high-signal' defects that is generally far greater than the incentive associated with the direct costs of accidents. We have not examined signal potential specifically in this study. As a result, we do not know how it relates to this two-factor space or to the functional taxonomy. We would specu-late that signal potential would increase as one goes from left to right and from bottom to top in the factor space. Further research, using questions specifically designed to assess signal potential (see Slovic, Lichtenstein et al, 1984), is re-quired to test these speculations. Research is also needed to determine exactly how to predict higher-order costs from signal potential and other characteristics of risk and how to incorporate these costs with the costs of injuries and damages in the context of a cost-benefit or risk analysis.

For example, one approach to risk analysis that incorporates both social and psychological considerations in a quantitative way has been developed by risk analysts in Switzerland (Bohnenblust, 1984; Bohnenblust & Schneider, 1984). Essentially, their model first develops a space of possible risk-reduction alter-natives that vary in effectiveness and cost. Alternatives having the greatest risk reduction for their cost form a non-dominated set. Social and psychological cri-teria based on risk perception factors are then applied as a basis for deciding which of the alternatives to select.

In conclusion, the present study demonstrates the possibility of characterizing and quantifying the perceived riskiness of automobile defects in ways that could prove important for decisions about safety design and recalls.

ACKNOWLEDGMENTS

We are grateful to Mark Layman, Leisha Sanders, and Geri Hanson for their help in various stages of this project. The writing of this paper was supported, in part, by the National Science Foundation under Grant SES 8517411 to Decision Research. Any opinions, findings, recommendations or conclusions expressed here are those of the authors and do not necessarily reflect the views of the National Science Foundation.

Appendix 12.A Automobile Recall Scenarios, Ordered by Perceived Level of Risk

Defect	Year	Compliance rate [a]	Code	Number of cars recalled	Description
6	1970		STEERLCK	6000	The locking bolt of the steering column lock may have been ineffectively secured in assembly. Under certain circumstances this could activate the lock, causing immediate loss of directional control of the vehicle.
23	1977		FUELRPTR		The fuel tank, placed directly behind the rear axle, may lack adequate protection from the rear-axle mounting brackets. In the event of a rear end collision, the fuel tank could be pushed into the mounting brackets with sufficient force to cause it to rupture, allowing fuel to escape. This could create the possibility of a fire and/or burn injuries to vehicle occupants and bystanders.
39	1981	74.0%	RBRKLOCK	47,371	The valve in the braking system that controls the amount of braking effort applied to each of the wheels may distribute greater braking force to the rear than to the front brakes. As a result, the rear brakes may lock up, potentially causing loss of vehicle control.
16	1971		COFUMES	679,900	Fumes in the direct air heating system may be transferred from the engine compartment to the passenger compartment. In some cases, such fumes contain carbon monoxide in sufficient concentration to harm or endanger the occupants of the vehicle.
36	1983	54.5%	ACLTRPIN	19,108	A retaining pin in the accelerator pump of the carburetor may come loose after repeatedly applying the throttle wide open. This could cause the control linkage to the accelerator pump to bind and prevent the throttle from closing. As a result, the speed of the car would remain constant even though the driver was no longer depressing the accelerator pedal.
9	1979	73.0%	FUELLINE	41,508	The connection between the fuel line and the engine may deteriorate, causing a gasoline leak. If a leak were to develop the gasoline could ignite, resulting in a fire under the hood of the vehicle.

Appendix 12.A *continued*

Defect	Year	Compliance rate [a]	Code	Number of cars recalled	Description
33	1971		FRWINDSH	10,711	There is the possibility that the front windshield has only marginal retention at the top edge. If the condition exists, air pressure may cause the glass to become disengaged from the windshield frame when the vehicle is moving at high speeds.
7	1979	74.9%	BRAKELIT	15,328	An incorrect lubricant may have been applied to the plunger that activates the brake light switch. This could result in excessive wear in the switch, possibly causing the switch plunger to stick. If the plunger were to stick, the rear brake lights would become inoperative and the cruise control, if activated, would stay engaged even after the brake pedal was pressed.
40	1980	85.4%	STERHOSE	25,463	The power steering hoses may deteriorate, resulting in leakage of power steering fluid onto the exhaust manifold. This condition could cause smoke or fire under the hood of the vehicle.
24	1980	84.0%	TRNSSCRW	18,881	The two screws securing the automatic transmission shift linkage bracket may loosen and fall out. As a result, the gear position indicated by the transmission selector may differ from the actual gear position of the transmission. In addition, when starting the vehicle with the selector in the "neutral" or "park" position, the transmission may actually be in gear, and the vehicle may move forward or backward when the engine is started.
21	1971		THRTLOPN	6,682,084	The motor mount may separate from the chassis, thus allowing the motor to lift. If this condition were to occur, the movement of the motor would affect the throttle linkage. As a result, the throttle may momentarily increase, possibly opening to full throttle, causing the vehicle to become difficult to control.
15	1979	80.4%	TRNFLUID	224,892	The hoses carrying automatic transmission fluid to the transmission cooler may be defective. If a failure occurred, transmission fluid leakage could create the potential for a vehicle fire.

10	1970		FOOTSLIP	58,525	The brake pedal may bend when abnormal pressure is applied, such as during an emergency stop. If the pedal bends it may cause the driver's foot to slip off of the brake unexpectedly.
32	1982	73.1%	TANKLEAK	519,329	The hose clamps on the fuel-tank filler pipe and the fuel tank filler vent pipe could fracture, causing fuel leakage at any one of four pipe-to-hose connections. Leakage can occur during refueling, or while driving if the fuel tank is above ¾ full. This could create the possibility of a fire and/or burn injuries to persons in or near the vehicle.
28	1975		GASFUMES	6,037	Gasoline fumes may enter into the passenger compartment in sufficient concentration to harm or endanger the occupants of the vehicle.
30	1981	51.8%	RETRACTR	55,238	The seat-belt retractors in the rear seat, which cause the unused portion of the seat-belt to coil automatically, may not lock the seat belts from extending when used by smaller passengers. In a crash, the seat belts would not effectively restrain smaller passengers using them.
17	1979	63.4%	BELTBOLT	1,326,404	The heads of the bolts used to secure the front seat belts to the floor board may break off during normal operation, even though no unusual forces have been applied to them. The seat belts may appear to be normally attached, but might be only lightly secured to the floor. In the event of an accident, the anchor bolts may fail, increasing the probability of injury to the wearer of the belt.

Appendix 12.A *continued*

Defect	Year	Compliance rate [a]	Code	Number of cars recalled	Description
11	1979	74.4%	FRAXLDAM	1,896,222	The bearings in the front wheels might have inadequate lubrication. If the vehicle is operated in this condition over time, the wheel bearings might fail, causing damage to the front wheel axles and a loss of vehicle control.
4	1970		HOODOPEN	1292	The hood safety and main latches may have been misaligned. If the condition exists, the hood may open to a position that obstructs the driver's vision while the vehicle is in motion.
29	1976		PWRBRAKE	40,000	In cars equipped with power brakes, the power brake booster may contain a silencer pad that restricts input of air during pedal application. This condition could cause braking action delay on rapid pedal application, increasing stopping distance.
38	1983	55.6%	LITELOSS	25,053	A main fuse link in the electrical system may inadvertently open when subjected to the electrical load of the rear window defogger. An open fuse link may cause sudden loss of headlights. Loss of headlights under severe weather or nighttime driving conditions could reduce driver visibility.
5	1979	56.0%	ACLTRSTK	372,466	The accelerator pedal may have been manufactured with a small rubber flap extending from the base of the pedal. This pedal flap could become wedged under the accelerator in such a way that it would increase the engine speed. If this were to occur and the vehicle was shifted from "park" or "neutral" to "drive" or "reverse", the increased engine speed could produce an acceleration rate greater than the driver might expect.
35	1981	89.5%	STERBOLT	9070	The bolts securing the control arm may not have been tightened sufficiently. These bolts may loosen and come off during the course of normal vehicle operation, causing noticeable changes in steering control during acceleration and cornering. While it is unlikely that steering would be lost, reduced controllability of the vehicle could occur.

13	1979	STERGEAR	161,225	79.7%	The steering gear mechanism may become loose on vehicles with high mileage. If the condition exists, the driver may notice that the steering wheel can be turned several degrees before any change in the direction of the vehicle occurs. This could result in loss of vehicle control under conditions requiring full steering control of the vehicle.
1	1979	STEERDIF	172,000	67.8%	The engine mount support could become deformed if the vehicle is driven over speed bumps, pot holes or curbs at too high a speed. Should that occur, the engine mounting bracket might interfere with the steering linkage, making it more difficult to steer the vehicle.
19	1982	FUELVALV	24,455	84.0%	The fuel-tank ventilator valve may produce a loud and persistent "whistle" during the venting of the tank. If the fuel filler cap is removed while this condition exists and the tank is over ¾ full, gasoline may be forced out of the filler pipe and onto persons standing nearby. This could result in a fire and/or burn injuries.
18	1970	SEATRCLN	19,600		The front seat may unexpectedly recline if extreme pressure is exerted against the seat back. If this happens, the collapsing seat could make it difficult for the driver to control the vehicle.
26	1981	LITEDIM	105,130	77.4%	One of the main electrical cables connecting the engine to the body of the car may have been improperly designed. If the cable should break at a time when the electrical system is under heavy use, the headlights may suddenly dim. Sudden dimming of headlights under severe weather or nighttime driving conditions could reduce driver visibility.
3	1979	SUSPDAMG	23,725	98.8%	The front coil spring in the suspension system may be too large to sit properly on its support structure. Normal operation of the vehicle in this condition might cause the spring to slip over its mount, resulting in damage to the suspension system, brake hoses, and possibly even the tires.

Appendix 12.A *continued*

Defect	Year	Compliance rate [a]	Code	Number of cars recalled	Description
3	1979	98.8%	SUSPDAMG	23,725	The front coil spring in the suspension system may be too large to sit properly on its support structure. Normal operation of the vehicle in this condition might cause the spring to slip over its mount, resulting in damage to the suspension system, brake hoses, and possibly even the tires.
34	1975		AIRBAG	1293	The propellant for the air-bag restraint system on the driver's side may be insufficient to correctly inflate the driver's air cushion. If the vehicle should become involved in a frontal crash, the driver's air bag might not deploy normally, which could increase the severity of the injuries to the driver.
8	1970		FRNTSEAT	2017	The front-seat lock adjustment may, under extreme loading of the seat, fail to hold the seat in a firm position. As a result, the front seat may begin to slide backwards or forwards without warning, making the vehicle difficult to control.
31	1972		WDWIPERS	3,700,000	The set screw locking the windshield wiper arm to the driving shaft may work loose, causing erratic wiper operation and the possibility that wiper operation may cease entirely. The result would be reduced driver visibility under weather conditions requiring the use of the windshield wipers.
25	1967		PWRSTEER	745	There is a possible cracking or fracture of the rack portion of the piston and rack assembly of the power steering unit. This may result in loss of power assist; however, manual steering would not be affected.
2	1970		JACKFALL	81,932	Under some conditions the bumper jack hook may not properly engage the front bumper flange, and the vehicle may fall during jacking operations.

#	Year	Code	Number	Compliance	Description
37	1974	XHSTPIPE	8422		The exhaust pipe protector may be deformed as a result of hitting the protector on the ground in vehicle off-road use. Should the protector be crushed into the exhaust pipe, the shield surface temperature could rise to a point where dry grass could smolder. This could occur only if the vehicle is parked in tall dry grass and the grass is in contact with the protector.
22	1975	DEFROSTR	22,402		In models equipped with air conditioning, the heater-defroster system selector control may not always respond when shifting from certain heating, ventilation and air conditioning modes to the defrost mode. Should this occur, the mode door may not immediately move to defrost position and defrost air would not be directed to the windshield.
12	1972	SGNLSWTC	10,500		The screws which secure the turn signal operating switch, wiper/washer switch and overdrive switch to the steering column may loosen and come in contact with the steering hub. If the condition exists, it could cause momentary stiff operation of the switches.
20	1980	DECLINFO	81,158	59.6%	The decal on the rear edge of the left front door that contains information about the vehicle's tires may have omitted the tire rim size. Omission of this information could result in errors in tire and wheel maintenance to the vehicle.
14	73	HEATRVLV	60,000		The heater-hose water valve does not open and close properly. The result is that affected vehicles may not have full heater and defrosting capabilities and, thus, may not comply with Federal Motor Vehicle Safety Standards.

a Compliance rates, where available, were selected from automobile recall listings compiled by the US Department of Transportation (US Department of Transportation, 1967–1983).

13   Perception of Risk

Paul Slovic

The ability to sense and avoid harmful environmental conditions is necessary for the survival of all living organisms. Survival is also aided by an ability to codify and learn from past experience. Humans have an additional capability that allows them to alter their environment as well as respond to it. This capacity both creates and reduces risk.

In recent decades, the profound development of chemical and nuclear technologies has been accompanied by the potential to cause catastrophic and long-lasting damage to the Earth and the life forms that inhabit it. The mechanisms underlying these complex technologies are unfamiliar and incomprehensible to most citizens. Their most harmful consequences are rare and often delayed, hence difficult to assess by statistical analysis and not well suited to management by trial-and-error learning. The elusive and hard to manage qualities of today's hazards have forced the creation of a new intellectual discipline called risk assessment, designed to aid in identifying, characterizing and quantifying risk (for a comprehensive bibliography on risk assessment see Covello & Abernathy, 1984).

Whereas technologically sophisticated analysts employ risk assessment to evaluate hazards, the majority of citizens rely on intuitive risk judgments, typically called 'risk perceptions'. For these people, experience with hazards tends to come from the news media, which rather thoroughly document mishaps and threats occurring throughout the world. The dominant perception for most Americans (and one that contrasts sharply with the views of professional risk assessors) is that they face more risk today than in the past and that future risks will be even greater than today's (Harris, 1980). Similar views appear to be held by citizens of many other industrialized nations. These perceptions and the opposition to technology that accompanies them have puzzled and frustrated industrialists and regulators and have led numerous observers to argue that the American public's apparent pursuit of a 'zero-risk society' threatens the nation's political and economic stability. Wildavsky (1979, p32) commented as follows on this state of affairs:

Note: reprinted with permission from 'Perception of Risk' by P Slovic, *Science*, 236, 1987, pp280–5. Copyright 1987 American Association for the Advancement of Science.

How extraordinary! The richest, longest lived, best protected, most resourceful civilization, with the highest degree of insight into its own technology, is on its way to becoming the most frightened.

Is it our environment or ourselves that have changed? Would people like us have had this sort of concern in the past?... Today, there are risks from numerous small dams far exceeding those from nuclear reactors. Why is the one feared and not the other? Is it just that we are used to the old or are some of us looking differently at essentially the same sorts of experience?

During the past decade, a small number of researchers has been attempting to answer such questions by examining the opinions that people express when they are asked, in a variety of ways, to evaluate hazardous activities, substances and technologies. This research has attempted to develop techniques for assessing the complex and subtle opinions that people have about risk. With these techniques, researchers have sought to discover what people mean when they say that something is (or is not) 'risky', and to determine what factors underlie those perceptions. The basic assumption underlying these efforts is that those who promote and regulate health and safety need to understand the ways in which people think about and respond to risk.

If successful, this research should aid policy-makers by improving communication between them and the public, by directing educational efforts and by predicting public responses to new technologies (eg, genetic engineering), events (eg, a good safety record or an accident) and new risk management strategies (eg, warning labels, regulations, substitute products).

RISK PERCEPTION RESEARCH

Important contributions to our current understanding of risk perception have come from geography, sociology, political science, anthropology and psychology. Geographical research focused originally on understanding human behavior in the face of natural hazards, but it has since broadened to include technological hazards as well (Burton et al, 1978). Sociological (Short, 1984) and anthropological studies (Douglas & Wildavsky, 1982) have shown that perception and acceptance of risk have their roots in social and cultural factors. Short (1984) argues that response to hazards is mediated by social influences transmitted by friends, family, fellow workers and respected public officials. In many cases, risk perceptions may form afterwards, as part of the ex-post facto rationale for one's own behavior. Douglas and Wildavsky (1982) assert that people, acting within social groups, downplay certain risks and emphasize others as a means of maintaining and controlling the group.

Psychological research on risk perception, which shall be the focus of this chapter, originated in empirical studies of probability assessment, utility assessment and decision-making processes (Edwards, 1961). A major development in this area has been the discovery of a set of mental strategies, or heuristics, that people employ to make sense out of an uncertain world (Kahneman, Slovic & Tversky, 1982). Although these rules are valid in some circumstances, in others they lead to large and persistent biases, with serious implications for risk assessment. In particular, laboratory research on basic perceptions and cognitions has shown that difficulties in understanding probabilistic processes, biased media coverage, misleading personal experiences, and the anxieties generated by life's gambles cause uncertainty to be denied, risks to be misjudged (sometimes overestimated and sometimes underestimated) and judgments of fact to be held with unwarranted confidence. Experts' judgments appear to be prone to many of the same biases as those of the general public, particularly when experts are forced to go beyond the limits of available data and rely on intuition (Henrion & Fischhoff, 1986; Kahneman et al, 1982).

Research further indicates that disagreements about risk should not be expected to evaporate in the presence of evidence. Strong initial views are resistant to change because they influence the way that subsequent information is interpreted. New evidence appears reliable and informative if it is consistent with one's initial beliefs; contrary evidence tends to be dismissed as unreliable, erroneous or unrepresentative (Nisbett & Ross, 1980). When people lack strong prior opinions, the opposite situation exists – they are at the mercy of the problem formulation. Presenting the same information about risk in different ways (eg, mortality rates as opposed to survival rates) alters people's perspectives and actions (Tversky & Kahneman, 1981).

THE PSYCHOMETRIC PARADIGM

One broad strategy for studying perceived risk is to develop a taxonomy for hazards that can be used to understand and predict responses to their risks. A taxonomic scheme might explain, for example, people's extreme aversion to some hazards, their indifference to others, and the discrepancies between these reactions and the opinions of experts. The most common approach to this goal has employed the psychometric paradigm (Fischhoff, Slovic, Lichtenstein, Read et al, 1978; Slovic, Fischhoff et al, 1984), which uses psychophysical scaling and multivariate analysis techniques to produce quantitative representations or 'cognitive maps' of risk attitudes and perceptions. Within the psychometric paradigm, people make quantitative judgments about the current and desired riskiness of diverse hazards and the desired level of regulation of each. These judgments are then related to judgments about other properties, such as:

- the hazard's status on characteristics that have been hypothesized to account for risk perceptions and attitudes (eg, voluntariness, dread, knowledge, controllability);
- the benefits that each hazard provides to society;
- the number of deaths caused by the hazard in an average year; and
- the number of deaths caused by the hazard in a disastrous year.

The rest of this chapter will briefly review some of the results obtained from psychometric studies of risk perception and outline some implications of these results for risk communication and risk management.

REVEALED AND EXPRESSED PREFERENCES

The original impetus for the psychometric paradigm came from the pioneering effort of Starr (1969) to develop a method for weighing technological risks against benefits in order to answer the fundamental question, 'How safe is safe enough?' His 'revealed preference' approach assumed that, by trial and error, society has arrived at an 'essentially optimum' balance between the risks and benefits associated with any activity. One may therefore use historical or current risk and benefit data to reveal patterns of 'acceptable' risk–benefit trade-offs. Examining such data for several industries and activities, Starr concluded that:

- Acceptability of risk from an activity is roughly proportional to the third power of the benefits for that activity.
- The public will accept risks from voluntary activities (such as skiing) that are roughly 1000 times as great as it would tolerate from involuntary hazards (such as food preservatives) that provide the same level of benefits.

The merits and deficiencies of Starr's approach have been debated at length (Fischhoff et al, 1981). They will not be elaborated upon here, except to note that concern about the validity of the many assumptions inherent in the revealed preferences approach stimulated Fischhoff, Slovic, Lichtenstein, Read et al (1978) to conduct an analogous psychometric analysis of questionnaire data resulting in 'expressed preferences'. In recent years, numerous other studies of expressed preferences have been carried out within the psychometric paradigm (Gardner et al, 1982; DeLuca, Stolwijk & Horowitz, 1986; Johnson & Tversky, 1984; Lindell & Earle, 1983; Otway & Fishbein, 1976; Renn & Swaton, 1984; Slovic, Fischhoff & Lichtenstein, 1980c; Vlek & Stallen, 1981; von Winterfeldt et al, 1981).

These studies have shown that perceived risk is quantifiable and predictable. Psychometric techniques seem well suited for identifying similarities and differences among groups with regard to risk perceptions and attitudes (see Table 13.1). They have also shown that the concept 'risk' means different things to different people. When experts judge risk, their responses correlate highly with technical estimates of annual fatalities. Laypeople can assess annual fatalities if they are asked to (and produce estimates somewhat like the technical estimates). However, their judgments of 'risk' are related more to other hazard characteristics (eg, catastrophic potential, threat to future generations) and, as a result, tend to differ from their own (and experts') estimates of annual fatalities.

Another consistent result from psychometric studies of expressed preferences is that people tend to view current risk levels as unacceptably high for most activities. The gap between perceived and desired risk levels suggests that people are not satisfied with the way that market and other regulatory mechanisms have balanced risks and benefits. Across the domain of hazards, there seems to be little systematic relationship between perceptions of current risks and benefits. However, studies of expressed preferences do seem to support Starr's argument that people are willing to tolerate higher risks from activities seen as highly beneficial. But, whereas Starr concluded that voluntariness of exposure was the key mediator of risk acceptance, expressed preference studies have shown that other (perceived) characteristics such as familiarity, control, catastrophic

Table 13.1 *Ordering of Perceived Risk for 30 Activities and Technologies*

	LOWV	College students	Active club members	Experts
Nuclear power	1	1	8	20
Motor vehicles	2	5	3	1
Handguns	3	2	1	4
Smoking	4	3	4	2
Motorcycles	5	6	2	6
Alcoholic beverages	6	7	5	3
General (private) aviation	7	15	11	12
Police work	8	8	7	17
Pesticides	9	4	15	8
Surgery	10	11	9	5
Fire fighting	11	10	6	18
Large construction	12	14	13	13
Hunting	13	18	10	23
Spray cans	14	13	23	26
Mountain climbing	15	22	12	29
Bicycles	16	24	14	15
Commercial aviation	17	16	18	16
Electric power	18	19	19	9
Swimming	19	30	17	10
Contraceptives	20	9	22	11
Skiing	21	25	16	30
X-rays	22	17	24	7
High-school and college football	23	26	21	27
Railroads	24	23	20	19
Food preservatives	25	12	28	14
Food coloring	26	20	30	21
Power mowers	27	28	25	28
Prescription antibiotics	28	21	26	24
Home appliances	29	27	27	22
Vaccinations	30	29	29	25

Note: The ordering is based on the geometric mean risk ratings within each group. Rank 1 represents the most risky activity or technology.

potential, equity and level of knowledge also seem to influence the relationship between perceived risk, perceived benefit and risk acceptance (Fischhoff, Slovic, Lichtenstein, Read et al, 1978; Slovic, Fischhoff & Lichtenstein, 1980c).

Various models have been advanced to represent the relationship between perceptions, behavior and these qualitative characteristics of hazards. As we shall see, the picture that emerges from this work is both orderly and complex.

FACTOR-ANALYTIC REPRESENTATIONS

Many of the qualitative risk characteristics are correlated with each other, across a wide range of hazards. For example, hazards judged to be 'voluntary' tend also to be judged as 'controllable'; hazards whose adverse effects are delayed tend to be seen as posing risks that are not well known, and so on. Investigation of these relations by means of factor analysis has shown that the broader domain of characteristics can be condensed to a small set of higher order characteristics or factors.

The factor space presented in Figure 13.1 has been replicated across groups of laypeople and experts judging large and diverse sets of hazards. Factor 1, labeled 'dread risk', is defined at its high (right-hand) end by perceived lack of control, dread, catastrophic potential, fatal consequences and the inequitable distribution of risks and benefits. Nuclear weapons and nuclear power score highest on the characteristics that make up this factor. Factor 2, labeled 'unknown risk',

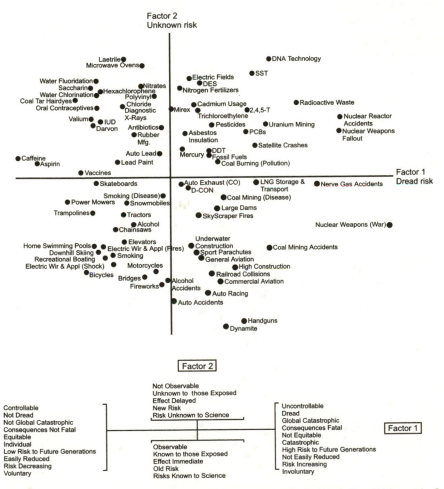

Source: 'Facts and Fears: Understanding perceived risk', by Slovic, P, Fischhoff, B and Lichtenstein, S in R C Schwing and W A Albers, Jr (eds) *Societal Risk Assessment: How Safe is Enough?* New York: Plenum, 1980, pp181-214. Copyright 1980 by Plenum Publishing. Reprinted with permission

Figure 13.1 *Location of 81 hazards on factors 1 and 2 derived from the interrelationships among 15 risk characteristics. Each factor is made up of a combination of characteristics, as indicated by the lower diagram*

is defined at its high end by hazards judged to be unobservable, unknown, new and delayed in their manifestation of harm. Chemical technologies score particularly high on this factor. A third factor, reflecting the number of people exposed to the risk, has been obtained in several studies. Making the set of hazards more or less specific (eg, partitioning nuclear power into radioactive waste, uranium mining and nuclear reactor accidents) has had little effect on the factor structure or its relationship to risk perceptions (Slovic et al, 1985).

Research has shown that laypeople's risk perceptions and attitudes are closely related to the position of a hazard within this type of factor space. Most important is the horizontal factor 'dread risk'. The higher a hazard's score on this factor (the further to the right it appears in the space), the higher its perceived risk, the more people want to see its current risks reduced, and the more they want to see strict regulation employed to achieve the desired reduction in risk (Figure 13.2). In contrast, experts' perceptions of risk are not closely related to any of the various risk characteristics or factors derived from these characteristics (Slovic et al, 1985). Instead, as noted earlier, experts appear to see riskiness as synonymous with expected annual mortality (Slovic, Lichtenstein et al, 1979). As a result, conflicts over 'risk' may result from experts and laypeople having different definitions of the concept.

The representation shown in Figure 13.1, while robust and informative, is by no means a universal cognitive mapping of the domain of hazards. Other psychometric methods (such as multidimensional scaling analysis of hazard-similarity judgments), applied to quite different sets of hazards, produce

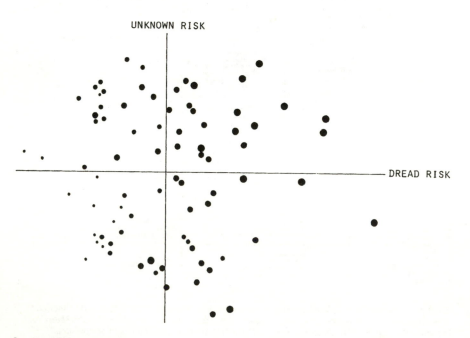

Source: Slovic et al (1985)

Figure 13.2 *Attitudes toward regulation of the hazards in Figure 13.1. (The larger the point, the greater the desire for strict regulation to reduce risk)*

different spatial models (Johnson & Tversky, 1984; Slovic, Fischhoff et al, 1984). The utility of these models for understanding and predicting behavior remains to be determined.

ACCIDENTS AS SIGNALS

Risk analyses typically model the impacts of an unfortunate event (such as an accident, a discovery of pollution sabotage, product tampering) in terms of direct harm to victims – deaths, injuries and damages. The impacts of such events, however, sometimes extend far beyond these direct harms and may include significant indirect costs (both monetary and non-monetary) to the responsible government agency or private company that far exceed direct costs. In some cases, all companies in an industry are affected, regardless of which company was responsible for the mishap. In extreme cases, the indirect costs of a mishap may extend past industry boundaries, affecting companies, industries and agencies whose business is minimally related to the initial event. Thus, an unfortunate event can be thought of as analogous to a stone dropped in a pond. The ripples spread outward, encompassing first the directly affected victims, then the responsible company or agency and, in the extreme, reaching other companies, agencies and industries.

Some events make only small ripples; others make larger ones. The challenge is to discover characteristics associated with an event and the way that it is managed that can predict the breadth and seriousness of those impacts (Figure 13.3). Early theories equated the magnitude of impact to the number of people killed or injured, or to the amount of property damaged. However, the accident at the Three Mile Island (TMI) nuclear reactor in 1979 provides a dramatic demonstration that factors other than injury, death and property damage impose serious costs. Despite the fact that not a single person died, and few if any latent cancer fatalities are expected, no other accident in our history has produced such costly societal impacts. The accident at TMI devastated the utility that owned and operated the plant. It also imposed enormous costs (EPRI, 1980) on the nuclear industry and on society, through stricter regulation (resulting in increased construction and operation costs), reduced operation of reactors worldwide, greater public opposition to nuclear power, and reliance on more expensive energy sources. It may even have led to a more hostile view of other complex technologies, such as chemical manufacturing and genetic engineering. The point is that traditional economic and risk analyses tend to neglect these higher order impacts; therefore, they greatly underestimate the costs associated with certain kinds of events.

Although the TMI accident is extreme, it is by no means unique. Other recent events resulting in enormous higher order impacts include the chemical manufacturing accident at Bhopal, India, the pollution of Love Canal, New York, and Times Beach, Missouri, the disastrous launch of the space shuttle *Challenger*, and the meltdown of the nuclear reactor at Chernobyl. Following these extreme events are a myriad of mishaps varying in the breadth and size of their impacts.

An important concept that has emerged from psychometric research is that the seriousness and higher order impacts of an unfortunate event are determined, in

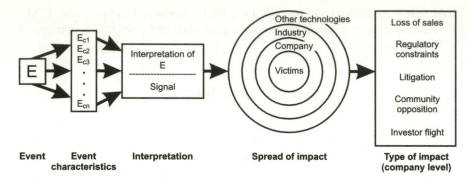

Figure 13.3 *A model of impact for unfortunate events*

part, by what that event signals or portends (Slovic, Lichtenstein et al, 1984). The informativeness or 'signal potential' of an event, and thus its potential social impact, appears to be systematically related to the characteristics of the hazard and the location of the event within the factor space described earlier (Figure 13.4). An accident that takes many lives may produce relatively little social disturbance (beyond that experienced by the victims' families and friends) if it occurs as part of a familiar and well-understood system (such as a train wreck). However, a small accident in an unfamiliar system (or one perceived as poorly understood), such as a nuclear reactor or a recombinant DNA laboratory, may have immense social consequences if it is perceived as a harbinger of further and possibly catastrophic mishaps.

The concept of accidents as signals was eloquently expressed in an editorial addressing the tragic accident at Bhopal (*New Yorker*, 1985).

> What truly grips us in these accounts is not so much the numbers as the spectacle of suddenly vanishing competence, of men utterly routed by technology, of fail-safe systems failing with a logic as inexorable as it was once – indeed, right up until that very moment – unforeseeable. And the spectacle haunts us because it seems to carry allegorical import, like the whispery omen of a hovering future.

One implication of the signal concept is that effort and expense beyond that indicated by a cost-benefit analysis might be warranted to reduce the possibility of 'high-signal accidents'. Unfortunate events involving hazards in the upper right quadrant of Figure 13.1 appear particularly likely to have the potential to produce large ripples. As a result, risk analyses involving these hazards need to be sensitive to these possible higher order impacts. Doing so would likely bring greater protection to potential victims as well as to companies and industries.

ANALYSIS OF SINGLE HAZARD DOMAINS

Psychometric analyses have also been applied to judgments of diverse hazard scenarios within a single technological domain, such as railroad transport (Kraus & Slovic, 1988b) or automobiles (Slovic et al, 1987). Kraus and Slovic (1988b) had people evaluate the riskiness of 49 railroad hazard scenarios that varied with respect to type of train, type of cargo, location of the accident and the nature and cause of the accident (eg, a high-speed train carrying passengers through a mountain tunnel derails due to a mechanical system failure). The results showed that these railroad hazards were highly differentiated, much like the hazards in Figure 13.1. The highest signal potential (and thus the highest potential for large ripple effects) was associated with accidents involving trains carrying hazardous chemicals.

A study by Slovic et al (1987) examined perceptions of risk and signal value for 40 structural defects in automobiles. Multivariate analysis of these defects, rated in terms of various characteristics of risk, produced a two-factor space. As in earlier studies with diverse hazards, the position of a defect in this space predicted judgments of riskiness and signal value quite well. One defect stood out much as nuclear hazards do in Figure 13.1. It was a fuel-tank rupture upon impact, creating the possibility of fire and burn injuries. This, of course, is similar to the notorious design problem that plagued Ford Pinto and that Ford allegedly declined to correct because a cost-benefit analysis indicated that the correction costs greatly exceeded the expected benefits from increased safety (*Grimshaw versus Ford Motor Co*, 1978). Had Ford performed a psychometric study, the analysis might have highlighted this particular defect as one whose seriousness and higher order costs (lawsuits, damaged company reputation) were likely to be greatly underestimated by cost-benefit analysis.

FORECASTING PUBLIC ACCEPTANCE

Results from studies of the perception of risk have been used to explain and forecast acceptance of and opposition to specific technologies (Slovic, Fischhoff & Lichtenstein, 1981b). Nuclear power has been a frequent topic of such analyses because of the dramatic opposition it has engendered in the face of experts' assurances of its safety. Research shows that people judge the benefits from nuclear power to be quite small and the risks to be unacceptably great. Nuclear power risks occupy extreme positions in psychometric factor spaces, reflecting people's views that these risks are unknown, dread, uncontrollable, inequitable, catastrophic and likely to affect future generations (Figure 13.1). Opponents of nuclear power recognize that few people have died thus far as a result of this technology. However, long before Chernobyl, they expressed great concern over the potential for catastrophic accidents.

These public perceptions have evoked harsh reactions from experts. One noted psychiatrist wrote that 'the irrational fear of nuclear plants is based on a mistaken assessment of the risks' (Dupont, 1981, p8). A nuclear physicist and leading advocate of nuclear power contended that. 'The public has been driven insane over fear of radiation [from nuclear power]. I use the word "insane" purposefully since one of its definitions is loss of contact with reality. The public's understanding of radiation dangers has virtually lost all contact with the actual dangers as understood by scientists' (Cohen, 1983a, p31).

Risk perception research paints a different picture, demonstrating that people's deep anxieties are linked to the reality of extensive unfavorable media coverage and to a strong association between nuclear power and the proliferation and use of nuclear weapons. Attempts to 'educate' or reassure the public and bring their perceptions in line with those of industry experts appear unlikely to succeed because the low probability of serious reactor accidents makes empirical demonstrations of safety difficult to achieve. Because nuclear risks are perceived as unknown and potentially catastrophic, even small accidents will be highly publicized and may produce large ripple effects (Figure 13.4).

Psychometric research may be able to forecast the response to technologies that have yet to arouse strong and persistent public opposition. For example, DNA technologies seem to evoke several of the perceptions that make nuclear power so hard to manage. In the aftermath of an accident, this technology could face some of the same problems and opposition now confronting the nuclear industry.

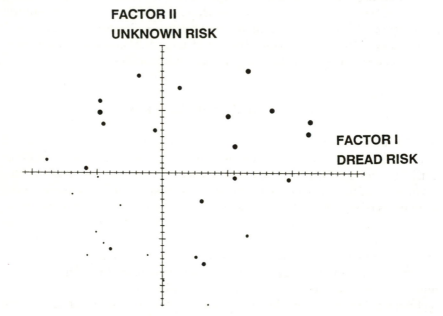

ACCIDENTS AS SIGNALS

Note: The larger the point, the greater the degree to which an accident involving that hazard was judged to 'serve as a warning signal for society, providing new information about the probability that similar or even more destructive mishaps might occur within this type of activity'. Media attention and the higher-order costs of a mishap are likely to be correlated with signal potential.

Source: Slovic, P, Lichtenstein, S and Fischhoff, B, 'Modeling the Societal Impact of Fatal Accidents', *Management Science,* 30(4), April 1994. Copyright 1994, The Institute of Management Sciences (currently INFORMS), 901 Elkridge Landing Road, Suite 400, Linthicum, MD 21090. Reprinted by permission

Figure 13.4 *Relationship between signal potential and risk characterization for 30 hazards in Figure 13.1*

PLACING RISKS IN PERSPECTIVE

A consequence of the public's concerns and its opposition to risky technologies has been an increase in attempts to inform and educate people about risk. Risk perception research has a number of implications for such educational efforts (Slovic, 1986).

One frequently advocated approach to broadening people's perspectives is to present quantitative risk estimates for a variety of hazards, expressed in some unidimensional index of death or disability, such as risk per hour of exposure, annual probability of death or reduction in life expectancy. Even though such comparisons have no logically necessary implications for acceptability of risk (Fischhoff et al, 1981), one might still hope that they would help to improve people's intuitions about the magnitude of risks. Risk perception research suggests, however, that these sorts of comparisons may not be very satisfactory even for this purpose. People's perceptions and attitudes are determined not only by the sort of unidimensional statistics used in such tables, but also by the variety of quantitative and qualitative characteristics reflected in Figure 13.1. To many people, statements such as, 'the annual risk from living near a nuclear power plant is equivalent to the risk of riding an extra 3 miles in an automobile', give inadequate consideration to the important differences in the nature of the risks from these two technologies.

In short, riskiness means more to people than 'expected number of fatalities'. Attempts to characterize, compare and regulate risks must be sensitive to this broader conception of risk. Fischhoff et al (1984) have made a start in this direction by demonstrating how one might construct a more comprehensive measure of risk. They show that variations in the scope of one's definition of risk can greatly change the assessment of risk from various energy technologies.

Whereas psychometric research implies that risk debates are not merely about risk statistics, some sociological and anthropological research implies that some of these debates may not even be about risk (Douglas & Wildavsky, 1982; Short, 1984). Risk concerns may provide a rationale for actions taken on other grounds or they may be a surrogate for other social or ideological concerns. When this is the case, communication about risk is simply irrelevant to the discussion. Hidden agendas need to be brought to the surface for discussion (Edwards & vonWinterfeldt, 1987).

Perhaps the most important message from this research is that there is wisdom as well as error in public attitudes and perceptions. Laypeople sometimes lack certain information about hazards. However, their basic conceptualization of risk is much richer than that of the experts and reflects legitimate concerns that are typically omitted from expert risk assessments. As a result, risk communication and risk management efforts are destined to fail unless they are structured as a two-way process. Each side, expert and public, has something valid to contribute. Each side must respect the insights and intelligence of the other.

ACKNOWLEDGMENTS

The text of this article draws heavily on the author's joint work with B Fischhoff and S Lichtenstein. Support for the writing of the article was provided by National Science Foundation Grant SES-8517411 to Decision Research.

14 The Social Amplification of Risk: A Conceptual Framework

Roger E Kasperson, Ortwin Renn, Paul Slovic, Halina S Brown, Jacque Emel, Robert Goble, Jeanne X Kasperson and Samuel Ratick

RISK IN MODERN SOCIETY

The investigation of risks is at once a scientific activity and an expression of culture. During the 20th century, massive governmental programs and bureaucracies aimed at assessing and managing risk have emerged in advanced industrial societies. Despite the expenditure of billions of dollars and steady improvements in health, safety and longevity of life, people view themselves as more rather than less vulnerable to the dangers posed by technology. Particularly perplexing is that even risk events with minor physical consequences often elicit strong public concern and produce extraordinarily severe social impacts, at levels unanticipated by conventional risk analysis.

Several difficult issues require attention:

- The technical concept of risk focuses narrowly on the *probability* of events and the *magnitude* of specific consequences. Risk is usually defined by multiplication of the two terms, assuming that society should be indifferent toward a low-consequence/high-probability risk and a high-consequence/low-probability risk with identical expected values. Studies of risk perception have revealed clearly, however, that most persons have a much more comprehensive conception of risk. Clearly, other aspects of the risk such as voluntariness, personal ability to influence the risk, familiarity with the hazard and the catastrophic potential shape public response (Renn, 1985; Slovic,

Note: reprinted from 'The Social Amplification of Risk: a Conceptual Framework', by R E Kasperson, O Renn, P Slovic, H S Brown, J Emel, R Goble, J X Kasperson & S Ratick, 1988, *Risk Analysis*, 8(2), pp177–87. Copyright 1988 Society for Risk Analysis. Reprinted with permission.

Fischhoff & Lichtenstein, 1982c). As a result, whereas the technical assessment of risk is essential to decisions about competing designs or materials, it often fails to inform societal choices regarding technology (Rayner & Cantor, 1987).

- Cognitive psychologists and decision researchers have investigated the underlying patterns of individual perception of risk and identified a series of heuristics and biases that govern risk perception (Slovic, 1987; Vlek & Stallen, 1981). Whereas some of these patterns of perception contrast with the results of formal reasoning, others involve legitimate concern about risk characteristics that are omitted, neglected or underestimated by the technical concept of risk. In addition, equity issues, the circumstances surrounding the process of generating risk and the timeliness of management response are considerations important to people, that are insufficiently addressed by formal probabilistic risk analysis (Doderlein, 1983; Kasperson, 1983).

- Risk is a bell-wether in social decisions about technologies. Because the resolution of social conflict requires the use of factual evidence for assessing the validity and fairness of rival claims, the quantity and quality of risk are major points of contention among participating social groups. As risk analysis incorporates a variety of methods to identify and evaluate risks, various groups present competing evidence based on their own perceptions and social agenda. The scientific aura surrounding risk analysis promotes the allocation of substantial effort to convincing official decision-makers, and the public, that the risk assessment performed by one group is superior in quality and scientific validity to that of others. Controversy and debate exacerbate divergences between expert and public assessment and often erode confidence in the risk decision process (Otway & von Winterfeldt, 1982; Wynne, 1984).

In short, the technical concept of risk is too narrow and ambiguous to serve as the crucial yardstick for policy-making.

Public perceptions, however, are the product of intuitive biases and economic interests and reflect cultural values more generally. The overriding dilemma for society is, therefore, the need to use risk analysis to design public policies on the one hand, and the inability of the current risk concepts to anticipate and explain the nature of public response to risk on the other. After a decade of research on the public experience of risk, no comprehensive theory exists to explain why apparently minor risk or risk events, as assessed by technical experts, sometimes produce massive public reactions, accompanied by substantial social and economic impacts and sometimes even by subsequently increased physical risks.[1] Explaining this phenomenon, and making the practice of risk analysis more sensitive to it, is one of the most challenging tasks confronting the societal management of risk. This chapter takes up that challenge.

The explanations that have emerged, while affording important insights, have been partial and often conflicting. The past decade has witnessed debates between the 'objectivist and subjectivist' schools of thought, between structuralistic and individualistic approaches, between physical and life scientists and social scientists. Even within the social sciences, psychologists see the roots of explanation in individual cognitive behavior (Fischhoff, Slovic, Lichtenstein, Read et al,

1978), a claim extensively qualified by anthropologists, who insist that social context and culture shape perceptions and cognition (Douglas & Wildavsky, 1982; Johnson & Covello, 1987), and by analysts of technological controversies, who see 'stakeholder' interaction and competing values as the keys (von Winterfeldt & Edwards, 1984). The assumption underlying these debates is that the interpretations are mutually invalidating. In fact, we will argue, the competing perspectives illuminate different facets of the public experience of risk.

A comprehensive theory is needed that is capable of integrating the technical analysis of risk and the cultural, social and individual response structures that shape the public experience of risk. The main thesis of this article is that risk events interact with psychological, social and cultural processes in ways that can heighten or attenuate public perception of risk and related risk behavior. Behavioral patterns, in turn, generate secondary social or economic consequences but may act also to increase or decrease the physical risk itself. Secondary effects trigger demands for additional institutional responses and protective actions, or, conversely (in the case of risk attenuation), impede needed protective actions. The social structures and processes of risk experience, the resulting repercussions on individual and group perceptions, and the effects of these responses on community, society and economy compose a general phenomenon that we term the *social amplification of risk*. This chapter sets forth an initial conceptualization of the elements, structure and processes that make up this phenomenon.

BACKGROUND

The technical assessment of risk typically models the impacts of an event or human activity in terms of direct harms, including death, injuries, disease and environmental damages. Over time, the practice of characterizing risk by probability and magnitude of harm has drawn fire for neglecting equity issues in relation to time (future generations), space (the so-called locally unwanted land use – LULU – or not in my backyard – NIMBY – issue), or social groups (the proletariat, the highly vulnerable, export of hazard to developing countries). It also has become apparent that the consequences of risk events extend far beyond direct harms to include significant indirect impacts (eg, liability, insurance costs, loss of confidence in institutions, or alienation from community affairs; Katzman, 1985). The situation becomes even more complex when the analysis also addresses the decision-making and risk-management processes. Frequently, indirect impacts appear to be dependent less upon the direct outcomes (ie, injury or death) of the risk event than on judgments of the adequacy of institutional arrangements to control or manage the risk, the possibility of assigning blame to one of the major participants, and the perceived fairness of the risk-management process.

The accident at the Three Mile Island (TMI) nuclear reactor in 1979 demonstrated dramatically that factors other than injury, death and property damage can impose serious costs and social repercussions. No one is likely to die from the release of radioactivity at TMI, but few accidents in US history have wrought such costly societal impacts. The accident devastated the utility that owned and operated the plant and imposed enormous costs – in the form of stricter regulations, reduced operation of reactors worldwide, greater public opposition to nuclear power, and a less viable role for one of the major long-term energy sources – on the entire nuclear industry and on society as a whole (Heising & George, 1986). This mishap at a nuclear power plant may even have increased public concerns about other complex technologies, such as chemical manufacturing and genetic engineering.

The point is that traditional cost-benefit and risk analyses neglect these higher order impacts and thus greatly underestimate the variety of adverse effects attendant on certain risk events (and thereby underestimate the overall risk from the event). In this sense, social amplification provides a corrective mechanism by which society acts to bring the technical assessment of risk more in line with a fuller determination of risk. At the other end of the spectrum, the relatively low levels of interest by the public in the risks presented by such well-documented and significant hazards as indoor radon, smoking, driving without seat belts, or highly carcinogenic aflatoxins in peanut butter serve as examples of the social attenuation of risk. Whereas attenuation of risk is indispensible in that it allows individuals to cope with the multitude of risks and risk events encountered daily, it also may lead to potentially serious adverse consequences from underestimation and underresponse. Thus, both social amplification and attenuation, through serious disjunctures between expert and public assessments of risk and varying responses among different publics, confound conventional risk analysis.

In some cases, the societal context may, through its effects on the risk assessor, alter the focus and scope of risk assessment. A case in point is the series of actions taken in 1984 by the Environmental Protection Agency with regard to a soil and grain fumigant, ethylene dibromide (EDB) (Sharlin, 1986). An atmosphere charged with intense societal concern about protecting the nation's food and groundwater supplies from chemical contaminants prompted the agency to focus primarily on these two pathways of population exposure to EDB, although it was well aware that emissions of EDB from leaded gasoline were a significant source of population exposure. Consequently, the first-line receivers of the risk information – the risk managers, the mass media, the politicians and the general public – heard from the start about cancer risks from tainted water and food, but not from ambient air. This example illustrates how the filtering of information about hazards may start as early as in the risk assessment itself and may profoundly alter the form and content of the risk information produced and conveyed by technical experts (Sharlin, 1986).

Other researchers have noted that risk sources create a complex network of direct and indirect effects that are susceptible to change through social responses (Hoos, 1980; Wynne, 1984). But because of the complexity and the transdisciplinary nature of the problem, an adequate conceptual framework for a theoretically based and empirically operational analysis is still missing. The lack of an integrative theory that provides guidelines on how to model and measure the complex relationships among risk, risk analysis, social response and socioeconomic effects has resulted in a reaffirmation of technical risk assessment, which at least provides definite answers (however narrow or misleading) to urgent risk problems.

The concept of social amplification of risk can, in principle, provide the needed theoretical base for a more comprehensive and powerful analysis of risk and risk management in modern societies. At this point, we do not offer a fully developed theory of social amplification of risk, but we do propose a fledgling conceptual framework that may serve to guide ongoing efforts to develop, test and apply such a theory to a broad array of pressing risk problems. Because the metaphor of amplification draws on notions in communications theory, we begin with a brief examination of its use in that context.

SIGNAL AMPLIFICATION IN COMMUNICATIONS THEORY

In communications theory, amplification denotes the process of intensifying or attenuating signals during the transmission of information from an information source to intermediate transmitters, and finally to a receiver (DeFleur, 1966). An information source sends out a cluster of signals (which form a message) to a transmitter or directly to the receiver. The signals are decoded by the transmitter or receiver so that the message can be understood. Each transmitter alters the original message by intensifying or attenuating some incoming signals, adding or deleting others, and sending a new cluster of signals on to the next transmitter or the final receiver where the next stage of decoding occurs.

The process of transmitting is more complex than the electronic metaphor implies. Messages have a meaning for the receiver only within a sociocultural context. Sources and signals are not independent entities but are perceived as a unit by the receiver who links the signal to the sources or transmitters and draws inferences about the relationship between the two. In spite of the problems of the source-receiver model, the metaphor is still powerful enough to serve as a heuristic framework for analyzing communication processes. In a recent literature review of 31 mass-communication textbooks, the source-receiver metaphor was, along with the concept of symbolic meaning, the predominant theoretical framework (Shoemaker, 1987).

Each message may contain factual, inferential, value-related, and symbolic meanings (Lasswell, 1948). The factual information refers to the content of the message (eg, the emission of an air pollutant is X milligrams per day) as well as the source of the message (eg, EPA conducted the measurement). The inferential message refers to the conclusions that can be drawn from the presented evidence (eg, the emission poses a serious health threat). Then those conclusions may undergo evaluation according to specific criteria (eg, the emission exceeds the allowable level). In addition, cultural symbols may be attached that evoke specific images (eg, 'big business', 'the military–industrial complex', 'high technology') that carry strong value implications.

Communication studies have demonstrated that the symbols present in messages are key factors in triggering the attention of potential receivers and in shaping their decoding processes (Hovland, 1948). If, for example, the communication source is described as an independent scientist, or a group of Nobel laureates, the content of the message may well command public attention. Messages from such sources may successfully pass through the selection filters of the transmitters or receivers and be viewed as credible. A press release by the nuclear industry, by contrast, may command much less credibility unless other aspects of the message compensate for doubts about the impartiality of the source.

Transmitters of signals may detect amplification arising from each message component (Sorensen & Mileti, 1987). A factual statement repeated several times, especially if by different sources, tends to elicit greater belief in the accuracy of the information. An elaborate description of the inference process may distract attention from the accuracy of the underlying assumptions. Reference to a highly appreciated social value may increase the receiver's tolerance for weak evidence. And, of course, a prestigious communication source can (at least in the short run) compensate for trivial factual messages. But adding or deleting symbols may well be the most powerful single means to amplify or attenuate the original message.

Amplification of signals occurs during both transmission and reception. The transmitter structures the messages that go to a receiver. The receiver, in turn, interprets, assimilates and evaluates the messages. But a transmitter, it should be noted, is also a new information source – one that transcribes the original message from the source into a new message and sends it on to the receiver, according to institutional rules, role requirements and anticipated receiver interests. Signals passing through a transmitter may therefore be amplified twice – during the reception of information and in recoding.

Signal amplification in communications, then, occupies a useful niche in the overall structure of the social amplification of risk. A discussion of the proposed conceptional framework takes up the next section of this chapter.

A STRUCTURAL DESCRIPTION OF THE SOCIAL AMPLIFICATION OF RISK

Social amplification of risk denotes the phenomenon by which information processes, institutional structures, social-group behavior and individual responses shape the social experience of risk, thereby contributing to risk consequences (Figure 14.1). The interaction between risk events and social processes makes clear that, as used in this framework, risk has meaning only to the extent that it treats how people think about the world and its relationships. Thus, there is no such thing as 'true' (absolute) and 'distorted' (socially determined) risk. Rather, the information system and characteristics of public response that compose social amplification are essential elements in determining the nature and magnitude of risk. We begin with the information system.

Like a stereo receiver, the information system may amplify risk events in two ways:

- intensifying or weakening signals that are part of the information that individuals and social groups receive about the risk; or
- filtering the multitude of signals with respect to the attributes of the risk and their importance.

Signals arise through direct personal experience with a risk object or through the receipt of information about the risk object (DeFleur, 1966). These signals

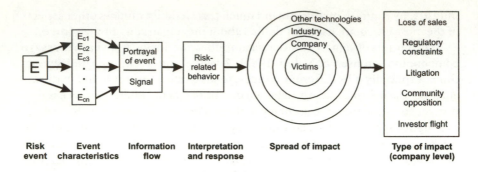

Figure 14.1 *Highly simplified representation of the social amplification of risk and potential impacts on a corporation*

are processed by social, as well as individual, amplification 'stations' that include the following:

- the scientist who conducts and communicates the technical assessment of risk;
- the risk-management institution;
- the news media;
- activist social organizations;
- opinion leaders within social groups;
- personal networks of peer and reference groups; and
- public agencies.

Social amplification stations generate and transmit information via communication channels (media, letters, telephones, direct conversations). In addition, each recipient also engages in amplification (and attenuation) processes, thereby acting as an amplification station for risk-related information. We hypothesize that the key amplification steps consist of the following:

- filtering of signals (eg, only a fraction of all incoming information is actually processed);
- decoding of the signal;
- processing of risk information (eg, the use of cognitive heuristics for drawing inferences);
- attaching social values to the information in order to draw implications for management and policy;
- interacting with one's cultural and peer groups to interpret and validate signals;
- formulating behavioral intentions to tolerate the risk or to take actions against the risk or risk manager; and
- engaging in group or individual actions to accept, ignore, tolerate or change the risk.

A fully-fledged theory of the social amplification of risk should ultimately explain why specific risks and risk events undergo more or less amplification or attenuation. Whether such a theory will carry the power to predict the specific kinds of public responses and the anatomy of social controversy that will follow the introduction of new risks must await the test of time. It may prove possible to identify and classify attributes of the risk source and of the social arena that heighten or attenuate the public response to risk.

Social amplifications of risk will spawn behavioral responses, which, in turn, will result in *secondary impacts*. Secondary impacts include the following effects:

- enduring mental perceptions, images and attitudes (eg, antitechnology attitudes, alienation from the physical environment, social apathy, stigmatization of an environment or risk manager);
- local impacts on business sales, residential property values, and economic activity;
- political and social pressure (eg, political demands, changes in political climate and culture);
- changes in the physical nature of the risk (eg, feedback mechanisms that increase or reduce the risk);
- changes in training, education, or required qualifications of operating and emergency-response personnel;
- social disorder (eg, protesting, rioting, sabotage, terrorism);
- changes in risk monitoring and regulation;
- increased liability and insurance costs; and
- repercussions on other technologies (eg, lower levels of public acceptance) and on social institutions (eg, erosion of public trust).

Secondary impacts are, in turn, perceived by social groups and individuals so that another stage of amplification may occur to produce third-order impacts. The impacts, therefore, may spread, or 'ripple', to other parties, distant locations or future generations. Each order of impact will not only disseminate social and political impacts but may also trigger (in risk amplification) or hinder (in risk attenuation) positive changes for risk reduction. The concept of social amplification of risk is hence dynamic, taking into account the learning and social interactions resulting from experience with risk.

The analogy of dropping a stone into a pond (see Figure 14.1) serves to illustrate the spread of the higher order impacts associated with the social amplification of risk. The ripples spread outward, first encompassing the directly affected victims or the first group to be notified, then touching the next higher institutional level (a company or an agency), and, in more extreme cases, reaching other parts of the industry or other social arenas with similar problems. This rippling of impacts is an important element of risk amplification because it suggests that amplification can introduce substantial temporal and geographical extension of impacts. The same graphic representation demonstrates the possibility that social amplification may, quantitatively and qualitatively, increase the direct impacts. In this case the inner circle changes its shape with each new round of ripples. Figure 14.2 depicts in greater detail the hypothesized stages of the social amplification of risk and its associated impacts for a hypothetical corporation.

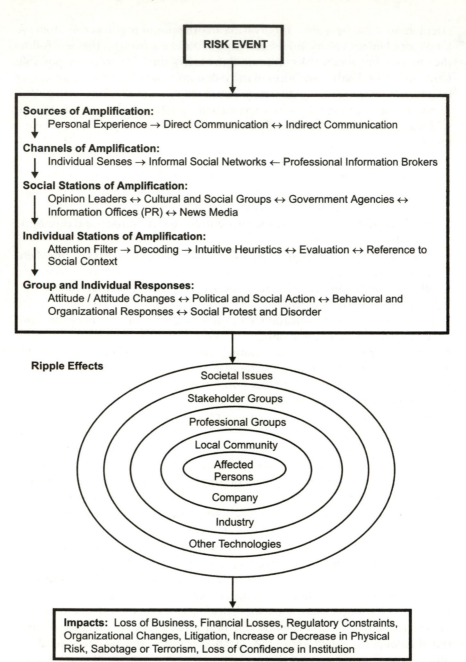

Figure 14.2 *Detailed conceptual framework of social amplification of risk*

Several examples illustrate the ripple effect of risk events. Following the Three Mile Island accident, nuclear plants worldwide were shut down and restarted more frequently for safety checks, although these phases of operations (as with aircraft take-offs and landings) are by far the riskiest operational stages.

In a more recent case of risk amplification, Switzerland recalled and ordered the incineration of 200 tons of its prestigious Vacherin Mont d'Or cheese because of bacterial contamination. Rival French cheesemakers at first celebrated their good fortune until it became apparent that public concern over the event had caused worldwide consumption of the cheese, from all producers, to plummet by over 25%. An entire industry, in short, suffered economic reversal from a specific risk event (Grunhouse, 1988).

Social amplification of risk, in our current conceptualization, involves two major stages (or amplifiers) – the transfer of information about the risk or risk event, and the response mechanisms of society.

INFORMATIONAL MECHANISMS OF SOCIAL AMPLIFICATION

The roots of social amplification lie in the social experience of risk, both in direct personal experience and in indirect, or secondary, experience, through information received about the risk, risk events and management systems. Direct experience with risky activities or events can be either reassuring (as with automobile driving) or alarming (as with tornadoes or floods). Generally, experience with dramatic accidents or risk events increases the memorability and imaginability of the hazard, thereby heightening the perception of risk (Slovic, 1986). But direct experience can also provide feedback on the nature, extent and manageability of the hazard, affording better perspective and enhanced capability for avoiding risks. Thus, whereas direct personal experience can serve as a risk amplifier, it can also act to attenuate risk. Understanding this interaction for different risks, for different social experiences and for different cultural groups is an important research need.

But many risks are not experienced directly. When direct personal experience is lacking or minimal, individuals learn about risk from other persons and from the media. Information flow becomes a key ingredient in public response and acts as a major agent of amplification. Attributes of information that may influence the social amplification are *volume*, the degree to which information is *disputed*, the extent of *dramatization* and the *symbolic connotations* of the information.

Independent of the accuracy and particular content of information, large volumes of information flow may serve as a risk amplifier. In an analysis of media coverage of Love Canal and Three Mile Island, Mazur (1984a) argued that the massive quantity of media coverage not only reported the events but defined and shaped the issues. Repeated stories, of course, direct public attention toward particular risk problems and away from competing sources of attention. Moreover, the news media tend to become battlegrounds where various participants vie for advantage. However balanced the coverage, it is unclear that reassuring claims can effectively counter the effects of fear-arousing messages (Sorensen, Soderstrom, Copenhaver, Carnes & Bolin, 1987). In Alvin Weinberg's (1977) metaphor, it is much harder to 'unscare' people than to scare them. High volumes of information also mobilize latent fears about a particular risk and enhance the recollection of previous accidents or management failures or enlarge the extent to which particular failures, events or consequences can be imagined. In this way, technologies or activities may come to be viewed as more dangerous (Kahneman et al, 1982; Renn, 1986).

The second attribute of information is the degree to which individuals or groups dispute factual information or inferences regarded as credible by interested members of the public. Debates among experts are apt to heighten public uncertainty about what the facts really are, increase doubts about whether the hazards are really understood and decrease the credibility of official spokespersons (Mazur, 1981). If the risks are already feared by the public, then increased concern is the likely result.

Dramatization, a third attribute, is undoubtedly a powerful source of risk amplification. The report during the Three Mile Island accident that a hydrogen bubble inside the reactor could explode within the next two days, blow the head off the reactor and release radioactive material into the atmosphere certainly increased public fears near the nuclear plant (and around the world). Sensational headlines ('Thousands Dead!') following the Chernobyl accident increased the memorability of that accident and the perceived catastrophic potential of nuclear power. If erroneous information sources find ready access to the mass media without effective antidotes, then large social impacts, even for minor events, become entirely possible.

The channels of information are also important. Information about risks and risk events flows through two major communication networks – the news media and more informal personal networks. The news media as risk articulators have received the bulk of scientific attention for their critical role in public opinion formation and community agenda setting (Mazur, 1981; National Research Council, 1980a). Because the media tend to accord disproportionate coverage to rare or dramatic risks, or risk events, it is not surprising that people's estimates of the principal causes of death are related to the amount of media coverage they receive (Combs & Slovic, 1979).

Informal communication networks involve the linkages that exist among friends, neighbors and coworkers, and within social groups more generally. Although relatively little is known about such networks, it is undoubtedly the case that people do not consider risk issues in isolation from other social issues or from the views of their peers. Because one's friends or co-workers provide reference points for validating perceptions but are also likely to share a more general cultural view or bias, the potential exists for both amplifying and attenuating information. If the risk is feared, rumor may be a significant element in forming public perceptions and attitudes. Within social group interaction, these interpretations of risks will tend to be integrated within larger frames of values and analysis and to become resistant to new, conflicting information. It should be expected, therefore, that interpersonal networks will lead to divergent risk perceptions, management preferences and levels of concern. Because experts also exhibit cultural biases in their selections of theories, methods and data, these variable public perceptions will also often differ as a group from those of experts.

Finally, specific terms or concepts used in risk information may have quite different meanings for varying social and cultural groups. They may also trigger associations independent of those intended (Blumer, 1969). Such symbolic connotations may entail 'mushroom clouds' for nuclear energy, 'dumps' for waste disposal facilities or feelings of 'warmth and comfort' for solar power technologies.

RESPONSE MECHANISMS OF SOCIAL AMPLIFICATION

The interpretation and response to information flow from the second major stage of social amplification of risk. These mechanisms involve the social, institutional and cultural contexts in which the risk information is interpreted, its meaning diagnosed and values attached. We hypothesize four major pathways to initiate response mechanisms:

1 *Heuristics and values.* Individuals cannot deal with the full complexity of risk and the multitude of risks involved in daily life. Thus people use simplifying mechanisms to evaluate risk and to shape responses. These processes, while permitting individuals to cope with a risky world, may sometimes introduce biases that cause distortions and errors (Kahneman et al, 1982). Similarly, the application of individual and group values will also determine which risks are deemed important or minor and what actions, if any, should be taken.

2 *Social group relationships.* Risk issues enter into the political agenda of social and political groups. The nature of these groups will influence member responses and the types of rationality brought to risk issues (Raynor & Cantor, 1987). To the extent that risk becomes a central issue in a political campaign or in a conflict among social groups, it will be vigorously brought to more general public attention, often coupled with ideological interpretations of technology or the risk-management process (Douglas & Wildavsky, 1982; Johnson & Covello, 1987). Polarization of views and escalation of rhetoric by partisans typically occur and new recruits are drawn into the conflicts (Mazur, 1981). These social alignments tend to become anchors for subsequent interpretations of risk management and may become quite firm in the face of conflicting information.

3 *Signal value.* An important concept that has emerged from research on risk perception is that the seriousness and higher order impacts of a risk event are determined, in part, by what that event signals or portends (Slovic, 1987). The informativeness or 'signal value' of an event appears to be systematically related to the characteristics of the event and the hazard it reflects. High signal events suggest that a new risk has appeared or that the risk is different and more serious than previously understood (see Table 14.1). Thus, an accident that takes many lives may produce relatively little social disturbance (beyond that experienced by the victims' families and friends) if it occurs as part of a familiar and well-understood system (such as a train wreck). A small accident in an unfamiliar system (or one perceived as poorly understood), such as a nuclear reactor or a recombinant-DNA laboratory, however, may elicit great public concern if it is interpreted to mean that the risk is not well understood, not controllable, or not competently managed, thus implying that further (and possibly worse) mishaps are likely. In sum, signals about a risk event initiate a process whereby the significance of the event is examined. If found to be ominous, these implications are likely to trigger higher order social and economic impacts.

4 *Stigmatization.* Stigma refers to the negative imagery associated with undesirable social groups or individuals (Goffman, 1963). But environments with heavy pollution, waste accumulation or hazardous technology may also come

Table 14.1 *Risk Events with Potentially High Signal Value*

Events	Messages
Report that chlorofluorocarbon releases are depleting the ozone layer.	A new and possible catastrophic risk has emerged.
Resignation of regulators or corporate officials in 'conscience'.	The managers are concealing the risks: they cannot be trusted.
News report of off-site migration at a hazardous waste site.	The risk managers are not in control of the hazard.
Scientific dispute over the validity of an epidemiological study.	The experts do not understand the risks.
Statement by regulators that the levels of a particular contaminant in the water supply involve only very low risks compared with other risks.	The managers do not care about the people who will be harmed; they do not understand long-term cumulative effects of chemicals.

to be associated with negative images. Love Canal, the Valley of the Thousand Drums, Times Beach and the Nevada Test Site evoke vivid images of waste and pollution. Because the typical response to stigmatized persons or environments is avoidance, it is reasonable to assume that risk-induced stigma may have significant social and policy consequences. Research is needed to define the role of risk in creating stigma, the extent of aversion that results and how durable such stigma become.

In addition to these four mechanisms, *positive feedback to the physical risk itself* can occur due to social processes. If a transportation accident with hazardous materials were to occur close to a waste-disposal site, for example, protests and attempted blockage of the transportation route could result. Such actions could themselves become initiating or coaccident events, thereby increasing the probabilities of future accidents or enlarging the consequences should an accident occur. Or, alternatively, an accident in waste handling at the facility could lead opponents, or a disgruntled worker, to replicate the event through sabotage. Especially where strong public concern exists over a technology or facility, a wide variety of mechanisms is present by which health and safety risks may be enlarged through social processes (Kasperson et al, 1987).

NEXT STEPS

Only partial models or paradigms exist for characterizing the phenomenon we describe as the social amplification of risk. Understanding this phenomenon is essential for assessing the potential impacts of projects and technologies, for establishing priorities in risk management, and for setting health and environmental standards. We put forth this conceptual framework to start building a comprehensive theory that explains why seemingly minor risks or risk events often produce extraordinary public concern and social and economic impacts, with rippling effects across time, space and social institutions. The conceptualization needs scrutiny, elaboration and competing views. Empirical studies, now beginning, should provide important tests and insights for the next stage of theory construction.

ACKNOWLEDGMENTS

This work was supported by the Nevada Nuclear Waste Project Office and by NSF Grant No SES 8796182 to Decision Research. We wish to thank Brian Cook, Christoph Hohenemser, Nancy Kraus, Sarah Lichtenstein, Steve Rayner and three anonymous reviewers for their constructive comments on earlier drafts of the manuscript.

NOTE

1   In this chapter, the term 'risk event' refers to occurrences that are manifestations of the risk and that initiate signals pertaining to the risk. Risk events thus include routine or unexpected releases, accidents (large and small), discoveries of pollution incidents, reports of exposures or adverse consequences. Usually such risk events are specific to particular times and locations.

15 The Perception and Management of Therapeutic Risk

Paul Slovic

INTRODUCTION

Technology has enhanced our ability to harness our environment, eradicate dread diseases and fashion a life of comfort and leisure. But it has become apparent that these benefits are accompanied by a variety of hazardous side effects. Hardly a day passes that does not reveal some new danger in our foods, our homes, our places of work, our leisure activities, our environment or our medical treatments.

In a world where more and more people are coming to see themselves as the victims rather than the beneficiaries of technology, it is not surprising that the control of hazards has become a major concern of society and a growing responsibility of government. Massive regulatory bureaucracies have been created and charged with answering myriad forms of the question: 'How safe is safe enough?'.

Yet despite this enormous effort, people in many industrialized nations feel increasingly vulnerable to the risks from technology and believe that the worst is yet to come (Harris, 1980). Regulatory agencies have become embroiled in rancorous conflicts, caught between a fearful and dissatisfied public on one side and frustrated technologists and industrialists on the other. Nuclear power was the focus of public concerns during the 1970s. During the 1980s, there has been great concern and increasing dissatisfaction with the production, use, transport and disposal of chemicals (Roper Reports, 1985). When people in the US are asked to report the first thing that comes to mind when they hear the word 'chemicals', the dominant response is 'dangerous' or some closely related term (toxic, hazardous, poison, harmful, deadly, pollution, risk). Beneficial aspects of chemical technologies are rarely mentioned.

Manufacturers and users of industrial and agricultural chemicals are virtually at war with the public and the regulatory authorities in many places. At the same

Note: originally published as part of the CMR International Annual Lecture Series, June 1989. Copyright 1989 by the Centre for Medicines Research. Reprinted with permission.

time, manufacturers of other important products of chemical technology – pharmaceutical medicines – are also concerned about what appears to be a changing social and political environment. The preface to a book reporting the proceedings of an international conference on the prescription and management of drug safety risks (Horisberger & Dinkel, 1989) summarized these concerns as follows:

> In the past two decades public debate about the risks, benefits and safety associated with drugs has intensified. Public disputes over risks are brought to court when individuals seek compensation for health problems attributed to a pharmaceutical product. The issue reaches legislatures and regulatory agencies when consumer advocates seek to influence the standards of drug usage. Front-page news tends to focus on accidents or other risk events with drugs.
>   Drug risk and drug safety have become an important political issue. Drug regulatory agencies have been instituted, and their responsibility has increased. The approval to market a drug is dependent on a set of sophisticated studies executed according to strict protocols and scientifically defined criteria. Drug surveillance activities have gained recognition, and reporting systems to identify drug safety problems have been strengthened. The understanding and management of drug safety is, nonetheless, beset by doubts, disagreements and disputes. Conflict occurs over the significance of risk, the adequacy of evidence, the methodologies used to evaluate and measure risk, the standards that guide regulation, and the optimal means of communicating risk information to the public.

At this same conference, Dr Walter von Wartburg (1989, p39) elaborated these concerns:

> Drug risks...constitute a major anxiety today ... If we look only at the 1980s, we see a phenomenon which was and still is difficult to explain. A number of old, established drugs have suddenly disappeared. We find quite a number of newly introduced 'wonder' drugs being withdrawn after a promising start. The number of drug issues has been rising rather dramatically.[1] And both manufacturers and drug regulatory authorities have come under increasing public criticism.

In part, von Wartburg argued, this change can be attributed to the emergence of new actors in the management of drug risks – patients, the public at large, politicians, the media, consumer organizations and special interest groups.

Working effectively with these new publics brings issues of perception and communication into prominence. Knowledge of perception has been shown to be vitally important in understanding how individuals and societies manage the risks of daily life (the Royal Society, 1983; Slovic, 1987). In medicine, perceptions of drug risks are likely to influence patients' treatment choices, their compliance with treatment regimens, their views on the acceptability of adverse reactions and the drugs that cause them, and their attitudes toward government regulation of drugs (Burley & Inman, 1988). Understanding perceptions is a prerequisite for designing better communication materials for patients and the public.

Risk Perception and the RAD-AR Program

Within the worldwide pharmaceutical industry, RAD-AR, standing for 'risk assessment of drugs-analysis and response', is a new program designed to improve the risk-management process. Research on the perception of risks has been designated as a priority topic within the RAD-AR program. To date, few studies have examined the perceptions of risk from pharmaceutical products. The RAD-AR program is attempting to remedy this deficiency by conducting a series of national surveys designed to meet the following objectives:

1   Describe precisely and quantitatively the public's perceptions of risk and benefit from the use of various kinds of prescription drugs.
2   Place perceptions of prescription drugs within a broader context of risk perceptions regarding many other activities (eg, driving, smoking) and technologies (eg, air travel, pesticides), including other medical technologies (eg, X-rays, surgery).
3   Allow comparisons to be made across populations from different nations and, within national samples, across important personal and demographic characteristics (eg, health status, age).
4   Provide baseline data that will allow the impact of new drug problems and controversies to be monitored and allow trends in relevant attitudes and perceptions to be followed over time.
5   Help pharmaceutical companies understand the influence of public perceptions on the sociopolitical environment in which they operate.

The first study in this series examined the attitudes and perceptions of a representative sample of the public in Sweden (Slovic et al, 1989). Parts of this survey were subsequently replicated in the UK using a large sample of patients suffering from ankylosing spondylitis (O'Brien, Elswood & Calin, 1989). A third survey of the general public in Canada is presently being completed and several additional studies in other nations are in the planning stages. I shall describe the results of the study in Sweden and, in less detail, the results of the patient survey in Britain.

THE SWEDISH SURVEY

Design of the Survey

The national survey of risk perception of prescription drugs, conducted in Sweden by Slovic et al (1989), was designed to apply concepts and methods taken from the literature described above. The survey had two separate components. Part I employed a traditional survey format in which respondents were asked to indicate their attitudes, perceptions and opinions in response to specific questions on the following topics:

- perceptions of risk today as compared to risks in the past;
- perceived frequency of drug side effects;
- the adequacy of performance by government regulators, drug manufacturers, doctors and pharmacists in insuring drug safety and efficacy;
- the respondent's personal experiences with drug side effects;
- perceived causes of drug side effects; and
- opinions in response to a vignette describing a drug controversy.

In addition, part I included a non-traditional task in which respondents were asked to read the words 'prescription drugs' which were printed six times on a card. Each time they read these words, they were instructed to write down the first association that came to their minds. This technique, called 'the method of continued associations', has been shown by Szalay and Deese (1978) to be a sensitive indicator of the imagery and meaning associated with people's mental representations for a wide variety of concepts. Of particular interest in the present context is the frequency and nature of negative associations and the ratio of positive to negative responses to prescription drugs.

Part I concluded with a series of demographic questions pertaining to the patient's age, sex, health status, cigarette smoking, occupation, income, marital status, medicine usage, health consciousness, attitude toward risk taking, attitude toward fate, and attitude toward using medicines.

Part II of the survey used the psychometric paradigm described earlier, in which people were asked to make quantitative judgments about the riskiness of various hazards. In the present survey, each of the 29 items shown in Table 15.1 was rated by each respondent on 7 characteristics of risk found to be important in prior studies of perceived risk. The 29 items included 15 pharmaceutical products, 5 medical devices or procedures and 9 non-medical items. The non-medical items were included to provide a broad context against which to compare the medical and pharmaceutical items. The pharmaceutical items were carefully selected according to several criteria, including importance, familiarity to the general public and diversity.

Respondents rated the perceived risk and perceived benefit for each item, the extent to which the risks are known to those exposed to them, the likelihood that people exposed to the risk would experience any degree of personal harm, the extent to which the risk associated with each item was new or old, the seriousness of harmful effects in the event of an accident or mishap, and the degree to which a mishap would serve as a warning sign indicating that the risk from this item might be greater than was thought before the problem occurred. All 29 hazard items were rated on one scale before the next scale was considered.

Table 15.1 *Hazard Items Studied in Part II of the Swedish Survey*

1 Pharmaceutical items

Vaccines	Sleeping pills	Herbal medicines
Laxatives	Antihypertensives	Vitamin pills
Antibiotic drugs	Antidepressants	Antiarthritics
Birth control pills	Anticancer drugs	Biotechnology drugs
Insulin	Aspirin	Drugs against AIDS

2 Medical procedures, tests and devices

Medical X-rays	Heart surgery	
IUDs	Acupuncture	Appendectomy

3 Non-medical hazards

Automobiles	Pesticides	Food additives
Travel by airplane	Household cleansers	Alcoholic beverages
Nuclear power plants	Artificial sweeteners	Cigarette smoking

Before starting this task, respondents were asked to examine a glossary that defined each term (eg, insulin – a drug used to treat diabetes). Respondents were allowed to refer to this glossary as necessary during the task.

Administration of the Survey

A representative sample of the Swedish adult population between the ages of 16 and 74 was interviewed in person in their own homes by personnel from SIFO, a leading survey and market research firm in Sweden. The interviews took place from 24 February through 19 March 1988. From 1234 persons contacted, 961 completed interviews were obtained, for a completion rate of 78 per cent.

Results

Characteristics of the sample

The sample was almost equally split between females (50.4%) and males (49.6%). About 28% of the respondents resided in Stockholm or Gothenberg; 17% resided in small villages (less than 3000 inhabitants) or rural areas; the remaining 55% came from towns and cities of intermediate size. Most of the respondents were between the age of 16 and 39 years (47.3%); 34.8% were between the ages of 40 and 59 years; and 17.9% were between 60 and 74 years of age. In these respects, the sample closely matched the characteristics of the Swedish adult population.

The majority of respondents rated their health as either excellent (34.6%) or very good (28.4%); 30.2% rated their health as fair and 6.6% as poor. When asked if they had a chronic illness or condition, 12.7% answered yes.

Some 20.9% of the sample said that they saw their doctor regularly; 40.2% replied that they had taken prescription drugs during the past four months, and 27.0% had bought a non-prescription medicine within the previous four months; 62.5% said they had benefited significantly during the last five years from taking a prescription drug.

Respondents were also asked to indicate the degree to which various statements about risk taking, health consciousness, fatalism and medicine taking described them personally. The results, shown in Figure 15.1, indicate that most of these individuals characterized themselves as not liking to take risks, being health conscious, not feeling comfortable about taking medicines, and resisting the use of medicine until they are absolutely forced to do so (92.2% said they were very well or somewhat well characterized by this last statement).

Images of prescription drugs

More than 3000 associations were produced in response to the stimulus concept 'prescription drugs'. The major types of associations are listed in Table 15.2 in order of their frequency. Names of drugs headed the list, followed closely by names of illnesses and types of drugs. Strong positive images (helpful, recovery, healing, effective, reliable) accounted for 259 responses. Strong negative imagery was somewhat more frequent and took two general forms: one form had to do with side effects, dangerousness, warning, allergic and other reactions

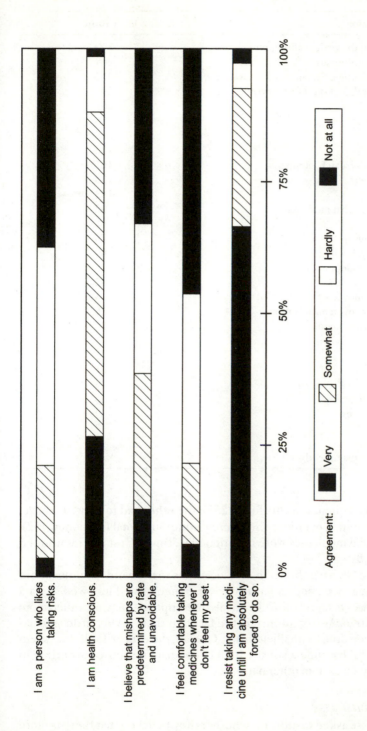

Agreement: ■ Very ⬚ Hardly ▨ Somewhat ■ Not at all

Source: Slovic et al, (1989)

Figure 15.1 *Attitudes toward health, risk, fate and medicines*

Table 15.2 *Associations with 'Prescription Drugs'*

Rank	Association	Count
1	Names of drugs (ie, valium, etc)	549
2	Names of illnesses	465
3	Types of drugs, eg, antibiotics, vitamins	412
4	'Medicine', ie, liquid form, syrup	299
5	Pills	261
6	Hospital	258
7	Doctor	222
8	Helpful	188
9	Industry, research, company	161
10	Side effects	136
11	Pharmacy	132
12	Natural, herbal medicine	92
13	Abuse	81
14	Dangerous	78
15	Recovery, healing	60
16	Addiction, dependence	45
17	Prescriptions	42
18	Price, money, cost	33
19	Overdose, overconsumption	26
20	Hypodermic needle	24
21	Bottles, jars, boxes	23
22	Warning	22
23	Profit	21
24	Paraphernalia (general)	18
25	Allergy, reactions	10
26	Preservatives	9
27	Death	7
28	Effective	7
29	Reliable, guaranteed	4

and death (total frequency of this form, 253); the other had to do with abuse, addiction, dependency, overdose and overconsumption (total frequency, 152). Natural and herbal medicines were mentioned 92 times. Cost was mentioned rather infrequently.

Surveys in the US have shown that associations to the word 'chemicals' are dominated by negative imagery (death, toxic, dangerous). The Swedish data show that responses to one class of chemicals, prescription drugs, are much more neutral and positive. Also of interest is the fact that there is very little association of prescription drugs with illicit drugs. Overall, the data in Table 15.2 seem to provide a useful baseline against which to compare responses over time in Sweden and responses from other nations.

Present and past risk

Respondents were asked to indicate whether they believed that there is more risk, less risk or about the same risk today than there was 20 years ago for each of several major sources of risk. The results, shown in Figure 15.2, indicate that

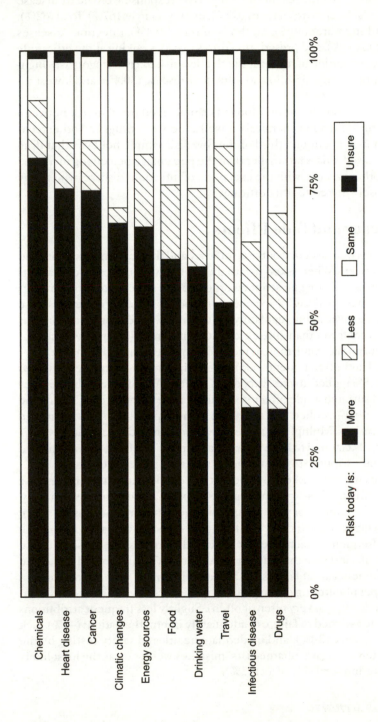

Figure 15.2 *Risk today versus 20 years ago*

Source: Slovic et al (1989)

the risks from chemicals were perceived to be greater today by 80% of the respondents. Other percentages for the 'more risk' response were heart disease (75%), cancer (74%), climate changes (69%), energy sources (67%), food (62%), quality of drinking water (60%), methods of travel (54%), infectious diseases excluding AIDS (35%), and prescription drugs (34%). Looking at the other side of the coin, the proportion of responses in the 'less risk today' category was highest for prescription drugs (35.8%) and infectious disease (30.4%) and lowest for climate changes (2.7%).

We thus see a strong differentiation in the perceived trend in risk between prescription drugs and other chemicals as well as between drugs and other technologies. Although about one third of the Swedish sample believes that drug risks have increased, this is far smaller than the percentage perceiving increased risk from the other hazards, with the exception of infectious disease, which may be seen as closely linked to drug efficacy.

Drug Efficacy and Side Effects

Several questions were asked about drug efficacy and the frequency, severity and causes of side effects. When asked to rate the job that various health-care agents were doing to make sure that prescription drugs are safe and effective, pharmacists received the highest marks (70% excellent or good), followed at quite a distance by doctors (56%), government regulatory agencies (50%) and drug manufacturers (40%). There were fewer than 20% excellent ratings in any category, which suggests that, in the public mind, there is room for improvement in this matter.

When asked how often patients taking prescription drugs experience *serious* side effects, 23.5% replied always, very often or often. When asked whether they personally had suffered a side effect from taking a prescription drug during the past five years, 19.9% replied that they had; of these people, 26.5% considered the side effect serious. Multiplying these two proportions indicates that only 5.3% of the total sample claimed to have suffered a serious side effect, a proportion far smaller than that attributed to other patients who take prescription drugs.

Respondents were also asked to indicate their opinions about the main cause of a drug side effect. Their spontaneous responses named patient sensitivity, improper drug prescription or wrong diagnosis, and non-compliance as the major causes. Following this question was a structured question that asked people to indicate how frequently each of eight specified factors is the cause of a side effect. The results indicate that patient sensitivity was again singled out as one of the most frequent causal factors (44.5% rated it always, very often or often a cause). Improper monitoring of the patient by the doctor was also rated as a frequent cause (45% always, very often or often). Slightly less frequent attributions of causality were assigned to failure to adequately inform the patient (41%), lack of patient compliance (38%), and inadequate health and safety testing by the manufacturer (38%). Again, pharmacists' mistakes were seen as the least likely causes of a drug-induced side effect (2%).

A *drug crisis scenario*

The following hypothetical scenario was posed to each respondent, indicating a possible link between a drug and some fatalities among its users.

Imagine that a new prescription drug becomes available in this country for treating a serious disease. Other drugs are also available for treating this disease. A study reveals that some people may have died from taking this drug. What do you think the government should do in this case?

- Leave the drug on the market.
- Take the drug off the market.
- Leave the drug on the market but warn the doctors and patients.
- Not sure.

In response to this question, 75% wanted the government to take the drug off the market, 1.8% wanted the drug left on the market, and another 21.8% wanted it left on the market with a warning.

Those who wanted the drug removed from the market or who were not sure (76.7% of the total sample) were asked to reconsider their answers, taking into account each of six possible extenuating circumstances. The results indicated that there is no circumstance that, by itself, would convince more than 16% of these people to leave the drug on the market as it was before. However, in combination with information warning doctors and patients about the possible problem, these circumstances led to considerable change in opinions. Knowledge that the risk affected only certain types of patients convinced 5.4% of these respondents to leave the drug on the market and another 52.6% to leave it on the market with a warning. Changes such as this also occurred when respondents were told that the drug is more effective than other similar drugs, or that the drug has fewer side effects for most patients than other similar drugs. Being told that the drug has been used safely and effectively for many years in another country produced somewhat fewer changes of opinion. The two circumstances that produced the least opinion change were the fact that the government and manufacturer are actively gathering more information about the problem, and the fact that the respondent had taken the drug for many months and was very satisfied with it.

The psychometric questionnaire

Ratings of each hazard item were averaged across all 961 respondents for each scale. The mean ratings for perceived risk, ordered from high to low, are shown in Figure 15.3. Three non-drug chemicals – cigarette smoking, pesticides and alcohol – stood out as highest in perceived risk, followed by two drug items – antidepressants and sleeping pills – which, surprisingly, were judged more risky than nuclear power. Vitamin pills, acupuncture and herbal medicines were judged lowest in risk.

The high level of concern about sleeping pills and antidepressant drugs may be due to extensive media publicity in Sweden regarding the risks of addiction and overdose from these and similar drugs. A subgroup analysis was conducted in which perceived risks and benefits for those persons ($N = 145$) associating prescription drugs with 'overdose', 'addiction' or 'abuse' were compared with judgments of persons not having any negative associations ($N = 776$). These two groups did not differ in their ratings of nuclear power, pesticides and other non-medical hazards. Nor did they differ much in their ratings of vaccines, antibiotics

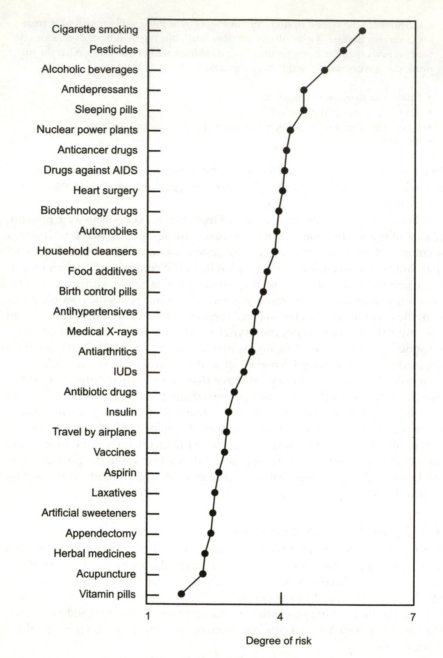

Cigarette smoking
Pesticides
Alcoholic beverages
Antidepressants
Sleeping pills
Nuclear power plants
Anticancer drugs
Drugs against AIDS
Heart surgery
Biotechnology drugs
Automobiles
Household cleansers
Food additives
Birth control pills
Antihypertensives
Medical X-rays
Antiarthritics
IUDs
Antibiotic drugs
Insulin
Travel by airplane
Vaccines
Aspirin
Laxatives
Artificial sweeteners
Appendectomy
Herbal medicines
Acupuncture
Vitamin pills

Degree of risk

Figure 15.3 *Perceived risk*

or cancer drugs. The group with these particular negative associations did, however, judge sleeping pills and antidepressants to have much greater risk and much lower benefits compared to persons without such associations. This evidence is congruent with the hypothesis that high levels of perceived risk associated with sleeping pills and antidepressants stem from concerns about overdose, addiction and abuse.

Additional analysis of specific subgroups of respondents showed that women perceived far higher risk from nuclear power than did men (mean rating, 4.86 for women and 3.53 for men; $p < .001$). This is a common finding in studies of perceived risk. However, no other differences between men and women exceeded .4. Those who claimed to have experienced any sort of side-effect from a prescription drug showed slightly higher mean perceptions of risk than those without side effect experience (the largest mean difference was .57 for antibiotics; $p < .001$). Perceptions of risk seemed unaffected by having experienced significant benefits from taking drugs.

Mean ratings of perceived benefit are shown in Figure 15.4. Unlike mean perceptions of risk, which exhibited a smooth, continuous decline from high to low values, benefits seemed to fall into three categories. High benefits were associated with cancer drugs, heart surgery, insulin, AIDS drugs, appendectomy, antibiotics, vaccines, X-rays, airplanes, automobiles and drugs to treat arthritis and hypertension, Moderate benefits were attributed to 11 items ranging from antidepressants to laxatives. Very low benefits were perceived for cigarettes, alcohol, food additives, pesticides, artificial sweeteners and sleeping pills. The perceived benefit of various drug items was only slightly higher for those claiming to have experienced significant benefits in the past five years than for those not claiming such beneficial experiences.

The risk and benefit means are superimposed in Figure 15.5. It is obvious that perceived risks and benefits were not positively related (the correlation was actually –.23). Appendectomy, insulin, vaccines and antibiotics stood out as being quite high in perceived benefit and low in perceived risk. Other drug items, with the notable exception of antidepressants and sleeping pills, showed a similar, though less extreme, pattern. Four non-drug chemical hazards – cigarettes, alcohol, pesticides and food additives – were judged extremely high in risk and low in benefit.

Although the scales are not strictly commensurable, it is instructive to create a net benefit score by subtracting the risk judgment from the benefit judgment for each item. Subgroup analysis on this measure showed that the perceived net benefits for antidepressants, birth control pills, sleeping pills and antihypertensives were higher for those persons claiming to be comfortable taking medicines than for those who are not comfortable doing so. However, these two groups of people did not differ in their net benefit ratings for such high benefit drugs as vaccines, antibiotics and insulin. Older respondents (ages 60 to 74) showed slightly higher net benefit ratings than younger respondents for antihypertensives, cancer drugs, antidepressants and artificial sweeteners.

The scales measuring likelihood of harm and seriousness of harm correlated highly with perceived risk. The scale values for knowledge of risk took an intermediate position for all items – there was rather little variation from the least well-known risks (biotechnology drugs, food additives) to the best known (airplanes, automobiles and cigarettes). There was much greater variation on the new versus old scale ranging from AIDS and biotechnology drugs (newest risks) to cigarettes and alcohol (oldest). The warning sign scale also showed rather small variation around the midpoint. Nuclear power and pesticides were highest on this scale, and automobiles and airplanes were lowest.

Correlation coefficients were calculated between the means of each pair of scales, across the 29 items. These correlations were subjected to a principal

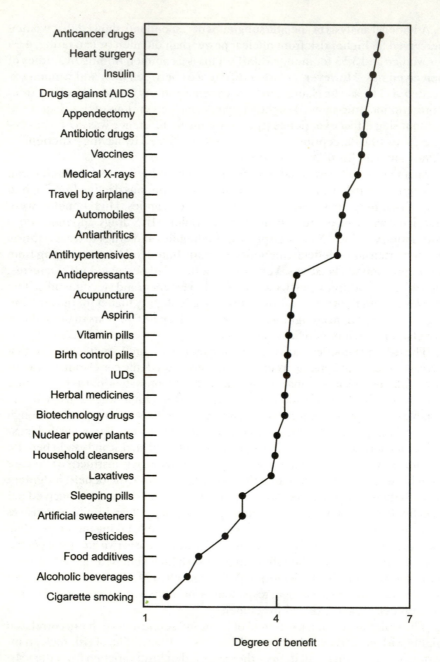

Figure 15.4 *Perceived benefit*

components factor analysis that uncovered two dominant, uncorrelated factors accounting for 71% of the variance in the scales. Factor I, which we will label 'risk', consisted of three scales: perceived risk, the likelihood of harm and the seriousness of harm, given a mishap. Factor II, which we will call 'warning', consisted of the scales pertaining to newness, knowledge and warning sign. Factor scores were computed for each hazard item by weighting the mean

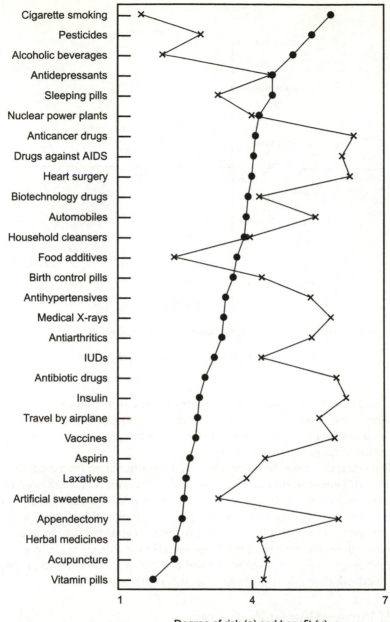

Figure 15.5 *Perceived risk and perceived benefit*

ratings on each scale proportionally to the importance of that scale for the factor and summing over all scales. The weighted sum gives each item a score that is an amalgamation of its ratings on the scales that define each factor. The factor scores for each item are plotted in Figure 15.6. As one moves from left to right in the factor space, the items are judged to have higher likelihood of causing harm, greater severity of harm in the event of a mishap, and overall, greater

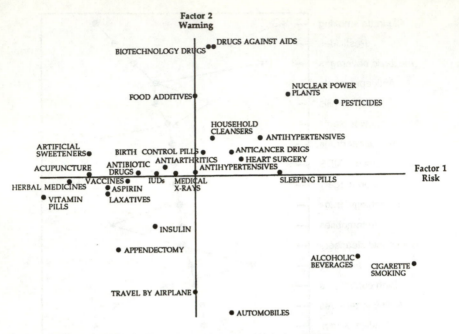

Source: Redrawn from Slovic, Kraus, Lappe, Letzel and Malmfors (1989).

Figure 15.6 *Perceptual map of risk factors*

perceived risk. As one goes from the bottom to the top of the space, the items are judged to have risks that are newer and less precisely known, and a mishap is judged as providing a stronger warning about the possibility that the risk is greater than was previously believed.

Most pharmaceutical products clustered together at an intermediate level on factor II. However, there was considerable differentiation on the risk factor, with sleeping pills and antidepressant drugs seen as extremely high in risk. Nuclear power and pesticides were judged to be new, unknown and high-risk technologies, and are located in the upper-right quadrant of the space, much as previous studies have shown. Drugs against AIDS and drugs made by means of biotechnology were seen as new and unknown risks, and relatively higher in perceived risk than most other pharmaceutical products.

Risk Perception in Patients

The Swedish survey was administered to members of the general public, few of whom were chronically ill. Would a survey of patients who were heavily dependent upon medicines produce similar results? Fortunately, there is some relevant data on this question, collected recently by O'Brien, Elswood and Calin (1989). These investigators administered a shortened and slightly revised version of the Swedish questionnaire to 1034 persons in the UK, all of whom were suffering from ankylosing spondylitis (AS), a chronic rheumatic disease. The average age of the respondents was 47 years; 72% of them were males. About 71% of these individuals were currently taking medications for AS.

As might be expected, a higher percentage of the AS patients reported experiencing a serious adverse drug reaction (ADR) (47%) than did the Swedish respondents (5%). Those AS patients who had experienced a serious ADR judged the incidence of ADRs from non-steroidal anti-inflammatory drugs (NSAIDs) as more frequent than did persons without such ADR experience. Those who had experienced serious ADRs were *more likely* than others to attribute the cause of the reaction to the patient's having inadequate information about the drug, to inadequate testing by the manufacturer, and to inadequate monitoring by the doctor; those who had experienced serious ADRs were *less likely* than others to blame the patient for a side effect.

Comparisons between the AS patients and the Swedish respondents are informative, though it must be recognized that these groups differed in nationality, average age (the Swedish respondents were younger) and ratio of men to women, as well as in their health status. The broad pattern of results were similar in the two groups, but there were certain sizable differences as well.

Both groups of respondents gave the highest ratings to pharmacists for making drugs safe and effective and the lowest ratings to government regulators and manufacturers. However, the AS patients gave about 10 to 15% fewer ratings in the combined categories 'excellent and good' than did the Swedish respondents.

There were sizable differences between groups in attributing the causes of a drug's side effect. The AS patients were much less likely to attribute the cause to patient noncompliance (19% said this was very often or often the cause) compared to the Swedish sample (38%). Similarly, the manufacturer was blamed only 23% of the time by the patients compared to 38% of the time in Sweden; wrong doses prescribed by the doctor were blamed only 8% of the time by the patients, compared with 28% by the Swedish sample. Lack of information for the patient was blamed 54% of the time by the patients compared with 40% in Sweden.

In response to the drug crisis scenario, 61% of the patients wanted the suspect drug taken off the market, compared to 75% in Sweden. In the follow-up questions, the patients responded much like the Swedish sample. Depending on the circumstances, between 21% and 47% of the patients were willing to have the drug left on the market if warning information was provided; between 25% and 52% of the Swedish sample responded this way.

In response to the question asking for comparisons between risks today and risks 20 years ago, the patients more frequently said that the various risks were the same as 20 years ago and the Swedish sample more frequently said that they were greater than they were 20 years ago. One striking exception was with infectious diseases, for which 16% of the patients said that the risks were about the same (32% in Sweden); 61% of the patients said that risks from infectious diseases were less, compared to 30% in Sweden.

RISK MANAGEMENT THROUGH PROVISION OF WARNINGS

Thus far the focus has been on perception, rather than management, of therapeutic risk. This concluding section shall briefly discuss one facet of risk management – that involving provision of risk information to patients.

There have been numerous surveys indicating that patients around the world strongly desire warning information pertaining to prescription drugs (eg, Fujino, 1989; Keown, Slovic & Lichtenstein, 1984; Malmfors et al, 1988). When the drug crisis scenario was evaluated by members of the public in Sweden (see Figure 15.4) and by patients in the UK, the results suggested that provision of warning information to patients may produce a much more tolerant attitude toward a beneficial but high-risk drug. In addition, the survey by O'Brien et al in the UK found that inadequate information was seen by patients as the major cause of ADRs.

Carpenter (1988) has argued that the provision of extensive, frank warnings and precautions is desirable because it affords the patient the opportunity for 'informed choice'. It also may help the patient to use the drug safely and effectively. The concept of informed choice is a powerful idea with the potential to revolutionize the role of risk and warning information in the marketing and use of prescription drugs. The concept is currently being implemented by the Alza Corporation in their marketing of the IUD, Progestasert (Carpenter, 1988), and by Hoffman-La Roche, Inc in their marketing of the anti-acne drug, Accutane. The results from these 'field tests' of informed choice will be very useful. However, additional information is needed to delineate the boundaries for the successful application of this approach. For which types of pharmaceutical or medical products will it be favorably received? Under what circumstances (or in which cultural or national environments) would such an approach be ill advised? Will extensive warnings lead to concerns that would deter some patients from taking essential medicines? Would such concerns lead to non-compliance with the prescription regimen? New studies, focused specifically on issues pertaining to informed choice, are needed to inform policy-makers about the merits of this approach.

We are currently studying attitudes toward precaution and warning information in a survey of the general public in Canada. In addition to replicating the Swedish survey, we have generated several new questions about information issues. One question was based on a study of perceptions of the risks from household chemicals (cleansers, bleaches, etc) conducted in the US by Kraus and Slovic (1988a). This study found that 59% of the respondents agreed and another 22% strongly agreed with the statement: 'I feel safer when I use a (household) product that has caution/ warning information on the label than I do when I use a similar product that does not have caution/warning information on the label'. Extent of agreement or disagreement with this statement is being asked in the Canadian survey with the words 'prescription drug' substituted for the word 'product'.

A second question in the Canadian survey is designed to assess attitudes toward one information strategy that is currently being used with Progestasert and Accutane. The question asks for degree of agreement or disagreement with the statement: 'When drugs have a potential for serious unwanted effects/side effects, patients should be required to read warning information and to sign a form indicating that they understand the risk before being allowed to take the drug'.

Additional questions in Canada are examining whether people believe that warnings and precautions give them greater ability to recognize and avoid problems when taking a drug and whether they feel that such information might make them uneasy and deter them from using a drug.

CONCLUSION

Recent surveys in Sweden and the UK provide insights into fundamental attitudes and perceptions regarding the risks and benefits of prescription drugs. Replication and extension of these studies in other countries with a variety of patient subgroups, as well as with the general public, should help pharmaceutical companies better understand patients' concerns, meet their needs for information and facilitate wiser and safer use of prescription drugs.

In the words of Medawar (1989), 'The key to making the progress that is needed [in drug risk management] is to identify with the people who take the risks. They will then identify with you.' Studies of risk perception will contribute significantly towards achieving this objective.

ACKNOWLEDGMENTS

Many people have contributed to the ideas and results discussed in this chapter. I am especially indebted to Nancy Kraus, Henner Lappe, Heintz Letzel, and Torbjörn Malmfors, who helped design the Swedish survey; to Walter von Wartburg, Gunter Lewandowski, David Taylor, Dana Miller and Peter Carpenter, who have supported and championed work on this topic; and to Bernie O'Brien, Judith Elswood and Andrei Calin, who have generously allowed me to describe their recent research results.

NOTE

1   Evidence for this claim is provided by Spriet-Pourra and Auriche (1988) who examined 77 cases in which medicines were withdrawn from the market in France, Germany, the UK and the US between 1961 and 1988. They found that withdrawals increased from a rate of 2.2 products per year prior to 1983 to 8.6 products per year thereafter.

16 Perception of Risk from Radiation

Paul Slovic

INTRODUCTION

How does the public perceive the risks associated with exposure to radiation? Perhaps the most important generalization from research in this domain is that there is no *uniform* or consistent perception of radiation risks. This is what makes this topic so fascinating to study. Public perception and acceptance is determined by the context in which radiation is used – and the very different reactions to different uses provide insight into the nature of perception and the determinants of acceptable risk.

A second generalization, and a disturbing one, is that in every context of use, with the exception of nuclear weapons, public perceptions of radiation risk differ from the assessments of the majority of experts on radiation and its effects. In some cases, members of the public see far greater risks associated with a radiation technology than do technical experts – in others, the public is much less concerned than the experts believe they should be. Although differences between perceptions of laypersons and those of experts cannot be attributed in any simple way to degree of knowledge, it is clear that better information and education about radiation and its consequences is needed. With the exception of studies that have designed brochures to help people understand their risk from radon, there has been little effort or progress made on the communication side.

There is a particularly urgent need to develop plans and materials for communicating with the public in the event of a radiological disaster. This point is driven home by the difficulties observed in Europe after Chernobyl, and in the chaos and disruption that reigned in Goiania, Brazil, after two scavengers unwittingly sawed open a capsule containing caesium that had been used for cancer therapy.

Note: reprinted from *Radiation Protection Dosimetry*, 68(3/4), pp165–80, 1996. Copyright 1996 by Nuclear Technology Publishing. Reprinted with permission.

PERCEPTION OF RADIATION RISK

Numerous psychometric surveys conducted during the past decade have examined perceptions of risk and benefit from various radiation technologies. This work shows that there is no general pattern of perception for radiation. Different sources of radiation exposure are perceived in different ways. This was evident in the first psychometric study (Fischhoff, Slovic, Lichtenstein, Read et al, 1978). There we saw that three groups of laypersons perceived nuclear power as having very high risk (ranks 1, 1 and 8 out of 30 hazards), whereas a group of risk-assessment experts had a mean risk rating that put nuclear power 20th in the hierarchy. Note also that the three groups of laypersons judged medical X-rays relatively low in risk (ranks 22, 17 and 24), whereas the experts placed it 7th. Thus, we see that two radiation technologies were perceived differently from one another and differently from the views of experts.

The risk-perception factor space presented in Slovic (1987) further illustrates the differences in perception of various radiation hazards. Note that nuclear-reactor accidents, radioactive waste and fallout from nuclear weapons testing are located in the upper-right quadrant of the factor space, reflecting people's perceptions that these technologies are uncontrollable, dread, catastrophic, lethal and inequitable in their distribution of risks and benefits. Diagnostic X-rays are perceived much more favorably on these scales, hence they fall in the upper-left quadrant of the space. Nuclear weapons fall in the lower-right quadrant, separating from nuclear-reactor accidents, nuclear waste and fallout on the scales measuring knowledge, immediacy of effects and observability of effects.

Although these data come from small and non-representative samples collected a decade or more ago, recent surveys of the general public in the US, Sweden and Canada show consistently that nuclear power and nuclear waste are perceived as extremely high in risk and low in benefit to society, whereas medical X-rays are perceived as very beneficial and low in risk (Kunreuther, Desvousges & Slovic, 1988; Slovic et al, 1989; Slovic, Kraus et al, 1991). Smaller studies in Norway and Hungary have also obtained these results (Engländer et al, 1986; Teigen et al, 1988).

Perceptions of risk associated with nuclear waste are even more negative than perceptions of nuclear power (Kunreuther et al, 1988; Flynn, Slovic, Mertz & Toma, 1990; Sjöberg & Drottz-Sjöberg, 1994a; 1994b; Slovic, Layman & Flynn, 1990; Slovic, Layman, Kraus et al, 1991). When asked to state whatever images or associations came to mind when they heard the words 'underground nuclear-waste storage facility', a representative sample of Phoenix, Arizona, residents could hardly think of anything that was not frightening or problematic. The disposal of nuclear wastes is a technology that experts believe can be managed safely and effectively. The discrepancy between this view and the images in people's minds is indeed startling.

The perception of nuclear power as a catastrophic technology was studied in depth by Slovic, Lichtenstein et al (1979). They found that, before the Three Mile Island (TMI) accident, people expected nuclear-power accidents to lead to disasters of immense proportions. Scenarios of reactor accidents were found to resemble scenarios of the aftermath of nuclear war. Replication of these studies after the TMI event found even more extreme 'images of disaster'.

The powerful negative imagery evoked by nuclear power and radiation is discussed from a historical perspective by Weart (1988). Weart argues that modern thinking about radioactivity employs beliefs and symbols that have been associated for centuries with the concept of transmutation – the passage through destruction to rebirth. In the early decades of the 20th century, transmutation images became centered on radioactivity, which was associated with 'uncanny rays that brought hideous death or miraculous new life; with mad scientists and their ambiguous monsters; with cosmic secrets of life and death ... and with weapons great enough to destroy the world' (p421).

But this concept of transmutation has a duality that is hardly evident in the imagery associated with nuclear power and nuclear wastes. Why has the evil overwhelmed the good? The answer undoubtedly involves the bombing of Hiroshima and Nagasaki, which linked the dread images to reality. The sprouting of nuclear power in the aftermath of the atomic bombing has led Smith (1988, p62) to observe:

> Nuclear energy was conceived in secrecy, born in war and first revealed to the world in horror. No matter how much proponents try to separate the peaceful from the weapons atom, the connection is firmly embedded in the minds of the public.

Additional insights into the special quality of nuclear fear are provided by Erikson (1990; 1991), who draws attention to the broad, emerging theme of toxicity, both radioactive and chemical, that characterizes a 'whole new species of trouble' associated with modern technological disasters. Erikson describes the exceptionally dread quality of technological accidents that expose people to radiation and chemicals in ways that 'contaminate rather than merely damage ... pollute, befoul and taint rather than just create wreckage ... penetrate human tissue indirectly rather than wound the surface by assaults of a more straightforward kind' (p120). Unlike natural disasters, these accidents are unbounded. Unlike conventional disaster plots, they have no end.

> Invisible contaminants remain a part of the surroundings – absorbed into the grain of the landscape, the tissues of the body and, worst of all, into the genetic material of the survivors. An 'all clear' is never sounded. The book of accounts is never closed (Erikson, p121).

Erikson's 'contamination model' may explain, in part, the reaction of the public to exposures to carcinogens. Numerous studies have found that a high percentage (60 to 75%) of people believe that if a person is exposed to a chemical that can cause cancer, that person will probably get cancer some day (Kraus, Malmfors & Slovic, 1992; Slovic, Flynn, Mertz & Mullican, 1993). A similarly high percentage believe that 'exposure to radiation will probably lead to cancer some day' (Slovic, Flynn, Mertz et al, 1993). The belief that *any* exposure to a carcinogen is likely to lead to cancer tends to coincide with the belief that it can never be too expensive to reduce such risks (Kraus et al, 1992). Therefore, it is not surprising to find in an analysis of more than 500 life-saving interventions by Tengs et al (1995) that radiation controls in industry were associated with the highest costs per year of life saved.

The deep fears and anxieties associated with radiation and with nuclear power make the cases in which radiation is responded to rather casually of particular interest. For example, Sandman, Weinstein and Klotz (1987) surveyed residents in the Reading Prong area of New Jersey, a region characterized by very high radon levels in many homes. They found that residents there were basically apathetic about the risk. Few had bothered to monitor their homes for radon. Most believed that, although radon might be a problem for their neighbors, their own homes did not pose any threat.

A striking contrast to the apathy regarding radon in homes is the strong public reaction that developed in many New Jersey cities when the state attempted to develop a landfill in which to place 14,000 barrels of mildly radioactive soil. The soil had been excavated from the former site of a radium watch-dial factory that had operated at the turn of the century. Over a period of several years, the state tried in vain to find a community that would accept the soil (Carlson, 1986).

Table 16.1 summarizes the status of perceived risk for six radiation technologies, contrasting the views of technical experts with the views of the general public. In addition to nuclear power, nuclear waste, X-rays, radon and nuclear weapons, food irradiation (Bord & O'Connor, 1990) and a source of non-ionizing radiation – electric and magnetic fields (EMF) – are included in the table, although there is relatively less information about perceptions of these two sources. We see that there is typically disagreement between the experts and the public regarding the level of risk and its acceptability. To my knowledge there have been only two published studies thus far of perceptions of risk from electric and magnetic fields. These studies by Morgan et al (1985) and MacGregor, Slovic and Morgan (1994) found that perceived risks associated with fields from home appliances and electric blankets were relatively low, and that perceived risks associated with large power lines were relatively high. Both studies also showed that, when the respondents were given a briefing about research on the health effects of electric fields (which said that many studies had been done but no

Table 16.1 *Summary of Perception and Acceptance of Risks from Diverse Sources of Radiation Exposure*

	Perceived risk	
	Technical experts	**Public**
Nuclear power/ nuclear waste	Moderate risk Acceptable	Extreme risk Unacceptable
X-rays	Low/moderate risk Acceptable	Very low risk Acceptable
Radon	Moderate risk Needs action	Very low risk Apathy
Nuclear weapons	Moderate to extreme risk Tolerance	Extreme risk Tolerance
Food irradiation	Low risk Acceptable	Moderate to high risk Acceptability questioned
Electric and magnetic fields	Low risk Acceptable	Significant concerns developing Acceptability questioned

adverse human health effects had yet been reliably demonstrated), their perceptions on subsequent retest shifted toward greater perceived risk. MacGregor et al found that this briefing (in the form of a brochure) also led to greater dread (particularly regarding power-line risks), less perceived equity, and greater concern regarding the effects of EMF on the nervous system, the immune system, cell growth and reproduction, chronic depression and cancer. These results imply that, as concerns (and reports of research) about the risks from electric and magnetic fields continue to be publicized, public fears will increase. The significance of the public's uneasiness about these fields is documented by Florig (1992), who estimated that the utility industry spends more than $1 billion annually attempting to mitigate public concerns.

Conspicuously missing from Table 16.1 is exposure from radiation medicine. An extensive search of Medline and six other data bases using key words such as radiation, risk perception, fear and nuclear medicine failed to uncover any studies of perception of risk regarding the use of radionuclides in medicine.

It is instructive to compare perceptions of risk and benefit for various radiation technologies with perceptions of various chemical technologies. Concerns about chemical risks have risen dramatically in the past decade, spurred by well-publicized crises at Love Canal, New York, Times Beach, Missouri and many

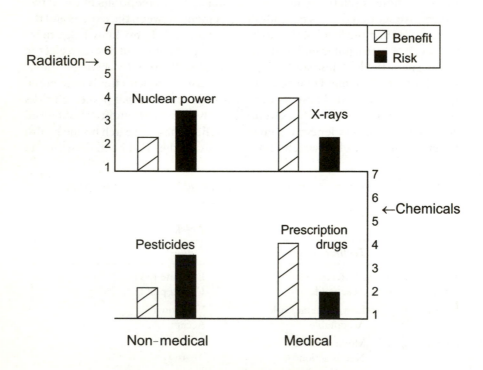

Note that medical sources of exposure have more favorable benefit/risk ratings.
Source: Data are from a national survey in Canada by Slovic, Kraus et al (1991).

Figure 16.1 *Mean perceived risk and perceived benefit for non-medical and medical sources of exposure to radiation and chemicals. (Each item was rated on two scales: perceived risk, ranging from 1 to 7 (very low to very high risk) and perceived benefit, ranging from 1 to 7 (very low to very high benefit))*

other waste sites; by major accidents at Seveso, Italy, Bhopal, India and Prince William Sound, Alaska; and by numerous other problems such as the contamination of ground water and flour with the pesticide ethylene dibromide (EDB) and the controversy regarding the use of Alar, a growth regulator, in apples. The image of chemical technologies is so negative that when you ask members of the general public to tell you what first comes to mind when they hear the word 'chemicals', by far the most frequent response is 'dangerous' or some synonym (eg, toxic, hazardous, poison, deadly). Chemicals, in general, and agricultural and industrial chemicals, in particular, are seen as very high risk and very low benefit, as are nuclear power and nuclear-waste technologies. However, just as medical uses of radiation (such as X-rays) are perceived in a very favorable way, differently from other radiation technologies, so are prescription drugs, which are a very potent and toxic category of chemicals to which we are often exposed at high doses. Figure 16.1, taken from a study in Canada (Slovic, Kraus et al, 1991), illustrates the parallels between nuclear power and non-medical chemicals (pesticides), seen as high in risk and low in benefit, and between X-rays and prescription drugs (high benefit/low to moderate risk). A national survey in Sweden has shown much the same results (Slovic et al, 1989).

Lessons

What does this research tell us about the acceptance of risk from radiation? There seem to be several lessons. First, although many technical experts have labeled public reactions as irrational or phobic, such accusations are clearly unjustified (Drottz-Sjöberg & Persson, 1993). There is a logic to public perceptions and behaviors that has become apparent through research. For example, the acceptance afforded X-rays and prescription drugs suggests that acceptance of risk is conditioned by perceptions of direct benefits and by trust in the managers of the technology, in this case the medical and pharmaceutical professions. The managers of nuclear power and non-medical chemical technologies are clearly less trusted and the benefits of these technologies are not highly appreciated, hence their risks are less acceptable. High risks from nuclear weapons are tolerated because of their perceived necessity (and probably also because people lack knowledge about how to intervene in military security issues; they do have such knowledge and opportunities to intervene in the management of nuclear power).

The apathetic response to the risk from radon appears to result from the fact that it is of natural origin, occurring in a comfortable, familiar setting, with no one to blame. Moreover, it can never be totally eliminated. Opposition to the burial of radioactive soil, on the other hand, likely derives from the fact that this hazard is imported, technological in origin, industry and the state are blameworthy, it is involuntary, has a visible focus (the barrels or the landfill), and can be totally eliminated by preventing the deposition in the landfill (Sandman et al, 1987).

THE IMPACTS OF PERCEPTIONS: STIGMA

It has become quite clear that, whether or not one agrees with public risk perceptions, they form a reality that cannot be ignored in risk management. Stigma associated with risk perception is a prime example of this. Substantial socio-economic impacts often result from the stigma associated with radiation contamination. The word stigma was used by the ancient Greeks to refer to bodily marks or brands that were designed to expose infamy or disgrace – to show, for example, that the bearer was a slave or criminal. As used today, the word denotes someone 'marked' as deviant, flawed, spoiled or generally undesirable in the view of some observer. When the stigmatizing characteristic is observed, the person is denigrated or avoided. Prime targets for stigmatization are members of minority groups, the aged, homosexuals, drug addicts, alcoholics and persons afflicted with physical or mental disabilities and deformities.

A dramatic example of stigmatization involving radiation occurred in September, 1987, in Goiania, Brazil, where two men searching for scrap metal dismantled a cancer therapy device in an abandoned clinic. In doing so, they sawed open a capsule containing 28 grams of caesium chloride. Children and workers nearby were attracted to the glowing material and began playing with it. Before the danger was realized, several hundred people became contaminated and four persons eventually died from acute radiation poisoning. Publicity about the incident led to stigmatization of the region and its residents (Petterson, 1988). Hotels in other parts of the country refused to allow Goiania residents to register, airline pilots refused to fly with Goiania residents on board, automobiles driven by Goianians were stoned, hotel occupancy in the region dropped 60% for six weeks following the incident, and virtually all conventions were canceled during this period. The sale prices of products manufactured in Goiania dropped by 40% after the first news reports and remained depressed for a period of 30 to 45 days despite the fact that no items were ever found to have been contaminated.

Risk Communication: Placing Radiation Risks in Perspective

Given the importance of risk perceptions and the extraordinary divergence between perceptions of experts and laypersons in the domains of chemical and radiation technologies, it is not surprising that there has been a burgeoning interest in the topic of 'risk communication'. Much has been written about the need to inform and educate people about risk and the difficulties of doing so (Covello, Sandman & Slovic, 1988; Covello, von Winterfeldt & Slovic, 1988; 1986; Hance, Chess & Sandman, 1988; Krimsky & Plough, 1988; Sandman, 1986; Slovic, 1981; 1986; Slovic et al, 1980b).

One of the few 'principles' in this field that seems to be useful is the assertion that comparisons are more meaningful than absolute numbers or probabilities, especially when these absolute values are quite small. Sowby (1965) argued that to decide whether or not we are responding adequately to radiation risks we need to compare them to 'some of the other risks of life'. Rothschild (1978) observed, 'There is no point in getting into a panic about the risks of life until you have compared the risks which worry you with those that don't, but perhaps should.'

Typically, such exhortations are followed by elaborate tables and even 'catalogs of risks' in which diverse indices of death or disability are displayed for a broad spectrum of life's hazards. Thus, Sowby (1965) provided extensive data on risks per hour of exposure, showing, for example, that an hour riding a motorcycle is as risky as an hour of being 75 years' old. Wilson (1979) developed a table of activities (eg, flying 1000 miles by jet, having one chest X-ray), each of which is estimated to increase one's annual chance of death by one in one million. Cohen and Lee (1979, p720) rank-ordered many hazards in terms of their reduction in life expectancy on the assumption that:

> ...to some approximation, the ordering should be society's order of priorities. However, we see several very major problems that have received very little attention ... whereas some of the items near the bottom of the list, especially those involving radiation, receive a great deal of attention.

A related exercise by Reissland and Harries (1979) compared loss of life expectancy in the nuclear industry with that in other occupations.

Although such risk comparisons may provide some aid to intuition, they do not educate as effectively as their proponents have assumed. A statement such as 'the annual risk from living near a nuclear power plant is equivalent to the risk of riding an extra 3 miles in an automobile' fails to consider how these two technologies differ on the many qualities that people believe to be important. As a result, such statements are likely to produce anger rather than enlightenment and they are not likely to be convincing in the face of criticism (Huyskens, 1994; Slovic, Kraus & Covello, 1990).

In sum, comparisons across diverse hazards may be useful tools for educating the public. Yet the facts do not speak for themselves. Comparative analyses must be performed with great care to be worthwhile.

Fortunately, radiation risks can be compared in a number of useful and defensible ways. Radiation emissions can be measured and comparisons can be made between actual or potential exposure levels of concern and familiar, everyday exposures from natural sources of radiation or medical X-rays and treatments. By making comparisons from one source of radiation to another, one avoids the apples versus oranges comparisons that befuddle and anger people.

Wilson (1987) used comparisons with natural sources of radiation to put the risks from the Chernobyl accident into perspective for the two million people living downwind from the reactor in Byelorussia. He noted that the estimated increased lifetime dose was .7 roentgen equivalent man (rem) for each of these persons and that this is considerably less than the difference in the lifetime external dose a person receives on moving from New York to Denver. It is also less than the difference in the dose a person receives from inhaled radon if he or she moves from an average New England house to an average Pennsylvania house.

When radiation from Chernobyl reached the US, the Inter-Agency Task Force, chaired by Environmental Protection Agency (EPA) administrator Lee Thomas, used similar comparisons to illustrate the low level of risk involved. Media stories pointed out that exposures in the US were a small fraction of the exposure from a chest X-ray. A news story from Portland, Oregon, indicated that readings of 2.9 picocuries of iodine-131 per cubic meter of air were insignificant compared to the 2700 picocurie level that would trigger concern.

This discussion is not meant to imply that we already know how to communicate radiation risks effectively. Communication about Chernobyl was dreadful in Europe (Drottz & Sjöberg, 1990; Gadomska, 1994; Hohenemser & Renn, 1988; Otway, Haastrup, Connell, Gianitsopoulas & Paruccini, 1988; Wynne, 1989). Information messages were peppered with different terms (roentgens, curies, bequerels, rads, rems, sieverts, grays) which were explained poorly or not at all. Public anxiety was high and not always related to actual threat. Public officials were at odds with one another and inconsistent in their evaluations of risks from consuming various kinds of food or milk. Comparisons with exposure to natural radiation from familiar activities were not well received because the media and the public did not trust the sources of such information. Other comparisons (eg, with background cancer rates) fared even worse. Many of the statements made by officials to calm the public confused and angered them instead. Although communications in the US effectively maintained a calm perspective, one could say that US officials had a relatively easy job. All they had to do was convince people that minuscule levels of radiation were not a threat. Had there been higher levels and 'hot spots' as in the Soviet Union and western Europe, the job of communicating would have been far tougher and it is not clear that proper perspectives on risk would have been achieved.

The good news is that enough is known about radiation and about risk communication to enable us to craft useful risk comparisons, if we devote proper attention and resources to doing so (see, for example, the effort by Johnson, Fisher, Smith & Desvousges, 1988, to inform homeowners about their risks from radon; and the recommendations by Adelstein, 1987).

Mental Models

An important new development is the use of mental models to guide risk communication efforts (Atman et al, 1994; Bostrom, Atman, Fischhoff & Morgan, 1994). Mental models are detailed representations of a person's knowledge and beliefs about a hazard and its consequences. These models are elicited by means of an interview procedure, beginning with open-ended questions (eg, 'What do you know about radon?') and proceeding to more specific questions about exposure, effects and mitigation issues. Ultimately, the person's valid knowledge and misconceptions are identified and risk communication is designed to fill knowledge gaps and correct misconceptions. This technique has been applied, with some success, in the design of brochures to inform people about the risks of radon (Atman et al, 1994; Bostrom et al, 1994).

Framing Effects

It would be comforting to believe that risk attitudes and perceptions, if erroneous, would respond to informational and educational programs. Unfortunately, psychological research demonstrates that people's beliefs change slowly and are extraordinarily persistent in the face of contrary evidence (Nisbett & Ross, 1980). Once formed, initial impressions tend to structure the way that subsequent evidence is interpreted. New evidence appears reliable and informative if it is consistent with one's initial belief; contrary evidence is dismissed as unreliable, erroneous or unrepresentative.

Table 16.2 *A Framing Effect: Surgery or Radiation Therapy*

	Mortality rates		Survival rates	
	Surgery (%)	*Radiation (%)*	*Surgery (%)*	*Radiation (%)*
Treatment	10	0	90	100
One year	32	23	68	77
•				
•				
•				
Five years	66	78	34	22
Percent choice of radiation therapy	44		18	

Source: McNeil, Pauker, Sox and Tversky (1982)

When people lack strong prior opinions, the opposite situation exists – they are at the mercy of the way that the information is presented. Subtle changes in the way that risks are 'framed' or expressed can have a major impact on perceptions and decisions. One dramatic example of framing in the context of medical decision-making comes from a study by McNeil et al (1982), who asked people to imagine that they had lung cancer and had to choose between surgery or radiation therapy. The two treatments were described in some detail. Then, some respondents were presented with the cumulative probabilities of surviving for varying lengths of time after the treatment. Other respondents received the same cumulative probabilities framed in terms of dying rather than surviving (eg, instead of being told that 68% of those having surgery will have survived after one year, they were told that 32% will have died – see Table 16.2). Framing the statistics in terms of dying dropped the percentage of respondents choosing radiation therapy over surgery from 44% to 18%. The effect was as strong for physicians as for laypersons.

Numerous other examples of 'framing effects' have been demonstrated by Tversky and Kahneman (1981) and others. The fact that subtle differences in how risks are presented can have such marked effects suggests that those responsible for information programs have considerable ability to manipulate perceptions and behavior. This possibility raises ethical problems that must be addressed by any responsible risk-information program.

IMPLICATIONS FOR RADIATION MEDICINE

In 20 years of research on perception and acceptance of technological risks, there has been remarkably little attention given to the medical uses of radiation – quite a contrast to the hundred or more studies of perceptions of nuclear power and nuclear waste. This lack of attention is surprising, given the importance of radiation medicine and the fact that some procedures, such as mammography screening for younger women, have been the source of much concern and controversy.

In the absence of studies specifically directed at radiation medicine, one can only speculate about public views based on more general findings. The use of radiation for diagnosis and therapy will likely stand apart from other radiation technologies because people see great benefits from medical radiation and they have relatively high trust in the medical profession. Where the need is particularly evident (eg, cancer therapy), tolerance of risk will be quite high, as shown by the strong desire of AIDS patients to have access to new, potentially dangerous medicines (Levi, 1991). But acceptance of radiation exposures will undoubtedly come with anxieties, due to the association of such exposures with the cause of cancer as well as the cure. Moreover, the public will likely support strict controls over radiation medicine regardless of costs and they will react strongly to incidents of improper or incompetent administration.

Ultimately, the best way to understand the public's view of radiation medicine is to ask people directly – by means of one-on-one interviews, focus groups and structured surveys. In this way we can obtain a 'clear image' of people's mental models pertaining to various diagnostic and therapeutic procedures, including their knowledge and misconceptions, their perceptions of risk and benefit, and their attitudes toward the use and regulation of these procedures.

Such data are really quite easy to collect. The methods are developed and the costs are reasonable. In the past, focused surveys have rarely failed to provide insights that are useful for education and policy.

17

Perceived Risk, Trust and the Politics of Nuclear Waste

Paul Slovic, James Flynn and Mark Layman

By the year 2000, the US will have a projected 40,000 metric tons of spent nuclear fuel stored at some 70 sites and awaiting disposal. By 2035, after all existing nuclear plants have completed 40 years of operation, there will be approximately 85,000 metric tons (Nuclear Waste Technical Review Board, 1991). The US Department of Energy (DOE) has been under intense pressure from congress and the nuclear industry to dispose of this accumulating volume of high-level waste since the passage of the Nuclear Waste Policy Act in 1982 and its amendment in 1987, at which time Yucca Mountain, Nevada, was selected as the only candidate site for the nation's first nuclear waste repository. The lack of a suitable solution to the waste problem is widely viewed as an obstacle to further developing nuclear power and a threat to the continued operation of existing reactors, besides being a safety hazard in its own right.

Yet, at this time, the DOE program has been brought nearly to a halt by overwhelming political opposition, fueled by perceptions of the public that the risks are immense (Dunlap, Kraft & Rosa, 1993; Flynn, Slovic, Mertz & Burns, 1990; Kasperson, 1990; Kunreuther et al, 1988; Nealey & Hebert, 1983; Slovic, 1991). These perceptions stand in stark contrast to the prevailing view of the technical community, which argues that nuclear wastes can be disposed of safely in deep underground isolation (Cohen, 1985b; Lewis, 1990; USDOE, 1986). Officials from the DOE, the nuclear industry and their technical experts are profoundly puzzled, frustrated and disturbed by public and political opposition that many of them consider to be based on irrationality and ignorance. Lewis (1990), for example, argued that the risk from a properly constructed repository 'is as negligible as it is possible to imagine... It is embarrassingly easy to solve the technical problems, yet impossible to solve the political problems... High-level nuclear waste disposal is a non-risk' (pp245–6).

Note: reprinted with permission from 'Perceived Risk, Trust, and the Politics of Nuclear Waste' by P Slovic, J Flynn & M Layman, *Science*, 254, 1991, pp1603–7. Copyright 1991 American Association for the Advancement of Science.

A number of important events during the past several years underscore the seriousness of this problem.

1　Official opposition by the State of Nevada has increased substantially. In June 1989, the Nevada Legislature passed Assembly Bill 222, making it unlawful for any person or governmental entity to store high-level radioactive waste in the state. The state attorney general subsequently issued an opinion that the Yucca Mountain site had been effectively vetoed under a provision of the Nuclear Waste Policy Act. The governor instructed state agencies to disregard the DOE's applications for environmental permits necessary to investigate the site. The state and the DOE initiated federal lawsuits over continuance of the program and issuance of the permits needed for on-site studies. In September 1990, the 9th US Circuit Court of Appeals ruled that the state had acted improperly and ordered Nevada officials to issue the permits. Nevada appealed to the US Supreme Court, which let stand the prior ruling. Although state officials have, under duress, begun to accept and process DOE permit applications, the governor and other elected officials have announced that their opposition to the repository will not diminish.

2　In November 1989, the DOE, admitting dissatisfaction with its technical assessments of the Yucca Mountain site, announced that it would essentially start over with, 'for the first time', an integrated, responsible plan. This plan would subject technical studies to close outside scrutiny to ensure that decisions about Yucca Mountain would be made 'solely on the basis of solid scientific evidence' (W H Moore, 1989).

3　In July 1990, the National Research Council's board on radioactive waste management issued a strong critique of the DOE program, charging that the DOE's insistence on doing everything right the first time has misled the public by promising unattainable levels of safety under a rigid schedule that is 'unrealistic given the inherent uncertainties of this unprecedented undertaking', and thus vulnerable to 'show stopping' problems and delays that could lead to a further deterioration of public and scientific trust' (National Research Council, 1990, p1). The board recommended, instead, a more flexible approach, permitting design and engineering changes as new information becomes available during repository construction and operation.

Perceptions of risk from radiation, nuclear power and nuclear waste play a pivotal role in this story and need to be thoroughly understood if we are to make any progress in resolving the current impasse. In this chapter, we summarize research designed to penetrate the surface veneer of nuclear fear and opposition and provide insight into the nature of people's concerns, the origins of these concerns, the emotions that underlie them and their implications for policy.

ATTITUDE AND OPINION SURVEYS

There have been more than a dozen surveys conducted during the past five years to assess public attitudes and opinions regarding the management of high-level radioactive wastes (Desvousges, Kunreuther & Slovic, 1993; Dunlap et al, 1993; Flynn, Slovic, Mertz & Toma, 1990; Kunreuther et al, 1988; Mountain West, 1989). The picture that emerges is uniformly negative.

One of the more extensive surveys was conducted in the autumn of 1989 by Flynn, Slovic, Mertz and Toma (1990). More than 2500 respondents were questioned by telephone about their perceptions of the risks and benefits associated with a nuclear-waste repository, their support of or opposition to the DOE repository program, their trust in the ability of the DOE to manage the program, and their views on a variety of other issues pertaining to radioactive waste disposal. In addition to a national survey, data were collected from two other populations of special interest: residents of Nevada, the state selected as the site for the proposed national repository, and residents of southern California, the major source of tourism and migration to Nevada.

When asked to indicate the closest distance they would be willing to live from each of ten facilities, the median distance from an underground nuclear-waste repository was 200 miles in each of the three surveys, twice the distance from the next most undesirable facility, a chemical waste landfill, and three to eight times the distances from oil refineries, nuclear power plants and pesticide manufacturing plants. In response to the statement, 'Highway and rail accidents will occur in transporting the wastes to the repository site', the percentage of respondents who agreed or strongly agreed was 77.4% in Nevada, 69.2% in California, and 71.6% nationally. Similar expectations of problems were expressed with regard to future earthquake or volcanic activity at the site, contamination of underground water supplies and accidents while handling the material during burial operations.

When asked whether a state that does not produce high-level nuclear wastes should serve as a site for a nuclear waste repository, 67.9% of the southern California and 76.0% of the national respondents answered 'no' (the question was not asked in Nevada). A majority of those polled in the southern California and national surveys judged a single national repository to be the least fair of five disposal options (the other options were storage at each nuclear plant, in each state, in each of several regions, and dual repositories in the East and West).

Strong distrust of the DOE was evident from the responses to statements such as, 'The US Department of Energy can be trusted to provide prompt and full disclosure of any accidents or serious problems with their nuclear-waste management programs.' In southern California, 67.5% either somewhat or strongly disagreed with this statement. The corresponding rate of disagreement in the national survey was 68.1%.

Nevadans were asked whether they would vote in favor of a repository at Yucca Mountain; 69.4% said they would vote against it, compared to 14.4% who would vote for it. About 68% of the Nevadans surveyed said they agreed strongly with the statement: 'The State of Nevada should do all it can to stop the repository'; another 12.5% agreed somewhat with this statement. Only 16.0% disagreed. When asked whether they favored Assembly Bill 222, making it illegal to dispose of high-level nuclear waste in Nevada, 74% were in favor and 18.4% were opposed. Finally, 73.6% of Nevadans said that the state should continue to do all it can to oppose the repository even if that means turning down benefits that may be offered by the federal government; 19.6% said the state should stop fighting and make a deal.

Follow-up surveys of Nevada residents in October 1990 and March 1991 suggest that opposition and distrust have risen (Flynn, Mertz & Slovic, 1991). The percentage of Nevadans who would vote against a repository at Yucca Mountain increased from 69.4 to 80.2%. In responses to a request to indicate 'how much you trust each of the following to do what is right with regard to a nuclear waste repository at Yucca Mountain', the governor of Nevada topped the list of officials, agencies and institutions. DOE, the Nuclear Regulatory Commission (NRC) and the US Congress were the least trusted entities. Between 1989 and 1991, strong increases in trust were evident for the governor of Nevada and the Nevada state legislature. In contrast, trust in DOE and NRC declined between 1989 and 1991.

IMAGERY AND PERCEPTION

Before answering any of the attitude or opinion questions, respondents in the national, Southern California and Nevada surveys, along with respondents in a survey of 802 residents of Phoenix, were asked to associate freely about the concept of a nuclear waste repository (Slovic, Layman & Flynn, 1991). The method of continued associations (Szalay & Deese, 1978) was used to evoke images, perceptions and affective states related to a repository. Respondents were asked to indicate the first thoughts or images that come to mind when they think of an underground nuclear-waste repository.

The 3334 respondents in the four surveys produced a combined total of exactly 10,000 word-association images to the repository stimulus. The associations were examined and assigned to 13 general categories.[1] All but one general category contained subcategories. In all, there were 92 distinct subcategories. Many of these contained multiple associations, judged to have similar meanings. For example, the subcategory labeled 'dangerous/toxic', within the general category labeled 'negative consequences', included the terms 'danger, dangerous, unsafe, disaster, hazardous, poisonous' and so on.

The two largest categories, 'negative consequences' and 'negative concepts', and their combined frequencies across all four samples are shown in Table 17.1. The subcategories are also shown, ordered by frequency within their superordinate category. The most arresting and most important result is the extreme negative quality of these images. These two largest categories accounted for more than 56% of the total number of images. The dominant subcategory, 'dangerous/toxic', contained almost 17% of the total number of images. The five largest subordinate categories – 'dangerous/toxic, death/sickness, environmental damage, bad/negative and scary' – were thoroughly negative in affective quality and accounted for more than 42% of the total number of images. The four most frequent single associations were 'dangerous' ($n = 539$), 'danger' ($n = 378$), 'death' ($n = 306$), and 'pollution' ($n = 276$).

Positive imagery was rare. A general category labeled 'positive' accounted for only 1% of the images. Other positive concepts, 'necessary', 'employment', and 'money/income' combined to total only 2.5% of the images. The response 'safe' was given only 37 times (.37%). In addition, there were 232 associations pertaining to war, annihilation, weapons and things military. The famous NIMBY

Table 17.1 *Dominant Images of a Nuclear Waste Repository: Totals for Four Surveys*

Image category	n
Negative consequences	
Dangerous/toxic	1683
Death/sickness	783
Environmental damage	692
Leakage	216
Destruction	133
Pain and suffering	18
Uninhabitable	7
Local repository area consequences	6
Negative consequences – other	8
Total	*3546*
Negative concepts	
Bad/negative	681
Scary	401
Unnecessary/opposed	296
Not near me	273
War/annihilation	126
Societally unpopular	41
Crime and corruption	40
Decay/slime/smell	39
Darkness/emptiness	37
Negative towards decision-makers and process	32
Commands to not build or to eliminate them	24
Wrong or bad solution	19
No nuclear, stop producing	15
Unjust	14
Violence	10
Prohibited	5
Negative – other	15
Total	*2068*

position (not in my backyard) was expressed in 273 images. Associations indicative of distrust appeared in the category 'negative towards decision-makers and process,' and in another subcategory dealing with mistakes. A number of images in the 'bad/negative' category also seemed to reflect lack of trust (eg, 'stupid', 'dumb', 'illogical').

Jones et al (1984) have attempted to characterize the key dimensions of stigma. Two such defining characteristics are peril and negative aesthetic qualities (ugliness and repulsion). These qualities dominate the repository images. Peril is pervasive throughout the 'negative consequences' category and negative aesthetics and repulsion form the bulk of 'negative concepts' (see Table 17.1). Indeed, the large subcategory 'bad/negative' is remarkable in this reflection of antagonism and hostility toward the repository concept. Common responses in this category were 'terrible', 'ugly', 'disgusting', 'anger', 'evil', 'insane', 'hate it', and, simply, 'bad' (107 responses). Associations indicating locations ('desert', 'Nevada', 'underground') and concepts such as 'radiation', 'nuclear' and 'chemicals' made up the bulk of the responses not covered in Table 17.1.

The images were similar in content and frequency from one survey to another. Demographic differences were also small. The negativity of repository images was remarkably consistent across men and women of different ages, incomes, educational levels and political persuasions.

After free-associating to the repository stimulus, each respondent in the Nevada survey rated the affective quality of his or her associations on a five-point scale ranging from extremely negative to extremely positive. These affective ratings were highly correlated with the respondent's attitudes and perceptions of risk. For example, more than 90% of the persons whose first image was judged very negative said they would vote against a repository at Yucca Mountain; more than half of the persons whose first image was judged positive would vote in favor of the repository. A similarly strong relationship was found between affective ratings of images and a person's judgment of the likelihood of accidents or other problems at a repository. Negativity of the image rating was also strongly related to support for the state of Nevada's opposition to the repository program.

What was learned by asking 3334 people to associate freely to the concept of a nuclear waste repository? The most obvious answer is that people do not like nuclear waste. However, these images (as well as the responses to the attitude and opinion questions) demonstrate an aversion so strong that to label it a 'dislike' hardly does it justice. What these responses reveal are pervasive qualities of dread, revulsion and anger – the raw materials of stigmatization and political opposition.

Because nuclear waste is a by-product of an impressive technology capable of producing massive amounts of energy without contributing to greenhouse gases, one might expect to find associations to energy and its benefits – electricity, light, heat, employment, health, progress, the good life – scattered among the images. Almost none were observed.

Moreover, people were not asked to reflect on nuclear waste; instead, they were asked about a storage facility or repository. One might expect, following the predominant view of experts in this field, to find a substantial number of repository images reflecting the qualities 'necessary' and 'safe'. Few images of this kind were observed.

How Did It Get this Way?

Imagery and attitudes so negative and so impervious to influence from the assessments of technical experts must have very potent origins. Weart's (1988) historical analysis shows that nuclear fears are deeply rooted in our social and cultural consciousness. He demonstrates that modern thinking about nuclear energy employs beliefs and symbols that have been associated for centuries with the concept of transmutation – the passage through destruction to rebirth. In the early decades of the 20th century, transmutation images became centered on radioactivity, which was associated with uncanny rays that brought hideous death or miraculous new life. This concept of transmutation has a duality that is hardly evident in the imagery observed in the surveys. Why has the destructive aspect predominated? The answer likely involves the bombings of Hiroshima and Nagasaki, which linked the frightening images of nuclear energy to reality.

Research supports this assertion. Fiske, Pratto and Pavelchak (1983) elicited people's images of nuclear war and obtained results that were similar to the repository images described above. A study by Slovic, Lichtenstein et al (1979) found that, even before the accident at Three Mile Island, people expected nuclear reactor accidents to lead to disasters of immense proportions. When asked to describe the consequences of a 'typical reactor accident', people's scenarios were found to resemble scenarios of the aftermath of nuclear war.[2] The shared imagery of nuclear weapons, nuclear power and nuclear waste may explain why a nuclear waste repository is judged by the public to pose risks at least as great as a nuclear power plant or a nuclear weapons test site (Kunreuther et al, 1988).

Further insights into the special quality of nuclear fear are provided by Erikson (1990), who describes the exceptionally dread quality of accidents that expose people to radiation. Unlike natural disasters, these accidents have no end. 'Invisible contaminants remain a part of the surroundings – absorbed into the grain of the landscape, the tissues of the body and, worst of all, into the genetic material of the survivors. An "all clear" is never sounded. The book of accounts is never closed' (p121).

Another strong determiner of public perceptions is the continuing story of decades of mishandling of wastes at the nation's military weapons facilities, now operated by the DOE (National Academy of Sciences, 1989). Leakage from these facilities has resulted in widespread contamination, projected to require more than $150 billion for cleanup over the next 30 years. The recent revelation of unprecedented releases of radiation from the Hanford, Washington, weapons plant in the 1940s and 1950s (Marshall, 1990) will certainly compound the negative imagery associated with a nuclear-waste repository and further undermine public trust in government management of nuclear-waste disposal.

A CRISIS OF CONFIDENCE

The fear and revulsion evoked in the general public by the thought of a nuclear waste repository stand in contrast to the confidence that most technical analysts and engineers have in their ability to dispose of radioactive materials safely. Even the report of the National Research Council (1990), highly concerned with the difficulties of predicting the long-term performance of a repository, conceded that 'these uncertainties do not necessarily mean that the risks are significant, nor that the public should reject efforts to site the repository' (p13).

Starr (1985) has argued that 'acceptance of any risk is more dependent on public confidence in risk management than on the quantitative estimates of risk' (p98). Public fears and opposition to nuclear-waste disposal plans can be seen as a 'crisis of confidence', a profound breakdown of trust in the scientific, governmental and industrial managers of nuclear technologies. The breakdown of trust was clearly evident at the time that the Nuclear Waste Policy Act was signed

(Jacob, 1990; US Office of Technology Assessment, 1985) and has been documented repeatedly in subsequent public opinion surveys (Dantico, Mushkatel & Pijawka, 1991; Dunlap & Baxter, 1988; Dunlap et al, 1993; Flynn, Slovic, Mertz & Toma, 1990; Rothman & Lichter, 1987).

Viewing the nuclear waste problem as one of distrust in risk management gives important insights into its intractability. Social psychological studies (Rothbart & Park, 1986) have validated 'folk wisdom' by demonstrating that trust is a quality that is quickly lost and slowly (if ever) regained. A single act of embezzlement is enough to convince us that our bookkeeper is untrustworthy. A subsequent opportunity to embezzle that is not taken would likely do little to reduce the degree of distrust. Indeed, 100 subsequent honest actions would probably do little to restore our trust in this individual.

In this light, the attempt by the DOE to regain the confidence of the public, congress and the nuclear industry by rearranging its organizational chart and promising to do a better job of risk management and science in the future (W H Moore, 1989) was naive. Trust, once lost, cannot so easily be restored. Similarly naive is the aim professed by DOE officials and other nuclear industry leaders to change perceptions and gain support by letting people see firsthand the safety of nuclear-waste management. The nature of any low-probability, high-consequence threat is such that adverse events will demonstrate riskiness, but demonstrations of safety (or negligible risk) will require a very long time, free of damaging incidents. The intense scrutiny given to nuclear power and nuclear waste issues by the news media (Slovic, 1987; Mazur, 1984b) ensures that a stream of problems, occurring all over the world, will be brought to the public's attention, continually eroding trust.

WHERE NEXT FOR NUCLEAR WASTE?

Although everyone recognizes the sophisticated engineering required to store nuclear wastes safely, the political requirements necessary to design and implement a repository have not similarly been appreciated. As a result, Jacob (1990) notes, 'While vast resources have been expended on developing complex and sophisticated technologies, the equally sophisticated political processes and institutions required to develop a credible and legitimate strategy for nuclear-waste management have not been developed' (p164).

In the absence of a trustworthy process for siting, developing and operating a nuclear-waste repository, the prospects for a short-term solution to the disposal problem seem remote. The report of the National Research Council (1990) is quite sensitive to issues of risk perception and trust, but makes the strong assumption that trust can be restored by a process that openly recognizes the limits of technical understanding and does not aim to 'get it right the first time'. It seems likely that such open admission of uncertainty and refusal to guarantee safety might well have opposite effects from those intended – increased concern and further deterioration of trust. Moreover, the National Research Council statement also assumes that the DOE will continue to manage the nuclear waste program, thus failing to come to grips with the difficulties that the agency will face in restoring its tainted image.

The lack of a trustworthy process for siting, developing and operating a nuclear waste repository has evoked numerous other comments and suggestions. Weinberg (1989) draws an analogy between fear of witches during the 15th through the 17th centuries and today's fear of harm from radiation. He hypothesizes that 'rad-waste phobia' may dissipate if the intelligentsia (read environmentalists) say that such fears are unfounded, much as eventually happened with fears of witches. Carter (1987) argues that 'trust will be gained by building a record of sure, competent, open performance that gets good marks from independent technical peer reviewers and that shows decent respect for the public's sensibilities and common sense' (p416). Others have called for more radical changes, such as creating new organizations to take over the DOE's management role (Creighton, 1990; US DOE, 1984) and developing procedures to ensure that state, local and tribal governments have a strong voice in siting decisions and oversight of actual repository operations (Bella, Mosher & Calvo, 1988b; Bord, 1987; Jacob, 1990). In this spirit, an official of the Canadian government has argued for making repository siting in that country voluntary by requiring public consent as an absolute prerequisite for confirming any decision (Frech, 1991).

Whatever steps are taken, it is unlikely that the current 'crisis in confidence' will be ended quickly or easily. We must anticipate a long effort to restore the public trust. Krauskopf (1990) has argued that postponing the repository to an indefinite future can be defended on a variety of technical grounds and points out that the choice between repository construction or postponement ultimately rests on the shoulders of the public and their elected representatives. The problems of perception and trust described above imply that postponement of a permanent repository may be the only politically viable option in the foreseeable future.

In an address to the National Association of Regulatory Utility Commissioners in November 1990, Joseph Rhodes, Jr, a commissioner from Pennsylvania, pointed out the implications of the polls indicating that most Nevadans oppose the siting of a repository anywhere in Nevada and want state leaders to oppose such siting with any means available.[3] 'I can't imagine', said Rhodes, 'that there will ever be a usable Yucca Mountain repository if the people of Nevada don't want it... There are just too many ways to delay the program' (p6).

What are the options in the light of insurmountable public opposition to a permanent underground repository? Rhodes lists and rejects several:

- Continuing on the present path in an attempt to site a permanent repository is a costly and doomed effort.
- Permanent on-site storage is unsafe.
- Deploying a monitored retrievable storage (MRS) program is also politically unacceptable. Without a viable program to develop a permanent repository, the MRS would be seen, in effect, as the permanent site.
- Reprocessing the spent nuclear fuel is also politically unacceptable because of concerns over nuclear weapons proliferation. Moreover, reprocessing reduces but does not eliminate high-level wastes, and the record of managing reprocessing residues at West Valley, Hanford, and other sites is hardly encouraging (Carter, 1987; National Academy of Sciences, 1989; US Office of Technology Assessment, 1992).

Rhodes concludes, and we concur, that the only viable option is to postpone the siting of a permanent repository and store the wastes on site in the interim – employing dry-cask storage that has been certified by the NRC as being as safe as geological storage for 100 or more years (US Nuclear Regulatory Commission, 1990). Should this course of action be followed, technical knowledge will undoubtedly advance greatly during this interim period. Perceptions of risk and trust in government and the nuclear industry may change greatly, too, if the problem of establishing and maintaining trust is taken seriously.

Notes

1   A complete categorized listing of all 10,000 images is available from the authors.
2   The fact that the earliest technical risk assessments for nuclear power plants portrayed 'worst-case scenarios' of tens of thousands of deaths and devastation over geographic areas the size of Pennsylvania likely contributed to such extreme images (Ford, 1977). These early projections received enormous publicity, as in the movie *The China Syndrome*.
3   Rhodes' assertion echoes an earlier statement made by former DOE official John O'Leary in an interview with Luther Carter: 'When you think of all the things a determined state can do, it's no contest', O'Leary told me, citing by way of example the regulatory authority a state has with respect to its lands, highways, employment codes and the like. The federal courts, he added, would strike down each of the state's blocking actions, but meanwhile years would roll by and in a practical sense DOE's cause would be lost (Carter, 1987, p185).

18 Intuitive Toxicology: Expert and Lay Judgments of Chemical Risks

Nancy Kraus, Torbjörn Malmfors and Paul Slovic

INTRODUCTION

Human beings have always been 'intuitive toxicologists', relying on their senses of sight, taste and smell to detect harmful or unsafe food, water and air. During the past several years, we have been studying the perception of risks from chemicals, based on this concept of intuitive toxicology.

As we have come to recognize that our senses and intuitions are not adequate to assess the dangers inherent in exposure to a chemical substance, we have created the sciences of toxicology and risk assessment to perform this function. Massive regulatory establishments have been formed to oversee the use of these sciences for standard-setting and policy-making in the interests of protecting public health.

Yet despite this enormous effort, people in many industrialized nations feel increasingly vulnerable to the risks from technology and believe that the worst is yet to come (Harris, 1980). Regulatory agencies have become embroiled in rancorous conflicts, caught between angry environmentalists on one side and frustrated technologists and industrialists on the other. The lay public is anxious and confused. Nuclear power has long been a focus of public concerns. Today, there is great concern and dissatisfaction with the production, use, transport and disposal of chemicals. The lay public has clearly not been satisfied with, or persuaded by, scientific assessments of risk for either nuclear power or chemical hazards.

Industrialists and scientists are equally dissatisfied with the public, whose concerns they equate with ignorance or, worse, irrationality. Industry leaders see an urgent need to educate and inform the public in order to erase the 'fear and sensationalism' that has tarnished the image of chemicals and the chemical

Note: Reprinted from 'Intuitive Toxicology: Expert and Lay Judgments of Chemical Risks' by N Kraus, T Malmfors & P Slovic, 1992, *Risk Analysis*, 12(2), pp215–32. Copyright 1992 by the Society for Risk Analysis. Reprinted with permission.

industry (Callis, 1990; Pimentel, 1989). Many have turned to the young field of risk communication in search of guidance that might make conflicts over technological decisions easier to resolve (National Academy of Sciences, 1983; Ruckelshaus, 1984). Much of the public unease and social conflict may be traceable to the inherent limitations of the science itself, which is short on knowledge of the mechanisms by which chemicals harm living organisms. In the absence of mechanistic knowledge, risk assessment must rely upon indirect methods, which infer human health effects from bacterial and animal responses to chemical exposures. These indirect methods have become the primary bases for government regulation and policy. Although the limitations and uncertainties underlying these methods are readily acknowledged, it is assumed that, used conservatively, they can identify chemical threats and estimate the upper bounds on risk with enough accuracy to adequately protect public health. Behind this orderly facade of what Efron (1984) has labeled 'regulatory science', in the trenches of 'basic science', the field of risk assessment has been in a state of intense controversy for more than a decade (Ames & Gold, 1990; Efron, 1984; Freedman & Zeisel, 1988; Graham, Green & Roberts, 1988; Malmfors, 1981; Marx, 1990). A number of investigators have argued that the ambiguities and uncertainties of risk assessment are fertile grounds for influence from political and ideological considerations (Clarke, 1988; Dietz & Rycroft, 1987; Gormley, 1986; Graham et al, 1988; Johnson & Covello, 1987; Lynn, 1987; Mazur, 1981; Swaen & Meijers, 1988; Whittemore, 1983). For example, Lynn (1987) found that attitudes of occupational health specialists toward fundamental issues in risk assessment were strongly related to whether they worked in industry, government or academia and whether they had voted Democratic or Republican in the previous presidential election. Graham et al (1988) have illustrated these kinds of biases in their detailed description of the controversies surrounding the regulation of benzene and formaldehyde.

A committee of the National Academy of Sciences has responded to this problem by calling for procedural changes designed to improve the scientific basis of risk assessment and insulate scientific analyses and interpretations from political influence (1983). It is significant that this committee highlighted the inherent subjectivity in toxicological risk assessment, noting that the procedures scientists follow and the interpretations they make 'rest, to various degrees, on a mixture of scientific fact and consensus, on informed scientific judgment, and on policy determinations (eg, the appropriate degree of conservatism)' (p36). The Academy report further indicated the need to examine the subjective and intuitive elements of expert and lay risk assessments – both to shore up the foundations of scientific analyses and to improve communication between scientists and the lay public.

Objectives of this Research

The National Academy of Sciences report acknowledged the subjective nature of risk assessment, but did not fully come to grips with its implications. One such implication is that different assumptions, conceptions and values, in addition to (or instead of) disagreements about facts, might underlie much of the discrepancy between expert and lay views of chemical risks.

The objective of the present study is to address this issue by exploring the cognitive models, assumptions and inference methods that comprise laypeople's 'intuitive toxicological theories' and by comparing these theories with cognitive models, assumptions and inference methods of scientific toxicology and risk assessment. Such comparisons should expose the specific similarities and differences within the expert community as well as the similarities and differences between lay perceptions and expert views. We hope that the knowledge gained from these comparisons will provide a valuable starting point around which to structure discussion, education and communication about the assessment of risks from chemicals and the management of those risks.

Questionnaire Development

We began by identifying several fundamental principles and judgmental components within the science of risk assessment. Questions were developed based on these fundamentals in order to determine the extent to which laypeople and experts share the same beliefs and conceptual framework. Our questions addressed the following four topics:

- category 1: dose-response sensitivity;
- category 2: trust in animal and bacterial studies;
- category 3: attitudes toward chemicals;
- category 4: attitudes toward reducing chemical risks.

Questions on these topics were incorporated within a single questionnaire, designed for both experts and the public. Respondents were instructed to think of the term 'chemicals' as including 'all chemical elements and compounds, including pesticides, food additives, industrial chemicals, household cleaning agents, prescription and non-prescription drugs, etc'. Tables 18.1 through 18.5 present the specific questions used, categorized according to four major topic areas and a miscellaneous set of items (category 5).[1] All but one of the questions were posed as statements to be evaluated by an agree/disagree response.[2]

Each question was designed, whenever possible, according to a guiding hypothesis about how experts and 'lay toxicologists' might respond. For example, perhaps the most important principle in toxicology is the fact that 'the dose makes the poison'.[3] Any substance can cause a toxic effect if the dose is great enough. Thus, we expected experts to be quite sensitive to considerations of exposure and dose when responding to the five items in category 1. In contrast, the often observed concerns of the public regarding very small exposures or doses of chemicals led us to hypothesize that the public would have more of an 'all or none' view of toxicity and would be rather insensitive to concentration, dose and exposure (thus, equating exposure with harm) when responding to items in category 1. We also expected laypersons to view natural substances as less toxic than synthetic substances (question 5a), and experts to recognize the potential toxicity of natural substances as well as synthetic ones (Ames, 1983).

With regard to category 2, we hypothesized that, because the science of toxicology and the discipline of risk assessment rely so heavily upon animal studies, experts would have a more favorable view than laypersons regarding the value of such studies. The prediction that laypersons lack sensitivity to dose-response considerations and thus fear even small exposures to toxic or carcinogenic substances led us to expect that they would exhibit far more negative attitudes toward chemicals than experts when responding to the questions in category 3. Similarly, we expected that laypersons' concerns about small exposures would cause them, more than experts, to want reduction and even elimination of chemical risks, regardless of cost (category 4).

Turning to category 5, we expected that laypersons would perceive chemicals in prescription drugs as less toxic than chemicals used in pesticides (question 5b). Further, we expected that laypersons' direct experiences with medicines and their knowledge of the risk of overdose would make them more likely to recognize that the dose makes the poison for prescription drugs than for chemicals in general (see the two forms of question 5e). Similarly, for question 5f, we expected that a 1 in 10 million lifetime risk would be less worrisome if it came from taking a prescription drug than if it came from exposure to a chemical.

Question 5h examined the interpretation of evidence pertaining to the cause of birth defects observed in a region where pesticides had been used. We hypothesized that experts would believe that the evidence presented was not sufficient to indict pesticides as the cause of the observed malformations, whereas laypersons would be more inclined to view the association between pesticides and birth defects as causal (see Jenkins and Ward, 1965, who demonstrated the difficulty people have in dissociating covariation from causality). We had no strong prior hypothesis about how either experts or laypersons would judge the relative vulnerability of animals and humans to adverse chemical effects. Differing views can be found in the scientific literature. Some argue that humans are less vulnerable than the particularly sensitive strains of animals used in many bioassays. Humans are also exposed to far smaller amounts of chemicals than the test animals. Others argue that humans are more vulnerable, because of their slower metabolic processes, their great genetic diversity and their exposure to a greater number of carcinogenic substances than laboratory animals. Regulatory policies typically assume that humans are more sensitive to adverse effects than animals.

Administration of the Survey

Expert sample

The sample of experts was selected from the 1988 membership directory of the Society of Toxicology (SOT). Only full members of the society residing in the US were considered for inclusion in the study. The names of these full SOT members were categorized into three subgroups based on the type of organization with which they were affiliated: academic, industrial or regulatory. Random numbers were used to select 120 names from each of the three affiliated subgroups. The survey was mailed to each of these persons, along with a cover letter from the past president of the SOT.

In all, 360 questionnaires were mailed in October 1988, and 170 completed questionnaires were returned, for an overall response rate of 47%. Subgroup response rates were consistent with this overall rate; 44% of those from the academic subgroup returned their questionnaires, along with 49% of those affiliated with industry, and 48% of those affiliated with regulatory agencies. Those who responded were highly educated (91% had a PhD degree and 2.4% an MD degree); 84.6% of the respondents were male; 58.9% were between the ages of 33 and 48; 37.5% were ages 49–64; and 3.6% were younger than 32 or older than 64 years.

Public sample

A sample of the general public was selected from the Portland, Oregon, metropolitan area. A professional listing organization provided a sampling frame organized by zip code. This population listing was screened for a minimum annual household income of $20,000, and 1100 households were randomly selected for the mailing, which took place on 25 October, 1988. Those who had not replied by 15 November, 1988 were sent another copy of the survey instrument.

Of the approximately 975 deliverable questionnaires, 262 usable questionnaires were returned, for a response rate of about 27%. These individuals were non-representative of the Portland general population in several ways. Specifically, respondents were more likely to be male (58.0% versus 48.6% in the population); well educated (95.7% high-school graduates in the sample and 23.1% with graduate-school training versus 78.7% and 9.9%, respectively, in the population); and high income (24.6% of the sample had household incomes greater than $50,000 versus 5.0% of the population in 1980 – corrected for 42.9% cumulative inflation between 1980 and 1988). Most (96.5%) of the respondents were white (versus 92.8% of the population); 24.1% were between the ages of 16 and 32; 46.4% were ages 33 to 48; 14.9% were ages 48 to 64; and 14.6% were older than 64 years.

RESULTS

Expert versus Layperson Comparisons

We expected that the toxicologists would differ greatly from the laypersons in their responses to most questions. However, there was striking agreement on question 5g, which asked respondents whether they agreed with the statement: 'I think I should know as much as I can about the chemicals around me. The more I know, the more I can control the risks that these chemicals pose to my health and to the environment.' The percentage of respondents who agreed or strongly agreed with this statement was 94.6% among the toxicologists and 93.4% among the public. Thus, though their perceptions and attitudes may differ, the stated motivations of experts and laypersons to understand and control chemical risks appear to be remarkably similar.

Category 1: dose-response sensitivity

Table 18.1 presents the responses for the five questions that were designed to assess sensitivity to the view that 'the dose makes the poison'. For each question, members of the public exhibited much less appreciation of this view than did the toxicologists. Specifically, the public respondents were more likely than the toxicologists to agree that:

Table 18.1 Responses of Toxicologists and Laypersons to Questions about Dose-Response Relationships (Category 1)[a]

Questions		Strongly disagree	Disagree	Agree	Strongly agree	Don't know/no opinion
1a If you are exposed to a toxic chemical substance, then you are likely to suffer adverse health effects.	T	14.0	53.7	24.4	4.3	3.7
	P	3.1	9.3	51.2	34.3	1.9
1b If you are exposed to a carcinogen, then you are likely to get cancer.	T	25.7	62.3	7.8	0.6	3.6
	P	5.1	42.6	25.4	9.0	17.2
1c For pesticides, it's not how much of the chemical you are exposed to that should worry you, but whether or not you are exposed to it at all.	T	61.5	33.1	1.8	2.4	1.2
	P	11.9	47.3	29.2	6.9	4.6
1d A chemical was found in a city's supply of drinking water in a concentration of 30 parts per million...The water was filtered by a process that was able to reduce, but not eliminate, the chemical concentration in the water. Under most circumstances, this means that the danger associated with drinking the water has also been reduced.	T	1.2	6.5	56.8	31.4	4.1
	P	3.8	18.8	63.2	7.3	7.1
1e There is no safe level of exposure to a cancer-causing agent.	T	27.7	47.0	13.9	4.8	6.6
	P	6.6	28.1	35.5	18.4	11.3

[a] Cell entries are percentages. Unless otherwise noted, differences between groups in this and all subsequent tables were significant at $p < .01$

T = toxicologists
P = public

- Exposure to a toxic chemical makes one likely to suffer adverse health effects.
- Exposure to a carcinogen makes one likely to get cancer.
- The fact of exposure to a pesticide is the critical concern, rather than the amount of exposure.
- Reducing the concentration of a possibly harmful chemical in a city's drinking water would not reduce the danger associated with drinking that water.
- There is no safe level of exposure to a cancer-causing agent.

Note that these views, though much more common in the public sample, were not always held by a majority of the public. Note also the high percentage (17.2%) of the public who marked 'don't know' or 'no opinion' regarding whether exposure to a carcinogen implies that one is likely to contract cancer (question 1b).

Category 2: trust in animal studies

Comparisons with regard to trust in animal studies are shown in Table 18.2. There was relatively little difference in the responses of the public and toxicologists to questions 2a, 2b and 2c (see Table 18.2). Both groups of respondents were greatly divided in their opinions about whether animal reactions to a chemical are reliable predictors of human reactions to the same chemical (question 2a). About 41% of the experts and 46% of the public disagreed with that assertion. There was very little agreement, in either group, with the propositions that proper animal studies could identify all possible harmful effects of a chemical (2b) and that laboratory studies could allow scientists to make accurate predictions about the amount of chemical exposure needed to cause human harm (2c).

The contrast between questions 2a and 2d is instructive. The confidence of toxicologists in predicting human harm from animal studies decreased when a chemical was found to be a carcinogen in animals (agreement decreased from 55.4% in 2a to 40.6% in 2d). However, the public respondents became much more confident in the prediction of human harm from an animal test when the test was said to produce evidence of carcinogenicity in animals (agreement rose from 43.7 to 69.4%). As a result, the two groups differed considerably on question 2d.

Categories 3 and 4: attitudes toward chemicals and risk reduction

Many of the public respondents in this study appeared to believe that if large exposures to a chemical are harmful, then small exposures are also harmful, and that animal tests can give little guidance about risk – except when they imply harm. Given these views, we would expect these individuals to be consistently negative in their general attitudes toward chemical risks (category 3) and to be strongly in favor of extreme measures to reduce such risks, regardless of cost. The data in Tables 18.3 and 18.4 support this expectation. The majority of the public respondents:

Table 18.2 Responses of Toxicologists and Laypersons to Questions about Trust in Animal Studies (Category 2)

Questions		Strongly disagree	Disagree	Agree	Strongly agree	Don't know/ no opinion
2a The way that an animal reacts to a chemical is a reliable predictor of how a human would react to the same chemical.	T	1.9	38.9	50.3	5.1	3.8
	P	5.5	40.2	40.2	3.5	10.6
2b Laboratory studies of a chemical's harmful effects on animals will, if properly done, identify all possible harmful effects of that chemical.	T	26.8	56.1	15.2	1.2	0.6
	P	17.1	60.7	11.3	2.3	8.6
2c Laboratory studies of a chemical's harmful effects on animals allow scientists to accurately determine how much of the chemical it takes to cause similar harm in humans.	T	12.2	55.5	29.3	1.2	1.8
	P	11.7	50.0	28.9	0.8	8.6
2d If a scientific study produces evidence that a chemical causes cancer in animals, then we can be reasonably sure that the chemical will cause cancer in humans.	T	10.3	47.3	39.4	1.2	1.8
	P	1.9	22.9	64.0	5.4	5.8

T = Toxicologists
P = Public

Table 18.3 *Responses of Toxicologists and Laypersons to Questions about Attitudes Toward Chemicals (Category 3)*

Questions		Strongly disagree	Disagree	Agree	Strongly agree	Don't know/ no opinion
3a Our society has perceived only the tip of the iceberg with regard to the risks associated with chemicals.	T	10.9	36.4	37.6	8.5	6.7
	P	1.6	9.0	50.2	33.7	5.5
3b The land, air and water around us are, in general, more contaminated now than ever before.	T	3.6	24.8	53.3	13.9	4.2
	P	1.5	8.1	45.2	43.2	1.9
3c Use of chemicals has improved our health more than it has harmed it.	T	0.0	3.0	59.4	33.3	4.2
	P	7.9	26.0	41.7	5.5	18.9
3d People are unnecessarily frightened about very small amounts of pesticides found in groundwater and on fresh food.	T	1.8	26.8	53.0	14.0	4.3
	P	13.1	55.6	20.1	3.9	7.3
3e People worry unnecessarily about what chemicals can do to their health.	T	3.6	53.3	33.9	4.2	4.8
	P	27.1	60.1	8.1	1.6	3.1
3f Chemicals are a major force behind technological advancement.	T	0.0	1.8	61.1	35.9	1.2
	P	1.9	12.4	55.4	13.2	17.1
3g Chemical risks are too scary. I don't even like to think about them.	T	74.6	24.9	0.6	0.0	0.0
	P	37.5	46.5	11.7	3.6	0.8
3h I do everything I can to avoid contact with chemicals and chemical products in my daily life.	T	44.0	46.4	6.0	3.6	0.0
	P	11.7	47.5	31.1	8.9	0.8

T = Toxicologists
P = Public

Table 18.4 *Responses of Toxicologists and Laypersons to Questions about Attitudes Toward Risk Reduction (Category 4)*

Questions		Strongly disagree	Disagree	Agree	Strongly agree	Don't know/ no opinion
4a While we should always try to minimize the risks we take by using chemicals, it is unrealistic to expect that we can completely eliminate those risks.	T	0.6	1.2	45.8	52.4	0.0
	P	2.8	14.2	65.8	15.0	2.3
4b It can never be too expensive to reduce the risks associated with chemicals.	T	27.7	54.2	12.7	3.0	2.4
	P	2.7	28.7	43.4	18.2	7.0
4c All use of prescription drugs must be risk free.	Td	54.8	39.9	3.6	0.6	1.2
(Alternative form: All use of chemicals must be risk free.)	Pd	13.4	64.2	12.7	4.5	5.2
	Pc	8.9	52.8	22.8	6.5	8.9

T = Toxicologists
P = Public
Td = Toxicologists, prescription drugs
Pd = Public, prescription drugs
Pc = Public, chemicals

- agreed that we have perceived only the tip of the chemical risk iceberg (83.9% agree or strongly agree);
- agreed that contamination is greater now than ever before (88.4%);
- disagreed that people are unnecessarily frightened about small amounts of pesticides in groundwater and food (68.7%);
- disagreed that people worry unnecessarily about chemicals (87.1%);
- agreed that chemical risks are too scary and they do not like to think about them (84.0%); and
- agreed that it can never be too expensive to reduce the risks associated with chemicals (61.6%).

Although not a majority view, a surprisingly high percentage of the public sample agreed that they do everything they can to avoid contact with chemicals and chemical products (40.0%) and agreed that all use of prescription drugs (17.2%) and chemicals (29.3%) must be risk-free.

In comparison with the public sample, the toxicologists conveyed more favorable attitudes toward chemicals on every question in category 3. In most cases these differences were substantial. The story was similar with respect to questions in category 4, with toxicologists showing much less agreement with the assertions that use of chemicals must be risk free regardless of cost.

Category 5: additional comparisons

The results for question 5a in Table 18.5 confirm the commonly held belief that the public has much more confidence in the safety of natural (as opposed to synthetic) chemicals than do the experts. Answers to questions 5b, 5e and 5f show that the public respondents had a much more favorable view of chemicals and were more tolerant of chemical risks if the chemicals were in the form of prescription drugs. Similarly, people were more likely to recognize that the risk from a prescription drug is dependent upon dose than they were to recognize dose dependence of chemicals in general (question 5e). Question 4c, shown in Table 18.4, also found a more tolerant public attitude toward risks from prescription drugs than for risks from chemicals in general. The toxicologists' versions of these questions used only the term prescription drugs, due to an error in printing the questionnaire. Compared to the public, toxicologists were not as likely to see prescription drugs as less toxic than pesticides (question 5b), more likely to recognize the dependence of drug risk on dose (5e), and more likely to agree that a 1 in 10 million risk of cancer from taking a prescription drug is too small a risk to worry about (5f).

There was considerable disagreement among both toxicologists and members of the public about whether pesticides are generally more harmful than fertilizers (question 5c). The toxicologists agreed with this statement more than the public did, the latter producing many more 'don't know or no opinion' responses (27.4%).

Question 5d is similar to the questions about trust in animal studies (category 2; Table 18.2). Toxicologists almost unanimously disagreed (89.6%) that microorganisms are reliable indicators of human reactions to a chemical. Members of the public sample also tended to disagree with this statement but exhibited an extremely high percentage of 'don't know/no opinion' responses (34.9%).

Results for question 5h confirmed the hypothesis that the public would be much more likely than the toxicologists to view an association between pesticide use and birth defects as a causal relationship (48.5% agreement among the public versus 5.5% among the toxicologists). The percentage of 'don't know/no opinion' responses to this question was high in both groups. Results from question 5i (not shown in Table 18.5) indicated that toxicologists were about equally split between the views that humans are more, equally or less vulnerable to adverse effects of chemicals than are animals. The dominant response in the public sample was equal vulnerability (35.0%). More than 20% in both samples marked the 'don't know/no opinion' response.

Predicting Perceptions and Attitudes

Comparisons between toxicologists and the public sample showed that these two groups differed greatly with regard to appreciation of dose-response relationships and attitudes toward chemical risks and risk reduction, but did not differ much regarding trust in animal testing. From these data, it appears that dose-response views and attitudes may be closely related but that neither type of response is related to trust in animal testing.

A separate analysis was done to test these relationships at the level of the individual respondent in the public sample. The items within each of the first four categories (Tables 18.1 through 18.4) were assigned scores on a four-point scale of agreement corresponding to the four responses (strongly disagree = 1; disagree = 2; agree = 3; strongly agree = 4). Responses of each person in the public sample were scored, and the scores were summed across all items in the category to produce four scale-scores per person:

- dose-response sensitivity (high score indicates high sensitivity to dose);
- trust in animal studies (high score indicates high trust);
- attitude toward chemicals and their risks (high score indicates a pro-chemical view);
- attitude toward risk-reduction (high score indicates acceptance of some degree of risk from chemicals).

The correlations between scales were computed across members of the public sample. The pattern of correlations indicated that laypersons who believed that exposure and dose mediate chemical risks were likely to be more favorable toward chemicals and relatively less concerned about their risks ($r = .68$) and less concerned about the necessity of reducing chemical risks ($r = .47$). Attitudes toward chemical risks and attitudes toward risk reduction were also positively correlated ($r = .55$). Trust in animal studies did not correlate significantly with any of the other scales.

Multiple regression analyses were performed to predict scale scores from demographic characteristics of the public sample. Examination of variables making a statistically significant contribution to the regression equation showed that scores on the attitude toward chemical risks scale could be predicted moderately well ($R = .49$) on the basis of education, gender and scientific training. Scientific training, more education, better health and male gender were all

Table 18.5 *Responses of Toxicologists and Laypersons to the Miscellaneous Questions in Category 5*

Questions		Strongly disagree	Disagree	Agree	Strongly agree	Don't know/no opinion
5a Natural chemicals, as a rule, are not as harmful as man-made chemicals.	T	45.6	40.2	11.2	2.4	0.6
	P	10.8	34.0	37.8	7.3	10.0
5b In general, chemicals used in prescription drugs are less toxic than chemicals used in pesticides.	T	22.8	47.9	21.6	6.6	1.2
	P	11.5	32.7	37.7	6.9	11.2
5c In general, chemicals used as pesticides are potentially more harmful than are chemicals used as fertilizers.	T	6.0	30.5	52.1	6.6	4.8
	P	5.4	30.9	32.8	3.5	27.4
5d How microorganisms (eg, bacteria) react to a chemical is a reliable indicator of how humans would react to the same chemical.	T	38.4	51.2	5.5	1.2	3.7
	P	12.4	43.4	7.8	1.6	34.9
5e Some prescription drugs are harmful if they are taken in large doses, but are not harmful if taken in small doses. (Alternate form: Some chemicals are harmful if people are exposed to them in large amounts, but are not harmful if people are exposed to them in small amounts.)	Td	1.2	11.4	50.0	34.9	2.4
	Pd	2.2	12.7	65.7	14.2	5.2
	Pc	2.4	28.0	50.4	7.2	12.0
5f A 1 in 10 million lifetime risk of cancer from taking a particular prescription drug is too small a risk to worry about. (For perspective the lifetime risk of dying in a car accident is 1 in 100.) (Alternative form: A 1 in 10 million lifetime risk of cancer from exposure to a particular chemical is too small a risk to worry about. – For perspective the lifetime risk of dying in a car accident is 1 in 100.)	Td	1.8	4.2	53.0	40.0	1.2
	Pd	1.5	14.3	65.4	14.3	4.5
	Pc	3.3	26.8	52.8	6.5	10.6
5g I think that I should know as much as I can about the chemicals around me. The more I know, the more I can control the risks that those chemicals pose to my health and to the environment.	T	0.6	4.1	47.9	46.7	0.6
	P	0.8	4.7	53.9	39.5	1.2

Table 18.5 *continued*

Questions		Strongly disagree	Disagree	Agree	Strongly agree	Don't know/ no opinion
5h	Residents of a small community (30,000 people) observed that several malformed children had been born there during each of the past few years. The town is in a region where agricultural pesticides have been used during the past decade. It is very likely that these pesticides were the cause of the malformations.					
	T	22.2	59.3	4.3	1.2	13.0
	P	3.9	23.4	39.5	9.0	24.2

T = Toxicologists
P = Public
Td = Toxicologists, prescription drugs
Pd = Public, prescription drugs
Pc = Public, chemicals

predictive of more favorable attitudes. Dose-response sensitivity was predictable ($R = .40$) on the basis of health status, education and age. Being older, well-educated and in good health was predictive of greater dose-response sensitivity. Trust in animal testing was not very predictable ($R = .22$) on the basis of demographic variables.

Education

It is instructive to assess the influence of the important demographic variables by examining data from specific questions. Table 18.6 presents items on which the college educated and non-college educated respondents showed statistically significant differences. In general, respondents with a college degree had more favorable attitudes toward chemicals, greater appreciation of the mediating role of dose and exposure and less concern about risks. In these respects, the college-educated respondents appeared to be somewhat more similar to the toxicologists than were the non-college educated persons. Examination of Table 18.6 indicates that college-educated respondents were:

- less likely to agree that worries about pesticides should depend only upon whether or not one was exposed at all (1c);
- more likely to see reduction in the concentration of a possibly harmful chemical in water as reducing risk (1d);
- less likely to agree that there is no safe level of exposure to a cancer-causing agent (2e);
- more likely to agree that use of chemicals has improved our health more than it has harmed it (3c);
- more likely to agree that chemicals are a major force behind technological advancement (3f); and
- less likely to agree that it can never be too expensive to decrease the risk associated with chemicals (4b).

Table 18.6 also illustrates that respondents who did not have a college degree were far more likely to answer 'don't know/no opinion' on certain of these items (lb, 1d, 3f).

Gender

Within the public sample, women were consistently more concerned about chemical risks than men, and they had less favorable attitudes regarding the benefits of chemicals. Questions for which gender differences were largest are shown in Table 18.7. Note that differences were particularly large for the attitudinal questions – 3c, 3f and 4b. Women were much less likely to agree that the use of chemicals has improved our health more than it has harmed it (3c) and less likely to agree that chemicals are a major force behind technological advancement (3f). Note also the high percentage of 'don't know/no opinion' responses among women for these questions. On question 4b, women were more likely than men to agree that it can never be too expensive to reduce chemical risks. On the other questions, women were more likely than men to:

Table 18.6 *Comparisons between Responses of College and Non-college Educated Persons in the Public Sample* [a]

Questions		Strongly disagree	Disagree	Agree	Strongly agree	Don't know/ no opinion
1b If you are exposed to a carcinogen, then you are likely to get cancer.	NC	3.3	38.5	23.0	9.0	26.2
	C	7.0	46.9	28.1	9.4	8.6
1c For pesticides, it's not how much of the chemical you are exposed to that should worry you, but whether or not you are exposed to it at all.	NC	8.9	40.3	39.5	5.6	5.6
	C	15.4	53.8	19.2	7.7	3.8
1d A chemical was found in a city's supply of drinking water in a concentration of 30 parts per million . . . the water was filtered by a process that was able to reduce, but not eliminate, the chemical concentration in the water. Under most circumstances this means that the danger associated with drinking the water has also been reduced.	NC	4.8	23.2	60.8	0.8	10.4
	C	3.1	13.8	65.4	13.8	3.8
1e There is no safe level of exposure to a cancer-causing agent.	NC	2.5	23.8	38.5	22.1	13.1
	C	10.2	31.3	32.8	15.6	10.2
3c Use of chemicals has improved our health more than it has harmed it.	NC	9.2	34.2	32.5	3.3	20.8
	C	7.0	18.8	49.2	7.8	17.2
3f Chemicals are a major force behind technological advancement.	NC	3.3	15.4	51.2	5.7	24.4
	C	0.8	10.1	58.9	20.2	10.1
4b It can never be too expensive to reduce the risks associated with chemicals.	NC	0.0	23.6	52.0	16.3	8.1
	C	5.4	33.3	34.9	20.2	6.2

The differences between college and non-college educated respondents on question 1e were significant at $p < .05$. All other comparisons were significant at $p < .01$.
NC = Non-College
C = College

Table 18.7 *Responses of Men and Women in the Public Sample to Selected Questions* "

Questions		Strongly disagree	Disagree	Agree	Strongly agree	Don't know/ no opinion
1c For pesticides, it's not how much of the chemical you are exposed to that should worry you, but whether or not you are exposed to it at all.	M	14.4	54.1	20.5	7.5	3.4
	W	9.3	37.4	41.1	6.5	5.6
3c Use of chemicals has improved our health more than it has harmed it.	M	6.9	21.4	51.7	8.3	11.7
	W	8.8	33.3	27.5	1.0	29.4
3f Chemicals are a major force behind technological advancement.	M	1.4	8.2	61.6	19.2	9.6
	W	2.9	19.0	46.7	3.8	27.6
3h I do everything I can to avoid contact with chemicals and chemical products in my daily life.	M	15.8	50.7	27.4	6.2	0.0
	W	6.7	44.8	34.3	12.4	1.9
4b It can never be too expensive to reduce the risks associated with chemicals.	M	4.1	34.7	40.8	14.3	6.1
	W	1.0	19.2	46.2	25.0	8.7
5h Residents of a small community (30,000 people) observed that several malformed children had been born there during each of the past few years. The town is in a region where agricultural pesticides have been used during the past decade. It is very likely that these pesticides were the cause of the malformations.	M	4.9	29.9	36.1	5.6	23.6
	W	2.9	14.3	43.8	14.3	24.8

" Gender differences were significant at $p < .05$ for questions 3h and 4b, and at $p < .01$ for questions 1c, 3c, 3f and 5h

M = Men

W = Women

- agree that, for pesticides, one should worry about whether or not they were exposed at all (1c);
- agree that they do everything they can to avoid contact with chemicals and chemical products in their daily life (3h); and
- agree that pesticides caused the malformations in the children (5h).

Gender differences were less evident in the sample of toxicologists, perhaps because the number of women was too small ($n = 26$) to measure them reliably. However, female toxicologists appeared to be more concerned about chemical risks and less favorably impressed with the benefits of chemicals than were male toxicologists, though the differences between men and women toxicologists were smaller than the differences between men and women in the public sample. In other words, men and women exhibited different response patterns in both samples, although women toxicologists were far more similar to men toxicologists than they were to women members of the public.

Affiliation Effects

The three subgroups of toxicologists responded similarly to many of the questions. However, there were also important differences between the groups on a number of questions, as shown in Table 18.8. Question 1e demonstrates that toxicologists from industry were much less likely than others to agree with the assertion that there is no safe level of exposure to a cancer-causing agent. With regard to the reliability and accuracy of animal tests, industrial toxicologists were somewhat more favorably inclined toward the tests (questions 2b and 2c) than other toxicologists, though the differences were not statistically significant and are not shown in the table. However, if a study produced evidence that a chemical caused cancer in animals (question 2d), the industrial toxicologists were much less confident than academic or regulatory scientists in the ability to extrapolate to humans (22.0% agreement versus 48.9% and 52.7% in the other two groups). Similarly, industrial toxicologists were much more likely than others to see humans as less vulnerable than animals to adverse effects of chemicals (question 5i).

Industrial toxicologists also had the most favorable attitudes toward chemicals and their risks (questions 3a and 3d), and they were the group of toxicologists who most often disagreed with the statement that pesticides were the likely cause of the observed malformations in question 5h.

Are Public/Toxicologist Differences Merely Demographic?

The toxicologists in our survey tended, for the most part, to be highly educated white males. We have seen that, within the general public, attitudes toward chemical risks are influenced by education and gender. Is it possible that these factors, and not expertise in toxicology, account for the observed differences between toxicologists and the public? Two kinds of analyses were performed to address these questions. First, multiple regression analyses were conducted to predict answers to questions on which the two groups disagreed, using gender,

Table 18.8 *Responses of Toxicologists According to Affiliation*[a]

Questions		Strongly disagree	Disagree	Agree	Strongly agree	Don't know/ no opinion
1e There is no safe level of exposure to a cancer-causing agent.	A	18.0	46.0	22.0	12.0	2.0
	I	45.8	42.4	5.1	0.0	6.8
	R	17.5	52.6	15.8	3.5	10.5
2d If a scientific study produces evidence that a chemical causes cancer in animals, then we can be reasonably sure that the chemical will cause cancer in humans.	A	4.1	44.9	46.9	2.0	2.0
	I	18.6	57.6	22.0	0.0	1.7
	R	7.0	38.6	50.9	1.8	1.8
3a Our society has perceived only the tip of the iceberg with regard to the risks associated with chemicals.	A	8.0	26.0	46.0	12.0	8.0
	I	19.0	44.8	24.1	8.6	3.4
	R	5.3	36.8	43.9	5.3	8.8
3d People are unnecessarily frightened about very small amounts of pesticides found in groundwater and on fresh food.	A	2.1	35.4	45.8	14.6	2.1
	I	0.0	16.9	61.0	20.3	1.7
	R	3.5	29.8	50.9	7.0	8.8
5h Residents of a small community (30,000 people) observed that several malformed children had been born there during each of the past few years. The town is in a region where agricultural pesticides have been used during the past decade. It is very likely that these pesticides were the cause of the malformations.	A	20.8	58.3	2.1	4.2	14.6
	I	29.3	63.8	1.7	0.0	5.2
	R	16.1	55.4	8.9	0.0	19.6

Questions		More vulnerable	Equally vulnerable	Less vulnerable	Don't know/ No opinion
5i In general humans are (more, equally, less) vulnerable to adverse effects of chemicals than are laboratory animals.	A	15.2	21.7	23.9	39.1
	I	19.6	21.4	44.6	14.3
	R	26.3	33.3	17.5	22.8

[a] Differences among groups were significant at $p < .05$ for questions 2d, 3a, 3d, and 5h, and at $p < .01$ for questions 1e and 5i.

A = Academic toxicologists

I = Industry toxicologists

R = Regulatory toxicologists

Table 18.9 *Responses of College-educated White Males*

Questions		Strongly disagree	Disagree	Agree	Strongly agree	Don't know/ no opinion
1b If you are exposed to a carcinogen, then you are likely to get cancer.	P	9.2	44.7	28.9	7.9	9.2
	A	27.3	59.1	9.1	0.0	4.5
	I	33.3	57.8	4.4	0.0	4.4
	R	28.2	66.7	2.6	0.0	2.6
2d If scientific study produces evidence that a chemical causes cancer in animals, then we can be reasonably sure that the chemical will cause cancer in humans.	P	0.0	28.6	63.6	3.9	3.9
	A	4.8	45.2	45.2	2.4	2.4
	I	20.0	55.6	22.2	0.0	2.2
	R	10.0	47.5	37.5	2.5	2.5

P = Public
A = Academic toxicologist
I = Industry toxicologists
R = Regulatory toxicologists

race, education and group status (member of the public versus toxicologist) as predictors. These regressions showed that group status was by far the most important predictor, with education, race and gender accounting for significant but small amounts of the variance in responses to the questions. This result can be illustrated concretely by comparing white male toxicologists with college-educated white male laypersons on two typical questions – lb and 2d. The results, presented in Table 18.9, show that the public sample still responds quite differently from each of the three groups of toxicologists, even when education, race and gender differences are minimized. Results from other questions were similar.

Toxicologists' Attitudes toward Public Concerns

We examined relationships between toxicologists' beliefs about the reliability of animal tests (question 2a) and their beliefs about whether people worry unnecessarily about chemicals (questions 3d and 3e). Comparing questions 2a and 3d, the proportion of toxicologists who agreed that people are unnecessarily frightened about small pesticide residues was about the same (70%) within the subsample who agreed that animal tests are reliable predictors as among those who disagreed with the assertion that animal tests are reliable (69.3% of whom agreed that people are unnecessarily frightened). Comparing questions 2a and 3e, those who distrusted animal tests were somewhat more likely (45.3%) to agree that people worry unnecessarily about what chemicals can do to their health than were those who trusted animal studies (33.3% of whom agreed that people worry unnecessarily).

These results raise a question. If distrust in animal studies is independent of or even positively related to toxicologists' beliefs that people worry unnecessarily about chemicals, what is the evidence, experience or belief on which such views are based?

At least a partial answer to this question can be found by examining responses to the questions about reliability (2a) and unnecessary fear (3e) in light of responses to a third question (5i) asking about the relative vulnerability of humans and laboratory animals. The results of this three-way comparison implicated perceptions about vulnerability as a key factor in mediating attitudes toward public fears and distrust in animal tests. Toxicologists who disagreed with the statement that animal tests are reliable predictors of human reactions and who also believed that humans are less vulnerable to adverse effects of chemicals than are laboratory animals were the persons most likely to believe that people are unnecessarily frightened about very small amounts of pesticides.

Additional Data: The EPA Baseline Survey

Concern about the low response rate (27%) and the limited geographic representation of our public sample caused us to collect additional data. We were fortunate to be able to add four questions to a telephone survey conducted by McCallum, Hammond, Morris and Covello (1990) for the US Environmental Protection Agency (EPA) in six communities across the US: Albuquerque, New Mexico; Cincinnati, Ohio; Durham, North Carolina; Middlesex County, New

Jersey; Racine, Wisconsin; and Richmond, Virginia. Several criteria guided the selection of these communities: the presence of major industries using, storing, processing or releasing chemicals; location of a Superfund or other hazardous waste sites nearby; existence of an active local emergency planning or environmental group; and previous experience with chemical-emissions problems. A total of 3129 completed interviews were obtained from the six communities (sample sizes in each community ranged from a low of 503 to a high of 604). The overall response rate was 59.1%, ranging from a high in Racine of 62.9% to a low in Middlesex County of 52.7%. Men and women were equally represented, by design. Comparison of the sample with community demographics indicated that the respondents were somewhat younger, better educated and more affluent than the general public as a whole.

We selected two questions pertaining to dose-response sensitivity (questions 1b and 1c), one attitude question (3c), and one from category 5 (5f). The wording was changed slightly in each case to improve clarity (eg, the term 'carcinogen' was replaced by the phrase 'chemical that can cause cancer') or to increase generality (eg, 'pesticide' was replaced by 'chemical' in question 1c).

The results from these new samples, shown in Table 18.10, differed even more from the responses of toxicologists than did the responses of the Portland public sample. For example, 73.3% either agreed somewhat or agreed strongly that 'if a person is exposed to a chemical that can cause cancer, then the person is likely to get cancer later in life', in contrast to 34.4% of the Portland sample and 8.4% of the toxicologists. The new version of question 1c also produced a much higher rate of agreement with an all-or-none view of toxicity ('It's not how much of a chemical you are exposed to that matters to your health'). Almost 63% agreed with this statement compared to 36.1% in the Portland sample and 4.2% of the toxicologists (on a version of the question that substituted pesticide for chemical). About 56% disagreed that some chemical risks are too small to worry about (compared to 30.1% in the Portland sample who responded to a 1 in 10 million risk). There was about an even split in the percentage of persons who agreed and the percentage who disagreed that 'chemicals have improved our health more than they have harmed it'. About 47% disagreed, compared with 33.9% in the Portland sample and 3% of the toxicologists.

The 'don't know/no opinion' response category was prominently displayed as an option in the written survey administered to the Portland survey but was not specifically mentioned as a response option in the EPA telephone survey. As a result, the frequency of 'don't know' responses was smaller in the EPA survey than in the Portland survey.

Further analysis of Table 18.10 shows that the overall response patterns for these questions varied rather little across communities, gender, education and age. As in the Portland sample, women's attitudes were somewhat less favorable toward chemicals than were men's and respondents with more formal education were more favorable toward chemicals than were less educated persons. Older respondents were more likely than younger persons to agree that it is not how much of a chemical that matters and to agree that some risks are too small to worry about. However, they were slightly less likely than younger persons to agree that exposure to a cancer-causing chemical will cause cancer later in life.

Table 18.10 *Responses from the EPA Baseline Survey*

	Total	Community						Gender		Education		Age in years		
		Richmond	Durham	Albuquerque	Cincinnati	Middlesex County	Racine County	Male	Female	High-school or less	Some college or more	< 30	30–50	> 50
1b If a person is exposed to a chemical that can cause cancer, then that person is likely to get cancer later in life.														
Strongly disagree	6.5	6.7	5.7	8.1	6.9	5.0	6.3	7.9	5.0	5.7	7.0	4.6	5.9	8.8
Somewhat disagree	18.3	19.0	20.0	21.1	17.4	15.3	17.2	20.4	16.2	11.7	22.8	17.7	19.0	17.6
Somewhat agree	35.8	34.8	38.4	34.6	34.1	35.6	37.3	35.2	36.5	31.3	39.0	43.5	37.0	27.6
Strongly agree	37.5	36.4	33.3	34.0	39.8	42.9	38.4	34.2	40.8	50.2	28.8	33.7	36.0	43.2
Don't know/no opinion	1.6	2.8	2.2	2.0	1.4	0.8	0.8	1.8	1.4	1.1	2.0	0.4	1.6	2.6
1c It's not how much of a chemical you are exposed to that matters to your health, it's whether or not you're exposed at all.														
Strongly disagree	18.6	16.6	22.0	17.4	20.6	19.7	16.1	18.7	18.5	19.8	17.8	19.2	18.7	17.7
Somewhat disagree	17.0	15.0	17.8	19.4	17.0	14.7	18.0	19.4	14.7	13.3	19.6	21.6	17.7	12.4
Somewhat agree	23.5	25.1	20.6	21.9	24.2	23.7	25.0	24.9	22.0	22.0	24.4	22.6	24.1	23.3
Strongly agree	39.2	40.9	38.2	39.7	36.8	40.2	39.6	35.7	42.8	43.3	36.5	36.2	38.2	43.3
Don't know/no opinion	1.7	2.4	1.4	1.6	1.4	1.7	1.3	1.3	2.0	1.6	1.7	0.4	1.3	3.3

Table 18.10 *continued*

	Total	Community						Gender		Education		Age in years		
		Rich-mond	Dur-ham	Albu-querque	Cincin-nati	Middlesex County	Racine County	Male	Female	High-school or less	Some college or more	< 30	30–50	> 50
3c Chemicals have improved our health more than they have harmed it.														
Strongly disagree	24.3	22.5	25.1	25.7	24.8	27.6	20.7	20.2	28.4	32.8	18.6	22.6	24.9	24.4
Somewhat disagree	22.9	23.5	23.6	19.4	20.0	25.6	24.8	19.9	25.9	22.9	22.9	26.9	24.0	18.0
Somewhat agree	34.4	36.2	31.7	35.0	35.0	30.0	37.7	37.3	31.5	28.3	38.5	37.2	34.0	32.8
Strongly agree	15.5	15.0	15.6	17.2	17.2	13.1	14.9	20.5	10.4	13.1	17.1	12.0	14.9	19.2
Don't know/no opinion	2.6	2.6	3.2	2.8	2.8	3.0	1.7	1.7	3.5	2.8	2.5	1.4	1.7	5.2
5f There are some chemical risks that are too small to worry about.														
Strongly disagree	35.3	36.0	36.2	31.6	33.5	38.6	35.8	30.7	39.9	41.0	31.5	37.0	34.5	34.9
Somewhat disagree	21.1	19.6	19.6	20.9	23.0	23.7	20.0	20.0	22.2	20.6	21.4	24.8	21.1	18.2
Somewhat agree	26.4	28.3	26.1	28.9	25.0	22.3	27.6	28.0	24.8	22.1	29.4	25.2	28.4	24.1
Strongly agree	16.8	16.2	16.6	18.0	18.2	15.5	16.6	21.1	12.5	15.6	17.6	13.0	15.6	22.0
Don't know/no opinion	0.4	0.0	1.5	0.6	0.3	0.0	0.0	0.2	0.6	0.7	0.1	0.0	0.4	0.8
Sample size	3,129	506	505	506	505	503	604	1,574	1,555	1,283	1,846	720	1,502	907

Source: McCallum, Hammond, Morris & Covello (1990)

DISCUSSION

Expert versus Public Views

Our primary objectives were to describe and compare responses of laypeople and toxicologists and to test a number of hypotheses about the differences between the public's views as 'intuitive toxicologists' and the views of experts. In general, we believe that this aspect of the study was successful. Toxicologists and laypeople were found to differ greatly, documenting some common assumptions (eg, that the public believes natural chemicals to be safer than synthetic ones) and verifying many of the other hypotheses that motivated the questionnaire.

Of particular importance is the pattern of responses to questions in category 1, which indicates that the public is much less sensitive than the experts to fundamental considerations of dose and exposure. Although the public recognizes the importance of these factors in some domains (eg, prescription drugs), they generally tend to view chemicals as either safe or dangerous and they appear to equate even small exposures to toxic or carcinogenic chemicals with almost certain harm. This orientation was found to be associated with high levels of concern regarding chemicals, including very small residues of chemicals on food, and a desire to reduce chemical risks at any cost. It is sobering to find that 40% of our public respondents said that they do everything they can to avoid contact with chemicals and chemical products in their daily lives. It is also remarkable to find that fewer than 50% of the public respondents in the Portland sample and fewer than 25% in the EPA sample recognized that exposure to a chemical that is carcinogenic does not make one likely to get cancer later in life.

Several other findings were noteworthy:

- the public's tendency to attribute causality to a temporal association between pesticide use and birth defects;
- the strong negative attitudes of the public toward chemicals and their risks;
- the relatively favorable perceptions of prescription drugs;
- the finding that 30% of the public respondents did not agree that a 1 in 10 million lifetime risk of cancer from exposure to a chemical was too small to worry about; and
- the finding that men and more highly educated persons were somewhat less concerned about chemical risks – in general, responses of college-educated persons were slightly more similar to responses of toxicologists than were responses of persons with less education.[5,6]

One of the major surprises in the data was the lack of difference between the public and toxicologists with regard to their confidence in extrapolation from animal studies. Both groups were divided in their opinions, and the high percentage of experts who lacked confidence in animal studies is particularly noteworthy in light of the extensive reliance on such studies in risk management. The public's trust in extrapolation from animal studies increased greatly when these studies were said to produce evidence of carcinogenicity. It is well known that people (scientists included) trust information more when it is congruent with their a priori expectations or theories (Koehler, 1989; Ross & Lepper, 1980). The reaction of our lay respondents to evidence of carcinogenicity is consistent with this view if we can assume that laypeople expect most chemicals to be carcinogenic in humans. The credibility that our public respondents gave to evidence of carcinogenicity is also consistent with a basic tenet of 'regulatory' science which gives much greater weight to positive results than to negative findings (US EPA, 1986). The confidence of our toxicologists in extrapolation from animal studies did not appear to be influenced by a positive finding (of carcinogenicity).

Additional Data: The New Jersey Study

Further evidence that the public perceptions and attitudes observed in the present study are widespread comes from a telephone survey of 500 residents in 31 New Jersey communities conducted in November 1987 by Weinstein (1988). This survey produced strong evidence for dose-response insensitivity and an 'all-or-none' conception of toxicity. Specifically, 78.4% of the respondents agreed strongly (and 6.6% agreed moderately) with the statement: 'If even a tiny amount of a cancer-producing substance were found in my water, I wouldn't drink it'. The statement: 'When some chemical is discovered in food, I don't want to hear statistics, I just want to know if its dangerous or not' elicited strong agreement from 62.0% and moderate agreement from 21.6% of the respondents. The New Jersey respondents also recognized limitations in the knowledge of experts. The statement, 'Although experts are willing to make estimates of the risk from hazardous waste, no one really knows how big the risks really are', elicited 84.9% agreement. About 78% agreed with the statement: 'For a lot of chemicals, we don't know enough to make decisions'. As in the other studies described earlier, women held more negative attitudes than men about chemical risks and more highly educated individuals were less likely to see chemical risks as 'all-or-none' phenomena.

Understanding the Origins of Public Attitudes and Concerns

What accounts for the public's insensitivity to dose and strong concerns about even minute exposures to toxic or carcinogenic chemicals? Psychological and anthropological research on the concept of 'contagion' may provide one possible explanation. Frazer (1890/1959) and Mauss (1902/1972) described a belief, widespread in many cultures, that things that have been in contact with each other may influence each other through transfer of some of their properties via an 'essence'. Thus, 'once in contact, always in contact', even if that contact (exposure) is brief. Rozin, Millman and Nemeroff (1986) show that this belief system, which they refer to as a 'law of contagion', is common in our present culture. The implication of this work is that even a minute amount of a toxic substance in one's food will be seen as imparting toxicity to the food; any amount of a carcinogenic substance will impart carcinogenicity, and so forth. The 'essence of harm' that is contagious is typically referred to as contamination. Being contaminated clearly has an all-or-none quality to it – like being alive or pregnant. When a young child drops a sucker on the floor, the brief contact with 'dirt' may be seen as contaminating the candy, causing the parent to throw it away rather than washing it off and returning it to the child's mouth. This all-or-none quality irrespective of the degree of exposure is evident in the observation by Erikson (1990) that: 'To be exposed to radiation or other toxins … is to be contaminated in some deep and lasting way, to feel dirtied, tainted, corrupted' (p122). A contagion or contamination model is obviously very different from the scientist's model of how contact with a chemical induces carcinogenesis or other adverse effects. Further examination of the concepts of contagion and contamination may help us better understand the origins of the public's concerns about very small exposures to chemicals.

Alternatively, the intuitive toxicologist may conceive of a toxic chemical as equivalent to a highly dangerous virus or bacteria such as botulism, salmonella or hepatitis. Early and influential writers such as Rachel Carson (1962) may have spawned this perception by drawing analogies between carcinogens and infectious diseases and referring to epidemics of cancer.[7] Exposure to the regulatory philosophy that there is no safe dose of a carcinogen may also have contributed to the public attitudes we observed here. In any event, it is clear that we need to probe further to understand the determiners of public attitudes and the mechanisms by which laypeople believe chemicals induce various kinds of harm.

Disagreement among Toxicologists

Among the most important findings in this study was the great divergence of opinion among the toxicologists themselves about fundamental issues in risk assessment and, in particular, the high percentage of toxicologists who doubted the validity of the animal and bacterial studies that form the backbone of their science. These results provide a quantitative description of the criticisms and disagreements that are clearly evident in statements of individual scientists (Clarke, 1988; Freedman & Zeisel, 1988) and in detailed case studies of specific chemical controversies (Graham et al, 1988). These results also clash with the messages given to the public. For example, the American Chemical Society's carefully written public information pamphlet on *Chemical Risk: Personal Decisions* informs people that 'toxic effects found in rodents usually occur in humans exposed to the same chemical'. Although acknowledging the fact that prediction for humans is not certain, the pamphlet concludes that 'they are the best predictors we have'.[8] The impression given the public by this authoritative source is, we submit, quite different from the impression gleaned from questions in category 2 of our survey or from the many strong criticisms of animal testing in the scientific literature.

The affiliation bias we observed is particularly noteworthy, indicating that toxicologists working for industry see chemicals as more benign than do their counterparts in academia and government. Industrial toxicologists were somewhat more confident than other experts in the general validity of animal tests – except when those tests provided evidence for carcinogenicity – in which case many of the industrial experts changed their opinions.

An earlier study of 136 occupational health specialists by Lynn (1987) obtained remarkably similar data demonstrating the effect of affiliation on opinions about the value of animal data and the existence of thresholds for carcinogens. She found that only 27% of respondents working for industry agreed that 'a substance which is shown conclusively to cause tumors in animals should be considered a carcinogen, thereby posing a risk to humans', whereas 69% and 52% of government and university employees agreed. Of the industry respondents, 80% agreed that thresholds exist, in contrast to 61% of the academics and 37% of the government employees. She also found that these responses were correlated with political orientation (liberal/conservative) and with voting in the 1980 presidential election. Finally, Lynn showed that these differences were congruent with the public stances of industrial and regulatory representatives in a number of major risk-management controversies. Data from the present study, and the data presented by Lynn, contribute to a substantial literature documenting the strong influence of the social and political context on risk assessment (Clarke, 1988; Dietz & Rycroft, 1987; Gormley, 1986; Graham et al, 1988; Jasanoff, 1986; Johnson & Covello, 1987; Swaen & Meijers, 1988; Whittemore, 1983).

Some reviewers of this manuscript have argued that the affiliation differences we and others have observed reflect the fact that toxicologists in industry tend to work with less harmful chemicals than toxicologists in regulatory or academic settings and thus have a lower base rate expectancy for chemical risks. We cannot rule this interpretation out, although, in response to the statement: 'Most chemicals cause cancer', industrial toxicologists in our study did not disagree more than other toxicologists (96.4% of all toxicologists disagreed or strongly disagreed with this statement). The weight of evidence seems to us to favor a sociopolitical interpretation of the affiliation effect.

Limitations of Risk Assessment

One of the major motivations behind this study was to develop an understanding of the differences between the ways that professional toxicologists and laypersons assess chemical risks, in order to facilitate communication and perhaps reduce the 'gap' between expert and lay views. To a certain extent, some of the present results do point toward concepts that experts should clarify for the public. It is obvious that the words 'toxic' and 'carcinogenic' mean very different things to experts and laypersons. If scientists could impart a better understanding of these concepts, and their relationship to exposure, significant progress most certainly will have been achieved.

However, the present results also suggest that the controversies over chemical risks in our society may be fueled as much by weaknesses in the science of risk assessment as by misconceptions on the part of the public. Our data (and those of Lynn) indicate that scientists cannot agree whether or not their main method of testing is reliable or accurate in predicting human health effects and that scientists who work for industry see fundamental issues quite differently from their colleagues in academia and government.

These results place the problems of risk communication in a new light. Our risk-management processes are open and adversarial – we battle in courtrooms and community halls, in view of the media, with experts on each side of the issue attacking the other's credibility, models and data. The young science of risk assessment is too fragile, too indirect, to prevail in an adversarial atmosphere. As shown in surveys by Weinstein (1988) and Mitchell (1992), the public is well aware of the limitations of expertise in risk assessment. Risk assessment, though invaluable to regulators in the design of management strategies, is not at all convincing to the public. Perhaps this should not surprise us, given the many criticisms of risk assessment in the literature. Our survey indicates that these criticisms are not a minority view. The affiliation bias we and others have observed is a natural outgrowth of the scientific ambiguity – but a disturbing one nonetheless. It feeds the public sense of distrust.

Risk communication cannot take place without appropriate messages to communicate. The messages emanating from the risk-assessment community are contradictory and confusing. Do animal studies overestimate cancer risks to humans because of the use of particularly sensitive strains of animals or because of the effects of cell proliferation caused by extreme doses? Or do they underestimate the risks because of the greater genetic diversity in the human population, the slower rate of metabolism in humans, or the exposure of humans to a greater number of carcinogenic substances than laboratory animals are exposed to? Are there, or are there not, thresholds for carcinogens? Regulators have sought to justify their actions through reliance on scientific consensus, insulated from considerations of policy and politics. Said William Ruckelshaus, at the beginning of his second term as EPA administrator: 'Risk assessment at EPA must be based only on scientific evidence and scientific consensus. Nothing will erode public confidence faster than the suspicion that policy considerations have been allowed to influence the assessment of risk' (Ruckelshaus, 1983, pp1027–28). Outside of the regulatory arena, many of the scientific foundations and findings of risk assessment are under dispute and appear to be shaped by political factors. What, then, is the message that should be communicated?

Risk assessment has been oversold because of the need to rationalize decisions about chemicals. Even Ruckelshaus came to admit this toward the end of his second term. The attempt to quantify risks to human health and the environment from industrial chemicals is, he said, 'Essentially ... a kind of pretense; to avoid the paralysis that would result from waiting for "definitive" data, we assume that we have greater knowledge than scientists actually possess and make decisions based on those assumptions' (Ruckelshaus, 1985, p26).

The challenge to toxicologists and risk assessors is clear. These scientists must look anew at the strengths and limitations of their craft. They should work to develop stronger, more definitive ways to assess chemical risks. They should play a greater role in interpreting the health implications of their data for the public. In doing so, they should acknowledge the subjective elements, judgments and assumptions inherent in their analyses, as well as the degree of uncertainty in their conclusions. Above all, they must protect the young science of risk assessment from being misrepresented, misused and abused in the regulatory process. We concur with Graham et al (1988, p218) in the conclusions they drew from their analysis of the intense controversies surrounding efforts to regulate benzene and formaldehyde:

> We believe that a precise and honest view about the role of science in chemical regulation will strengthen both science and democracy. Modest expectations ...

can be realized, and that means strengthened public confidence in science in the long run. Modest expectations for science also foster and legitimize explicit political discussion in our democracy about how to cope with chemical hazards.

ACKNOWLEDGMENTS

Primary support for this research came from Grant SES-8722109 from the National Science Foundation to Decision Research. Any opinions, findings and conclusions or recommendations expressed in this chapter are those of the authors and do not necessarily reflect the views of the National Science Foundation. We are grateful for additional funding from the US Environmental Protection Agency, the Risk Science Institute, the Dow Chemical Company and the Monsanto Chemical Company. The students and faculty of the Risk Assessment Summer School (RASS) of the International Union of Toxicology patiently helped us pretest our questionnaire. Many persons have helped us by providing critiques of our work and other valuable services. Without implying that they concur in our findings and conclusions, we wish to thank Frederick Allen, Patricia Beattie, Vincent Covello, Michael Davidson, Anthony Dayan, Doug Easterling, Ann Fisher, Gary Flamm, William Freudenburg, James Gibson, Bernard Goldstein, John Graham, P J (Bert) Hakkinen, Cecelia Hagen, Carol Henry, Fred Hoerger, Daniel Krewski, Mark Layman, Birgitta Lewander, Sarah Lichtenstein, Frances Lynn, David McCallum, Leisha Mullican, A John Newman, Tom Osimitz, Emil Pfitzer, Peter Preuss, Sarah Spedden and James D Wilson.

NOTES

1   The actual survey contained several additional questions not discussed in this chapter because they were essentially made redundant with questions in Table 18.1.

2   This one question, not shown in Tables 18.1 throug 18.5, was as follows: 'In general, humans are (more, equally, less) vulnerable to adverse effects of chemicals than are laboratory animals' (question 5i).

3   In reference to the observation by Paracelsus that 'All substances are poisons; there is none that is not a poison. The risk dose differentiates a poison and a remedy' (as quoted in Casarett & Doull, 1975).

4   Unless otherwise noted in the tables, all of the reported differences between toxicologists and laypersons or between subgroups within either sample of respondents are statistically significant at $p < .01$ or $p < .001$ as determined by a chi-square test that included the 'don't know/no opinion' responses. Significance levels are not given in the text.

5   We attribute this to the fact that prescription drugs are familiar, high in perceived benefit and administered by highly trusted professionals. The more favorable view of prescription drugs relative to industrial and other chemicals is analogous to the more favorable perceptions of medical X-rays in comparison to industrial radiation technologies such as nuclear power and food irradiation (see Slovic, 1990).

6   Many policy-makers have argued that lifetime risks equal to or less than 1 in 1 million are *de minimus* – too small to worry about or to regulate (Whipple, 1987). The present results suggest that many laypersons would object to this view.

7   Carson may have been a major influence behind another popular view of our public respondents – that natural chemicals are not as harmful as synthetic chemicals. In *Silent Spring* she observed that although 'natural cancer-causing agents are still a factor in producing malignancy... they are few in number and they belong to that ancient array of forces to which life has become accustomed from the beginning' (p195). She contrasts these natural chemicals with synthetic agents of the industrial era against which 'man had no protection' (p196).

8   A survey of other presentations of toxicology designed to educate the public shows that this relatively favorable view of the validity of animal tests is typical.

19   Perceived Risk, Trust and Democracy

Paul Slovic

INTRODUCTION

My objective in this chapter is to examine the interplay between several remarkable trends within our society pertaining to the perception and management of risk.

The first of these trends is the fact that during a 20-year period during which
our society has grown healthier and safer on average and spent billions of dollars and immense effort to become so, the American public has become more –
rather than less – concerned about risk. We have come to perceive ourselves as
increasingly vulnerable to life's hazards and to believe that our land, air and
water are more contaminated by toxic substances than ever before.

A second dramatic trend – that I believe is closely related to the first – is the
fact that risk assessment and risk management (like many other facets of our
society) have become much more contentious. Polarized views, controversy
and overt conflict have become pervasive. Frustrated scientists and industralists
castigate the public for behaviors they judge to be based on irrationality or ignorance. Members of the public feel similarly antagonistic toward industry and
government. A desperate search for salvation through risk-communication efforts began in the mid 1980s – yet, despite some localized successes, this effort
has not stemmed the major conflicts or reduced much of the dissatisfaction with
risk management.

Early studies of risk perception demonstrated that the public's concerns could
not simply be blamed on ignorance or irrationality. Instead, research showed that
many of the public's reactions to risk could be attributed to a sensitivity to technical, social and psychological qualities of hazards that were not well-modeled
in technical risk assessments (eg, qualities such as uncertainty in risk assessments, perceived inequity in the distribution of risks and benefits, and aversion to being exposed to risks that were involuntary, not under one's control

Note: reprinted from 'Perceived Risk, Trust and Democracy' by P Slovic, 1993, *Risk Analysis*, 13(6), pp675–82. Copyright 1993 by the Society for Risk Analysis. Reprinted with permission.

or dreaded). The important role of social values in risk perception and risk acceptance thus became apparent (Slovic, 1987).

More recently, another important aspect of the risk-perception problem has come to be recognized. This is the role of trust. In recent years there have been numerous articles and surveys pointing out the importance of trust in risk management and documenting the extreme distrust we now have in many of the individuals, industries and institutions responsible for risk management. This pervasive distrust has also been shown to be strongly linked to risk perception and to political activism to reduce risk (Bord & O'Connor, 1990; Flynn, Burns, Mertz & Slovic, 1992; Jenkins-Smith, 1992; Mushkatel & Pijawka, 1992; Slovic, Flynn et al, 1991).

In this chapter I shall look beyond current perceptions of risk and distrust and attempt to explain how they came to be this way. My explanation begins with the idiosyncrasies of individual human minds, befitting my background as a psychologist. However, individual psychology is not fully adequate to account for risk perception and conflict. A broader perspective is necessary, one that includes the complex mix of scientific, social, political, legal, institutional and psychological factors operating within our society's risk-management system.

THE IMPORTANCE OF TRUST

Everyone knows intuitively that trust is important for all forms of human social interaction. Perhaps because it is such a familiar concept, its importance in risk management has not been adequately appreciated. However, numerous recent studies clearly point to *lack of trust* as a critical factor underlying the divisive controversies that surround the management of technological hazards (Bella, 1987; Bella, Mosher & Calvo, 1988a; Bella et al, 1988b; Cvetkovich & Earle, 1992; US Department of Energy, 1992; English, 1992; Flynn & Slovic, 1993; Freudenburg, 1993; Johnson, 1992; Kasperson, Golding & Tuler, 1992; Laird, 1989; Mitchell, 1992; Pijawka & Mushkatel, 1992; Raynor & Cantor, 1987; Renn & Levine, 1991).

To appreciate the importance of trust, it is instructive to compare those risks that we fear and avoid with those we casually accept. Starr (1985) has pointed to the public's lack of concern about the risks from tigers in urban zoos as evidence that acceptance of risks is strongly dependent upon confidence in risk management. Similarly, risk-perception research (Slovic, 1990) documents that people view *medical* technologies based on use of radiation and chemicals (ie, X-rays and prescription drugs) as high in benefit, low in risk and clearly acceptable. However, they view *industrial* technologies involving radiation and chemicals (ie, nuclear power, pesticides, industrial chemicals) as high in risk, low in benefit and unacceptable. Although X-rays and medicines pose significant risks, our relatively high degree of trust in the physicians who manage these devices makes them acceptable. Numerous polls have shown that the government and industry officials who oversee the management of nuclear power and non-medical chemicals are not highly trusted (Flynn, Burns et al, 1992; McCallum et al, 1990; Pijawka & Mushkatel, 1992; Slovic, Flynn et al, 1991).

During the past several decades, the field of risk assessment has developed to impart rationality to the management of technological hazards. Risk assessment has its roots in epidemiology, toxicology, systems analysis, reliability theory and many other disciplines. Probably more than $1 billion has been spent to conduct innumerable animal bioassays and epidemiological studies to assess the human health consequences of exposure to radiation and chemicals and to develop probabilistic risk analyses for nuclear reactors, dams, hazardous waste treatment and other engineered facilities. The US Environmental Protection Agency, the US Nuclear Regulatory Commission and numerous other government agencies have made risk assessment the centerpiece of their regulatory efforts (Levine, 1984; US Nuclear Regulatory Commission, 1983; Ruckelshaus, 1983).

It is now evident that public perceptions and acceptance of risk from nuclear and chemical technologies are not much influenced by technical risk assessments. Nowhere is this phenomenon more dramatically illustrated than in the unsuccessful struggle, across many years, to dispose of the accumulating volume of spent fuel from the nation's commercial nuclear reactors. The US Department of Energy's program to establish a national repository has been stymied by overwhelming public opposition, fueled by public perceptions that the risks are immense and unacceptable (Slovic, Flynn et al, 1991). These perceptions stand in stark contrast to the prevailing view of the technical community, whose risk assessments assert that nuclear wastes can be disposed of safely in an underground repository (see Table 19.1). Public fears and opposition to nuclear-waste disposal plans can be seen as a 'crisis in confidence', a profound breakdown of trust in the scientific, governmental and industrial managers of nuclear technologies. It is clear that the US Department of Energy (DOE) and the US Congress have not adequately appreciated the importance of (dis)trust in the failure of the nuclear-waste program, nor have they recognized the implications of this situation (US DOE, 1992; Slovic, Flynn et al, 1991). Analogous crises of confidence can be demonstrated in numerous controversies surrounding exposures to chemicals. Again, risk assessment, in these situations based primarily on toxicology, is often impotent when it comes to resolving conflict about chemical risks (Graham et al, 1988).

Because it is impossible to exclude the public in our uniquely participatory democracy, the response of industry and government to this crisis of confidence has been to turn to the young and still primitive field of risk communication in search of methods to bring experts and laypeople into alignment and make conflicts over technological decisions easier to resolve (see, for example, William Ruckelshaus' stirring speeches on this topic, 1983, 1984; the National Academy of Sciences report on risk communication, National Research Council, 1989; and the Chemical Manufacturer's Association communication manual for plant managers, Covello, Sandman et al, 1988). Although attention to communication can prevent blunders that exacerbate conflict, there is rather little evidence that risk communication has made any significant contribution to reducing the gap between technical risk assessments and public perceptions, or to facilitating decisions about nuclear waste or other major sources of risk conflict. The limited effectiveness of risk-communication efforts can be attributed to the lack of trust. If you trust the risk manager, communication is relatively easy. If trust is

Table 19.1 *Viewpoints on the Risks from Nuclear-waste Disposal*

Quote	Source
'Several years ago... I talked with Sir John Hill ... chairman of the UK's Atomic Energy Authority. "I've never come across any industry where the public perception of the problem is so totally different from the problems as seen by those of us in the industry", Hill told me. In Hill's view, the problem of radioactive waste disposal was, in a technical sense, comparatively easy.'	L J Carter, *Nuclear Imperatives and Public Trust.* Resources for the Future, Inc, Washington DC, 1987, p9
'Nuclear wastes can be sequestered with essentially no chance of any member of the public receiving a non-stochastic dose of radiation ... Why is the public's perception of the nuclear waste issue at such odds with the experts' perception?'	A M Weinberg, *Public Perceptions of Hazardous Technologies and Democratic Political Institutions.* Paper presented at Waste Management 1989, Tucson, Arizona, 1989, pp1–2
'The fourth major reason for public misunderstanding of nuclear power is a grossly unjustified fear of the hazards from radioactive waste ... there is general agreement among those scientists involved with waste management that radioactive waste disposal is a rather trivial technical problem.'	B L Cohen, *Before It's Too late: A Scientist's Case for Nuclear Energy.* Plenum, New York, 1983, p119
'The risk is as negligible as it is possible to imagine ... It is embarrassingly easy to solve the technical problems, yet impossible to solve the political ones.'	H W Lewis, *Technological Risk.* W W Norton, New York, 1990, pp245–246

lacking, no form or process of communication will be satisfactory (Fessenden-Raden, Fitchen & Heath, 1987). Thus, trust is more fundamental to conflict resolution than is risk communication.

CREATION AND DESTRUCTION OF TRUST

One of the most fundamental qualities of trust has been known for ages. Trust is fragile. It is typically created rather slowly, but it can be destroyed in an instant – by a single mishap or mistake. Thus, once trust is lost, it may take a long time to rebuild it to its former state. In some instances, lost trust may never be regained. Abraham Lincoln understood this quality. In a letter to Alexander McClure he observed: 'If you *once* forfeit the confidence of your fellow citizens, you can *never* regain their respect and esteem' (emphasis added).

The asymmetry between the difficulty of creating trust and the ease of destroying it has been studied by social psychologists within the domain of interpersonal perception. For example, Rothbart and Park (1986) had people rate 150 descriptive traits (adventurous, gentle, lazy, trustworthy, etc) in terms of the number of relevant behavioral instances necessary to establish or disconfirm the trait. Favorable traits (such as trustworthiness) were judged to be hard to acquire (many behavioral instances needed) and easy to lose. Unfavorable traits were judged to be easier to acquire and harder to lose. The number of behavioral instances required to disconfirm a negative quality (eg, dishonesty) was greater than the number required to disconfirm a positive trait. As Abraham Lincoln might have predicted, trustworthiness stood out among the 150 traits as requiring a relatively large number of confirming instances to establish the trait and a relatively small number of relevant instances to disconfirm it. (Note that data here were *judgments* of the number of instances that would be required as opposed to data documenting the number of instances that actually confirmed or disconfirmed a trait.)

The fact that trust is easier to destroy than to create reflects certain fundamental mechanisms of human psychology that I shall call 'the asymmetry principle'. When it comes to winning trust, the playing field is not level. It is tilted toward distrust, for each of the following reasons:

1   Negative (trust-destroying) events are more visible or noticeable than positive (trust-building) events. Negative events often take the form of specific, well-defined incidents such as accidents, lies, discoveries of errors or other mismanagement. Positive events, while sometimes visible, more often are fuzzy or indistinct. For example, how many positive events are represented by the safe operation of a nuclear power plant for one day? Is this one event? Dozens of events? Hundreds? There is no precise answer. When events are invisible or poorly defined, they carry little or no weight in shaping our attitudes and opinions.

2   When events do come to our attention, negative (trust-destroying) events carry much greater weight than positive events. This important psychological tendency is illustrated by a study in which my colleagues and I asked 103 college students to rate the impact on trust of 45 hypothetical news events pertaining to the management of a large nuclear power plant in their community (Slovic, Flynn, Johnson & Mertz, 1993). Some of these events were designed to be trust increasing, such as:

- There have been no reported safety problems at the plant during the past year.
- There is careful selection and training of employees at the plant.
- Plant managers live near the plant.
- The county medical examiner reports that the health of people living near the plant is better than the average for the region.

Other events were designed to be trust decreasing, such as:
- A potential safety problem was found to have been covered up by plant officials.
- Plant safety inspections are delayed in order to meet the electricity production quota for the month.
- A nuclear power plant in another state has a serious accident.
- The county medical examiner reports that the health of people living near the plant is worse than the average for the region.

The respondents were asked to indicate, for each event, whether their trust in the management of the plant would be increased or decreased upon learning of that event. After doing this, they rated how strongly their trust would be affected by the event on a scale ranging from 1 (very small impact on trust) to 7 (very powerful impact on trust).

The percentages of category 7 ratings, shown in Figure 19.1, dramatically demonstrate that negative events are seen as far more likely to have a powerful effect on trust than are positive events. The data shown in Table 19.2 are typical. The negative event, reporting plant neighbors' health as *worse* than average, was rated 6 or 7 on the impact scale by 5% of the respondents. A matched event, reporting neighbors' health to be *better* than average was rated 6 or 7 by only 18.3% of the respondents.

Only one event was perceived to have any substantial impact on increasing trust. This event stated that: 'An advisory board of local citizens and environmentalists is established to monitor the plant and is given legal authority to shut the plant down if they believe it to be unsafe.'

This strong delegation of authority to the local public was rated 6 or 7 on the impact scale by 38.4% of the respondents. Although this was a far stronger showing than for any other positive event, it would have been a rather average performance in the distribution of impacts for negative events.

The reasons for the greater impact of trust-destroying incidents are complex, and I shall not discuss them here except to note that the importance of an event is at least in part related to its frequency (or rarity). An accident in a nuclear plant is more informative with regard to risk than is a day (or even a large number of days) without an accident. Thus, in systems where we are

Table 19.2 *Judged Impact of a Trust-increasing Event and a Similar Trust-decreasing Event* [a]

	Impact on Trust						
	Very small						Very powerful
	1	2	3	4	5	6	7
Trust-increasing event: The county medical examiner reports that the health of people living near the plant is *better* than average.	21.5	14.0	10.8	18.3	17.2	16.1	2.2
Trust-decreasing event: The county medical examiner reports that the health of people living near the plant is *worse* than average.	3.0	8.0	2.0	16.0	21.0	26.0	24.0

[a] Cell entries indicate the percentage of respondents in each impact rating category.

Local board authority to close plant
Evacuation plan exists
On-site government inspector
Rewarded for finding problems
Responsive to any sign of problems
Effective emergency action taken
Local advisory board established
Public encouraged to tour plant
Mandatory drug testing
No problems for five years
Hold regular public hearings
Employees carefully trained
Conduct emergency training
Community has access to records
Serious accident is controlled
Nearby health is good
Monitor radioactive emissions
Employees informed of problems
Neighbors notified of problems
No evidence of withholding information
Contribute to local charities
Employees closely supervised
Try to meet with public
Managers live nearby
Operates according to regulations
No problems in past year
Record keeping is good

TRUST INCREASING

TRUST DECREASING

Don't contribute to local charities
No public hearings
Little communication with community
Emergency response plans not rehearsed
Officials live far away
Poor record keeping
Accident occurs in another state
Accused of releasing radiation
Denied access to records
Employees not informed of problems
Delayed inspections
Public tours not permitted
Health nearby worse than average
Official lied to government
Serious accident is controlled
No adequate emergency response plan
Plant covered up problem
Employees drunk on job
Records were falsified

60%   40%   20%   0%   20%   40%   60%

Percent very powerful impact

Note: Only the percentage of respondents giving category 7 ratings (very powerful impact) are shown here.

Figure 19.1 *Differential impact of trust-increasing and trust-decreasing events*

concerned about low-probability/high-consequence events, problematic events will increase our perceptions of risk to a much greater degree than favorable events will decrease them.

3   Adding fuel to the fire of asymmetry is yet another idiosyncrasy of human psychology – sources of bad (trust-destroying) news tend to be seen as more credible than sources of good news. For example, in several studies of what

we call 'intuitive toxicology' (Kraus et al, 1992), we have examined people's confidence in the ability of animal studies to predict human health effects from chemicals. In general, confidence in the validity of animal studies is not particularly high. However, when told that a study has found that a chemical is carcinogenic in animals, people express considerable confidence in the validity of this study for predicting health effects in humans. Regulators respond like the public. Positive (bad news) evidence from animal bioassays is presumptive evidence of risk to humans; negative evidence (eg, the chemical was not found to be harmful) carries little weight (Efron, 1984).

4   Another important psychological tendency is that distrust, once initiated, tends to reinforce and perpetuate distrust. This occurs in two ways. First, distrust tends to inhibit the kinds of personal contacts and experiences that are necessary to overcome distrust. By avoiding others whose motives or actions we distrust, we never get to see if these people are competent, well-meaning and trustworthy. Second, initial trust or distrust colors our interpretation of events, thus reinforcing our prior beliefs. Persons who trusted the nuclear power industry saw the events at Three Mile Island as demonstrating the soundness of the 'defense in depth' principle, noting that the multiple-safety systems shut the plant down and contained most of its radiation. Persons who distrusted nuclear power prior to the accident took an entirely different message from the same events, perceiving that those in charge did not understand what was wrong or how to fix it and that catastrophe was averted only by sheer luck.

'THE SYSTEM DESTROYS TRUST'

Thus far, I have been discussing the psychological tendencies that create and reinforce distrust in situations of risk. Appreciation of those psychological principles leads us toward a new perspective on risk perception, trust and conflict. Conflicts and controversies surrounding risk management are not due to public irrationality or ignorance but, instead, can be seen as expected side effects of these psychological tendencies, interacting with our remarkable form of participatory democratic government, and amplified by certain powerful technological and social changes in our society. The technological change has given the electronic and print media the capability (effectively utilized) of informing us of news from all over the world – often right as it happens. Moreover, just as individuals give greater weight and attention to negative events, so do the news media. Much of what the media reports is bad (trust-destroying) news (Lichtenberg & MacLean, 1992). This is convincingly demonstrated by Koren and Klein (1991), who compared the rates of newspaper reporting of two studies, one providing bad news and one good news, published back to back in the 20 March 1991 issue of the *Journal of the American Medical Association*. Both studies examined the link between radiation exposure and cancer. The bad news study showed an increased risk of leukemia in white men working at the Oak Ridge National Laboratory. The good news study failed to show an increased risk of cancer in people residing near nuclear facilities. Koren and Klein found that subsequent newspaper coverage was far greater for the study showing increased risk.

The second important change, a social phenomenon, is the rise of powerful special interest groups – well funded (by a fearful public) and sophisticated in using their own experts and the media to communicate their concerns and their distrust to the public in order to influence risk policy debates and decisions (Fenton, 1989). The social problem is compounded by the fact that we tend to manage our risks within an adversarial legal system that pits expert versus expert, contradicting each other's risk assessments and further destroying the public trust.

The young science of risk assessment is too fragile, too indirect, to prevail in such a hostile atmosphere. Scientific analysis of risks cannot allay our fears of low-probability catastrophes or delayed cancers unless we trust the system. In the absence of trust, science (and risk assessment) can only feed distrust by uncovering more bad news. A single study demonstrating an association between exposure to chemicals or radiation and some adverse health effect cannot easily be offset by numerous studies failing to find such an association. Thus, for example, the more studies that are conducted looking for effects of electric and magnetic fields or other difficult-to-evaluate hazards, the more likely it is that these studies will increase public concerns, even if the majority of these studies fail to find any association with ill health (MacGregor, Slovic & Morgan, 1994; Morgan et al, 1985). In short, such risk-assessment studies tend to increase perceived risk.

WHERE NEXT? RISK AND DEMOCRACY

Although the study of risk perception and trust has not yet led to a solution to our risk-management problems, it appears to be leading to a more adequate diagnosis of the root causes of risk concerns and risk conflicts. As we begin to understand the complexity of risk conflicts, we recognize the need for new approaches to risk management. The road branches in two very different directions (Fiorino, 1989). One direction leads toward less public participation and more centralized control. One might call this the French model. France leads the world in the percentage of electricity generated by nuclear power (73% in 1991, compared to 21% for the US). France, like the US, was rocked by strong anti-nuclear protests during the late 1970s, but the state acted forcefully to repress these protests and the anti-nuclear movement never gained favor with the political parties in power. Today, surprisingly, the perception of risk from nuclear power remains extremely high in France – as high as in the US, according to national surveys my colleagues and I recently conducted in both countries. However, French citizens, while recognizing that they have little control over risks to their health and safety, have a high degree of trust in their government and in the experts who design and operate nuclear power plants. Americans, in contrast, combine their similarly high degree of perceived risk with a distrust of government, science and industry and a belief that they do have some ability to control risks. In fact, the American system does provide individual citizens and citizen groups considerable freedom to intervene in administrative proceedings, to question expert judgments of government agencies and to force changes in policy through litigation (Jasanoff, 1986).

Political scientists have recognized that, in a climate of strong distrust, the French approach, in which policy formation and implementation is not accessible to public intervention, is expedient (Morone & Woodhouse, 1989). Campbell (1988), for example, argues that formal democratic institutions providing political access to nuclear critics may be fundamentally incompatible with the commercial success of nuclear power.

What works in France, however, is unlikely to be achievable in the US. The French nuclear power program is run by the state, not private industry. Electricité de France has long had a strong reputation for being competent and putting service above profits. The French have a tradition of looking to a scientific elite for guidance in policy matters. Jasper (1990), noting that the word as well as the image of a 'technocrat' arose in France, observed that 'Perhaps no other political system provides as large a role for people to exercise power on the basis of technical training and certification' (p83).

America, since Thomas Jefferson, has had a different approach to democracy, and it is not surprising that attempts to restrict citizens' rights to intervene directly in national risk-management policies have been vigorously opposed. A recent example is the unsuccessful attempt in congress to strip the state of Nevada of its rights to issue environmental and safety permits for nuclear-waste studies at Yucca Mountain (Batt, 1992).

Given that the French approach is not likely to be acceptable in the US, restoration of trust may require a degree of openness and involvement with the public that goes far beyond public relations and 'two-way communication' to encompass levels of power-sharing and public participation in decision-making that have rarely been attempted (Flynn, Kasperson, Kunreuther & Slovic, 1992; Kunreuther, Fitzgerald & Aarts, 1993; Leroy & Nadler, 1993). Even this, however, is no guarantee of success (Bord, 1988; Nelkin & Pollak, 1979). In many situations, we may have to recognize that relationships are so poisoned that trust and conflict resolution cannot realistically be achieved in the short run. The bitter conflict over the proposed nuclear-waste repository in Nevada is a prime example of such a situation. To preserve the form of democracy we value so highly, we will need to develop ways to work constructively in situations where we cannot assume that trust is attainable (Kasperson et al, 1992).

We have a long way to go in improving our risk-management processes. Although we have expended massive amounts of time, money and resources on scientific studies designed to identify and quantify risks, we have failed to expend the effort needed to learn how to manage the hazards that science is so good at identifying. Gerald Jacob (1990, p164) frames the challenge well in the context of nuclear-waste disposal, and his words are also relevant to many other risk problems:

> While everyone can appreciate that complex, highly sophisticated engineering is required to safely store nuclear materials for thousands of years, few have appreciated the political requirements necessary to design and implement such a solution. While vast resources have been expended on developing complex and sophisticated technologies, the equally sophisticated political processes and institutions required to develop a credible and legitimate strategy for nuclear-waste management have not been developed. The history of high-level radioactive waste management describes repeated failure to recognize the need for institutional reform and reconstruction.

Some may view the analysis in this chapter as a depressing one. I do not. Understanding the root causes of social conflict and recognizing the need to create better risk-management processes are essential first steps toward improving the situation. It is far more depressing, in my view, to fail to understand the complex psychological, social, cultural and political forces that dictate the successes and failures of risk management.

ACKNOWLEDGMENTS

This is a revised version of the address given upon receipt of the Distinguished Contribution Award of the Society for Risk Analysis at Baltimore, Maryland, in December 1991.

Preparation of this paper was supported by the Alfred P Sloan Foundation, the Electric Power Research Institute and the National Science Foundation under Grant No SES-91-10592.

I wish to thank my colleagues at Decision Research for their contributions to the ideas and work underlying this paper. Jim Flynn, C K Mertz and Leisha Mullican deserve special thanks in this regard. Marc Poumadere and Claire Mays assisted in the collection of the French data reported here. Howard Kunreuther provided valuable comments on the manuscript.

20 Adolescent Health-threatening and Health-enhancing Behaviors: A Study of Word Association and Imagery

Alida Benthin, Paul Slovic, Patricia Moran, Herbert Severson, C K Mertz and Meg Gerrard

Adolescents engage in many high-risk behaviors including alcohol and drug use (Jessor, 1984; Johnston, O'Malley & Bachman, 1987; McLaughlin, Baer, Pokorny, Burnside & Fairlie, 1985). These have been shown to be correlated with other risk behaviors such as sexual risk taking (Benthin et al, 1993; Centers for Disease Control, 1988; 1990; Donovan, Jessor & Costa, 1988; Hedges, Gerrard & Gibbons, 1995; Novello, 1988).

Why do adolescents engage in behaviors that pose considerable risk to their health and well-being? In addressing this question, Jessor (1984) suggested that adolescents' risk-taking behavior is instrumental toward the attainment of certain goals, such as coping with feelings of anxiety or gaining admission into a peer group. Empirical efforts to identify psychological functions of health-threatening behaviors among adolescents have primarily focused on outcome expectancies. Outcome expectancies are cognitions about the relationship between behavior and its perceived consequences. Expectancies are thought to be acquired through direct and vicarious experiences with risky behaviors (Goldman, Brown, Christiansen & Smith, in press). Expectancy items studied are usually derived through content analysis of interviews and then factor analyzed to specify domains of expectancies. For example, Brown, Christiansen and Goldman (1987) used this approach to identify seven basic factors in adolescents' alcohol-related expectancies:

Note: reprinted by permission of Elsevier Science from 'Adolescent Health-threatening and Health-enhancing Behaviors: A Study of Word Association and Imagery' by A Benthin, P Slovic, P Moran, H Severson, C K Mertz & M Gerrard, *Journal of Adolescent Health*, 17, pp143–52, copyright 1995 by The Society for Adolescent Medicine.

1   global positive changes;
2   changes in social behavior;
3   improved cognitive and motor ability;
4   sexual enhancement;
5   cognitive and motor impairment;
6   increased arousal; and
7   relaxation and tension reduction.

Although the outcome expectancy literature has been successful in identifying some of the outcomes adolescents associate with alcohol use, expectancies have not been identified for other adolescent risk behaviors (eg, sexual risk taking, reckless driving). Therefore, one goal of the current study is to expand this litera-ture to include additional risk-taking behaviors. Furthermore, it has been sug-gested that even the listings of the psychological functions of alcohol use among adolescents require further empirical validation (Jessor, 1984; Millstein, 1989).

The current study employs a word association methodology to explore ado-lescents' conceptual images and outcome expectancies related to a variety of health-threatening behaviors, including the use of alcohol. In addition, it seeks to examine adolescents' images and outcome expectancies associated with various health-enhancing behaviors. By examining a broad spectrum of health-threatening and health-enhancing activities, we hope to gain a more complete understanding of the ways in which perceived risks and benefits relate to a wide variety of health-relevant actions.

One assumption of this research is that word associations provide a useful approach for examining the images and outcomes adolescents associate with health-threatening and health-enhancing behaviors. This assumption rests on previous research that shows that word association techniques encompass effi-cient ways of determining the contents and representational systems of human minds without requiring those contents to be expressed in the full discursive structure of human language (Szalay & Deese, 1978). Therefore, a word asso-ciation method may allow adolescents to express themselves quickly and eas-ily in ways they might otherwise find difficult (Szalay & Deese, 1978).

Recent studies utilizing word association techniques have demonstrated a strong link between imagery and behavior. For example, Slovic, Layman and Kraus et al (1991) showed that the content of subjects' images of cities and states predicted their preferences for places in which to vacation. Places associated with positive imagery were more likely to be selected as vacation sites than places with negative imagery. The results from such studies lead us to expect that the content of word associations will reflect some of the important reasons, justifications and experiences that motivate adolescents to participate in both health-threatening and health-enhancing behaviors.

The current study examines several predictions:

1   Different health-threatening behaviors will stimulate similar associations. This prediction is suggested by empirical findings indicating a problem-behavior syndrome during adolescence. That is, many of the health-threaten-ing behaviors of adolescents have been found to be interrelated rather than

being a collection of independent activities (Jessor, 1984; Benthin et al, 1993; Hedges et al, 1995). Moreover, it has been suggested that although each type of health-threatening behavior has unique determinants and situational rein-forcers, different risk behaviors may be serving similar psychological functions, and thus may have common social and personal meanings (Jessor, 1987). We might expect the same to be true for health-enhancing behaviors.

2   Participants in health-threatening behaviors are more likely than non-participants to associate positive concepts and outcomes with such behav-iors and less likely to associate negative concepts and outcomes with them. This prediction is derived from the outcome expectancy literature and the risk perception literature, both of which found that adolescents who partici-pate in risk-taking behaviors think more positively about those behaviors compared to non-participants. Studies of adolescents (Brown et al, 1987; Christiansen, Goldman & Brown, 1985; Christiansen, Smith, Roehling & Goldman, 1989) have consistently demonstrated a relationship between al-cohol outcome expectancies and alcohol consumption. Findings from the risk perception literature are consistent with those from the outcome expectancy literature. For example, Benthin et al (1993) found that adolescent partici-pants in health-threatening behaviors were more likely than non-participants to judge such behaviors as providing greater benefits than risks.

3   Participants in health-enhancing behaviors also are more likely than non-participants to associate positive concepts and outcomes with those behav-iors and less likely to associate negative concepts and outcomes with them.

4   Images associated with health-threatening behaviors and health-enhancing behaviors will be linked with positive and negative affective evaluations, and these affective values will be predictive of participation in those behaviors. This prediction is suggested by a study by Gerrard, Gibbons & Boney-McCoy (1993) indicating a correlation between positive affect and engaging in sexual activity. Likewise, Gerrard (1987) demonstrated that negative affect toward sex is related to inhibited sexual behavior.

METHOD

Sample

Participants were recruited through a high-school (grades 9 through 12) located in a small coastal town in Oregon. The sample consisted of all the students who attended school on a regular school day ($N = 411$). The age range was between 14 and 20 years. Fifty-one percent ($n = 209$) of the sample were female, 47% ($n = 195$) were male, and 2% of the sample ($n = 7$) did not report gender. Approxi-mately 78% of the participants were Caucasian, 12% Native American, 4% His-panic, 1% African American and 6% 'other'.

Procedure

Parent permission slips were sent home with the students several weeks prior to data collection. Subjects responded to a self-report questionnaire during one regular classroom period (50 minutes). Participation was voluntary and responses were anonymous. Completed questionnaires were collected by the researchers – the regular classroom teachers were not present.

Questions examined in the current study were part of a larger questionnaire that assessed risk perceptions for 16 different activities, several personality measures (eg, the Sensation Seeking Scale – Zuckerman, Kolin, Price & Zoab, 1964 – an ego control scale – Shedler & Block, 1990) and values for academic achievement and independence.

Information about participation in health-threatening activities and health-enhancing activities was obtained for each subject by asking, 'How many times have you done this activity during the past six months (never, occasionally, frequently)?' Subjects were then given the Teen Imagery Survey with the following introductory instructions:

> We all have images and ideas about things. Often when people hear about certain behaviors, they develop certain images in their mind about the meaning of these behaviors. We are interested in the meaning of certain behaviors to people your age.
>
> In answering these questions, please make your judgments on the basis of what these behaviors mean to you. Work at a fairly high speed through this test. Do not worry or puzzle over your answers. It is your first impressions, your immediate thoughts that we want. On the other hand, please do not be careless, because we want your true impressions.
>
> It is important that, in answering these questions, you always focus on the specific behavior that we ask about. For example, if we ask you about thoughts that come to your mind when you think about playing sports, it is important that you think about playing sports each time you write down a new thought about playing sports.

Subjects were asked to associate to each of eight behaviors. For example, for the stimulus behavior *drinking beer*, the instructions were as follows: 'Think for a moment about *drinking beer*. We are interested in the first *FIVE* thoughts that come to mind when you think about *drinking beer*.'

The eight behaviors included five considered to be health-threatening behaviors and three behaviors considered to be health enhancing. The health-threatening behaviors were drinking beer, drinking liquor (eg, vodka, mixed drinks), smoking cigarettes, smoking marijuana and having sexual intercourse. The three health-enhancing behaviors were exercising, wearing a seat belt and using a condom during sexual intercourse. These behaviors were selected on the basis of prevalence and importance from a health standpoint.

Following the elicitation of image associations for each particular behavior, the subject was asked to indicate the affective meaning for each image:

> Now that you have thought about five images that come to your mind when you think about *drinking beer*, we want to be sure we understand if these images mean something positive or something negative to you.
>
> So, please rate your images in the order in which you gave them on the scales below. Circle one number for each image.
>
> Be sure to RATE ONLY YOUR IMAGES and *not drinking beer* itself.

The rating scale went from 1 (very negative/very bad) to 5 (very positive/very good) with 2 = somewhat negative, 3 = neutral and 4 = somewhat positive.

As noted by Isen and Diamond (1988), there are two ways in which affect has been conceptualized in the psychological literature. Affect may be viewed as a feeling state that people experience, such as happiness or sadness. Affect may also be viewed as a quality – valence – assigned to a stimulus. For example, stimuli can be rated with regard to their degree of goodness or badness, attractiveness or unattractiveness, pleasantness or unpleasantness. It is the second conception – affect as valence – that this rating scale measures. A further analysis of image content, performed by the investigators and explained in the next section, attempts to assess both conceptions of affect.

RESULTS

Imagery

The 411 respondents provided a total of 15,650 word association images to the eight stimulus behaviors. The greatest number of word associations (n = 1895) was given for the stimulus *drinking beer*, and the fewest number (n = 1562) was given for the stimulus *using a condom*. The content of these associations was examined for each stimulus behavior, and the researchers developed a classification scheme to assign the associations to various content categories.

This content analysis resulted in five general or superordinate categories for each stimulus behavior: positive concepts or positive descriptions of the behavior (eg, nice, awesome), positive outcomes associated with the behavior (eg, fun, social facilitation), negative concepts or negative descriptions of the behavior (eg, dirty, ugly), negative outcomes associated with the behavior (eg, accident, disease), and miscellaneous associations (eg, references to family members, friends; see Table 20.1). Positivity and negativity were determined by the judges who did the content analysis. A reliability check was performed by having a second coder independently categorize a randomly selected set of 40 associations for each of the eight behaviors (approximately 20% of the total sample of associations). The second coder agreed with the first coder's assignment of superordinate categories in 85% of the cases. There were almost no instances of disagreement as to whether an association was positive or negative. Agreement on the distinction between a concept and an outcome was 93% for positive associations and 91% for negative associations. A complete list of images organized by stimulus behavior and by content categories is available on request from the second author.

All superordinate categories contained subordinate categories. In all, there were 265 distinct subordinate categories across all eight stimulus behaviors. Table 20.2 presents the category structure for two activities, drinking beer and having sexual intercourse. Many of the subordinate categories contained multiple associations, evaluated to have similar meanings. For example, the category *intimacy/affiliation*, within the superordinate category *positive outcomes* for having sex, included terms such as intimacy, sharing, togetherness and closeness.

The 40 superordinate categories (five for each behavior) and their 265 subordinate categories contained 14,005 word association images. A total of 1645

Table 20.1 *Percentages of Associations in Each Superordinate Category*

Behavior	Positive concepts	Positive outcomes	Negative concepts	Negative outcomes	Miscella-neous	Uncate-gorized	n
Beer	4.3	25.9	21.3	24.0	13.9	10.7	1895
Liquor	4.5	17.5	23.3	28.6	15.1	11.0	1820
Cigarettes	1.6	5.6	30.6	41.5	12.8	7.9	1822
Marijuana	2.9	11.2	33.7	29.2	14.6	8.5	1708
Sexual intercourse	10.5	36.0	8.2	10.6	19.7	15.0	1741
Condom use	40.5	14.7	13.6	14.0	4.7	12.4	1562
Exercise	7.9	45.6	7.5	7.3	22.8	8.8	1868
Seat belt	17.8	34.5	29.6	3.8	6.1	8.1	1663

Table 20.2 *Image Category Structure for Drinking Beer and Having Sexual Intercourse*

			Drinking beer		Having sexual intercourse
1	Positive	1a	Good taste	1a	Awesome/good
	concepts	1b	Cold/refreshing	1b	Erotic/sexy
		1c	Socially accepted	1c	Special
		1d	Other		
2	Negative	2a	Bad taste	2a	Dangerous/scary
	concepts	2b	Bad smell	2b	Other
		2c	Expensive		
		2d	Illegal		
		2e	Dangerous/scary		
		2f	Other		
3	Positive	3a	Fun/pleasure	3a	Fun/enjoyment
	outcomes	3b	Positive affective change	3b	Intimacy/affiliation
		3c	Relaxation	3c	Love/romance
		3d	Arousal/sensation seeking	3d	Arousal
		3e	Sexual facilitation	3e	Gratification/orgasm
		3f	Social facilitation	3f	Positive affective change
				3g	Relaxation
				3h	Social facilitation
4	Negative	4a	Negative affective change	4a	Social stigma/impairment
	outcomes	4b	Cognitive impairment	4b	Negative affective change
		4c	Social impairment	4c	Pain
		4d	Bad breath	4d	Abortion
		4e	Weight gain	4e	AIDS / STDs / disease
		4f	Violence/crime	4f	Punishment
		4g	Hangover	4g	Other
		4h	Health damage		
		4i	Accidents		
		4j	Punishment		
		4k	Emotional disinhibition		
		4l	Addiction		
		4m	Death		
		4n	Other		

(10.5%) associations were not categorized. For example, for the stimulus behavior *smoking cigarettes*, 144 (7.9%) out of a total of 1822 images were not categorized. These images were either ambiguous in content, did not clearly fit into any of the 310 distinct categories for the total images, or did not indicate meaningful categories of their own. Specific image associations for *smoking cigarettes* that were treated in this manner included words such as ashes, ashtrays and puffs.

Examination of Table 20.1 shows that each behavior elicited a mix of positive and negative imagery. Negative imagery (concepts and outcomes) accounted for at least 45% of the associations to each of the health-threatening behaviors, with the exception of sexual intercourse. Both sexual intercourse and drinking beer had a high percentage of images categorized as positive outcomes (Table 20.2). Positive concepts and outcomes predominated for the health-enhancing behaviors, although seat belt use had a high percentage (29.6%) of associations categorized as negative concepts. These included concepts such as difficult to remember, inconvenient, uncomfortable, boring and dangerous. Condom use was associated with a high percentage (40.5%) of positive concepts such as easy, good idea, smart, wise, safe and careful.

Similarity of Associations across Different Health-threatening Behaviors

The content analysis showed that, as predicted, the various health-threatening behaviors, despite their different nature, had similar outcome associations. For example, all five risk behaviors were associated with having fun, social facilitation, physiological arousal and physical relaxation (Table 20.3). Furthermore,

Table 20.3 *Percentages for Types of Positive Outcomes Associated with Five Health-threatening Behaviors*

Positive outcomes	Beer	Liquor	Cigarettes	Marijuana	Sexual intercourse
Social					
Fun/pleasure	30.1	25.0	11.8	25.6	41.0
Social facilitation	45.0	44.2	38.2	24.6	2.5
Love/romance	—	—	—	—	16.6
Sexual facilitation	4.7	8.8	—	4.2	—
Intimacy/affiliation	—	—	—	—	7.8
Physical					
Arousal	7.1	10.3	16.7	5.7	16.6
Relaxation	6.7	5.0	33.3	27.2	1.9
Physical gratification	—	—	—	—	4.9
Emotional					
Positive affect	6.3	6.5	—	11.5	8.5
Other	—	—	—	1.0	—
n =	491	287	102	191	626

Note: Percentages are based on the total number of positive outcomes for each behavior.

all health-threatening behaviors, with the exception of cigarette smoking, were associated with positive affect (eg, feeling good, being in a good mood, feeling happy).

Table 20.3 also indicates differences across risk behaviors in the relative frequency of various associations. For example, relaxation was most often associated with cigarette smoking and marijuana use, and social facilitation was most often associated with alcohol use.

Negative outcomes differed across behaviors. For drinking beer and drinking liquor the dominant negative outcomes were hangover, cognitive and motor impairment, social impairment, punishment, accidents, violence and negative affective feelings (eg, feeling bad, feeling angry). Health damage was a rare associate. For smoking cigarettes, disease, social stigma and feeling sick were the major associates, followed by addiction and death. Smoking marijuana was associated primarily with cognitive and motor impairment, social impairment, disease, death and feeling sick. Sexual intercourse was associated primarily with disease and to a far lesser extent with social stigma and negative affective feelings.

Unlike the results for positive outcomes of health-threatening behaviors, there was little similarity in content across health-enhancing behaviors. Exercising was associated with physical and psychological well-being (eg, improved physical health, increased energy, stress reduction, positive affective change) as well as with fun and peer approval. Seat-belt use was primarily associated with life saving and protection, and, to a lesser extent, with peer and parental approval and avoidance of punishment (eg, in the form of traffic tickets). Condom use was associated with disease and pregnancy prevention as well as with reduced worry and social approval. Interestingly, condom use, unlike seat belts, was not associated with saving lives.

Finally, although the images associated with the three health-enhancing behaviors were predominantly positive in tone, the behaviors were also associated with a variety of negative outcomes. Condom use was associated with physical discomfort, reduced pleasure and intimacy, mood interruption and embarrassment. Exercise was associated with fatigue and pain, and seat belt use was associated with death, the danger of being trapped in an accident and social stigma.

Imagery and Behavior

About one half of the respondents said that they participated occasionally or frequently in drinking beer, drinking liquor and sexual intercourse; participation was lower for smoking cigarettes and marijuana. Each of the health-enhancing behaviors was engaged in by more than 75% of the respondents.

Do those who participate in a particular activity produce different kinds of associations to that activity than do non-participants? Figure 20.1 addresses this question by comparing the associations of persons who said they never engaged in the various behaviors with the associations of those who had frequently taken part in these activities. It is clear that, for frequent participants, a much higher percentage of associations took the form of positive outcomes, as compared to non-participants. For example, 41.4% of the images given by adolescents who frequently drank beer were categorized as positive outcomes. In comparison,

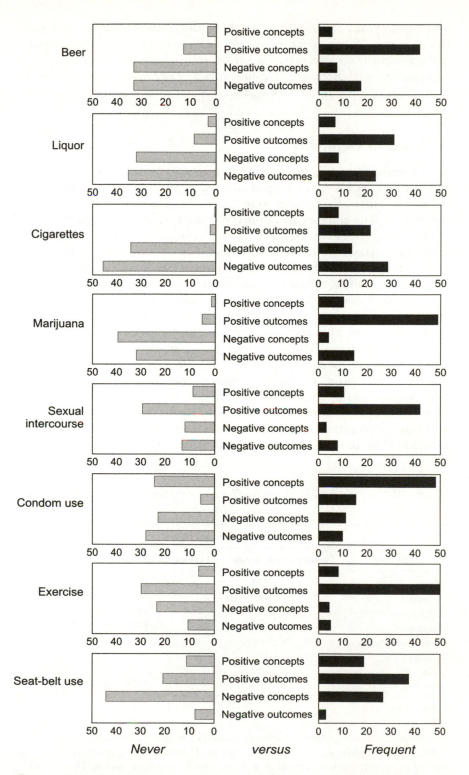

Figure 20.1 *Percentages for each superordinate image category by participation (never versus frequent) during the six months prior to the survey*

only 12.9% of the images given by non-beer drinkers were categorized as positive outcomes. Positive concepts did not differ as much between participants and non-participants, except for condom use (much higher positive concept percentage for users). Both negative outcomes and negative concepts formed a much higher percentage of the image sets for non-participants than for participants.

Affect and Behavior

In addition to examining the content categories, we also analyzed the relationship between the affective ratings of images and participation in health-related behaviors. These affect ratings were assigned by the respondents to each of their associations, and they are distinct from the assignment of the associations to positive and negative categories by the investigators. These ratings sometimes differed from the investigators' assignments. For example, an association such as 'dangerous' may be rated positively by some respondents and negatively by others. In addition, the ratings lend themselves nicely to quantitative analysis, as shown below. Table 20.4 presents the results of regression analyses in which positive and negative image scores were used to predict frequency of participation (coded 0, 1 and 2 for never, occasionally and frequently) for each of the eight behaviors. The positive (negative) image score is calculated for each respondent by summing all of the positive (negative) ratings given by that person. Positive ratings were stronger than negative ratings for predicting participation in drinking liquor, smoking marijuana, having sexual intercourse and exercising; negative ratings were stronger predictors for cigarette smoking and seat-belt use; negative and positive ratings were about equally important in predicting beer drinking and condom use. Overall predictability, as indicated

Table 20.4 *Standardized Regression Coefficients for Predicting Participation in Health-related Behaviors*

	Predictor variables		
Behavior	*Positive image score*	*Negative image score* [a]	*R²*
Beer	.32**	.27**	.29
Liquor	.46**	.13*	.31
Cigarettes	—	.41**	.14
Marijuana	.40**	.18**	.29
Sexual intercourse	.38**	—	.14
Condom use	.19	.19	.11
Exercise	.36**	.17**	.23
Seat-belt use	—	.20**	.05

* $p < .05$.
** $p < .01$.
[a] Because the negative ratings by definition carried a negative sign, higher scores reflected less negative (ie, more positive) ratings. Therefore, the regression coefficients would be expected to have a positive sign when predicting participation. This, in fact, occurred, as is shown in this column of the table.

by R^2, was highest for drinking liquor, drinking beer and smoking marijuana and was lowest for seat-belt use, which had a very skewed distribution for participation.

To gain additional perspective on the association between imagery and behavior, a second multiple regression analysis was performed to predict participation in each behavior (participation was again coded 0, 1 or 2). In this analysis, imagery was represented by the average rating given to the associations a person produced to a particular behavioral stimulus. Age and gender were also entered into the regression equation whenever they were statistically significant. Average image rating was always a highly significant predictor. The resulting R^2 values were similar to those in Table 20.4.

The regression equations resulting from this analysis were used to generate a behavioral participation index. The distribution of scores on this index was dichotomized at a point that maximized the combined number of correct predictions for never participating and frequently participating persons. The results are shown in Table 20.5 for three behaviors: drinking beer, sexual intercourse and condom use. Entries in the cells of the table are frequencies. The column headings differentiate those who fall below the cutting score (labeled 'no' for predicted non-participant) and those above the cutting score (labeled 'yes').

Table 20.5 indicates the degree of association between the predictions based on the regression equations and the self-reported frequencies of behavior. It is clear that there is quite a distinct separation between never participating and frequently participating persons. Among those who never participated in a behavior, some 77% to 91% had index scores below the cutting score. For example, 166 out of 182 or 91.2% of those who said they had not had sexual intercourse were below the cutting score. Among those who frequently participated in the behaviors, between 42% (sexual intercourse) and 82% (drinking beer) were categorized as participants. Adopting a lower cutting score for sexual intercourse would correctly classify 96% of those who reported frequent sexual intercourse and include 84% of those who reported occasional sexual intercourse, at the cost, however, of including in the predicted 'yes' category 60% of those who reported no sexual intercourse. Most of the predictability in these data came

Table 20.5 *Association Between Predicted and Self-reported Participation in Three Health-threatening Behaviors*

Self-report	Drinking beer [a] prediction		Sexual intercourse [b] prediction		Condom use [c,d] prediction	
	No	Yes	No	Yes	No	Yes
Never	108	11	166	16	56	17
Occasionally	110	73	61	30	47	23
Frequently	17	80	58	42	10	33

[a] Prediction equation included average image rating and age: $R^2 = .31$.
[b] Prediction equation included average image rating, gender and age: $R^2 = .20$.
[c] Prediction equation included average image rating and gender: $R^2 = .16$.
[d] Includes only those who had sexual intercourse during six months prior to survey.

from the average image-rating score. Deleting age and gender from the equations made only a small difference in the numbers.

The point of this exercise was not to validate a prediction equation; we used no holdout sample for cross-validation. Moreover, the sample of young adults in this study cannot be considered representative of other populations. Rather, the point was to illustrate the rather striking degree of association between the affective quality of five words or phrases, quickly written on a page, and self-reported participation in three important health-related behaviors.

DISCUSSION

The present study employed a word association technique to assess adolescents' thoughts and feelings associated with a variety of health-threatening and health-enhancing behaviors. The fact that the results are generally orderly and meaningful suggests that the association method provides a useful technique for investigating adolescents' thinking about health-related behaviors. In addition, the current study has demonstrated that the method is useful for eliciting positive and negative affect associated with adolescents' behaviors.

Previous work suggests that adolescents' participation in risky behaviors is instrumental in attaining specific goals and outcomes (Jessor, 1984). Findings from the current study are consistent with this view. For example, functional associations for drinking beer were fun, positive affective change, relaxation, arousal, sexual enhancement and social facilitation. These outcome associations are consistent with those identified in the literature on alcohol expectancies. In addition, the current study was successful in expanding the outcome expectancy literature by identifying outcomes and other image concepts that are associated with health-threatening behaviors other than alcohol consumption. For example, sexual intercourse was associated with positive outcomes such as fun, positive affective change, physical gratification and intimacy, as well as with negative outcomes such as social stigma, pain, disease and punishment.

Costa, Jessor and Donovan (1989) suggested that health-enhancing behaviors during adolescence may be associated with outcomes aside from physical well-being. Findings from the present study support this suggestion. For example, although exercising was associated with improved physical health, it was predominantly associated with fun. In fact, out of 852 images given in response to exercising that were classified as positive outcomes, 656 pertained to outcomes other than physical health (eg, fun, positive affective change, social facilitation, improved physical appearance). In addition, the current study was able to identify some of the negative outcomes adolescents associate with health-enhancing behaviors. For example, seat-belt use was associated with social stigma and physical danger (eg, being trapped in case of an accident).

Previous studies have suggested that different risk-taking behaviors may serve similar functions for the adolescent (Jessor, 1984; Mechanic, 1979). The present study was unique in that it focused on several risk behaviors and thus allowed a comparison of associations across these behaviors. The results showed considerable overlap among the positive outcomes associated with the five health-threatening behaviors. For example, 'fun' and 'social facilitation' were associated with all five health-threatening behaviors. This supports the idea that different risk-taking behaviors may indeed serve similar psychological functions and therefore carry similar meaning for the adolescent.

There was also uniqueness in the imagery. Among positive outcomes, relaxation was most frequently associated with cigarettes and marijuana. Positive outcomes were quite different for each of the three health-enhancing behaviors. Patterns of negative outcomes were also quite different across the various behaviors we studied.

Previous research on outcome expectancies and risk perceptions has indicated that those who participate in a health-threatening behavior are more likely to anticipate positive outcomes and less likely to anticipate harmful consequences of the behavior than those who do not participate (Benthin et al, 1993; Brown et al, 1987). Consistent with previous findings, the current study found participants in risky behavior to be much more likely than non-participants to associate the behavior both with positive outcomes and positive concepts. Participants were also less likely than non-participants to associate negative concepts and negative outcomes with the behavior. These relationships held for the affective coding of responses by the participants as well as for the affective categorization performed by the investigators.

Research exploring the antecedents of adolescents' risk-taking behavior typically has focused on the role of cognition. The finding that the affective quality of imagery served as a strong predictor for participation in health-threatening and health-enhancing behaviors suggests that affect also plays an important role in adolescent risk taking.

Implications for Future Research

A number of directions for research are indicated by the present findings. For example, it would be of interest to investigate whether adolescents differ from adults with respect to the images and associations associated with health-threatening and health-enhancing behaviors. In addition, adolescents may value some of the possible outcomes differently than do adults.

Another direction for research lies in longitudinal research. Adolescents who engage in a given health-threatening or health-enhancing behavior may adjust their associational imagery to be consistent with their actions. In addition, some kinds of positive outcomes of health-threatening behaviors may only become accessible to participants in these activities while negative outcomes may be evident to both participants and non-participants. Only smokers, for example, may know much about the relaxing effects of smoking. Longitudinal studies should be conducted to assess the development of imagery and to determine whether the imagery specific to a given health-threatening or health-enhancing behavior occurs prior to participation in the behavior (thus enabling it to be used to predict the onset), or whether it occurs after the behavior has begun.

Implications for Prevention/Intervention Programs

The finding that health-threatening behaviors were associated with specific positive outcomes for adolescents engaging in these behaviors has implications for programs designed to deter adolescents from engaging in risk behavior. Such programs should acknowledge that risk behavior fulfills important functions for adolescents and, therefore, offers less hazardous means to meet adolescents' needs.

Adolescents' positive affect toward health-threatening behaviors also carries important implications for educational programs. For example, Ross, Lepper and Hubbard (1975) demonstrated that affect often persists even after complete invalidation of its original cognitive basis. Consequently, educational programs need to determine how to address affective as well as cognitive components in adolescents' behaviors.

Finally, where specific images and feelings are linked to participation in health-related behaviors, advertising and other messages can be evaluated to see whether they change imagery in a desirable or undesirable manner. For example, for years cigarette companies have said that their advertisements are not designed to make smoking more attractive to young people. The imagery analysis presented here provides a method for testing the impact of such advertising.

ACKNOWLEDGMENT

This study was sponsored by a grant from the Alcoholic Beverage Medical Research Foundation.

21   Technological Stigma

Robin Gregory, James Flynn and
Paul Slovic

The word 'stigma' was used by the ancient Greeks to refer to a mark placed on an individual to signify infamy or disgrace. A person thus marked was perceived to pose a risk to society. Within the social sciences, there exists an extensive literature on the topic of stigma as it applies to people (eg, Goffman, 1963; Jones et al, 1984). By means of its association with risk, the concept of stigma recently has been generalized to technologies, places and products that are perceived to be unduly dangerous.

Stigma plays out socially in opposition to many technological activities, particularly those involving the use of chemicals and radiation, and in the large and rapidly growing number of lawsuits claiming that one's property has been devalued by perceptions of risk. For example, in 1993 in *Criscuola et al versus New York Power Authority* (1993), the New York State Court of Appeals ruled that landowners whose property is taken for construction of high-voltage power lines can collect damages if the value of the rest of their property falls because of public fears about safety, regardless of whether that fear is reasonable. In *City of Santa Fe versus Komis* (1992), the Supreme Court of New Mexico in 1992 upheld the award of $337,815 to a Santa Fe couple for diminished property value resulting from the proximity of their land to a proposed transportation route for transuranic wastes. These and other similar cases have received national attention because they explicitly link public perceptions of a technological hazard with monetary compensation for a possible future decline in economic value.

This form of stigma has risen to prominence as a result of increasing concern about the human and ecological health risks associated with the use of technology. But stigma goes beyond conceptions of hazard. It refers to something that is to be shunned or avoided not just because it is dangerous but because it overturns or destroys a positive condition; what was or should be something good is now marked as blemished or tainted. As a reporter for *Time Magazine* commented in reference to a food contamination scare, 'The most deep-seated fears are

Note: reprinted from 'Technological Stigma' by R Gregory, J Flynn & P Slovic, 1995, *American Scientist*, 83(3), pp220–3. Copyright 1995 by Sigma Xi. Reprinted with permission.

engendered when the benign suddenly turns menacing' (Carlson, 1989, p24). As a result, technological stigmatization is a powerful component of public opposition to many proposed new technologies, products and facilities. It represents an increasingly significant factor influencing the development and acceptance of scientific and technological innovations and, therefore, presents a serious challenge to policy-makers.

Stigma reminds us that technology, like the Roman god Janus, offers two faces: one shows the potential for benefit, the other shows the potential for risk. The existence of stigma reflects a widespread social concern about the risks from technology and provides evidence of an expectation that has not been met or a reputation that has become tarnished.

In this sense, scientific and technological prestige might be viewed as the opposite of stigma. For example, the fierce nationwide competition for the superconducting supercollider project was motivated, in part, by the prestige of hosting one of the world's most advanced scientific and technological research facilities. This shows that stigma is not an inevitable outcome of technological advance; it exists only when something has gone awry, so that prestige is replaced by fear and disappointment.

CHARACTERISTICS OF STIGMA

The impetus for stigmatization is often some critical event, accident or report of a hazardous condition. This initial event sends a strong signal of abnormal risk. Kasperson et al (1988) have shown that the perceived risks of certain places, products and technologies are amplified by the reporting power of the mass media. Negative imagery and negative emotional reactions become closely linked with the mere thought of the product, place or technology, motivating avoidance behavior. A theoretical model developed by Slovic, Layman and Kraus et al (1991) demonstrates how images of a place or product affect its desirability or undesirability, consistent with models used in the marketing and advertising world.

Stigmatized places, products and technologies tend to share several features. The source of the stigma is a hazard with characteristics, such as dread consequences and involuntary exposure, that typically contribute to high perceptions of risk (Slovic, 1987). Its impacts are perceived to be inequitably distributed across groups (eg, children or pregnant women are affected disproportionately) or geographical areas (one city bears the risks of hazardous waste storage for an entire state). Often the impacts are unbounded, in the sense that their magnitude or persistence over time is not well known. A critical aspect of stigma is that a standard of what is right and natural has been violated or overturned because of the abnormal nature of the precipitating event (crude oil on pristine beaches and the destruction of valued wildlife) or the discrediting nature of the consequences (innocent people are injured or killed). As a result, management of the hazard is brought into question with concerns about competence, conflicts of interest or a failure to apply proper values and precautions. Specific examples of technological stigmatization demonstrate the importance of these features and the sometimes devastating effects of stigma.

Public evaluations of advanced technologies tend to be ambiguous, are often inaccurate and can, as such, contribute to the stigmatization of the technologies. It is not surprising that nuclear energy – touted so highly in the 1950s for its promise of cheap, safe power – is today subject to severe stigmatization, reflecting public perceptions of abnormally great risk, distrust of management and the disappointment of failed promises. Certain products of biotechnology also have been rejected in part because of perceptions of risk; milk produced with the aid of bovine growth hormone (BGH, or bovine somatotrophin, BST) is one example, with many supermarket chains refusing to buy milk products from BGH-treated cows (Elmer-Dewitt, 1994). Startling evidence of stigmatization of one of the modern world's most important classes of technology comes from studies by Slovic and others asking people to indicate what comes to mind when they hear or read the word 'chemicals'. The most frequent response tends to be 'dangerous' or some closely related term such as 'toxic', 'hazardous', 'poison', or 'deadly' (Slovic, 1992; Slovic, Flynn, Mertz et al, 1993).

Stigmatization of places has resulted from the extensive media coverage of contamination at sites such as Times Beach, Missouri, and Love Canal, New York. Other well-known examples of environmental stigmatization include Seveso, Italy, where dioxin contamination following an industrial accident at a chemical plant resulted in local economic disruptions estimated to be in excess of $100 million, and portions of the French Riviera and Alaskan coastline in the aftermath of the *Amoco Cadiz* and *Exxon Valdez* oil spills. The impacts of environmental stigma have been well documented by Edelstein (1988).

Because stigmatization is based on perceptions of risk, places can suffer stigma in advance of or in the absence of any demonstrated physical impacts. More than a dozen surveys we conducted in Nevada during the past decade show that a majority of Nevadans are worried that the Las Vegas tourist industry might suffer from negative imagery associated with plans to construct the nation's first geologic repository for high-level nuclear wastes at nearby Yucca Mountain (Flynn et al, 1991; Slovic, Layman and Kraus et al, 1991). In Tennessee, opposition by the governor and state legislature to a locally supported monitored retrievable storage (MRS) facility for high-level nuclear wastes was based on their fear that announcement of the facility would impose a negative and economically harmful image on the Oak Ridge region (Sigmon, 1987). The governors of Utah and Wyoming have both cited potential tourism losses as reasons for rejecting proposals for locating an MRS facility in their states (Leavitt, 1993; Sullivan, 1992).

The stigmatization of products has resulted in severe losses stemming from consumer perceptions that the products were inappropriately dangerous. A dramatic example is that of the pain reliever Tylenol. Mitchell (1989) estimated that, despite swift action on the part of the manufacturer, Johnson and Johnson, the seven tampering-induced poisonings that occurred in 1982 cost the company more than $1.4 billion. Another well-known case of product stigmatization played out in the spring of 1989, when millions of consumers stopped buying apples and apple products because of their fears that the chemical Alar (used then as a growth regulator by apple growers) could cause cancer. Apple farmers saw wholesale prices drop by about one third and annual revenues decline by more than $100 million (Rosen, 1990).

PUBLIC POLICY IMPLICATIONS

Technological stigma raises the specter of gridlock for many important private and public initiatives. The current practice of litigating stigma claims under the aegis of tort law does not seem to offer an efficient or satisfactory solution but rather points to a lack of policy options.

Project developers can, of course, simply pay whatever is asked for as compensation. However, for several reasons this option seems unwise. First, the pay-and-move-on option fails to distinguish between valid claims for compensation and strategic demands based on greed or politically motivated attempts to oppose a policy or program. Second, claims are often made for economic losses predicted to take place years or even decades into the future, despite the many difficulties inherent in forecasting future economic activities or social responses. Finally, this option fails to help us learn, as a society, to understand stigma and to manage it more effectively.

Another option is for proponents or developers to abandon projects threatened by stigma. This would be unfortunate in the many cases where the risks of proceeding are in fact reasonable. Our society's continued economic and social strength depends on its willingness to accept reasonable risks. The search for safer means to store hazardous wastes and to produce new goods for the marketplace requires us to face difficult trade-offs between new and old sources of risks, costs and benefits.

One recent response has been to restrict communications that might produce or contribute to stigma. Apple growers in Washington State are suing CBS for broadcasting what they claim were false messages about Alar on the network's '60 Minutes' program. The Alar scare has led the Florida legislature to pass a bill allowing Florida growers to sue anyone who says in public that fruits, vegetables and other food products are unsafe for consumption but who cannot substantiate their claims with scientific evidence (Associated Press, 1994). Whatever their merits for specific cases, these anti-disparagement efforts are problematic for policy because they threaten the constitutional right of free speech and may inadvertently limit the ability of people and the media to discuss legitimate concerns about the safety of a product or technology.

Stigma effects might be lessened if public fears could be addressed effectively through risk-communication efforts. However, such a simple solution seems unlikely. In our view, risk communication efforts often have been unsuccessful because they failed to address the complex interplay of psychological, social and political factors that creates a profound mistrust of government and industry and results in high levels of perceived risk (Flynn, Slovic & Mertz, 1993; Slovic, 1993).

We believe the best response is to recognize that stigma is the outcome of widespread fears and perceptions of risk, lack of trust in the management of technological hazards, and concerns about the equitable distribution of the benefits and costs of technology. Technological stigma should be seen as a rational social response to the multiple influences that produce it and therefore as subject to a variety of rational solutions. These solutions must involve thoughtful public policies and active public support. Adopting more open and participatory decision processes could provide valuable early information about potential sources of stigmatization and invest the larger community in understanding and managing technological hazards. This approach might even remove the basis for the blame and outrage that often occurs in the event of an accident or problem. Rather than being seen as unethical or evil, an industry might be viewed as unlucky or even shortsighted, avoiding the moral tainting that exacerbates a stigmatizing event. The active involvement of stakeholders, for example, might have enabled the nuclear industry to begin at a much earlier stage to plan for the disposal of nuclear wastes and to operate within a much less adversarial process.

In recent years, Rodney Fort and others have discussed the idea of offering insurance against the realization of potential stigma effects (Fort, Rosenman & Bud, 1993; Kunreuther, 1987). We are not aware of any currently existing stigma-insurance markets. However, improvements over time in the ability of researchers to identify and define those factors contributing to stigmatization may make it possible to predict the magnitude or timing of expected economic losses. This could open the door to the creation of new insurance markets and to efforts for mitigating potentially harmful stigma effects.

In cases where fears are great and impacts are extraordinarily difficult to forecast, the developer may have to provide protection against potential losses from stigma. The creation of a stigma-protection option by the New Mexico state government, for example, could guarantee that the value of properties lying along the proposed nuclear waste transportation route would be maintained according to acceptable measures of the market. Such an indemnification strategy would provide an opportunity to monitor expected versus actual market behavior over time: will the average sale prices of homes near nuclear-waste transportation routes actually fall? Will buyers really go elsewhere? In addition, the existence of a program that guarantees market-based values for properties along a transportation route may in itself act to ease public fears and thereby diminish stigma.

Most importantly, the societal institutions responsible for risk management must meet public concerns and conflicts with new norms and new methods for addressing stigma issues. The goal should be to create arenas for resolving these conflicts based on values of equity and fairness. This undoubtedly will require a major reorientation for risk management, reducing the heavy reliance on technical expertise and creating new forms of partnership that allow the public expanded roles in decision-making and effective oversight of the risk-management process.

Over time, these and other new policy initiatives may decrease the significance of technological stigma. At the moment, however, stigma effects loom large. In some cases, technological stigma may be so strong as to rule out the use of entire technologies, products or places. The experience of the past decade has been difficult. The years ahead are likely to add to the growing list of technological casualties unless innovative public policy and risk-management processes are developed and implemented.

ACKNOWLEDGMENTS

This chapter has been funded by a grant from the Alfred P Sloan Foundation and a shared Public/Private Sector Initiative award to Decision Research from the National Science Foundation (Grant No SES-91-10592) and the Electric Power Research Institute.

22

Probability, Danger and Coercion: A Study of Risk Perception and Decision-making in Mental Health Law

Paul Slovic and John Monahan

Analyses of how people perceive risk of harm and how they make decisions based on those perceptions have proven fruitful in many topical areas such as the management of technological and natural hazards (eg, Krimsky & Golding, 1992; National Research Council, 1989; Slovic et al, 1974) and promotion of safe sex, use of seat belts and other personal protective behaviors (Weinstein, 1987a). One area in which, to date, risk perception and decision-making methodologies have not often been applied is mental health law (see Wexler & Winick, 1991, for an exception). This is unfortunate, since some of the key issues in mental health law appear highly amenable to being enlightened by a risk-perception and decision-making framework. In this chapter, we explore the manner in which people perceive one kind of risk – the risk that a person with a mental disorder will be violent – and the effects of those perceptions on their willingness to impose involuntary mental hospitalization on the individual.

Perhaps the clearest example of an issue in mental health law that might be illuminated by a risk-perception and decision-making framework is what has come to be known as 'the dangerousness standard' for involuntary mental hospital admission. In 1969, California changed its legal test for admitting a person to a mental hospital against his or her will: the person must be mentally disordered and 'dangerous to self or others' (see Brooks, 1978). Most states have adopted the California 'dangerous' language (Brakel, Parry & Weiner, 1985), but others refer to the 'likelihood' that the individual will cause 'serious harm' (Brakel et al, 1985, p34). The American Psychiatric Association (1983) recommends similar language – 'likely to cause harm to others' – in one of its model tests for civil commitment. The National Center for State Courts' Guidelines

Note: Reprinted from 'Probability, Danger and Coercion' by P Slovic & J Monahan, 1995, *Law and Human Behavior*, 19(1), pp49–65. Copyright 1995 by Plenum Publishing Corporation. Reprinted with permission.

for Involuntary Civil Commitment (1986), on the other hand, speaks of 'predictions of violence', and the American Bar Association (1989) recommends that the civil commitment of persons acquitted of crime by reason of insanity be limited to those who are mentally disordered and 'as a result, pose a substantial risk of serious bodily harm to others' (Standard 7–7.3). Finally, one influential court decision phrased the issue in terms of a 'high probability of substantial injury' (*Cross versus Harris*, 1969, p1097).

'Dangerousness', 'likelihood', 'prediction', 'risk' and 'probability', therefore, have been used interchangeably to refer to the undesirable outcomes that are anticipated to occur if some mentally disordered persons are left at liberty. However, the extensive literature in the area of risk perception and behavioral decision theory has uncovered many subtle and anomalous effects which suggest that these various terms may not be fungible. They may, in fact, have differential effects on the judgments that are rendered by clinicians and courts (eg, Slovic, Fischhoff & Lichtenstein, 1982a). The equivalence of concepts such as probability of doing harm and dangerousness is examined in the present study.

A second pivotal issue in mental health law that follows directly from the 'dangerousness standard' issue is the use of the coercive power of the state to impose mental health treatment (Bennett et al, 1993). Once a person is perceived as mentally disordered and as dangerous – the legal test for commitment in most American states – a decision must be made as to whether he or she is 'sufficiently' mentally disordered and dangerous to qualify for involuntary mental hospitalization, unless the person voluntarily admits him or herself into the hospital (Hoge et al, 1993; Rogers, 1993).

The present study represents an initial attempt to provide insight into two questions fundamental to the relationship between dangerousness and coercion in mental health law:

1   How are judgments of probability of doing harm and dangerousness formed, and to what extent are these two concepts equivalent?
2   How much danger is enough danger to trigger coercive intervention?

STUDY 1

Method

Hypothetical case vignettes were constructed from the following eight dichotomous cues:

1   gender (M/F);
2   prior hospitalization (1 or 3);
3   delusions (no/yes);
4   prior assaultiveness (never/yes);
5   anger (often/rarely);
6   impulsivity (frequent/seldom);
7   psychopathy (little empathy or concern/much empathy or concern); and
8   social support (many friends and family members/few friends and family members).

These cues are believed to be, in fact, related to the likelihood of future violence. They are among the cues being researched in the MacArthur Risk Assessment Study (Steadman et al, 1994). There are 256 patterns of 'cases' that can be formed from all 2^8 combinations of these cues. Thirty-two of these patterns were selected for study, based on a $\frac{1}{8}$ fractional replication design. Across these 32 cases, all pairs of cues are uncorrelated and each one takes each of its two levels 16 times. In addition to the eight cues, each case was assigned an age (between 25 and 29 years) and occupation. One of the 32 cases is given at the beginning of Appendix A. Participants were told that each vignette provided a brief description of a person who has been examined by a psychiatrist or psychologist and has been diagnosed as having some form of mental illness.

Participants were asked to make three consecutive judgments about each vignette, as shown in Appendix A. First, they were asked to indicate 'the probability that this person will harm someone else during the three years following the examination'. This judgment, designated P_h was made on an 11-category scale ranging from 0 (*no chance*) to 100 (*certain to harm*) in increments of 10.

Second, participants were asked to indicate whether they would describe the patient as dangerous (yes or no). Finally, they were asked whether they believed coercion should be used to ensure hospitalization and treatment for the patient in the event that the patient refused to enter the hospital. This, too, was a dichotomous judgment (yes or no). The judgments of dangerousness and coercion will hereafter be labeled D and C, respectively.

A second group of participants judged the 32 cases in the same three ways except that the probability scale included five small probabilities: less than 1 chance in 1000, 1 in 1000, 1%, 2%, and 5%. These changes were made to allow the respondent to differentiate at the low end of the probability scale instead of being forced to use either 0% or 10% to express a small probability. In addition, the high end of the scale was labeled 'greater than 40%'. The instructions for this scale are shown in Appendix B. Hereafter, we shall differentiate the two probability formats by referring to the first as condition LP (for large probability) and the second as condition SP (for small probability).

In a medical judgment task, Mazur and Merz (1994) found that use of a small-probability scale (such as that used in condition SP) led to much lower probabilities being assigned to complications from surgery described as 'rare' (in comparison with results obtained from a scale such as that in condition LP). It is important, therefore, to examine possible probability scale effects in the present study.

Participants

Participants were 95 women and 96 men who answered an advertisement in the University of Oregon student newspaper. Most of these individuals were university students. Their mean age was 21 years (range = 18 to 49 years). They were paid for participating in the study. Ninety-five participants judged the vignettes using the 0 to 100 probability scale (condition LP) and 96 used the scale that allowed various small probabilities to be assigned (condition SP).

Results

Probability and dangerousness judgments

Table 22.1 presents the relationship between judged probability of harming someone (denoted P_h) and the judgment of dangerousness in condition LP. It is apparent that there is a close functional relationship between these two judgments. When judged probability of harm is .20 or less, the person is rarely judged dangerous. When the judged probability is .70 or greater, dangerousness is almost always ascribed to the individual in the vignette. As P_h increases from .20 to .70, the probability that the label 'dangerous' will be assigned increases quite rapidly.

Table 22.1 presents group data, from all respondents in condition LP. What might the relationship look like for individual respondents? One possibility is that individual subjects will exhibit functions that look more or less similar to the group function. A second hypothesis is that the individual data resemble step functions, with the stimulus patient being judged not dangerous ($D = 0$) whenever judged probability of harm was less than some transition level (denoted P_{ht}) and dangerous whenever $P_h \geq P_{ht}$. After arranging all the P_h judgments in ascending order, a step function might look like this (hypothetical data):

Judge 1 P_h judgment   10   10   20   30   30   30   40   40   50   50   50

Dangerousness   0   0   0   1   1   1   1   1   1   1   1
judgment
                                                      ↑
                                                     P_{ht}

where 0 represents not dangerous and 1 represents dangerous, and the transition point (P_{ht}) occurs at .30.

Table 22.1 *Judgments of Probability, Dangerousness and Coercion in Condition LP*

Judged probability of doing harm	N	Percent of total judgments	Percent judged dangerous	Percent judged coerce
0	47	1.6	00	15
10	277	9.2	01	14
20	421	13.9	04	19
30	438	14.5	13	36
40	382	12.6	24	44
50	462	15.3	32	59
60	383	12.7	69	63
70	314	10.4	85	80
80	184	6.1	90	90
90	93	3.1	97	72
100	20	0.7	90	85
	3021			

Another judge might have a different transition point, say P_{ht} = .50, as in the following example:

Judge 2 P_h judgment   10   20   20   30   30   40   40   50   60   70

         Dangerousness   0   0   0   0   0   0   0   1   1   1
         judgment   ↑
                                                             P_{ht}

Combining data across judges whose step functions differ only with respect to the point of transition between not dangerous and dangerous could produce group data similar to the data in Table 22.1.

The step-function hypothesis was tested by examining respondents' dangerousness judgments to see whether they indeed made a clean transition as shown in the examples above. The 32 responses for each judge were coded as 0 (not dangerous) or 1 (dangerous) and arranged in a vector ordered in terms of the probability of harm judgments that preceded each dangerousness judgment, as in the examples just given.[1] Guttman's *coefficient of reproducibility* (Guttman, 1944) was computed to indicate the percent of responses that would have to be changed in order to produce a perfect step function for each respondent. This was done for each respondent. The results provided strong support for the step-function hypothesis. The median coefficient of reproducibility was .93; 64 of 86 participants (74%) had coefficients of .88 or greater, meaning that reversal of 3 or fewer responses out of 32 would give them a perfect step function relating P_h to D.

Examination of the transition values of P_h calculated for subjects with coefficients of reproducibility above .88, indicated that the switch from not dangerous to dangerous occurred as low as P_h = .30 for some respondents and as high as P_h = .90 for others, with median and modal value being P_h = .60.

Examination of the step function relationship between P_h and D for individual subjects showed that virtually all had the characteristics of the hypothetical step functions shown earlier. That is, there were multiple values of P_h assigned to patients judged not dangerous (up to the threshold possibility), and multiple values of P_h within the set of patients judged as dangerous (ie, above the threshold). Thus, whereas a judgment of probability leads rather precisely to a judgment of dangerousness, the converse does not hold. Judgments of dangerousness do not lead to a precise judgment of probability.

Coercion judgments

The relationship between coercion judgments (C) and judged P_h is also shown in Table 22.1. The relationship between P_h and C would be S-shaped if plotted. Some patients (15%) were judged in need of coercion even when P_h = 0 and some (again 15%), for whom P_h was 100, were not judged to need coercion.

An analysis was carried out to determine whether the relationship between P_h and coercion could also be modeled by a step function. Twenty-three participants could not be modeled because they did not vary their judgment across cases. Of the remaining 73 participants, only 58% had coefficients of reproducibility ≥ .88

Table 22.2 *Dangerousness and Coercion in Condition LP*

		Coerce		
		No	Yes	
Dangerous	No	70.4	29.6	63.0
	Yes	19.2	80.8	37.0
		51.4	48.6	$N = 3027$

Note: Cell entries are row percentages. For example, of those who judged a patient not dangerous, 70.4% did not believe the patient should be coerced.

for coercion (compared to 74% for the dangerousness judgments). The median coercion threshold was .60 for these individuals, the same median as the dangerousness threshold.

We next examined the relationship between the two dichotomous judgments, dangerousness and coercion, for each of the 32 stimulus cases. The relationship is shown in Table 22.2. Table 22.2 indicates that across all respondents, the mental patient was judged dangerous in 37.0% of the cases and was judged in need of coercion in 48.6% of the cases. There was a strong relationship between dangerousness and coercion judgments. However, patients judged not dangerous were still judged in need of coercion in 29.6% of the cases and patients judged dangerous were not judged in need of coercion 19.2% of the time, indicating that dangerousness was not the sole criterion for the coercion judgment.

Influence of the P_h response scale

In condition LP, P_h was judged by marking an 11-point scale from 0 to 100 in units of 10. This scale gave the judge no opportunity to provide small values of P_h other than 0 or 10. What happened to judgments of P_h, D and C, and the relationship between them in condition SP, in which the scale was changed to allow distinctions to be made among small values of P_h?

Table 22.3 gives the distribution of P_h judgments and the proportion of cases at each P_h level that were judged dangerous and in need of coercion in condition SP. If we compare this table with the data from condition LP in Table 22.1, we see an immense effect due to the change in the probability response scale. Condition SP offered six probability response categories equal to or less than 10% (< 1/1000, >1/1000, 1%, 2%, 5% and 10%), and these six categories accounted for 67.7% of the total responses. This can be compared to 10.8% of cases assigned a $P_h \leq 10$ in condition LP. Offering small-probability responses led our subjects to make many more assignments of small values of P_h. Across the 32 case vignettes, the mean probability of doing harm was .44 in condition LP and .12 in condition SP.[2]

The relationship of dangerousness judgments and coercion judgments to P_h was also greatly altered by the change in response scale. For example, when $P_h =$ .10, only 1% of the cases in condition LP were judged dangerous and only 14%

Table 22.3 *Judgments of Probability, Dangerousness and Coercion in Condition SP*

Judged probability of doing harm	N	Percent of total judgments	Percent judged dangerous	Percent judged coerce
< 1/1000	148	4.8	00	18
1/1000	244	8.0	04	19
1%	406	16.0	09	17
2%	407	13.3	12	20
5%	457	15.0	18	35
10%	323	10.6	25	55
15%	250	8.2	31	46
20%	186	6.1	42	56
25%	151	4.9	64	64
30%	168	5.5	77	74
35%	102	3.3	85	77
40%	104	3.4	97	61
> 40%	105	2.6	95	81
	3051			

were judged in need of coercion (see Table 22.1), compared to 25% judged dangerous and 55% coerced in condition SP when $P_h = .10$ (Table 22.3). Similar differences between conditions LP and SP occurred when P_h was .20, .30 and .40.

Table 22.3 shows that the relationships between P_h and D and between P_h and C were strongly affected by the response categories for P_h. Does the overall incidence of dangerous and coercion judgments also change? The answer to this question is 'yes'.

There were fewer judgments of dangerousness in condition SP (30.5% versus 37.0%). Coercion judgments were also less frequent in condition SP (40.4% versus 48.6%). However, the relationship between dangerousness and coercion was quite similar within each condition. Of those judged dangerous in condition SP, 79.4% were judged in need of coercion (compared to 80.8% in condition LP); of those judged not dangerous in condition SP, only 22.3% were judged in need of coercion (compared to 29.6% in condition LP).

Would the step-function relationships between P_h and D and P_h and C hold as well for condition SP, with its many small probabilities? The step-function model fit the dangerousness judgments moderately well, as indicated by the fact that 67% of the respondents had coefficients of reproducibility equal to or greater than .88. As in condition LP, precise step functions were less frequent among the coercion judgments, with only 53% of the subjects exhibiting coefficients $\geq .88$.[3]

The respondents in condition SP whose judgments were well fitted by step functions had threshold values that were similar for both dangerousness and coercion. The switch from not dangerous to dangerous and from do not coerce to coerce occurred as low as $P_h = 1/1000$ for some respondents and as high as $P_h > 40$ for others. The median threshold was .20 for both types of judgments. These median thresholds were considerably lower than the median threshold of .60 obtained for both dangerousness and coercion using the 0, 10, 20 ... 100 response scale in condition LP. In both conditions, the median threshold was about 60% up the length of the scale.

Condition SP, with its numerous small-probability response categories, caused many more judges to rate all 32 cases as not dangerous and all cases as not in need of coercion. Specifically, the percentage of respondents judging all 32 cases as 'not dangerous' was 17.7% in condition SP and 3.2% in condition LP. The percentage of respondents wanting none of the 32 cases coerced was 19.8% in condition SP and 9.5% in condition LP.

Case-by-case mean values of P_h, D and C were computed by averaging across all judges in each condition (LP and SP). The mean P_h value was far higher in condition LP for every case. However, the percentage of judges who rated a case as dangerous or in need of coercion was not as dramatically different in the two conditions, despite the widely discrepant judgments of P_h. Take case 4, for example. The mean P_h was .51 in condition LP and only .13 in condition SP, yet the proportion of subjects who judged this patient as dangerous was .44 versus .32 in the two conditions, and the coercion percentages were .48 and .39, respectively.

Although the mean values of P_h varied greatly between conditions LP and SP, their relative magnitudes across cases were almost identical. The correlation between P_h in condition LP and in condition SP was .95. The correlation between the dangerousness percentages in the two conditions was also .95; for the two sets of coercion percentages it was .89. In sum, our respondents' probability responses were much higher in condition LP, but in a relative sense (relative to P_h in condition SP and to the dangerousness and coercion judgments) interrelationships across cases were changed little.

Modeling judgments of P_h, D and C

We developed an equation to predict the mean judgments of P_h, D and C for each case, based on a weighted additive combination of the eight attributes in the vignette (see, for example, Hoffman, Slovic & Rorer, 1968). Because the 32 cases were constructed by means of a fractional replication design, pairs of attributes are uncorrelated and standardized regression weights for each of the eight attributes are equivalent to the correlations between the attributes and the judgments across the 32 vignettes. These weights are shown in Table 22.4,

Table 22.4 *Standardized Weights in Linear Models to Predict Mean Judgments in Conditions LP and SP*

Judgment:	Condition LP			Condition SP		
	P_h	D	C	P_h	D	C
R^2	.96	.92	.90	.90	.92	.85
Gender	−.11	−.14	−.08	−.04	−.09	−.09
Prior hospitalization	.14	.06	.13	.23	.16	.35
Delusions	.19	.20	.37	.24	.28	.29
Assaultiveness	.77	.78	.72	.69	.68	.54
Anger	−.40	−.37	−.37	−.32	−.43	−.45
Impulsivity	−.21	−.20	−.14	−.23	−.25	−.25
Psychopathy	−.28	−.21	−.13	−.35	−.30	−.26
Social support	.16	.14	.21	.19	.09	.12

along with the R^2 value indicating the overall predictability of the mean judgments from the model. The results indicate that the 32 vignette means were highly predictable from these simple weighted additive models, with R^2 values ranging between .85 and .96. Prior assault was the most heavily weighted attribute in every model, with anger being next most important. Gender and support from friends and family were given relatively small weights. The models for P_h and D were quite similar. The weight given to delusions was substantially higher in the coercion model for condition LP, and slightly higher for the coercion model for condition SP. The weight given to prior hospital admissions was substantially higher in the coercion model for condition SP.

Discussion of Study 1

Study 1 produced a number of substantive findings relevant to the central issues of violence and coercion in mental health law. First, the judged probability that a patient will harm someone was strongly related to the judgment that the patient is 'dangerous'. Second, whereas group data on the relationship between judged probability of harm and dangerousness could be represented nicely by an S-shaped curve, the relationship appeared to be a step function for many of our individual subjects: below a given probability value, the patient was rarely designated dangerous, and above that value, the patient was almost always designated dangerous. That 'transition value' varied greatly across subjects, from as low as a .30 probability of harm to as high as a .90 probability of harm when the response options included larger probabilities, and from a probability of 1 in 1000 to .40 when the response options included smaller probabilities.

Third, the judged probability that a patient will harm another, and the ascription of dangerousness, were both strongly related to the judgment that the patient should, if necessary, be coerced into mental hospital admission. In the condition employing large probabilities, for example, subjects would coerce into treatment 29.6% of the patients seen as not dangerous, and 80.8% of the patients seen as dangerous.

Fourth, it was possible using attributes of the case vignettes to create highly accurate models to predict judgments of probability of harm, dangerousness and need to coerce. Prior assault was the most heavily weighted attribute, with anger being the next most important, in models predicting all three judgments. The three models were similar except that prior hospital admissions and the presence of delusions weighed more heavily in judgments that coercive treatment was necessary than in judgments of probability of harm or dangerousness.

Fifth, the response scale used to structure judgments of the probability of harm had an enormous effect on the judgments that were rendered. When two probabilities equal to or less than 10 (ie, 0 and 10) were provided, 10.8% of the cases were assigned to one of these categories. When six response options equal to or less than a 10% probability of harm were provided, those response categories together accounted for 67.7% of all responses. Rating probability of harm on a scale with small-probability options reduced the tendency to subsequently judge the patient as being dangerous and reduced the tendency to want coercion used. Scales with small probabilities seemed to induce more people never to label someone as dangerous and never to desire any patient to be coerced.

Although the numerical probability judgment was greatly affected by the response scale, mean judgments of probability for each case correlated quite highly (.95) across the 32 cases despite being elicited with two different response scales.

STUDY 2

Participants in study 1 had no professional expertise in judging the dangerousness of mental patients. It is perhaps not surprising that they exhibited little consistency in assigning probabilities to cases when the response scale was altered. Would mental health professionals behave similarly? We addressed this question in study 2, which was a partial replication of study 1.

Method

The participants in study 2 were 137 forensic clinicians (55% men, 45% women) attending the semiannual Forensic Symposium of the Institute of Law, Psychiatry and Public Policy at the University of Virginia. The majority of these clinicians (68%) were psychologists; 13% were psychiatrists and 11% were social workers. The number of years these people had been in practice ranged from 1 to 45 with a mean and median of 12 years.

Each participant was given the same task used in study 1 except that only the first eight of the 32 vignettes were included in the questionnaire. Seventy persons were assigned to condition LP; 67 were assigned to condition SP.

Results

Influence of the P_h response scale

Tables 22.5 and 22.6 present the distribution of responses in conditions LP and SP, respectively. As in study 1, the scale format had a strong influence on the judged values of P_h. In condition SP, the six response categories equal to or less than 10% accounted for 49.3% of the total responses. This contrasts sharply with the 20.0% of the cases assigned to $P_h \leq 10$ in condition LP. Offering small probability responses led even these professionals to make many more assignments of small values of P_h.

The relationship between dangerousness judgments and coercion judgments to P_h was also greatly altered by the change in response scale. In condition LP, few cases were judged dangerous or in need of coercion until P_h reached .50. In condition SP, the rapid increase in dangerousness and coercion judgments began when P_h reached 15. Additional perspective on the response-scale effect is gained by examining specific levels of P_h. For example, when $P_h = .20$, only 2% of the cases in condition LP were judged dangerous, and only 6% were judged in need of coercion, compared to 53% judged dangerous and 55% in need of coercion at $P_h = .20$ in condition SP. Providing small-probability response options greatly increased judgments of dangerousness and coercion at specific values of P_h.

Table 22.5 *Judgments of Probability, Dangerousness and Coercion in Condition LP, Study 2*

Judged probability of doing harm	N	Percent of total judgments	Percent judged dangerous	Percent judged coerce
0	17	3.0	00	12
10	95	17.0	00	11
20	87	15.5	02	06
30	69	12.3	10	19
40	39	7.0	13	15
50	66	11.8	41	44
60	53	9.5	74	55
70	65	11.6	74	75
80	36	6.4	83	75
90	30	5.4	83	80
100%	3	0.5	100	100
	560			

Table 22.6 *Judgments of Probability, Dangerousness and Coercion in Condition SP, Study 2*

Judged probability of doing harm	N	Percent of total judgments	Percent judged dangerous	Percent judged coerce
< 1/1000	8	1.5	00	12
1/1000	37	6.9	03	11
1%	52	9.7	00	06
2%	36	6.7	03	14
5%	76	14.1	05	14
10%	56	10.4	09	20
15%	36	6.7	25	28
20%	38	7.1	53	55
25%	36	6.7	61	55
30%	40	7.5	80	70
35%	22	4.1	55	64
40%	47	8.8	64	49
> 40%	47	8.8	83	77
	531			

As in study 1, there was a strong relationship between the two dichotomous judgments, dangerousness and coercion – and this relationship was almost identical in the two probability conditions. Moreover, despite the different values of P_h assigned in the two conditions, the overall percentage of cases judged dangerous and the percentage judged in need of coercion were almost identical in the two conditions (about 33% dangerous and 35% in need of coercion).

Table 22.7 *Mean Probability of Harm and Proportion of Dangerousness and Coercion Judgments in Study 2*

Case number	Condition LP			Condition SP		
	P_h	Danger	Coercion	P_h	Danger	Coercion
1	.15	.00	.03	.03	.01	.06
2	.62	.64	.69	.35	.57	.73
3	.52	.54	.55	.27	.45	.60
4	.52	.44	.34	.27	.55	.39
5	.63	.69	.62	.38	.74	.55
6	.22	.06	.11	.04	.03	.03
7	.26	.09	.31	.05	.03	.25
8	.39	.23	.17	.15	.29	.21
Mean	.41	.33	.35	.19	.33	.35

The case-by-case assignments of P_h, D and C across all judges in each condition are shown in Table 22.7. The mean value of P_h is considerably higher in condition LP for each case.[4] However, as in Study 1, the percentage of clinicians who judged a case to be dangerous or in need of coercion was not much different in the two conditions, despite the large mean differences in P_h. Across the eight cases, the mean values of P_h in the two conditions correlated .99, showing that the ordering was preserved although the mean values differed.

In study 1, condition SP appeared to cause more judges to rate none of the 32 cases as dangerous and none of the cases as needing coercion. This finding did not replicate with the experienced clinician respondents in study 2. The proportion of respondents who judged none of the eight cases as dangerous or none in need of coercion was almost identical in the two response-scale conditions.

GENERAL DISCUSSION

The results of study 2, with experienced clinicians as participants, were remarkably similar to the results obtained in study 1, with naive participants. Together, these studies underscore the central importance of violence to others in current mental health law (Appelbaum, 1988). Whether expressed as 'probability of harm' or 'dangerousness', the higher a person's perceived risk of violence, the more likely that both the public and the clinicians will want the person treated in a mental hospital, coercively so if voluntary admission is refused.

At the same time, it should be recognized that violence, while a dominating concern, is not the only issue in involuntary hospitalization. In study 1, between one quarter and one third of the cases that were not judged as dangerous to others were nonetheless recommended as candidates for involuntary hospital admission (the comparable percentage in study 2 was about 15%). Among the attributes of these 'not dangerous to others, but coercible' cases in study 1 were the presence of delusional beliefs and multiple hospital admissions. Participants responding to such cases may have been concerned more with 'danger to self'. Such a *parens patriae* concern with danger to self (or the passive form of danger to self called 'grave disability') has always been part of mental health law (Monahan & Shah, 1989).

Perhaps the most striking result in the two studies was the effect of the response scale on judged probability of harm. A scale that finely differentiated among small probabilities led to far lower probabilities being assigned to the cases, much as had been found earlier in a medical judgment context (Mazur & Merz, 1994). The response-scale effect was almost as large among experienced clinicians in study 2 as with naive participants in study 1. Naive participants, who were induced by the response scale to assign lower P_h values to a case, were somewhat less likely to label the patient as dangerous or in need of coercion. However, the mental health professionals appeared immune to such influence. The likelihood that a clinician would judge a patient to be dangerous or in need of coercion was not systematically affected by the response scale and its effect on P_h.

Our respondents appear to have used the probability response scales as if they were rating scales, numbered from 1 to 11 or 1 to 13, with no meaning to the numbers other than their rank. This behavior is more than just a methodological artifact. It strongly implies that the concept 'probability of harm' was not represented in our respondents' minds in a consistent, quantitative way. The numbers circled on the probability scale appear to have been meaningless in an absolute sense, though they were consistent and meaningful in a relative sense. In other words, if a respondent circled 10% as the probability for case 1 and 20% for case 2, we can be confident that he or she perceived case 2 as having a greater probability of harming someone. We cannot have confidence in the values 10% and 20%. Small changes in response scale can cause these two cases to be judged as having very different values of P_h (although the order will likely be preserved).

If this interpretation of the response-scale effect is correct, it has profound implications for the manner in which risk assignments are formulated by psychiatrists and psychologists for use by the legal system. Judged probabilities that an individual will be violent cannot be trusted, except in an ordinal sense. It has long been advocated (eg, Monahan & Wexler, 1978) that mental health professionals offer courts their probability estimates that violent behavior will occur, and not impose summary labels of 'dangerous' or 'not dangerous' on these estimates. From our data, however, ascriptions of 'dangerousness' actually appear more stable than numerical judgments of probability! We do not, however, recommend a return to the era when clinicians offered conclusory statements about 'dangerousness' to courts. Rational decision-making must ultimately depend on an appreciation of the probability that the patient (or prospective patient) will become violent. To use an example from study 2 – with experienced clinician respondents – it should make a difference in decision-making, at least in the marginal case, whether the probability of violence is .27 or .52 (which were the obtained mean probabilities in conditions SP and LP, respectively, for vignette 4; see Table 22.7). Ordinal judgments alone (eg, 'Of the eight people I have recently evaluated, I would rank him as the third or fourth most likely to be violent', which was also true for vignette 4, in both conditions SP and LP) will not suffice.

Rather than resurrect the respectability of summary labels, the conclusion that numerical probability judgments by clinicians are unreliable points to the need for probability assessments guided by actuarial studies (eg, Klassen & O'Connor, 1988; Lidz, Mulvey & Gardner, 1993; Steadman et al, 1994). Indeed, if numerical probability judgments are as unstable as our studies have shown them to be, one might question the ethicality of making such judgments in a clinical setting without relying on actuarial guidelines, despite the acknowledged difficulties of the actuarial approach (Grisso & Appelbaum, 1992; 1993; Litwack, 1993).

Such a strong conclusion may, however, be premature. One can argue that study 2 placed clinicians at a severe disadvantage by asking them to rate hypothetical vignettes in an unnatural context. Clinicians, in their actual practice, judging real patients, might be better able to apply their knowledge and experience to the task of assessing probabilities. We suspect, however, that our well-structured hypothetical cases are easier to judge than are real patients, whose history and attributes are not so clearly defined. Nevertheless, it is important that additional studies be conducted to determine the impact of scale effects in the clinician's natural assessment setting.

Additional studies should also employ procedures for structuring the assessment task that have been found to facilitate probabilistic thinking. Such procedures range from instruction about the meaning of probability and practice in making probability judgments (eg, Fong, Krantz & Nisbett, 1986; Lichtenstein & Fischhoff, 1980; Morgan & Henrion, 1990) to asking about relative frequencies ('Of 100 patients with this set of characteristics or symptoms, how many would be violent?') instead of asking for the 'probability that this particular person will be violent' (eg, Cosmides & Tooby, 1996; Gigerenzer, 1994).

There may be other structural changes in the assessment task that would infuse quantitative meaning into clinicians' probability assessments. For example, assuming that the clinician could judge probability reliably at the ordinal level, he or she could be asked to insert the stimulus case into a probability scale whose numerical values were linked with (or calibrated against) other kinds of events, whose probabilities or relative frequencies were well known and agreed upon. Alternatively, the scale might be calibrated with verbal expressions of probability (Hamm, 1991) or descriptions of other 'marker' patients located on the scale by expert consensus.

In sum, the strong effect of scale format has important implications for research and practice in mental health law. It remains to be seen whether the continued use of quantitative clinical judgments of the probability of violent behavior can be justified.

POSTSCRIPT

Slovic, Monahan and MacGregor (2000) conducted a series of new studies to address some of the questions raised by the original Slovic and Monahan study described in this chapter. The new study replicated, with case summaries of actual patients as stimuli, the response-scale effects found by Slovic and Monahan (1995). Providing clinicians with response scales offering more smaller probabilities again led patients to be judged as posing lower probabilities of committing harmful acts. This format effect was not eliminated by having clinicians judge relative frequencies rather than probabilities or by providing them with instruction in how to make these types of judgments. In addition, frequency scales led to lower mean likelihood judgments than did probability scales but, at any given level of likelihood, a patient was judged as posing higher risk if that likelihood was derived from a frequency scale (eg, 10 out of 100) than if it was derived from a probability scale (eg, 10%). Similarly, communicating a patient's dangerousness as a relative frequency (eg, 2 out of 10) led to much higher perceived risk than did communicating a comparable probability (eg, 20%). The different reactions to probability and frequency formats appear to be attributable to the more frightening images evoked by frequencies and the reliance upon affect as a cue for making risk judgments (see Chapter 26).

These results have important implications for assessing and communicating the risk of violence (and other forms of risk as well). They suggest that probabilities and frequencies each come with a complex set of advantages and disadvantages. Neither is inherently superior to, or less susceptible to bias, than the other. One option, therefore, would be that clinicians employ *multiple* formats for communicating violence risk. For example, a risk communication might read: 'Of every 100 patients similar to Mr Jones, 20 are expected to be violent to others. In other words, Mr Jones is estimated to have a 20% likelihood of violence'. If multiple formats were used in violence risk communication, the biases associated with any given risk communication format might, at least to some extent, cancel each other.

A second option is that suggested by Monahan and Steadman (1996). They related violence prediction to weather prediction, as practiced by the National Weather Service. The Service communicates the risk of rarer and more severe events, such as tornadoes and hurricanes, by using a *categorical* format (eg, a hurricane 'watch' or a tornado 'warning'). Monahan and Steadman give illustrative examples of categorical violence risk communications, ranging from *Low violence risk* ('Few risk factors are present. No further enquiry into violence risk or special preventive actions is indicated'), to *Very high violence risk* ('Many key risk factors are present. Enough information is available to make a decision. Take preventive action now (eg, intensive case management or treatment, voluntary or involuntary treatment, and warning the potential victim)'). Of course, the decision maker who received such a categorical communication would also have to be informed about what behaviors constituted violence, what time period was at issue, what specific risk factors were present, and what cut-off scores were used to generate the risk categories.

As alternatives to the unsatisfactory choice between probability and frequency formats, the use of multiple formats, and of categorical formats, bears further empirical examination.

APPENDIX A

Case 1–6

TD, a 25-year-old male, is employed as a bus driver. Records reveal that this is his first admission to a mental hospital. He is not experiencing any delusional beliefs. Relatives report that he has never been assaultive in the past.

Among the characteristics of his personality noted in the mental health examination are that he rarely becomes very angry, that he seldom acts impulsively and that he has much empathy or concern for others.

TD has many friends and family members to help him with his problems.

- Please indicate your judgment of the probability that this person will harm someone during the three years following the examination. (Circle the appropriate probability.)

0   10   20   30   40   50   60   70   80   90   100

no   certain

chance   to harm

- Would you describe this individual as *dangerous*? (Check one.)
  - ☐   No.
  - ☐   Yes.
- Sometimes it is necessary to coerce a mentally disturbed person into entering a hospital and receiving treatment. If this person were to refuse hospitalization and treatment, do you believe that coercion should be used to ensure that proper treatment is received? (Check one.)
  - ☐   No. Do not coerce.
  - ☐   Yes. Coercion should be used.

APPENDIX B

One of the questions asks you to judge the probability that the person described would harm someone during the three years following the examination. The response scale begins with very low probabilities:

- less than 1 chance in 1000;
- 1/1000 (meaning 1 chance in 1000);
- 1% (meaning 1 chance in 100);
- 2% (meaning 2 chances in 100 or 1 chance in 50);
- 5% (meaning 5 chances in 100 or 1 chance in 20);

and progresses to higher probabilities, as shown below:

less than   1/1000 1% 2%   5% 10% 15% 20% 25% 30% 40%   greater

1 chance   than

in 1000   40%

Circle the appropriate probability for each case.

ACKNOWLEDGMENTS

This research was supported by the Research Network on Mental Health and the Law of the John D and Catherine T MacArthur Foundation. We are grateful to Paul Appelbaum, Thomas Grisso, Steven K Hoge, Sarah Lichtenstein, Allan Murphy and Henry Steadman for their comments on the manuscript, and to C K Mertz, Leisha Mullican and Kari Nelson for their assistance in data analysis and preparation of the manuscript.

NOTES

1   This analysis included only respondents who gave both kinds of judgments ($D = 0$ and $D = 1$). Nine persons who judged every one of the 32 cases identically were excluded because no threshold could be calculated for them.
2   When computing means in condition SP, responses $< 1/1000$ and $1/1000$ were assigned the value 0, and the response > 40 was assigned the value 70, which is above the median of the categories greater than 40 in condition LP (see Table 22.1).
3   As before, these analyses included only subjects who gave both kinds of judgments (D and $\bar{D}$ and C and $\bar{C}$). Twenty-six persons who judged all 32 cases identically with respect to dangerousness and 41 persons who judged all cases identically with respect to coercion were excluded because no threshold could be calculated for them.
4   Means for condition SP were computed as in study 1; see note 2.

23   Do Adolescent Smokers Know the Risks?

Paul Slovic

After many years of intense publicity about the hazards of smoking cigarettes, it is generally believed that every teenager and adult in the US knows that smoking is hazardous to one's health. Perhaps the best known empirical demonstration of this 'fact' comes from research by Viscusi on perceptions of risks from smoking as reported in several articles (Viscusi, 1990; 1991; 1998) and a book (Viscusi, 1992).

The data reported in Viscusi's book are derived from a national telephone survey of more than 3000 persons age 16 or older. Respondents were asked: 'Among 100 cigarette smokers, how many of them do you think will get lung cancer because they smoke?' The mean response was 43 out of 100, considerably higher than the actuarial rate of lung cancer among smokers. Viscusi thus concluded that people greatly overestimated the probability of a smoker getting lung cancer.[1] Viscusi's sample of respondents also overestimated overall mortality rates from smoking and loss of life expectancy from smoking. Moreover, young people aged 16 to 21 overestimated these risks to an even greater extent than did older people. Perceptions of risk from smoking were also found to be predictive of whether and how much people smoked, for young and old alike.

Viscusi has argued that these and other data support a rational learning model in which consumers respond appropriately to information, making trade-offs between the costs and benefits of smoking. With respect to young people, he concluded that his findings 'strongly contradict the models of individuals being lured into smoking at an early age without any cognizance of the risks' (Viscusi 1992, p143). Viscusi further concluded that young people are so well informed that there is little sense in informational campaigns designed to boost their awareness. Finally, he observed that social policies that allow smoking only after age 18 'run little risk of exposing uninformed decision-makers to the potential hazards of smoking' (p149). Viscusi's data and conclusions thus appear to lend support to the defense used by cigarette companies to fend off lawsuits from diseased smokers: these people knew the risks and made an informed, rational choice to smoke.

Note: reprinted with modifications from *Duke Law Journal*, 47(6), 1998, pp1133–41. Copyright 1998 by *Duke Law Journal*. Reprinted with permission.

In so concluding, Viscusi assumed that people's knowledge of the risks of cigarette smoking is adequately represented by their judgments that cigarettes will cause cancer (or some other disease) in *n* out of 100 smokers. I disagree with this assumption.

My disagreement is based on five failings I perceive in Viscusi's analyses. The first is the faulty assumption that one knows the 'risk' of an activity if one knows the *probability* of an adverse outcome of that activity, even if one does not fully comprehend the *severity* of such an outcome. The second is the failure to consider the optimism bias that leads people to see themselves as less at risk than others. The third is the fact that the quantitative judgments Viscusi elicits are unreliable. The fourth is the failure to consider the repetitive nature of cigarette smoking and the cumulative nature of its risks. The fifth is the failure to consider young people's misperceptions of the probability of becoming addicted to smoking.

Risk as Probability

Both laypeople and experts use the word 'risk' inconsistently, sometimes using it to mean a hazardous activity ('bungee jumping is a serious risk'), sometimes to mean an adverse consequence ('the risk of letting your parking meter expire is getting a ticket,)' and sometimes to mean probability ('What is the annual risk of death at age 80?'). It is this last concept, risk as probability, that Viscusi embraces when he equates risk perception with answers to the question: 'Among 100 cigarette smokers, how many of them do you think will get lung cancer because they smoke?'.

There is a fourth definition of risk that, to my mind, is more appropriate than any of the preceding three. According to this definition, 'risk' is a blend of the probability and the severity of consequences.

The inadequacy of equating risk with the probability of an adverse consequence is shown by data from Sjöberg (1999), who asked people to judge the relative risk from 43 adverse consequences. This form of questioning leads people to judge risk in terms of probability. As a result, in Sjöberg's study, 'trivial risks' such as the risk of getting a cold or being bothered by a drunk person in the subway emerged as the highest 'risks' of all, far higher than risks from smoking, alcohol, motor vehicles or AIDS. This is because the perceived probabilities of the trivial consequences were higher. In a subsequent study, the questions were rephrased to induce people to think also of the magnitude of a danger or threat and thus to attend to both probability and severity of consequences (eg, 'What is the risk of an activity that might lead to AIDS?' or 'What is the risk of an activity that might cause a cold?'). With these sorts of questions, hazards imposing trivial consequences were judged less risky than those associated with more serious consequences (Slovic, 1999).

My point is a simple one. Appreciating the risks of smoking means appreciating the nature of the consequences as well as the probabilities of those consequences. I have seen no evidence to show that young people have realistic knowledge of what it is like to experience lung cancer, chronic obstructive pulmonary disease, or any of the other fates awaiting smokers that many would consider 'worse than death'.

The difficulty of appreciating the unfamiliar consequences of one's decisions has long been recognized by doctors attempting to inform patients about treatment risks. For example, one can convey to a patient deciding whether to undergo a laryngectomy for throat cancer that it is almost certain that normal speech will be lost, but it is quite difficult to convey what it feels like to experience that loss. Do most patients adapt well to it? Are they satisfied or regretful after having that surgery? Personal contact or videotaped interviews with patients who are experiencing such outcomes appear to help convey the meaning of such outcomes (Barry, Fowler, Mulley, Henderson & Wennberg, 1995).

The Optimism Bias

Viscusi relies upon questions that ask individuals to judge the risks to '100 smokers', not the risks to themselves. Numerous studies have found that people consistently believe that their personal risk is less than the risk faced by others in the same situation (Weinstein, 1989). Research has not only demonstrated the existence of such 'optimistic biases' for a wide range of health and safety hazards, but has identified types of hazards for which biases are likely to be especially great (Weinstein, 1987b). Optimism biases are greatest for hazards judged to be controllable by personal action, such as lifestyle risks. Biases are also likely to be large when people think that signs of vulnerability will appear early, because people then think that an absence of present signs means they are exempt from future risks (Weinstein, 1987b). Because smoking fits in both of these categories, it is not surprising that strong optimism biases have been found in cigarette smokers (Lee, 1989; Segerstrom, McCarthy, Caskey, Gross & Jarvik, 1993; McKenna, Warburton & Winwood, 1993). Young smokers are highly likely to judge themselves as less at risk from cigarettes than they judge the 100 hypothetical smokers asked about in Viscusi's survey questionnaire.

Viscusi's Quantitative Judgments Are Unreliable

Viscusi's failure to take account of optimism bias pales in comparison with an even more serious deficiency: the quantitative estimates of risk that he relies upon for his conclusions are so heavily influenced by the wording and content of the elicitation questions as to be completely untrustworthy.

That quantitative estimates of probability and risk depend upon the way the question is asked has been known for a long time. Viscusi (1992) was even aware of this, citing a classic study by Fischhoff and MacGregor (1983) as a cautionary note. That study showed that judged lethality rates for diseases and accidents varied greatly across logically equivalent ways of eliciting responses. Viscusi attempted to test the sensitivity of his key question to such biases by conducting additional studies in which he varied the format slightly, asking, for example, how many of 1000 smokers could get lung cancer (rather than how many of 100). The fact that many people responded to this 1000 smoker question by giving a percentage, gave him false confidence in the robustness of his answers to the 100 smoker question.

Tversky and Koehler (1994) presented an impressive theoretical and empirical analysis of the tendency for probability judgments to be highly sensitive to the ways in which the events being evaluated are described. In one study they found that, focusing the respondent on only one outcome or one outcome set, as Viscusi did, leads to significant overestimation of the probability of that outcome.

The strong effect of outcome focusing is demonstrated in the following experiment I conducted with 49 students from the University of Oregon. Each student was given a two-page questionnaire. On page one they were asked to 'Consider 100 individuals, 50 men and 50 women, who smoke one pack of cigarettes per day for all of their adult lives.' Next, they were asked to 'Please make a judgment about how many of these 100 people are likely to die of lung cancer.' The mean response was *56* and the median response was *60*. Both values are at least as high as the values Viscusi has obtained in his surveys with similar focused questions.

On page two of the questionnaire, the same respondent was again asked to consider these 100 smokers and to judge how many of these people were likely to die from *each* of 15 causes of death (eg, car accident, homicide, suicide) including lung cancer (there was also an 'all other causes' category). These second estimates for lung cancer decreased for 45 of the 49 respondents, often precipitously (mean = *20* and median = *20*).[2] Moreover, the correlation between the estimate a person gave to lung cancer alone (page one) and the estimate given to lung cancer as part of a larger set (page two) was only .21.

The point of this exercise is to demonstrate that, consistent with the theoretical and empirical work of Tversky and Koehler, one can get almost any estimate one wishes for lung cancer (or other smoking-induced causes of death) simply by varying the number of other causes that are also being judged.

The Cumulative Nature of Risks from Smoking

Cigarette smoking takes place one cigarette at a time. A person smoking one pack of cigarettes every day for 40 years smokes about 300,000 cigarettes. I question whether most smokers appreciate how health risks from smoking accumulate across these many single acts. Little is known about this aspect of 'knowing a risk'. However, Diamond (1990), in an experimental study, found that subjects were more willing to expose themselves to a fictional risk from a chemical carcinogen described as cumulative ('the poison builds up in your body') than to take a statistically equivalent risk described as a series of independent exposures ('the poison does not build up – if a dose does not make you sick it will pass right through you without doing any harm'). It appeared that people making decisions about a cumulative hazard tended to believe that the first few exposures would be safe. This tendency was less apparent among subjects making decisions about independent exposures, despite the fact that both groups were told that the first five exposures would make the risk of succumbing to the toxin equal to 50%.

One might hypothesize that young people, like the experimental subjects in Diamond's study, believe they can get away with some amount of smoking before the risk takes hold. Adolescent smokers may tend to believe that smoking the 'very next cigarette' poses little or no risk to their health or that smoking for only a few years poses negligible risk. And there is evidence that young smokers are more prone to believe in the safety of short-term smoking than are young non-smokers. In the 1989 Teenage Attitudes and Practices Survey, 21% of smokers in the 12 to 18 age range said that they believed it was safe to smoke for only a year or two compared to 3% of those who had never smoked (Allen, Moss, Giovino, Shopland & Pierce, 1993).

I also tested this hypothesis in a survey of high-school students (grades 9 to 12) located in a small coastal town in Oregon. The survey asked whether the respondent smoked, and if so, how many cigarettes he or she smoked every day, on average. Next, respondents were asked to evaluate the following statements:

> Consider the following statements about the effects of a person's smoking one package of cigarettes each day, starting at age 16, and indicate whether you agree or disagree with each statement.
>
> 1 There is really no risk at all for the first few years.
> 2 Every single cigarette smoked causes a little bit of harm.
> 3 Although smoking may eventually harm this person's health, the *very next single cigarette* he or she smokes will probably not cause any harm.
> 4 Harmful effects of smoking rarely occur until a person has smoked steadily for many years.
> 5 Smoking at the daily rate of one package of cigarettes each day will eventually harm this person's health.

Respondents evaluated these statements on a scale labeled strongly agree, agree, disagree, strongly disagree and don't know/no opinion.

Figure 23.1 contrasts the survey responses of 50 smokers (defined as those who said they smoked six or more cigarettes per day), 48 light smokers (one to five cigarettes per day) and 223 non-smokers (zero cigarettes per day).

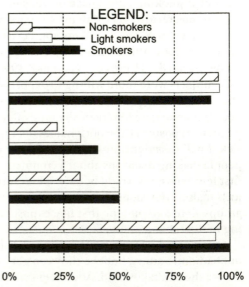

Figure 23.1 *Percent agreement for non-smokers, light smokers and smokers in response to statements about the risk of smoking*

Figure 23.1 indicates that almost every non-smoker and every smoker agreed that smoking a package of cigarettes each day will eventually harm a person's health (statement 5). High percentages of agreement were also found for the statement that every single cigarette smoked causes a little bit of harm (statement 2). However, the picture changes for each of the other questions pertaining to the near-term risks for smoking. The smokers in this study were considerably more likely than non-smokers to agree with statements denying short-term risks. Responses from light smokers fell between the responses of non-smokers and smokers for statements 1 and 3 and were equal to those of smokers for statement 4. Looking at statement 1 in Figure 23.1, we see that about one third of those who smoked more than six cigarettes per day believed that there is 're-ally no risk at all' from smoking a pack of cigarettes daily for the first few years after starting to smoke, and about 40% saw no harm associated with the very next cigarette smoked (statement 3). Fifty percent of the smokers believed that harmful effects of smoking rarely occur until a person has smoked steadily for many years (statement 4).

The results of this study verify the contention of cigarette manufacturers and the results of previous investigations by Viscusi (1992), Leventhal, Glynn and Fleming (1987), and others indicating that most young people acknowledge that extensive smoking is likely to harm one's health. Young smokers appear to acknowledge this to the same extent as non-smokers. However, the present study also demonstrates a degree of denial about the short-term risks from smoking – and this denial is considerably more prevalent among smokers.

The Risk of Addiction

Belief in the near-term safety of smoking may combine insidiously with a tendency of young smokers to underestimate or be uninformed about the difficulty of stopping smoking. Many young people regret their decisions to start smoking and unsuccessfully attempt to stop. The 1989 Teenage Attitudes and Practices Survey found that 74% of adolescent smokers reported they had seriously thought about quitting, and that 49% had tried to quit in the previous six months (Allen et al, 1993). A longitudinal survey conducted as part of the University of Michigan's Monitoring the Future Study (reported in US Department of Health and Human Services, 1994) found that high-school seniors, at all levels of cigarette consumption, greatly overestimated the likelihood that they would no longer be smoking five years after high-school (see Table 23.1). Among those smoking more than one cigarette per day during their senior year who predicted they would quit smoking in the next five years, fewer than half actually quit. Of those who smoked one to five cigarettes per day as seniors, only 30% had quit and 44% had actually increased their cigarette consumption. Other researchers found that adolescent smokers were less knowledgeable than their non-smoking peers about the problems of addiction (Leventhal et al, 1987).

Viscusi has argued that smokers are well informed and making rational decisions that are in their best interest, given their preferences. However, the high percentage of young smokers who say they have seriously thought about quitting contradicts this assertion. Further evidence for this change in perspective comes from a recent survey in which 58 University of Oregon students who

Table 23.1 *Smoking Prevalence Five Years After High-School by Senior-year Smoking Status*

Senior-year smoking	Percent who predicted they would not be smoking in five years	Percent actually not smoking five years later
< 1 cigarette/day	85%	58%
1 – 5 cigarettes/day	60%	30%
About half a pack/day	41%	18%
≥ 1 pack/day	32%	13%

Source: US Department of Health and Human Services (1994)

smoked cigarettes daily were asked: 'If you could go back to the time when you first began to smoke, would you decide to smoke again?' The answer was *no* for 55% of the smokers and *yes* for only 36%. Among those who had smoked for five years or more, 65% said they would not decide to smoke again compared to 27% who said they would (unpublished study by the author, May 1998). The fact that those who had smoked for a longer period of time and were still smoking were least satisfied with their decision attests to the difficulty they were having in stopping this behavior.

The finding that longer duration of smoking was associated with less satisfaction with the initial decision to smoke was replicated in a study of 135 smokers who took part in a representative survey of Oregonians age 18 or older during the autumn of 1998. The median age of these individuals was 40 years and the median length of time they had been smoking was 24 years. As expected, they were even less satisfied than the college students with their initial decision. When asked if they would 'decide to smoke again', 83.0% said 'no' and only 11.8% said 'yes'. The high percentage of people who are dissatisfied with their decision to begin smoking invalidates Viscusi's claim that such decisions are fully informed and in the individual's best interests.

Conclusion

Many young smokers perceive themselves to be at little or no risk from smoking because they expect to stop smoking before any damage to their health occurs. In reality, a high percentage of young smokers continue to smoke over a long period of time and are placed at risk by this behavior.

Being knowledgeable about the risks from cigarettes means more than just knowing the probabilities of contracting disease after decades of heavy smoking. It means appreciating the severity of the disease consequences, appreciating the cumulative nature of smoking risks, and appreciating the difficulty of stopping the behavior once it has been initiated. By failing to appreciate the severe and cumulative consequences of an addictive behavior, young people underestimate the risks of smoking.

ACKNOWLEDGMENTS

Herbert Severson was instrumental in providing access to the subject population studied here. In addition, he and Richard J Bonnie helped greatly with their advice and encouragement. Linda Schrader's help in collecting the data is also gratefully acknowledged.

NOTES

1 At one point, Viscusi (1992, p141) states that consumer perception of the lung-cancer risk from smoking '*dwarfs* scientists' estimates of the actual risk level' (emphasis added).

2 The second estimate for lung cancer, although relatively low, was likely biased upward by the fact that the respondent had just given a higher estimate on page one of the questionnaire.

24 Insensitivity to the Value of Human Life: A Study of Psychophysical Numbing

David Fetherstonhaugh, Paul Slovic, Stephen M Johnson and James Friedrich

Nobelist Albert Szent-Gyorgi once observed, 'I am deeply moved if I see one man suffering and would risk my life for him. Then I talk impersonally about the possible pulverization of our big cities, with a hundred million dead. I am unable to multiply one man's suffering by a hundred million.' Most people seem to at least tacitly appreciate the kind of insensitivity toward loss of human life articulated in Szent-Gyorgi's statement. We recognize the need for creative attempts to drive home the severity of catastrophic losses. One activist group lobbied Congress by placing 38,000 pairs of shoes, boots and sneakers around the Capitol building to sensitize representatives to the 38,000 gunshot fatalities the US experiences annually (*The Register Guard*, 1994). Another example is given by Rummel (1995), who asked people to consider this century's total democide (state sanctioned killing, aside from warfare) of 170 million by imagining a chain of bodies laid head to toe reaching from Honolulu, across the Pacific and the continental US, to Washington DC and then back again more than 16 times. Losses of life framed in these ways attempt to mitigate the insensitivity that seems to occur so naturally when we try to comprehend past tragedies or think rationally about how to mitigate or prevent large losses of life in the future.

What psychological principles lie behind this insensitivity? In the 19th century, E H Weber and Gustav Fechner discovered a fundamental psychophysical principle that describes how we perceive and discriminate changes in our physical environment. They found that people's ability to detect changes in a physical stimulus decreases rapidly as the magnitude of the stimulus increases (Fechner, 1860; Weber, 1834). What is known today as 'Weber's law' states that in order for a change in a stimulus to become *just noticeable*, a fixed percentage must be

Note: reprinted from 'Insensitivity to the Value of Human Life: A Study of Psychophysical Numbing' by D Fetherstonhaugh, P Slovic, S M Johnson & J Friedrich, 1997, *Journal of Risk and Uncertainty*, 14, pp283–300. Copyright 1997 by Kluwer Academic Publishers; with kind permission from Kluwer Academic Publishers.

added. Thus, perceived difference is a relative matter. To a small stimulus, only a small amount must be added. To a large stimulus, a large amount must be added to be equally noticeable. Fechner proposed a logarithmic law to model this non-linear growth of sensation. Numerous empirical studies by S S Stevens (1975) have demonstrated that the growth of sensory magnitude (ψ) is best fit by a power function of the stimulus magnitude ϕ:

$$\psi = k\phi^{\beta}$$

where the exponent β is typically less than one for measurements of phenomena such as loudness, brightness and even the value of money (Galanter, 1962).[1] For example, if the exponent is .5 as it is in some studies of perceived brightness, a light that is four times the intensity of another light will be judged only twice as bright.

Our cognitive and perceptual systems seem to be designed to sensitize us to small changes in our environment, possibly at the expense of making us less able to detect and respond to large changes. As the psychophysical research indicates, constant increases in the magnitude of a stimulus typically evoke less and less of a change in response. Applying this principle to the valuing of human life suggests that a form of *psychophysical numbing* may result from our inability to appreciate losses of life as they become more catastrophic – a phenomenon that could impair our ability to make consistent, equitable and wise decisions.[2]

Evidence of psychophysical numbing comes from a study by Summers, Slovic, Hine and Zuliani (1998) who hypothesized that people may exhibit a systematic distortion in perception of death tolls from wars not unlike the systematic distortion found in many traditional experiments in sensory psychophysics. They found that deaths from wars were perceived according to a power function where $\beta = .32$. Thus, respondents in these experiments perceived a war that claimed eight times more lives than a second war to be only about two times greater in magnitude. The degree of psychophysical numbing changed in these experiments as a function of how the losses were framed. Respondents' insensitivity was reduced ($\beta = .99$) when the same total number of casualties was presented as 'deaths per day' rather than 'deaths per war'.

Kahneman and Tversky (1979) have incorporated this psychophysical principle of decreasing sensitivity into prospect theory, a descriptive theory of decision-making under uncertainty. A major element of prospect theory is the value function, which relates subjective value to actual gains or losses. The function is concave for gains and convex for losses. When applied to human lives, the value function implies that the subjective value of saving a specified number of lives is greater for a smaller tragedy than for a larger one (when the life-saving effort is framed as reducing a loss). Such psychophysical numbing may have dramatic implications for the judgments and decisions people make. For example, an intervention that reduces the number of deaths in a tragedy from 2000 to 1000 may be judged substantially more valuable than one that reduces deaths from 99,000 to 98,000. Even though both interventions save the *same* number of lives, in the former people may decide to act, while in the latter they may not, perhaps under the impression that saving 1000 lives out of 2000 is a significant proportion but saving 1000 out of 99,000 is merely 'a drop in the bucket'.

How should we value the saving of a life? We believe that, in most circumstances, 'a life is a life' – the value of saving a certain number of people from death should not be affected by the number or proportion of others who remain unsaved. This perspective presumes a linear relationship between the number of lives one can save in a given situation and the value associated with saving them. Thus, an effort saving 200 lives would have twice the value of another that saves 100 lives in the same circumstances. This would lead decision-makers to prefer the intervention that saves the greatest number of lives even if that number is proportionally smallest when compared to the number at risk. Stated differently, we argue that the value of lives saved should be based on the *number* an intervention can save, and should therefore be independent of the size of the population from which the saved lives originate.

Under a one-to-one correspondence between the number and value of saved lives, the value of a life-saving effort should also be independent of when in the process those lives are saved. For example, the value of saving the first 100 individuals in a tragedy should not change if, instead, these individuals happened to be the last 100 saved. According to prospect theory's curved value function, however, the value of saving lives will, in many cases, depend upon when in the process those lives are saved. For example, the value of reducing deaths by 100 early in an intervention would not likely be equivalent to that of an identical reduction later in the process; a reduction in loss of life that brings the death toll closer to zero might appear more valuable.

Other than the study by Summers et al (1998) and a demonstration by Tversky and Kahneman (1981) showing that the non-linear value function does seem to apply to gains and losses of life, little empirical work has been conducted that investigates psychophysical numbing in the domain of life saving. The three studies reported here explored how people value life-saving interventions. We hypothesized that respondents' judgments would exhibit psychophysical numbing by responding to life-saving interventions in a manner consistent with prospect theory's value function. Studies 1 and 2 examined how the perceived benefit of saving lives changed when interventions saving the *same* number of people are implemented in tragedies that differ in magnitude. We predicted that such life-saving interventions would be valued more highly when the number of lives at risk was small than when the number at risk was large. We also predicted that saving lives later in an intervention, bringing the death toll closer to zero, would be valued more highly. Study 3 examined how the total number of people at risk influenced people's estimates of the number of lives an intervention must save to justify a *fixed* amount of funding. We predicted that, when the number at risk was larger, the intervention would be required to save more lives.

STUDY 1

Method

Materials and procedure

Undergraduate volunteers ($n = 54$) from two sections of an economics statistics course were instructed in a short questionnaire to imagine themselves as a government official of a small developing country and were asked to evaluate four government programs (programs A, B, C and D) being considered for funding. Each of the programs 'cost about the same' and addressed the following issues: the employment problem in their country; the transportation problem in their country; and the life-threatening refugee problem in Rwanda.[3] The transportation program proposed to remedy poor road conditions, and the employment program proposed to decrease the jobless rate. There were two Rwandan refugee programs, each proposing to provide enough clean water to save the lives of 4500 refugees suffering from cholera in neighboring Zaire. The Rwandan programs differed only in the size of the refugee camps where the water would be distributed; one program proposed to offer water to a camp of 250,000 refugees and the other proposed to offer it to a camp of 11,000.

Respondents evaluated the programs in pairs, one pair per page. Because the two Rwandan programs were never paired together, only five of the six possible pairings appeared in the booklets. All respondents evaluated the same paired comparisons, presented in one of two randomized orders. Each page contained brief descriptions of two programs being compared, followed by a response scale such as that shown below for programs A and B.

Program A												Program B
6	5	4	3	2	1	0	1	2	3	4	5	6
Strong preference for A				Slight preference for A		No preference	Slight preference for B					Strong preference for B

On the last page, participants responded to several questions designed to verify whether they perceived that the *same* number of refugees would be saved by either of the Rwandan programs. The final item requested respondents to briefly explain whether it was better to save lives in the smaller or the larger refugee camp, and why.

Results and Discussion

The manipulation checks verified that most respondents correctly perceived that the two Rwandan programs saved the *same* number of lives.

Ratings on the 13-point preference scale constituted the dependent measure. For the four pairings containing a Rwandan program, participants' responses were subsequently recoded so that a preference for the Rwanda program in a pair was indicated by a positive number and a preference for the *non*-Rwandan program in a pair was coded as a negative number. For example, in a pair containing the large-camp program and the transportation program, if a participant circled a '2' to indicate a slight preference for the transportation program, the rating would have been recoded as a '–2'. Thus, participants' recoded responses ranged from –6 to +6. Because responses in the transportation versus employment program comparison were not of theoretical interest, they were excluded from the analysis. An analysis of variance (ANOVA) on respondents' preferences revealed no effects due to respondents' gender or to the order in which the paired comparisons were presented. Data were therefore combined without regard for these variables.

We predicted that preference ratings would be greater for the small-camp program than the large-camp program. Because these programs were never paired together, however, we compared respondents' ratings for the two Rwandan programs in pairings that shared a common *non*-Rwandan program. For example, we compared respondents' ratings in the transportation versus the small-camp pairing with their ratings in the transportation versus the large-camp pairing. We expected that the recoded rating for the small-camp pairing would be greater than the rating for the large-camp pairing.

This prediction was tested using a within-subjects, 2 x 2 analysis of variance on preference ratings, varying comparison program type (transportation or employment) and Rwanda camp size (large or small). As predicted, the results revealed a camp-size main effect, $F(1, 52) = 8.24, p < .01$ (see Figure 24.1). Even though most respondents realized that the same number of refugees could be saved in either camp, they preferred the small-camp program ($M = .45$) over the large-camp program ($M = -.20$) when paired with either the transportation or employment programs.

The same ANOVA was conducted on the preferences of 22 respondents who indicated on the last page of the booklet that saving 4500 lives in the large camp was neither better nor worse than saving 4500 lives in the small camp. Even these respondents, who indicated no preference between one life-saving Rwandan program and the other when asked directly, preferred the small-camp program ($M = .93$) over the large-camp program ($M = .41$) when evaluations were masked by paired comparisons, $F(1, 21) = 3.92; p = .06$.

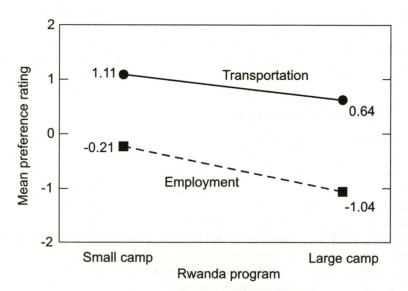

Note: Ratings were made on a 13-point scale (-6 to +6). Positive numbers indicate preference for a Rwanda program over a non-Rwanda program.

Figure 24.1 *Main effects in study 1 for Rwanda camp size (11,000 or 250,000) and program type (transportation or employment) using preference ratings from paired comparisons*

One last question asked respondents whether it was better to save lives in the smaller or the larger refugee camp, and to state why. About 44% of respondents reported that it was better to save lives in the smaller camp. As perhaps the strongest evidence for the psychophysical numbing hypothesis thus far, this result is quite remarkable, especially considering that the life-saving potential of each Rwandan program was reinforced by the preceding question in which nearly all respondents reported that the interventions would save the same number of lives. Approximately 42% of respondents reported no preference between the two programs and 14% indicated that it was better to save lives in the larger camp.

We suggest that the sizable proportion of respondents who preferred to save lives in the smaller camp reflects people's general tendency to become desensitized to the life-saving potential of interventions applied to larger tragedies. However, what appears to be psychophysical numbing might not be caused by insensitivity at all, but actually by respondents' sensitivity to preventing further casualties among refugees – an eminently reasonable goal. Respondents might have preferred the small-camp program because of the increased hazard of administering a limited supply of a scarce commodity to a large and desperately needy group of people, as might likely be found in a large camp. Not only might such an effort incur additional casualties through the riot it could spark, but people could be at greater risk of infection or later reinfection due to the increased tendency for water-borne diseases to spread in a larger compared to a smaller refugee camp. We have labeled these explanations the riot and contagion hypotheses, respectively.

Evidence in the present study suggested that most respondents considered neither the riot nor the contagion hypotheses. In fact, only one participant mentioned the riot hypothesis as a rationale when responding to the final question (ie, whether it was better to save lives in the small or the large refugee camp, and why). Seven respondents, however, did cite some form of the contagion hypothesis, although several used it to support their preference for saving lives in the larger camp. The fact that even the 22 respondents who stated that saving lives in the larger camp was neither better nor worse than saving lives in the small camp exhibited psychophysical numbing also speaks against these hypotheses. Unless a substantial portion of respondents used, but failed to report, one or both of these hypotheses as part of their rationale, we believe it unlikely that either hypothesis could be widely responsible for the effects found in the above analyses.

Furthermore, the next study reports data that not only replicates the present study, but provides evidence that essentially rules out both the riot and the contagion hypotheses as alternative explanations for psychophysical numbing.

STUDY 2

Study 2 retained much of the content and structure of the previous study. Participants first read a cover story about the Rwandan refugee crisis and then evaluated one small country's life-saving intervention proposed for several refugee camps. For each camp, all respondents answered two questions:

1   How beneficial would sending the aid be?
2   Should aid be sent or not?

Study 2, however, differed from the previous study in several respects. In study 2, comparisons between the Rwandan scenarios were easier, which would presumably lessen psychophysical numbing among respondents. Whereas study 1 paired each Rwandan scenario with a 'dummy' scenario, making direct comparisons between Rwandan scenarios more difficult, study 2 omitted dummy scenarios and had respondents evaluate Rwandan scenarios individually.

Though easier in this regard, study 2 was generally more complex because it contained a more detailed cover story and incorporated two additional independent variables. As well as camp-size manipulation found in the previous study, study 2 manipulated *when* in the life-saving process the humanitarian aid was distributed. We predicted that saving a portion of lives near the end of a crisis would be valued more highly than saving an equal portion near the beginning of a crisis, because the former solves virtually all the problem whereas the latter does not. Study 2 also manipulated the '*reliability*' of the equipment used to administer the aid (ie, purified water). We included this variable to discourage respondents from rating the intervention as maximally beneficial in every scenario.

Method

Overview of design

The present study manipulated three within-subjects variables: size of refugee camp (11,000 or 250,000); amount of pure-water aid a camp was receiving *before* a water-purification plane was sent (low or high); and reliability of the plane (60% or 100%). This yielded the eight different scenarios participants read and it allowed us to analyze their responses in a $2 \times 2 \times 2$ repeated-measures factorial design.

All respondents evaluated the same eight scenarios. Half received the block of four 100%-reliable plane scenarios first and the block of four 60%-reliable plane scenarios second, and half received the blocks of four in the reverse order. Within each block of four scenarios, the 'camp-size' and 'prior help' variables were mixed according to a Latin-square design.

There were two dependent variables:
1   the rated benefit of sending a plane; and
2   a yes/no decision on whether or not to send a plane.

Materials and procedure

University of Oregon students ($n = 162$) were paid $4 to complete an 11-page questionnaire about the Rwandan refugee crisis. The cover story of the questionnaire informed respondents that the UN High Commissioner for Refugees was coordinating a massive humanitarian aid campaign by requesting that able countries send assistance to the Rwandan refugees in Zaire. Many refugees had a water-borne disease and would die if purified water did not soon become available. One small country was considering sending one of two Dash-

8 water-purification planes to Zaire. Although each water system was capable of producing only a small fraction of the water needed, each could keep about 1500 disease victims alive every day. The purification system in one plane was 100% reliable, and the system in the other plane was only 60% reliable – reliable in the sense that there was only a '60% chance that the system would work once it got to Zaire'. Once a plane was operating in a camp, respondents were informed that, 'aid-workers will distribute the clean water to designated disease victims, which usu-ally saves the victims' lives'. The cost to this small country of delivering and operating these purification systems was significant in light of its economy.

The following pages contained eight scenarios about the four refugee camps (see Table 24.1 for a summary of information given in the eight scenarios). Each scenario was identically structured. For example, on one page respondents read the following scenario (scenario 1):

> The city of Moga in Zaire now has about 11,000 Rwandan refugees. Few water purification systems from other countries are now in place. 5% of the clean water needed for disease victims in this camp is currently being met. If the 100%-reli-able Dash-8 water purification plane is sent to Moga, 50% of this camp's water need for disease victims would be met.

For scenarios using the 60%-reliable plane, the following phrase was added: 'provided the purification system works'.

In the other small-camp scenarios (Fizi 1 and Fizi 2 – see Table 24.1), 50% of the clean water need was currently being met, so the aid increased this to 95%, provided the system worked.

Table 24.1 *Summary of Information in the Eight Scenarios Given to All Respondents in Study 2*

Scenario number	Zairian refugee camp	Camp size	Plane reliability (%)	Prior aid (%)	Post aid (%)
1	Moga 1	11,000	100	5	50
2	Moga 2	11,000	60	5	50
3	Fizi 1	11,000	100	50	95
4	Fizi 2	11,000	60	50	95
5	Uvira 1	250,000	100	5	7
6	Uvira 2	250,000	60	5	7
7	Kalehe 1	250,000	100	93	95
8	Kalehe 2	250,000	60	93	95

Note: The prior-aid variable indicates the amount of pure water need being met for disease victims in a camp *before* the aid was delivered. Post-aid indicates the water need that would be met for disease victims after the aid was provided. Within each level of plane reliability, the intervention in each camp was capable of keeping the same number of disease victims (1,500) alive each day (which usually saves the victims' lives).

In the two scenarios involving the large (250,000 refugees) camp, Uvira, the prior aid met 5% of the water need and the additional aid would bring this to 7%. In the scenarios involving the Kalehe camp (scenarios 7 and 8), 93% of the water need was being met and the additional aid would bring this to 95%. Thus, the intervention proposed to save 2% of disease victims in a given large camp and 45% of disease victims in a given small camp. Recall, however, that the same absolute number of lives (1500) would be saved in each case, regardless of camp size.

Each scenario was followed by two questions. First, 'What would be the benefit of sending this Dash-8 plane to this camp?' Respondents answered this question on a nine-point Likert scale, titled 'benefit', anchored at the ends by: 0 ('extremely low benefit') and 8 ('extremely high benefit'). Second, they were asked, 'Given the benefit indicated on the scale above, would it be worth sending the plane to this camp?' Respondents circled either 'yes' or 'no'. On each page, participants were reminded that responses to each scenario should be independent of their responses to the other scenarios.

After completing this task, participants responded to a question designed to assess whether they correctly perceived that the same number of lives would be saved by an intervention, regardless of the size of camp where it was implemented.

Results and Discussion

A check on subjects' understanding of the problem revealed that 60% of respondents correctly perceived that the water systems would save about the same number of lives regardless of refugee camp size, 23% believed that substantially more lives would be saved in the larger camp, and 17% believed that substantially more lives would be saved in the smaller camp. The analyses reported below omitted this last group of respondents because their belief could have quite reasonably lead them to prefer implementing the intervention in the small camps, not because of psychophysical numbing but simply because it could have saved more lives.

A $2 \times 2 \times 2$ within-subjects ANOVA on respondents' benefit ratings provided strong support for the psychophysical numbing hypothesis (see Figure 24.2). A significant main effect for camp size, $F(1, 132) = 160.5, p < .001$, indicated that respondents believed sending the planes to small camps was more beneficial ($M = 6.46$) than sending them to large camps ($M = 4.54$). A main effect for the prior-aid variable, $F(1, 132) = 15.35, p < .001$, indicated that respondents believed sending the planes to camps that were already satisfying a substantial portion of their clean-water need was more beneficial ($M = 5.73$) than sending them to camps that were only satisfying a small portion of their water need ($M = 5.27$). And, not surprisingly, the results revealed a main effect for plane reliability, $F(1, 132) = 12.01, p < .001$, indicating that respondents believed the 100%-reliable plane ($M = 5.67$) was more beneficial than the 60%-reliable plane ($M = 5.33$). No other effects were significant.

As predicted, respondents appeared to favor interventions more when implemented in the later stages of the life-saving process. For example, respondents thought it was more beneficial to save 2% of those at risk when the threat of a

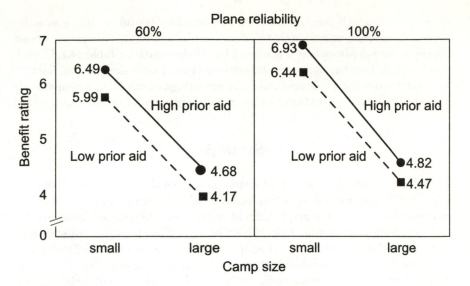

Note: Benefit rating was scored on a scale from 0 (low) to 8 (high).

Figure 24.2 *Main effects in study 2 for the three within-subjects variables: Camp size (11,000 or 250,000), prior aid (low or high), and plane reliability (60% or 100%)*

tragedy was nearly contained than when it was just beginning to take its toll. As the absence of interaction effects indicated, this was as true for small camps as it was for large.

A $2 \times 2 \times 2$ ANOVA on respondents' dichotomous decisions about whether or not to send the planes to the camps also revealed a significant main effect for camp size, $F(1, 130) = 105.4$, $p < .001$, indicating that respondents decided to send the planes to small camps more often (93%) than to large camps (59%). A main effect for plane reliability, $F(1, 130) = 4.61$, $p < .05$, indicated that respondents decided to send the reliable plane to the camps slightly more often (78%) than the unreliable plane (74%). Interestingly, the main effect for prior aid was not significant, $F(1, 130) = .47$, $p = .50$. Respondents decided to send the planes 75% of the time to camps receiving little prior aid, and 77% of the time to camps receiving substantial prior aid. No other effects were significant.

The above analyses show that respondents' judgments and decisions about sending aid to refugee camps differed greatly depending upon camp size. It is possible that such responses could be justified if they were based on some rationale such as the riot hypothesis or the contagion hypothesis. However, in addition to the evidence against the riot and contagion hypotheses from study 1, data from the present study provided strong evidence that neither of these alternative hypotheses were widely considered. If respondents had considered such explanations, one would have expected them to substantially devalue the interventions for those scenarios in which the risk of rioting or reinfection was the greatest – namely, large camps in the early stages of the life-saving process. In these scenarios, respondents were faced with implementing an intervention whose supply of aid was particularly inadequate for the demand (see Table 24.1, Uvira 1 and Uvira 2). The data, however, did not reflect this interaction pattern. Rather, respondents devalued interventions to the same degree both in large camps needing little additional aid and large camps needing massive additional aid.

STUDY 3

In the previous studies, we asked respondents to make evaluations about *one* type of intervention (saving a *fixed* number of lives) applied to several tragic circumstances varying in magnitude. In study 3 we asked respondents to estimate the minimum number of lives each of several interventions must save to merit a *fixed* amount of money. If people tend to view an amount of assistance in a large tragedy as less valuable than an equivalent amount in a small tragedy, as was shown in the previous studies, then they should require more life-saving assistance to be 'added' to the large tragedy to make the assistance in each of equal value. In the present study, therefore, we predicted that respondents' estimates of the minimum number of lives each intervention would have to save would be greater for the larger than the smaller tragedies.

Method

Materials and procedure

University of Oregon students ($n = 165$) were paid $4 to complete a questionnaire asking them to imagine that they were the chairperson on the board of 'Science For Life', a charitable foundation in charge of distributing large sums of money to research institutions that develop treatments for serious diseases. Each respondent was asked to determine which medical institutions Science For Life should fund with its limited resources. The three medical institutions (X, Y and Z) who were requesting support each proposed to implement a new treatment that would significantly reduce the annual number of deaths caused by a particular disease.

Respondents were also instructed to assume that:

1   The treatments will induce a cure for some people and thus 'save their lives'.
2   The people who are not cured will experience no other beneficial effect; that is, the treatment will not improve their 'quality of life'.

Respondents completed two tasks: an estimation task and a ranking task. The first task required them to estimate for each disease: 'How large a reduction in yearly deaths makes [the] institution worthy of funding?'.

Each respondent made estimates for all three medical institutions. Each page of the questionnaire presented information about one medical institution, X, Y or Z, and information about the number of deaths caused in the previous year by the disease for which the institution proposed treatment, disease A, B or C,

Table 24.2 *Information Given to Respondents in Task 1 and Task 2 of Study 3*

Medical institution	Disease treated	Task 1 [a]	Task 2 [b]	
		Number of deaths last year	Number of deaths this year	Number of deaths next year
X	A	15,000	15,000	5000
Y	B	160,000	160,000	145,000
Z	C	290,000	290,000	270,000

[a] Respondents were asked to indicate the minimum number of lives the treatment would have to save to merit $10 million in funding.
[b] Respondents were asked to rank order the three programs with regard to priority for receiving $10 million in support.

respectively (see 'Task 1 Information' in Table 24.2). Thus, on each page respondents read the following:

> Medical institution (X) [Y] {Z} has developed a treatment for disease (A) [B] {C} and now requests $10 million from Science For Life. Last year, people with disease (A) [B] {C} did not have access to this treatment and (15,000) [160,000] {290,000} died from the disease. Given Science For Life's shrinking budget, what is the minimum number of lives this treatment would have to save next year in order for medical institution (X) [Y] {Z} to merit funding?

Respondents recorded their estimates on a blank line provided on each page. Six versions of the questionnaire were distributed, reflecting all possible orderings of the three stimulus scenarios.

The second task asked the same respondents to imagine that they must now choose which proposal among the three submitted should receive the $10 million. They were told that partial funding was not possible and they must rank order the three medical institutions. Before giving their preference order, respondents were told that:

- Institution X would reduce deaths from disease A from approximately 15,000 per year to about 5000 per year.
- Institution Y would reduce deaths from disease B from approximately 160,000 per year to about 145,000 per year.
- Institution Z would reduce deaths from disease C from approximately 290,000 per year to about 270,000 per year (see 'Task 2 Information' in Table 24.2).

Thus, there was an inverse relationship between 'number of lives saved' and 'proportion of lives saved': disease C deaths were to be reduced by the greatest number (20,000) but by the smallest percentage (7%), whereas disease A deaths were to be reduced by the smallest number (10,000) but by the greatest percentage (67%). Respondents were asked to rank the three proposals from *most worthy* to *least worthy* to receive the $10 million funding.

Results and Discussion

The results from task 1 indicated that a majority of respondents exhibited psychophysical numbing (see Table 24.3). When estimating the minimum number of lives an institution's treatment must save to merit a $10 million award, 65% of participants gave estimates that increased as the size of the population at risk increased. Approximately 28% required that the same number be saved, regardless of size, and 7% gave either varied or decreasing estimates. We also calculated the medians and geometric means, which are less affected by extreme values. Table 24.3 shows that the arithmetic means, medians and geometric means all reflect a substantial effect consistent with psychophysical numbing.

For those who responded in accord with the numbing hypothesis, the median number of lives institution Y's treatment was required to save (median = 60,000) was more than six times greater than that of X's treatment (median = 9000), whereas the median estimate for Z's treatment (median = 100,000) was more than 11 times greater than the estimate for X's treatment. Interestingly, for the 28% of respondents whose estimates did not vary with disease size, the median estimate was only 100, far less than that of the psychophysical numbing respondents' estimates for even the small-scale disease (median = 9000).

Figure 24.3 shows the *proportion* of lives that respondents required each disease treatment to save. Three clearly defined groups emerged from the analysis: 16 respondents (10%) made estimates such that the proportion of lives saved remained constant across disease size; 91 respondents (55%) made estimates such that, as disease size increased, the proportion saved decreased, but at a rate where the number required to be saved was greater for larger diseases; and 47 respondents (28%) made estimates such that, as the disease size increased, the proportion saved decreased at a rate such that the number of lives saved remained constant. The remaining 11 individuals (7%) exhibited no consistent pattern and were therefore not included in any of the three groups mentioned.

These results suggest that respondents evaluated the interventions using two evaluation strategies. Some respondents appeared to employ a *proportion rule*; some, an absolute *number rule*; and still others seemed to employ some

Table 24.3 *Estimated Minimum Number of Lives Each Institution Would be Required to Save in Task 1 of Study 3*

Institution:	Psychophysical numbing respondents, n = 107 (65%)			Consistent respondents, n = 47 (28%)
	X	Y	Z	X, Y and Z
Arithmetic mean	7746	63,780	111,625	3047
Geometric mean	4701	32,678	56,707	100
Median	9000	60,000	100,000	100
Lower quartile	3000	16,000	29,000	1
Upper quartile	10,000	100,000	200,000	5000

Note: Institutions X, Y and Z each proposed treatment for a disease that caused 15,000, 160,000 and 290,000 annual deaths, respectively.

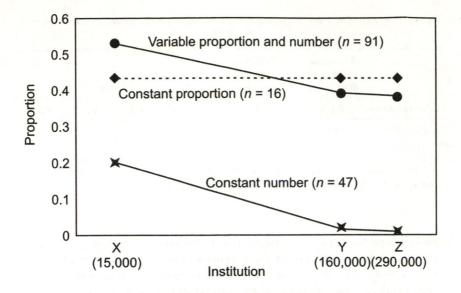

Figure 24.3 *Respondents' estimates in terms of the proportion of lives that each institution should save (study 3)*

combination of the two. That is, some respondents believed a given institution to be 'worthy' of funding only if the ratio of number of lives saved to total number of lives at risk reached some proportion threshold (proportion rule). Those who followed the number rule also held a threshold, but one that was based on an absolute number of lives saved rather than a proportion saved. The majority of respondents, however, fell into a third group that made estimates in a manner consistent with an anchoring and adjustment process. In such a process, for example, one might choose a reasonable proportion threshold for the smallest disease treatment, say 'must save at least 50% of those at risk', and then adjust this threshold downward for the treatments of larger diseases, say 'save 47%' for the medium disease and 'save 45%' for the largest disease. In fact, many of the 55% of respondents who appeared in this category imposed proportion thresholds that were within 5% across the three disease treatments.

In task 2, we gave information about the annual expected reduction in deaths for each of the three disease treatments (see 'Task 2 information' in Table 24.2). Respondents then rank-ordered the treatments from 'most worthy' to 'least worthy' to receive funding. The results were quite different from those of task 1 (see Table 24.4). More than 60% of respondents preferred to fund disease treatments that maximized the number of lives saved, preferring institution Z (20,000 saved) over institution Y (15,000 saved) over institution X (10,000 saved). Approximately 16% preferred treatments that maximized the proportion of lives saved, choosing the preference order XYZ. The remaining 34% of respondents fell somewhere in between the above two groups, choosing preference orders that maximized neither the number of lives saved nor the proportion of lives saved.

The three groups that emerged in task 2 roughly corresponded to those that emerged in task 1, though the proportion of respondents in each did not. In task 2, a majority of respondents seemed to employ the absolute number rule by

Table 24.4 *Task 2 in Study 3: Frequency and Percentage of Respondents' Preference Orders (N = 164)*

	Maximize number of lives saved	Maximize proportion of lives saved	Other			
Preference order:	Z Y X	X Y Z	X Z Y	Y X Z	Y Z X	Z X Y
Frequency	99	26	15	9	7	8
Percentage	60%	16%	9%	5%	4%	5%

Note: Institutions X, Y and Z each proposed a treatment to reduce annual deaths of those at risk by 10,000 (67%), 15,000 (9%) and 20,000 (7%), respectively.

consistently preferring to save a greater number of lives; others seemed to employ a proportion rule by consistently preferring to save a greater proportion of lives; and about one third seemed to attempt some combination of the two strategies.

The results of task 2 underscore two important points. First, the task format can significantly influence the degree of psychophysical numbing. Second, even in the rather simple and transparent format studied here, psychophysical numbing does not disappear.

GENERAL DISCUSSION

Evidence from the present studies shows that people often judge the value of life-saving efforts in much the same way that they judge the intensity of stimuli in traditional psychophysical experiments. Just as a fixed decrease in brightness seems greater when the original intensity is small than when it is large, an intervention saving a fixed number of lives seems more valuable when fewer lives are at risk to begin with – when the saving is a larger proportion of the number at risk. When such psychophysical numbing occurs, the value of a life-saving intervention is inversely proportional to the magnitude of the threat rather than being determined by the absolute number of lives the intervention can save.

A significant portion of the respondents in each of the present studies exhibited psychophysical numbing. Many respondents in the first two studies judged interventions serving larger refugee camps to be considerably less valuable than ones serving smaller camps, even though the interventions could save the same number of lives. Furthermore, when respondents in task 1 of study 3 estimated the number of lives several proposed disease treatments would have to save to be equally worthy of a fixed amount of funding, median estimates were more than 11 times greater for the intervention that treated the disease killing 290,000 annually than the one killing 15,000 annually.

Although psychophysical numbing was present in each study, its prevalence varied. This is important because it shows that the incidence of the phenomenon is mutable. For example, over 67% of participants responded psychophysically in task 1 of study 3, whereas only 16% responded psychophysically in task 2. In addition, study 3 suggested that those most likely to see the value of an intervention as independent of a problem's size were also the ones who attached the greatest value to saving lives generally. For example, psychophysical respondents in study 3 required over 1000 times as many lives to be saved (median estimate) in the largest disease category than respondents who gave consistent responses (see Table 24.3)!

There are several other features in the present studies that may have affected the degree to which psychophysical numbing occurred. First, the way information about life-saving interventions was framed changed the degree of numbing. In study 3, for example, numbing was frequent when information about the interventions highlighted the magnitude of each tragedy (task 1), but far less frequent when the information emphasized the magnitude of each intervention's life-saving potential (task 2). Thus, descriptions of events that focus on the outcomes of the intervention rather than the tragedy it serves appear to reduce the degree of psychophysical numbing.

Second, the ease of comparison between different interventions may have also contributed to the degree of numbing respondents exhibited. In task 2 of study 3, where the numbing incidence was low, information on each intervention and tragedy was presented side-by-side, whereas in task 1, information about each tragedy was presented on separate pages. Study 1 also showed that ease of comparison may have been a factor. Those who, when asked directly, reported no preference between two interventions that saved the same number of lives, nevertheless preferred the intervention serving the smaller tragedy in the previous task where direct comparisons were more difficult.

Despite this variability, however, the present studies suggest that psychophysical numbing is a robust phenomenon – ingrained in the workings of our cognitive and perceptual systems, which seem geared to sensitize us to small changes in our environment, perhaps at the cost of making us less able to appreciate and respond adequately to large changes. When we contemplate nuclear war, for example, and its immense capability for death and destruction, it may be difficult to escape psychophysical numbing as we attempt to grasp the significance of the difference between 10,000, 100,000 or a million or more deaths. Where we lack perceptual sensitivity, we might also expect to find that our language is also inadequate to discriminate among degrees of harm or destructiveness. Thus John Hersey's elegant chronicle of the aftermath of the Hiroshima bombing (which killed about 140,000 people) simply refers to the scene as *havoc* (Hersey, 1946, p5) and *terrible* (p86). Lifton (1967) refers to Hiroshima as a *disaster*, a term commonly applied to events that are far less severe. *Holocaust, catastrophe, calamity, tragedy* ... the vocabulary of disaster seems sparse indeed. Can the potential deaths of large numbers of people really be comprehended without an adequate vocabulary of destructiveness?

Some who have worried about the incomprehension of mass destruction are pessimistic. Humphrey (1981, pp21–2), for example, writes of our ability to be moved greatly by the plight of single human beings at the expense of insensitivity to 'giant dangers'. He says:

In a week when 3000 people are killed by an earthquake in Iran, a lone boy falls down a well shaft in Italy – and the whole world grieves. Six million Jews are put to death in Hitler's Germany, and it is Anne Frank trembling in her garret that remains stamped in our memory.

We must live with this... It will not change. I do not expect my dog to learn to read *The Times*, and I do not expect myself or any other human being to learn the meaning of nuclear war or to speak rationally about megadeaths.

Yet writers such as Hersey, Lifton, Jonathan Schell (1982) and many others do have the power to move us emotionally with their eloquent descriptions of individual and societal tragedies despite the lack of adequate one-word descriptors. Is that a sign that we can, indeed, comprehend these tragedies in a way that will help us to make good decisions about preventing them or managing their risks?

Modern technology has great power to cause, prevent and alleviate mass human suffering. Yet the psychophysical numbing we have observed in our studies is strong enough and pervasive enough to raise some disturbing questions about our ability to make rational decisions when many lives are at stake. Further research is clearly needed to illuminate the dynamics of psychophysical numbing and to determine its effects on decision-making.

ACKNOWLEDGMENTS

We acknowledge with thanks support from the National Science Foundation under Grant No SBR-9422754 to Decision Research and a Graduate Research Fellowship granted to the first author. Any opinions, findings, conclusions or recommendations expressed in this chapter are those of the authors and do not necessarily reflect the views of the National Science Foundation. We also thank Sarah Lichtenstein for her comments on the manuscript and Leisha Mullican for her technical assistance in the preparation of the report.

NOTES

1   A striking example of psychophysical insensitivity to money was Ronald Reagan's assertion that a $4.6 billion job program 'would add virtually nothing to the federal budget' (*Eugene Register-Guard*, 25 March 1983).
2   Lifton (1967) used the term 'psychic numbing' to refer to the accommodation and reduced sensitivity to shocking and emotionally overwhelming threats and experiences, such as those created by nuclear war. Hiroshima survivors, for example, said that they very quickly 'ceased to feel'. Whereas psychic numbing is adaptive, enabling survivors and rescue workers to cope with trauma, psychophysical numbing may degrade our ability to appreciate the consequences of our actions.
3   In the summer of 1994, when these data were collected, ethnic warfare in Rwanda had resulted in over a million refugees fleeing into neighboring Zaire. The brutal nature of the civil war, as well as the problems of disease and hunger that plagued the refugees, had made the Rwandan conflict the topic of considerable print, radio and television news attention (Cooper, 1994;

Purvis, 1994; 'World News Tonight', 1994a; 1994b). Participants' likely familiarity with the Rwanda crisis should have helped to make the potential loss of life addressed in the judgment task particularly salient and realistic.

25

Trust, Emotion, Sex, Politics and Science: Surveying the Risk-assessment Battlefield

Paul Slovic

INTRODUCTION

The practice of risk assessment has steadily increased in prominence during the past several decades as risk managers in government and industry have sought to develop more effective ways to meet public demands for a safer and healthier environment. Dozens of scientific disciplines have been mobilized to provide technical information about risk, and billions of dollars have been expended to create this information and distill it in the context of risk assessments.

Ironically, as our society and other industrialized nations have expended this great effort to make life safer and healthier, many in the public have become more, rather than less, concerned about risk. These individuals see themselves as exposed to more serious risks than were faced by people in the past, and they believe that this situation is getting worse rather than better. Nuclear and chemical technologies (except for medicines) have been stigmatized by being perceived as entailing unnaturally great risks (Gregory, Flynn & Slovic, 1995). As a result, it has been difficult, if not impossible, to find host sites for disposing of high-level or low-level radioactive wastes, or for incinerators, landfills and other chemical facilities.

Public perceptions of risk have been found to determine the priorities and legislative agendas of regulatory bodies such as the US Environmental Protection Agency (US EPA), much to the distress of agency technical experts who argue that other hazards deserve higher priority. The bulk of the EPA's budget in recent years has gone to hazardous waste primarily because the public believes that the cleanup of Superfund sites is the most serious environmental priority for the country. Hazards such as indoor air pollution are considered more

Note: this is a slightly revised version of 'Trust, Emotion, Sex, Politics and Science: Surveying the Risk-assessment Battlefield' by P Slovic in *Environment, Ethics and Behavior* (pp277–313), by M Bazerman, D Messick, A Tenbrunsel & K Wade-Benzoni (eds), 1997, San Francisco: New Lexington Press. Reprinted with permission.

Table 25.1 *Costs of a Year of Life Saved by Various Interventions*

Intervention	Cost ($)
Flu shots	500
Water chlorination	4000
Pneumonia vaccination	12,000
Breast cancer screening	17,000
All medical interventions	19,000
Construction safety rules	38,000
All transportation interventions	56,000
Highway improvement	60,000
Home radon control	141,000
Asbestos controls	1.9 million
All toxin controls	2.8 million
Arsenic emission controls	6.0 million
Radiation controls	10.0 million

Source: Adapted from Tengs et al, (1995).

serious health risks by experts but are not perceived that way by the public (US EPA, 1987).

Great disparities in monetary expenditures designed to prolong life, as shown in Table 25.1, may also be traced to public perceptions of risk. The relatively small sums expended to reduce mundane hazards such as automobile accidents are as noteworthy as the large sums of money devoted to protection from radiation and chemical toxins. Other studies have shown that serious risks from natural disasters such as floods, hurricanes and earthquakes generate relatively little public concern and demand for protection (Palm, 1990; Kunreuther, 1996).

Such discrepancies are seen as irrational by many harsh critics of public perceptions. These critics draw a sharp dichotomy between the experts and the public. Experts are seen as purveying risk assessments, characterized as objective, analytic, wise and rational – based on the *real* risks. In contrast, the public is seen to rely on *perceptions of risk* that are subjective, often hypothetical, emotional, foolish and irrational (see, for example, DuPont, 1980; or Covello, Flamm, Rodricks & Tardiff, 1983). Weiner (1993) defends the dichotomy, arguing that 'This separation of reality and perception is pervasive in a technically sophisticated society, and serves to achieve a necessary emotional distance' (p495).

In sum, polarized views, controversy and overt conflict have become pervasive within risk assessment and risk management. A desperate search for salvation through risk-communication efforts began in the mid 1980s – yet, despite some localized successes, this effort has not stemmed the major conflicts or reduced much of the dissatisfaction with risk management. This dissatisfaction can be traced, in part, to a failure to appreciate the complex and socially determined nature of the concept *risk*. In the remainder of this chapter, I shall describe several streams of research that demonstrate this complexity and point toward the need for new definitions of risk and new approaches to risk management.

THE NEED FOR A NEW PERSPECTIVE

New perspectives and new approaches are needed to manage risks effectively in our society. Social science research has provided some valuable insights into the nature of the problem that, without indicating a clear solution, do point to some promising prescriptive actions.

For example, early studies of risk perception demonstrated that the public's concerns could not simply be blamed on ignorance or irrationality. Instead, research has shown that many of the public's reactions to risk (including reactions that may underlie the data in Table 25.1) can be attributed to a sensitivity to technical, social and psychological qualities of hazards that are not well-modeled in technical risk assessments (eg, qualities such as uncertainty in risk assessments, perceived inequity in the distribution of risks and benefits, and aversion to being exposed to risks that are involuntary, not under one's control or dreaded). The important role of social values in risk perception and risk acceptance has thus become apparent (Slovic, 1987).

More recently, another important aspect of the risk-perception problem has come to be recognized. This is the role of trust. In recent years there have been numerous articles and surveys pointing out the importance of trust in risk management and documenting the extreme distrust we now have in many of the individuals, industries and institutions responsible for risk management (Slovic, 1993). This pervasive distrust has also been shown to be strongly linked both to the perception that risks are unacceptably high and to political activism to reduce those risks.

A third insight pertains to the very nature of the concept *risk*. Current approaches to risk assessment and risk management are based on the traditional view of risk as some objective function of probability (uncertainty) and adverse consequences. I shall argue for a conception of risk that is starkly different from this traditional view. This new approach highlights the subjective and value-laden nature of risk and conceptualizes risk as a game in which the rules must be socially negotiated within the context of a specific problem.

The Subjective and Value-laden Nature of Risk Assessment

Attempts to manage risk must confront the question: 'What is risk?'. The dominant conception views risk as 'the chance of injury, damage, or loss' (*Webster's New Twentieth Century Dictionary*, second edition, 1983). The probabilities and consequences of adverse events are assumed to be produced by physical and natural processes in ways that can be objectively quantified by risk assessment. Much social science analysis rejects this notion, arguing instead that risk is inherently subjective (Funtowicz & Ravetz, 1992; Krimsky & Golding, 1992; Otway, 1992; Pidgeon, Hood, Jones, Turner & Gibson, 1992; Slovic, 1992; Wynne, 1992). In this view, risk does not exist 'out there', independent of our minds and cultures, waiting to be measured. Instead, human beings have invented the concept risk to help them understand and cope with the dangers and uncertainties of life. Although these dangers are real, there is no such thing as 'real risk' or 'objective risk'. The nuclear engineer's probabilistic risk estimate for a nuclear

Table 25.2 *Some Ways of Expressing Mortality Risks*

- Deaths per million people in the population.
- Deaths per million people within x miles of the source of exposure.
- Deaths per unit of concentration.
- Deaths per facility.
- Deaths per ton of air toxic released.
- Deaths per ton of air toxic absorbed by people.
- Deaths per ton of chemical produced.
- Deaths per million dollars of product produced.
- Loss of life expectancy associated with exposure to the hazard.

accident, or the toxicologist's quantitative estimate of a chemical's carcinogenic risk, are both based on theoretical models whose structure is subjective and assumption-laden, and whose inputs are dependent upon judgment. As we shall see, non-scientists have their own models, assumptions and subjective assessment techniques (intuitive risk assessments), which are sometimes very different from the scientists' models.

One way in which subjectivity permeates risk assessments is in the dependence of such assessments on judgments at every stage of the process, from the initial structuring of a risk problem to deciding which endpoints or consequences to include in the analysis, identifying and estimating exposures, choosing dose-response relationships and so on. For example, even the apparently simple task of choosing a risk measure for a well-defined endpoint such as human fatalities is surprisingly complex and judgmental. Table 25.2 shows a few of the many different ways that fatality risks can be measured. How should we decide which measure to use when planning a risk assessment, recognizing that the choice is likely to make a big difference in how the risk is perceived and evaluated?

An example taken from Crouch and Wilson (1982) demonstrates how the choice of one measure or another can make a technology look either more or less risky. For example, between 1950 and 1970, coal mines became much less risky in terms of deaths from accidents per ton of coal, but they became marginally riskier in terms of deaths from accidents per employee. Which measure one thinks more appropriate for decision-making depends upon one's point of view. From a national point of view, given that a certain amount of coal has to be obtained to provide fuel, deaths per million tons of coal is the more appropriate measure of risk, whereas from a labor leader's point of view, deaths per thousand persons employed may be more relevant.

Each way of summarizing deaths embodies its own set of values (National Research Council, 1989). For example, 'reduction in life expectancy' treats deaths of young people as more important than deaths of older people, who have less life expectancy to lose. Simply counting fatalities treats deaths of the old and young as equivalent; it also treats as equivalent deaths that come immediately after mishaps and deaths that follow painful and debilitating disease. Using 'number of deaths' as the summary indicator of risk implies that it is as important to prevent deaths of people who engage in an activity by choice and have been benefiting from that activity as it is to protect those who are exposed to a hazard involuntarily and get no benefit from it. One can easily imagine a range of arguments to justify different kinds of unequal weightings for different kinds of deaths, but to arrive at any selection requires a value judgment concerning which deaths one considers most undesirable. To treat the deaths as equal also involves a value judgment.

Framing the Risk Information

After negiotiating a risk analysis through all the subjective steps of defining the problem and its options, selecting and measuring risks in terms of particular outcomes, determining the people at risk and their exposure parameters and so on, one presents this information to the decision-maker, often referred to as *framing*. This process of presentation is also rife with subjectivity.

Numerous research studies have demonstrated that different (but logically equivalent) ways of presenting the same risk information can lead to different evaluations and decisions. One dramatic example of this comes from a study by McNeil et al (1982), who asked people to imagine that they had lung cancer and had to choose between two therapies, surgery or radiation. The two therapies were described in some detail. Then one group of subjects was presented with the cumulative probabilities of surviving for varying lengths of time after the treatment. A second group of subjects received the same cumulative probabilities framed in terms of dying rather than surviving (eg, instead of being told that 68% of those having surgery will have survived after one year, they were told that 32% will have died). Framing the statistics in terms of dying changed the percentage of subjects choosing radiation therapy over surgery from 18% to 44%. The effect was as strong for physicians as for laypersons.

Equally striking changes in preference result from framing the information about consequences in terms of either lives saved or lives lost (Tversky & Kahneman, 1981) or from describing an improvement in a river's water quality as a *restoration* of lost quality or an *improvement* from the current level (Gregory, Lichtenstein & MacGregor, 1993).

We now know that every form of presenting risk information is a frame that has a strong influence on the decision-maker. Moreover, when we contemplate the equivalency of lives saved versus lives lost, mortality rates versus survival rates, restoring lost water quality versus improving water quality and so forth, we see that there are often no 'right frames' or 'wrong frames' – just 'different frames'.

Multidimensionality of Risk

As noted, research has also shown that the public has a broad conception of risk, qualitative and complex, that incorporates considerations such as uncertainty, dread, catastrophic potential, controllability, equity, risk to future generations and so forth into the risk equation. In contrast, experts' perceptions of risk are not closely related to these dimensions or the characteristics that underlie them. Instead, studies show that experts tend to see riskiness as synonymous with expected mortality, consistent with the definition given above and consistent with the ways that risks tend to be characterized in risk assessments (see, for example, Cohen, 1985a). As a result of these different perspectives, many conflicts over 'risk' may result from experts and laypeople having different definitions of the concept. In this light, it is not surprising that expert recitations of 'risk statistics' often do little to change people's attitudes and perceptions.

There are legitimate, value-laden issues underlying the multiple dimensions of public risk perceptions, and these values need to be considered in risk-policy decisions. For example, is risk from cancer (a dreaded disease) worse than risk from auto accidents (not dreaded)? Is a risk imposed on a child more serious than a known risk accepted voluntarily by an adult? Are the deaths of 50 passengers in separate automobile accidents equivalent to the deaths of 50 passengers in one airplane crash? Is the risk from a polluted Superfund site worse if the site is located in a neighborhood that has a number of other hazardous facilities nearby? The difficult questions multiply when outcomes other than human health and safety are considered.

The Risk Game

There are clearly multiple conceptions of risk (Shrader-Frechette, 1991). Thompson and Dean (1996) note that the traditional view of risk characterized by event probabilities and consequences treats the many subjective and contextual factors described above as secondary or accidental dimensions of risk, just as coloration might be thought of as a secondary or accidental dimension of an eye. Accidental dimensions might be extremely influential in the formation of attitudes toward risk, just as having blue or brown coloration may be influential in forming attitudes toward eyes. Furthermore, it may be that all risks possess some accidental dimensions, just as all organs of sight are in some way colored. Nevertheless, accidental dimensions do not serve as criteria for determining whether someone is or is not at risk, just as coloration is irrelevant to whether something is or is not an eye.

I believe that the multidimensional, subjective, value-laden, frame-sensitive nature of risky decisions, as described above, supports a very different view, which Thompson and Dean call 'the contextualist conception'. This conception places probabilities and consequences on the list of relevant risk attributes along with voluntariness, equity and other important contextual parameters. On the contextualist view, the concept of risk is more like the concept of a game than the concept of the eye. Games have time limits, rules of play, opponents, criteria for winning or losing and so on, but none of these attributes is essential to the concept of a game, nor is any of them characteristic of all games. Similarly, a contextualist view of risk assumes that risks are characterized by some combination of attributes such as voluntariness, probability, intentionality, equity and so on, but that no one of these attributes is essential. The bottom line is that, just as there is no universal set of rules for games, there is no universal set of characteristics for describing risk. The characterization must depend upon which risk game is being played.

SEX, POLITICS AND EMOTION IN RISK JUDGMENTS

Given the complex and subjective nature of risk, it should not surprise us that many interesting and provocative things occur when people judge risks. Recent

studies have shown that factors such as gender, race, political worldviews, affiliation, emotional affect and trust are strongly correlated with risk judgments.
Equally important is that these factors influence the judgments of experts as
well as judgments of laypersons.

Sex

Sex is strongly related to risk judgments and attitudes. Several dozen studies
have documented the finding that men tend to judge risks as smaller and less
problematic than do women (Brody, 1984; Carney, 1971; DeJoy, 1992; Gutteling
& Wiegman, 1993; Gwartney-Gibbs & Lach, 1991; Pillisuk & Acredolo, 1988;
Sjöberg & Drottz-Sjöberg, 1993; Slovic, Flynn, Mertz et al, 1993; Slovic et al,
1989; Spigner, Hawkins & Loren, 1993; Steger & Witte, 1989; Stern, Dietz &
Kalof, 1993). A number of hypotheses have been put forward to explain sex
differences in risk perception. One approach has been to focus on biological
and social factors. For example, women have been characterized as more concerned about human health and safety because they are socialized to nurture and
maintain life (Steger & Witte, 1989). They have been characterized as physically
more vulnerable to violence, such as rape, and this may sensitize them to other
risks (Baumer, 1978; Riger, Gordon & LeBailly, 1978). The combination of
biology and social experience has been put forward as the source of a 'different
voice' that is distinct to women (Gilligan, 1982; Merchant, 1980).

A lack of knowledge and familiarity with science and technology has also been
suggested as a basis for these differences, particularly with regard to nuclear and
chemical hazards. Women are discouraged from studying science and there are
relatively few women scientists and engineers (Alper, 1993). However, Barke,
Jenkins-Smith and Slovic (1997) have found that female physical scientists judge
risks from nuclear technologies to be higher than do male physical scientists.
Similar results with scientists were obtained by Slovic et al (1997), who found
that female members of the British Toxicological Society were far more likely
than male toxicologists to judge societal risks as moderate or high (see Figure
25.1). Certainly, the female scientists in these studies cannot be accused of lacking knowledge and technological literacy. Something else must be going on.

Hints about the origin of these sex differences come from a study by Flynn
et al (1994) in which 1512 Americans were asked, for each of 25 hazard items,
to indicate whether the hazard posed:

- little or no risk;
- slight risk;
- moderate risk; or
- high risk to society.

Figure 25.2 shows the difference in the percentage of males and females who
rated a hazard as a high risk. All differences are to the right of the 0% mark,
indicating that the percentage of high-risk responses was greater for women on
every item. A similar graph (Figure 25.3) shows that the percentage of high-risk
responses was greater among people of color than among white respondents for
every item studied.

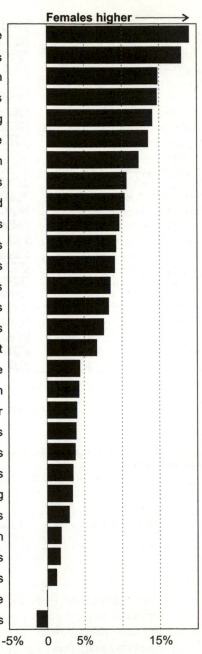

Females higher ⟶

Nuclear waste
Nuclear power reactors
Outdoor air pollution
Alcoholic beverages
Suntanning
Environmental tobacco smoke
Ozone depletion
Non-prescription drugs
Pesticides in food
Dioxins
Breast implants
Asbestos
Waste incinerators
Contraceptive pills
Prescription drugs
Chemical pollution in the environment
Crime and violence
Indoor air pollution
Tap water
Food additives
EMFs
Medical X-rays
Cigarette smoking
Mercury in fillings
Food irradiation
Motor vehicle accidents
Radon in homes
Chemical pollution in the workplace
Burning fossil fuels

-5%   0   5%   15%

Difference in percent of moderate-
and high-risk responses

Note: Percent difference is percent female moderate- and high-risk responses minus
percent male moderate- and high-risk responses (*N* = 92 females and 208 males).

Source: Slovic et al (1997).

Figure 25.1 *Perceived health risk to the average exposed British by gender:
Different between male and female members of the British Toxicological Society*

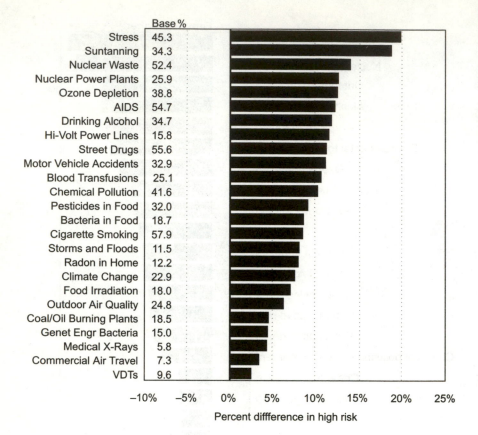

	Base %
Stress	45.3
Suntanning	34.3
Nuclear Waste	52.4
Nuclear Power Plants	25.9
Ozone Depletion	38.8
AIDS	54.7
Drinking Alcohol	34.7
Hi-Volt Power Lines	15.8
Street Drugs	55.6
Motor Vehicle Accidents	32.9
Blood Transfusions	25.1
Chemical Pollution	41.6
Pesticides in Food	32.0
Bacteria in Food	18.7
Cigarette Smoking	57.9
Storms and Floods	11.5
Radon in Home	12.2
Climate Change	22.9
Food Irradiation	18.0
Outdoor Air Quality	24.8
Coal/Oil Burning Plants	18.5
Genet Engr Bacteria	15.0
Medical X-Rays	5.8
Commercial Air Travel	7.3
VDTs	9.6

Percent diffference in high risk

Note: Base percent equals male high-risk response. Percent difference is female high-risk response minus male high-risk response.

Source: Flynn et al (1994)

Figure 25.2 *Perceived health risk to American public by gender: Difference between males and females*

Perhaps the most striking result from this study is shown in Figure 25.4, which presents the mean risk ratings separately for white males, white females, non-white males and non-white females. Across the 25 hazards, white males produced risk-perception ratings that were consistently much lower than the means of the other three groups. Although perceived risk was inversely related to income and educational level, controlling for these differences statistically did not reduce much of the white-male effect on risk perception. Figure 25.5 shows, for example, that white males exhibited far lower perceived risk at each of three levels of income and educational status.

When the data underlying Figure 25.4 were examined more closely, Flynn et al observed that not all white males perceived risks as low. The 'white-male effect' appeared to be caused by about 30% of the white-male sample who judged

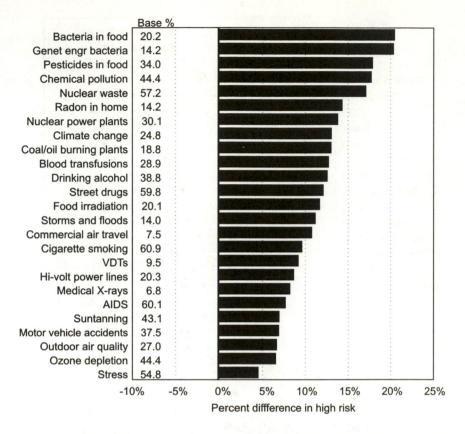

	Base %
Bacteria in food	20.2
Genet engr bacteria	14.2
Pesticides in food	34.0
Chemical pollution	44.4
Nuclear waste	57.2
Radon in home	14.2
Nuclear power plants	30.1
Climate change	24.8
Coal/oil burning plants	18.8
Blood transfusions	28.9
Drinking alcohol	38.8
Street drugs	59.8
Food irradiation	20.1
Storms and floods	14.0
Commercial air travel	7.5
Cigarette smoking	60.9
VDTs	9.5
Hi-volt power lines	20.3
Medical X-rays	6.8
AIDS	60.1
Suntanning	43.1
Motor vehicle accidents	37.5
Outdoor air quality	27.0
Ozone depletion	44.4
Stress	54.8

Percent diffference in high risk

Note: Base percent equals white high-risk response. Percent difference is non-white high-risk response minus white high-risk response.

Source: Flynn et al (1994)

Figure 25.3 *Perceived health risks to American public by race: Difference between whites and non-whites*

risks to be extremely low. The remaining white males were not much different from the other subgroups with regard to perceived risk.

What differentiated these white males who were most responsible for the effect from the rest of the sample, including other white males who judged risks as relatively high? When compared to the remainder of the sample, the group of white males with the lowest risk-perception scores were better educated (42.7% college or postgraduate degree versus 26.3% in the other group), had higher household incomes (32.1% above $50,000 versus 21%), and were politically more conservative (48% conservative versus 33.2%).

Particularly noteworthy is the finding that the low risk-perception subgroup of white males also held very different attitudes than the other respondents. Specifically, they were *more likely* than the others to:

- agree that future generations can take care of themselves when facing risks imposed upon them from today's technologies (64.2% versus 46.9%);

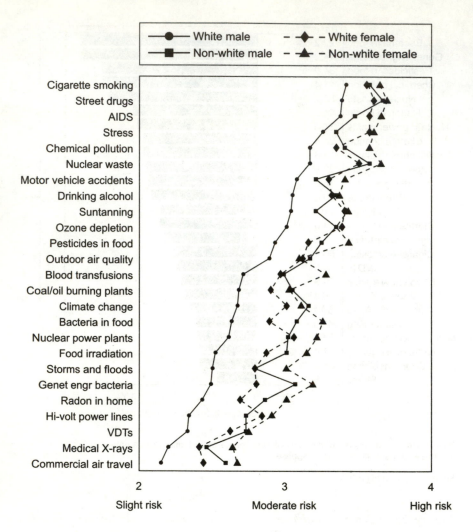

Source: Flynn et al (1994)

Figure 25.4 *Mean risk-perception ratings by race and gender*

- agree that if a risk is very small it is okay for society to impose that risk on individuals without their consent (31.7% versus 20.8%);
- agree that science can settle differences of opinion about the risks of nuclear power (61.8% versus 50.4%);
- agree that government and industry can be trusted with making the proper decisions to manage the risks from technology (48.0% versus 31.1%);
- agree that we can trust the experts and engineers who build, operate, and regulate nuclear power plants (62.6% versus 39.7%);
- agree that we have gone too far in pushing equal rights in this country (42.7% versus 30.9%);
- agree with the use of capital punishment (88.2% versus 70.5%);

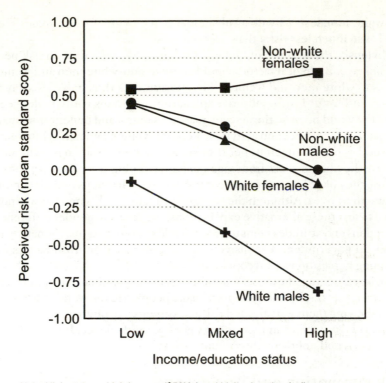

Figure 25.5 *Risk-perception index by race, gender, income and education*

- disagree that technological development is destroying nature (56.9% versus 32.8%);
- disagree that they have very little control over risks to their health (73.6% versus 63.1%);
- disagree that the world needs a more equal distribution of wealth (42.7% versus 31.3%);
- disagree that local residents should have the authority to close a nuclear power plant if they think it is not run properly (50.4% versus 25.1%);
- disagree that the public should vote to decide on issues such as nuclear power (28.5% versus 16.7%).

In sum, the subgroup of white males who perceive risks to be quite low can be characterized by trust in institutions and authorities and by anti-egalitarian attitudes, including a disinclination toward giving decision-making power to citizens in areas of risk management.

The results of this study raise new questions. What does it mean for the explanations of gender differences when we see that the sizable differences between white males and white females do not exist for non-white males and non-white females? Why do a substantial percentage of white males see the world as so much less risky than everyone else sees it?

Obviously, the salience of biology is reduced by these data on risk perception and race. Biological factors should apply to non-white men and women as well as to white men and women. The present data thus move us away from biology and toward sociopolitical explanations. Perhaps white males see less risk in the world because they create, manage, control and benefit from many of the major technologies and activities. Perhaps women and non-white men see the world as more dangerous because in many ways they are more vulnerable, because they benefit less from many of its technologies and institutions, and because they have less power and control over what happens in their communities and their lives. Although the survey conducted by Flynn et al was not designed to test these alternative explanations, the race and gender differences in perceptions and attitudes point toward the role of power, status, alienation, trust, perceived government responsiveness and other sociopolitical factors in determining perception and acceptance of risk.

To the extent that these sociopolitical factors shape public perception of risks, we can see why traditional attempts to make people see the world as white males do, by showing them statistics and risk assessments, are often unsuccessful. The problem of risk conflict and controversy goes beyond science. It is deeply rooted in the social and political fabric of our society.

Risk Perception and Worldviews

The influence of social, psychological and political factors also can be seen in studies examining the impact of worldviews on risk judgments.

Worldviews are general social, cultural and political attitudes that appear to have an influence over people's judgments about complex issues (Buss, Craik & Dake, 1986; Dake, 1991; Jasper, 1990). Dake (1991) has conceptualized worldviews as 'orienting dispositions', because of their role in guiding people's responses. Some of the worldviews identified to date are listed below, along with representative attitude statements:

- fatalism (eg, 'I feel I have very little control over risks to my health');
- hierarchy (eg, 'Decisions about health risks should be left to the experts');
- individualism (eg, 'In a fair system, people with more ability should earn more');
- egalitarianism (eg, 'If people were treated more equally, we would have fewer problems');
- technological enthusiasm (eg, 'A high-technology society is important for improving our health and social well-being').

People differ from one another in these views. Fatalists tend to think that what happens in life is preordained and one cannot change that. Hierarchists like a society organized so that commands flow down from authorities and obedience flows up the hierarchy. Egalitarians prefer a world in which power and wealth are more evenly distributed. Individualists like to do their own thing, unhindered by government or any other kind of constraints.

Table 25.3 *Agreement or Disagreement with an Individualism Worldview Is Associated with Percentage of Respondents Who Support Building New Nuclear Power Plants*

Individualism worldview: In a fair system people with more ability should earn more	Build new nuclear power plants (percent agree) [a]
Strongly disagree	37.5
Disagree	37.7
Agree	47.2
Strongly agree	53.4

[a] The precise statement was: 'If your community was faced with a potential shortage of electricity, do you agree or disagree that a new nuclear power plant should be built to supply that electricity?'

Table 25.4 *Agreement or Disagreement with an Egalitarian Worldview Is Associated with Percentage of Respondents Who Support Building New Nuclear Power Plants*

Egalitarian worldview: What this world needs is a more equal distribution of wealth	Build new nuclear power plants (percent agree) [a]
Strongly disagree	73.9
Disagree	53.7
Agree	43.8
Strongly agree	33.8

[a] The precise statement was: 'If your community was faced with a potential shortage of electricity, do you agree or disagree that a new nuclear power plant should be built to supply that electricity?'

Dake (1991; 1992), Jenkins-Smith (1993) and others have measured worldviews with survey techniques and found them to be strongly linked to public perceptions of risk. My colleagues and I have obtained similar results. Peters and Slovic (1996), using the same national survey data analyzed for race and gender effects by Flynn et al (1994), found particularly strong correlations between worldviews and attitudes toward nuclear power. Egalitarians tended to be strongly anti-nuclear; persons endorsing fatalist, hierarchist and individualistic views tended to be pro-nuclear. Tables 25.3 and 25.4 illustrate these findings for one individualism item (Table 25.3) and one egalitarian item (Table 25.4). When scales measuring the various worldviews were combined into a regression equation, they exhibited considerable ability to predict perceptions of risk from nuclear power and attitudes toward accepting a new nuclear power plant in one's community (see Figure 25.6).

Risk Perception and Affect

The studies described in the preceding section illustrate the role of worldviews as orienting mechanisms. Research suggests that affect is also an orienting mechanism that directs fundamental psychological processes such as attention, memory and information processing. Zajonc (1980), for example, argued that affective

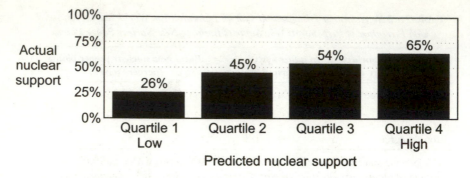

Note: Actual nuclear support was based on the percent agreeing that, if their community was faced with a potential shortage of electricity, a new nuclear power plant should be built to supply that electricity.

Figure 25.6 *Relationship between predictions of nuclear support based on fatalism, hierarchism, individualism and egalitarian worldviews and actual nuclear support*

reactions to stimuli are often the very first reactions, occurring without extensive perceptual and cognitive encoding and subsequently guiding information processing and judgment. According to Zajonc, all perceptions may contain some affect. 'We do not just see 'a house:' We see "a *handsome* house", "an *ugly* house" or "a *pretentious* house"' (p154). He later adds, 'We sometimes delude ourselves that we proceed in a rational manner and weigh all the pros and cons of the various alternatives. But this is probably seldom the actual case. Quite often "I decided in favor of *X*" is no more than "I liked *X*" ... We buy the cars we "like", choose the jobs and houses we find "attractive", and then justify these choices by various reasons' (p155).

If Zajonc is correct regarding the primacy and automaticity of affect, then affective reactions may also serve as orienting dispositions. Affect and worldviews may thus be functionally similar in that both may help us navigate quickly and efficiently through a complex, uncertain and sometimes dangerous world. This view is schematized in Figure 25.7, which indicates that people's perceptions of risk, their acceptance of risk and their trust in risk management are based on knowledge and experience. But the model in this figure also assumes that knowledge, experience and ultimately our risk evaluations are themselves colored by two overarching phenomena – worldviews and affect.

One demonstration of the influence of affect on risk perception comes from a study by Johnson and Tversky (1983). They found that reading about a tragic death increased people's frequency estimates for many other causes of death. Johnson and Tversky interpreted this as an indication that the negative affect generated by the tragic story influenced all the subsequent estimates, regardless of the similarity between the tragic event and other fatal events.

Support for the conception of affect as an orienting mechanism also comes from a study by Alhakami and Slovic (1994). They observed that, whereas the risks and benefits to society from various activities and technologies (eg, nuclear power, commercial aviation) tend to be *positively* associated in the world, they are *inversely* correlated in people's minds (higher perceived benefit is associated with

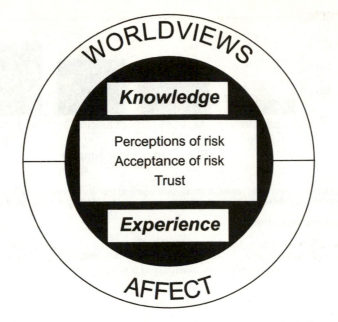

Figure 25.7 *Schematic model of worldviews and affect as orienting dispositions*

lower perceived risk; lower perceived benefit is associated with higher perceived risk). This inverse relationship had been observed previously in numerous studies of risk perception (eg, Fischhoff, Slovic, Lichtenstein, Read et al, 1978; Slovic, Kraus et al, 1991). Alhakami and Slovic found that this inverse relationship was linked to people's reliance on general affective evaluations when making risk-benefit judgments. When the affective evaluation was favorable (as with automobiles, for example), the activity or technology being judged was seen as having high benefit and low risk; when the evaluation was unfavorable (eg, as with pesticides), risks tended to be seen as high and benefits as low. It thus appears that the affective response is primary, and the risk and benefit judgments are derived (at least partly) from it (see also Chapter 26).

Slovic, Flynn, et al (1991) and Slovic, Layman, Kraus, et al (1991) studied the relationship between affect and perceived risk for hazards related to nuclear power. For example, Slovic, Flynn, et al asked respondents: 'What is the first thought or image that comes to mind when you hear the phrase "nuclear waste repository?"' After providing up to three associations to the repository stimulus, each respondent rated the affective quality of these associations on a five-point scale, ranging from extremely negative to extremely positive.

Although most of the images that people evoke when asked to think about nuclear power or nuclear waste are affectively negative (eg, death, destruction, war, catastrophe), some are positive (eg, abundant electricity and the benefits it brings). The affective values of these positive and negative images appear to sum in a way that is predictive of our attitudes, perceptions and behaviors. If the balance is positive, we respond favorably; if it is negative, we respond unfavorably. For example, the affective quality of a person's associations to a nuclear waste repository was found to be related to whether the person would vote for or

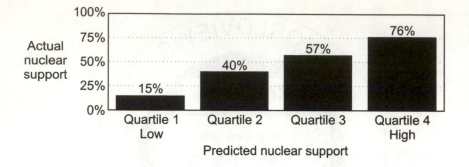

Note: Actual nuclear support was based on the percent agreeing that, if their community was faced with a potential shortage of electricity, a new nuclear power plant should be built to supply that electricity.

Source: Peters and Slovic (1996)

Figure 25.8 *Relationship between predictions of nuclear support based on affect and worldviews and actual nuclear support*

against a referendum on a nuclear waste repository and to their judgments regarding the risk of a repository accident. For example, more than 90% of those people whose first image was judged very negative said that they would vote against a repository in Nevada; fewer than 50% of those people whose first image was positive said they would vote against the repository (Slovic, Flynn et al, 1991).

Using data from the national survey of 1500 Americans described earlier, Peters and Slovic (1996) found that the affective ratings of associations to the stimulus 'nuclear power' were highly predictive of responses to the question: 'If your community was faced with a shortage of electricity, do you agree or disagree that a new nuclear power plant should be built to supply that electricity?' Among the 25% of respondents with the most positive associations to nuclear power, 69% agreed to the building of a new plant. Among the 25% of respondents with the most negative associations, only 13% agreed. A comparison of these percentages with those in the extreme quartiles of Figure 25.6 (65% and 26%, respectively) shows that affect was even more powerful as a predictor of nuclear power support than the combined worldviews. When affect plus the various worldviews were combined into one prediction equation, the ability to predict support for nuclear power was even stronger (see Figure 25.8).

Worldviews, Affect and Toxicology

Affect and worldviews seem to influence the risk-related judgments of scientists, as well as laypersons. Evidence for this comes from studies of 'intuitive toxicology' that Torbjörn Malmfors, Nancy Neil, Iain Purchase and I have been conducting in the US, Canada and the UK during the past eight years. These studies have surveyed both toxicologists and laypersons on a wide range of concepts relating to risks from chemicals. We have examined judgments about the effects of chemical concentration, dose and exposure on risk. We have also

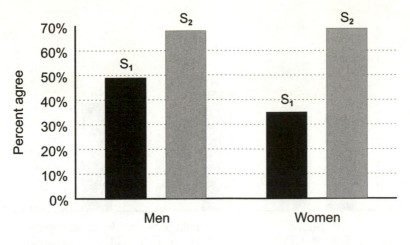

Source: Kraus et al (1992)

Figure 25.9 *Agreement among members of the US public (1988) for statements S_1 and S_2*

questioned our respondents about the value of animal studies for predicting the effects of chemicals on humans. Before showing how worldviews and affect enter into toxicologists' judgments, a brief description of some basic results will be presented.

Consider two survey items that we have studied repeatedly. One is statement S_1: 'Would you agree or disagree that the way an animal reacts to a chemical is a reliable predictor of how a human would react to it?' The second statement, S_2, is a little more specific: 'If a scientific study produces evidence that a chemical causes cancer in animals, then we can be reasonably sure that the chemical will cause cancer in humans'.

When members of the American and Canadian public responded to these items, they showed moderate agreement with S_1; about half the people agreed and half disagreed that animal tests were reliable predictors of human reactions to chemicals. However, in response to S_2, which stated that the animal study found evidence of cancer, there was a jump in agreement to about 70% among both male and female respondents (see Figure 25.9). The important point about the pattern of response is that agreement was higher on the second item.

What happens if toxicologists are asked about these two statements? Figure 25.10 shows that toxicologists in the US and toxicologists in the UK responded similarly to the public on the first statement but differently on the second. They exhibited the same rather middling level of agreement with the general statement about animal studies as predictors of human health effects.[1] However, when these studies were said to find evidence of carcinogenicity in animals, then the toxicologists were less likely to agree that the results could be extrapolated to humans. Thus, the same findings that lead toxicologists to be less willing to generalize to humans lead the public to see the chemical as more dangerous for humans.[2]

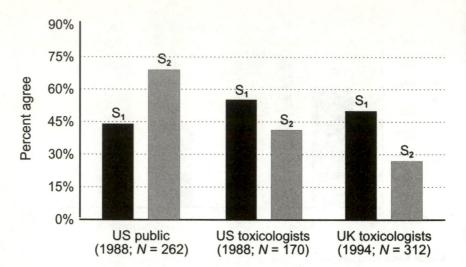

Figure 25.10 *Agreement with two statements, S₁ and S₂, regarding the extrapolation of chemical effects in animals to chemical effects in humans*

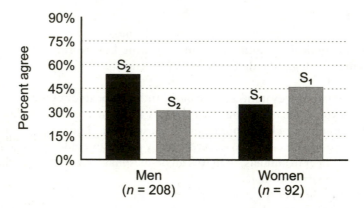

Figure 25.11 *Agreement of men and women toxicologists in the UK with two statements regarding extrapolation of chemical effects in animals to chemical effects in humans*

Figure 25.11 presents the responses for S_1 and S_2 among men and women toxicologists in the UK (208 men and 92 women). Here we see another interesting finding. The men agree less on the second statement than on the first, but the women agree more, just like the general public. Women toxicologists are more willing than men to say that one can generalize to humans from positive carcinogenicity findings in animals.

We created a change score between statements S_1 and S_2, with each individual getting a score of increasing agreement, decreasing agreement or no change. Selected correlations between this change score and other items in the survey of British toxicologists are shown in Table 25.5. A positive change score (meaning greater agreement with S_2 than with S_1) was associated with:

Table 25.5 *Correlations with the S_2-S_1 Change Score*

• Belief that there is a threshold dose for nongenotoxic carcinogens	−.33
• Risk Perception Index (average across 25 items)	.26
• Pesticides: Bad–Good rating	−.26
• Industrial chemicals: Bad–Good rating	−.25
• Sex: female	.25
• Age: young	−.23
• Agree to accept some risk to strengthen economy	−.23
• I have little control over health risks	.22
• Respondent works in an academic position	.19
• Technology is important for social well being	−.17
• Economic growth is necessary for quality of life	−.17
• Respondent works in industry	−.16

Note: All correlations are significant at $p < .01$

- disagreeing that there is a threshold dose for carcinogens;
- higher mean perceptions of risk across 25 hazards (the risk-perception index);
- rating pesticides and industrial chemicals as 'bad' on a task in which various items were rated on a scale ranging from *good* to *bad*;
- being female;
- being younger;
- agreeing that 'I have little control over risks to my health';
- holding an academic position rather than a position in industry;
- disagreeing that 'technology is important for social well-being'; and
- disagreeing that 'economic growth is necessary for good quality of life'.

These studies of intuitive toxicology have yielded a number of intriguing findings. One is the low percentage of agreement that animal studies can predict human health effects. Another is that toxicologists show even less confidence in studies that find cancer in animals resulting from chemical exposure. The public, on the other hand, has high confidence in animal studies that find cancer. Disagreements among toxicologists are systematically linked to gender, affiliation (academic versus other), worldviews and affect. Thus affective and sociopolitical factors appear to influence scientists' risk evaluations in much the same way as they influence the public's perceptions.[3]

TRUST

The research described above has painted a portrait of risk perception influenced by the interplay of psychological, social and political factors. Members of the public and experts can disagree about risk because they define risk differently, have different worldviews, different affective experiences and reactions or different social status. Another reason why the public often rejects scientists' risk assessments is lack of trust. Trust in risk management, like risk perception, has been found to correlate with gender, race, worldviews and affect.

Social relationships of all types, including risk management, rely heavily on trust. Indeed, much of the contentiousness that has been observed in the risk-management arena has been attributed to a climate of distrust that exists between the public, industry and risk-management professionals (eg, Slovic, 1993; Slovic, Flynn et al, 1991). The limited effectiveness of risk-communication efforts can be attributed to the lack of trust. If you trust the risk manager, communication is relatively easy. If trust is lacking, no form or process of communication will be satisfactory (Fessenden-Raden et al, 1987).

How Trust Is Created and Destroyed

One of the most fundamental qualities of trust has been known for ages. Trust is fragile. It is typically created rather slowly but it can be destroyed in an instant – by a single mishap or mistake. Thus, once trust is lost, it may take a long time to rebuild it to its former state. In some instances, lost trust may never be regained. Abraham Lincoln understood this quality. In a letter to Alexander McClure, he observed: 'If you *once* forfeit the confidence of your fellow citizens, you can *never* regain their respect and esteem' [emphasis added].

The fact that trust is easier to destroy than to create reflects certain fundamental mechanisms of human psychology called here 'the asymmetry principle'. When it comes to winning trust, the playing field is not level. It is tilted toward distrust (Slovic, 1993; see also Chapter 19).

RESOLVING RISK CONFLICTS: WHERE DO WE GO FROM HERE?

Technical Solutions to Risk Conflicts

One prominent proposal by Justice Stephen Breyer (1993) attempts to break what he sees as a vicious circle of public perception, congressional overreaction and conservative regulation that leads to obsessive and costly preoccupation with reducing negligible risks as well as to inconsistent standards among health and safety programs. Breyer sees public misperceptions of risk and low levels of mathematical understanding at the core of excessive regulatory response. His proposed solution is to create a small centralized administrative group charged with creating uniformity and rationality in highly technical areas of risk management. This group would be staffed by civil servants with experience in health and environmental agencies, the US Congress and the US Office of Management and Budget. A parallel is drawn between this group and the prestigious Conseil d'Etat in France.

Similar frustration with the costs of meeting public demands led the 104th US Congress to introduce numerous bills designed to require all major new regulations to be justified by extensive risk assessments. Proponents of this legislation argue that such measures are necessary to ensure that regulations are based on 'sound science' and effectively reduce significant risks at reasonable costs.

The language of this proposed legislation reflects the traditional narrow view of risk and risk assessment based 'only on the best reasonably available scientific data and scientific understanding'. Agencies are further directed to develop a systematic program for external peer review using 'expert bodies' or 'other devices comprised of participants selected on the basis of their expertise relevant to the sciences involved' (US Senate, 1995, pp57–8). Public participation in this process is advocated, but no mechanisms for this are specified.

The proposals by Breyer and the 104th US Congress are typical in their call for more and better technical analysis and expert oversight to rationalize risk management. There is no doubt that technical analysis is vital for making risk decisions better informed, more consistent and more accountable. However, value conflicts and pervasive distrust in risk management cannot easily be reduced by technical analysis. Trying to address risk controversies primarily with more science is, in fact, likely to exacerbate conflict.

Process-oriented Solutions

A major objective of this chapter has been to demonstrate the complexity of risk and its assessment. To summarize the earlier discussions, danger is real but risk is socially constructed. Risk assessment is inherently subjective and represents a blending of science and judgment with important psychological, social, cultural and political factors. Finally, our social and democratic institutions, remarkable as they are in many respects, breed distrust in the risk arena.

Whoever controls the definition of risk controls the rational solution to the problem at hand. If you define risk one way, then one option will rise to the top as the most cost-effective or the safest or the best. If you define it another way, perhaps incorporating qualitative characteristics and other contextual factors, you will likely get a different ordering of your action solutions (Fischhoff et al, 1984). Defining risk is thus an exercise in power.

Scientific literacy and public education are important, but they are not central to risk controversies. The public is not irrational. The public is influenced by emotion and affect in a way that is both simple and sophisticated. So are scientists. The public is influenced by worldviews, ideologies and values. So are scientists, particularly when they are working at the limits of their expertise.

The limitations of risk science, the importance and difficulty of maintaining trust and the subjective and contextual nature of the 'risk game' point to the need for a new approach – one that focuses on introducing more public participation within both risk assessment and risk decision-making in order to make the decision process more democratic, improve the relevance and quality of technical analysis and increase the legitimacy and public acceptance of the resulting decisions. Work by scholars and practitioners in Europe and North America has begun to lay the foundations for improved methods of public participation within deliberative decision processes that include negotiation, mediation, oversight committees and other forms of public involvement (English, 1992; Kunreuther et al, 1993; National Research Council, 1996; Renn, Webler & Johnson, 1991; Renn, Webler & Wiedemann, 1995).

Recognizing interested and affected citizens as legitimate partners in the exercise of risk assessment is no short-term panacea for the problems of risk management. But serious attention to participation and process issues may, in the long run, lead to more satisfying and successful ways to manage risk.

ACKNOWLEDGMENT

Preparation of this chapter was supported by the Alfred P Sloan Foundation, the Electric Power Research Institute and the National Science Foundation under Grants No 91-10592 and SBR 94-122754. Portions of the text appeared in H Kunreuther & P Slovic (1996). *Science, Values, and Risk: the Annals of the American Academy of Political and Social Science*, 545, pp116-25.

NOTES

1   This is actually a very surprising result, given the heavy reliance on animal studies in toxicology.

2   This pattern suggests that animal studies may be scaring the public without informing science.

3   Although we have focused only on the relationship between toxicologists' reaction to chemicals and their responses to S_1 and S_2, there were many other links between affect and attitudes in the survey. For example, very simple bad–good ratings of pesticides correlated significantly ($r = .20$) with agreement that there is a threshold dose for non-genotoxic carcinogens. The same ratings correlated $-.27$ with the belief that synergistic effects of chemicals cause animal studies of single chemicals to underestimate risk to humans.

26 The Affect Heuristic in Judgments of Risks and Benefits

Melissa L Finucane, Ali Alhakami,
Paul Slovic and Stephen M Johnson

Although affect has long played a key role in many behavioral theories, it has rarely been recognized as an important component of human judgment and decision-making. Perhaps befitting its rationalistic origins, the main focus of descriptive decision research has been cognitive, rather than affective. When principles of utility maximization appeared to be descriptively inadequate, Simon (1956) oriented the field toward problem-solving and information-processing models based upon bounded rationality and concepts such as satisficing (as opposed to maximizing). The work of Tversky and Kahneman (1974) demonstrated how boundedly rational individuals employed heuristics such as availability, representativeness and anchoring and adjustment to make judgments, and how they used simplified strategies such as 'elimination by aspects' to make choices (Tversky, 1972). Other investigators elaborated the cognitive strategies underlying judgment and choice through models of constructed preferences (Slovic, 1995; Payne, Bettman & Johnson, 1992), dominance structuring (Montgomery, 1983) and comparative advantages (Shafir, Osherson & Smith, 1989). In 1993, the entire volume of the journal *Cognition* was dedicated to the topic of reason-based choice, in which it was argued that 'Decisions ... are often reached by focusing on reasons that justify the selection of one option over another' (Shafir, Simonson & Tversky, 1993, p34). Similarly, a recent state-of-the-art review was entitled 'Decision Making from a Cognitive Perspective' (Busemeyer, Hastie & Medin, 1995). In keeping with its title, it contained almost no references to the influence of affect on decisions.

Despite this cognitive emphasis, the importance of affect is being acknowledged increasingly by decision researchers.[1] A limited role for affect was acknowledged by Shafir et al (1993) who conceded that: 'People's choices may

---

Note: reprinted from *Journal of Behavioral Decision Making*, 2000, 13, 1–17. Copyright 2000 © John Wiley & Sons Limited. Reproduced with permission.

occasionally stem from affective judgments that preclude a thorough evaluation of the options' (p32, emphasis added).

A strong early proponent of the importance of affect in decision-making was Zajonc (1980), who argued that affective reactions to stimuli are often the very first reactions, occurring automatically and subsequently guiding information processing and judgment. According to Zajonc, all perceptions contain some affect. 'We do not just see "a house": we see a *handsome* house, an *ugly* house or a *pretentious* house' (p154). He later adds, 'We sometimes delude ourselves that we proceed in a rational manner and weigh all the pros and cons of the various alternatives. But this is probably seldom the actual case. Quite often "I decided in favor of X" is no more than "I liked X" ... We buy the cars we "like", choose the jobs and houses we find "attractive", and then justify these choices by various reasons' (p155).

One of the most comprehensive and dramatic theoretical accounts of the role of affect in decision-making is presented in Damasio's (1994) somatic marker hypothesis. In seeking to determine 'what in the brain allows humans to behave rationally', Damasio argues that thought is made largely from images, broadly construed to include perceptual and symbolic representations. A lifetime of learning leads these images to become 'marked' by positive and negative feelings linked directly or indirectly to somatic or bodily states. When a negative somatic marker is linked to an image of a future outcome, it sounds an alarm. When a positive marker is associated with the outcome image, it becomes a beacon of incentive. Damasio hypothesized that somatic markers increase the accuracy and efficiency of the decision process and the absence of such markers, observed in people with certain types of brain damage, degrades decision performance.

Other theorists give affect a direct role in motivating behavior, asserting or implying that we integrate positive and negative feelings according to some sort of automatic, rapid 'affective algebra', whose operations and rules remain to be discovered. Epstein's (1994, p716) view on this is clear, although he gives no clue as to how feelings are integrated:

> The experiential system is assumed to be intimately associated with the experience of affect ... which refer[s] to subtle feelings of which people are often unaware. When a person responds to an emotionally significant event ... the experiential system automatically searches its memory banks for related events, including their emotional accompaniments ... If the activated feelings are pleasant, they motivate actions and thoughts anticipated to reproduce the feelings. If the feelings are unpleasant, they motivate actions and thoughts anticipated to avoid the feelings.

Also emphasizing the motivational role of affect, Mowrer (1960a; b) conceptualizes conditioned emotional responses to images as prospective gains and losses that directly 'guide and control performance in a generally sensible adaptive manner' (1960a, p30). He criticizes theorists who postulate purely cognitive variables such as expectancies as intervening between stimulus and response, reiterating the concern of Guthrie (1952) that we must be careful not to leave the organism at the choice point 'lost in thought'. Mowrer's solution is to view expectancies more dynamically as conditioned emotions such as hopes and fears, which serve as motivating states leading to action.

Despite the increasing popularity of affect in research programs and recent attempts to acknowledge the importance of the interplay between affect and cognition, little progress has been made in developing a theory about the role of affect in judgment and decision-making. Drawing on ideas about affect marking images (eg, Damasio, 1994), which in turn motivates behavior (eg, Epstein, 1994; Mowrer, 1960a; b), we propose that affect is an essential component in many forms of judgment and decision-making. The ideas articulated below are intended as a first step toward encouraging the development of theory about, and methods for exposing, the role of affect in judgment.

The basic tenet in this paper is that images, marked by positive and negative affective feelings, guide judgment and decision-making.[2] Specifically, we propose that people use an *affect heuristic* to make judgments. That is, representations of objects and events in people's minds are tagged to varying degrees with affect. People consult or refer to an 'affective pool' (containing all the positive and negative tags associated with the representations consciously or unconsciously) in the process of making judgments. Just as imaginability, memorability and similarity serve as cues for probability judgments (eg, the availability and representativeness heuristics), affect may serve as a cue for many important judgments. Using an overall, readily available affective impression can be far easier – more efficient – than weighing the pros and cons or retrieving from memory many relevant examples, especially when the required judgment or decision is complex or mental resources are limited. This characterization of a mental short-cut leads us to label the use of affect a 'heuristic'.

To illustrate the role of affect in judgment and show how we can ascertain people's use of the affect heuristic, we focus on a specific problem, namely, trying to explain the often observed inverse relationship between judgments of risk and benefit.

Using the Affect Heuristic to Explain the Inverse Relationship between Perceived Risk and Perceived Benefit

Within an analytic view of judgment and decision-making, risk and benefit are distinct concepts. The nature of the gains attained from pursuit of a hazardous activity or technology is qualitatively different from the nature of the risks. For instance, the benefit gained from using roller blades (eg, entertaining pastime) is different from the risk (eg, injury from a car collision). Driving to work, eating beef and using a cellular phone are other examples of activities with distinct benefits and risks. Though distinct, risks and benefits generally tend to be positively correlated. Whereas activities that bring great benefits may be high or low in risk, activities that are low in benefit are unlikely to be high in risk (if they were, they would be proscribed), suggesting the positive correlation in Figure 26.1.

Although risk and benefit may be positively correlated in the environment, numerous studies have shown them to be negatively related in peoples' minds. For example, Fischhoff, Slovic, Lichtenstein and Read et al (1978), Slovic, Kraus et al (1991), and McDaniels, Axelrod, Cavanagh and Slovic (1997) reported that for many hazards the greater the perceived benefit, the lower the

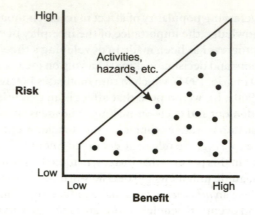

Figure 26.1 *Hypothesized relationship between risk and benefit in the environment. Risk and benefit are positively correlated across activities*

perceived risk, and vice versa. Smoking, alcoholic beverages and food additives tend to be seen as very high in risk and relatively low in benefit, while vaccines, antibiotics and X-rays tend to be seen as very high in benefit and relatively low in risk.

A study by Alhakami and Slovic (1994) suggested that risk and benefit may be inversely related in people's minds because an affective feeling is referred to when the risk or benefit of specific hazards is judged. Specifically, Alhakami and Slovic observed that the relationship between perceived risk and perceived benefit was linked to an individual's general affective evaluation of a hazard. If an activity was 'liked', people tended to judge its risks as low and its benefits as high. If the activity was 'disliked', the judgments were opposite – high risk and low benefit. The model implied by this behavior is similar to the model Zajonc proposed in 1980. Our model assumes that affect comes prior to, and directs, judgments of risk and benefit. See Figure 26.2.

Despite supporting evidence of the role of affect in judgment and decision-making, a cognitive interpretation of Alhakami and Slovic's (1994) results cannot be excluded completely. Their experimental design cannot rule out the possibility that risk and benefit judgments are correlated negatively because

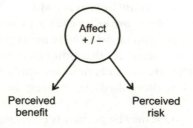

Figure 26.2 *A model of the affect heuristic explaining the risk/benefit confounding observed by Alhakami and Slovic (1994). (Judgments of risk and benefit are assumed to be derived by reference to an overall affective evaluation of the stimulus item)*

individuals approach the judgment tasks analytically, producing a 'net riskiness' or 'net benefit' judgment rather than independent judgments of risk and benefit. That is, individuals may be making judgments (regardless of whether the rating scale focuses only on risk or on benefit) by deliberating on what the net difference between risk and benefit is for any particular item.

STUDY 1: RISK AND BENEFIT JUDGMENTS UNDER TIME PRESSURE

Study 1 attempted to rule out the possibility of a cognitive explanation for the inverse risk-benefit relationship by using a 'time-pressure' methodology (see Benson & Beach, 1996; Ordóñez & Benson, 1997). Inducing time pressure when individuals are making judgments has two main consequences compatible with the goal of exposing the importance of affect in judgment. As outlined by Maule and Svenson (1993), perception that time is limited may influence judgment by:

- inducing affective changes via a generally increased arousal level (making 'hot' affective processes more salient than analytical cognitive processes);
- reducing cognitive resources available for analytical deliberation during risk and benefit judgments (because the awareness of time pressure demands that resources are allocated to monitoring the time available).

Most time-pressure research has examined how cognitive processes and outcomes change as a result of the minimization of cognitive effort (see Beach & Mitchell, 1978; Edland & Svenson, 1993; Kerstholt, 1994; Payne, Bettman & Johnson, 1988; Svenson, Edland & Slovic, 1990). However, from our perspective the methodology is most relevant because of its potential for manipulating individuals' heuristic reliance on affect when making judgments.

So far, few researchers have exploited the potential of time-pressure studies to highlight the use of affectively-based heuristics. One exception was an examination of the influence of attitudes and stereotypes on judgments of people belonging to particular social categories by Dijker and Koomen (1996). They found greater differences between 'ingroup' and 'outgroup' targets when judgments were made under time pressure, suggesting that when processing is difficult people tend to use an 'acceptability heuristic' (ie, the tendency to produce socially acceptable judgments; see Tetlock, Skitka & Boettger, 1989). Dijker and Koomen reported that under time pressure, subjects seemed to base their judgments on both positive and negative aspects of their attitudes; they concluded that emotional responses toward social groups are important components in judgments. Similarly, we anticipated that reliance on affect in the domain of judgments about hazards could be exposed by inducing time pressure.

According to the affect heuristic, people may judge the risks and benefits of hazards by accessing a pool of positive and negative feelings that they associate with the hazards. The affect heuristic is more efficient than analytic processing. Thus, compared with individuals not under any time pressure, we expected those under time pressure to rely more heavily on affect because efficiency is important. Stronger negative correlations between risk and benefit judgments were expected for participants in the *time-pressure* than in the *no time-pressure* condition.

Method

Participants

Fifty-four first-year psychology students from the University of Western Australia (mean age 19 years) participated in the study for course credit. Females constituted 78% of the sample.

Design

Participants were randomly assigned to one of two conditions (time pressure or no time pressure) and to one of two counterbalancing orders (risk judgments followed by benefit judgments, or vice versa).

Apparatus

Stimuli were presented via computer, using MetaCard 2.1.2 on an IBM 486 (DX-4100) with a 15-inch monitor.

Stimuli and Procedure

All instructions were presented on the computer monitor. First, participants learned that they would be making judgments about the risk (or benefit) of various activities and technologies for Australian society as a whole, on a seven-point scale ranging from *not at all risky (beneficial)* to *very risky (beneficial)*. The scale was shown and the end point labels flashed in yellow to attract participants' attention. The participants were then shown how to move the mouse and click on the scale to make a rating. For the time-pressure condition, the instructions next indicated, in capital letters, that only a short time would be available for participants to click on the scale for each item and that a response must be made before a clock shown at the bottom of the screen ticked down completely from green to red. A demonstration of the clock ticking down was given. For the no time-pressure condition, participants were instructed to take as much time as they wanted to complete the ratings; no clock was present.

Participants were presented with eight hazardous facilities or activities for rating in practice trials, and 23 items for the experimental trials (eg, cars, chemical plants). The beginning of each trial was signaled by the computer with the sound of a bell, at which time the name of the item was shown in the middle of the monitor (and the clock in the time-pressure condition began to tick down). Pilot testing ($n = 10$) under the no time-pressure condition showed that about 5.2 seconds was one standard deviation faster than the mean times for risk and benefit ratings. Thus, in the time-pressure condition the clock was set to run out of time after 5.2 seconds for each item, at which point a yellow sign flashed above the scale saying 'You MUST click on the scale NOW', and the computer made a beeping sound until a rating was made.

Each participant received the items in a different random order. When all items had been rated on the first scale (either risk or benefit), the instructions were shown for the second (benefit or risk) scale, and all items were presented in a different random order again for rating.

Results

Manipulation Check

As expected, participants in the time-pressure condition took significantly less time to do the risk judgments than did participants in the no time-pressure condition (M = 101.24 seconds, sd = 15.94 versus M = 127.27 seconds, sd = 29.12); $t(52)$ = 4.11, $p<.001$. The same was true for the benefit judgments (M = 100.71 seconds, sd = 14.16 versus M = 126.57 seconds, sd = 34.57); $t(52)$ = 3.65, $p<.001$.

Correlations

The correlation between judged risk and judged benefit across the 23 items based on mean ratings was −.80 for the time-pressure condition and −.75 for the no time-pressure condition. Both these correlations are heavily influenced by two extreme items, cigarettes (benefit M = 1.29, risk M = 6.22 for time pressure; benefit M = 1.79, risk M = 6.33 for no time pressure) and solar power (benefit M = 6.26, risk M = 1.68 for time pressure; benefit M = 6.21, risk M = 1.55 for no time pressure). There were no other means less than 2.37 and only two other means greater than 5.88 (air travel, benefit M = 6.10 for no time pressure and risk M = 6.02 for time pressure). Nonetheless, correlations calculated after eliminating cigarettes and solar power showed the same results: negative relationships between judged risk and judged benefit, with correlations of −.69 under time pressure and −.62 under no time pressure.

Correlations calculated on each individual's ratings across the 21 items showed the same pattern. For the time-pressure condition, the mean correlation was −.45; the range was from −.95 to +.28; 27 of the 28 participants' correlations in this condition were negative (96%). For the no time-pressure condition, the mean correlation was −.33; the range was from −.73 to +.30; 22 of the 26 participants' correlations were negative (85%). The difference between the two mean correlations approached significance; $t(52)$ = 1.64, p = .05, 1-tailed.

Another way of looking at these data is via individual differences. If people use the affect heuristic, then a person who has a positive feeling about, say, cellular phones, will rate it higher on benefit and lower on risk than will another person whose affect is not so positive. This will induce a negative correlation between risk and benefit ratings for cellular phones across participants.

As shown in Table 26.1, correlations across participants between rated risk and rated benefit were negative for all but one of the 23 items in the time-pressure condition, and for all but four items in the no time-pressure condition. As expected, the correlations were more strongly negative under time pressure than under no time pressure for most items (19 out of 23). For the time-pressure condition, 13 correlations were significantly negative (eight at the .01 level, and five at the .05 level), while only two items showed a significant negative correlation for the no time-pressure condition. The highest negative correlations under time pressure were found for alcoholic beverages (r = −.71), water fluoridation (r = −.68), chemical plants (r = −.62), eating beef (r = −.53), food preservatives (r = −.52), cars (r = −.48), cigarettes (r = −.48), and pesticides

Table 26.1 *Correlations Across Participants between Perceived Risk and Perceived Benefit Under Time Pressure (N = 28) and No Time-pressure (N = 26) Conditions*

Item	Time pressure	No time pressure
Alcoholic beverages	-.71**	.07
Water fluoridation	-.68**	-.33
Chemical plants	-.62**	-.10
Eating beef	-.53**	-.30
Food preservatives	-.52**	-.24
Cars	-.48**	-.36*
Cigarettes	-.48**	-.24
Pesticides	-.47**	-.07
Natural gas	-.41*	.13
Chemical fertilizers	-.41*	-.07
Explosives	-.39*	-.10
Cellular phones	-.36*	-.44*
Food irradiation	-.35*	-.01
Roller blades	-.31	-.02
Nuclear power plants	-.30	-.07
Surfing	-.28	.01
Swimming pools	-.27	-.28
Solar power	-.27	-.03
Railroads	-.25	-.02
Air travel	-.22	.21
Motorcycles	-.20	-.16
Microwave ovens	-.06	-.23
Bicycles	.02	-.04
Mean r	-.37	-.12

* $p<.05$ (1-tailed)
** $p<.01$ (1-tailed)

($r = -.47$). In contrast, the highest negative correlations under no time pressure were more modest, including cellular phones ($r = -.44$), cars ($r = -.36$), and water fluoridation ($r = -.33$). See Table 26.1. At the item level, the difference between the correlation under time pressure and the correlation under no time pressure was statistically significant for alcoholic beverages ($p < .001$), and for water fluoridation, chemical plants, natural gas and pesticides ($p < .05$).

Discussion of Study 1

Study 1 investigated the inverse relationship between risk and benefit judgments under conditions designed to limit the use of analytical thought and enhance the use of the affect heuristic. As expected, we found that the inverse relationship strengthened when time pressure was introduced. The stronger inverse relationship under time pressure was demonstrated in terms of more negative correlations between perceived benefit and perceived risk, within individuals over hazards and within hazards over individuals. The results are consistent with theories suggesting that people use affect to make judgments (Zajonc, 1980) and that affect is an important evaluation mechanism in risk perception (eg, Alhakami & Slovic, 1994; Peters & Slovic, 1996; Slovic, 1997).[3]

Reliance on the affect heuristic seems to be exposed more clearly when people's opportunity for analytic deliberation is reduced and an efficient mode of judgment is needed. The results are consistent with Dijker and Koomen's (1996) report that time pressure reduces people's use of data-driven, attribute-based processing strategies and increases reliance on a more holistically evaluative strategy (in their case, attitudes). Although Dijker and Koomen refer to reliance on attitudes as a schema-driven strategy, which seems to have a cognitive connotation, their discussion underlines the importance of considering the affective components (emotional responses) of attitudes that affect judgments. Likewise, we suggest that reliance on affective processes to make quick judgments when cognitive processing is difficult is exhibited in our time-pressure condition and is an underexplored explanation of time-pressure effects.

Finally, of note is that the correlations found in study 1 in the no time-pressure condition are smaller for many items (ie, less negative) than those found previously (eg, water fluoridation; Alhakami & Slovic, 1994). The discrepancies may be due to methodological differences. In the present study we urged participants in the no time-pressure condition 'to take as much time as desired', whereas participants in the Alhakami and Slovic study worked quickly through the ratings as part of a longer experiment. Making the task part of a larger set of demands may implicitly induce some sense of time pressure for participants. Cultural differences may also have contributed to the results. Alhakami and Slovic used American participants, but the present study was conducted in Australia where the risks and benefits of hazards may be experienced or perceived differently from the risks and benefits found in an American context (Finucane & Maybery, 1996; Rohrmann, 1994).

STUDY 2: MANIPULATING AFFECT BY PROVIDING RISK AND BENEFIT INFORMATION

Study 1 tested the affect heuristic by experimentally manipulating time pressure to force greater reliance on affect. Study 2 carried out another, but very different, experimental test of the affect model. The basic idea is simple. If people consult their overall affective evaluation of an item (say nuclear power) when judging its risk and benefit, then raising or lowering the favorability of the affective impression should alter both the risk and benefit judgments derived from that impression. That is, we expect risk and benefit judgments for a hazard to be congruent with the overall affective evaluation of the hazard.

One way to alter the favorability of the overall impression is through provision of information. For example, nuclear power could take on a more favorable affective evaluation as a result of information indicating that it has high benefit or, alternatively, that it has low risk.

According to the affect model, information indicating that the benefit is high should lead to a more favorable affective impression and thus to lower judgments of risk (because risk would be derived from the more favorable overall impression and a more attractive technology would be judged to have lower risk). Similarly, information that the risk is low should lead to an inference that the benefit is high (again because the technology has been made more attrac-

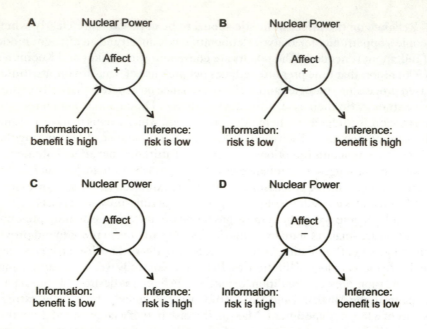

Figure 26.3 *Model showing how information about benefit (A) or information about risk (B) could increase the global affective evaluation of nuclear power and lead to inferences about risk and benefit that are affectively congruent with the information input. (Similarly, information could decrease the global affective evaluation of nuclear power as in C and D, resulting in inferences that are opposite from those in A and B)*

tive overall). These two predictions are summarized in parts A and B of Figure 26.3 and in rows 1 and 4 of Table 26.2. In parallel fashion, overall positive affect toward nuclear power could be decreased by information indicating that benefit is low or risk is high, as shown in parts C and D of Figure 26.3. The model predicts that decreasing the overall affective favorability of nuclear power by decreasing perceived benefit would lead to an increase in perceived risk. Similarly, decreasing favorability by increasing perceived risk should lead to a decrease in judgments of benefit. These predictions are summarized in rows 2 and 3 of Table 26.2.

We can contrast these predictions, based upon the affect heuristic, with an alternative prediction derived from a cognitive analysis. Since care is taken in this design to provide information only about risk or only about benefit, it should

Table 26.2 *Manipulations of Benefit and Risk Information and Predicted Effects on the Non-manipulated Attribute*

Information content	Predicted effect on non-manipulated attribute
1 Benefit is high	Decrease perceived risk
2 Benefit is low	Increase perceived risk
3 Risk is high	Decrease perceived benefit
4 Risk is low	Increase perceived benefit

be difficult for the respondent to analytically derive a congruent judgment (eg, benefit is high) from the information given (eg, risk is low). Therefore, one might expect the non-manipulated attribute (benefit in this case) to remain unchanged upon receipt of information pertaining to the other attribute (risk in this case). This explanation would thus predict little or no systematic effect of the information on benefit, the non-manipulated attribute.

Method

Participants
Two hundred and nineteen undergraduate students from the University of Oregon (mean age 21 years) participated in the study. Females constituted 49 % of the sample.

Design
A mixed, 4 (affective information: high risk/low risk/high benefit/ low benefit) x 3 (technologies: nuclear power/natural gas/food preservatives) design was used, with the first factor between subjects and the second factor within subjects. Participants were randomly assigned to one of the four experimental conditions that corresponded to the use of vignettes designed to increase or decrease perceived risk and perceived benefit. The high-risk and high-benefit conditions each included 56 participants; for the low-risk and low-benefit conditions there were 54 and 53 participants, respectively. Three vignettes were given to participants in each condition: one each about nuclear power, natural gas and food preservatives.

Stimuli and Procedure
Participants completed a questionnaire as part of a larger series of judgment studies. Initially, ratings of each technology's benefits and risks were elicited. For example, participants were asked: 'In general, how beneficial do you consider the use of natural gas to be to US society as a whole?' and made ratings on 10-point scales ranging from *not at all beneficial* to *very beneficial*. A similar question and scale was used for eliciting risk ratings.

Next, instructions indicated to participants that the subsequent pages contained some general information about the benefits (risks) associated with each of several technologies, and even though it was recognized that there were some risks (benefits) associated with these technologies, the latter would not be dealt with at this time (see the appendix at the end of this chapter for examples from the nuclear power series). Participants were told that after they had read the information they would be asked to make several judgments about each technology. The questions and 10-point scales used to collect risk and benefit ratings following the vignettes were identical to those that preceded the vignettes.

Results

Ratings of risk and benefit before and after the information manipulation was presented were averaged across participants. The effect of the manipulation was assessed by, first, taking the mean difference in the ratings for the *manipulated* attribute and dividing by the standard error of the mean to produce a *t* value; and, second, calculating a similar *t* value for the *non-manipulated* attribute.

For example, the brief paragraph about nuclear power given to 56 subjects in the low-risk condition (see the appendix) led the mean judged risk from nuclear power to decrease from 7.48 (prior to information) to 6.61 (post information); $t = -2.54$; $p < .01$. The judged benefits of nuclear power increased, as predicted, after receipt of the information about low risk, moving from 5.25 (prior to information) to 6.02 (post information); $t = 3.33$; $p < .01$. All 12 such *t* values (three technologies by four experimental conditions) are plotted in Figure 26.4. The affect model predicts that the non-manipulated attribute would change in a direction affectively congruent with the manipulation. That is, if the manipulation was designed to decrease perceived risk, then perceived benefit should increase, leading to an inverse relationship between the manipulated and non-manipulated attributes. As predicted, the non-manipulated attribute generally changed in the direction affectively congruent with the manipulation (the only exceptions were food LB and nuclear LB). The correlation across the 12 data points was –.75.

Perhaps more informative than the aggregated data in Figure 26.4 are the reactions of individual subjects to the information manipulations. Recall that each of the 219 subjects received three vignettes, making a total of $219 \times 3 = 657$ attempted manipulations of affect and response. As noted in the bottom row of Table 26.3, the manipulation worked for 50% of the attempts (judgments of perceived risk increased after receipt of information saying risk was high; judgments of perceived benefit decreased after receipt of information saying benefit was low; etc). The judgment remained unchanged after receipt of information for 33% of the attempts and the judgment changed in the wrong direction 16% of the time. The success of the manipulation was slightly higher in

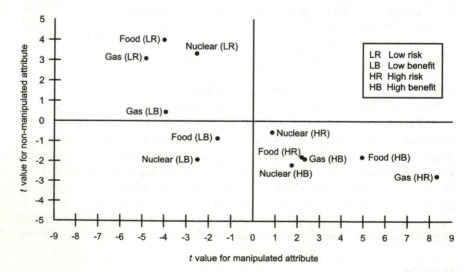

Figure 26.4 *t values for manipulated versus non-manipulated attributes for four information manipulations (high risk, low risk, high benefit and low benefit) about three technologies (nuclear power, natural gas and food preservatives)*

the low-risk condition (58%) and for the natural gas information set (57%). The manipulation was somewhat less successful for nuclear power (45%).

Table 26.4 shows the change in judgments regarding the *non-manipulated* attribute, after the information manipulation occurred. Note that for the 331 cases in which the information worked as intended on the manipulated attribute, the effect on the non-manipulated attribute was in the affectively congruent direction (as predicted) for 45% of the cases. There was no change in the non-manipulated attribute for 31% of those cases and there was a change that went in the same direction as the manipulation (opposite the prediction) for 23% of the cases. In sum, when the information manipulation worked, the judgment of the non-manipulated attribute tended to move in the predicted direction. The results clearly differ from what would be predicted from a cognitive model that recognized the lack of direct relevance between the information provided about risk (or benefit) and the judgment requested regarding the non-manipulated attribute. Such a model would have predicted that the no-change responses would be dominant, a result that did not occur.

The predicted response was much less frequent when the manipulation failed to cause a change in judgment (in Table 26.4, compare the first column of data in row 2 with the first data column in row 1). Interestingly, when the information produced a change in the manipulated attribute that was in the wrong direction (row 3 of the table), the judgment of the non-manipulated attribute moved in a direction opposite (but affectively congruent with) the change in the first judgment on 33% of the occasions, giving further indication of the tendency for risk and benefit judgments to move in inverse relationship to one another.[4]

Discussion of Study 2

The results of study 2 confirmed the prediction that evaluative judgments on one affective attribute can be influenced by experimentally manipulating information on another affective attribute. The findings are generally consistent with the idea that people use the affect heuristic to make judgments about risk and benefit.

Importantly, study 2 showed that the inverse relationship between perceived risk and perceived benefit found in study 1 and other previous studies (eg,

Table 26.3 *Effect of the Manipulation on the Attribute that was Manipulated*

Condition	Percent of trials that manipulation worked	Percent of trials that effect was opposite manipulation	Percent of trials no change
High benefit	50	16	34
Low benefit	47	19	35
High risk	47	18	35
Low risk	58	13	29
Natural gas	57	11	32
Nuclear power	45	21	34
Food preservatives	49	17	33
Overall ($N = 657$)	50	16	33

Table 26.4 *Effect of the Risk and Benefit Manipulations on Judgments about the Non-manipulated Attribute*

	Effect on the non-manipulated attribute		
Effect on the manipulated attribute	Percent of trials prediction confirmed	Percent of trials change was opposite of prediction	Percent of trials no change
Manipulation worked N = 331 (50.4%)	45[a]	23	31
No change N = 218 (33.2%)	20	15	64
Change was contrary to manipulation N = 108 (16.4%)	26	33	41
Total N = 657	34	22	44

[a] The corresponding percentages for natural gas, nuclear power and food preservatives were 46, 41 and 49 respectively.

Alhakami & Slovic, 1994) is causally determined. That is, the study demonstrated a causal relationship by means of a direct experimental manipulation of risk and benefit. When the manipulation worked (ie, when information increased perceived risk or benefit) the expected affectively congruent but inverse effect was found on the non-manipulated attribute (ie, perceived benefit or risk decreased).

The results demonstrate a phenomenon in risk perception that is similar to the halo effect, a tendency toward affectively consistent judgments. Previous researchers have found that the favorability of the overall impression of an attitude object is a good predictor of how strongly positive or negative qualities are ascribed to the object (Klauer & Stern, 1992). For example, an object judged favorably overall tends to be given more positive than negative evaluations on specific dimensions. The results of the present study demonstrate a similar effect: changing people's perception of one attribute (eg, increasing risk) tended to influence ratings on another attribute (eg, decreasing benefit). Thus, a confounding between risk and benefit judgments is revealed, which we believe occurs because people are consulting their overall affective evaluation of the item when judging its risk and benefit.

GENERAL DISCUSSION

In this chapter we have used two different approaches to study the affect heuristic. Neither approach rules out the use of cognitive strategies by individuals, but together the studies strongly suggest that affect plays an important role in the types of risk-benefit judgments investigated here. We do not claim that this paper represents a comprehensive or exhaustive approach, merely a beginning. Ultimately, synthesis of findings from diverse methodologies will clarify our understanding of the role of affect in judgment. For now, the present studies highlight the importance of considering affect in judgment processes, and specifically suggest that the inverse relationship between risk and benefit judgments can be explicated at least partially by reference to the affect heuristic.

The present studies present two lines of evidence suggesting that risk and benefit are linked in people's perceptions and consequently in their judgments. The first line shows strong inverse relationships between risk and benefit judgments for hazards with qualitatively different risks and benefits; the second line shows the influence of information about one attribute of hazards (either risk or benefit) on judgments about the other unmentioned attribute. Based on recent work emphasizing the crucial role in judgment of images marked by positive and negative feelings (Damasio, 1994), and research documenting the fundamental influence of affect as a motivator of behavior (Epstein, 1994; Mowrer, 1960a; b), it is plausible that perceived risk and benefit are linked via some sort of affective commonality. Specifically, a parsimonious explanation is that the positive and negative feelings attached to the images people associate with hazards are available and influential when risk and benefit are judged. That is, representations of objects and events in people's minds are tagged to varying degrees with affect, and the affective pool is consulted to make quick evaluations. In this way, judgments of risk and benefit are guided and linked by affect. Reliance on affect probably ebbs and flows according to various contextual factors, including the extent to which stimuli evoke images that are tagged clearly with positive or negative feelings. Which situations are most influenced by the affect heuristic is an empirical question.

Future researchers need to explore more deeply the underlying affective mechanisms by which judgments are made, as well as the interplay between affect and cognition in reasoning. One suggestion is that researchers examine the relationship between the affect and availability heuristics. To date the availability heuristic has been portrayed typically as a cognitive judgment strategy, in that it works by increasing deliberation about reasons that bias probability judgments. However, the reasons that come to mind may be analytic or tinged with positive and negative affective tags, or both. Thus, the availability heuristic may be working through cognitive *or* affective processes. The extent to which each process is evoked is unclear; the challenge is to begin hypothesizing about and testing models of judgment that elucidate the role of both cognition and affect.

ACKNOWLEDGMENTS

This research was supported by the US National Science Foundation under Grants SBR 9422754 and SBR 9709307 to Decision Science Research Institute. We are grateful to the Department of Psychology, University of Western Australia, for the laboratory space and equipment used in study 1. We thank Sarah Lichtenstein, Lisa Ordóñez and two anonymous reviewers for valuable comments on the manuscript, and C K Mertz for assistance with the data analysis. We also thank Janet Douglas and Leisha Mullican for their assistance in preparation of the manuscript.

APPENDIX:
VIGNETTES ABOUT NUCLEAR POWER FOR AFFECTIVE INFORMATION MANIPULATIONS IN STUDY 2

High-risk Condition

Nuclear power creates significant hazards to human health. Because each plant requires tons of enriched uranium to operate, the nuclear fuel cycle produces radioactive hazards and waste at every stage. Radiation hazards start with mining and milling, continue through fabrication, to transportation, to operation and finally to waste storage. In addition, the plants themselves are extremely complicated and can fail in ways that are both hard to predict and impossible to control. The accidents at Three Mile Island and at Chernobyl illustrate the dangers of plant operation. Even more serious accidents have been narrowly avoided in the past and could occur in the future. Finally, after the nuclear plants that created the waste have served out their life and been shut down, the waste they have generated will need to be stored and protected for thousands of years. This waste is highly radioactive and contaminated with plutonium, a deadly element that can be reprocessed from such waste and turned into nuclear weapons.

Low-risk Condition

Nuclear power has a good safety record and an accident rate that is comparable with other industries that produce electricity. Part of the reason that risks have been low in the nuclear power industry is that the industry is heavily monitored and regulated by the federal government. All nuclear power plants have on-site federal regulators. The plants are also built to resist accidents. Even the most serious nuclear accident in US history, Three Mile Island, did not harm anyone's health.

High-benefit Condition

Nuclear power has many advantages over other methods of producing electricity. For example, nuclear power does not depend upon a diminishing supply of fossil fuels, as do coal, oil and natural-gas power plants. Consequently, nuclear power can be produced without dependence upon oil imports from distant countries.

Nuclear power can be produced in an almost unlimited amount. It already produces a substantial proportion of all electricity used in the US. As our society grows and develops, nuclear power will be able to meet increasing demands for electricity and thus contribute greatly to our nation's economic development and prosperity.

Low-benefit Condition

Nuclear power today produces only a small percentage of our nation's electricity. New methods of generating electricity, such as geothermal, solar power and wind turbines, could eventually replace nuclear power. In addition, the application of energy-conservation methods could save more energy than is produced by nuclear power. Finally, the addition of electrical generators to the boilers of factories all over the US could produce more power than is supplied by nuclear power, without the construction of any more power plants of any sort.

NOTES

1 Affect may be viewed as a feeling state that people experience, such as happiness or sadness. It may also be viewed as a quality (eg, goodness or badness) associated with a stimulus. These two conceptions tend to be related. This chapter will be concerned with both of these aspects of affect.

2 This is not meant to imply that *only* affect influences judgment and decision-making. Clearly, many other cognitive operations have been shown to be important (Payne, Bettman & Johnson, 1993) and need to be integrated with our emerging understanding of the role of affect in judgments.

3 A perceptive reviewer of this manuscript has questioned whether the results we observed may have been due to simple mechanical factors such as smaller movements from starting points or anchors in the time-pressure condition. We believe this to be unlikely because there was no anchor to start from for each trial, and because there is no obvious relationship between the physical demands of the task and the changes in response necessary to produce increased negative correlations under time pressure.

4 An example of this would be the case where information indicating that the risk of nuclear power was low led a subject to increase his or her judgment of the risk from nuclear power (a change contrary to the manipulation) and then to decrease the judged benefit of nuclear power. The benefit judgment moved in a direction opposite from that predicted by the information manipulation, but it changed in a way that was affectively consistent with the increased judgment of nuclear risk.

References

Acton, J P (1973, January). *Evaluating public programs to save lives: The case of heart attacks* (Report R-590-RC). Santa Monica, CA: Rand Corporation

Adelstein, S J (1987). 'Uncertainty and relative risks of radiation exposure'. *Journal of the American Medical Association*, 258, 655–657

Alfidi, R J (1971). 'Informed consent: A study of patient reaction'. *Journal of the American Medical Association*, 216, 1325

Alhakami, A S & Slovic, P (1994). 'A psychological study of the inverse relationship between perceived risk and perceived benefit'. *Risk Analysis*, 14(6), 1085–1096

Allen, K A, Moss, A, Giovino, G A, Shopland, D R & Pierce, J P (1993). 'Teenage tobacco use: Data estimates from the Teenage Attitudes and Practices Survey, United States, 1989'. *Advance Data*, 224, 1

Alper, J (1993). 'The pipeline is leaking women all the way along'. *Science*, 260, 409–411

Alpert, M & Raiffa, H (1968). A progress report on the training of probability assessors. Unpublished manuscript. Cambridge, MA: Harvard University. Also in D Kahneman, P Slovic & A Tversky (eds) (1982) *Judgment under uncertainty: Heuristics and biases* (pp294–305). Cambridge University Press

American Bar Association (1989). *ABA criminal justice mental health standards*. Chicago: American Bar Association

American Psychiatric Association (1983). 'Guidelines for legislation on the psychiatric hospitalization of adults'. *American Journal of Psychiatry*, 140, 672–679

Ames, B (1983). 'Dietary carcinogens and anticarcinogens'. *Science*, 221, 1256–1264

Ames, B N & Gold, L S (1990). 'Too many rodent carcinogens: Mitogenesis increases mutagenesis'. *Science*, 249, 970–971

Anderson, D R (1974). 'The national flood insurance program: Problems and potential'. *Journal of Risk and Insurance*, 41, 579–599

Appelbaum, P (1988). 'The new preventive detention: Psychiatry's problematic responsibility for the control of violence'. *American Journal of Psychiatry*, 145, 779–785

Arrow, K J (1971). *Essays in the theory of risk bearing*. Chicago: Markham

Associated Press (1994, 6 May). 'Florida outlaws critics of its fruit'. *The Register-Guard*, p9B

Atman, C J, Bostrom, A, Fischhoff, B & Morgan, M G (1994). 'Designing risk communications: Completing and correcting mental models of hazards processes, part I'. *Risk Analysis*, 14(5), 779–788

Atomic Energy Commission (1975). 'Reactor safety study: An assessment of accident risks in US commercial power plants (WASH 1400)'. Washington, DC: Atomic Energy Commission

Bakan, P (1960). 'Response tendencies in attempts to generate random binary series'. *American Journal of Psychology*, 73, 127–131

Barke, R, Jenkins-Smith, H & Slovic, P (1997). 'Risk perceptions of men and women scientists'. *Social Science Quarterly*, 78(1), 167–176

Barry, N J, Fowler, F J, Jr, Mulley, A G, Jr, Henderson, J V, Jr & Wennberg, J E (1995). 'Patient reactions to a program designed to facilitate patient participation in treatment decisions for benign prostatic hyperplasia'. *Medical Care*, 33(8), 771–782

Barton, A H (1970). *Communities in disaster*. New York: Anchor Books

Batt, T (1992, 23 July). 'Nevada claims victory in Yucca deal'. *Las Vegas Review-Journal*, pp1A–3A

Baumann, D D & Sims, J H (1972). 'The tornado threat: Coping styles of the North and South'. *Science*, 176, 1386–1392

Baumer, T L (1978). 'Research on fear of crime in the United States'. *Victimology*, 3, 254–264

Beach, L R & Mitchell, T R (1978). 'A contingency model for the selection of decision strategies'. *Academy of Management Review*, 3, 439–449

Becker, G M, De Groot, M H & Marschak, J (1964). 'Measuring utility by a single-response sequential method'. *Behavioral Science*, 9, 226–232

Bella, D A (1987). 'Engineering and erosion of trust'. *Journal of Professional Issues in Engineering*, 113, 117–129

Bella, D A, Mosher, C D & Calvo, S N (1988a). 'Establishing trust: Nuclear waste disposal'. *Journal of Professional Issues in Engineering*, 114, 40–50

Bella, D A, Mosher, C D & Calvo, S N (1988b). 'Technocracy and trust: Nuclear waste controversy'. *Journal of Professional Issues in Engineering*, 114, 27–39

Bennett, N, Lidz, C, Monahan, J, Mulvey, E, Hoge, S, Roth, L & Gardner, W (1993). 'Inclusion, motivation, and good faith: The morality of coercion in mental hospital admission'. *Behavioral Sciences and the Law*, 11(3), 295–306

Benson, L, III & Beach, L (1996). 'The effects of time constraints on the pre-choice screening of decision options'. *Organizational Behavior and Human Decision Processes*, 67, 222–228

Benthin, A, Slovic, P, Moran, P, Severson, H, Mertz, C K & Gerrard, M (1995). 'Adolescent health-threatening and health-enhancing behaviors: A study of word association and imagery'. *Journal of Adolescent Health*, 17, 143–152

Benthin, A, Slovic, P & Severson, H (1993). 'A psychometric study of adolescent risk perception'. *Journal of Adolescence*, 16, 153–168

Berkson, J, Magath, T B & Hurn, M (1940). 'The error of estimate of the blood cell count as made with the hemocytometer'. *American Journal of Physiology*, 128, 309–323

Berman, D M (1978). 'How cheap is a life?' *International Journal of Health Sciences*, 8, 79–99

Bernoulli, D (1954). 'Specimen theoriae novae de mensura sortie'. *Econometrica*, 22, 22–36 (original work published 1738, St Petersburg)

Bernstein, G K (1972). *A bill to amend the National Flood Insurance Act of 1968 to increase flood insurance coverage of certain properties, to authorize the acquisition of certain properties, and for other purposes* (Testimony before the US Senate Subcommittee on Housing and Urban Affairs, 92nd Congress, S 2791). Washington, DC: US Government Printing Office

Bick, T, Hohenemser, C & Kates, R (1979). 'Target: Highway risks, II. The government regulators'. *Environment*, 21(2), 6–15, 29–38

Bick, T & Kasperson, R E (1978, October). 'Pitfalls of hazard management: The consumer product safety commission experiment'. *Environment*, 20(8), 30–42

Biomedical Computer Program (1979). 'Program BMDP:P4M'. In W J Dixon & M B Brown (eds), *BMDP, P-series, 1979*. Los Angeles: University of California Press

Blumer, H (1969). *Symbolic interactionism: Perspective and method*. Englewood Cliffs, NJ: Prentice-Hall

Bohnenblust, H (1984). *Safety of high-speed railway tunnels: Application of a risk-based decision model* (unpublished working paper). Zurich, Switzerland: Ernst Basler and Partners

Bohnenblust, H & Schneider, T (1984, October). *Risk appraisal: Can it be improved by formal models?* Paper presented at the Annual Meeting of the Society for Risk Analysis, Knoxville, TN

Borch, K H (1968). *The economics of uncertainty*. Princeton, NJ: Princeton University

Bord, R J (1987). 'Judgments of policies designed to elicit local cooperation on LLRW disposal siting: Comparing the public and decision makers'. *Nuclear and Chemical Waste Management*, 7, 99–105

Bord, R J (1988). 'The low-level radioactive waste crisis: Is more citizen participation the answer?' In M A Burns (ed), *Low-level radioactive waste regulation: Science, politics, and fear* (pp193–213). Chelsea, MI: Lewis

Bord, R J & O'Connor, R E (1990). 'Risk communication, knowledge, and attitudes: Explaining reactions to a technology perceived as risky'. *Risk Analysis*, 10, 499–506

Borton, T E et al (1970). *The Susquehanna communication participation study*. Springfield, VA: FSTI

Bostrom, A, Atman, C J, Fischhoff, B & Morgan, M G (1994). 'Evaluating risk communications: Completing and correcting mental models of hazards processes, part II'. *Risk Analysis*, 14(5), 789–798

Bostrom, A, Fischhoff, B & Morgan, M G (1992). 'Characterizing mental models of hazardous processes: A methodology and an application to radon'. *Journal of Social Issues*, 48(4), 85–110

Bostrom, A, Morgan, M G, Fischhoff, B & Read, D (1994). 'What do people know about global climate change? 1. Mental models'. *Risk Analysis*, 14(6), 959–970

Boyd, D W et al (1971). *Decision analysis of hurricane modification* (Final report: Project 8503). Menlo Park, CA: Stanford Research Institute (This report is available through the National Technical Information Service, US Department of Commerce, Washington, DC, accession number COM-71-00784.)

Brakel, S J, Parry, J & Weiner, B A (1985). *The mentally disabled and the law* (3rd ed). Chicago: American Bar Foundation

Brehmer, B (1974). 'Hypotheses about relations between scaled variables in the learning of probabilistic inference tasks'. *Organizational Behavior and Human Performance*, 11, 1–27

Brenot, J, Bonnefous, S & Marris, C (1998). 'Testing the cultural theory of risk in France'. *Risk Analysis*, 18(6), 729–739

Breyer, S (1993). *Breaking the vicious circle: Toward effective risk regulation*. Cambridge, MA: Harvard University

Brody, C J (1984). 'Differences by sex in support for nuclear power'. *Social Forces*, 63, 209–228

Brooks, A (1978). 'Notes on defining the dangerousness of the mentally ill'. In C Frederick (ed), *Dangerous behavior: A problem in law and mental health* (pp37–60). Washington, DC: Government Printing Office

Brown, S, Christiansen, B & Goldman, M (1987). 'The alcohol expectancy questionnaire: An instrument for the assessment of adolescent and adult alcohol expectancies'. *Journal of Studies on Alcohol*, 48, 483–491

Brown, R A & Green, C H (1980). 'Precepts of safety assessment'. *Journal of the Operational Research Society*, 31, 563–571

Brown, R V, Kahr, A S & Peterson, C (1974). *Decision analysis for the manager.* New York: Holt, Rinehart & Wilson

Bruner, J S, Goodnow, J J & Austin, G A (1956). *A study of thinking.* New York: Wiley

Burger, E J, Jr (1984). *Health risks: The challenge of informing the public.* Washington, DC: The Media Institute

Burley, D & Inman, W H W (eds) (1988). *Therapeutic risk: Perception, measurement, management.* Chichester: Wiley

Burton, I (1972). 'Cultural and personality variables in the perception of natural hazards'. In J F Wohlwill & D H Carson (eds), *Environment and the social sciences: Perspectives and applications* (pp184–195). Washington, DC: American Psychological Association

Burton, I & Kates, R W (1964). 'The perception of natural hazards in resource management'. *Natural Resources Journal*, 3, 412–414

Burton, I, Kates, R W & White, G F (1968). *The human ecology of extreme geophysical events* (Natural Hazards Working Paper No 1). Toronto: University of Toronto, Department of Geography

Busemeyer, J, Hastie, R & Medin, D L (eds). (1995). *Decision making from a cognitive perspective*. San Diego: Academic

Burton, I, Kates, R W & White, G F (1978). *The environment as hazard*. New York: Oxford University Press

Business Week (1978) 'Special report: Nuclear dilemma'. (25 December). *Business Week* pp54–68

Buss, D M, Craik, K H & Dake, K M (1986). 'Contemporary worldviews and perception of the technological system'. In V T Covello, J Menkes & J L Mumpower (eds), *Risk evaluation and management* (pp93–130). New York: Plenum

Callis, C F (1990). 'Improving the public understanding of science'. *Environmental Science and Technology*, 24, 410–411

Campbell, J L (1988). *Collapse of an industry: Nuclear power and the contradictions of US policy*. Ithaca, NY: Cornell University

Campbell, B I, O'Neill, B & Tingley, B (1974). *Comparative injuries to belted and unbelted drivers of subcompact, compact, intermediate and standard cars*. Chapel Hill, NC: University of North Carolina Highway Safety Research Center

Carlson, E (1986, 23 December). 'Suburban radium lode gives New Jersey a headache'. *Wall Street Journal*, p23

Carlson, M (1989, 27 March). 'Do you dare to eat a peach?' *Time Magazine*, pp24–27

Carney, R E (1971). 'Attitudes toward risk'. In R E Carney (ed), *Risk taking behavior: Concepts, methods, and applications to smoking and drug abuse*. Springfield, IL: Charles C Thomas

Carpenter, P F (1988). 'Responsibility, risk, and informed consent'. In K B Ekelmen (ed), *New medical devices: Invention, development, and use*. (Series on Technology and Social Priorities, pp138–145). Washington, DC: National Academy Press

Carson, R (1962). *Silent Spring*. New York: Houghton Mifflin (quotations herein taken from the paperback version, Fawcett, 1962)

Carter, L J (1979). 'An industry study of TSCA: How to achieve credibility'. *Science*, 203, 247–249

Carter, L (1987). *Nuclear imperatives and public trust: Dealing with radioactive waste*. Washington, DC: Resources for the Future

Casarett, L J & Doull, J (1975). *Toxicology: The basic science of poisons*. New York: MacMillan

Casper, B N (1976). 'Technology policy and democracy'. *Science*, 194, 29–35

Centers for Disease Control (1988). *Morbidity and mortality weekly report*, 37, 709–711

Centers for Disease Control (1990). *HIV/AIDS surveillance report*, pp1–18

Chapanis, A (1975). 'Random number guessing behavior [Abstract]'. *American Psychologist*, 8, 332

Chapman, L J & Chapman, J P (1969). 'Illusory correlation as an obstacle to the use of valid psychodiagnostic signs'. *Journal of Abnormal Psychology*, 74, 271–280

Chemical and Engineering News (1978, 22 January). p7

Christiansen, B, Goldman, M & Brown, S (1985). 'The differential development of adolescent alcohol expectancies may predict adult alcoholism'. *Journal of Addictive Behaviors*, 10, 299–306

Christiansen, B, Smith, G, Roehling, P & Goldman, M (1989). 'Using alcohol expectancies to predict adolescent drinking behavior after one year'. *Journal of Consulting and Clinical Psychology*, 57, 93–99

Cirino, R (1971). *Don't blame the people: How the news media use bias, distortion and censorship to manipulate public opinion*. New York: Random House

City of Santa Fe versus Komis (1992). *P2d*, 845, 753, NM

Clarke, L (1988). 'Politics and bias in risk assessment'. *The Social Science Journal*, 25, 155–165

Cohen, B L (1983a). *Before it's too late: A scientist's case for nuclear energy*. New York: Plenum

Cohen, B L (1983b, February). 'Lies, damned lies, and news reports'. *Policy Review*, pp70–74

Cohen, B L (1985a). 'Criteria for technology acceptability'. *Risk Analysis*, 5, 1–2

Cohen, B L (1985b). 'A simple probabilistic risk analysis for high-level waste repositories'. *Nuclear Technology*, 68, 73–76

Cohen, B L & Lee, I S (1979). 'A catalog of risks'. *Health Physics*, 36, 707–722

Cohen, J & Hansel, C E M (1956). *Risk and gambling*. London: Longmans Green

Coleman, W T, Jr (1976, April). *The national highway safety needs report*. Washington, DC: US Department of Transportation

Combs, B & Slovic, P (1979). 'Newspaper coverage of causes of death'. *Journalism Quarterly*, 56(4), 837–843, 849

Coombs, C H, Dawes, R M & Tversky, A (1970). *Mathematical psychology*. Englewood Cliffs, NJ: Prentice-Hall

Cooper, A (1994, 25 July). *All things considered*. Washington, DC: National Public Radio

Cosmides, L & Tooby, J (1996). 'Are humans good intuitive statisticians after all? Rethinking some conclusions from the literature on judgment under uncertainty'. *Cognition*, 58(1), 1–7

Costa, F M, Jessor, R & Donovan, J E (1989). 'Value on health and adolescent conventionality: A construct validation of a new measure in problem-behavior theory'. *Journal of Applied Social Psychology*, 19, 841–861

Council for Science and Society (1977). *The acceptability of risks*. London

Covello, V & Abernathy, M (1984). 'Risk analysis and technological hazards: A policy-related bibliography'. In P F Ricci, L A Sagan & C G Whipple (eds), *Technological risk assessment* (pp283–363). Nijhoff: The Hague

Covello, V T, Flamm, W G, Rodricks, J V & Tardiff, R G (1983). *The analysis of actual versus perceived risks*. New York: Plenum

Covello, V T, Sandman, P M & Slovic, P (1988). *Risk communication, risk statistics, and risk comparisons: A manual for plant managers*. Washington, DC: Chemical Manufacturers Association

Covello, V T, von Winterfeldt, D & Slovic, P (1986). 'Risk communication: A review of the literature'. *Risk Abstracts*, 3, 171–182

Covello, V T, von Winterfeldt, D & Slovic, P (1988). *Risk communication: Research and practice*. New York: Columbia University, School of Public Health

Creighton, J (1990). 'Siting means safety first'. *Forum for Applied Research on Public Policy*, 5(2), 97–98

Criscuola et al versus New York Power Authority (1993) NY Lexis 3254 (NY Cir 12 October, 1993)

Crouch, E A C & Wilson, R (1982). *Risk/Benefit analysis*. Cambridge, MA: Ballinger

Cross versus Harris (1969). 418 F2d 1095

Culliton, B J (1978). 'Toxic substances legislation: How well are laws being implemented?' *Science*, 201, 1198–1199

Cvetkovich, G & Earle, T C (1992, December). *Social trust and value similarity: New interpretations of risk communication in hazard management*. Paper presented at the Annual Meeting of the Society for Risk Analysis, San Diego, CA

Cyert, R M & March, J G (1963). *A behavioral theory of the firm*. Englewood Cliffs, NJ: Prentice-Hall

Dacy, D C & Kunreuther, H C (1969). *The economics of natural disasters*. New York: Free Press

Dake, K (1991). 'Orienting dispositions in the perception of risk: An analysis of contemporary worldviews and cultural biases'. *Journal of Cross-Cultural Psychology*, 22, 61–82

Dake, K (1992). 'Myths of nature: Culture and the social construction of risk'. *Journal of Social Issues*, 48, 21–27

Damasio, A R (1994). *Descartes' error: Emotion, reason, and the human brain*. New York: Avon

Dantico, M K, Mushkatel, A H & Pijawka, K D (1991). *Public response to the siting of the high-level nuclear waste repository in Nevada: Analysis of risk and trust perceptions*. Tempe: Arizona State University, Office of Hazard Studies

David, E E (1975). 'One-armed scientists?' *Science*, 189, 891

DeFleur, M L (1966). *Theories of mass communication*. New York: D McKay

DeJoy, D (1992). 'An examination of gender differences in traffic accident risk perception'. *Accident Analysis and Prevention*, 24, 237–246

DeLuca, D R, Stolwijk, J A & Horowitz, W (1986). 'Public perceptions of technological risk: A methodological study'. In V T Covello, J Menkes & J L Mumpower, (eds), *Risk evaluation and management* (pp25–67). New York: Plenum

Denenberg, H S (1974, 25 November). 'Nuclear power: Uninsurable'. *Congressional Record*. Washington, DC: US Government Printing Office

Desvousges, W H, Kunreuther, H, Slovic & Rosa, E A (1993). 'Perceived risk and attitudes toward nuclear wastes: National and Nevada perspectives'. In R E Dunlap, M E Kraft & E A Rosa (eds), *Public reactions to nuclear waste: Citizens' views of repository siting* (pp175–208). Durham, NC: Duke University

Diamond, W D (1990). 'Effects of describing long-term risks as cumulative or noncumulative'. *Basic & Applied Social Psychology*, 11(4), 405–419

Dietz, T M & Rycroft. R W (1987). *The risk professionals*. New York: Russell Sage

Dijker, A J & Koomen, W (1996). 'Stereotyping and attitudinal effects under time pressure'. *European Journal of Social Psychology*, 26, 61–74

Dillon, J L (1971). 'An expository review of Bernoullian decision theory in agriculture: Is utility futility?' *Review of Marketing and Agricultural Economics*, 39, 3–80

Doderlein, J M (1983). 'Understanding risk management'. *Risk Analysis*, 3, 17–21

Donovan, J, Jessor, R & Costa, F (1988). 'Syndrome of problem behavior in adolescence: A replication'. *Journal of Consulting and Clinical Psychology*, 56, 762–765

Douglas, M & Wildavsky, A (1982). *Risk and culture: An essay on the selection of technological and environmental dangers*. Berkeley: University of California Press

Drottz, B-M & Sjöberg, L (1990). 'Risk perception and worries after the Chernobyl accident'. *Journal of Environmental Psychology*, 10, 135–149

Drottz-Sjöberg, B-M & Persson, L (1993). 'Public reaction to radiation: Fear, anxiety or phobia?' *Health Physics*, 64, 223–231

Dunlap, R E & Baxter, R K (1988). *Public reaction to siting a high-level nuclear waste repository at Hanford: A survey of local area residents* (For Impact Assessment, Inc). Pullman: Washington State University, Social and Economic Sciences Research Center

Dunlap, R E, Kraft, M E & Rosa, E A (eds). (1993). *Public reactions to nuclear waste: Citizens' views of repository siting*. Durham, NC: Duke University

DuPont, R L (1980). *Nuclear phobia—Phobic thinking about nuclear power*. Washington, DC: The Media Institute

Dupont, R L (1981, 7 September). 'The nuclear power phobia'. *Business Week*, pp14–16

Earle, T C & Cvetkovich, G T (1995). *Social trust: Toward a cosmopolitan society*. Westport, CT: Praeger

Edelstein, M R (1988). *Contaminated communities: The social and psychological impacts of residential toxic exposure*. Boulder, CO: Westview

Edland, A & Svenson, O (1993). 'Judgment and decision making under time pressure'. In O Svenson & A J Maule (eds), *Time pressure and stress in human judgment and decision making* (pp27–40). New York: Plenum

Edwards, W (1961). 'Behavioral decision theory'. In P R Farnsworth, O McNemar & Q McNemar (eds), *Annual Review of Psychology* (vol 12, pp473–498). Palo Alto, CA: Annual Reviews, Inc

Edwards, W (1968). 'Conservatism in human information processing'. In B Kleinmuntz (ed), *Formal representation of human judgment* (pp17–52). New York: Wiley

Edwards, W & von Winterfeldt, D (1984). *Public values in risk communication.* University of Southern California: Institute for Systems and Safety Management

Edwards, W & von Winterfeldt, D (1987). Public values in risk debates. *Risk Analysis,* 7(2), 141–158

Efron, E (1984). *The apocalyptics.* New York: Simon & Schuster

Einhorn, H J & Hogarth, R M (1981). 'Behavioral decision theory: Processes of judgment and choice'. *Annual Review of Psychology,* 32, 53–58

Electric Power Research Institute (EPRI) (1980). 'Assessment: The impact and influence of TMI'. *EPRI Journal,* 5(5), 24–33

Elmer-Dewitt, P (1994, 14 February). 'Brave new world of milk'. *Time Magazine,* p31

Engländer, T, Farago, K, Slovic, P & Fischhoff, B (1986). 'A comparative analysis of risk perception in Hungary and the United States'. *Social Behaviour: An International Journal of Applied Social Psychology,* 1, 55–66

English, M R (1992). *Siting low-level radioactive waste disposal facilities: The public policy dilemma.* New York: Quorum

Epstein, S (1994). 'Integration of the cognitive and the psychodynamic unconscious'. *American Psychologist,* 49, 709–724

Ericson, J E, Shirahata, H & Patterson, C C (1979, 26 April). 'Skeletal concentrations of lead in ancient Peruvians'. *New England Journal of Medicine,* 300(17), 946–951

Erikson, K (1990, January–February). 'Toxic reckoning: Business faces a new kind of fear'. *Harvard Business Review,* pp118–126

Erikson, K (1991, March). 'Radiation's lingering dread'. *The Bulletin of the Atomic Scientists,* pp34–39

Eugene Register Guard (1976, 14 January). 'Doubts linger on cyclamate risks', p9A

Evans, N & Hope, C (1984). *Nuclear power: Futures, costs, and benefits.* Cambridge, UK: Cambridge University

Fairfax, S K (1978). 'A disaster in the environmental movement'. *Science,* 199, 743–748

Fechner, G T (1860). *Elemente der psychophysik.* Leipzig: Breitkopf und Härtel

Fenton, D (1989, 3 October). 'How a PR firm executed the Alar scare'. *Wall Street Journal,* pA22

Ferreira, J & Slesin, L (1976, October). *Observations on the social impact of large accidents* (Technical Report No 122). Massachusetts: Massachusetts Institute of Technology, Operations Research Center

Fessenden-Raden, J, Fitchen, J M & Heath, J S (1987). 'Providing risk information in communities: Factors influencing what is heard and accepted'. *Science Technology and Human Values,* 12, 94–101

Fhanér, G & Hane, M (1973). 'Seat belts: Factors influencing their use: A literature survey'. *Accident Analysis and Prevention,* 5, 27–43

Fhanér, G & Hane, M (1974). 'Seat belts: Relations between beliefs, attitudes and use'. *Journal of Applied Psychology,* 59, 472–482

Finucane, M L & Maybery, M T (1996). 'Risk perceptions in Australia'. *Psychological Reports,* 79, 1331–1338

Finucane, M L, Slovic, P, Mertz, C K, Flynn, J & Satterfield, T A (2000). 'Gender, race, and perceived risk: The 'white male' effect'. *Health, Risk & Society,* 2, 159–172

Fiorino, D (1989). 'Technical and democratic values in risk analysis'. *Risk Analysis*, 9, 293–299

Fischhoff, B (1974). 'Hindsight: Thinking backward?' *Oregon Research Institute Research Monograph*, 14(1)

Fischhoff, B (1975). 'Hindsight ≠ foresight: The effect of outcome knowledge on judgment under uncertainty'. *Journal of Experimental Psychology: Human Perception and Performance*, 1, 288–299

Fischhoff, B (1977). 'Cost-benefit analysis and the art of motorcycle maintenance'. *Policy Sciences*, 8, 177–202

Fischhoff, B (1980). 'Clinical decision analysis'. *Operations Research*, 28, 28–43

Fischhoff, B (1983). 'Informed consent for transient nuclear workers'. In R Kasperson (ed), *Equity issues in radioactive waste management* (pp302–328). Cambridge, MA: Oelgeschlager, Gunn & Hain, Inc

Fischhoff, B (1985a). 'Cognitive and institutional barriers to "informed consent"'. In M Gibson (ed), *To breathe freely* (pp169–185). Totowa, NJ: Rowan & Allanheld

Fischhoff, B (1985b, Winter). 'Protocols for environmental reporting: What to ask the experts'. *The Journalist*, pp11–15

Fischhoff, B & Beyth, R (1975). '"I knew it would happen": Remembered probabilities of once-future things'. *Organizational Behavior and Human Performance*, 13, 1–16

Fischhoff, B, Hohenemser, C, Kasperson, R E & Kates, R W (1978). 'Can hazard management be improved?' *Environment*, 20(7), 16–20, 32–37

Fischhoff, B, Lichtenstein, S, Slovic, P, Derby, S L & Keeney, R L (1981). *Acceptable risk*. New York: Cambridge University Press

Fischhoff, B & MacGregor, D G (1983). 'Judged lethality: How much people seem to know depends upon how they are asked'. *Risk Analysis*, 3, 229–236

Fischhoff, B, Slovic, P & Lichtenstein, S (1977). 'Knowing with certainty: The appropriateness of extreme confidence'. *Journal of Experimental Psychology: Human Perception and Performance*, 3, 552–564

Fischhoff, B, Slovic, P & Lichtenstein, S (1978). 'Fault trees: Sensitivity of estimated failure probabilities to problem representation'. *Journal of Experimental Psychology: Human Perception and Performance*, 4, 330–344

Fischhoff, B, Slovic, P & Lichtenstein, S (1980). 'Knowing what you want: Measuring labile values'. In T Wallsten (ed), *Cognitive processes in choice and decision behavior* (pp117–141). Hillsdale, NJ: Erlbaum

Fischhoff, B, Slovic, P, Lichtenstein, S, Read, S & Combs, B (1978). 'How safe is safe enough? A psychometric study of attitudes towards technological risks and benefits'. *Policy Sciences*, 9, 127–152

Fischhoff, B, Watson, S & Hope, C (1984). 'Defining risk'. *Policy Sciences*, 17, 123–139

Fiske, S T, Pratto, F & Pavelchak, M A (1983). *Journal of Social Issues*, 39, 41

Florig, H K (1992). 'Containing the costs of the EMF program'. *Science*, 257, 468–492

Flynn, J, Burns, W, Mertz, C K & Slovic, P (1992). 'Trust as a determinant of opposition to a high-level radioactive waste repository: Analysis of a structural model'. *Risk Analysis*, 12, 417–430

Flynn, J, Kasperson, R, Kunreuther, H & Slovic, P (1992, Summer). 'Time to rethink nuclear waste storage'. *Issues in Science and Technology*, 8(4), 42–48

Flynn, J, Mertz, C & Slovic, P (1991). *The 1991 Nevada State Telephone Survey: Key Findings* (Report No NWPO-SE-036-91). Carson City: State of Nevada, Nuclear Waste Project Office

Flynn, J & Slovic, P (1993). 'Nuclear wastes and public trust'. *Forum for Applied Research and Public Policy*, 8, 92–100

Flynn, J, Slovic, P & Mertz, C K (1993). 'The Nevada Initiative: A risk communication fiasco'. *Risk Analysis*, 13(5), 497–502

Flynn, J, Slovic, P & Mertz, C K (1994). 'Gender, race, and perception of environmental health risks'. *Risk Analysis*, 14(6), 1101–1108

Flynn, J, Slovic, P, Mertz, C K & Carlisle, C (1999). 'Public support for earthquake risk mitigation in Portland, Oregon'. *Risk Analysis*, 19(2), 205–216

Flynn, J, Slovic, P, Mertz, C K & Burns, W (1990). *Some policy implications resulting from public perceptions of radioactive wastes* (Report No 91-1). Eugene, OR: Decision Research

Flynn, J, Slovic, P, Mertz, C K & Toma, J (1990). *Evaluations of Yucca Mountain: Survey findings* (Report No NWPO-SE-029-90). Carson City, NV: Nuclear Waste Project Office

Fong, G T, Krantz, D H & Nisbett, R E (1986). 'The effects of statistical training on thinking about everyday problems'. *Cognitive Psychology*, 18, 253–292

Ford, D F (1977). *The history of federal nuclear safety assessment: From WASH 740 through the reactor safety study*. Cambridge, MA: Union of Concerned Scientsts

Fort, R, Rosenman, R & Budd, W (1993). 'Perception costs and NIMBY'. *Journal of Environmental Management*, 38, 185–200

Frazer, J G (1959). *The new golden bough: A study in magic and religion*. New York: MacMillan (original work published in 1890)

Frech, E R (1991). 'How can we deal with NIMBY in nuclear waste management?' In *High level radioactive waste management: Proceedings of the second annual international conference, Las Vegas, Nevada, 28 April–3 May, 1991* (vol 1, pp442–446). La Grange, IL and New York: American Nuclear Society and American Society of Civil Engineers

Freedman, D A & Zeisel, H (1988). 'From mouse-to-man: The quantitative assessment of cancer risks'. *Statistical Science*, 3, 3–56

Freedman, K, Wood, R & Henderson, M (1974). *Compulsory seat belts: A survey of public reaction and stated usage*. New South Wales: Department of Motor Transport

Friedman, M & Savage, L J (1948). 'The utility analysis of choices involving risk'. *Journal of Political Economy*, 56, 279–304

Friemuth, V S, Greenberg, R H, De Witt, J & Romano, R (1984). 'Covering cancer: Newspapers and the public interest'. *Journal of Communication*, 34, 62–73

Freudenburg, W R (1993). 'Risk and recreancy: Weber, the division of labor, and the rationality of risk perceptions'. *Social Forces*, 71(4), 909–932

Fuchs, V R (1976). 'From Bismarck to Woodcock: The "irrational" pursuit of national health insurance'. *Journal of Law and Economics*, 19, 47–59

Fujino, S (1989). 'Risk perception of prescription drugs: Report on surveys in Japan'. In B Horisberger & R Dinkel (eds), *The perception and management of drug safety risks* (pp112–116). Berlin: Springer-Verlag

Funtowicz, S O & Ravetz, J R (1992). 'Three types of risk assessment and the emergence of post-normal science'. In S Krimsky & D Golding (eds), *Social theories of risk* (pp251–274). Westport, CT: Praeger

Gadomska, M (1994). 'Risk communication'. In Swedish Risk Academy (ed), *Radiation and society: Comprehending radiation risk* (vol 1, pp147–166). Vienna: International Atomic Energy Agency

Galanter, E (1962). 'The direct measurement of utility and subjective probability'. *American Journal of Psychology*, 75, 208–220

Galanter, E (1975, March). *Utility scales of monetary and non-monetary events* (Technical Report PLR-36). New York: Columbia University, Psychophysics Laboratory

Galanter, E & Pliner, P (1974). 'Cross-modality matching of money against other continua'. In H R Moskowitz et al (eds), *Sensation and measurement* (pp65–76). Dordrecht-Holland: Reidel

Gans, H J (1980). *Deciding what's news*. New York: Vintage

Gardner, G T, Tiemann, A R, Gould, L C, DeLuca, D R, Doob, L W & Stolwijk, J A J (1982). 'Risk and benefit perceptions, acceptability judgments, and self-reported actions toward nuclear power'. *Journal of Social Psychology*, 116, 179–197

Gerrard, M (1987). 'Sex, sex guilt, and contraceptive use revisited: Trends in the 1980s'. *Journal of Personality and Social Psychology*, 52, 975–980

Gerrard, M, Gibbons, F & Boney-McCoy, S (1993). 'Emotional inhibition of effective contraception'. *Anxiety, Stress, and Coping*, 6, 73–88

Gigerenzer, G (1994). 'Why the distinction between single-event probabilities and frequencies is important for psychology and vice versa'. In G Wright & P Ayton (eds), *Subjective probability* (pp129–160). New York: Wiley

Gillette, R & Walsh, J (1971). 'San Fernando earthquake study: NRC panel sees premonitory lessons'. *Science*, 172, 140–143

Gilligan, C (1982). *In a difference voice: Psychological theory and women's development.* Cambridge, MA: Harvard University Press

Goffman, E (1963). *Stigma.* Englewood Cliffs, NJ: Prentice-Hall

Golant, S & Burton, I. (1969). *Avoidance response to the risk environment* (Natural Hazards Research Working Paper No 6). Canada: University of Toronto, Department of Geography

Goldman, M, Brown, S, Christiansen, B & Smith, G (in press). 'Alcohol etiology and memory: Broadening the scope of alcohol expectancy research'. *Psychological Bulletin*

Goodwin, R (1978). 'Uncertainty as an excuse for cheating our children: The case of nuclear wastes'. *Policy Sciences*, 10, 25–43

Gori, G B (1980). 'The regulation of carcinogenic hazards'. *Science*, 208, 256–261

Gormley, W T (1986). *Professionalism within environmental bureaucracies: The policy implications of personnel choices* (Occasional Paper No 1). Madison, WI: University of Wisconsin, Robert M Lafollette Institute of Public Affairs

Goszczynska, M, Tyszka, T & Slovic, P (1991). 'Risk perception in Poland: A comparison with three other countries'. *Journal of Behavioral Decision Making*, 4, 179–193

Gould, L C, Gardner, G T, Deluca, D R, Tiemann, A R, Doob, L W & Stolwijk, J A J (1988). *Perceptions of technological risks and benefits.* New York: Russell Sage Foundation

Graham, J D., Green, L C & Roberts, M J (1988). *In search of safety: Chemicals and cancer risk.* Cambridge, MA: Harvard University

Green, A E & Bourne, A J (1972). *Reliability technology.* New York: Wiley Interscience

Green, C H (1974). *Measures for safety.* Unpublished manuscript. University of Illinois, Urbana, Center for Advanced Study

Green, C H (1980). 'Risk: Beliefs and attitudes'. In D Canter (ed), *Fires and human behaviour* (pp277–291). Chichester, England: Wiley

Green, C H & Brown, R A (1980). *Through a glass darkly: Perceiving perceived risks to health and safety* (Research paper). Scotland: University of Dundee, Duncan of Jordanstone College of Art, School of Architecture

Green, P G (1976). 'Ontario's buckle-up law is paying off'. *Traffic Safety*, 76, 8–11, 34–35

Greene, M R (1963). 'Attitudes toward risk and a theory of insurance consumption'. *Journal of Insurance*, 30, 165–182

Greene, M R (1964). 'Insurance mindedness—implications for insurance theory'. *Journal of Insurance*, 31, 27–38

Greenwood, D R, Kingsbury, G L & Cleland, J G (1979). *A handbook of key federal regulations and criteria for multimedia environmental control* (EPA-600/7-79-175). Washington, DC: US Environmental Protection Agency

Gregory, R, Flynn, J & Slovic, P (1995). 'Technological stigma'. *American Scientist*, 83, 220–223

Gregory, R, Lichtenstein, S & MacGregor, D G (1993). 'The role of past states in determining reference points for policy decisions'. *Organizational Behavior and Human Decision Processes*, 55, 195–206

Grether, D M & Plott, C R (1979). 'Economic theory of choice and the preference reversal phenomenon'. *American Economic Review*, 69, 623–638

Grimshaw versus Ford Motor Co (1978). No 19776, Superior Court, Orange County, CA, February 6, 1978

Grisso, T & Appelbaum, P S (1992). 'Is it unethical to offer predictions of future violence?' *Law and Human Behavior*, 16, 621–633

Grisso, T & Appelbaum, P S (1993). 'Structuring the debate about ethical predictions of future violence'. *Law and Human Behavior*, 17, 482–485

Grunhouse, S (1988, 1 January). 'French and Swiss fight about tainted cheese'. *New York Times*, p2

Gustafson, P E (1998). 'Gender differences in risk perception: Theoretical and methodological perspectives'. *Risk Analysis*, 18(6), 805–811

Guthrie, E R (1952). *The psychology of learning* (Rev ed). New York: Harper & Bros

Gutteling, J M & Wiegman, O (1993). 'Gender-specific reactions to environmental hazards in the Netherlands'. *Sex Roles*, 28, 433–447

Guttman, L (1944). 'A basis for scaling qualitative data'. *American Sociological Review*, 9, 139–150

Gwartney-Gibbs, P A & Lach, D H (1991). 'Sex differences in attitudes toward nuclear war'. *Journal of Peace Research*, 28, 161–174

Haas, J E (1971). 'Factors in the human response to earthquake risk'. In *Earthquake risk: Proceedings of the Conference of the California Legislature Joint Committee on Seismic Safety.* (available from the Joint Committee, State Capitol, Sacramento, CA)

Hamm, R M (1991). 'Selection of verbal probabilities: A solution for some problems of verbal probability expression'. *Organizational Behavior and Human Decision Processes*, 48, 193–223

Hammerton, M (1973). 'A case of radical probability estimation'. *Journal of Experimental Psychology*, 101, 252–254

Hance, B J, Chess, C & Sandman, P M (1988). *Improving dialogue with communities: A risk communication manual for government.* Trenton: New Jersey Department of Environmental Protection

Harding, C M & Eiser, J R (1984). 'Characterizing the perceived risk of some health issues'. *Risk Analysis*, 4, 131–141

Harris, L (1980). *Risk in a complex society* (Public opinion poll). New York: for the Marsh and McClennan Company

Harriss, R C, Hohenemser, C & Kates, R W (1978, September). 'Our hazardous environment'. *Environment*, p6

Hedges, T, Gerrard, M & Gibbons, R (1995). 'Psychosocial factors affecting rural adolescent alcohol use'. In R R Watson (ed), *Substance abuse during pregnancy and childhood.* Totowa, NJ: Humana Press

Heising, C D & George, V P (1986). 'Nuclear financial risk: Economy-wide costs of reactor accidents'. *Energy Policy*, 14, 45–51

Henrion, M & Fischhoff, B (1986). 'Uncertainty assessment in the estimation of physical constants'. *American Journal of Physics*, 54, 791–798

Herrero, S (1970). 'Human injury inflicted by grizzly bears'. *Science*, 170, 593–597

Hersey, J (1946). *Hiroshima*. New York: Bantam

Hershey, J C & Schoemaker, P J H (1980). 'Risk taking and problem context in the domain of losses: An expected-utility analysis'. *Journal of Risk and Insurance*, 47, 111–132

Higbee, K L (1969). 'Fifteen years of fear arousal: Research on threat appeals, 1953–1968'. *Psychological Bulletin*, 72, 426–444

High, C & Richards, P (1972). 'The random walk drainage simulation model as a teaching exercise'. *Journal of Geography*, 71, 41–51

Hinman, G W, Rosa, E A, Kleinhesselink, R R & Lowinger, T C (1993). 'Perceptions of nuclear and other risks in Japan and the United States'. *Risk Analysis*, 13, 449–455

Hodson-Walker, N. J (1970). 'The value of safety belts: A review'. *Canadian Medical Association Journal*, 102, 391

Hoffman, P J, Slovic, P & Rorer, L G (1968). 'An analysis-of-variance model for the assessment of configural cue utilization in clinical judgment'. *Psychological Bulletin*, 69, 338–349

Hoge, S, Lidz, C, Mulvey, E, Roth, L, Bennet, N., Siminoff, L, Arnold, R & Monahan, J (1993). 'Patient, family, and staff perceptions of coercion in mental hospital admission: An exploratory study'. *Behavioral Sciences and the Law*, 11(3), 281–294

Hohenemser, C, Goble, R, Kasperson, J X., Kasperson, R E, Kates, R W, Collins, P & Goldman, A (1983, October). *Methods for analyzing and comparing technological hazards: Definitions and factor structures* (CENTED Research Report No 3). Worcester, MA: Clark University, Center for Technology, Environment, and Development

Hohenemser, C & Renn, O (1988). 'Chernobyl's other legacy: Shifting public perceptions of nuclear risk'. *Environment*, 30, 3

Holdren, J P (1982). 'Energy hazards: What to measure, what to compare'. *Technology Review*, 85(3), 32–38

Holmes, R A (1970). 'On the economic welfare of victims of automobile accidents'. *American Economic Review*, 60, 143–152

Holmes, R C (1961). 'Composition and size of flood losses'. In G F. White (ed), *Papers on flood problems* (Research Paper No 70, pp7–20). University of Chicago, Department of Geography

Hoos, I (1980). 'Risk assessment in social perspective'. In *Perceptions of risk* (pp37–85). Washington, DC: National Council on Radiation Protection and Measurement

Horisberger, B & Dinkel, R (eds). (1989). *The perception and management of drug safety risks*. Berlin: Springer-Verlag

Hovland, C J (1948). 'Social communication'. *Proceedings of the American Philosophical Society*, 92, 371–375

Howard, R A (1968a). 'The foundations of decision analysis'. *IEEE Transactions on Systems Science and Cybernetics*, 4, 211–219

Howard, R A (1968b). 'Decision analysis: Applied decision theory'. In D B Hertz & J Melese (eds), *Proceedings of the Fourth International Conference on Operational Research*. New York: Wiley

Howard, R A, Matheson, J E & Miller, K E (1976). *Readings in decision analysis*. Menlo Park, CA: Stanford Research Institute

Howard, R A, Matheson, J E & North, D W (1972). 'The decision to seed hurricanes'. *Science*, 176, 1191–1202

Howard, R A, Matheson, J E & Owen, D L (1978). 'The value of life and nuclear design'. In D Okrent & E Cramer (eds), *Probabilistic analysis of nuclear reactor safety*. LaGrange Park, IL: American Nuclear Society

Humphrey, N (1981). 'Four minutes to midnight'. Quoted in R J Lifton & N. Humphrey (eds), *In a Dark Time* (pp21–22). Cambridge, MA: Harvard University

Huyskens, C (1994). 'Problems in risk comparisons'. In Swedish Risk Academy (ed), *Radiation and society: Comprehending radiation risk* (vol 1, pp131–146). Vienna: International Atomic Energy Agency

Hynes, M & Vanmarcke, E (1976). 'Reliability of embankment performance predictions'. In *Proceedings of the ASCE Engineering Mechanics Division Special Conference*. Ontario, Canada: University of Waterloo Press

Inhaber, H (1979). *Risk of energy production* (Report AECB 1119, Ed 4). Ottawa, Ontario: Atomic Energy Control Board

Isen, A M (1993). 'Positive affect and decision making'. In M Lewis & J M Haviland (eds), *Handbook of emotions* (pp261–277). New York: The Guilford Press

Isen, A & Diamond, G (1988). 'Affect and automaticity'. In J Vleman & J Bargh (eds), *Unintended Thought* (pp124–152). New York: Guilford

Jacob, G (1990). *Site unseen: The politics of siting a nuclear waste repository*. Pittsburgh, PA: University of Pittsburgh

Janis, I L & Mann, L (1977). *Decision making*. New York: The Free Press

Jarvik, M E (1951). 'Probability learning and a negative recency effect in the serial anticipation of alternative symbols'. *Journal of Experimental Psychology*, 41, 291–297

Jasanoff, S (1986). *Risk management and political culture*. New York: Russell Sage

Jasper, J M (1990). *Nuclear politics: Energy and the state in the United States, Sweden, and France*. Princeton, NJ: Princeton University Press

Jenkins, H M & Ward, W C (1965). 'Judgment of contingency between responses and outcomes'. *Psychological Monographs: General and Applied*, 79(1), 594

Jenkins-Smith, H C (1992, December). *Culture, trust, ideology and perceptions of the risks of nuclear waste: A causal analysis*. Paper presented at the Annual Meeting of the Society for Risk Analysis, San Diego, CA

Jenkins-Smith, H C (1993). *Nuclear imagery and regional stigma: Testing hypotheses of image acquisition and valuation regarding Nevada* (technical report). Albuquerque, NM: University of New Mexico, Institute for Public Policy

Jessor, R (1984). 'Adolescent development and behavioral health'. In J D Matarazzo, S M Weiss, J A Herd & N. E Miller (eds), *Behavioral health: A handbook of health enhancement and disease prevention* (pp69–90). New York: Wiley

Jessor, R (1987). 'Problem-behavior theory, psychosocial development, and adolescent problem drinking'. *British Journal of Addiction*, 82, 331–342

Johnson, B B (1992, December). *Trust in theory: Many questions, few answers*. Paper presented at the Annual Meeting of the Society for Risk Analysis, San Diego, CA

Johnson, B B & Covello, V T (eds) (1987). *The social and cultural construction of risk*. Dordrecht, The Netherlands: Reidel

Johnson, E J & Tversky, A (1983). 'Affect, generalization, and the perception of risk'. *Journal of Personality and Social Psychology*, 45, 20–31

Johnson, E J & Tversky, A (1984). 'Representations of perceptions of risk'. *Journal of Experimental Psychology: General*, 113, 55–70

Johnson, E M & Huber, G P (1977). 'The technology of utility assessment'. *IEEE Transactions on Systems, Man, and Cybernetics*, SMC-7, 311–325

Johnson, F R, Fisher, A, Smith, V K & Desvousges, W H (1988). 'Informed choice or regulated risk? Lessons from a study in radon communication'. *Environment*, 30(4), 12–15, 30–35

Johnston, L D, O'Malley, P M & Bachman, J G (1987). *National trends in drug use and related factors among American high school students and young adults: 1975–1986*. Rockville, MD: US Department of Health and Human Services, National Institute on Drug Abuse

Jones, E E, Farina, A, Hastorf, A H, Markus, H, Miller, D T, Scott, R A & French, R D (1984). *Social stigma: The psychology of marked relationships*. New York: W H Freeman

Kahneman, D, Slovic, P & Tversky, A, (eds) (1982). *Judgment under uncertainty: Heuristics and Biases*. New York: Cambridge University Press

Kahneman, D & Snell, J (1990). 'Predicting utility'. In R M Hogarth (ed) *Insights in decision making* (pp295–310). Chicago: University of Chicago Press

Kahneman, D & Tversky, A (1975, June). *Value theory: An analysis of choices under risk*. Paper presented at a conference on public economics, Jerusalem, Israel

Kahneman, D & Tversky, A (1972). 'Subjective probability: A judgment of representativeness'. *Cognitive Psychology*, 3, 430–454

Kahneman, D & Tversky, A (1973). 'On the psychology of prediction'. *Psychological Review*, 80, 237–251

Kahneman, D & Tversky, A (1979). 'Prospect theory: An analysis of decision under risk'. *Econometrica*, 47, 263–291

Kasper, R G (1980). 'Perceptions of risk and their effects on decision making'. In R C Schwing & W A Albers, Jr. (eds), *Societal risk assessment: How safe is safe enough?* (pp71–84). New York: Plenum

Kasperson, R E (ed) (1983). *Equity issues in radioactive waste management.* Cambridge, MA: Oelgeschlager, Gunn & Hain, Inc

Kasperson, R E (1990). 'Social realities in high-level radioactive waste management and their policy implications'. In *High level radioactive waste management: Proceedings of the international topical meeting* (vol 1, pp512–518). La Grange, IL and New York: American Nuclear Society and American Society of Civil Engineers

Kasperson, R E, Emel, J, Goble, R, Hohenemser, C, Kasperson, J X & Renn, O (1987). 'Radioactive wastes and the social amplification of risk'. In R G Post (ed), *Waste management '87.* Tucson: Arizona Board of Regents, University of Arizona

Kasperson, R, Golding, D & Tuler, S (1992, Winter). 'Social distrust as a factor in siting hazardous facilities and communicating risks (individual and collective responses to risk)'. *Journal of Social Issues*, 48(4), 161–188

Kasperson, R, Renn, O, Slovic, P, Brown, H, Emel, J, Goble, R, Kasperson, J & Ratick, S (1988). 'The social amplification of risk: A conceptual framework'. *Risk Analysis*, 8, 177–187

Kates, R W (1962). *Hazard and choice perception in flood plain management* (research paper no 78). University of Chicago, Department of Geography

Kates, R W (1970). *Natural hazard in ecological perspective: Hypotheses and models* (natural hazards research working paper no 14). Toronto: University of Toronto, Department of Geography

Kates, R W (1975). *Risk assessment of environmental hazard* (SCOPE Report 8). Paris: International Council of Scientific Unions

Kates, R W (1977). 'Summary report'. In R W Kates (ed), *Managing technological hazards: Research needs and opportunities* (pp1–48). Boulder: University of Colorado, Institute of Behavioral Science

Kates, R W (1978). *Risk assessment of environmental hazard.* New York: Wiley

Katzman, M T (1985). *Chemical catastrophes: Regulating environmental risk through pollution liability insurance.* Springfield, IL: R D Irwin

Keeney, R L (1977). *Evaluation involving potential fatalities.* Unpublished report, Woodward Clyde Consultants, San Francisco

Keown, C F (1989). 'Risk perceptions of Hong Kongese vs. Americans'. *Risk Analysis*, 9(3), 401–405

Keown, C, Slovic, P & Lichtenstein, S (1984). 'Attitudes of physicians, pharmacists, and laypersons toward seriousness and need for disclosure of prescription drug side effects'. *Health Psychology*, 3, 1–11

Kersholt, J H (1994). 'The effect of time pressure on decision-making behaviour in a dynamic task environment'. *Acta Psychologica*, 86, 89–104

Kidner, R & Richards, K (1974). 'Compensation to dependants of accident victims'. *Economic Journal*, 84, 130–142

Kinchin, G H (1978). 'Assessment of hazards in engineering work'. *Proceedings of the Institute of Civil Engineers*, Part I, 64, 431–438

Kirkby, A V (1972). *Perception of rainfall variability and agricultural and social adaptation to hazard by peasant cultivators in the valley of Oaxaca, Mexico.* Paper presented at the 22nd International Geographical Congress, Calgary, AL, Canada

Klassen, D & O'Connor, W (1988). 'A prospective study of predictors of violence in adult male mental health admissions'. *Law and Human Behavior*, 12, 143–158

Klauer, K C & Stern, E (1992). 'How attitudes guide memory-based judgments: A two-process model'. *Journal of Experimental Social Psychology*, 28, 186–206

Kleinhesselink, R R (1992). 'Risk perceptions, risk regulatory motivations, and personality: US/Japan comparisons'. *International Journal of Psychology*, 27, 308–311

Kleinhesselink, R R & Rosa, E A (1991). 'Cognitive representations of risk perceptions: A comparison of Japan and the United States'. *Journal of Cross-Cultural Psychology*, 22, 11–28

Knapper, C K, Cropley, A J & Moore, R J (1976). 'Attitudinal factors in the non-use of seat belts'. *Accident Analysis and Prevention*, 8, 241–246

Knight, F. H (1965). *Risk, uncertainty, and profit.* New York: Harper & Row (original work published 1921)

Koren, G & Klein, N (1991). 'Bias against negative studies in newspaper reports of medical research'. *Journal of the American Medical Association*, 266, 1824–1826

Koehler, J J (1989). *Judgments of evidence quality among scientists as a function of prior beliefs and commitments.* Unpublished doctoral dissertation, University of Chicago

Kraus, N, Malmfors, T & Slovic, P (1992). 'Intuitive toxicology: Expert and lay judgments of chemical risks'. *Risk Analysis*, 12, 215–232

Kraus, N & Slovic, P (1988a). *Consumer risk perceptions of household chemicals* (Report No 89-2). Eugene, OR: Decision Research

Kraus, N & Slovic, P (1988b). 'Taxonomic analysis of perceived risk: Modeling individual and group perceptions within homogeneous hazard domains'. *Risk Analysis*, 8(3), 435–455

Krauskopf, K (1990). 'Disposal of high-level nuclear waste: Is it possible?' *Science*, 249, 1231–1232

Krewski, D, Slovic, P, Bartlett, S, Flynn, J & Mertz, C K (1995a). 'Health risk perception in Canada I: Rating hazards, sources of information and responsibility for health protection'. *Human and Ecological Risk Assessment*, 1(2), 117–132

Krewski, D, Slovic, P, Bartlett, S, Flynn, J & Mertz, C K (1995b). 'Health risk perception in Canada II: Worldviews, attitudes and opinions'. *Human and Ecological. Risk Assessment*, 1(3), 231–248

Krimsky, S & Golding, D (eds). (1992). *Social theories of risk.* Westport, CT: Praeger-Greenwood

Krimsky, S & Plough, A (1988). *Environmental hazards: Communicating risks as a social process.* Dover, MA: Auburn House

Kristiansen, C M (1983). 'Newspaper coverage of diseases and actual mortality statistics'. *European Journal of Social Psychology*, 13, 193–194

Kunreuther, H (1968). 'The case for comprehensive disaster insurance'. *Journal of Law and Economics*, 11, 133–163

Kunreuther, H C (1972). *Risk-taking and farmer's crop growing decisions* (Report No 7219). University of Chicago, Center for Mathematical Studies in Business and Economics

Kunreuther, H C (1973a). *Recovery from natural disasters: Insurance or federal aid?* Washington, DC: American Enterprise Institute for Public Policy Research

Kunreuther, H C (1973b). 'Values and costs'. In R Wright, S Kramer & C Culver (eds), *Building practices for disaster mitigation* (Building Science Series 46, pp41–62). Washington, DC: US Department of Commerce, National Bureau of Standards

Kunreuther, H C (1974). 'Economic analysis of natural hazards: An ordered choice approach'. In G F White (ed), *Natural hazards: Local, national, global* (pp206–214). New York: Oxford University Press

Kunreuther, H C (1976). 'Limited knowledge and insurance protection'. *Public Policy*, 24, 227–261

Kunreuther, H (1987). 'Gridlock in environmental insurance: The failure of EIL coverage'. *Environment*, 29, 18–35

Kunreuther, H (1996). 'Mitigating disaster losses through insurance'. *Journal of Risk and Uncertainty*, 12(2–3), 171–187

Kunreuther, H, Desvousges, W H & Slovic, P (1988). 'Nevada's predicament: Public perceptions of risk from the proposed nuclear waste repository'. *Environment*, 30(8), 16–20, 30–33

Kunreuther, H, Easterling, D, Desvousges, W & Slovic, P (1990). 'Public attitudes toward siting a high-level nuclear waste repository in Nevada'. *Risk Analysis*, 10, 469–484

Kunreuther, H, Fitzgerald, K & Aarts, T D (1993). 'Siting noxious facilities: A test of the facility siting credo'. *Risk Analysis*, 13, 301–318

Kunreuther, H C, Ginsberg, R, Miller, L, Sagi, P, Slovic, P, Borkin, B & Katz, N (1977). *Limited knowledge and insurance protection: Implications for natural hazard policy.* New York: Wiley

Kunreuther, H C, Ginsberg, R, Miller, L, Sagi, P, Slovic, P, Borkin, B & Katz, N (1978). *Disaster insurance protection: Public policy lessons.* New York: Wiley

Kunreuther, H & Slovic, P (in press). 'Coping with stigma: Challenges and opportunities'. In J Flynn, P Slovic & H Kunreuther (eds), *Risk, media, and stigma.* London: Earthscan

Kuyper, H & Vlek, C (1984). 'Contrasting risk judgments among interest groups'. *Acta Psychologica*, 56, 205–218

Laird, F N (1989). 'The decline of deference: The political context of risk communication'. *Risk Analysis*, 9, 543–550

Langer, E J (1975). 'The illusion of control'. *Journal of Personality and Social Psychology*, 32, 311–328

Lasswell, H D (1948). 'The structure and function of communication in society'. In L Bryson (ed), *The communication of ideas: A series of addresses* (pp32–35). New York: Cooper Square

Lave, L B (1968). 'Safety in transportation: The role of government'. *Law and Contemporary Problems*, 33, 512–535

Lave, L (1972). 'Risk, safety, and the role of government'. In *Perspectives on benefit-risk decision making* (pp96–108). Washington, DC: National Academy of Engineering, Committee on Public Engineering Policy

Lave, L B (1981). 'Conflicting objectives in regulating the automobile'. *Science*, 212, 893

Lave, L B & Weber, W E (1970). 'A benefit-cost analysis of auto safety features'. *Applied Economics*, 2, 265–275

Lawless, E W (1977). *Technology and social shock.* New Brunswick, NJ: Rutgers University Press

Leavitt, M D (1993, 13 January). *Policy statement on monitored retrievable storage.* Salt Lake City, UT: Office of the Governor

Lee, C (1989). 'Perceptions of immunity to disease in adult smokers'. *Journal of Behavioral Medicine*, 12(3), 267–277

Leroy, D H & Nadler, T S (1993). 'Negotiate way out of siting dilemmas'. *Forum for Applied Research and Public Policy*, 8, 102–107

Leventhal, H, Glynn, K & Fleming, R (1987). 'Is the smoking decision an "informed choice?" Effect of smoking risk factors on smoking beliefs'. *Journal of the American Medical Association*, 257, 3373–3376

Levi, J (1991). 'Unproven AIDS therapies: The Food and Drug Administration and DDI'. In K E Hanna (ed), *Bio-medical politics* (pp9–37). Washington, DC: National Academy

Levine, S (1984). 'Probabilistic risk assessment: Identifying the real risks of nuclear power'. *Technology Review*, 87, 40–44

Lewis, H W (1990). *Technological risk.* New York: Norton

Lichtenberg, J & MacLean, D (1992). 'Is good news no news?' *The Geneva Papers on Risk and Insurance*, 17, 362–365

Lichtenstein, S & Fischhoff, B (1980). 'Training for calibration'. *Organizational Behavior and Human Performance*, 26, 149–171

Lichtenstein, S, Fischhoff, B & Phillips, L D (1982). 'Calibration of probabilities: The state of the art to 1980'. In D Kahneman, P Slovic & A Tversky (eds), *Judgment under uncertainty: Heuristics and biases* (pp306–334). Cambridge, England: Cambridge University Press

Lichtenstein, S & Slovic, P (1971). 'Reversals of preference between bids and choices in gambling decisions'. *Journal of Experimental Psychology*, 89, 46–55

Lichtenstein, S & Slovic, P (1973). 'Response-induced reversals of preference in gambling: An extended replication in Las Vegas'. *Journal of Experimental Psychology*, 101, 16–20

Lichtenstein, S, Slovic, P, Fischhoff, B, Layman, M & Combs, B (1978). 'Judged frequency of lethal events'. *Journal of Experimental Psychology: Human Learning and Memory*, 4, 551–578

Lichtenstein, S, Slovic, P & Zink, D (1969). 'Effect of instruction in expected value on optimality of gambling decisions'. *Journal of Experimental Psychology*, 79, 236–240

Lidz, C, Mulvey, E & Gardner, W (1993). 'The accuracy of predictions of violence to others'. *Journal of the American Medical Association*, 269, 1007–1011

Lifton, R J (1967). *Death in life: Survivors of Hiroshima*. New York: Random House

Lindblom, C E (1964). 'The science of "muddling through"'. In W J Gore & J W Dyson (eds), *The making of decisions: A reader in administrative behavior* (pp155–169). New York: The Free Press

Lindell, M K & Earle, T C (1983). 'How close is close enough: Public perceptions of the risks of industrial facilities'. *Risk Analysis*, 3, 245–254

Linnerooth, J (1975, July). *The evaluation of life saving: A survey* (Research Report 75–21). Laxenburg, Austria: International Institute for Applied Systems Analysis

Liska, A E (ed) (1975). *The consistency controversy*. New York: Wiley

Litai, D, Lanning, D D & Rasmussen, N. C (1983). 'The public perception of risk'. In V T Covello, G W Flamm, J V Rodricks, & R G Tardiff (eds), *The analysis of actual versus perceived risks* (pp213–224). New York: Plenum

Litwack, T R (1993). 'On the ethics of dangerousness assessments'. *Law and Human Behavior*, 17, 479–482

Loewenstein, G (1996). 'Out of control: Visceral influences on behavior'. *Organizational Behavior and Human Decision Processes*, 65, 272–292

Loewenstein, G F, Weber, E U, Hsee, C K & Welch, E S (1999, April). *Risk as feelings*. Philadelphia, PA: Carnegie Mellon University, Department of Social and Decision Sciences

Lowrance, W W (1976). *Of acceptable risk: Science and the determination of safety*. Los Altos, CA: William Kaufman

Luce, R D (1977). 'The choice axiom after twenty years'. *Journal of Mathematical Psychology*, 15, 215–233

Luce, R D & Raiffa, H (1957). *Games and decisions*. New York: Wiley

Lynn, F M (1987). 'OSHA's carcinogens standard: Round one on risk assessment models and assumptions'. In B B Johnson & V T Covello (eds), *The social and cultural construction of risk* (pp345–358). Dordrecht, The Netherlands: Reidel

Lyon, D & Slovic, P (1976). 'Dominance of accuracy information and neglect of base rates in probability estimation'. *Acta Psychologica*, 40, 287–298

MacGill, S M (1983). 'Exploring the similarities of different risks'. *Environment and Planning B: Planning and Design*, 10, 303–329

MacGregor, D G & Slovic, P (1986). 'Perceived acceptability of risk analysis as a decision-making approach'. *Risk Analysis*, 6, 245–256

MacGregor, D G & Slovic, P (1989). 'Perception of risk in automotive systems'. *Human Factors*, 31, 377–389

MacGregor, D G & Slovic, P (1995). 'The planetary exploration survey: What society members think about planetary protection'. *Planetary Report*, XV(2), 4–6

MacGregor, D G, Slovic, P, Berry, M & Evensky, H R (1999). 'Perception of financial risk: A survey study of advisors and planners'. *Journal of Financial Planning*, 12(8), 68–86

MacGregor, D G, Slovic, P, Mason, R G, Detweiler, J, Binney, S E & Dodd, B (1994). 'Perceived risks of radioactive waste transport through Oregon: Results of a state-wide survey'. *Risk Analysis*, 14(1), 5–14

MacGregor, D G, Slovic, P & Morgan, M G (1994). 'Perception of risks from electromagnetic fields: A psychometric evaluation of a risk-communication approach'. *Risk Analysis*, 14(5), 815–828

MacLean, D (1982). 'Risk and consent: Philosophical issues for centralized decisions'. *Risk Analysis*, 2, 59–67

Malmfors, T (1981). 'Toxicology as a science'. *Trends in Pharmacological Sciences*, 2(1), I–IV

Malmfors, T, Slovic, P, Kraus, N N, Wiström, G, Lappe, H & Letzel, H (1988). 'Allmänhetens uppfattning au risker och läkemedelsbehandling' [The general public's conceptions of risks and treatment with drugs]. *Svensk Farmaceutisk Tidskrift*, 92(11), 31–37

Marshall, E (1990). 'Radiation exposure: Hot legacy of the cold war'. *Science*, 249, 474

Marx, J (1990). 'Animal testing challenged'. *Science*, 250, 743–745

Marzoni, P (1971). *Motivating factors in the use of restraint systems*. Philadelphia: National Analysts. (NTIS No DOT HS-80C 585)

Matheson, J E (1969–1970). 'Decision analysis practice: Examples and insights'. In J Lawrence (ed), *Proceedings of the Fifth International Conference on Operational Research*. London: Tavistock

Maugh, T H (1978). 'Chemical carcinogens: The scientific basis for regulation'. *Science*, 201, 1200–1205

Maule, A J & Svenson, O (1993). 'Concluding remarks'. In O Svenson & A J Maule (eds), *Time pressure and stress in human judgment and decision making* (pp323–329). New York: Plenum

Mauss, M (1972). *A general theory of magic*. New York: Norton (original work published in 1902)

May, W W (1982). '$s for lives: Ethical considerations in the use of cost/benefit analysis by for-profit firms'. *Risk Analysis*, 2, 35–46

Maynard, W S, Nealey, S M, Hebert, J A & Lindell, M K (1976, June). *Public values associated with nuclear waste disposal* (Report BNWL-1977-UC-70). Seattle, WA: Battelle Memorial Institute, Human Affairs Research Center

Mazur, A (1973). 'Disputes between experts'. *Minerva*, 11, 243–262

Mazur, A (1981). *The dynamics of technical controversy*. Washington, DC: Communications Press

Mazur, A (1984a). 'The journalist and technology: Reporting about Love Canal and Three Mile Island'. *Minerva*, 22, 45–66

Mazur, A (1984b). 'Media influences on public attitudes toward nuclear power'. In W R Freudenburg & E Rosa, A (eds), *Public reactions to nuclear power* (pp97–114). Boulder, CO: Westview

Mazur, A (1984c). *Perception and communication of risk: Sociological issues*. Syracuse University, Department of Sociology

Mazur, D J & Merz, J F (1994). 'How age, outcome severity, and scale influence general medicine clinic patients' interpretations of verbal probability terms'. *Journal of General Internal Medicine*, 9(5), 268–271

McCallum, D B, Hammond, S L, Morris, L A & Covello, V T (1990). *Public knowledge and perceptions of chemical risks in six communities* (Report No 230-01-90-074). Washington, DC: US Environmental Protection Agency

McDaniels, T L, Axelrod, L J, Cavanagh, N S & Slovic, P (1997). 'Perception of eco- logical risk to water environments'. *Risk Analysis*, 17(3), 341–352

McDaniels, T L, Axelrod, L J & Slovic, P (1995). 'Characterizing perception of eco- logical risk'. *Risk Analysis*, 15(5), 575–588

McGinty, L & Atherly, G (1977). 'Acceptability versus democracy'. *New Scientist*, 74, 323–325

McGrath, P E (1974). *Radioactive waste management* (Report EURFNR 1204). Karlsruhe, Germany

McKenna, F P, Warburton, D M & Winwood, M (1993). 'Exploring the limits of opti- mism: The case of smokers' decision making'. *British Journal of Psychology*, 84, 389–394

McLaughlin, R, Baer, P, Pokorny, A, Burnside, M & Fairlie, A (1985). *Age-graded preva- lence of alcohol use during adolescence*. ERIC Document Reproduction Service No ED 257 020

McNeil, B J, Pauker, S G, Sox, H C, Jr & Tversky, A (1982). 'On the elicitation of preferences for alternative therapies'. *New England Journal of Medicine*, 306(21), 1259– 1262

McNeil, B J, Weichselbaum, R & Pauker, S G (1978). 'The fallacy of the five year sur- vival in lung cancer'. *New England Journal of Medicine*, 299, 1397–1401

Mechanic, D (1979). 'The stability of health and illness behavior: Results from a 16- year follow-up'. *American Journal of Public Health*, 69, 1142–1145

Mechitov, A I & Rebrick, S B (1990). 'Studies of risk and safety perception in the USSR'. In K Borcherding, D I Larichev & D M Messick (eds), *Contemporary issues in decision making* (pp261–270). Amsterdam: Elsevier

Medawar, C (1989). 'Professional drug information: A consumer perspective'. In B Horisberger & R Dinkel (eds), *The perception and management of drug safety risks* (pp135– 140). Berlin: Springer-Verlag

Meehl, P E & Rosen, A (1955). 'Antecedent probability and the efficiency of psycho- metric signs, patterns, or cutting scores'. *Psychological Bulletin*, 52, 194–216

Mellers, B A, Schwartz, A, Ho, K & Ritov, I. (1996). *Elation and disappointment: Emo- tional responses to risky options*. Columbus, OH: Ohio State University, Department of Psychology

Merchant, C (1980). *The death of nature: Women, ecology, and the scientific revolution*. New York: Harper & Row

Miller, G A (1956). 'The magical number seven, plus or minus two: Some limits on our capacity for processing information'. *Psychological Review*, 63, 81–97

Millstein, S (1989). 'Adolescent health'. *American Psychologist*, 44, 837–842

Mitchell, J V (1992). 'Perception of risk and credibility at toxic sites'. *Risk Analysis*, 12, 19–26

Mitchell, M L (1989, October). 'The impact of external parties on brand-name capital: The 1982 Tylenol poisonings and subsequent cases'. *Economic Inquiry*, 27, 601–618

Moatti, J P, Stemmelen, E & Fagnani, F (1984, October). *Risk perception, social conflicts and acceptability of technologies (an overview of French studies)*. Paper presented at the Annual Meeting of the Society for Risk Analysis, Knoxville, TN

Monahan, J & Shah, S (1989). 'Dangerousness and commitment of the mentally dis- ordered in the United States'. *Schizophrenia Bulletin*, 15, 541–553

Monahan, J & Steadman, H J (1996) 'Violent storms and violent people: How meteo- rology can inform risk communication in mental health law'. *American Psychologist*, 51, 931–938

Monahan, J & Wexler, D (1978). 'A definite maybe: Proof and probability in civil com- mitment'. *Law and Human Behavior*, 2, 37–42

Montgomery, H (1983). 'Decision rules and the search for a dominance structure: To- wards a process model of decision making'. In P Humphreys, O Svenson & A Vari (eds), *Analysing and aiding decision processes* (pp343–369). Amsterdam: North-Holland

Moore, J A (1989, May–June). 'Speaking of data: The Alar controversy'. *EPA Journal*, 15, 5–9

Morgan, K Z (1969). 'Present status of recommendations of the International Commission on Radiological Protection, National Council on Radiation Protection and Federal Radiation Council'. In A M F Duhamel (ed), *Health physics*. New York: Pergamon

Morgan, M G & Henrion, M (1990). *Uncertainty*. New York: Cambridge University

Morgan, M G, Slovic, P, Nair, I, Geisler, D, MacGregor, D G, Fischhoff, B, Lincoln, D & Florig, K (1985). 'Powerline frequency electric and magnetic fields: A pilot study of risk perception'. *Risk Analysis*, 5, 139–149

Morone, J F & Woodhouse, E J (1989). *The demise of nuclear energy? Lessons for a democratic control of technology*. New Haven, CT: Yale University

Morris, L A, Mazis, M B & Barofsky, I (eds) (1980). *Product labeling and health risks* (Report No 6). Cold Spring Harbor, NY: Cold Spring Harbor Laboratory

Morrison, D, Chapman, C R & Slovic, P (1994). 'The impact hazard'. In T Gehrels (ed), *The hazards of impacts by comets and asteroids* (pp59–91). Tucson: University of Arizona

Mountain West (1989, June). *Yucca Mountain socioeconomic project: An interim report* (NWPO-SE-024-89). Carson City, NV: NWPO

Mowrer, O H (1960a). *Learning theory and behavior*. New York: John Wiley & Sons, Inc

Mowrer, O H (1960b). *Learning theory and the symbolic processes*. New York: John Wiley & Sons, Inc

Murphy, A H & Winkler, R H (1971). 'Forecasters and probability forecasts: Some current problems'. *Bulletin of the American Meteorological Society*, 52, 239–247

Murray, M L (1971). 'A deductible selection model-development and application'. *Journal of Risk and Insurance*, 38, 423–436

Murray, M L (1972). 'Empirical utility functions and insurance consumption decisions'. *Journal of Risk and Insurance*, 39, 31–41

Mushkatel, A H & Pijawka, K D (1992). *Institutional trust, information, and risk perceptions: Report of findings of the Las Vegas metropolitan area survey, 29 June–1 July, 1992* (NWPO-SE-055-92). Carson City, NV: Nevada Nuclear Waste Project Office

Najarian, T (1978). 'The controversy over the health effects of radiation'. *Technology Review*, 81, 74–82

National Academy of Sciences (1983). *Risk assessment in the federal government: Managing the process*. Washington, DC: National Academy Press

National Academy of Sciences (1989). *The nuclear weapons complex: Management for health, safety, and the environment*. Washington, DC: National Academy Press

National Center for State Courts (1986). 'Guidelines for involuntary civil commitment'. *Mental and Physical Disability Law Reporter*, 10, 409–514

National Research Council; Committee on Water (1966). *Alternatives in water management: a report* (National Research Council Publication 1408). Washington, DC: National Academy of Sciences–National Research Council

National Research Council (1980a). *Disasters and the mass media*. Washington, DC: National Academy of Sciences Press

National Research Council; Committee on Nuclear and Alternative Energy Systems (1980b). *Energy in transition*, 1985-2010. San Francisco: Freeman

National Research Council; Committee on the Institutional Means for Assessment of Risks to Public Health (1983). *Risk assessment in the Federal Government: Managing the process*. Washington, DC: National Academy Press

National Research Council (1989). *Improving risk communication*. Washington, DC: National Academy Press

National Research Council; National Academy of Sciences; Board on Radioactive Waste Management (1990). *Rethinking high-level radioactive waste disposal: A position statement of the Board on Radioactive Waste Management.* Washington, DC: National Academy Press

National Research Council; Committee on Risk Characterization (1996). *Understanding risk: Informing decisions in a democratic society,* P C Stern & H V Fineberg, (eds). Washington, DC: National Academy Press

National Safety Council (1977). *Accident facts.* Chicago: National Safety Council

Nealey, S M & Hebert, J A (1983). 'Public attitudes toward radioactive wastes'. In C A Walker, L C Gould, & E J Woodhouse (eds), *Too hot to handle: Social and policy issues in the management of radioactive wastes* (pp94–111). New Haven, CT: Yale University

Nelkin, D (1974). 'The role of experts on a nuclear siting controversy'. *Bulletin of the Atomic Scientists,* 30, 29–36

Nelkin, D & Pollak, M (1979, August/September). 'Public participation in technological decisions: Reality or grand illusion?' *Technology Review,* pp55–64

Neter, J & Williams, C A, Jr (1971). 'Acceptability of three normative methods in insurance decision making'. *Journal of Risk and Insurance,* 38, 385–408

Neter, J, Williams, C A, Jr & Whitmore, G A (1968). 'Comparison of independent and joint decision making for two insurance decisions'. *Journal of Risk and Insurance,* 35, 87–106

New Yorker (1985). 'The talk of the town'. *New Yorker,* 60(53), 29–30

Newell, A & Simon, H A (1972). *Human problem solving.* Englewood Cliffs, NJ: Prentice-Hall

Nisbett, R E, Borgida, E, Crandall, R & Reed, H (1976). 'Popular induction: Information is not necessarily informative'. In J S Carroll & J W Payne (eds), *Cognition and social behavior* (pp113–133). Hillsdale, NJ: Erlbaum

Nisbett, R & Ross, L (1980). *Human inference: Strategies and shortcomings of social judgment.* Englewood Cliffs, NJ: Prentice-Hall

Novello, A (1988). *Final report of secretary's working group on pediatric HIV infection and disease.* Washington, DC: US Department of Health and Human Services

Nuclear Waste Technical Review Board (1991). *Third report to the US Congress and the US Secretary of Energy.* Arlington, VA: Nuclear Waste Technical Review Board

O'Brien, B J, Elswood, J & Calin, A (1989). *Risk perception of medicines: A survey of patients with ankylosing spondylitis.* Uxbridge, Middlesex, UK: Brunel University, Health Economics Research Groups

Ordóñez, L & Benson, L, III (1997). 'Decisions under time pressure: How time constraint affects risky decision making'. *Organizational Behavior and Human Decision Processes,* 71(2), 121–140

O'Riordan, T (1974). 'The New Zealand natural hazard insurance scheme: Application to North America'. In G F White (ed), *Natural hazards: Local, national, global* (pp217–219). New York: Oxford University Press

Otway, H (1975, February). *Risk assessment and societal choices* (Research Memorandum 75-2). Laxenburg, Austria: International Institute for Applied Systems Analysis

Otway, H (1992). 'Public wisdom, expert fallibility: Toward a contextual theory of risk'. In S Krimsky & D Golding (eds), *Social theories of risk* (pp215–228). Westport, CT: Praeger

Otway, H J & Cohen, J J (1975, March). *Revealed preferences: Comments on the Starr benefit-risk relationships* (Research Memorandum 75-5). Laxenburg, Austria: International Institute for Applied Systems Analysis

Otway, H J & Fishbein, M (1976). *The determinants of attitude formation: An application to nuclear power* (Technical Report No RM-76-80). Laxenburg, Austria: International Institute for Applied Systems Analysis

Otway, H, Haastrup, P, Connell, W, Gianitsopoulas, G & Paruccini, M (1988). 'Risk communication in Europe after Chernobyl: A media analysis of seven countries'. *Industrial Crisis Quarterly*, 2, 31–35

Otway, H J, Maderthaner, R & Gutzman, G (1975, May). *Avoidance response to the risk environment: A cross cultural comparison* (Research Report No 75–14). Laxenburg, Austria: International Institute for Applied Systems Analysis

Otway, H J, Maurer, D & Thomas, J (1978). 'Nuclear power: The question of public acceptance'. *Futures*, 10(2), 109–118

Otway, H J & Pahner, P D (1976). 'Risk assessment'. *Futures*, 8, 122–134

Otway, H J & von Winterfeldt, D (1982). 'Beyond acceptable risk: On the social acceptability of technologies'. *Policy Sciences*, 14, 247–256

Palm, R I (1990). *Natural hazards: An integrative framework for research and planning.* Baltimore: Johns Hopkins

Parra, C G (1971). 'Perception of past droughts in Ticul, Yucatan'. In *Proceedings of the Great Plains—Rocky Mountain Meeting of the American Association of Geographers*, Colorado Springs

Pashigian, B P, Schkade, L L & Menefee, G H (1966). 'The selection of an optimal deductible for a given insurance policy'. *Journal of Business*, 39, 35–44

Patton, D J (ed) (1970). *From geographic discipline to inquiring student: Final report on the high school geography project.* Washington, DC: Association of American Geographers

Payne, J W, Bettman, J R & Johnson, E J (1988). 'Adaptive strategy selection in decision making'. *Journal of Experimental Psychology: Learning, Memory, and Cogition*, 14, 534–552

Payne, J W, Bettman, J R & Johnson, E J (1992). 'Behavioral decision research: A constructive processing perspective'. *Annual Review of Psychology*, 43, 87–131

Payne, J, Bettman, J & Johnson, E (1993). *The adaptive decision maker.* New York: Cambridge

Payne, J W & Braunstein, M L (1971). 'Preferences among gambles with equal underlying distributions'. *Journal of Experimental Psychology*, 87, 13–18

Peters, E & Slovic, P (1996). 'The role of affect and worldviews as orienting dispositions in the perception and acceptance of nuclear power'. *Journal of Applied Social Psychology*, 26, 1427–1453

Petterson, J S (1988). 'Perception vs. reality of radiological impact: The Goiania model'. *Nuclear News*, 31(14), 84–90

Pidgeon, N, Hood, C, Jones, D, Turner, B & Gibson, R (1992). 'Risk perception'. In Royal Society Study Group (ed), *Risk: Analysis, perception and management* (pp89–134). London: The Royal Society

Piehler, H R, Twerski, A D., Weinstein, A & Donaher, W A (1974). 'Product liability and the technical expert'. *Science*, 186, 1089–1093

Pijawka, K D & Mushkatel, A H (1992). 'Public opposition to the siting of the high-level nuclear waste repository: The importance of trust'. *Policy Studies Review*, 10(4), 180–194

Pillisuk, M & Acredolo, C (1988). 'Fear of technological hazards: One concern or many?' *Social Behavior*, 3, 17–24

Pimentel, G C (1989). 'Chemistry at a crossroad'. *Chemical and Engineering News*, 67(18), 53–55

Preston, F & Shortridge, R (1973). 'A study of restraint use and effectiveness'. *HIT Lab Reports*, 3(8), 1–27

Purvis, A (1994, 13 June). 'All the hatred in the world'. *Time*, pp36–37

Raiffa, H (1968). *Decision analysis: Introductory lectures on choices under uncertainty.* Reading, MA: Addison-Wesley

Rappaport, E B (1974, November). *Economic analysis of life-and-death decision making* (Appendix 2 in Report No Eng 7478). University of California, Los Angeles, School of Engineering and Applied Science

Rappaport, E B (1981). *The demand for improvements in mortality probabilities*. Unpublished doctoral dissertation, University of California, Los Angeles

Rasmussen, N C (1974). *An assessment of accident risks in US commercial nuclear power plants* (WASH-1400). Washington, DC: US Atomic Energy Commission

Rayner, S & Cantor, R (1987). 'How fair is safe enough? The cultural approach to societal technology choice'. *Risk Analysis*, 7, 3–9

The Register-Guard (1994, 21 September). '38,000 shoes stand for loss in lethal year', p6A

Reissland, J & Harries, V (1979). 'A scale for measuring risks'. *New Scientist*, 83, 809–811

Renn, O (1981, June). *Man, technology, and risk: A study on intuitive risk assessment and attitudes towards nuclear power* (Report Jul-Spez 115). Julich, Federal Republic of Germany: Nuclear Research Center

Renn, O (1986). 'Risk perception: A systematic review of concepts and research results'. In *Avoiding and managing environmental damage from major industrial accidents: Proceedings of the Air Pollution Control Association International Conference* (pp377–408). Pittsburgh, PA: The Association

Renn, O (1991). 'Premises of risk communication: Results of two participatory experiments'. In R E Kasperson & P J Stallen (eds), *Communicating risks to the public: International perspectives* (pp457–481). Amsterdam and New York: Kluwer Academic

Renn, O & Levine, D (1991). 'Credibility and trust in risk communication'. In R E Kasperson & P J M Stallen (eds), *Communicating risks to the public: International perspectives* (pp175–218). Amsterdam and New York: Kluwer Academic

Renn, O & Swaton, E (1984). 'Psychological and sociological approaches to studying risk perception'. *Environment International*, 10, 557–575

Renn, O, Webler, T & Johnson, B B (1991, Summer). 'Public participation in hazard management: The use of citizen panels in the US'. *Risk – Issues in Health and Safety*, 2(3), 197–226

Renn, O, Webler, T & Wiedemann, P (1995). *Fairness and competence in citizen participation*. Dordrecht, The Netherlands: Kluwer

Riger, S, Gordon, M T & LeBailly, R (1978). 'Women's fear of crime: From blaming to restricting the victim'. *Victimology*, 3, 274–284

Robertson, L S (1976). 'The great seat belt campaign flop'. *Journal of Communication*, 26, 41–45

Robertson, L S, Kelley, A B, O'Neill, B, Wixom, C W, Elswirth, R S & Haddon, W, Jr (1974). 'A controlled study of the effect of television messages on safety belt use'. *American Journal of Public Health*, 64, 1071–1080

Rogers, A (1993). 'Coercion and "voluntary" admission: An examination of psychiatric patient views'. *Behvaioral Sciences and the Law*, 11(3), 259–268

Rohrmann, B (1994). 'Risk perception of different societal groups: Australian findings and cross-national comparisons'. *Australian Journal of Psychology*, 46(3), 150–163

Roper Reports (1985). Public opinion poll conducted for the Environmental Protection Agency

Rosen, J D (1990). 'Much ado about Alar'. *Issues in Science and Technology*, 7(1), 85–90

Rosenberg, J (1978). 'A question of ethics: The DNA controversy'. *American Educator*, 2(1), 27–30

Ross, L (1977). 'The intuitive psychologist and his shortcomings: Distortions in the attribution process'. In L Berkowitz (ed), *Advances in experimental social psychology* (vol 10, pp174–220). New York: Academic Press

Ross, L & Lepper, M R (1980). 'The perseverence of beliefs: Empirical and normative considerations'. *New Directions for Methodology of Social and Behavioral Science*, 4, 17–36

Ross, L, Lepper, M R & Hubbard, M (1975). 'Perseverance in self-perception and social perception: Biased attributional processes in the debriefing paradigm'. *Journal of Personality and Social Psychology*, 32, 880–892

Ross, B M & Levy, N (1958). 'Patterned predictions of chance events by children and adults'. *Psychological Reports*, 4, 87–124

Rothbart, M & Park, B (1986). 'On the confirmability and disconfirmability of trait concepts'. *Journal of Personality and Social Psychology*, 50, 131–142

Rothman, S & Lichter, S (1987). 'Elite ideology and risk perception in nuclear energy policy'. *American Political Science Review*, 81, 383–405

Rothschild, N (1978, November). 'Coming to grips with risk'. Address presented on BBC television; reprinted in the Wall Street Journal

Rowe, W D (1977). *An anatomy of risk*. New York: Wiley

The Royal Society (1983). *Risk assessment: A study group report*. London: The Royal Society

Rozin, P, Haidt, J & McCauley, C R (1993). 'Disgust'. In M Lewis & J M Haviland (eds), *Handbook of Emotions* (pp575–594). New York: Guilford

Rozin, P, Millman, L & Nemeroff, C (1986). 'Operation of the laws of sympathetic magic in disgust and other domains'. *Journal of Personality and Social Psychology*, 50, 703–712

Ruckelshaus, W D (1983). 'Science, risk, and public policy'. *Science*, 221, 1026–1028

Ruckelshaus, W D (1984). 'Risk in a free society'. *Risk Analysis*, 4, 157–162

Ruckelshaus, W D (1985). 'Risk, science, and democracy'. *Issues in Science and Technology*, 1(3), 19–38

Rummel, R J (1970). *Applied factor analysis*. Evanston, IL: Northwestern University Press

Rummel, R J (1995, June). 'The holocaust in comparative and historical perspective'. Paper delivered at the Conference on the 'Other' as Threat – Demonization and Antisemitism. Hebrew University of Jerusalem

Sandman, P M (1986). *Explaining environmental risk*. (Report No TS-799). Washington, DC: Environmental Protection Agency, Office of Toxic Substances

Sandman, P M, Weinstein, N D & Klotz, M L (1987). 'Public response to the risk from geological radon'. *Journal of Communication*, 37, 93–108

Savage, L J (1954). *The foundations of statistics*. New York: Wiley

Schell, J (1982). *The fate of the earth*. New York: Alfred A Knopf

Schelling, T C (1968). 'The life you save may be your own'. In S B Chase, Jr (ed), Problems in public expenditure analysis (pp127–176). Washington, DC: Brookings Institute

Schiff, M (1970). *Some theoretical aspects of attitudes and perception*. (working Paper No 15). Toronto: Natural Hazards Research

Schlaifer, R (1969). *Analysis of decisions under uncertainty*. New York: McGraw-Hill

Schoemaker, P J H (1977). 'Experimental studies on individual decision making under risk: An information processing approach'. Unpublished doctoral dissertation. The Wharton School, University of Pennsylvania, Philadelphia

Schoemaker, P J H & Kunreuther, H C (1979). 'An experimental study of insurance decisions'. *Journal of Risk and Insurance*, 46, 603–618

Schwing, R C (1979). 'Longevity benefits and costs of reducing various risks'. *Technological Forecasting and Social Change*, 13, 333–345

Segerstrom, S C, MacCarthy, W J, Caskey, N H, Gross, T M & Jarvik, M E (1993). 'Optimistic bias among cigarette smokers'. *Journal of Applied Social Psychology*, 23(19), 1606–1618

Selvidge, J (1975). 'A three-step procedure for assigning probabilities to rare events'. In D Wendt & C A Vlek, J (eds), *Utility, subjective probability, and human decision making* (pp199–216). Dordrecht, Holland: Reidel

Shafir, E, Osherson, D & Smith, E (1989). 'An advantage model of choice'. *Journal of Behavioral Decision Making*, 2, 1–23

Shafir, E, Simonson, I & Tversky, A (1993). 'Reason-based choice'. *Cognition*, 49, 11–36

Sharlin, H I. (1986). 'EDB: A case study in the communication of health risk'. *Risk Analysis*, 6, 61–68

Shedler, J & Block, J (1990). 'Adolescent drug use and psychological health: A longitudinal perspective'. *American Psychologist*, 45, 612–629

Shoemaker, P J (1987). 'Mass communication by the book: A review of 31 texts'. *Journal of Communication*, 37(3), 109–131

Short, J F, Jr (1984). 'The social fabric at risk: Toward the social transformation of risk analysis'. *American Sociological Review*, 49, 711–725

Shrader-Frechette, K S (1991). *Risk and rationality: Philosophical foundations for populist reforms*. Berkeley: University of California

Siegel, S (1956). *Nonparametric statistics for the behavioral sciences*. New York: McGraw-Hill

Sigmon, E (1987). 'Achieving a negotiated compensation agreement in siting: The MRS case'. *Journal of Policy Analysis and Management*, 6(2), 170–179

Simon, H A (1956). 'Rational choice and the structure of the environment'. *Psychological Review*, 63, 129–138

Simon, H (1957). *Models of man*. New York: Wiley

Simon, H A (1959). 'Theories of decision making in economics and behavioral science'. *American Economic Review*, 49, 253–283

Simon, H A (1960). *The new science of management decision*. New York: Harper & Row

Sinclair, C, Marstrand, P & Newick, P (1972). *Innovation and human risk*. London: Centre for the Study of Industrial Innovation

Sinsheimer, R L (1971). 'The brain of Pooh: An essay on the limits of mind'. *American Scientist*, 59, 20–28

Sjöberg, L (1997). 'Explaining risk perception: An empirical evaluation of cultural theory'. *Risk Decision and Policy*, 2(2), 113–130

Sjöberg, L (1999). 'Consequences of perceived risk: Demand for mitigation'. *Journal of Risk Research*, 2, 129–149

Sjöberg, L & Drottz-Sjöberg, B M (1993, August). *Attitudes toward nuclear waste* (Rhizikon Research Report No 12). Sweden: Stockholm School of Economics, Center for Risk Research

Sjöberg, L & Drottz-Sjöberg, B-M (1994a). 'Risk perception'. In Swedish Risk Academy (ed), *Radiation and society: Comprehending radiation risk* (vol 1, pp29–60). Vienna: International Atomic Energy Agency

Sjöberg, L & Drottz-Sjöberg, B-M (1994b). *Risk perception of nuclear waste: Experts and the public* (Rhizikon Risk Research Report No 16). Stockholm: Stockholm School of Economics, Center for Risk Research

Slovic, P (1972). 'From Shakespeare to Simon: Speculation – and some evidence – about man's ability to process information'. *Oregon Research Institute Research Monograph*, 12(2)

Slovic, P (1975). 'Choice between equally valued alternatives'. *Journal of Experimental Psychology: Human Perception and Performance*, 1, 280–287

Slovic, P (1981). 'Informing the public about the risks from ionizing radiation'. *Health Physics*, 41, 589–598

Slovic, P (1982). 'Toward understanding and improving decisions'. In W C Howell & E A Fleishman (eds), *Human performance and productivity: Vol 2: Information processing and decision making* (pp157–183). Hillsdale, NJ: Erlbaum

Slovic, P (1986). 'Informing and educating the public about risk'. *Risk Analysis*, 6(4), 403–415

Slovic, P (1987). 'Perception of risk'. *Science*, 236, 280–285

Slovic, P (1989, June). 'The perception and management of therapeutic risk'. In *CMR Annual Lecture*. Carshalton, Surrey, England: Centre for Medicines Research

Slovic, P (1990). 'Perception of risk from radiation'. In W K Sinclair (ed), *Proceedings of the Twenty-fifth Annual Meeting of the National Council on Radiation Protection and Measurements, Vol 11: Radiation protection today: The NCRP at sixty years* (pp73–97). Bethesda, MD: NCRP

Slovic, P (1992). 'Perception of risk: Reflections on the psychometric paradigm'. In S Krimsky & D Golding (eds), *Social theories of risk* (pp117–152). New York: Praeger

Slovic, P (1993). 'Perceived risk, trust, and democracy'. *Risk Analysis*, 13, 675–682

Slovic, P (1995). 'The construction of preference'. *American Psychologist*, 50, 364–371

Slovic, P (1997). 'Trust, emotion, sex, politics, and science: Surveying the risk-assessment battlefield'. In M H Bazerman, D M Messick, A E Tenbrunsel & K A Wade-Benzoni (eds), *Environment, ethics, and behavior* (pp277–313). San Francisco: New Lexington

Slovic, P (1998). 'Do adolescent smokers know the risks?' *Duke Law Journal*, 47, 1133–1141

Slovic, P (1999). 'Are trivial risks the greatest risks of all? Comment on Sjöberg'. *Journal of Risk Research*, 2, 281–288

Slovic, P, Fischhoff, B & Lichtenstein, S (1976). 'Cognitive processes and societal risk taking'. In J S Carroll & J W Payne (eds), *Cognition and social behavior* (pp165–184). Potomac, MD: Erlbaum

Slovic, P, Fischhoff, B & Lichtenstein, S (1977). 'Behavioral decision theory'. *Annual Review of Psychology*, 28, 1–39

Slovic, P, Fischhoff, B & Lichtenstein, S (1978). 'Accident probabilities and seat belt usage: A psychological perspective'. *Accident Analysis and Prevention*, 10, 281–285

Slovic, P, Fischhoff, B & Lichtenstein, S (1979). 'Rating the risks'. *Environment*, 21(3), 14–20, 36–39

Slovic, P, Fischhoff, B & Lichtenstein, S (1980a). *Expressed preferences* (Report No 80–1). Eugene, OR: Decision Research

Slovic, P, Fischhoff, B & Lichtenstein, S (1980b). 'Informing people about risk'. In L A Morris, M B Mazis & I Barofsky (eds), *Product labeling and health risks* (Report No 6, pp165–181). Cold Spring Harbor, NY: Cold Spring Harbor Laboratory

Slovic, P, Fischhoff, B & Lichtenstein, S (1980c). 'Facts and fears: Understanding perceived risk'. In R C Schwing & W A Albers, Jr (eds), *Societal risk assessment: How safe is safe enough?* (pp181–216). New York: Plenum

Slovic, P, Fischhoff, B & Lichtenstein, S (1981a). 'Perceived risk: Psychological factors and social implications'. In F. Warner & D H Slater (eds), *The assessment and perception of risk* (pp17–34). London: The Royal Society

Slovic, P, Fischhoff, B & Lichtenstein, S (1981b). 'Perception and acceptability of risks from energy systems'. In A Baum & J E Singer (eds), *Advances in environmental psychology* (vol 3, pp157–169). Hillsdale, NJ: Erlbaum

Slovic, P, Fischhoff, B & Lichtenstein, S (1982a). 'Facts versus fears: Understanding perceived risk'. In D Kahneman, P Slovic & A Tversky (eds), *Judgment under uncertainty: Heuristics and biases* (pp463–489). New York: Cambridge University

Slovic, P, Fischhoff, B & Lichtenstein, S (1982b). 'Response mode, framing, and information-processing effects in risk assessment'. In R M Hogarth (ed), *New directions for methodology of social and behavioral science: No 11. Question framing and response consistency* (pp21–36). San Francisco: Jossey-Bass

Slovic, P, Fischhoff, B & Lichtenstein, S (1982c). 'Why study risk perception?' *Risk Analysis*, 2, 83–93

Slovic, P, Fischhoff, B & Lichtenstein, S (1984). 'Behavioral decision theory perspectives on risk and safety'. *Acta Psychologica*, 56, 183–203

Slovic, P, Fischhoff, B & Lichtenstein, S (1985). 'Characterizing perceived risk'. In R W Kates, C Hohenemser, & J X. Kasperson (eds), *Perilous progress: Technology as hazard* (pp91–123). Boulder, CO: Westview

Slovic, P, Fischhoff, B, Lichtenstein, S, Corrigan, B & Combs, B (1977). 'Preference for insuring against probable small losses: Insurance implications'. *Journal of Risk and Insurance*, 44, 237–258

Slovic, P, Flynn, J, Johnson, S M & Mertz, C K (1993). *The dynamics of trust in situations of risk* (Report No 93–2). Eugene, OR: Decision Research

Slovic, P, Flynn, J & Layman, M (1991). 'Perceived risk, trust, and the politics of nuclear waste'. *Science*, 254, 1603–1607

Slovic, P, Flynn, J, Mertz, C K, Mays, C & Poumadère, M (1996). *Nuclear power and the public: A comparative study of risk perception in France and the United States* (Report No 96–6). Eugene, OR: Decision Research

Slovic, P, Flynn, J, Mertz, C K & Mullican, L (1993). *Health risk perception in Canada* (Report No 93-EHD-170). Ottawa: Department of National Health and Welfare

Slovic, P, Kraus, N & Covello, V T (1990). 'What *should* we know about making risk comparisons?' *Risk Analysis*, 10(3), 389–392

Slovic, P, Kraus, N N, Lappe, H, Letzel, H & Malmfors, T (1989). 'Risk perception of prescription drugs: Report on a survey in Sweden'. *Pharmaceutical Medicine*, 4, 43–65

Slovic, P, Kraus, N, Lappe, H & Major, M (1991). 'Risk perception of prescription drugs: Report on a survey in Canada'. *Canadian Journal of Public Health*, 82, S15–S20

Slovic, P, Kunreuther, H C & White, G (1974). 'Decision processes, rationality and adjustment to natural hazards'. In G F White (ed), *Natural hazards: Local, national, global* (pp187–205). New York: Oxford University Press

Slovic, P, Layman, M & Flynn, J (1990). *Images of a place and vacation preferences: Report of the 1989 surveys* (Report No NWPO-SE-030-90). Carson City: Nevada Nuclear Waste Project Office

Slovic, P, Layman, M & Flynn, J (1991). 'Risk perception, trust, and nuclear waste: Lessons from Yucca Mountain'. *Environment*, 33, 6–11, 28–30

Slovic, P, Layman, M, Kraus, N, Flynn, J, Chalmers, J & Gesell, G (1991). 'Perceived risk, stigma, and potential economic impacts of a high-level nuclear waste repository in Nevada'. *Risk Analysis*, 11, 683–696

Slovic, P & Lichtenstein, S (1968). 'The importance of variance preferences in gambling decisions'. *Journal of Experimental Psychology*, 78, 646–654

Slovic, P & Lichtenstein, S (1983). 'Preference reversals: A broader perspective'. *American Economic Review*, 73, 596–605

Slovic, P, Lichtenstein, S & Edwards, W (1965). 'Boredom-induced changes in preferences among bets'. *American Journal of Psychology*, 78, 208–217

Slovic, P, Lichtenstein, S & Fischhoff, B (1979). 'Images of disaster: Perception and acceptance of risks from nuclear power'. In G Goodman & W Rowe (eds), *Energy risk assessment* (pp223–245). London: Academic

Slovic, P, Lichtenstein, S & Fischhoff, B (1984). 'Modeling the societal impact of fatal accidents'. *Management Science*, 30, 464–474

Slovic, P, MacGregor, D G & Kraus, N N (1987). 'Perception of risk from automobile safety defects'. *Accident Analysis and Prevention*, 19(5), 359–373

Slovic, P & MacPhillamy, D J (1974). 'Dimensional commensurability and cue utilization in comparative judgment'. *Organizational Behavior and Human Performance*, 11, 172–194

Slovic, P, Malmfors, T, Krewski, D, Mertz, C K, Neil, N & Bartlett, S (1995). 'Intuitive toxicology. II. Expert and lay judgments of chemical risks in Canada'. *Risk Analysis*, 15(6), 661–675

Slovic, P, Malmfors, T, Mertz, C K, Neil, N & Purchase, I F H (1997). 'Evaluating chemical risks: Results of a survey of the British Toxicology Society'. *Human & Experimental Toxicology*, 16, 289–304

Slovic, P & Monahan, J (1995). 'Probability, danger, and coercion: A study of risk perception and decision making in mental health law'. *Law and Human Behavior*, 19(1), 49–65

Slovic, P, Monahan, J & MacGregor, D G (2000). 'Violence risk assessment and risk communication: The effects of using actual cases, providing instruction, and employing probability versus frequency formats'. *Law and Human Behavior*, 24(3), 271–296

Slovic, P & Peters, E (1998). 'The importance of worldviews in risk perception'. *Risk Decision and Policy*, 3(2), 165–170

Smedslund, J (1963). 'The concept of correlation in adults'. *Scandinavian Journal of Psychology*, 4, 165–173

Smith, K (1988). 'Perception of risks associated with nuclear power'. *Energy Environment Monitor*, 4(1), 61–70

Sorensen, J H & Mileti, D S (1987). 'Decisionmaking uncertainties in emergency warning system organizations'. *International Journal of Mass Emergencies and Disasters*, 5(1), 33–61

Sorensen, J, Soderstrom, J, Copenhaver, E, Carnes, S & Bolin, R (1987). *Impacts of hazardous technology: The psycho-social effects of restarting TMI-1* (L W Milbrath, ed). SUNY Series in Environmental Public Policy. Albany: State University of New York Press

Sowby, F D (1965). 'Radiation and other risks'. *Health Physics*, 11, 879–887

Spigner, C, Hawkins, W & Loren, W (1993). 'Gender differences in perception of risk associated with alcohol and drug use among college students'. *Women and Health*, 20, 87–97

Spriet-Pourra, C & Auriche, M (1988). *Drug withdrawal from sale: An analysis of the phenomenon and its implications*. Richmond, UK: PJB Publications Ltd

Starr, C (1969). 'Social benefit versus technological risk'. *Science*, 165, 1232–1238

Starr, C (1972). 'Benefit-cost studies in sociotechnical systems'. In *Perspectives on benefit-risk decision making* (Report of the Committee on Public Engineering Policy, pp17–42). Washington, DC: National Academy of Engineering

Starr, C (1985). 'Risk management, assessment, and acceptability'. *Risk Analysis*, 5, 97–102

Starr, C, Rudman, R & Whipple, C (1976). 'Philosophical basis for risk analysis'. *Annual Review of Energy*, 1, 629–662

Steadman, H, Monahan, J, Appelbaum, P, Grisso, T, Mulvey, E, Roth, L, Robbins, P & Klassen, D (1994). 'Designing a new generation of risk assessment research'. In J Monahan & H Steadman (eds), *Violence and mental disorder: Developments in risk assessment* (pp297–318). Chicago: University of Chicago

Steger, M A & Witte, S L (1989). 'Gender differences in environmental orientations: A comparison of publics and activists in Canada and the US'. *Western Political Quarterly*, 42, 627–649

Steinbrugge, K V, McClure, F E & Snow, A J (1969). *Studies in seismicity and earthquake damage statistics* (Report COM-71-00053, Appendix A). Washington, DC: US Department of Commerce

Stern, P C, Dietz, T & Kalof, L (1993). 'Value orientations, gender, and environmental concern'. *Environment and Behavior*, 25, 322–348

Stevens, S S (1958). 'Problems and methods of psychophysics'. *Psychological Bulletin*, 55, 177–196

Stevens, S S (1975). *Psychophysics*. New York: Wiley

Stokey, E & Zeckhauser, R (1978). *A primer for policy analysis*. New York: Norton

Sullivan, M (1992, 21 August). Letter to the Fremont County Commissioners. Cheyenne, WY: Office of the Governor

Summers, C, Slovic, P, Hine, D & Zuliani, D (1998). '"Psychophysical numbing": An empirical basis for perceptions of collective violence'. In C Summers & E Markuson (eds), *Collective violence: Harmful behavior in groups and government*. Lanham: Rowman & Littlefield

Svenson, O (1977). *Risks of road transportation from a psychological point of view* (Report 3-77 of the Risk Project). Stockholm: Committee for Future Oriented Research

Svenson, O (1984). 'Managing the risks of the automobile'. *Management Science*, 30, 486–502

Svenson, O, Edland, A & Slovic, P (1990). 'Choices and judgments of incompletely described decision alternatives under time pressure'. *Acta Psychologica*, 75, 153–169

Swaen, G M H & Meijers, J M M (1988). 'Influence of design characteristics on the outcome of retrospective cohort studies'. *British Journal of Industrial Medicine*, 45, 624–629

Swalm, R D (1966). 'Utility theory–insights into risk taking'. *Harvard Business Review*, 44, 123–136

Szalay, L B & Deese, J (1978). *Subjective meaning and culture: An assessment through word associations*. Hillsdale, NJ: Erlbaum

Taft, R, Jr. (1973). 'Testimony before the US Senate Subcommittee on Housing and Urban Affairs, 92nd Congress, S 2794. Washington, DC: US Government Printing Office

Teigen, K H, Brun, W & Slovic, P (1988). 'Societal risks as seen by a Norwegian public'. *Journal of Behavioral Decision Making*, 1, 111–130

Tengs, T O, Adams, M E, Pliskin, J S, Safran, D G, Siegel, J E, Weinstein, M C & Graham, J D (1995). 'Five-hundred life-saving interventions and their cost effectiveness'. *Risk Analysis*, 13, 369–390

Tetlock, P E, Skitka, L & Boettger, R (1989). 'Social and cognitive strategies for coping with accountability: Conformity, complexity, and bolstering'. *Journal of Personality and Social Psychology*, 57, 632–640

Thaler, R & Rosen, S (1976). 'The value of saving a life: Evidence from the labor market'. In N. Terleckyj (ed), *Household production and consumption*. Studies in income and wealth, vol 40. New York: National Bureau of Economic Research

Thompson, P B & Dean, W R (1996). 'Competing conceptions of risk'. *Risk: Health, Safety and Environment*, 7, 361–384

Thorndike, E L (1913). *The psychology of learning*. New York: Teachers College

Torrance, G W (1970). *A generalized cost-effectiveness model for the evaluation of health programs* (Research Series No 101). Hamilton, Ontario: McMaster University, Faculty of Business

Tribe, L H, Schelling, C S & Voss, J (1976). *When values conflict: Essays on environmental analysis, discourse and decision*. Cambridge, MA: Ballinger

Tuller, J (1985). 'Economic costs and losses'. In R W Kates, C Hohenemser & J X. Kasperson (eds), *Perilous progress: Managing the hazards of technology* (pp157–174). Boulder, CO: Westview

Tversky, A (1969). 'Intransitivity of preferences'. *Psychological Review*, 76, 31–48

Tversky, A (1972). 'Elimination by aspects: A theory of choice'. *Psychological Review*, 79, 281–299

Tversky, A & Kahneman, D (1971). 'Belief in the law of small numbers'. *Psychological Bulletin*, 76, 105–110

Tversky, A & Kahneman, D (1973a). 'Availability: A heuristic for judging frequency and probability'. *Cognitive Psychology*, 5, 207–232

Tversky, A & Kahneman, D (1973b). 'Anchoring and calibration in the assessment of uncertain quantities'. *Oregon Research Institute Research Bulletin*

Tversky, A & Kahneman, D (1974). 'Judgment under uncertainty: Heuristics and biases'. *Science*, 185, 1124–1131

Tversky, A & Kahneman, D (1981). 'The framing of decisions and the psychology of choice'. *Science*, 211, 453–458

Tversky, A & Kahneman, D (1982). 'The framing of decisions and the psychology of choice'. In R M Hogarth (ed), *New directions for methodology of social and behavioral science: No 11. Question framing and response consistency* (pp3–20). San Francisco: Jossey-Bass

Tversky, A & Koehler, D J (1994). 'Support theory: A nonextensional representation of subjective probability'. *Psychological Review*, 101(4), 547–567

Tyler, A R, Masuda, M & Holmes, T H (1968). 'Seriousness of illness rating scale'. *Journal of Psychosomatic Research*, 11, 363–374

US Committee on Government Operations (1976). *Teton dam disaster.* Washington, DC: US Government Printing Office

US Department of Energy (US DOE) (1984). *Draft report to the secretary of energy on the conclusions and recommendations of the advisory panel on alternative means of financing and managing (AMFM) radioactive waste management facilities.* Washington, DC: US DOE.

US Department of Energy (US DOE) (1986, May). *Environmental assessment: Yucca Mountain site* (Report No RW-0073, vols 1–3). Washington, DC: US DOE

US Department of Energy (US DOE) (1992, December). *Draft final report of the Secretary of Energy Advisory Board Task Force on radioactive waste management.* Washington, DC: US DOE

US Department of Health and Human Services (1994). *Preventing tobacco use among young people: A report of the Surgeon General* (S/N 017-001-00491-0). Washington, DC: Government Printing Office

US Department of Transportation (1967–1983). *Motor vehicle safety defect recall campaigns – Detailed reports from National Highway Traffic Safety Administration.* Washington, DC: US Department of Transportation

US Department of Transportation (1967–1983). *Safety needs report.* Washington, DC

US Environmental Protection Agency (US EPA) (1986) *Guidelines for carcinogen risk assessment*, 51 Fed Reg 992-34, 005

US Environmental Protection Agency (US EPA); Office of Policy Analysis (1987, February). *Unfinished business: A comparative assessment of environmental problems.* Washington, DC: US EPA

US Nuclear Regulatory Commission (1975, October). *Reactor safety study: An assessment of accident risks in US commercial nuclear power plants* (WASH 1400 NUREG-75/014). Washington, DC: US Nuclear Regulatory Commission

US Nuclear Regulatory Commission (1978a, 6 February) 7590-01 Fed Reg 4865. (10 CFR Parts 19 and 20)

US Nuclear Regulatory Commission (1978b, September). *Risk assessment review group report to the US Nuclear Regulatory Commission* (NUREG/CR-0400). Washington, DC: US Nuclear Regulatory Commission

US Nuclear Regulatory Commission (1983, May). *Safety goals for nuclear power plant operation* (NUREG-0880). Washington, DC: US Nuclear Regulatory Commission

US Nuclear Regulatory Commission (1990, 18 July) 55 Fed Reg 29181 (10 CFR Parts 50, 72 and 170)

US Office of Technological Assessment (1985). *Managing the nation's commercial high-level radioactive waste* (OTA-O-171). Washington, DC: Government Printing Office

US Office of Technological Assessment (1992). *Complex cleanup: The environmental legacy of nuclear weapons production.* Washington, DC: Government Printing Office

US Senate (1995, June). *The comprehensive regulatory reform act of 1995* Dole/Johnson discussion draft of S 5343. Washington, DC: US Government Printing Office

Vaughn, C K (1971). *Notes on insurance against loss from natural hazards* (Natural hazards research: Working Paper No 21). Toronto: University of Toronto, Department of Geography

Viscusi, W K (1990). 'Do smokers underestimate risks?' *Journal of Political Economy*, 98, 1253–1269

Viscusi, W K (1991). 'Variations in risk perceptions and smoking decisions'. *The Review of Economics and Statistics*, 73, 577–588

Viscusi, W K (1992). *Smoking: Making the risky decision.* New York: Oxford University

Viscusi, W K (1998). 'Constructive cigarette regulation'. *Duke Law Journal*, 47, 1095–1131

Vlek, C A J & Stallen, P J (1981). 'Judging risk and benefits in the small and in the large'. *Organizational Behavior and Human Performance*, 28, 235–271

von Neumann, J & Morgenstern, O (1947). *Theory of games and economic behavior* (second ed). Princeton, NJ: Princeton University Press

von Wartburg, W P (1989). 'Overview of the drug safety issue and Ciba-Geigy's response: RAD-AR'. In B Horisberger & R Dinkel (eds), *The perception and management of drug safety risks* (pp37–44). Berlin: Springer-Verlag

von Winterfeldt, D & Edwards, W (1984). *Understanding public disputes about risky technologies* (technical report). New York: Social Science Research Council

von Winterfeldt, D, John, R S & Borcherding, K (1981). 'Cognitive components of risk ratings'. *Risk Analysis*, 1, 277–288

Ward, R M (1974). 'Decisions by Florida citrus growers and adjustments to freeze hazards'. In G F White (ed), *Natural hazards: Local, national, global* (pp137–145). New York: Oxford University Press

Ward, W C & Jenkins, H M (1965). 'The display of information and the judgment of contingency'. *Canadian Journal of Psychology*, 19, 231–241

Water Resources Council (1971). 'Proposed principles and standards for planning water and related land resources'. *Federal Register*, 36, 245

Weart, S (1988). *Nuclear fear: A history of images*. Cambridge, MA: Harvard

Weber, E H (1834). 'De pulsu, resorptione, auditu et tactu'. In *Annotationes anatomical et physiological*. Leipzig: Koehler

Weinberg, A (1977). 'Is nuclear energy acceptable?' *Bulletin of the Atomic Scientists*, 33(4), 54–60

Weinberg, A M (1989). 'Public perceptions of hazardous technologies and democratic political institutions'. In R G Post (ed), *Waste management '89: Waste processing, transportation, storage and disposal, technical programs and public education: Proceedings of the Symposium on Waste Management at Tucson, Arizona, 26 February–2 March, 1989* (pp121–124). Tucson: Arizona Board of Regents

Weiner, R F (1993). 'Comment on Sheila Jasanoff's guest editorial'. *Risk Analysis*, 13, 495–496

Weinstein, N D (1979). 'Seeking reassuring or threatening information about environmental cancer'. *Journal of Behavioral Medicine*, 2, 125–139

Weinstein, N D (ed). (1987a). *Taking care: Understanding and encouraging self-protective behavior*. New York: Cambridge University

Weinstein, N D (1987b). 'Unrealistic optimism about susceptibility to health problems: Conclusions from a community-wide sample'. *Journal of Behavioral Medicine*, 10, 481–500

Weinstein, N D (1988). *Attitudes of the public and the department of environmental protection toward environmental hazards* (final report). New Jersey. New Jersey Department of Environmental Protection

Weinstein, N D (1989). 'Optimistic biases about personal risks'. *Science*, 246, 1232–1233

Wexler, D & Winick, B (1991). *Essays in therapeutic jurisprudence*. Durham, NC: Carolina Academic

Whipple, C (1987). *De minimus risk*. New York: Plenum

White, G F (1945). *Human adjustment to floods: A geographical approach to the flood problem in the United States* (Department of Geography Research Paper No 29). Chicago: University of Chicago

White, G F (1961). 'The choice of use in resource management'. *Natural Resources Journal*, 1, 23–40

White, G F (1964). *Choice of adjustment to floods* (Department of Geography Research Paper No 93). University of Chicago

White, G F (1966). 'Optimal flood damage management: Retrospect and prospect. In A V Kneese & S C Smith (eds), *Water Research* (pp251–269). Baltimore: Johns Hopkins Press

White, G F (1970). 'Flood-loss reduction: The integrated approach'. *Journal of Soil and Water Conservation*, 25,172–176

White, G F, Bradley, D & White, A (1972). *Drawers of water: Domestic water use in east Africa*. Chicago: University of Chicago

Whittemore, A S (1983). 'Facts and values for environmental toxicants'. *Risk Analysis*, 3, 23–33

Wiggins, J H, Jr (1972). 'Earthquake safety in the city of Long Beach based on the concept of balanced risk'. In *Perspectives on benefit-risk decision making* (pp87–95). Washington, DC: National Academy of Engineering

Wiggins, J H (1974). 'Toward a coherent natural hazards policy'. *Civil Engineering—ASCE*, pp74–76

Wildavsky, A (1979). 'No risk is the highest risk of all'. *American Scientist*, 67, 32–37

Williams, C A (1966). 'Attitudes toward speculative risks as an indicator of attitudes toward pure risks'. *Journal of Risk and Insurance*, 33, 577–586

Wilson, R (1975). 'The costs of safety'. *New Scientist*, 68, 274–275

Wilson, R (1979). 'Analyzing the daily risks of life'. *Technology Review*, 81, 40–46

Wilson, R (1987, 7 May). Testimony before the Subcommittee on Nuclear Regulation, Committee on the Environment and Public Works. Washington, DC: US Senate

Wilson, T D, Lisle, D J, Schooler, J W, Hodges, S D., Klaaren, K J & LaFleur, S J (1993, June). 'Introspecting about reasons can reduce post-choice satisfaction'. *Personality and Social Psychology Bulletin*, 19(3), 331–339

Wisner, B & Mbithi, P M (1974). 'Drought in eastern Kenya: Nutritional status and farmer activity'. In G F White (ed), *Natural hazards: Local, national, global* (pp87–97). New York: Oxford University Press

World News Tonight (1994a, 22 July). 'Many Rwandan refugees are dying of cholera'. New York and Washington, DC: American Broadcasting Corporation

World News Tonight (1994b, 26 July). 'US Army begins water purification in Rwanda'. New York and Washington, DC: American Broadcasting Corporation

Wynne, B (1984). 'Public perceptions of risk'. In J Surrey (ed), *The urban transportation of irradiated fuel* (pp246–259). London: Macmillan

Wynne, B (1989, March). 'Sheepfarming after Chernobyl: A case study in communicating scientific information'. *Environment*, 31(2), 10–15, 33–39

Wynne, B (1992). 'Risk and social learning: Reification to engagement'. In S Krimsky & D Golding (eds), *Social theories of risk* (pp275–300). Westport, CT: Praeger

York, H (1970). *Race to oblivion: A participant's view of the arms race*. New York: Simon & Schuster

Zajonc, R B (1980). 'Feeling and thinking: Preferences need no inferences'. *American Psychologist*, 35, 151–175

Zuckerman, M, Kolin, E, Price, L & Zoob, I (1964). 'Development of a sensation-seeking scale'. *Journal of Consulting Psychology*, 28, 477–482

Index